MODERN SOUTH INDIA

A HISTORY *from the* 17TH CENTURY *to our* TIMES

RAJMOHAN GANDHI

ALEPH

ALEPH

ALEPH BOOK COMPANY
An independent publishing firm
promoted by Rupa Publications India

First published in India in 2018
by Aleph Book Company
7/16 Ansari Road, Daryaganj
New Delhi 110 002

ISBN: 978-93-88292-22-1

3 5 7 9 10 8 6 4 2

Printed by Parksons Graphics Pvt. Ltd., Mumbai

That they may know more the South Indian in them, this book is affectionately offered to my daughter Supriya, grandson Anoush, and son Debu; sister Tara; brother Gopu; niece Sukanya and her son Vidur; nephew Vinayak and his daughters Ananya, Anoushka and Andrea; niece Leela; niece Divya and her daughter Ava; niece Amrita and her daughters Siya and Radha—offspring all of their Tamil forebear, my mother, Lakshmi Devadas Gandhi, 1912–1983.

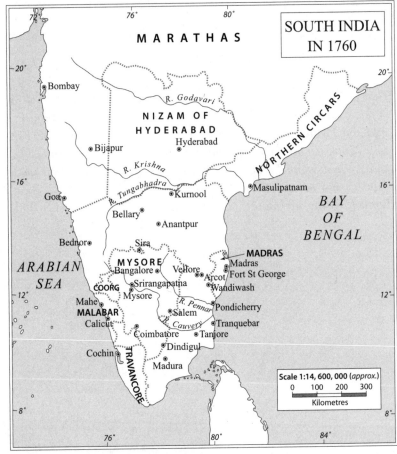

SOUTH INDIA
IN 1760

MARATHAS

Bombay

R. Godavari

NIZAM OF
HYDERABAD

Hyderabad

Bijapur

R. Krishna

NORTHERN CIRCARS

Goa

R. Tungabhadra

Kurnool

Masulipatnam

Bellary

Anantpur

BAY
OF
BENGAL

Bednor

Sira

MYSORE

Bangalore

Vellore

Srirangapatna

Arcot

MADRAS

Madras

Fort St George

Wandiwash

COORG

Mysore

R. Pennar

Pondicherry

Mahe

MALABAR

Salem

R. Cauvery

Calicut

Tranquebar

Coimbatore

Tanjore

Cochin

TRAVANCORE

Dindigul

Madura

ARABIAN
SEA

Scale 1:14, 600, 000 (approx.)

0   100   200   300

Kilometres

© Government of India, Copyright, 2018

The responsibility for the correctness of internal details rests with the publisher.

The coastlines of India agree with the Record/Master Copy certified by Survey of India.

The state boundaries between Uttarakhand & Uttar Pradesh, Bihar & Jharkhand and Chattisgarh & Madhya Pradesh have not been verified by the Governments concerned.

The spellings of names in this map, have been taken from various sources.

The territorial waters of India extend into the sea to a distance of twelve nautical miles measured from the appropriate base line.

TIPU'S MYSORE 1791

NIZAM OF HYDERABAD

Bijapur

Hyderabad

R. Godavari

R. Krishna

Goa

R. Tungabhadra

Kurnool

Bellary

Anantpur

Bednor

Sira

ARABIAN SEA

Vellore

Madras

Bangalore

Arcot

Fort St George

Srirangapatna

Wandiwash

Mahe

Mysore

R. Pennar

Pondicherry

Calicut

Salem

BAY OF BENGAL

COORG

MALABAR

R. Kaveri

Coimbatore

Tranquebar

Tanjore

Cochin

Dindigul

TRAVANCORE

Madura

Scale 1:14, 600, 000 (approx.)
0   100   200   300
Kilometres

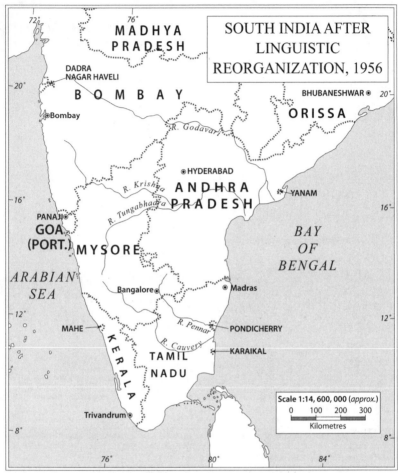

SOUTH INDIA AFTER LINGUISTIC REORGANIZATION, 1956

MADHYA PRADESH

DADRA NAGAR HAVELI

BOMBAY

Bombay

BHUBANESHWAR ⊙

ORISSA

R. Godavari

⊙ HYDERABAD

ANDHRA PRADESH

R. Krishna

R. Tungabhadra

PANAJI ⊙

GOA (PORT.)

MYSORE

YANAM

BAY OF BENGAL

ARABIAN SEA

Bangalore ⊙

⊙ Madras

MAHE

R. Pennar

PONDICHERRY

R. Cauvery

KARAIKAL

KERALA

TAMIL NADU

Trivandrum ⊙

Scale 1:14, 600, 000 (approx.)

0   100   200   300

Kilometres

© Government of India, Copyright, 2018

The responsibility for the correctness of internal details rests with the publisher.

The coastlines of India agree with the Record/Master Copy certified by Survey of India.

The state boundaries between Uttarakhand & Uttar Pradesh, Bihar & Jharkhand and Chattisgarh & Madhya Pradesh have not been verified by the Governments concerned.

The spellings of names in this map, have been taken from various sources.

The territorial waters of India extend into the sea to a distance of twelve nautical miles measured from the appropriate base line.

CONTENTS

PREFACE

Four years ago, in 2014, David Davidar reminded me that after the publication in 1955 of K. A. Nilakanta Sastri's classic work, which began with pre-historic times and ended with the fall of Vijayanagara, not many have tried to convey South India's story in a single study. David next asked if I would attempt a fresh history of the region.

At first I quailed. Emboldened, however, by the welcome accorded in the previous year to my history of another large region, the undivided Punjab of the pre-1947 era, I agreed.

Aware of my limitations, I knew I could only dare to confront South India's modern period. Its ancient history was beyond my powers. On the other hand, writing on South India from, say, the European advent to present times might turn out to be, if I proved lucky, a doable project, in fact an exciting one. I plunged into the deep waters of such an exercise.

Readers will find out if what I have emerged with is of interest. If they want a rationale for the account, the Introduction that follows tries to spell it out.

For writing this book, I turned to libraries and archives, newspapers and journals, and published works. I also talked to a great many persons.

This book's pages reveal the immense amount I owe to the authors and researchers of studies tapped by me. In most cases, the authors did not seek the broad picture I was after, but their details, often so rich with meaning, have helped me construct it.

Putting the matter slightly differently, if the weaving of this cloth is mine, most of the threads that constitute it were produced by the toil, often inspired, of scores of others.

As must be true for anyone delving into a subject of wide and long-standing interest, I marvelled at the skill and perseverance of previous researchers who went after its different aspects. Their sensitive toil humbled me, apart from also providing knowledge.

A number of these scholars were not Indian by birth. Some were British, belonging to the race that ruled over India and Indians. I do not hold the circumstances of their birth against them. What was dug out was more important than who did the digging.

No matter their nationality, whether it was Indian, British, American, European, Japanese or something else, I deeply thank the scholars, many from earlier centuries, whose information, findings or perspectives I have read and in many cases cited. The bibliography at the end names them.

Libraries or archives I was able to consult include the Tamil Nadu Archives in Chennai; National Archives in New Delhi; British Library in London (which houses the collections of the old India Office Library); and libraries at the University of Illinois at Urbana-Champaign, Michigan State University in East Lansing, Michigan, Yale University in New Haven, Connecticut, Indian Institute of Technology, Gandhinagar, Indian Institute of Technology, Bombay, Vemana University, Kadapa, Centre for Development Studies, Thiruvananthapuram, and India International Centre, New Delhi. For these opportunities, I express thanks.

Enormously helpful, too, were conversations with numerous historians, scholars and knowledgeable persons in different parts of southern India. In some cases, the circumstances (and travels) that enabled the conversations were as interesting as the knowledge they shared. These seemed to provide material for a separate book, if only I could put it together! To all of them, my great thanks anyway. These generous helpers included:

Hasanuddin Ahmed, Fatima Attari, N. P. Bhatt, Kesavanarayana Boyanapalli, P. J. Cherian, Raghu Cidambi, Maria Couto, J. Devika, Ganesh and Surekha Devy, Gopalkrishna Gandhi, Asim Kumar Ghosh, Ashok Gladston, Luis Gomes, Margaret Gonzalves, V. Gopal, Janaki Govindarajan, Venu Madhav and Neeta Govindu, Rajan Gurukkal,

Shankar Halagatti, Neelambar Hatti, Gopal Kadikodi, Manorama Kamat, Vaman Kamat, Girish Karnad, C. V. Krishnaswamy, Sanjeev Kulkarni, K. Lakshmi Narayan, Pampayya Malemath, Sunil Mani, Mammen Mathew, Damodar and Shaila Mauzo, K. Ramachandra Murthy, Usha Murthy, (the late) Venkatesh Murthy, S. Muthiah, M. G. S. Narayanan, M. D. and Vinaya Okkund, Nidhin Olikara, Gautam Pingle, Urmila Pingle, Rajendra Poddar,

K. S. Radhakrishnan, A. Raghuramaraju, 'Kalki' Rajendran, P. Yenadi Raju, Vakula Ramakrishna, Biju Rao, Kandoba Rao, Pandu Ranga Rao, Ram Mohan Rao, Surendra and Geetha Rao, Vidya Sagar and Deepika Rao, Vikram Rao, D. Chandresekhar Reddy, S. Jaipal Reddy, A. R. Ramachandra Reddy, G. Siva Reddy, Srinivas Reddy, Dr Thummalapally Dharma Reddy, Rev. Dr Packiam Samuel, T. L. Sankar, P. Saraswathi, S. C. Sardeshpande, E. A. S. and Rani Sarma, Vikhar Ahmed Sayeed, A. Sethumadhavan, Vasanthi Srinivasan, V. Sriram, Rahamath Tarikere, Matthew Thomas, A. R. Venkatachalapathy, K. R. and Lakshmi Venugopal, Rafael Vieras, Vijay Kumar of Emesco, T. Vijay Kumar, G. Vijay Mohan, and Mallamma Yalawar and daughter Tejaswani.

To kind helpers somehow unnamed, my apologies! I want to thank them too.

Like all histories, this one, too, is personal and unavoidably selective. I cannot claim that the material I studied added up to a complete or totally fair picture, or that the persons I interviewed are a representative cross-section of knowledgeable South Indians.

In the end, despite a wish to absorb all viewpoints, this book is only one person's understanding of information obtained from a large number of documents or human sources, at times reached by accident or circumstance, and not always because I knew beforehand that they would lead me to the bottom of a subject.

Possible 'subjects' for a South Indian history were so many that I could not possibly deal with them all. What was left out is bound to strike some as being more important than what has been taken up. I would be more than delighted if this effort encourages others in their own studies of South India's modern history, focusing on what is unaddressed here.

Every writer of a South Indian story runs into the challenge of variety (and change) in the spelling of names and places. Bangalore or Bengaluru? Tanjore or Thanjavur? Trivandrum or Thiruvananthapuram? Trichy, Trichinopoly or Tiruchirappalli? Iyer, Iyyer, Aiyer, Aiyar or Ayyar?

Consistency is almost impossible, especially when you also want to cite from earlier texts. There are similar choices when it comes to miles and kilometres. Where a writer cannot be consistent, readers may be tolerant. I beseech their indulgence.

Acknowledged on the dedication page, the South-Indian-ness of my mother was part of the pull for writing this book. I must recall three other South Indians: K. Santhanam (1895–1980), T. Sadasivam (1902–97) and C. R. Narasimhan (1909–89). They are long gone, but I am indebted to them for asking me, way back in 1973, to attempt a biography of Chakravarti Rajagopalachari. I have been on a boat on history's river ever since.

But for David Davidar I would not have ventured on this book. Thank you, David. I don't know how you continue to come up with one exciting (and difficult) idea after another. And thank you, editor Pujitha Krishnan. As before, you demanded clarity, asked necessary questions, made many a beneficial suggestion, and took great pains.

By offering, for multiple weeks, their gracious Bengaluru home as a base for my research for this study, Jitinder and Chand have contributed crucially to it. Thank you both.

Organizing travels for this study, often accompanying me, often sharing the exercise of interviewing the knowledgeable, identifying persons to meet and material to read, ensuring that I remained fit and fed, and playing other critical roles, Usha is once more a co-creator of a book where I am called the author. I don't know how to say thanks to her.

Rajmohan Gandhi, Urbana, Illinois
4 October 2018

MODERN SOUTH INDIA

INTRODUCTION

Imagine a traveller in the year 1600 who, starting, say, from Vizag (Vishakhapatnam), sails all the way along South India's lengthy eastern, southern and western shores, and then, after reaching Goa, rides over the peninsula's land, first along a perimeter not very far from the seas and then on an inner 'circle', ending his journey, which perhaps consumes a year or more, in Bengaluru.

What does the traveller take in on this enormous snail-shaped route?

The Vizag area, where he starts his southward sail, contains undulating coastal land and, close to it, red or black hills, some reaching up to 5,000 feet, 'whale-backed in outline and appearing to follow one another in procession', as the author of a 1907 gazetteer would put it.[1]

Politically, in 1600, this hilly coastal tract is under a weak regional chief appointed by the Muslim ruler of Golconda (later to become Hyderabad city). This ruler is nominally subject to Delhi's reigning Mughal but belongs to a Deccan confederacy that thirty-five years previously had defeated the grand Vijayanagara Empire to its south.

South of Vizag along this Coromandel coast is the major port of Machilipatnam in the delta formed by the river Krishna as it enters the Bay of Bengal.

Small or large ports line the long coast. Perhaps our traveller gets off his boat for a day or two when it enters the natural harbour of Pulicat, where the Portuguese had established a base *a century earlier*, in 1502. Nine years into the future, in 1609, the Dutch would displace Pulicat's Portuguese.

About 38 miles down the coast from Pulicat is the town of San Thome, set up by the Portuguese in the 1540s. Right next to San Thome is the much older native town of Mylapore, with which Europe and the Arabs have long been familiar. There is no Madras city as yet.

Farther south, down a vertically straight section of the continuing coast, is the ancient trading port of Nagapattinam, where the traveller in the year 1600 finds traders from distant places as well as native ones, including Muslims descended from ninth-century Arab immigrants.

Later, after the coastline makes a sudden ninety-degree turn westward, faint outlines of northern Sri Lanka emerge on the horizon to the left of the moving boat. As the boat proceeds through what the future would call the Palk Straits, the island of Pamban surfaces, barely separated from the peninsula, from where, in the Ramayana, Rama launched his bid to recover a Lanka-confined Sita.

Exporting pearls fished up in adjacent waters, the old port of Tuticorin (Thoothukudi) shows up as the boat continues to sail southwest. Beyond Tuticorin, at Kanyakumari, the Bay of Bengal becomes the Arabian Sea, and our traveller now sails north.

Going past the land where Thiruvananthapuram would rise in the future, he steps ashore at Kochi (Cochin), where the population includes Christians whose forebears may have arrived more than a thousand years earlier. Later, when the traveller walks on land again at the port of Kozhikode (Calicut), he runs into scores of Arab and European traders, finds Malayalam-speaking Muslims with centuries-old ties to India, and hears of Vasco da Gama's visit more than a hundred years previously.

In Kochi, in Kozhikode and all along his northward voyage, he senses green hills not very far from the shoreline to his right. Landing in the port of Mangaluru, he hears new tongues and sees brisk commercial activity. He may not have realized it, but the languages he has so far heard from the peninsula's natives include Telugu, Tamil, Malayalam, Kannada and Tulu, more or less in that order.

When he arrives in Goa, our traveller runs into a flourishing Portuguese-run city, where Konkani and Marathi are among the languages spoken.

His sea travels over, from Goa he starts a land journey to traverse the vast acreage between the two coasts. The expedition is not comfortable or risk-free: the narrow roads are mountainous much of the time, rough all the time, and on occasion attacked by men or animals, and the bumping bullock carts are creaky as well.

Now proceeding in a *northeasterly direction,* our plucky traveller manages to trek through villages and impressive cities like Bijapur, Gulbarga, Golconda, and Warangal, whose sultans had recently joined hands to defeat Vijayanagara, but are now suspicious of one another and even more of the Mughal in far-to-the-north Delhi.

In Golconda, he looks at a few sparkling diamonds. In Warangal, where the Kakatiyas ruled from the twelfth to the fourteenth centuries, he stares at an immense water reservoir.

Here he changes direction and proceeds *southwards*, encountering places on a long line parallel to the peninsula's eastern shores, including Vijayawada, Guntur, Nellore, the great temple towns of Tirupati and Kanchipuram, the mountain fort of Gingee, the rich and well-watered city of Thanjavur (from where the Cholas ruled in a distant past), and prestigious Madurai, the deep-south seat of earlier Pandian kings.

On this extensive land journey, the sounds he hears seem to change again, first from Goa's Konkani to Kannada, then from Kannada to Telugu, and finally from Telugu to Tamil, though even in Thanjavur and Madurai the ruling class seems to speak Telugu.

When, on meeting a resident, our traveller asks, 'Who is your ruler?' he receives a variety of responses. A few speak of the Delhi Mughal, most say 'our nayaka' or 'our sultan', usually without naming him. In the year 1600, the peninsula as a whole has no clear ruler.

At Madurai, our traveller swings again and journeys *northwest* towards Coimbatore, starting another 'circle', this time a smaller one. His stops on this perimeter include, in clockwise order, Coimbatore, Srirangapatna (not far from where the Hoysalas ruled between the eleventh and fourteenth centuries), Madikeri (the town of the Coorgs) and Shivamogga (Shimoga), where our traveller turns northeast.

At and around Hampi, he runs into destroyed palaces of the Vijayanagara kings who ruled from there during the fourteenth, fifteenth and sixteenth centuries. At Bellary (Ballari) he alters direction, journeying *southeast* towards Kurnool and Kadapa (Cuddapah). Languages have shifted on this route too: Tamil to Kannada to Kodava to Kannada to Telugu.

At Kadapa, our traveller turns *southwest* in the direction of recently-founded Bengaluru.

At Bengaluru, the snail-shaped journey ends. Yet our traveller has so far seen only a portion of the coastal and hinterland tracts of peninsular India. The four-century story, from 1600 to our times, of the people inhabiting this varying, intricate peninsula is what this book tries to study.

◆

Although no political realm named South India ever existed, a cultural, geographical and geopolitical space of that description was long recognized. Thus the Deccan, Dakkan or Dakhan (from the Sanskrit 'dakshin' or the Prakrit 'dakkin', meaning south) was a widely used term in the not so distant past. It connoted the region south of the Vindhya mountains which, in the fifteenth century, was dominated by two entities—the Bahmani Sultanate and the Vijayanagara Empire.

Writing in 1918, S. Krishnaswami Aiyangar, professor of history and archaeology at Madras University, spoke of 'South India: A Distinct Entity in Indian History'.[2] Since then innumerable works have illuminated aspects of the history of the Kannada, Malayali, Tamil or Telugu worlds, as also of other cultures in the region.

Yet the number of scholars embracing the whole of South India is not large.

The South India story attempted here is of a peninsular region influenced by the oceans, not by the Himalayas. Yet it is more than that.

It is a story of facets of four powerful cultures—Kannada, Malayali, Tamil and Telugu, to name them again in alphabetical order—and yet more than that, for Kodagu, Konkani, Marathi, Oriya and Tulu cultures have also influenced it, as also other older and possibly more indigenous cultures often seen as 'tribal', as well as cultures originating in other parts of India and the world.

With South India's Malayalam region being (in modern times) the most 'balanced' in terms of religion and also the most literate, its Kannada zone occupying South India's geographical centre and containing the sites of the Vijayanagara kingdom and also the kingdom of Haidar and Tipu, its Telugu portion the largest in area and holding the most people, and its Tamil part the most Dravidian and possessing the oldest literature, the four principal cultures are, unsurprisingly, competitive. But they are also complementary.

This is a Dravidian story, and also more than that.

It is a story involving four centuries, the seventeenth, eighteenth, nineteenth and twentieth, yet other periods intrude upon it.

Largely excluded from this story are happenings in the adjacent regions of Maharashtra and Odisha. In some ways these are arbitrary omissions, for the Marathi world has usually been linked to the Deccan, while the Oriya world, too, has frequently interacted with it.

Stern laws of time and space have enforced these absences.

◆

A North Indian looking southwards sees the peninsula narrowing until it becomes a mere point, enabling the oceans on either side of India's landmass to finally embrace each other. A South Indian looking northwards sees the peninsula widening until the Bay of Bengal and the Arabian Sea lose consciousness of each other and retreat separately from the swelling landmass.

Going east, the peninsula's land dips gently, so that many of its rivers fall into the Bay of Bengal, not the Arabian Sea. South India's hills, older and shorter than the Himalayas, seem on maps to hug the two coastlines. While the western hills or ghats form an almost continuous line parallel to the Malabar coast, the eastern hills are more scattered if also analogous to the Coromandel shore.

Capturing the more predictable, more continuous, and more inclusive southwest monsoon, usually active from June to September, the Western Ghats relay to the peninsula most of its water. By contrast, the northeast monsoon, which may strike any time between October and December, brings, on days of its choosing, heavy downpours to random places on the east coast, giving the South most of its thunder, lightning and floods.

Or, by failing to appear, its famines.

Much of the South is a plateau. Some of it can be arid. Different parts provide memorable views of magnificent rocks sculpted by time and balanced precariously by gravity. There are flowering trees across the region, luxuriant rice fields in the deltas, plants and trees in the moist soil between the Arabian Sea and the Western Ghats, as well as waterfalls, rivers, oceans.

Everyone knows the southern aromas and flavours: jasmine and coffee, tamarind and coconut, the dosai, idli, and appam, and accompaniments that burn the tongue but cannot be resisted. For the eyes and ears, the South provides lamps, bells, temples, churches, mosques and shrines, the sounds of its music and the movements of its dances.

And the movements and voices, also of its homemakers, fishermen, boatmen, weavers, cobblers and others who toil. Above all, South India today contains hundreds of millions of people, speaking in one or more of several, usually connected, languages, each individual vulnerable and valiant in a unique way, all living in a range of easy or difficult relationships with one another and the world.

This study of South India's life can merely hope to capture a few fragments of their common story. With luck, and in very broad terms, it may indicate how today's South India was made.

◆

The story is not easy to gather, for the seventeenth-, eighteenth- and nineteenth-century forebears of today's South Indians did not leave many clear records. We can feel thankful for those individuals, Indian and foreign, who left material, or preserved, collected or interpreted it.

For example, but for the French who salvaged his diaries and the British who published them (in Madras in 1904), Indians might not have known of the Coromandel coast merchant, Ananda Ranga Pillai.

If, to give a second example, a century and half after Yusuf Khan's death in Madurai, the Briton Samuel Charles Hill had not conducted his research in the Tamil country and among the papers (in London and Madras) of the British East India Company and its armies, we, might not have known the first thing about the early life of this unusual character.

S. Muthiah, whose painstaking researches (in the twentieth and twenty-first centuries) have saved parts of Chennai's past for us, points out that descendants of the merchant-dubashes, whose role in starting Fort St George was not smaller than that of their better-known British associates, have provided little or no information regarding their noteworthy forebears.

We can be grateful for those who from old sites, old inscriptions, old ballads, or old coins have recovered a lost story, or by microscopic study of crumbling files in our country's fading archives have saved other stories from oblivion.

This book does not seek to unearth hidden knowledge about the past. By now, accessible material is in fact vast; selection is a bigger challenge than excavation. It hopes, nevertheless, that by switching on a couple of neglected lamps, and studying available material in their light, something fresh might be observed.

In addition to feeling that they are Kannadigas or Malayalis, Tamils or Telugus, many feel they are 'South Indian', and many in the rest of India and the world recognize that some people and some things, including ways of expression, languages, songs and foods, are 'South Indian'. The 'South Indian' lamp was waiting to be switched on.

It is a reality, moreover, that the different cultural or linguistic portions of South India (which exceed the four mentioned) are often poorly informed or even prejudiced about one another. In the second edition of his famed *Comparative Grammar of South Indian Languages,* first published in the 1850s, Robert Caldwell praised 'the intellectual capacity of a people amongst whom wonderful organ[s] of thought'— the various southern languages—had grown, but he went on to regret that the South's native scholars had 'never attempted to compare their own languages with others—not even with other languages of the same family'.[3]

The scene has not dramatically improved in the 150 years since Caldwell's study first appeared. 'Know your neighbour' was a second lamp waiting to be switched on. Perhaps a portrayal of South Indian history would help enhance the understanding South Indians have of one another.

◆

For context, we should briefly recall earlier history. Enterprising Chola and Pandian rulers were known to Asoka in his BCE time, and Pallava rulers had Mamallapuram's rock-cut temples carved during the sixth and seventh centuries. Much later, in the thirteenth century, the Yadavas ruled the Marathi world and the Kakatiyas the Telugu world, while the Kannadiga and Tamil worlds were ruled, respectively, by the Hoysalas and the Pandians. Earlier ruled by its Cheras, Kerala struggled to re-find its feet.

For conquerors, Kanyakumari always seemed a stronger magnet than the Himalayas. Many a covetous eye in northern India peered southwards, there were fewer south-to-north invasions than in the opposite direction.

In the first half of the fourteenth century, armies led by commanders of Delhi's Turkic rulers, swept down deep into the South, unseating kings in their way, destroying palaces and temples, and establishing their hegemony. But Delhi's rule was not easily established in the South. What emerged was an independent Bahmani Sultanate of the Deccan, which separated into at least five distinct units under chiefs who ruled from modern Karnataka's Gulbarga, Bidar and Bijapur, from Maharashtra's Ahmadnagar, or from Golconda (Hyderabad) in Telangana.

To the south of the Bahmani kingdoms rose the Vijayanagara Empire, which flourished from the middle of the fourteenth century. Governed for much of its impressive history from the Bellary area in modern Karnataka, this empire lasted until 1565, when a combination of Bahmani chiefs destroyed it.

It was only at the end of the seventeenth century, after Aurangzeb had devoted years of his life and the bulk of the Mughal empire's resources to overpower the Deccan sultanates that rule by Delhi encompassed the greater part of southern India. By this time the Marathas too were pushing into southern India. More significantly, so were European powers.

For retaining perspective, it may be helpful to keep four dates in mind:

- the year 1498, when Vasco da Gama arrived in Kerala on the Malabar coast;
- the year 1565, when, having lost the Battle of Talikota in the Kannada country, the Vijayanagara Empire started to disintegrate;
- the year 1639, when Fort St George was launched on the Coromandel coast by the English East India Company;
- and the year 1687, when, forcing the independent Sultan of Golconda to surrender, Aurangzeb enforced Mughal authority in the South.

We are ready now to begin the story.

Chapter 1

SAILS ON THE HORIZON: 1498–1697

After combining to defeat Vijayanagara in 1565, the Deccan sultanates of Bijapur, Ahmadnagar, Golconda and Bidar had fallen apart. Though Akbar, who would live until 1605, had significantly expanded the Mughal empire, he was headquartered too far to the north, in Delhi or Agra, to think of running the southern peninsula.

While different native chiefs—sultans or nayakas—controlled pieces of the southern hinterland, admirals and priests of a small European country, Portugal, had long established themselves in pockets on both coasts. Leading a four-ship fleet armed with cannon, Vasco da Gama had landed on the Malayali shore 102 years before the seventeenth century arrived. His voyage taking more than nine months, he arrived in Kozhikode on 20 May 1498.

Until then no one had sailed all the way from Europe to India. A century and ten years later, in 1608, the Dutch arrived at Pulicat on the east coast. In 1620, a Danish fleet landed in Tranquebar (Tharangambadi), also on the east coast, a good deal south of Pulicat. The British and the French were not far behind.

If horses—the sound of their hooves and the dust they kicked up—announced the outside world to northern India, slowly expanding sails on the horizon were thus alerting coastal South Indians to a visit by strangers.

Sponsored by monarchs, these ships from Europe brought traders who established 'factories' in several coastal places with apparent ease. Incoming and outgoing merchandise was stored in these 'factories' where a fort, too, was usually built, inside which European and Indian retainers protected their European masters and their goods. In the initial decades, South Indian merchants entering the fort dealt on equal terms with their European counterparts.

When Vasco da Gama landed on Kerala's coast, Kozhikode (Calicut) had a strong ruler, the Zamorin, with whom the Portuguese trader-explorer had to negotiate. A fair distance inland, northeast of

1

Kozhikode, lay Hampi, capital of a Vijayanagara Empire then at its zenith. Its umbrella covered large portions of what we think of today as Karnataka, Telangana, Andhra Pradesh and Tamil Nadu. As the historian Burton Stein would put it:

> Whether the Vijayanagara rulers are to be regarded as essentially Kannadigas or Telugus or whether they are to be regarded as both from the very beginning, the territorial scope of their power included the entire southern peninsula.[1]

Ascending the throne eleven years after da Gama's landing, Krishnadevaraya, Vijayanagara's greatest emperor, reigning from 1509 to 1529 and a poet in Telugu, was in fact of Tulu[2] origin.

After Vijayanagara's defeat, the Dutch, Danish, British and French traders wishing to set up a 'factory' or fort in South India had to obtain permission from a nayaka or a surviving Deccan sultan.

Places in the Tamil country like Trichy (Tiruchirappalli), Thanjavur (Tanjore) and Madurai (Madura) were under separate nayaka dynasties, mostly of Telugu origin, whose entry into these Tamil territories in the fourteenth and fifteenth centuries had been accompanied by a significant southward migration of Telugu-speaking agrarian castes.

Whether characterized as viceroyalties or kingdoms, the nayaka territories in South India that followed the Vijayanagara decline saw the construction of stone walls, thick forts, market towns and temples. As the fortification implies, the period also saw numerous destructive battles. In fact, fighting in the nayaka period was 'more or less incessant'.[3]

Some wars were on a truly large scale. The Jesuit Manuel Barradas, who travelled in parts of the South at the beginning of the seventeenth century and noticed, close to the city of Thanjavur, shade-giving trees as well as strong walls and a moat, wrote of a war occurring in the Trichy region in 1616 or 1617 *which according to him was fought by 'as many as a million soldiers'*.[4] Barradas may have exaggerated, but war among even a tenth of that number would have consumed a great quantity of blood and grain.

The nayakas of Thanjavur, Madurai and Gingee were evidently among those involved in this immense land war, as also the Portuguese, who seem to have assisted one side, and the Dutch (possibly joined by recruits from Jaffna in Sri Lanka), who helped the other.

The picture one gets of post-Vijayanagara South India is of power vacuums and struggles for supremacy involving natives but also outsiders. We have scant information on conflicts in the first quarter of the seventeenth century. The soldiers' castes or ethnicities are not known. European mercenaries, 'Turks' (probably Muslims from the Deccan sultanates) and even Abyssinians feature in some accounts, but most soldiers would have come from within the region.

From the sixteenth century, cannons (first brought into India by the Turks) were beginning to be cast in South Indian foundries, at times with the aid of a European mercenary, but these native products were of uncertain quality. Maintaining war elephants (including some imported from Burma and Thailand) and buying warhorses from Arabia was a huge expense, as was putting together a large infantry and cavalry.

The nayaka period also saw a steady cultural output in poetry, painting and sculpture, often explicitly erotic, at times witty, at other times merely crass. In some instances, making love and making war were seen as two essential parts of a ruler's dharma, even though the ruler himself did not enter the battlefield.

Feeding Brahmins en masse was viewed as the ruler's duty, but Brahmins were not central to the installation of the nayaka rulers or viceroys, who in most cases were descendants of Telugu-speaking warriors from peasant castes proud of their Sudra origin. Yet peasants and artisans did not seem to be their ruler's first concern. The courtesan's smile interested him more than the contentment of the peasant's wife or the pride of the artisan's mother.[5]

Rivalries between South Indian chiefs and between European companies led to battles where one Indo–European alliance clashed against another brown-white alliance. These alliances shifted from year to year, or even week to week.

After elimination and sifting, two European powers, the French and the British, would eventually remain to fight it out, in association with native chiefs.

Indian forces interested in filling the seventeenth-century's southern vacuum seemed to be, broadly speaking, of four kinds. There were, first, the Mughals in the north, who under Aurangzeb made a big southern push in the century's last quarter. A second group of claimants to power consisted of the Deccan sultanates resisting the Mughals, including the Telugu country's Golconda and, to its west, Bijapur. Nayakas to the south of the sultanates were a third set.

The Marathas comprised the fourth element. Having long soldiered for the Bijapur Sultanate, the Marathas wished to become rulers themselves.

◆

Vasco da Gama was not the first outsider seen in South India. Marco Polo had arrived over *two hundred years* before him, in 1292, and stopped with his ship at Pulicat, and at the place that later became Madras, and along the Malabar coast. *Twelve hundred years* earlier, Saint Thomas, the doubting apostle, had, it seems, landed in South India. Well before the Vasco da Gama visit, Arab traders lived in ports on the Malabar and the Coromandel coasts, as did seafarers of different races.

Indian traders also lived beyond the seas, some of whom Vasco da Gama encountered in eastern Africa before commencing the final leg of his voyage to the Malabar coast.

Traders came to India for wealth, and mariners for jobs, because of 'the magnificence of the richest empire of the globe', to quote the words written in the 1760s by Robert Orme, Robert Clive's companion and imperial historian.[6]

In the seventeenth and eighteenth centuries, India was the go-to land for bold spirits seeking a fortune, just as the United States was in the twentieth century.

India's trade with Africa and the Arab worlds, with Europe, and with Southeast and East Asia, was, however, an old story, connected to the influence beyond the seas of Chola, Pallava and other South Indian rulers.

The pearl fishery in the Pandian dominions was 'well known to the Greeks and Romans of the first century' and Pliny, a famous Roman of that century, was aware that 'the Pandian king resided at Madura in the interior'. In 1851, five headloads of Roman gold coins were found near Cannanore (Kannur) on the Malabar coast.[7] Fifty years earlier, in 1800, near the Tamil town of Karur, 'a pot was dug up containing a great many Roman coins of the reigns of Augustus and Tiberius'.[8]

A history of India published by the British in 1906 would say: 'It is…certain that the Pandya state, during the early centuries of the Christian era, shared along with the Chera kingdom of Malabar a very lucrative trade with the Roman empire, and was in exclusive possession of the much prized pearl fishery.'[9]

In a subsequent period, 'as early as the eighth or ninth century AD'—so the scholar Susan Bayly writes—'Arab traders and navigators settled along the Coromandel coast, and their numbers increased as the region began to play a central role in the international textile trade which linked south India to the entrepôts of west Asia and the Indonesian archipelago'.[10] These Muslim traders also settled on the Malabar coast.

Trade was large, ships were small, and roads were scarce. Therefore, on both coasts, ports were numerous and close to one another. In the mid-thirteenth century, the Kakatiya king, Ganapati, displayed this inscription in Motupalli, today a coastal village in Andhra's Prakasam district, but probably a leading port at the time:

> This inscribed guarantee has been granted by His Majesty the King Ganapatideva to sea-traders going back and forth en route to all continents, countries and towns. In the past, kings forcibly seized all the cargo such as gold, elephants, horses, jewels, etc. when sea-going vessels…were caught in storms, wrecked and cast on shore.
>
> But We, for the sake of our reputation and religious merit and out of pity for those who have incurred the grave risk of a sea-voyage [and] thinking that wealth is more valuable even than life, give up all but the customary tariff.[11]

◆

The Dutch were conspicuous for decades in seventeenth-century South India. As an India-based Briton would later put it:

> In Europe the great merchants were the Dutch… In 1610 the Dutch erected the fort at Pulicat, 23 miles north of Madras. In 1660 they took Negapatam from the Portuguese. In 1663 they took Cochin in like manner. Thus they became the great merchant princes of the East, possessing important settlements on both coasts, of Coromandel and Malabar.

The 17th century was indeed the golden period of Dutch commerce. Without any native produce to export, and without even a piece of timber fit for shipbuilding, the foreign trade of Holland was at this period greater than that of all Europe besides.[12]

Until the eighteenth century, and for much of that century as well, India's exports (calico* and other cotton textiles, cotton yarn, indigo, spices, pearls and more) greatly exceeded in value its imports (including horses for the armies of India's numerous chiefs, woollen cloth, swords and knives, mirrors and vermilion). As a result, gold and silver accumulated in India, including in its southern half.

Echoing other European comments at the time, François Bernier, the French doctor who served under Dara Shukoh and Aurangzeb, observed: 'Gold and silver, after circulating in every other quarter of the globe, come at length to be absorbed in Hindostan.'[13]

The seventeenth century dominance of Indian textiles was studied by the American scholar Bennet Bronson, who examined old records of the Dutch and English East India companies. Writes Bronson:

> [T]he Dutch and British East India Companies...followed the Portuguese into Asia in the early 1600s and almost immediately found that they had to use Indian textiles to buy spices in Indonesia [*which were in great demand in Europe*], [but] the growers were not interested in cash or, seemingly, in most other commodities.
>
> The Dutch and English companies both, therefore, became involved in exporting Indian textiles, at first to consumer markets within Asia but soon to consumers in Europe, Africa and the Americas as well... [I]n 1684 Indian exports to all points totalled more than 100 million yards.
>
> [With] the spectacular nature of Indian export growth...the European textile industry was already in an uproar by the late 1670s... Public relations men and concerned citizens (among them Daniel Defoe, the author of...*Robinson Crusoe*) produced a flood of pamphlets and newspaper articles claiming...that hundreds of thousands of European textile workers were about to starve and their national economies irreparably damaged...

---

*Derived from Calicut (Kozhikode), calico at this time signified unbleached, strong and inexpensive Indian cloth.

Yet it was not as if the East India companies were using cheap Indian labour to undercut European textile-makers.

At the time, the East India companies had little real control within India. The weavers and dyers were not their employees, and neither were the wealthy middlemen with whom they contracted each year for delivery of given amounts of cloth; the companies' factories often had to buy their supplies on the open market just like anyone else. They were not even the biggest buyers in that market.

Native Indian merchants owned ships as large as the Europeans and regularly carried more cloth and other goods to some of the major foreign markets.

Explaining the seventeenth-century popularity of Indian textiles, Bronson adds:

[T]he Indian cloth was actually better: at least as beautiful, more practical, and a good deal cheaper than anything comparable on the market... [India's textiles] came in colors which could be washed repeatedly without fading. Being mainly of cotton and cotton-silk mixtures, they were far more comfortable for wear in warm weather and indoors than were the traditional woolens and linens of Europe... Many were outstandingly cheap, and even the most expensive types were more durable than any non-Indian cloth that could be sold at a comparable price.

In Bronson's view, Indian textiles were, in addition, more hygienic than European ones.[14]

FORT ST GEORGE

[W]hen the British founded a fort at Madras in 1639, India was then at the center of an economic and cultural 'world system', with something like a quarter of the world's total manufacturing capacity located within its peninsular boundaries.[15]

In 1639, Francis Day and Andrew Cogan of the East India Company, hitherto employed in the port of Machilipatnam, and two Indians, the merchant Beri Thimmanna (also called Thimmappa) and Nagabattan (who made gunpowder), began building what would soon be called

Fort St George on a strip facing the beach in Madras, except that it wasn't known as Madras yet.

Having been pushed out by Dutch ships and soldiers from Pulicat, about 23 miles north of this site, the English company—'the Grandest Society of Merchants in the Universe'[16]—was hungry for a base where ships could land and exchange merchandise.

It obtained the new strip, measuring around 4 miles by 1 mile, from the Raja of Chandragiri, to which a Vijayanagara branch had repaired after the kingdom's defeat in the 1560s. Close to the great temple at Tirupati, Chandragiri lay 60 miles northwest of the Madras-to-be.

Cogan became the Company's first chief at Fort St George, Day the second. Called 'agents' to begin with, chiefs were later referred to as 'presidents' and 'governors'.

Thimmanna, an important player in Fort St George's early years, was the sort of Indian merchant Bronson was speaking of, holding his own in dealings with the Company, bilingual, and bold. We can assume that it was he who clinched the deal with the Chandragiri nayaka.

A man coping with more than one language or bhasha was a 'dubash' or 'dubashi', a name also given to a European trader's native domestic if the latter was similarly competent. But dubashes of Thimmanna's rank were more than linguistically skilled. They read the winds, seized opportunities, and took risks.

Also bold were the Company's Britons at Fort St George, who sought to create in an alien land a long-term establishment including a fort, a governor, a harbour and more. Arriving in Madras after a long and uncertain voyage past Africa's western, southern and eastern coasts, across the Arabian Sea, and into the Bay of Bengal, these adventurers from Britain were hungry for money.

Buying and selling for the Company, which gave them salaries, they also bought and sold for themselves as individuals. Provided they did not die in India of disease or accident (a few of them did), they had a good prospect of returning home with a fortune.

To have textiles to sell in Madras, 'Francis Day and Beri Thimmanna brought in cloth-makers in 1639 when they founded the city and dumped them by the North River and let them fend for themselves'.[17] South of the Fort, other 'weavers and painters in the employment of the Factory...erected a little village for themselves; while the fishermen at the mouth of the Triplicane river were living, marrying and dying—catching fish, making nets, and celebrating their...festivals'.[18]

The remarkably detailed records kept at Fort St George right from its inception tell us a good deal about its British chiefs and councillors, very little, it would seem, about men like Thimmanna,* much less about men like the gunpowder-maker Nagabattan, and nothing at all about the cloth-makers whose skills and sweat contributed in 1689 to the global sale of 100 million yards of Indian textiles.

These records inform us that Thimmanna was designated the Company's 'chief merchant', given a 'seat in Council', and deemed entitled to a five-gun salute. When he died in 1678, he was succeeded as the chief merchant by Kasi Viranna, who started 'Cassa Verona and Co', which may have been India's first joint-stock company.[19]

Influential Hindus in growing Madras built temples but Viranna, who had cultivated good relations in the Telugu country with the Sultan of Golconda (one of the Deccan states that had combined to defeat Vijayanagara in the sixteenth century), built a mosque as well and gave himself a Muslim name, Hasan Khan.

Power in the neighbourhood was changing hands. Not long after giving the land to the Company, the Raja of Chandragiri, threatened by the Sultan of Golconda, retired to Mysore, and the English placated the Golconda court with presents, usually conveyed through an Indian dubash.

The Golconda sultan became lord of a fair part of the South Indian region and thus critically important for the Company and for merchants like Viranna. In 1676, doubtless with Viranna's help, the Company rented Triplicane, close to Fort St George, from the sultan; Viranna leased Triplicane from the Company and invited many Muslims to live there.[20]

When he died in 1680, Viranna's wife wished to perish on his pyre, but Streynsham Master, the Fort's chief who ordered a thirty-gun salute in the dying merchant's honour, prevented the sati.[21] Thimmanna's brother Pedda Venkatadri followed Viranna as chief merchant.

---

*Venkatachari Jagannathan states that a Thimmanna descendant, K. Venkataswami Naidu, became minister for religious endowments in Rajaji's 1952 ministry and that other descendants formed a pharmaceutical firm, Appah and Company, *Madras Musings*, Vol. 2, No. 17, 16–31 Dec. 1992.

In 1689, Venkatadri was followed in this position by Alangatha Pillai, described as 'the most outstanding of the early dubashes', whose accomplishments included building 'the nucleus of the Sri Ekambareswarar Temple'.[22]

When, in 1690, the authorities of Fort St George decided to erect a court of judicature in Madras, Alangatha Pillai, who was considered 'a wise and able Jentue', was made a justice 'for Natives, as well Jentues, Moores and Mallabars'. So we are told by a Fort St George minute dated 16 June 1690.[23]

'Jentue' at the time meant 'Hindu', 'Moor' was 'Muslim', and for a while 'Mallabar' was the European word in Madras for a Tamil-speaker rather than (or in addition to) a name for the peninsula's western coast, or for the northern part of the Malayalam country.

Though not spoken of as a dubash, another prominent Madras merchant in the late seventeenth century was Pachaiyappa Mudaliar, after whom the well-known college is named.[24]

◆

These Indian merchants were among the period's celebrities and innovators. If the Fort St George records do not tell us more about these risk-taking pioneers, later chronicles of the city ignore them altogether. However, *Sarvadevavilasa*, an anonymous Sanskrit text apparently written in the late eighteenth century, portrays merchant-dubashes in Madras city as associates of the British, eminent trustees of temples, patrons of poets, musicians and dancers, and hosts at parties in the gardens of their large houses.[25]

These Indian elites of seventeenth-century Madras formed a diverse circle. Its Telugu- and Tamil-speaking members belonged to a range of trading and land-owning castes, worshipped Siva and/or Vishnu, and donated to popular temples that employed Brahmin priests and also linked the elites to the broader community.

Counterparts of Madras's merchant-dubashes existed in the other European settlements on the Malabar and Coromandel coasts. In the next chapter, we will look at one of them in particular, Ananda Ranga Pillai, chief dubash in the eighteenth century to Joseph François Dupleix, governor of Pondicherry, where—following Portuguese, Dutch and English examples—the French established a settlement in 1674.

Unlike fellow dubashes on South India's coasts, Ananda Ranga Pillai entered observations into his diary, enabling us to know him and his times.

A suggestive glimpse of the South Indian economy in the seventeenth and eighteenth centuries has been provided by the scholars V. Narayana Rao, David Shulman and Sanjay Subrahmanyam in their 2001 study, *Textures of Time*. These three see the dubashes we have mentioned as part of a South Indian political economy which went down from the courts of rajas, nobles and foreign trading companies to 'the humble village with its peasants'.

In the middle of this hierarchy were small 'centres' where different 'service groups and artisan castes found their livelihood, and these centres were also the fulcra of a significant market- and cash-economy'. These intermediary towns 'performed a variety of roles, some of a primarily economic nature' (presumably such as weekly or periodic marketing, information-gathering or revenue-raising), 'others more sociopolitical or cultural'.[26]

◆

Fort St George was not the first European settlement in the Madras area, and the urban world of Indian communities that quickly grew around the Fort was hardly the area's first native town.

A century earlier, and only about 3 miles south of the Fort St George strip, the Portuguese had set up the town of San Thome, around Thomas the Apostle's presumed tomb. Right next to San Thome was the old town of Mylapore, which Arabs had known of in the eleventh century. Later, in 1572, Luís de Camões, Portugal's national poet, wrote of 'Meliapor' as the place adjacent to San Thome.

A *much* earlier resident of Mylapore was the weaver Tiruvalluvar, author (possibly in the first century) of the verses of the *Kural*, possibly a Jaina and more than familiar with the Gita, whose aphorisms would be encountered throughout the Tamil country by visiting or governing Europeans.[27]

When the Portuguese established San Thome, Mylapore became known as its Black Town. Similarly, while only whites resided in Fort St George, the space immediately to its north became Madras's Black Town, later to be called George Town.

Merchants lived on streets close to Fort St George. Those who wove, washed or dyed cloth, or toiled in other ways for wages from the Company or an Indian merchant, lived farther off, including in Washermanpet.

Portuguese control over San Thome was shaky. To British alarm, the Dutch seized it for a while. Later, Golconda asserted its dominion over San Thome. But Aurangzeb was pressing hard into the Deccan, and in 1687, after he had conquered Ahmednagar and Bijapur, Golconda fell to him.

Just prior to Golconda's fall, Chinna Venkatadri, who was Thimmanna's younger brother and one of Madras's leading merchants, had rented San Thome from Madananta Pantulu, the Golconda kingdom's Brahmin governor for a region that included Madras.[28]

The Fort's confidential records refer to its Indian agents and spies in Golconda and in the camp, about 100 miles southwest of Madras, of the Mughal commander Zulfiqar Khan, who from the late 1680s was laying siege to the Maratha-occupied Gingee Fort that sat like a crown on three hills joined at the top.

There is, for instance, mention of 'the Brahmin who superintended the affairs of the English at the court of Golconda',[29] while 'letters received weekly from the spy Brahmin at the Camp (at Gingee) claimed that the French and the Portuguese continue their solicitations...' 'Our spy Brahmin at the camp...' is referred to, but the loyalty of 'Narrain the spy Brahmin' is questioned.[30]

Marching south via Golconda, where he sought the sultan's alliance, Shivaji had captured Gingee in 1677 from the Bijapur Sultanate. Fort St George noted that the Maratha ruler had 'passed close to Madras on his way to the capture of Gingee'.[31] Shivaji's brother, Rajaram, escaped from the Gingee stronghold before the Mughals finally took it in 1698, following a prolonged siege.

◆

Despite shake-ups across South India, Fort St George had expanded. Here is a description of life in its early years, the 1640s:

> Members of the Council rode about in bullock bandies (carts), and the guards of the President were armed with bows and arrows, swords and shields... [G]entlemen wore large hose doublets,

preposterous breeches and hats with conical crowns and bunches of feathers... [L]adies, very few in number, wore long-waisted stomachers and powerfully starched ruffs...

[T]he Fort was...a fortified Factory in which the Factors and Merchants bought and sold; all took their meals together, attended daily prayers, and lived like a little brotherhood...who, but for the attractions of burnt wine, punch, native beauty and occasional quarrels...lived sober and God-fearing lives.[32]

The Fort saw a military hospital emerge in 1664 and a bank in 1683. On 30 December 1687, under the governorship of Elihu Yale (whose subsequent donation would give Yale University its name), a Royal Charter established the Madras Corporation, the first city body to be set up in India. Three Indians were among the twelve aldermen named to the body: Chinna Venkatadri, Mudda Viranna (probably related to Kasi), and the previously mentioned Alangatha Pillai.

In 1692, the Company was authorized by Prince Kam Baksh, one of Aurangzeb's sons, to mint gold mohurs and silver rupees in Fort St George. Through negotiations with the Marathas who in 1674 had captured the throne of Thanjavur, Yale also secured trading and settlement rights for the Company in Porto Novo (Parangipettai) and Cuddalore on the east coast, considerably to the south of Madras.[33]

Immediately to the north of Cuddalore, Yale built Fort St David, a sanctuary which would give the Company a toehold in India in 1746, when the French threw the English out of Fort St George.

In January 1693, Nathaniel Higginson, Yale's successor as Governor of Madras, wrote to Aurangzeb that the English had placed their dependence on him and were praying for a favourable firman.[34] In consequence, the Mughal court in Delhi, rather than someone in a southern seat of influence, authorized a grant to the Company of Tondiarpet, Purasawalkam and Egmore, 'villages' central to Madras city in the future.

So in the seventeen-year period between 1676 and 1693, *four* different authorities, the Sultan of Golconda, Prince Kam Baksh, the Marathas of Thanjavur and Emperor Aurangzeb, leased lands in South India to the East India Company, which in 1639 had obtained the Fort St George strip from a *fifth* authority, the Raja of Chandragiri, a Vijayanagara descendant.

The East India Company was beginning to look like a stable island in a volatile sea.

◆

By the 1690s, a beautiful building of brick, polished lime and teak had emerged in Fort St George, St Mary's Church, which remains one of South India's finest and most evocative structures.

To the horror of some of the Fort's British residents, a Catholic church for meeting the needs of a significant Portuguese population had come up before St Mary's was built. A few Armenians, too, were allowed within the Fort, as also a handful of Jewish traders, who exported diamonds to England and imported silver.

The Armenians were resourceful enough to secure, from India's Muslim rulers, a few trading monopolies and the right to travel for trade into interior India. These Armenians owned ships that went as far out to sea as Manila in the Philippines, used Danish ships to trade with Europe and Persia (Iran), and kept offices in Madras city, in the coastal town of Nagapattinam, and in the interior city of Srirangapatna in the Kannada country.[35]

But travel was hard, even within Madras city. Those who could ride hired ponies. 'Pegu' ponies, imported from pre-colonial Burma, were prized for their stamina. Those with money could also hire palanquins. Usually eight palanquin bearers, four porters and two torchbearers accompanied a palanquin, which sometimes came with a portable hookah.[36]

For years after Fort St George had been created, Madras had no pier or harbour. Arriving sailing ships dropped anchor some distance from the shore, and passengers were transferred first to masula-boats made from timber-planks tied together by coir created from coconut fibre, and then, for the final yards of surf, onto 'the backs of sturdy fishermen'.[37]

After a six-month voyage from England (during which passengers could not have bathed) ladies apparently landed in Madras in 'mountainous flouncy skirts, many petticoats beneath', and men in 'tight trousers, top hats, starched collars that reached high up their cheeks, and the inevitable waistcoats'.[38]

While we thus have a picture of what South India's tiny European minority may have looked like in the seventeenth century, individual Indians of that period, whether merchants, weavers, dyers, fishermen or whatever, must be imagined almost wholly from scratch.

However, nuggets of information have been excavated from literature. In their joint 1992 study, *Symbols of Substance,* the previously mentioned trio, Rao, Shulman and Subrahmanyam, translate a Sanskrit poem, written by an orthodox Srivaishnava Tamil Brahmin named Venkatadhvarin, which describes mid-seventeenth-century southern India from the vantage point of gandharvas (heavenly beings) who 'fly' into several places.

One of these is Madras. Through his gandharvas, the poet finds it to be a 'populated city filled with evil' whose 'Hunas, devoid of all virtue', 'treat Brahmins with contempt' and 'care nothing for rules of purity'.[39] The poem goes on to say that the Hunas (its term for European merchants) 'punish offenders in their own manner, according to rule'.

The last clause, 'according to rule', is significant, as we will shortly see.

The three scholars note the poet's wide range and his awareness that politics is intertwined with language, religion and caste. The Tamil world shown in the poem is governed by numerous nayakas and is exposed to 'the Andhra, Karnata and Maharashtra' spheres of influence, 'which impinge upon the far south with very real political and military pressures'.

Turushkas or Yavanas (the word Muslim is not used in the poem) are seen as desecrators of shrines, but the poem concedes that they 'have an unparalleled claim to the virtue of heroism'.

The poem also says that 'in every village the Sudra lives like a lord, while at his side the Brahmin turned into a servant recites his accounts' or 'is scouring someone's dirty pots'—he is an account-keeper or a pot-washing cook. According to the scholars, the poem portrays a 'Nayaka ideology of Sudra pride and Sudra power', but the poet seems troubled by that pride and power.

Rao, Shulman and Subrahmanyam present another Tamil folktale, 'The Subahdar of the Cot', written by one Natesa Sastri at the end of the seventeenth century or the start of the eighteenth, which acknowledges Mughal Delhi 'as the ultimate power-centre, even vis-à-vis Tanjavur' and sees Tamil Nadu as descending from 'the Vijayanagara state-system'.[40]

Thus, apart from an oral tradition, there also existed, in different South Indian languages, at least a small body of written work penned on paper, palm leaves or copper plates. This was evidently true even in the sixteenth century. Moreover, there were South Indians before the European arrival who wrote in several languages and translated from one to the other.[41]

This suggests that the bilingual or multilingual dubashes linked to places like Fort St George were only following an established tradition. They added up to a network of South Indians of different linguistic, caste and religious backgrounds who at times worked in the same court of an Indian prince or for the same European company.

A British civil servant, Samuel Charles Hill, would later write of 'the facility with which natives of southern India acquire foreign languages'.[42] Hill was referring to the eighteenth century but the remark may have also applied to the seventeenth.

How important was linguistic identity in the seventeenth century or earlier? According to Cynthia Talbot, a student of medieval Andhra, 'At least at the level of elite cultural practice, there was a clear consciousness of affiliation with one regional language rather than another and even a certain degree of pride.'[43]

Another well-regarded scholar of India's languages and regions, Sheldon Pollock, offers a seemingly contrary view: 'There is no evidence whatever for linguism in South Asia before modernity... People were simply bearers of language, they were not defined by language.'[44]

Clearly, there were linguistic regions where one language predominated. Yet many migrated to regions where theirs was not the main language. There were a few 'cusp' areas: the Kanyakumari region containing Tamils and Malayalis; Palakkad in the Malayalam country where many Tamil Brahmins had moved from Thanjavur in the sixteenth century if not earlier; the Mangalore region where Tulu, Kannada and Konkani were spoken; the Bellary area containing Kannadigas and Telugu speakers; around Tirupati, where three languages were heard (Telugu, Kannada and Tamil); Nellore where Tamil speakers lived close to Telugu speakers; and so forth.

No doubt people felt more at ease amidst people speaking their language, but was 'linguism' a political sentiment? We do not know. In any case, an area's ruler frequently spoke a language different from that of its majority.

◆

We may look at two other broad pictures of the period. Citing Subrahmanyam, Cynthia Talbot suggests that agrarian settlement and demographic increase led to a large growth of trade in the sixteenth and seventeenth centuries,[45] the very period when European companies strove for factory rights in South Indian ports.

Within India, goods were transported by bullock cart, by pack bullocks, or as human headloads. Pack bullocks negotiated difficult terrain better than carts, and a herder guided pack bullocks moving in herds to graze and feed their hunger from the ground they treaded.[46]

Guns, horses and New World crops like tobacco and chillies, quickly adopted and accepted as indigenous, were among the major imports.

◆

By 1687, Madras city had a population of around 300,000![47] Some newcomers were Muslims evidently drawn to the city by Mughal victories over the Deccan's sultans.[48] Hindus, Muslims and Armenians invested money with the English in Fort George, all of whom were involved in private trade. Large profits were quickly made by many Britons and Indians.

But racial separation was complete. Two hundred years later (in 1886), Talboys Wheeler would write of the 1680s:

Within forty years of the building of the British factory, Madras was the pride and glory of the East India Company. Fort St. George, or White Town, was a European city in miniature. The primitive factory in the centre was replaced by a stately mansion with a dome, which was known as the Governor's House, but included a town hall, a council-chamber and sundry offices. It was seated in an open square, having a strong wall along each of its sides...and bastions at each corner mounted with cannon. Outside the fortification were little streets, paved with pebbles, containing about fifty European houses...

The whole of White Town was environed by an outer wall, sufficiently fortified to keep off an Indian army. None but Britons, or Europeans under British protection, were permitted to reside in White Town. The garrison consisted of two companies of European soldiers, and a large number of native guards, who were known as peons.[49]

The seventeenth-century trade conducted from Fort St George included trafficking in slavery. Issued under instructions from London, a Fort order of 18 September 1683 is revealing (italics added):

> There being *a great number of slaves* yearly exported from this place, to the great grievance of many persons whose children are *very commonly privately stolen away* from them, by those who are *constant traders in this way*, the Agent and Council, considering the great scandal that might accrue to the Government, and the great loss that many parents may undergo...have ordered that no more slaves be sent off the shore again.[50]

Dealing with Mughal rule became a major challenge for the masters of Fort St George, whose strategy was to profess great respect for the Great Mughal, acknowledge his paramountcy over India, and yet claim that the transfer of land from the Raja of Chandragiri remained valid and had no end date. As far as they were concerned, the territory of Fort St George belonged to the English monarch.

Their confidence was half feigned but also half real. The latter part stemmed from the sea in front of the Fort, the ships anchored there, and the guns they possessed. If push came to shove, they would fight their way to the safety of their boats and try to sail away to their faraway home.

Joined to this trust in a precarious escape route was the encouraging knowledge that Indians around Fort St George were showing them respect. Some of this respect was for European guns.

> Men like Sir Edward Winter and Mr. Streynsham Master [two of the Fort's seventeenth-century chiefs] could see very plainly what Clive and Dupleix saw sixty years later, that an exhibition of force was necessary in all dealings with natives. [They were willing to] display...Anglo-Saxon pluck in [an] hour of danger.[51]

Respect was also being gained, however, by what may be described as 'a rule of law' visible in Fort St George and in some other European establishments. Guns backed this rule of law and large profits financed it, yet it existed.

For all the private trade briskly carried on by every Company official, including presidents of Fort St George (a diamond that Thomas

Pitt, president from 1698 to 1709, bought at a small price from a Golconda jeweller was afterwards sold by him to the regent of France for 135,000 sterling),[52] and for all the bitter rivalry among the officials, the word of London, which arrived regularly by boat (in an envelope sealed more than six months earlier) was, it seems, always accepted throughout the Fort's career, even if, for example, that word asked the president opening the envelope to resign.

Though ambitious and money-loving men officered Fort St George, from the start they referred to their set-up as a 'government'; and they governed the territory on the Company's behalf and in the king's name. To Indian associates and employees in Black Town, and elsewhere in Madras, the Britons of the East India Company seemed to belong to a system with rules, which is what the Brahmin poet Venkatadhvarin, critical of the 'Hunas' of Fort St George, was conceding.

These rules were, indeed, being constantly broken, except for the one of obeying London, but punishment often followed. Indians were impressed and became eager to work for the Company.

In bygone Vijayanagara times, Mylapore belonged to a remote periphery, and Hampi, situated in an imposing hinterland in what today would be called North Karnataka, was South India's capital. In the 1670s, it looked as if a city rapidly growing on the shores of the Bay of Bengal would become South India's centre.

That divide-and-rule could consolidate its early gains was quickly realized by the Company. The faultlines of South Indian society were not concealed in the seventeenth century: even half-opened eyes could notice tensions between Hindus and Muslims, Brahmins and non-Brahmins, and the so-called left-hand and right-hand castes. Variously explained, this last divide perplexed the British but did not endure, except in some parts.

In 'about 1676', when an unnamed Indian told a Company officer, Dr Fryer, 'that the antagonism [between the so-called 'hands'] was planned by the Brahmans to keep the lower castes in subjection',[53] Fryer and his colleagues would have absorbed the hint. If the cards were rightly played, a long period of British rule was possible.

◆

We noted earlier that Madras's Armenian merchants kept an office in Srirangapatna in Kannada country. In the last quarter of the seventeenth century, Mysore, comprising much of the Kannada plateau and rich in forests, sandalwood and elephants, was ruled by Chikka Devaraja, successor to Vijayanagara vassals who had become independent kings following that empire's decline.

Not possessing a coastline, Devaraja, who had extended the boundaries of his kingdom, faced no European trading companies, but he had to cope with the southward expansion by land of the Mughals and the Marathas. To give himself room, Devaraja tried to advance towards the Arabian Sea, but the chiefs of Kodagu (Coorg) and the Keladi rulers of Ikkeri in coastal Kannada country blocked him.

By the end of the century, the Mughals had procured Mysore as a tributary. Devaraja sent an embassy to Aurangzeb and received an ivory crown as an emblem of Mysore's autonomy, which was aided by continuing Maratha pressure. Playing the Marathas against the Mughals, Devaraja, 'a shrewd politician' and a 'consummate warrior', exercised a fair degree of independence.[54]

◆

Kerala, the Malayalam country, was another story. It was on a narrow belt by the Arabian Sea that the Malayalis lived. From Kerala's southernmost point, the Bay of Bengal, too, was not all that far. Situated at the tail end of any north–south invasion route, protected also by mountains and blessed with numerous streams flowing westwards from the hills to the sea, the green land of the Malayalis was never annexed by a sultan or emperor living in Delhi.

But Malayalis saw sails ominously expand on their western horizon. After Vasco da Gama's 1498 visit, Portuguese ships called regularly in the sixteenth and seventeenth centuries, and rival Dutch ships appeared from the beginning of the seventeenth century. Long-lasting rivalry between the Zamorin of Kozhikode and the Raja of Kochi eased European entry.

The Malayalam country had for long entertained an indigenous Christian presence, possibly from the first century onwards, as also a respectable numbers of Jews. A ninth-century copper plate, identified in the nineteenth century and written in Old Malayalam, evidently speaks of a bishop, a trader and a sailor from outside, all of them clearly Christian, who were given land and shelter. Warehousing and fortification followed, a pattern replicated centuries later by European trading companies.[55]

Part of the Indian subcontinent, Kerala was always also a province of the world, an image the poet Balamani Amma (1909–2004) would later seek to convey through a provocative upside-down portrait of a Malayali woman with her back to India, face towards the Arab world, and feet towards northern India. A calmer, if also evocative, simile for Kerala is a banana leaf spread out before a hill.[56]

The ocean and the hills did not wholly explain Kerala's distinctiveness. The sea was not a barrier to movement, and mountains had passes. It was the abundance of water and its availability in diverse places—not, as in other parts of South India, only from a single village well—that made a Kerala village different.[57]

Unlike most villages in the Kannada, Tamil and Telugu countries, a typical Malayali village contained dispersed settlements that were never abandoned. Malayalis had no need to go elsewhere in search of water. How to get rid of excess water was generally the challenge.[58]

To continue in metaphors, the Kerala terrain encountered by arriving Portuguese consisted of three adjoining ribbons that ran parallel to the hills and the coast. There was a hilly, eastern strip where spices were grown and the tribals lived. Next to it, along the valley, was a middle ribbon where lower-caste tenants or labourers grew a prestigious crop—rice—on lands owned by Nambudiri Brahmins who had obtained these as gifts from rajas.

The third strip, running along the coast, was where Syrian Christians, Jews, Muslims, Gujaratis and Chettis lived, trading with Malayalis, with one another, and with the world. These immigrant communities filled the merchant's role, for there seemed to be no Malayali trader caste.[59]

But Kerala's seemingly uniform topography was accompanied by political fragmentation. Rivers flowing into the Arabian Sea, often bringing spices from the hills, divided the land into numerous pockets ruled by autonomous rajas. Flooding rivers made it impossible for horses to cross, or for one ruler to control more than his area.[60]

Many local rulers made room in their coastal tracts for immigrants, whether Christian, Jew or Arab.[61] Immigrating groups were considered additional jaatis, not parties in a religious contestation. Thus the eighteenth century would even see a Nasrani (Christian) Jaati Aikya Sangha.[62]

◆

Malayalis had been observing ships for centuries, mostly Arab dhows and a few Turkish sailing ships too, but those earlier boats were smaller than the ones now arriving under a European flag. Moreover, earlier sailors did not set up forts on the Kerala coast or carry cannons.

The Hindu Zamorin's old friendship with Arabs and local Muslims was an obstacle to the Portuguese, who, influenced by the Crusades, seemed opposed to Islam and its adherents. Kozhikode's Muslim warriors, the Kunhali Marakkars, gained fame in the sixteenth century by creating a navy with which the Zamorin fought the Portuguese.

But the real fight was over Kerala's pepper, in which the Arabs had traded for ages. Eventually, the Portuguese won the fight and captured the spice trade, and the Zamorin made his peace with them.

From the start a Portuguese ally, the Kochi raja enabled them to build, in the sixteenth century's opening decades, a strong fort in Kochi, where a Portuguese viceroy, no less, reigned. Other Portuguese fortresses followed up and down the coast.

Kerala's local Christians did not impress the Portuguese, who disapproved of the Syrian or West Asian branches of Orthodox Christianity to which the locals belonged. New churches submitting to the Pope in Rome were built by the Portuguese.

If seventeenth-century Kerala was distinctive in South India because of its Christian, Muslim and Jewish numbers (including so-called Black Jews, perhaps born to local women) its majority Hindus also appeared to differ from Hindu communities elsewhere in the South.

Prohibitions imposed on lower castes and 'untouchables' seemed harsher in Kerala than in other places, yet Hindus from many castes, including the lowest, appeared to subscribe to the legend that the Malayalam country belonged to Parasurama, mythical restorer of Brahmin rule and Vishnu's axe-wielding incarnation, but also, and more importantly, the hero who reclaimed the Malayali land from the ocean.

Despite the unique status they gave to Vishnu's incarnation, Siva seemed the more popular god of the Malayalis, to note another paradox. It seemed that Kerala's Ezhavas, to whom some ascribed a Sri Lankan origin, did not affirm a link with Parasurama, but everyone appeared to accept the caste hierarchy, where Nambudiri Brahmins were placed at the top.

◆

Though Portuguese merchant-soldiers remained for long in Kerala, they did not strike permanent roots. After a series of seventeenth-century fights, the Dutch, backed by groups of Malayalis, became the dominant European force in the Malayalam country, edging out the Portuguese, who, too, had local supporters. The climax was a bitter 1662–63 battle ending with the Dutch capture of Kochi and its fort.

The mostly Protestant Dutch enjoyed, in comparison with the Portuguese, an easier relationship with Kerala's Syrian Christians. They also seemed more tolerant towards Hindu Malayalis.

The Netherlands' affairs in India and Sri Lanka, which also saw substantial Dutch involvement, were managed by the Vereenigde Oostindische Compagnie, or United East India Company, from Batavia, as Jakarta was known until the twentieth century. The company was capable of looking beyond markets. Between 1686 and 1703, Dutch and Indian scholars associated with it produced in Amsterdam, twelve volumes on plants grown in the land of the Malayalis that amaze us even today.[63]

Well aware of the Malayalam country, and wanting to lay hands on it, the British East India Company announced its stake in 1695 by building a coastal fort in Anjengo (Attingal), only a few miles north of modern Thiruvananthapuram.

◆

Also on the coast but well to the north of the Malayalam country, north also of Mangaluru and the rest of the Tulu region, was Port Goa, which the Portuguese had seized early in the sixteenth century from the Adilshahis of the Bijapur Sultanate.

With the Portuguese controlling the Arabian Sea, including the strategic Gulf port of Hormuz, and forbidding ships from sailing in its waters without a Portuguese cartaz or licence, Goa quickly developed into a lively European colony.

Emerging also as Christianity's eastern centre and the capital of Portuguese in India, the city evidently saw its population grow in the 1540s to the 200,000 mark. But bigotry linked to the Inquisition in Europe raised its head in Goa. Many Hindus and Muslims fled, taking the Konkani language further south along the western coast.

As in Kerala, in Goa, too, the Dutch challenged the Portuguese. This pressure early in the seventeenth century from another European power brought relief to the Adilshahis, who ruled their sultanate from Bijapur (now in northern Karnataka), which lay inland about 200 miles northeast of Goa, and whose control over other west coast ports was threatened by the Portuguese.

Though able to fend off the Dutch in Goa, the Portuguese were obliged to sign a treaty with the Adilshahis, who provided many seamen for Portuguese ships.

The Adilshahis built extraordinary monuments in Bijapur, where Kannada flourished alongside Persian. In the early part of the seventeenth century, an Iranian scholar residing there, Abul Qasim 'Firishta', wrote a history of India's dynasties to which scholars continue to turn.

But a plague that followed Aurangzeb's conquest in the late 1680s destroyed much of Bijapur, eliminated innumerable residents, including Aurangzeb's wife, and removed all traces of where someone like Firishta might have lived.

Adilshahi decline had begun before the plague. Shivaji, son of an Adilshahi chieftain, rebelled, rose to become the Maratha king in 1674, and captured several ports from the sultanate. While Portuguese control continued over Goa, where impressive churches were built, the city was ravaged by malaria, cholera and plague, and the population fell to a few thousands by the end of the century.

◆

Another major power was the Golconda Sultanate, which took its name from the city and fort of Golconda, about 200 miles east of Bijapur and equidistant between the Arabian Sea and the Bay of Bengal. Golconda's diamond mines were fabled worldwide.

Like the Adilshahis of Bijapur, Golconda's rulers, the Qutbshahis, were successors to the large Bahmani kingdom of earlier times. As was also true of the Adilshahis, many Qutbshahis were Shia. In the 1560s, Golconda, Bijapur and other Bahmani successors joined hands to end the Vijayanagara kingdom. In 1591, Golconda's Qutbshahi ruler, Muhammad Quli, marked the end of a plague epidemic by building the famed Char Minar Mosque about 5 miles east of Golconda Fort, and naming Hyderabad, the mosque's location, as his new capital.

Telugu was Golconda's official language and one of the languages in which Quli wrote his poems, the other being the Urdu-related Dakkani or Dakhni. 'Administrative and revenue papers at local levels in the Qutbshahi Sultanate were prepared largely in Telugu', while the last Qutbshahi sultan, Abul Hasan 'Tana Shah', often 'issued his orders only in Telugu'.[64]

The existence of the Deccan sultanates was a standing affront to Mughal pride. By acknowledging Mughal suzerainty, the sultanates had averted an invasion. But in the 1680s first Bijapur, and then Golconda, submitted to Aurangzeb's forces, in each case after a prolonged siege.

Throughout the sixteenth and seventeenth centuries, arriving European interests had to reckon with Golconda. After the Qutbshahis were eliminated by the Mughals in 1687, European companies in South India's ports and cities had to negotiate with Mughal officers assigned to Golconda or with their agents.

One of the east coast's oldest ports, frequented in earlier centuries by Arab traders and in the seventeenth century by Portuguese, Dutch, British and French ships (mainly for the region's textiles) was Machilipatnam (Masulipatam). This was where the Krishna River, starting near the west coast and journeying across the peninsula, entered the Bay of Bengal. Golconda held sway over this port city.

The language spoken around Machilipatnam was Telugu, which was also true of Golconda, even though the ruling class spoke Hindustani or Dakhni. Because of Machilipatnam's trade and its value to Golconda, Muhammad Quli had named Char Minar's eastern gate after this port city.

After seizing it from the Qutbshahis and controlling it for about a dozen years, the Portuguese left Machilipatnam in 1610. The British East India Company built a fort there in 1611, but by the 1630s the

Company had decided to make Madras its principal base.

The Mughals' southern successes in the last quarter of the century did not hurt the European companies. An empire directed from a distant capital was easier to deal with than a sturdy local chiefdom like that of the Qutbshahis.

The Telugu country stretched north from Machilipatnam to and beyond the coastal city of Vishakhapatnam (Vizag), which was held until the 1680s by Golconda and later by the Mughals, and south towards Pulicat and Madras.

Populations south of Madras generally spoke Tamil, including in the ports of Nagapattinam and Thoothukudi, which also witnessed the Portuguese/ Dutch/ British sequence.

◆

In the latter part of the seventeenth century, the nayaka lands of the Tamil country were penetrated by Indian forces marching a fair distance from their homes. These soldiers belonged to Shivaji's Marathas or to the Adilshahis of Bijapur, to whom Shivaji's father Shahaji had been a feudatory.

In 1674, the throne of Thanjavur, for long the gateway to the rich delta of the Kaveri and the seat of the ancient Cholas, was captured from its nayaka occupant by Shivaji's Bhonsle kinsmen, who arrived as Bijapur's agents. Shaking off their Adilshahi employers, the Bhonsles would keep the Thanjavur throne for more than a century and patronize an impressive development in the arts.

Controlling the trading port of Nagapattinam, which linked the delta to the Moluccas (Maluku islands) and other resource-rich parts of southeast Asia, Thanjavur was a major prize. A nayaka dynasty continued to rule over Trichy, which lay to Thanjavur's west, and another over Madurai, historic seat of the Pandian kingdom, which was situated south of both.

Madurai had witnessed another sort of entry from without when the Italian Jesuit, Roberto de Nobili, preached Christianity there for some years. Unlike other European priests who stressed Christianity's principle of equality before Hindu society's lowest castes, de Nobili aimed at the higher castes.

'Exchang[ing] his priestly garb for the robe of a Brahmin sanyasi and adopt[ing] the sanyasi's rigorous lifestyle and dietary customs', he presented himself as 'a Roman aristocrat' to Madurai's Brahmin pandits. Studying Hinduism's sacred scriptures in both Tamil and Sanskrit, de Nobili debated 'on equal terms with the city's pandits' and made a notable impact.[65]

South of Madurai, in the Ramanathapuram (Ramnad) territory ruled by the Setupati of Ramnad, the success in 1692 of another European Jesuit, John de Britto, in converting to Christianity four 'poligars', including the head of the warrior Maravas of Siruvalli, resulted in the priest's execution by the setupati's order.[66]

Used widely for a local chief, 'poligar' was Europeanized from the Kannada palegara, the Telugu palegadu and the Tamil palaiyakkarar. A poligar commanded a palaiyam, Tamil for a military camp or fort, and often also the territory surrounding it.

South India in the seventeenth century's second half was thus a site where numerous local chiefs, and forces spanning wider areas—the Mughals, Marathas, Adilshahis and Qutbshahis —and the Europeans (chiefly Dutch and British) battled for control. By now confined to Goa and its satellites on the west coast, the Portuguese, who had abandoned Kerala earlier, had been pushed out of the Bengal delta as well by Aurangzeb.

◆

From the 1660s, the multi-party contest for South India was joined also by the French. While the English and Dutch trading companies had been formed in 1600 and 1602, respectively, it was only several decades later—and in tandem with François Bernier's service at the Mughal court—that the French East India Company emerged.

The first French factory in India was set up in Surat in 1668. A year later, another rose in Machilipatnam. Four years thereafter, in 1673, the French acquired a coastal area about 100 miles south of Madras called Pondicherry (Puducherry).

With whom did the French negotiate for this 'fishing village', as it was described at the time? With nearby Valikondapuram's qiladar or fort-controller, who was an agent/officer of the weakening Adilshahi Sultan of Bijapur.

The Bijapur sultan was thus the *sixth* ruler in southern India with whom a foreign company negotiated for land in the seventeenth century: earlier, we had counted five different authorities who granted land to the British. In 1674, François Martin, the first governor of the 'fishing village', launched projects to raise there the flourishing port town of Pondicherry.

The period was turbulent. On land, the Mughals were marching to crush the Deccan sultanates. On the west coast, Shivaji was seizing Bijapur's ports. South of Pondicherry, his kinsmen were capturing Thanjavur towards the east coast. Along both shores of the peninsula, European forces were jockeying against one another.

It could not have been a great surprise when, in 1693, the Dutch captured Pondicherry from the French. A realignment in Europe intervened, however, and in 1697, by the Treaty of Ryswick, the French received Pondicherry back from the Dutch.

Chapter 2

CANNONS ON THE GROUND: 1700–1761

As South Indians entered the eighteenth century, the curious among them, including outsiders in their midst, may have tried to imagine the years that lay ahead. A local dubash in Golconda, or a Gujarati trader in Madras (there were a few of these before the year 1700),[1] a European missionary in the hinterland (there were some of them too), a Dutch merchant on the Malabar coast (also present and visible), or someone else on the peninsula may have wondered about the future.

Aurangzeb was past eighty but alive. Under him, the Mughals had crushed the Deccan sultanates and added new territories and numbers to their empire. European companies were soliciting his favours.

Our nameless visualizer in the year 1700 may have expected the Mughal grip to tighten and, Shivaji having died in 1680, the Maratha eruption to subside. In the coastal contest among Europeans, he or she might have predicted a tussle between the British and the Dutch, for the latter had secured their presence in the Malayalam country and in Sri Lanka.

However, history rolled out differently. First, Mughal power weakened and, by the 1740s, the Marathas were energized. Second, instead of an Anglo–Dutch rivalry, the sixty-year period covered by this chapter witnessed a roller-coaster battle between the French and the British.

Third, the period saw the emergence, at times through alliance with Europeans, of a few powerful local individuals. Finally, towards this period's end, Europeans widened their nets beyond trade and their control beyond the coast: they started to extract revenue from South Indian land.

◆

In early 1702, Aurangzeb sent Nawab Daud Khan Panni, his Afghanorigin subahdar of the Carnatic,* to besiege and blockade Fort St George. Three months later, after Governor Thomas Pitt** sued for peace, the siege was lifted.

Daud Khan's siege, during which the city was plundered, is described in *Annals of the Madras Presidency, 1639–1702,* written by Talboys Wheeler, a nineteenth-century British East India Company officer. Backed by elephants, horses and a threatening entourage, the subahdar had visited the fort before the siege. Wheeler informs us that Daud Khan posed a question to the 'Moollah' employed by the Fort: if the British 'were merchants, what need had [they] of such a Fortification and so many Guns?'

In discussions during the siege, Pitt argued that the Company was assisting 200,000 Mughal subjects; its income, he claimed, was being generated by benevolent rule. He would record on 4 February 1702:

> As to our revenues, we ordered our Moollah to tell [Daud Khan] they were only raised upon our own people, and such acquired considerable fortunes in our service; and that we are ready to demonstrate not only that we daily give subsistence to at least two hundred thousand subjects of the Mogul, but that there also arose yearly by the trade of the place a vast sum to the King's treasury; and whereas we imported a great amount of silver and gold, we exported nothing but the produce of the country and the labour of his people.[2]

Pitt and his British associates did not realize it at the time, but the empire on whose behalf Daud Khan had shown up was beginning to decline. Not only would Aurangzeb's successors prove less resolute than him, the empire they inherited was also overstretched and overburdened. A heavy toll had been taken by Aurangzeb's Deccan wars, in which, along with thousands of elephants, horses, and soldiers, entire tent-

---

*Muslim armies first entering the South in the thirteenth century came across Karnataka and thought of the entire south as 'the Carnatic'. Following suit, Europeans later employed 'the Carnatic' for the whole of the Tamil country plus the Telugu district of Nellore. See C. Hayavadana Rao, (ed.), *Mysore Gazetteer,* Vol. 1, Bangalore, 1926, p. 256.
**William Pitt the Elder (1708–1778) and his son William Pitt the Younger (1759–1806), both prime ministers of Britain, were related to this Thomas Pitt.

cities were required to move from one theatre of war to another in the peninsula's vastness.

The expensive successes of Aurangzeb, who died in 1707, redrew the political map of South India. Golconda became a top-tier Mughal province with a viceroy called the nizam; its capital, Hyderabad, was named the chief city of Mughal South India. Other Telugu zones under Mughal control or suzerainty included the 'Circars', districts washed by the Bay of Bengal, and interior 'Karnul' and 'Kurpa' (Cuddapah or Kadapa).

In the Kannada country, a new province called Sira was created in what today, roughly speaking, would be Central Karnataka. South of Sira, Devaraja's Mysore was labelled a Mughal tributary. To Mysore's west lay tracts governed by Hindu chiefs, where Tulu was among the languages spoken. Some of these tracts extended to the Arabian Sea.

The Tamil area south and east of Mysore was declared a Mughal province—in theory answerable to Golconda—and called 'Carnatic' or 'Arcot', the latter after the city selected as its Mughal-controlled capital. Now an important town, Arcot attracted many, including 'European vagabonds and Jesuits'.[3]

Today we know where Karnataka is, but in 1700 and for a century or more thereafter it was the Tamil country that was called 'the Carnatic', while Kannada-speakers lived in three tracts: 'Mysore', Mughal-administered 'Sira', and Hindu-governed 'Bednor', which embraced the Arabian Sea.

Coorg or Kodagu was a separate political unit (under a Hindu chief), with a language of its own, as was Portuguese-run Goa, where Konkani was a prominent language. The Malayalam country, which included Malabar and Cochin, had several Hindu rulers, and a new political space called Travancore was emerging.

Ere long the Marathas would foray again into Telugu, Kannada and Tamil lands, but for a while they lost ground in South India. Gingee Fort, their possession from 1677, was yielded to the Mughals in 1698. In 1707 Daud Khan defeated the Marathas at Vellore Fort and the town close to it, Arcot—sites the Marathas had taken from the Adilshahis in 1678.

Even after Aurangzeb had redrawn it, the South India map remained a changeable mosaic. As the new century progressed, Mughal governors in the south found it easier to ignore or even defy a weakening and remote Delhi, as was dramatically shown in Golconda, where Mir Qamaruddin, whose loyal service in the imperial capital had won for him the viceroyalty of the South, began in 1724 a kingship later referred to as Hyderabad's Asaf Jahi dynasty.

◆

Situated about 35 miles northwest of Pondicherry and about 75 miles southwest of Chennai, Gingee Fort may have originated in Chola times, perhaps in the ninth century. Strengthened by later occupants, including Vijayanagara nayakas and Shivaji, it has been called 'a site meant for a heroic stand' by the three authors of *Textures of Time*, an illuminating study containing, among other things, a 1714 story which has become part of Tamil folklore.

Few places in the world may be spelt as variously in English as Gingee. Versions employed include Chandi, Chenji, Jinji, Senchi and Senji, which last is the form adopted by the authors of *Textures*, who remind us that 'Senji' is 'one of the most melodramatic of all South Indian landscapes—a huge stony mountain rising out of the paddy fields and continuous with a neighbouring range of boulder-strewn hills and ridges'.

After Daud Khan had played his role over Fort St George, Saadatullah Khan became the chief Mughal officer in the Tamil country. He was called Nawab of the Carnatic or, at times, the Nawab of Arcot, a city lying 45 miles north of Gingee.

In 1714, claiming arrears of tribute, the nawab led an attack on Gingee Fort, held at the time by a young Bundela Rajput, Tej Singh, whose father was one of numerous Rajputs serving in the Mughal armies that marched to the South in the 1670s and 1680s.

Convinced that the Mughal emperor desired either his father, who had recently died, or himself to possess the fort, Tej Singh resisted Saadatullah Khan and his Arcot army, which included many Portuguese soldiers. Evidently, the Marathas remaining in the region backed Saadatullah's force.

Formidable research enables the authors of *Textures* to cite several accounts of the battle that ensued. Some depictions are from British, Dutch and French sources 'watching' the contest from their bases on the Coromandel coast. Others are from Marathi texts recovered about a century later in a South Indian project launched by a Company officer called Colin Mackenzie. There is, too, an undated Tamil poem 'restored from damaged palm-leaf' and probably composed in the eighteenth century, and a poem in Persian from an Arcot-based North Indian Brahmin, Jaswant Rai, who also wrote a biography of his master, Saadatullah Khan.

These different accounts allow us to glimpse the numerous languages, cultures and interests intersecting with one another in early eighteenth-century South India, a vignette as instructive as the story of the 1714 Battle of Gingee.

Almost all accounts quoted in *Textures*, whether of Indian or European origin, agree on the details of the final close encounter. Tej Singh gets his favourite horse to mount its forelegs on the forehead of the nawab's elephant and is about to lance the nawab to death, but the nawab's men standing beneath the elephant smash one hindleg of the horse, causing it to collapse to the ground, whereupon Tej Singh is killed.

A French report prepared at the time in Pondicherry and a contemporaneous British account penned in Fort St George offer the same core story of the climax. Tej Singh's alter ego and bosom friend, Mahabat Khan (Movuttakaran in Tamil), was also killed after a ferocious battle, as was the horse. All three, the horse included, received samadhis or graves in Gingee that attract visitors to this day.

Depending on who describes it, Tej Singh's heroic end is either a classic to-the-death defiance by a young, handsome, newly-married hero who spurns the wedding bed and nearly defeats the stronger enemy, or the tragic tale of an immature youth who rejects the option of a compromise that would have avoided destruction. The latter is what Jaswant Rai conveyed, but the people of the Gingee country, for whom Tej Singh is Desingu Raja, have been singing the former tale for up to three hundred years.[4]

We may mark that the year 1714 also saw the arrival, in a Protestant mission in Danish-held Tranquebar, of a small German-made printing press, southern India's first, plus a set of Tamil fonts, also cast in Germany.[5]

A year after Gingee's horse–elephant duel, a Frenchman in his teens, Joseph François Dupleix (1697–1763), landed in India on a vessel of the French East India Company. Five years later, in 1720, young Dupleix became a member of Pondicherry's Superior Council.

By 1742, Dupleix, an officer with a commanding physique, was the Governor of Pondicherry and Governor General of French India, which was starting to look extensive. Having acquired Chandernagore (Chandannagar) at about the time they leased Pondicherry (1673), the French had gone on to obtain Mahe on the Malabar coast in the 1720s; Yanam, a weaving town about 25 miles north of Machilipatnam on the Andhra coast, in 1731; and the port of Karaikal, south of Pondicherry, in the late 1730s.

Together with Ananda Ranga Pillai (1709–61), a Madras-born merchant who conducted his affairs in and from Pondicherry, where he also served as Dupleix's dubash and counsellor, the Frenchman formed what for the eighteenth century was an exceptional Indo-European duo.

Pillai's connection with Pondicherry was older than Dupleix's. In 1716, his father, Tiruvengada Pillai, a successful merchant in British-run Madras, had moved to the French settlement, where his brother-in-law was the chief Indian merchant. Seven-year-old Ananda Ranga Pillai moved too.

Much of what we know about Pillai comes from the uncommon diary he would write later, containing entries from 1736 to 1761, when he died, and from the introduction written for its 1904 publication in English by the Madras civil servant who translated the diary and researched Pillai's life, J. Frederick Price.

From Price's introduction, we learn that Ranga Pillai's merchant father traded on a large scale. 'The affairs of the [French] Company grew and prospered' from the time when Tiruvengada Pillai 'and five other wealthy and capable merchants' returned to Pondicherry after a time of absence.

The son exceeded the father's success. The 'large trading posts' that Ranga Pillai 'established at his own cost' in two inland cities (Arcot was one of them) 'were soon carrying on a brisk business in the exchange of European goods for the merchandise of the country' (1: viii).

Evidently able to speak Tamil, Telugu, Hindustani, French and

English, Ranga Pillai wrote his diary entries in Tamil 'in bound volumes of the size of large account books'. While most entries were hand-written, some were dictated.

It was years after his death that the 'account books' were discovered. Not all of them however—many had been lost. A French translation was published before the English. From the two translations, the world learnt what a talented South Indian saw and felt in the middle of the eighteenth century. Observed Price, more than a hundred years ago:

> It is very clear that [the diary] was never written with the slightest view to publication... It stands unique as a record of the inmost thoughts and reflections of an extremely able, level-headed Oriental, and of his criticisms—which at times are of the freest character—of his fellows and masters.
>
> His influence with M. Dupleix—which he apparently exercised honestly and with judgment—was very marked, and he was evidently treated by that great man with full trust in his integrity and capacity.
>
> He then became, amongst the natives—if not the Europeans also—the right-hand man of his illustrious master, and was in constant personal communication with him.

Simultaneously competing for the governor's attention, Pillai and Mme Dupleix (Jeanne Albert was the widow of a councillor of the French Company when she married the governor) found each other difficult. Mme Dupleix's keenness to promote Christianity was a major irritant.

A bigger challenge for Pillai had been the conversion to Christianity, in France, of his older cousin Guruva Pillai, whose father had been responsible for Tiruvengada's original move to Pondicherry. 'Made much of in France,' as Price puts it, and appointed not only 'a knight of St. Michael' but also 'head of the Indian subjects of the French' in Pondicherry, Guruva, however, died in Pondicherry in 1724, when Ranga was seventeen.

The acceptance of Christianity by another prominent Pondicherry merchant, Kanakaraya Mudali, was a factor in Ranga Pillai's long-standing rivalry with Mudali. Both desired proximity to the governor and the 'chief dubash' title. It was not until 1747 that Ranga Pillai, who had become Dupleix's confidant well before this, received the designation.

Pillai's diary entries for 23 May 1739 tell us how news of Nadir Shah's momentous invasion of northern India that year reached the South:

> M. Dupleix's ship, *Chandernagore*, arrived this day from Surat, and brought the following intelligence. [Nadir Shah], of the tribe of Iran, who was...the Shah of Persia, left Isfahan in 1738 with 60,000 cavalry...marched against Lahore...proved victorious... next marched against Delhi, captured the city, made the Emperor Muhammad Shah and the nobles prisoners...commanded that coins should be struck in his name...and that [the name] of Muhammad Shah should be obliterated from the current money.
>
> The Nawab of Surat was directed to suppress the coins struck by Muhammad Shah and to issue new ones bearing the legend, By the grace of God, Nadir Shah, Emperor
>
> This stunning news, says the diary, 'was made known by [Pondicherry's] Governor' at the time, Pierre Dumas. Another entry on the same day conveys news as received by Armenian merchants in Pondicherry: Nadir Shah has left for Persia, his son taking with him a daughter of the Delhi emperor as a wife, and that 'between 100,000 and 150,000 men and women have perished' in Delhi by the sword or by suicide.

According to the diary, the Armenians alleged that 'the Nizam (*of Hyderabad*) was secretly in league with the invader'.

Receiving word (we are not told how) from Delhi, persons in Surat relay it to the French in Pondicherry by a boat that goes down the long western coast of India before turning east and north up to the French settlement, with stops at several ports en route. Interestingly, the Armenian merchants of Pondicherry, also perhaps getting a report via the same ship, have newer information.

In 1739, men like Pillai, and governors like Dumas, must make what they can of news (originating months previously) that the mighty Mughal empire—a constant for all their lives—has fallen, and then of a correction that quickly follows: no, it has not fallen, only taken a near-fatal blow. They must also chew over the possibility that Nizam Asaf

Jah I, South India's chief lord, had clandestinely backed Nadir Shah.*
Whether European or Indian, persons in eighteenth-century South
India had to be ready each day for any contingency.

◆

In his diary dated 30 November 1745, Pillai comments on a feast given
by his rival Kanakaraya Mudali, probably the chief dubash at this
time, to celebrate the construction of a new church in Reddipalaiyam
village near Pondicherry.

'Brahmans, Vellazhas, Komutis, Chettis, goldsmiths, weavers, oil-
mongers and other castes' were invited, and Europeans as well, but
caste rules were strictly observed. Different kitchens prepared food
separately for the different castes, and one distinct kitchen served only
Europeans.

Conceding that the guests were pleased, Pillai nonetheless objects
to a Christian host making 'Hindu' differentiations while offering a
feast and adds:

> If [Kanakaraya Mudali] wished to conform to the rules of his
> church, and the commands of his scriptures, he should have
> entertained only the Europeans, Native Christians, Pariahs and
> such others (1: 293–94).

In other words, while Christians, whether foreign or native, and 'Pariahs'
could eat together, caste Hindus should not be mixed with them in a
common reception.

◆

Ten months later, in September 1746, Pillai told Dupleix—so we learn
from the diary—that verses recording the governor's feats were being
sung in the streets of Pondicherry, and that the emperor in Delhi, his
throne's prestige evidently restored seven years after the humiliation
inflicted by Nadir Shah, had heard of those feats.

Dupleix responded by telling Pillai, '*You* must have caused these
to be composed, and sung; for no others knew of these matters.' Pillai

---

*Asaf Jah I, who died in 1748, wrote in his last testament that he had spurned
an offer of Delhi's sultanate from Nadir Shah and that the latter had appreciated
his response. See Bawa, *Last Nizam*, p. 12.

did not dispute the remark (2: 315). The songs celebrated the French capture of Fort St George.

Dupleix was not the only Frenchman behind this dramatic takeover. In fact, it was the naval officer Mahé de la Bourdonnais (arriving from his command post at distant Mauritius, home to numerous French ships) who had quickly and without much of a fight obtained the British surrender in September 1746.

Events of this Anglo–French clash on the Coromandel coast were recorded by the British East India Company's historiographer, India-born Robert Orme (1728–1801). Serving on the Madras Council in the 1750s, Orme was a friend of another European officer for whom praises would soon be sung—Robert Clive, who first arrived in India in 1744.

In the 1760s and 1770s, Orme wrote his multi-volume *History of the Military Transactions of the British Nation in Indostan*. He informs us that on 3 September 1746, a French force of 1,100 Europeans, 400 'Caffres'* and '400 Indian natives, disciplined in the European manner', landed in Madras, while 1,800 European mariners remained on the ships that brought the force (Orme, 1: 67). On 10 September, the British, whose armies were smaller, surrendered.

That day, Orme informs us, a messenger riding a camel arrived in Pondicherry with a letter for Dupleix from the 'Nabob' of Arcot, Anwaruddin Khan, in which the nawab expressed 'great surprize at the presumption of the French in attacking Madras without his permission'. In response, Dupleix directed his unnamed agent in Arcot 'to pacify the Nabob' by promising that the French would give him Madras, which the nawab could sell back to the British 'for a large sum of money' (Orme, 1: 69).

But in Madras a separate negotiation with the British for ransoming Fort St George was being conducted by Bourdonnais, a gifted admiral who was 'capable', Orme tells us, 'of building a ship from the keel and of conducting her to any part of the globe' (73).

On the night of 2 October, however, a great storm destroyed six of the French ships berthed in Madras, causing Bourdonnais to sail

---

*'Originally the Coffrees were African slaves trained as soldiers, in which capacity they distinguished themselves by their steadiness and courage.' Hill, *Yusuf Khan*, p. 27fn. 'Caffre' or 'Coffre' is seen as a derogatory term.

back all the way to Mauritius, 'the arsenal of all the French military expeditions to India'. Writes Orme, 'The storm to which the French squadron had been exposed ruined the maritime force of that nation in India' (73).

Even so, Dupleix now had unchallenged control over France's men in India.

REVELATION

Three weeks after the storm, a fight took place near the Adyar River in Madras between a small French force and a much larger army of the nawab. Given the destruction of the French fleet and the 'great respect and humility with which [the French] had carried themselves in all their transactions with the Mogul government', the nawab had concluded that the French were weak.

He expected to seize Madras from them.

However, on 22 October the artillery of a small number of Frenchmen routed the nawab's soldiers, who were astonished that a cannon could 'fire five or six times a minute'. Their own cannon only 'fired once in a quarter of an hour'. Losing seventy of their fellows, the nawab's men rapidly retreated; not one Frenchman was killed (75).

Even if India came up with large numbers of soldiers, even if a Mughal emperor controlled most of India, Europe's superior cannons could prove decisive. This was the startling and, for Dupleix's French and for the British in India, promising revelation from the Adyar battle of 22 October 1746.

Two days later, the French defeated the nawab's forces in San Thome, where they had taken refuge, and forced them to march back all the way to Arcot. However, a bid by Dupleix to capture Fort St David near Cuddalore, where the British and the nawab's forces had joined hands, failed, but in 1748 he protected Pondicherry against a British siege.

ROBERT CLIVE (1725–1774)

Sixteen when he first arrived in Madras in 1744, Robert Clive was one of many Britons confined by the French when they took the city two years later. Cleverly escaping, Clive took part in the successful defence of Fort St David and the unsuccessful siege of Pondicherry and emerged as Dupleix's British challenger.

The two would resume their contest, but for the time being a 1749 treaty signed in Europe produced a truce in India: Fort St George and Madras were returned to the British in exchange for a French fort captured by the British in North America.

Another external force revived in the Tamil country were the Marathas. Swift on their horses, they had raced down in 1740, killed Dost Ali Khan (Saadatullah Khan's successor as the Arcot nawab) and prominent associates, taken possession of Arcot, and gone further south to capture the fort of Trichy.

The fort's governor at the time, a charismatic noble described as Chanda Sahib, was seized by the Marathas and taken to the Marathi country.

A nephew of Saadatullah Khan, Chanda Sahib, whose real name was Shams-ud-daula Husain Dost Khan, was apparently born into the 'Navaiyat' branch of South India's Muslims. Arab forebears of Navaiyats like Chanda may have landed on a Konkani-speaking tract of the west coast before the tenth century.[7]

In 1734, Chanda Sahib had deposed Minaksi, the ruling nayaka rani of Madurai, and 'proclaimed himself heir and successor to the Hindu nayaka regime'.[8]

Two years after Chanda Sahib was removed to Maratha lands, Asaf Jah, the Nizam of Hyderabad, arrived in the Tamil country with a large army, whereupon the Marathas vacated all their positions there.

The Thanjavur exception apart, the Marathas descending on the South were more interested in taking away stores of treasure than in staying on a site and governing it. Writing in the 1760s of 'the rapidity of [the Marathas'] motions', Robert Orme would add:

> The Morattoes [are] the most enterprising soldiers of Indostan...
> Of late years they have often been at the gates of Delhi; sometimes
> in arms against the throne; at others, in defence of it. The strength
> of their armies consists in their numerous cavalry, which is more
> capable of resisting fatigue than any in India...
>   Great parsimony in their expences, and continued collection
> of treasure [by plunder and extortion] have been the principal

causes of raising them, in less than a century, from a people of inconsiderable note to a nation which at present strikes terror into all the countries between Delhi and Cape Comorin (40).

●

Pillai's diary, 15 October 1746: As the governor was engaged in council, I proceeded to my areca-nut storehouse and seated myself there. Wandiwash Tiruvengada Pillai then delivered to me a letter written on palmyra-leaf sent by Kandappan from Karikal (2: 392).

Pillai, trader in areca-nut and other merchandise, goes on to describe a discussion that ensued in which Pillai and six other Indians (all named) took part. The question was whether natives should defray expenses incurred in a recent skirmish seen in the French territory. Pillai adds that his views were conveyed in a letter that he wrote, 'sealed' and 'posted' to Kandappan.

Indians in the 1740s are thus involved in the affairs of the territory, writing to one another on palmyra leaves, and posting letters (2: 393).

The diary entry the next day is about disputes between Dupleix and Bourdonnais, who had acted independently of the governor before the storm that hit Madras but spared Pondicherry. The naval officer's conduct shocked Pillai, who had assumed that 'there is generally concord and good understanding amongst [senior] Europeans, and that they never disagree'. Writes Pillai:

16 October 1746: The ways of Europeans, who used always to act in union, have apparently now become like those of natives and Muhammadans (2: 395).

CHANDA SAHIB (d. 1752)

An entry fourteen months later, on 17 December 1747, indicates a partnership taking shape between the French in South India and the Muslim prince, Chanda Sahib, at the time a prisoner of the Marathas, who hoped to replace old Anwaruddin as the Arcot nawab, even as Chanda Sahib's ally Muzaffar Jung hoped to replace Nasir Jung as the nizam. Orme would write:

Chunda-saheb was esteemed the ablest soldier that had of late years appeared in the Carnatic. His contempt of the sordid means by which most of the Indian princes amass treasures had gained him the affections of the whole province; and an excellent understanding contributed to make his character universally revered (1: 123).

Chanda Sahib's wife and son were harboured in Pondicherry, and Pillai encouraged Dupleix's efforts to cultivate them. The diary entry of 17 December 1747 records Pillai telling Dupleix that if right gestures were made,

> You will be as powerful at Arcot as you are at Pondicherry, without any further trouble, once Chanda Sahib becomes Nawab, as you have planned (4: 276).

Pillai admits his flattery of the governor. Two months later, in February 1748, when Dupleix remarked that the previous governor, Dumas, 'though incapable, knew how to make money', Pillai responded by saying that Dupleix's 'glory' in defeating Anwaruddin and seizing Madras 'will endure as though written upon stone'. Glory 'dies not, but riches perish', Pillai added (4: 359).

Flattery was not a one-way street. On 23 June 1748, Dupleix said to Pillai, referring to a vacillating Muslim chief during an Anglo–French conflict, 'One can trust Europeans or Tamils but never Muhammadans' (5: 62). Pillai advised the governor to treat the chief courteously.

We can mark that both Pillai and Dupleix speak of *three* communities in their area: Europeans, Tamil natives and Muslims. While recognizing the exceptional nature of the Dupleix–Pillai connection, we also obtain an impression that, compared with British–Indian relations, Franco–Indian interactions saw a greater spirit of equality.

Another diary entry (11 August 1748) discusses Brahmins and Jesuits in the context of the British attack on Pondicherry, which had sparked something of an exodus. Dupleix told Pillai of a Jesuit priest's report that many, including Pillai's wife and children, had left. Present at the conversation, the priest, Father Gaston Cœurdoux, who was a gifted linguist, admitted that he too had removed images, windows and doors from a couple of churches. Pillai said to the governor:

Some poor people and Brahmans have gone, and some women born here but married to men elsewhere may have gone also. But otherwise people are going in and out as usual.

The diary adds:

[Dupleix] then asked if my womenfolk had gone. I told him that neither the boys nor the girls of my household had gone, and that he might send to see. [Dupleix] then turned to Father Cœurdoux and said, 'Whenever you are questioned about your mistakes, you always throw the blame upon others. When you yourself carry off even your windows for fear of an English attack, it is natural that ignorant Tamils should fly. But it is you who alarm[s] the town' (5: 188–89).

A month later, Pillai entered a remarkable allegation against Mme Dupleix.

19 September 1748: She sends Pariahs to live in the houses of Brahmans, Komuttis, Vellalas and other castes, in order to root out the religion of the Tamils and establish her own in its place. If any of these Pariahs are driven out...they complain to Madame, who sends for the accused and punishes them... I cannot describe [the Tamils'] alarm (5: 334–35).

♦

Writing in the 1760s of the response in India to the Anglo–French truce signed in Europe in 1748–49, Orme would comment that though 'the sword was sheathed' as between each other, the East India Companies of England and France could not 'refrain from...employing their arms in the contests of the princes of the country'.

Both companies now possessed troops in numbers 'greatly superior to any which either of the two nations had hitherto assembled in India' and felt the urge for 'enterprizes' (111).

While the English backed Nasir Jung for the throne of Golconda, and Anwaruddin, and later his son Muhammad Ali Walajah, for the throne of Arcot, the French put their weight behind Muzaffar Jung for Hyderabad and Chanda Sahib for Arcot.

Bribes from Dupleix to the Marathas, who were holding Chanda Sahib in Satara, and Chanda Sahib's promises to his captors resulted in his release in 1748, which was the year of the death of Qamaruddin, Golconda's nizam since 1724, an event that opened the floodgates for succession battles.

In theory, the Mughal in Delhi appointed the Golconda viceroy, but Hindostan was no longer what it was. In the late 1740s, the Mughal emperor still commanded unique prestige, but his power had greatly weakened. In Orme's view, a crucial role in breaking the Mughal spell was played by Dupleix, who grasped the weakness, first exposed in Adyar in 1746, of the armies of Hindostan.

> At a time when all other Europeans entertained the highest opinion of the strength of the Mogul government, suffering tamely the insolence of its meanest officers, rather than to make resistance against a power which they chimerically imagined to be capable of overwhelming them, [Dupleix] discovered and despised this illusion (379–80).

The Frenchman also nursed a big goal: winning as much of India as he could for France, by arms and diplomacy. Orme writes that Dupleix became 'as great an adept in the politics of Indostan, as if he had been educated a Mahomedan lord at the court of Delhi' (171). Building a French empire in India on the shoulders of the charismatic Chanda Sahib was the cornerstone of his strategy.

Marching south from Satara through Kannada country, where he collected recruits, Chanda Sahib took part in a conflict between the chiefs of Chitradurga and Bidanur (Nagara) in which Chanda's son was killed. After he reached the Tamil country, Chanda was joined by Dupleix's soldiers and those of Muzaffar Jung.

In the late summer of 1749, in the Battle of Ambur (about 50 miles west of Arcot), where Nawab Anwaruddin and the British confronted Chanda and his allies, old Anwaruddin was killed.

Chanda became the Carnatic nawab and Dupleix emerged as a white giant. The chiefs of South India, thus far 'accustomed (in Orme's words) to see Europeans assuming no other character than that of merchants, and paying as much homage to the Mogul government as [could be] exacted...were astonished at the rapid progress of the French arms, and beheld with admiration the abilities of Mr. Dupleix' (171). Gingee was captured by the French, the Pathan chiefs of Kurnool and Kadapa defected from Nasir Jung, and in early December 1750, Nasir Jung was killed in a battle.

Less than two weeks later, in a grand ceremony in Pondicherry, Muzaffar Jung was proclaimed the Nizam of Golconda, Chanda Sahib was honoured as the Nawab of the Carnatic, and Dupleix, appearing in the dress of a Muslim lord, was declared the Mughal emperor's governor for all the lands south of the Krishna (Orme, 165).

The French company received monetary and other rewards (the port of Machilipatnam was made over to it), riches were bestowed on Dupleix personally, and Muzaffar Jung, accompanied by a large army and a larger number of camp followers, began the long trek back to Hyderabad. They were joined by a band of Frenchmen and an officer deputed by Dupleix, Charles de Bussy.

En route, in Kadapa, the Pathan chiefs' forces and those of Muzaffar Jung fought wildly with one another. In the fracas, Jung was killed, as also the Nawab of Kadapa. Thanks in part to Bussy's intervention, Salabat Jung, Muzaffar's uncle and the oldest of Qamaruddin's surviving sons, was declared the Golconda throne's inheritor.

Advised of these events, kingmaker Dupleix acquiesced in the enthronement of Salabat, who was among the marchers returning to Hyderabad, while Salabat on his part confirmed the awards granted to the French.

MUHAMMAD ALI WALAJAH (1717–1795)

Muhammad Ali Walajah, Anwaruddin's son, eluding the forces of Dupleix and Chanda Sahib and claiming to be Arcot's rightful nawab, was not giving up. He was not only entrenched with supporters in Trichy Fort, about 150 miles south of Arcot; he was trying to mobilize support south of Trichy in Madurai and Tirunelveli.

In the summer of 1751, Dupleix and Chanda Sahib moved with their forces to crack Trichy, the strongest fort, as many thought, in the Tamil country (a fort, moreover, that Chanda Sahib had occupied in the late 1730s), but Robert Clive, now twenty-three, had other ideas. Moving from Madras, he would bid to capture Arcot, forcing the attackers to return to their capital, a plan first suggested, it appears, by Muhammad Ali.[9]

Assenting to the plan, Fort St George backed it with British and Indian soldiers and with 'two 18 pounders' sought by Clive. In August–September 1751, Arcot was taken with surprising ease by Clive and a small number of British soldiers and Indian sepoys who, we are told, were 'inflamed' by Clive's courage. When a Franco–Indian army laid siege to Arcot, its new owners defiantly held out. After fifty-three days, the besiegers withdrew (Orme, 187).

Walajah, meanwhile, had reached out to the regent of Mysore, a rich territory once eyed by Chanda Sahib and now under an infant king. Betting on the British and glad to have Arcot in his debt, the Mysore regent offered help, including by taking in his kingdom's pay several thousand Maratha soldiers, ready for battle and plunder, who were 'encamped at the foot of mountains 30 miles from Arcot' (196). In return, Ali promised Mysore much of his revenue and some of his major possessions, including Trichy Fort.[10]

Also declaring for Ali and the British were the Maratha ruler of Thanjavur and the chief of the 'Kallar' country between Thanjavur and Madurai. Though Alam Khan, the governor of Madurai, sided with Chanda Sahib, as did the poligar of the Marava country south of Thanjavur (212), the momentum had turned against him.

As Orme tells the story, in the 1752 summer, when it became clear he and the French were losing, Chanda Sahib sought terms for a clandestine escape from Mankoji, Thanjavur's army chief. Agreeing to a deal, Mankoji showed Chanda's emissary the palanquin in which the nawab would be quietly escorted to safety. When Chanda arrived, 'he was met by a guard who carried him with violence into a tent where they immediately put him into irons'.

Walajah, the Mysoreans and the Marathas all demanded the prisoner's custody. Unwilling to antagonize any of them, Mankoji chose the option of ending his prisoner's life. Ordered to do the deed, a Pathan in Mankoji's retinue first 'stabbed Chanda Sahib to the heart' and then 'severed his head from the body'. The head was sent to Muhammad Ali Walajah, now the unchallenged Nawab of Arcot (244–45).

◆

A friend of Chanda Sahib's, we may interject, was the Italian Jesuit, Constanzo Giuseppe Beschi (1680–1742), who served in the southern Tamil country around Madurai. Like de Nobili in the preceding century, Beschi adopted a cloak resembling that of a Brahmin pontiff, smeared his forehead with sandalwood paste, and converted many. Unlike de Nobili, Beschi also became a literary figure celebrated to this day in the Tamil world, which has honoured him with a statue on Chennai's Marina Beach.

Composing dictionaries and grammars in Tamil, and epic poems with Christian themes, Beschi was an ardent Jesuit inspired also by non-Christian Tamil texts, but perhaps he is most remembered for his 'Parramarta Kuruvi Katai', or the 'Tale of Guru Simpleton', which he brilliantly wove from elements in Indian and Western folklore.

Writing the tale first in Tamil, Beschi then translated it into Latin. Though the bilingual text was published only in 1822 (in London), the tale had become well known during Beschi's lifetime. The first Indian edition was published in 1845; new editions continue to appear. In the words of a modern scholar:

> One thing is certain: 'Guru Simpleton' marks the beginning of literary prose fiction in Tamil.[11]

◆

The Mysoreans were angered by Walajah's failure to fulfil the promise regarding Trichy Fort. Surviving as Pondicherry's governor, Dupleix noticed their reaction and succeeded in detaching them from the English alliance.

To protect the fort from the Mysoreans, and from the Marathas who were in Mysore's pay, the Company was obliged to place a garrison in it. Provisioning the garrison across the unfriendly country was a challenge that was met, on the Company's behalf, by an unusual sepoy called Muhammad Yusuf Khan.

Born around 1725 into the Vellala caste of landowners in the deep southern district of Ramanathapuram, and named Maruthanayagam Pillai, he spent some time in Pondicherry and then in Nellore in the Telugu country just north of Madras.

In Nellore, he became a Muslim, took the name Yusuf Khan, and enlisted in Chanda Sahib's army, where he rose to head a company of sepoys.[12] Following Chanda's defeat, he joined Clive's troops along with his company.[13] In 1754, according to Orme, the Company's convoys in the country around Trichy

> were much assisted by the activity and vigilance of Mahomed Issouf...he was a brave and resolute man, but cool and wary in action, and capable of stratagem; he constantly procured intelligence of the enemy's motions, and having a perfect knowledge of the country, planned the marches of the convoys so well, that by constantly changing the roads and the times of bringing the provisions out of the woods, not one of them was intercepted for three months (1: 349).

Because of his abilities, in March 1754 Yusuf Khan was made commandant of all the Indian sepoys of John Company. Precisely because of these skills, the Mysore regent appears to have plotted with a 'Brahmin linguist' named 'Poniapah', who was the chief interpreter for Major Stringer Lawrence, the head of the English army in India, to frame Yusuf Khan as an agent of Mysore and have him executed.

When, as arranged, letters incriminating Yusuf Khan were 'discovered', the sepoy commandant was confined, but investigations not only cleared him, Khan emerged from them with an enhanced reputation. It was 'Poniapah' (as Orme calls him in the 1760s), or 'Punniyappan', as the name is spelt by Samuel Charles Hill (who published a biography of Yusuf Khan in 1914), who 'was condemned, and some time after blown off from the muzzle of a cannon' (1: 355).

As Hill puts it, this was 'the usual military punishment for treachery' meted out by the Company.[14]

Referring to Yusuf Khan, Major (and future Major General) Stringer Lawrence pronounced that 'a better soldier of his colour I never saw in the country'.[15] We will see more of this Tamil soldier in the next chapter.

Holding Dupleix's ambitions responsible for defeat and financial loss, the French East India Company recalled him in 1754. In a treaty signed that year with the British, the French recognized Muhammad Ali as the Nawab of Arcot. Of Dupleix, Orme would write:

The haughtiness and arrogance of [Dupleix's] spirit disgusted all who approached him: he exhibited on all occasions the oriental pomp, and marks of distinction, which he assumed as the Great Mogul's viceroy in the counties south of the Kristna...

[Yet], had [Dupleix] been supplied with the forces he desired immediately after the death of Anwar-a-dean Khan, or had he afterwards been supported from France in the manner necessary to carry on the extensive projects he had formed, there is no doubt but that he would have placed Chunda-saheb in the Nabobship of the Carnatic, given law to the Soubah of the Decan, and perhaps [to] the throne of Delhi itself, and have established a sovereignty over many of the most valuable provinces of the emperor...

But military qualifications were wanting in his composition... [H]e had not received from nature that firmness of mind which is capable of contemplating instant and tumultuous anger with the serenity necessary to command an army (379–80).

It was Robert Clive, implies Orme, who possessed this cool daring. Dupleix died in neglect and want in France in 1763, seven years after the death of his wife.

Decades later, after his victories in southern and eastern India, England would punish Clive for enriching himself in its eastern colony, but in 2014 a British writer would call Clive 'a continental emperor', a rival in history of men like Alexander, Genghis Khan and Tamerlane.[16]

◆

Clearly, the European advent had caused excitement and alarm across South India. Tales of strange, pale-skinned men possessing terrifying guns but showing, within their fortified domains, an unusual rule of law must have raced like tremors across the peninsula. The claim of a few missionaries and other Europeans that equality in society could in time replace hierarchy would have been discussed in towns and villages, as also the ominous possibility of whites with peculiar customs replacing the South's indigenous rulers.

In some places, the landscape too was changing. Within the Europeans' fortified and steadily expanding domains, a fresh steeple or two rose skyward, roads became wider and more even, and spacious new offices admitted Indian merchants as well as other Indians working for the Company. Other glimpses, less favourable, were recorded in the 1750s by Charles Frederick Schwartz, a German missionary living in Tranquebar.

Evidently 'a wealthy old merchant who understood Danish, English and French'—apart from Tamil and, very likely, Telugu—told Schwartz: 'From what we daily observe and experience, [Europeans are] self-interested, proud, incontinent, full of illiberal contempt and prejudice[d] against us Hindoos.'

When, upon meeting 'a Hindoo dancing-master and his female pupil', Schwartz said to them, 'No unholy person shall enter the kingdom of heaven', the girl, it seems, responded, 'Alas, sir, in that case hardly any European will enter it,' and moved on, Schwartz would write.[17]

MARTHANDA VARMA (r. 1729–1758)

In the spice-rich Malayalam country, seemingly safe in its hill-to-sea corner from the armies of northern India, sea-borne influence in the first part of the eighteenth century largely belonged to the Dutch, who were strongly entrenched in and around the Kochi kingdom on the Kerala coast.

The scene changed noticeably with the reign of Marthanda Varma, who inherited, on the southern tip, a small remnant of an old kingdom called Venad, extended its boundaries into the north, and created a new kingdom called Travancore.

To obtain and keep the Venad throne which, by ancient convention in the matrilineal (and dominant) Nair community, had passed to him from his maternal uncle, Varma fought close relatives, escaped assassination, and outwitted well-entrenched clans.

Varma's Travancore benefited from a treaty signed in the 1720s with the British East India Company, which had followed up its fort built in 1695 in Anjengo (Attingal) in southern Kerala with a 1708 fort in Tellicherry (Thalassery) in Kolattiri country, north of Kozhikode. Also helpful for Travancore were good relations with the French, who in 1726 established a coastal fort in Mahe (also in Kolattiri country), and whose influence with Chanda Sahib restrained the latter during his attack on southern Kerala in 1740.

North to south, the Kerala land's major native rulers, often at odds with one another, were located in Kolattiri (around Cannanore or Kannur, where a feudatory named Ali Raja was also influential*), Kozhikode (Zamorin-ruled Calicut), Kochi (Cochin), which had grown weak, and Travancore. Varma kept at bay the energetic and strongly anti-Dutch Zamorins of Kozhikode who were keen to extend their rule southwards.

However, Varma's biggest external foe, antagonized by his interest in the pepper trade, was the Dutch East India Company, governed from Jakarta but with bases also in Sri Lanka, ruled by the Dutch from 1640. To the surprise of many, Travancore won a key battle in 1741 against the Dutch in the port of Colachel or Kulachal (12 miles north of Kanyakumari and now part of Tamil Nadu), from where the Dutch had hoped to storm the kingdom's centre. Gunpowder and weapons obtained by Varma with British aid played a role in the Colachel victory, but storms, a fire, and a siege enforced by Varma also contributed.[18]

This defeat was the beginning of the end of Dutch control. After Colachel, Varma, who had captured a fair portion of the pepper trade, practised 'shrewd diplomacy' alongside a 'show of strength'.[19] Two years before the raja's death, Sampati Rao, the nizam's diwan, would write to John Caillaud, one of the Company's military officers, that 'among black men he never met with so wise a one' as Marthanda Varma.[20] Rao's remark suggests that white superiority was an assumption that well-placed Indians were starting to internalize.

The raja enlisted the services of some Europeans taken prisoner at Colachel. The best known among them is Eustachius Benoit de Lannoy, a soldier-builder of Belgian origin who later commanded the Travancore army in victorious campaigns and constructed fortifications for the kingdom before dying in 1777.**

Marthanda Varma seems to have acted cruelly towards Nair chiefs and Brahmin priests who had combined in a bid to curb his influence.[21] But the ancient Vishnu temple of Sri Padmanabha Swamy, whose priests had tried unsuccessfully to resist Varma, won out on 3 January 1750, when Marthanda Varma dedicated the new state of Travancore to the deity and declared that he was only ruling it as Padmanabha's servant.

---

*The Ali Raja dynasty also controlled the Laccadive or Lakshadweep Islands.
**Lannoy's grave lies in Udayagiri Fort, now part of Tamil Nadu's Kanyakumari district.

It was in the cellars of this temple that treasures reportedly worth close to a trillion dollars (including diamonds, other jewels, gold statues and a large hoard of Roman gold coins) were discovered in the second decade of the twenty-first century.[22]

We may speculate that over time—before, during, and after Marthanda Varma's reign—captured treasure, heirlooms of insecure rulers, and inflows of specie for Indian exports joined the offerings of devotees to swell the wealth in the Sri Padmanabha Swamy vaults.

As in the Kerala country, ambitions clashed in the lands we now call Karnataka, which in the first half of the eighteenth century witnessed several Maratha incursions. In Mughal-established Sira (which included places like Dodballapur, Hoskote, Kolar and Penukonda), Dilavar Khan, the province's governor from 1726 to 1759, raised gardens, palaces and a fort in Sira town that may have inspired later versions in Srirangapatna and Bengaluru.[23]

A Maratha raid in 1757 was followed two years later by a return of precarious Mughal rule in Sira.

THE TELUGU COUNTRY

A glimpse of another facet of history in another part of South India is offered by an anonymous Telugu text completed 'in the beginning of the nineteenth century', *Dupati Kafiyatu** as it came to be called, which relates the story of a long-surviving farming clan possessing lands 'in the wilderness area of western Telangana'.

In the first quarter of the sixteenth century, the great Vijayanagara king, Krishnadevaraya, apparently gifted these lands to an ancestor of this clan, one Shayappa Nayadu.[24]

Dupati Kafiyatu shows successive rulers of the region, including the Qutbshahis of the sixteenth and seventeenth centuries and the eighteenth-century Asaf Jahis, recognizing the title to their lands of Shayappa Nayadu's successive descendants.

These descendants retain fair autonomy while remaining

---

*Derived from Persian, a kaifiyat or kafiyatu denoted a record of 'circumstances' or 'the situation'. In the early nineteenth century (see Chapter 6), the East India Company's Colin Mackenzie and his Indian aides collected thousands of kaifiyats in southern India.

pragmatically obedient to changing establishments. Moreover, they seem able to prove their rights to every new ruler by showing paper records and pointing to inscriptions of donations. In *Dupati Kafiyatu*'s three-century long story, the Nayadus are shown to have received legal and bureaucratic assistance from Niyogi (non-priestly) Brahmins.

Analysing *Dupati Kafiyatu*'s Telangana-based text, the Rao-Subrahmanyam-Shulman trio of scholars also brings flavours from the 1750s of another Telugu area: the 'Circars', the water-rich Mughal province, north of Madras and south of Odisha, along the east coast. This, they do by probing contemporaneous and later poems about 'the Bobbili war' of January 1757.

Occurring in the Srikakulam region of the Circars, this war involved two rajas, Ranga Raya of Bobbili and Vijaya Rama Raju of Vizianagaram, about 28 miles south of Bobbili. Showing that French interest in South India had not died with Chanda Sahib's death, Charles de Bussy, the previously encountered French officer, joined the war on Vizianagaram's side.

Evidently the name Bobbili, Telugu for sher or tiger, originated from a Sher Muhammad Khan who had conquered Srikakulam for Mughal overlords. One of Sher Muhammad Khan's aides from the region, Peddarayudu, seems to have founded the Bobbili line, while another aide, Madhava Varma, sired the Vizianagaram branch.

In 1756–57, a thirty-six-year-old Bussy, who has received a remarkable firman from the Delhi Mughal, confirmed by the Golconda nawab, *authorizing the French Company to farm the large territory of the Circars for land tax*, is eager to start the juicy process. Collecting a force of 174,000, no less, he leaves Hyderabad for the long eastward journey to rulers like Bobbili's Ranga Raya who have not paid revenue for years.[25]

When the army enters Vijayawada, two of Bussy's aides, Haidar Jung and Hasan Ali, send a demand to the local lord to show up at once and to 'come as you are'. The zamindar, Potteyya, arrives with gifts of meat, butter and foreign liquor, but Bussy asks for something more valuable: a dubash.

Potteyya says a good one may be found in Machilipatnam (known at the time simply as 'Bandar'* to everyone), the port that linked the

---

*Persian for port.

Circars to the world and was already in French possession. In Bandar, Somadasa Laksmana is found, a Telugu-speaker 'expert in Persian and English' and in painting cloth with kalamkari designs.

After crossing the river at Rajahmundry, Bussy sends Vizianagaram's Vijaya Rama Raju a letter announcing his arrival to collect revenue. A perturbed Raju proposes joint resistance to nearby zamindars, but Bobbili's Ranga Raya, who is Raju's old enemy, responds haughtily: 'There is no friendship between us.'[26]

Raju swears revenge. After Bussy arrives with his force in Vizianagaram, Laksmana the dubash meets the raja along with Haidar but without Bussy, warns Vijaya Rama Raju of Bussy's strength, and extracts a bribe for himself. Raju assures Laksmana and Haidar, who is also bribed, of more money if an attack on Bobbili can be arranged.

When Raju meets Bussy, he showers the Frenchman with presents and tells him untruthfully that Ranga Raya 'tore up the letters you sent': Ranga Raya had received a letter from Raju, not from Bussy. But the lie produces the desired effect. Bussy will attack Bobbili, joined by Raju's force.[27]

What follows contains epic-like ingredients: a classic letter to Raju (sent as from a sister and without Ranga Raya's knowledge) dictated by Ranga Raya's wife Mallamma, in which she pleads for the attack to be called off but does so from a perch of superiority (after all she and her husband are warrior Velamas); treachery from Haidar and Laksmana; the choice of death before dishonour made by the prince, his women and children, and (we must mark) by the palace's maids and servants as well; a defiant disdain of compromise; and more.

Led by Bussy, the Europeans, presented as greedy and foolish, are the story's principal villains, but there is also a Muslim villain (Bussy's aide Haidar Jung) and another who is a Hindu and possibly a Brahmin: Laksmana the dubash. One version sends Laksmana to death by trampling by elephants. This evidently was the order of the Golconda nizam.[28] We are reminded of Poniapah's fate three years earlier and of the oft-dangerous if financially alluring life of a dubash.

The great hero is Mallamma, who dictated that secret letter to Vijaya Rama Raju. Dignified even when pleading, this letter manages to humiliate the enemy lord by promising him cash in the future should he find himself in need. The letter is also memorable for a metaphor.

Bobbili and Vizianagaram are 'two pots balanced on the same pole', it says. 'Don't throw them off balance.'[29]

In the end, when all is lost, Mallamma demands that her husband behead her. He hesitates but is shamed by her into doing the deed. Then he kills himself. He, too, has tried earlier, in a brief lapse from heroics, for peace, but his court shouts him back into duelling.

Another hero in the poems is the sister of the Vizianagaram ruler, who warns her brother against marching to Bobbili. When the brother pays no heed, she drowns herself in a tank. The sister and her drowning are annually remembered in Vizianagaram, where, apparently, the 1757 attack on Bobbili is not justified.[30]

The only silver lining was the survival of Mallamma and Ranga Raya's boy. The mother had sent him on a deadly errand but, impressed by the boy's valour, Bussy foiled Raju's order to crush him under elephants. The Bobbili line was saved.

Our three scholars view the poems/ballads about the Bobbili battle as being largely faithful to what happened; the poets are accepted as credible historiographers.[31] Writing much earlier, the nineteenth-century British military historian G. B. Malleson, too, would observe that the Bobbili warriors offered 'resistance that was so determined, that the defenders stabbed their wives and children, and then threw themselves on the bayonets of the French, rather than surrender'.[32]

These accounts of the Bobbili battle are a reminder of the Mahabharata story, with similar excitements, twists, treacheries and valour, the quick taking of offence, and the dying sigh, 'It is avenged, I am satisfied.' The epic's justice is also repeated: a curse by Mallamma is followed by Raju being secretly attacked at night, Mahabharata style, while asleep in his well-guarded tent, and mercilessly killed.

Preoccupation with settling scores blinded these coastal Telugu nobles to the announced wish of the newly-arrived foreigner to collect taxes from Indian peasants and landlords. The native rival was the focus, not the incoming alien. Enmity enlarged the princes' heroics yet dimmed their sight.

Alluding to some of this, Rao, Subrahmanyam and Shulman write of 'the kind of meaningless slaughter that the case of Bobbili so powerfully exemplifies'.[33]

According to the *Bobbili-yuddha-katha,* one of the texts describing the battle, Ranga Raya, making a failed last-minute bid for peace, spoke as follows to his people:

> If we defeat [Bussy and Vijaya Rama Raju] today, tomorrow the Nizam will come. After the Nizam, the Delhi army will arrive. The Maratha cavalry will destroy our country. We cannot win by the sword.[34]

We learn a few other things about eighteenth-century Circars from the trio's examination of texts on the Bobbili battle. Neither Golconda's authority nor Mughal hegemony is being questioned: the Circars' princes and zamindars enjoy a close relationship with Golconda. There is mutual Hindu–Muslim prejudice, but no call to Hindus to unite against Golconda or Delhi, or to newly-arrived Europeans to liberate Hindus from Muslim rule. In the Circars, that rule is anyway remote. Locally, Hindu lords are running things.

Europeans are polluters, not liberators. When the Bobbili palace learns that French attackers are on their way, Ranga Raya shouts to his wife, 'In an hour or two we will have to eat French food!' He reaches for his sword to kill his son before the latter can be contaminated, but Mallamma stops him.[35]

There is nothing like acceptance of European or white superiority, that is to come later. On the administrative front, hundis or bankers' drafts are used in the 1720s and 1730s to remit collections from coastal districts to the Asaf Jahi ruler of Hyderabad.[36]

As for warfare, the Bobbili battle once more shows the decisive difference made by European artillery. Soldiers on the two Indian sides belong to diverse castes, though the Velama or warrior element is foregrounded. Ranga Raya's force includes men of Bundela Rajput and Turkic origin.[37]

Five months after Bobbili, we may note, Bussy would take Vizag from the British. The Frenchman had become 'really powerful' and was spoken of as 'the kingmaker' of the Telugu country.[38]

ASSESSING THE NATIVES

Robert Orme, who observed first-hand some of India's battles of the 1740s and 1750s, was struck by the speed of Indian infantrymen in the Company's army. 'The Sepoys, who formed the van of the English column, appeared outmarching the Europeans at a great rate,' he would write, referring to a 1752 battle near Trichy (1: 238).

Referring to the 'Colleries', as he called them (the 'Kallars' of southern Tamil Nadu), Orme noted their readiness to invite death and composure while facing it (1: 382–83). He wrote of a 1752 battle where 'the Colleries' of 'the Polygar Tondeman' had tipped the scales in favour of the British (1: 212).

When a pair of 'Kallar' brothers, hired by the Company for their skill in stealing enemy horses, instead stole all the chargers belonging to Clive and Lawrence, they were ordered to be hanged. If pardon was offered, responded one of them, he would bring back all the horses while his brother remained a hostage. He was allowed out to produce the horses. When he did not return, Lawrence told the hostage that unless the horses and his brother showed up that evening, he would be executed on the morrow.

He was surprised, the hostage replied, that the English were so weak as to imagine that he and his brother would return a booty, now possessed by their clan, for which they were more than willing to lose their lives. Did the English not know that 'Kallars' were willing to lose a life for a bet? While Lawrence laughed, Clive apparently said that the hostage should be released, which he was, without punishment (1: 382–83).

The South Indian battles portrayed by Orme reveal participation by numerous castes and ethnicities including European (Portuguese and other) mercenaries, Eurasians* and Africa-connected 'Caffres'. After reporting a successful French attack on an Arcot position, Orme comments:

> The Moors, as well as Indians, often defend themselves very obstinately behind strong walls; but it would seem that no advantages, either of number or situation, can countervail the terror with which they are struck when attacked in the night (1: 156).

At times a morning attack too seemed to surprise native soldiers:

---

*Often called Topasses, Eurasians generally descended from Portuguese men and Indian women and were at times counted among Europeans.

As it is the custom in an Indian army to make the great meal at night, and after it to smoke opium...the whole camp towards morning is generally in so deep and heavy a sleep that a handful of disciplined and determined men may beat up thousands before they recover alertness sufficient to make any vigorous resistance (1: 149).

Orme also claimed he found defeated soldiers willing to switch to the victorious side.

It is common in the wars of Indostan to see large bodies of troops going over to the enemy on the very field of battle (1: 49).

Sweepingly but perhaps not without truth Orme writes about non-combatants slowing down India's battle convoys:

Every common soldier in an Indian army is accompanied either by a wife or a concubine; the officers have several, and the generals whole seraglios; besides these the army is encumbered by a number of attendants and servants exceeding that of the fighting men; and to supply the various wants of this enervated multitude, dealers, pedlars, and retailers of all sorts follow the camp; to whom a separate quarter is allotted, in which they daily exhibit their different commodities in greater quantities and with more regularity than in any fair in Europe; all of them sitting on the ground in a line with their merchandise exposed before them... (1: 233).

His comments on the Pathans serving in various armies in the South are of interest.

The Pitans...are the bravest of the Mahomedan soldiery levied in Indostan. From a consciousness of this superiority, together with a reliance on the national connection which exists amongst them however dispersed into the services of different princes, they have acquired an insolence and audacity of manners which distinguishes them, as much as the hardness of their physiognomy, from every other race of men in the [Mughal] Empire... They treat even the lords they serve with very little of that respect which characterizes all the other dependents of a sovereign in Indostan (1: 55–56).

◆

Orme noticed ancient water-storage tanks and water-resisting dams in different parts of South India, and their role in the survival of the toiler and the peasant.

For this purpose [of supplying water in the dry season] vast reservoirs have been formed...

The Pakala Lake in Warangal district in eastern Telangana was probably built in the first half of thirteenth century—*five hundred years* before Orme's observation—by the son of a minister of the Kakatiya kingdom.[39] Adds Orme:

If the avarice of the prince withholds his hand from the preservation of these [tanks] and [yet he insists on the usual revenue]; then the farmer oppressed, oppresses the labourer, and the misery of the people becomes complete...of which the cruel parsimony of their ruler has been the principal cause (1: 54).

From Orme, we obtain other pictures of the countryside and human constructions upon it. He finds the lands near Dindigul of 'Polygar Lachenaig' to be 'fortified either by nature or art'. Separated craggy hills are covered with bushes and loose stones. Between the hills are 'works' consisting of

a thick wall composed of large stones laid upon one another flanked at proper distances by round towers made of earth, well rammed down; before the wall is a deep and road ditch, and in front of the ditch a broad hedge of bamboos, so thickly set that it cannot be penetrated without the hatchet or fire (1: 384).

◆

For whatever they are worth, we can also look at Orme's appraisements, offered in the 1760s, of the accomplishments and psychologies of India's people.

The Indian...shudders at the sight of blood and is of [extreme] pusillanimity...[but his] wife is of a decency of demeanour, of a solicitude in her family, and of a fidelity to her vows, which might do honour to human nature in the most civilized countries (1: 5–6).

It is to the suppleness with which the whole frame of an

Indian is endowed, and which is still more remarkable in the configuration of his hand, that we are indebted for the exquisite perfection of their manufactures of linen (1: 7).

At the same time, no ideas of taste or fine design have existed amongst them; and we seek in vain for elegance in the magnificence of the richest empire of the globe (1: 7).

It does not appear that [the Indians] had ever made a bridge of arches over any of their rivers, before the Mahomedans came amongst them (1: 7).

He cites an unnamed oriental poet for the view that in India's princely families 'parents have during the life of their sons, such overweening affection for their grandchildren, because they see in them the enemies of their enemies [i.e. their sons]' (1: 127). Orme also thought that

In Indostan, none but those of the royal blood are considered as hereditary nobility... The field of fortune is open to every man who has courage enough to make use of his sword, or to whom nature has given superior talents of mind (1: 54).

Apart from the Mughal in Delhi, no authority received wide respect. The only undisputed treason was to 'oppose the sovereign of sovereigns, the Great Mogul' (246). Every other execution or slaying was merely 'unfortunate' (1: 246).

Making a different point, Orme claims that Indian chiefs were reluctant to commit themselves.

The secrets of the princes of Indostan are very difficult to be discovered. In affairs of consequence, nothing, except in the most equivocal terms, is ever given by them in writing... So indefinite a commitment reserves to the lord who gives it the resource of disavowing the transaction of his agent (1: 59–60).

◆

A picture of transport in eighteenth-century southern India was painted early in the nineteenth century by the Company's officer, Talboys Wheeler:

In Southern India, there were neither caravan routes nor waterways of any moment. Hindu Rajas never opened out the country like the Mohammedans of Northern India. Hindu infantry and light Mahratta horsemen required no roads; and Rajas and other Hindu grandees were carried in palanquins.

Europeans travelled in palanquins...and were in no fear of robbers. Ladies and children were borne along through jungles and over rivers; leopards and tigers were kept off at night by lighted torches; and the sure feet of the half-naked coolies carried travellers safely over rocky heights and troubled waters.[40]

WANDIWASH (1760)

After arriving in India in the 1758 summer and taking charge as the Pondicherry governor, Thomas Arthur Lally, a Frenchman with Irish blood, had captured several English outposts including at Fort St David and Arcot in a swift campaign. In December, his forces besieged and almost took Madras but were obliged in the end to lift the siege. The year 1759 saw little fighting, but major differences arose between Lally and his deputy in the field, Bussy, who had been summoned from the Telugu country. This proved unwise, for the English filled the vacuum.

At the end of November 1759, Eyre Coote showed up with a siege army before the walls of Wandiwash, which was in French possession, compelled the French there to raise the white flag, and moved against Arcot. Lally responded 'by plundering the British supply depot' at Kanchipuram and by 'storming Wandiwash, with Lally himself one of the first over the wall'.

But the British inside the fort held out. On 21 January 1760, the British army was again in Wandiwash. The next day, two evenly matched armies, each with its Indian sepoys and a few hundred European soldiers, fought in the open fields of Wandiwash. At day's end, after substantial casualties on both sides, the French lost.

Lally made his way to Pondicherry but Bussy was captured. Writes Thomas Mullen Jr., a modern historian of this war:

A young British officer inside the besieged fort at Wandiwash wrote that at 7 in the morning (of 22 January) he and his companion heard cannon fire. He added with great prescience: 'Then followed the battle that gave us India.'[41]

Not everyone understood what had happened, and in any case the conflict continued for some more months, but the unnamed young officer's remark confirms that at least by 1760, three years after the famous battle in eastern India of Palashi (Plassey) and eight years after the death of Chanda Sahib, the thought of *possessing India* had entered the English mind in India. In his Pondicherry enclave, Lally hoped in vain for reinforcements from France or word of a peace settlement.

As far as Ananda Ranga Pillai was concerned, the fates were shaping India's future. The diary entry of 9 August 1760 of this high-caste non-Brahmin reveals his reaction to news that by the beleaguered governor's order a Brahmin charged with assisting the English had been hanged.

> In former times when a Brahman was about to be hanged, I would explain to the Governor that it was a great sin to kill a Brahman, so he would be let off, because the town was then destined to prosperity, but now a Brahman has been hanged, for the town is destined to ruin (12: 290–91).

We have previously come across hints of Pillai's scepticism about Brahmin loyalty but also his acceptance of traditional customs and beliefs. By hanging a Brahmin, the French confirm to Pillai what Wandiwash had shown: they are not aligned with the gods.

With supplies exhausted and the residents of Pondicherry unwilling to prolong their hardships, Lally (to quote Mullen again) 'surrendered what was left of his army and Pondicherry' on 15 January 1761. He was sent as a captive to Madras—a ship took him to England, from there he made it to France. In May of 1766, King Louis XV condemned Lally to death: apparently, the French company needed a scapegoat. Lally was beheaded like a common criminal.

The day following the surrender of Pondicherry, Ranga Pillai himself died there, aged fifty-one. Yet even as a chapter closed in Pondicherry, another story was brewing in Mysore, which had to do with a cavalryman there who had opposed Nawab Muhammad Ali Walajah and tried from the mid-1750s to assist the French—Haidar Ali.[42]

Chapter 3

FIRE IN THE MIND: 1761–1807

In the middle of the eighteenth century, the European powers confronting the peninsula's unstable political mosaic look strong with their ships and big guns. Privately the British desire to possess all of India. However, owning only a few coastal pockets in 1750, they are merely one of several contending forces.

Most Europeans at this juncture are supplicants still. The Indian merchant feels socially equal to the European agent, and an Indian prince or chief appears to be the paymaster of the whites. But Indian chiefs view one another as rivals or enemies, and they find a European company useful for destroying a native foe.

In the public, fear and dislike of European ascendancy is spreading. Five decades later, by when much of South India had fallen under British rule, a French priest called Jean-Antoine Dubois would say that the people of the Tamil and Kannada tracts where he had spent three decades 'hate and despise their [white] rulers from the bottom of their hearts'.

But, Abbé Dubois added, the people at the same time 'cherish and respect' the administrative machinery run by British officials.

Before the British had taken over (Dubois would go on to claim), the people 'cherished and respected' the Indian princes holding sway over them, but they hated the native administration which in his view was 'under the supremacy of the Brahmins'. In Dubois's assessment, 'the rule of all the Hindu princes, and often that of the Mahomedans, was, properly speaking, Brahminical rule, since all posts of confidence were held by Brahmins' (Dubois, 4).

In 1750, many rulers in South India are Muslim, and Muslims are a larger percentage in a chiefdom's soldiery than in the population, but there are no signs of Hindus wanting to join with the British to overthrow a Muslim ruler. Temples and mosques seem to stand at peace next to each other, and the army of every chief is a Hindu–Muslim mix.

Brahmins are influential in British-run pockets of South India. By the 1750s, many a Company officer, civil or military, refers to 'my Brahmin'—the man who keeps accounts, translates for the white officer, assists him in different ways and in effect becomes a (at times *the*) link between the officer and the South Indian public.

The people face a caste hierarchy, its rigidity varying by area, but seem resigned to it. Writing in the 1970s, the historian T. K. Ravindran would say:

> When the British [acquired] political ascendancy in the South... society was as feudal and caste-ridden as it was in the days of the medieval kingdoms... Every Hindu government was directed and led by a strong Brahmin minority, giving a highly orthodox theocratic character to the rule.[1]

From their Christian perspective, some arriving Europeans find the caste divide offensive. Not, however, all of them. Abbé Dubois, for example, would find virtue in the caste system. In any case, most Europeans feel they must acknowledge Indian hierarchies, even as India's Muslim rulers had done before them. In 1750, it seemed risky to try to overturn ancient customs.

YUSUF KHAN (1725–1764)

Of the early career with the English company of Yusuf Khan, the man who inspired Haidar Ali, John Malcolm (soldier, future governor of Bombay, and biographer of Clive) would write:

> Sepoys were first disciplined [in Fort St George] in 1748; they were at that period, and for some time afterwards, in independent companies under subadars or native captains. Muhammad Yusuf, one of the most distinguished of these officers, rose by his talents and courage to the general command of the whole.[2]

This commandant of the Company's Indian sepoys climbed to become, in the late 1750s, the governor of the Tamil country's southernmost region, where he was born. Apparently 'acquainted with more than one of the vernaculars in common use in the Carnatic', Khan spoke English and also, it seems, Portuguese, which was the language of his wife Maza and of the clerks he employed when ruling Madurai and Tirunelveli.[3]

Tasked to recover revenue from refractory poligars, Yusuf Khan had impressed the British with his drive and integrity. In theory, and on occasion in practice, the money Khan collected went to Muhammad Ali, the Trichy-based Carnatic nawab. More often it went to Ali's impatient creditor, the East India Company. The British and the nawab found it hard to extract 'the ruler's share' in this region. At times, British soldiers employed inflammatory methods. In 1755, a temple where rebels were hiding in the Kallar country was attacked, many Kallars were put to the sword, and 'the little images which the Kallans worshipped' were removed.

When an offer to return these for 5,000 rupees was refused, the images were placed amongst baggage to be sold as old brass for the benefit of the army. Driven to frenzy, the Kallars are said to have killed everyone connected to the army who fell into their hands, native or European, man, woman or child. The British responded with savage reprisals.[4]

After Yusuf Khan took over, one of his celebrated feats was the storming of the so-called 'Kallar barrier', made up of thorn-hedge barricades and earth-work fortifications, at Manapparai, 30 miles south of Trichy. The most powerful of the southern Kallar chiefs paid the full poligar tribute claimed by the nawab.[5]

This successful agent operating in his native turf was seen as a rival by Ali, but many Englishmen in India wished that the Carnatic as a whole belonged to Yusuf Khan rather than to Ali.

'One of Yusuf Khan's greatest strengths,' says the scholar Susan Bayly, 'was his ability to represent himself as heir to the Hindu nayaka rulers of Madurai'. In the sixteenth century, the southern country's poligars and their clansmen had submitted to a hero on horseback, Ariyanatha Mudaliar of Madurai. Two centuries later, their descendants yielded similarly to another Vellala warrior. Bayly adds:

> The men who served [Yusuf Khan] believed that he could bring them glory and plunder... These included Europeans.[6]

Khan recognized the usefulness of European discipline and European instructors, and prepared his own muskets, guns, cannon-balls and powder. Unlike most Indian chiefs of his time, he also realized the advantages of attacks by night.[7]

In March 1756, against payment of 'rent' to it, the Company allowed Yusuf Khan and Tittarappa Mudali, 'a wealthy inhabitant of Tinnevelly', to collect land revenue in Madurai and Tirunelveli. However, Mudali being 'a very timid person',[8] Yusuf Khan had in effect become the governor of the two tracts.

Won over by Yusuf Khan's exploits, many Kallar and Marava fighters,[9] previously his opponents, joined him. Also active in the region, however, were individuals claiming to be Chanda Sahib's successors and thus rulers of Madurai, including a Pathan named Nabi Khan Khattack, who lent support to poligars resisting Yusuf Khan.

Fleeing from a 1756 confrontation with Yusuf Khan, Nabi Khan made an attack on the temple of Srivilliputtur, about 40 miles southwest of Madurai. According to Khan's biographer, Samuel Hill,

> [Nabi Khan] would have taken and plundered [the temple] had not one of the temple Brahmans mounted the high tower of the gateway, and after cursing the assailants in a loud voice, thrown himself down, dashing his brains on the pavement, an act which so horrified and terrified Nabi Khan's followers that they left the town.[10]

Hill does not give us the name of the Brahmin who by this extreme measure evidently saved the temple and, it would seem, the town.

In October 1757, Yusuf Khan clashed with Haidar Ali near the town of Dindigul, thirty miles north of Madurai. Having first arrived in the Tamil country as a junior commander in the Mysorean army (for whose aid Muhammad Ali had begged), Haidar was now the faujdar or commander of Dindigul, which the Mysoreans held, and where a few Frenchmen worked under him.

Haidar tried to extend his boundary, but Yusuf Khan's resistance forced him back into Dindigul.[11]

By 1758, with the Company's backing, Yusuf Khan had taken over Madurai city. Visiting its old Meenakshi temple, Yusuf Khan was evidently 'so struck with its grandeur that he gave orders for its purification and the renewal of the usual worship'. A Muslim fakir who had planted his canopy on the temple's chief gateway was removed, as also the canopy, and the temple's revenues were restored.[12]

Later in 1758, Yusuf Khan gave critical assistance to the British when the French under Lally almost captured Madras. During that failed attempt, 'what most distressed Lally's army' were 'the constant attacks of Yusuf Khan's band of raiders', a fact 'universally acknowledged by Europeans as well as natives'.[13]

From 1759, Yusuf Khan was 'the acknowledged ruler of Madura and Tinnevelly'. 'Subject to the payment of rent, he was given absolute discretion in all matters civil and military.'[14] The men who fought or worked under his banner (which was also that of the English Company) included Indians of different stripes (Maravas and Kallars among them), Portuguese and other Europeans, and topasses, soldiers of mixed Portuguese and Indian descent.

If he brushed against Mysore's Haidar, the Malayalam country too lay close, just beyond the hills to Khan's west. Rama Varma, who in 1758 succeeded Marthanda Varma on the Travancore throne and was friendly with the British, allied with Yusuf Khan to fight some of the southern poligars. The raja, 'a man of craft, like his predecessor,'[15] obtained from Khan a large fertile district, Kalakadu, in 1759.

Of the many battles that Yusuf Khan waged to collect revenue, the only one he lost took place at a fort belonging to Puli Thevar (Pulidevar), seen as 'the most important of the western Poligars of Tinnevelly'.[16]

After referring to the ability of Puli Thevar's men to 'repair breaches steadily with palmeira and heaps of straw' and their 'inconceivable contempt of death', an English officer called Donald Campbell would say that in fighting skills they were 'as superior to other natives of the Carnatic as the best Europeans that ever were in the East Indies'.[17]

> The Travancoreans [*Hill tells us*] assisted Yusuf Khan to ravage the territory of the Pulidevar, and on the 4th of December 1759 Yusuf Khan laid siege to Vasudevanallur, one of the strongest of the Pulidevar's forts... The Pulidevar's men successfully resisted the siege, which was raised. The Travancoreans returned to their country and Yusuf Khan retired to Tinnevelly.
>
> Vasudevanallur was Yusuf Khan's only failure.[18]

Khan's fiscal skills were an asset for the British. In 1758, he told Captain John Caillaud of the Company: 'As it is not the harvest [time], I borrow money of the Saucers [sowcars] and pay the troops, and dispatch the business.'[19] Thus Gujarati (and possibly Marwari) moneylenders were active deep in the southern country, even in places close to fields of battle, in the 1750s and probably earlier.

From 1761 to 1764, when Yusuf Khan ruled over Madurai and Tirunelveli, rent or land revenues due to the government did not fall below 1,030,489 chakrams (about 25 lakh rupees). One year they amounted to 1,244,530 (about 30 lakh rupees). In 1770, under Nawab Muhammad Ali's subsequent rule, they would fall to 739,035 (about 19 lakh rupees). The figures were provided in 1802 by the Tirunelveli collector, Stephen Lushinghton.[20]

Khan was cordial with Hindus. While Hill saw 'no record of [Yusuf Khan] making direct gifts to the temples', he found that when the raja of Ramanathapuram and his pradhan (minister) presented Yusuf Khan with a golden cradle on the birth of his son in the early 1760s, Yusuf Khan 'acknowledged the gift by granting to the [minister], in jagir, the village of Sakkudi, which the pradhan presented to the temple of Sri Minakshi'.[21]

Two decades after Yusuf Khan's death, an English colonel called William Fullarton, who had worked with Khan, would write:

While he ruled those provinces his whole administration denoted vigour and effort: his justice was unquestioned, his word [was] unalterable; the guilty had no refuge from punishment. His maxim was that the labourer and the manufacturer should be the favourite children of the Sarkar.[22]

Fired, however, by a desire to be his own master, Yusuf Khan broke off his allegiance to Muhammad Ali and the British. Supporting him were Frenchmen living in port towns like Nagapattinam and Danish-controlled Tranquebar. These Frenchmen looked for careers and for a chance to avenge Wandiwash.

Pressed by the Madras Council to appear at Fort St George, Yusuf Khan dragged his feet. In April 1763, Major General Stringer Lawrence informed the Madras Council that Khan had 'thrown off his allegiance' and was receiving 'help from the French...and Haidar Naik's army'. Portraying Khan as a new Chanda Sahib in the making, Lawrence warned that Khan would prevent the nawab from clearing his debt to the Company.[23]

Travancore's Rama Varma tried to buttress the British position in the deep south but in a clash in February 1763, Yusuf Khan defeated Varma's army. In March, the raja wrote to the Council in Madras 'that he had been compelled to make peace'. The Company complained that though repeatedly asked to attack Khan and 'make a diversion', the raja 'never moved'.[24]

South of Madras, the strongest British base was in Trichy, headquarters of their ally, Nawab Muhammad Ali. In July 1763, Lawrence had a proclamation nailed to the gates of Trichy, which lay about 80 miles north of Madurai:

> I, Major-General Lawrence, do hereby give notice that I have joined the Nawab against the rebel Yusuf Khan. Whoever is taken with him will be deemed a rebel... But those who leave him...before his troops come into any action will be favourably received by the Nawab.[25]

The British had decided to finish Khan. In October 1763, Madurai was attacked and besieged by the Company's forces and the nawab's army, but Yusuf Khan and his force fought off the siege. In the spring of 1764 another costly siege was mounted. This one also failed. In the summer, the British and the nawab tried to storm the Madurai fort occupied by Yusuf Khan and his supporters. There was a fierce battle, but the fort held out and Khan again survived.

A total blockade was enforced in the autumn of 1764. Khan's camp was unable to obtain food and its supply of water ran dangerously low. Inside the fort 'dead horses, dead men, women and children [lay] unburied amongst the ruins',[26] and it was whispered among inmates that Khan and his family would escape in secret, leaving the rest to their fate.

Hill finds that a mutiny against Khan was led by his chief French collaborator, a Monsieur Marchand,[27] who in earlier years had soldiered in the Andhra country. Madurai's sealed-off, hungry fort saw numerous quarrels, and on one occasion,

> passion flamed so high that Yusuf Khan actually struck Marchand with his riding whip, an unpardonable insult never before offered to a European officer in this part of India. From that moment, Marchand...forgot his duty in his thirst for revenge.[28]

Survival was another impulse. If he delayed in betraying Khan, the Fort's troops might deliver both Marchand and Khan to the nawab. Encouraged by Marchand, two Indians, 'Srinavas Rao', a Thanjavur Brahmin who was Khan's chief adviser, and a Muslim confederate called 'Baba Sahib', who had been personally ill-treated, joined a conspiracy to 'seize Yusuf Khan and hand him over' to the enemy.[29]

At five in the evening of 13 October 1764, Marchand, Rao, Baba Sahib and a few others entered a private room where Khan was engaged in prayers. One of the intruders charged Khan with intending to desert those who had faithfully served him. Enraged at the insult, Khan drew his sword but was overpowered by the rest of the conspirators, who bound Khan with the cloth of his own turban.

Though he 'begged them to kill him there and then rather than deliver him to the Nawab', Khan was taken to Marchand's quarters. After Marchand secured a commitment from Charles Campbell, the head of the British forces surrounding the fort, that the lives of the besieged would be spared, Khan was handed over to the nawab's men.

A young aide called Mudali had managed to carry word of his master's plight to Maza, who sent Marchand a letter, offering him the fort and all the treasure in it if he released her husband, but Marchand refused. Mudali also tried to mobilize others in a bid to rescue Khan, but he was 'shot or cut down at once' by the mutineers.[30]

Since 'the records' usually leave out persons like Mudali, it is worth marking that in different places in his study Hill calls Mudali 'a brave young fellow', 'faithful' and 'unfortunate'. In a note that Marchand sent to the Madras Council on 17 October, the Frenchman refers to Mudali as 'this young dog'.[31] From his one-word name (which is all we have), we may infer that this trusty assistant belonged to Khan's caste.

The nawab had Yusuf Khan hanged on the evening of 15 October. Ten years earlier, Poniapah, the interpreter whose treachery against the Company was unearthed by Khan, had been blown from a cannon's mouth. Like Khan, Poniapah had been loyal for years before committing his fatal disloyalty. Hill, whose sources include diaries from officers involved in the blockade as also a long account written by Marchand himself, would write:

[Yusuf Khan's] long service and previous fidelity could not serve him any more than they had availed in the case of his enemy Punniyappan [Poniapah].

But, as Hill also points out,

As the servant of the company, [Khan] had been loyal when times were darkest and when rebellion would have been both easy and safe; when he did rebel, the Company had no other enemy in the field, and he had been bidden to consider himself no longer the servant of the Company but of his ancient enemy the Nawab.[32]

Hill's biography appeared 150 years after Khan's death, but Britons had acknowledged Khan's qualities much earlier. In 1818, John Malcolm would write of Khan:

The name of this hero, for such he was, occurs almost as often in the page of the English historian of India as that of Lawrence and Clive.

In his book on Robert Clive, Malcolm would comment on Khan's defeat and death:

The Company's troops were combined with those of the Nawab for his reduction, which was not however effected without great waste of blood and treasure, and at last accomplished by an act of treachery.[33]

A hundred and seventy years later, Susan Bayly would observe that Yusuf Khan 'still commands veneration across much of Madurai, Ramnad and Tirunelveli districts', including in countryside ballads, with Hindus as well as Muslims claiming him.[34]

The removal of Yusuf Khan satisfied Muhammad Ali's yearning but the nawab's proposal to enlist '21 companies of sepoys and about 200 topasses who had been in Yusuf Khan's service' was rejected by the Madras Council, which took a poor view of discipline in the nawab's army.

Many of Khan's fellow-inmates in the Madurai fort found employment under Haidar Ali. In 1780, Yusuf Khan's son would be seen in Mysore.[35]

Writes Hill:

> Haidar must have watched [Yusuf Khan's] career with keen
> attention and learned much from it, especially in regard to the
> adaptation of European methods of warfare to Indian armies...
> And the fate of [Yusuf Khan] taught him that if he valued his
> independence, not to mention his personal security, he must employ
> [Europeans] only in very subordinate capacities.[36]

HAIDAR ALI (1721–1782)

Born in 1721 or 1722 in a fort in Devanahalli (near Bengaluru),[37]
Haidar had an ancestry of which not much is known. His 'fair and
florid' complexion[38] may have hinted at remote West Asian origins,
but Haidar himself was a Mysorean whose forebears for generations
had soldiered for the Adilshahis of Bijapur, often against the Mughals.

Haidar's paternal grandfather, Muhammad Ali, had six brothers-
in-law employed in Adilshahi units. After all of them died in clashes
with the Mughals in the 1680s, Muhammad Ali left Bijapur for Kolar,
also in the Kannada country.

In 1697, his son Fath Muhammad (Haidar's father) moved from
Kolar to serve, first Arcot's Saadatullah Khan, next the Raja of Mysore,
and finally the Nawab of Sira.

When Haidar was about five, Fath Muhammad was killed in an
internal battle in Sira. Confined and harassed, along with her children,
by her husband's creditors, the mother sent word of her distress to
Haidar Sahib, a relative bearing her son's name and working for the
kingdom of Mysore, which, like Sira, was a Mughal tributary in the
1720s.

Approached by Haidar Sahib, Devaraja, the dalavai[39] of Mysore,
persuaded the Sira subedar to release the family, who moved to Mysore's
capital, Srirangapatna.

Trained by Haidar Sahib in their father's profession of 'arms and
horsemanship' and recruiting a band of warriors, Haidar and his older
brother Shahbaz worked for a spell for the Nawab of Chittoor before
returning to Srirangapatna, where Haidar Sahib introduced them to
Devaraja's younger brother Nanjaraja, who headed the Mysore army.

Like other armies at this time, the Mysore army included different

Indian ethnicities, Europeans and topasses.[40]

Sira, Kolar, Arcot and Chittoor were all located in a broad region where the Kannada, Tamil and Telugu worlds intersected. The 1740s had seen Maratha incursions into Mysore, Sira, Arcot and other principalities in the southern hinterland, which also attracted a growing interest from the East India Company, now firmly based on both coasts. In Mysore itself, ruled by successors of the ruler we previously looked at—Chikka Devaraja—real power was being exercised by the dalavai and his brother Nanjaraja, who quickly recognized Haidar's military skills.

In 1749, intervening in the dispute over the nizam's throne, Nanjaraja sent Haidar to support Nasir Jung against Muzaffar. When the victorious Muzaffar was assassinated on his journey back to Hyderabad, an ingenious Haidar laid hands on some of the treasure being carried and used it to augment his troops.

Hiring a few French deserters, Haidar trained his troops in a European manner. When, in 1752, Nanjaraja took the Mysorean army to the Trichy region to back Nawab Muhammad Ali and the English company against Chanda Sahib and the French, a major contingent was led by Haidar. Alienated by Ali's failure to cede Trichy, Nanjaraja switched to the French side. Returning himself to Srirangapatna, he made Haidar Mysore's faujdar in the Carnatic, based in Dindigul.

But Mysore was overextended and also targeted. The Marathas were again making incursions. So was the nizam. Srirangapatna not only became bankrupt, it saw a divide between the raja and his chief officers, another divide between Devaraja and Nanjaraja, and a third divide between soldiers who were not getting paid and the state.

Running from Dindigul, Haidar brought Devaraja and Nanjaraja together in Srirangapatna, assured the raja of his protection, and helped the soldiers get their pay. Now a major player, he was made commander-in-chief when, with overwhelming strength, the Marathas attacked Mysore in 1758.

Haidar's success in forcing the Marathas to raise their siege of Bengaluru made him a hero across the Kannada country. When he returned in triumph to Srirangapatna, the titular ruler, Krishnaraja, named him Nawab Haidar Ali Khan. With Devaraja dying in 1758 and Nanjaraja forced into retirement by soldiers who were again not getting paid, Haidar was installed as the dalavai.

A loyal associate of his for years, Khande Rao, fell out with Haidar and became the raja's dewan. Haidar was the victor in the violent clash that ensued, and Khande Rao spent the two last years of his life as a caged prisoner in Bengaluru.

By 1761, though reluctant to call himself raja or king, the thirty-nine-year-old Haidar was Mysore's unchallenged ruler, often spoken of as Sultan Haidar, and giving Mysore what the region had lacked for a long time—stable rule. But the state was being hemmed in by the British (with Travancore supporting them) on the Malabar coast as well as in Madras, by the Marathas to the northwest, the nizam to the northeast, and the Carnatic nawab to the southeast.

While the Marathas argued that 'as successors to the sovereignty of the Bijapur king...Mysore really belonged to them',[41] the nizam held that as the Mughal viceroy all of South India was his. Nawab Muhammad Ali, too, claimed rights over Mysore, and the British conveyed an ominous capability.

The number of adversaries and of points of entry into Mysore, and the fact that it was landlocked, made the domain a hard place to defend.

◆

Impressions of Haidar and Tipu are provided in the four volumes on Mysore's rulers written in the 1810s by Mark Wilks, who arrived in India as an eighteen-year-old soldier for the East India Company, joined the war against Tipu, helped run Mysore as a resident after Tipu's death, and then, as the Company's Governor of St Helena, oversaw Napoleon's internment on that remote South Atlantic island.

In 1816, Wilks discussed Britain's new possession in the east, India, with the defeated French emperor who had become his prisoner.

Modern Indian historians, including Mohibbul Hasan and Irfan Habib, have with good reason charged Wilks, a participant in a historic clash rather than its detached observer, with bias. Yet Wilks's long account contains images which, for all their one-sidedness, recall the times of Haidar and Tipu.

Another graphic source for that period is Francis Buchanan, also known as Francis Hamilton, an East India Company doctor asked by Lord Mornington (also known as Richard Wellesley), the Calcutta-based Governor General who planned the war that finally finished Tipu, to journey across Tipu's late domain and report on its castes, crops, minerals, and more.

Commenced within weeks of Tipu's downfall, Buchanan's journey led to a remarkable three-volume report that paints for us the 'Mysore, Canara and Malabar' of the year 1800. While as ill-disposed as Wilks towards Tipu, Buchanan made positive remarks about Tipu's father:

> That tyrant (Tipu) received the country in a very flourishing state from his father, of whom every native whom I have conversed with on the subject speaks in terms of the highest respect.[42]

We can bear in mind that as servants of the East India Company, Wilks and Buchanan had a stake in finding native divides, whether Hindu–Muslim, Brahmin–non-Brahmin, or father–son.

What Wilks tells us about Haidar, whom he never saw, was gathered from others:

> In person [Haidar] was tall and robust; his neck was long, and his shoulders were broad; his complexion inclining to fair and florid, with a prominent and rather aquiline nose, and small eyes; his countenance produced terror. He wore a turban of brilliant scarlet, projecting it by means of a cane frame...

Made up of 'a hundred cubits of fine turban web', the extended turban dominated Haidar's form.

> He was fond of show and parade, and on great occasions was attended by a retinue of one thousand spearmen splendidly clothed and armed, preceded by bards who sung his exploits in the Canarese language.
>
> [V]olunteers [who] engaged in single combat with the royal tiger in the public shews [were] confident of being preserved in the last extremity by the fusil of Hyder, from the balcony.

Wilks also wrote on Haidar's speaking and writing capacities:

> He could neither read nor write any language but [apart from] Hindoostanee, his mother tongue, he spoke with entire fluency the Canarese, Mahratta, Telegoo and Tamul languages. Of the Persic or Arabic he had no knowledge whatever.

And on Haidar's personality:

> [Haidar dealt with people] with [outward] frankness and perpetual suspicion.
>
> [He kept] a harem of six hundred women... But Hyder in... the harem had no feeling distinct from animal instinct. The mind was never permitted to wander from the most rigid attention to public business.
>
> On occasions apparently trivial, [Haidar] would pour forth a torrent of...obscene abuse...on persons of whatever rank; and there were perhaps not, in his whole court, six persons who had not on some one occasion sustained the actual lash of the long whip.

Of Haidar's court and administration, Wilks would say:

> [M]en of almost every country were attracted to his court and standard by brilliant prospects of advancement and wealth; but a person once engaged in his service was a prisoner for life... Official men had cause to tremble; but the mass of the population felt that the vigour of the government compensated for many ills and rendered their condition comparatively safe.
>
> In council he had no adviser and no confidant; he encouraged a free discussion of every measure suggested by himself or by others, but no person knew at its close what measures he would adopt.

On Haidar's beliefs and policies:

> Hyder was of all Mahommedan princes the most tolerant... It was his avowed and public opinion that all religions proceed from God, and are equal in the sight of God; and [he respected] the mediatory power represented by Runga Sawmy (Ranganathaswami of the Vishnu temple in Srirangapatna).
>
> He fixed his stedfast view upon the end, and considered simply the efficiency and never the moral tendency of the means. If he was cruel and unfeeling, it was for the promotion of his objects, and never for the gratification of anger or revenge.
>
> His European prisoners were in irons, because they were otherwise deemed unmanageable; they were scantily fed, because that was economical...but there was by his authority no wanton severity; there was no compassion but there was no resentment...

He converted the male children [of captured and executed rebels] into military slaves, because he expected them to improve the quality of his army... Everything was weighed in the balance of utility.[43]

◆

In 1790, seven years after Haidar's death, a twenty-eight-year-old Company lieutenant called Thomas Munro (he would acquire fame later as Governor of Madras) wrcte to his father in Scotland of the strength of the Mysore that Tipu was ruling at the time:

[Mysore has] the most simple and despotic monarchy in the world, in which every department, civil and military, possesses the regularity and system [created] by the genius of Hyder, which— [with] all independent chiefs and Zemindars subjected or extirpated [and] justice severely and impartially administered to every class of people, a numerous and well-disciplined army kept up—gives to the government a vigour hitherto unexampled in India.[44]

Well before Wilks, Buchanan and Munro penned their comments, in fact while Haidar was alive, Maistre de la Tour, a Frenchman who headed Haidar's artillery for a time, wrote a biography of his master.[45] Describing Haidar's appearance, the Frenchman reported that the ruler kept a moustache but no beard or whiskers. Every morning barbers plucked off the hairs on his chin, and he used a gold-headed cane while walking.

In de la Tour's account, Haidar's court in Srirangapatna 'is the most brilliant in India' (39). Jewels abound. The horse-guard is Abyssinian. Dazzling in beauty and skill, young dancing girls with 'bells on their feet' come from nearby temples to entertain Haidar's guests.

Swedes, Irishmen, Europeans of different kinds are in Haidar's service. He adjudicates quarrels among Europeans. One such quarrel is between a Madame Mequinez, widow of a Portuguese officer who had served Haidar, and a Jesuit priest. Haidar has made the lady 'colonel' of the topass regiment previously headed by her husband, but she tries to extort money by blackmailing the priest. Though exposed, Haidar spares her.

De la Tour writes also of a Hindu raja hosting Haidar who has not paid the expected tribute. 'I lack the wherewithal,' the raja says. When his water supply is stopped, the raja opens an underground treasure at the precise spot where Haidar has been put up (172).

Haidar spends time each day dictating letters to a clutch of Brahmin secretaries. If, however, he hears that a tiger has left its forest and entered the plains, he rides to hunt it down, escorted by men with spears and bucklers. The party surrounds the tiger.

When, to force an escape, the animal prepares to spring on one of the men, 'he is attacked by Hyder, to whom the honour of giving the first stroke is yielded, and in which he seldom fails' (44).

Europeans in Haidar's service have bilingual servants. Offering glimpses of South India's economic life during Haidar's time, de la Tour writes of bankers from 'Guzerat' found in different towns in the south who give letters of exchange which are honoured in cities where connected bankers exist. Where there are no bankers, cash is sent through reliable porters who charge by distance.

De la Tour relates a story he has heard of how caste-men of these money porters reimbursed a Madras banker the sum one of their number had run off with, and later brought to the banker the head of the offender, who had been tracked down in Malabar. Adds the Frenchman:

> Letters of exchange are far more ancient in India than in Europe; but they are not drawn to order [*they were drawn to the bearer*]... This difficulty is in some measure obviated by naming several persons in the same bill: 'Pay to John, or in his absence to Peter, or in his absence to James, &c' (73–75fn).

At Haidar's general audience, up to thirty or forty secretaries sit against a wall and write continually. At every station, letters are marked, and the time of arrival is noted. These 'posts have since been imitated by the British', claims de la Tour (32).

The Frenchman writes also of the Malayalam country's Syrian Christians involved with Haidar, including 'deputies who came to Coimbatoor: stout men with a ferocious manner; they had the figure of a small cross above their nose punctured in the skin, and a large scar on the right cheek, caused by the recoil of their musquets' (168).

According to de la Tour, 'The men of consequence [in Mysore] have agents, who are usually Bramins, who [at a general audience] solicit their affairs either with the prince or his ministers' (32). Too important to go themselves to a general audience, these 'men of consequence' send Brahmin vakils (agents) to ministers likely to be present there, or the ministers' principal secretaries.

These 'men of consequence' may meet Haidar over a dinner or an evening play, without, however, discussing any business with the prince, who dictates letters to secretaries while a performance takes place.

Haidar's interest in Coorg, at this stage subordinate to Bidanur, is referred to by de la Tour, who describes the tract as 'a small kingdom situated at the southern extremity of Canara, and separated from that kingdom as well as from the Malabar district, and the kingdom of Mysore, by mountains that entirely enclose it' (90).

The Frenchman also writes of Haidar's move in 1766 into Malabar. Reacting to bullying, the area's Nairs have killed some Mapillas, who welcome Haidar's cavalry. Many fleeing Nairs are slaughtered by Mapillas advancing in the wake of Haidar's cavalry.

Shaken by the slaughter and, it seems, suspected of betrayal by the rulers of Kochi and Travancore, the zamorin immolates himself, his family and his treasure (110).

Ruthless in punishing Nairs who had killed Frenchmen in his army, Haidar apparently ordered that the Nairs could not carry arms and must salute inferior castes. When that did not work, he said they could regain their privileges by becoming Muslim. Few Nairs took up the offer; most slipped away, beyond Haidar's reach, to Travancore (120–25).

In a 'most public place' in Bengaluru, de la Tour runs into the iron cage in which Khande Rao had died and finds the unfortunate man's bones still there (72–73).

◆

In 1763, Haidar captured Sira, which lay between Mysore and the Marathas, plus a tract, westward of Bangalore, around Bidanur, which led to the Arabian Sea. And he obtained sway also over the port city of Mangaluru.

Although the Marathas soon took Bidanur from him, Haidar retained Sira. In 1766, he seized the major Malayali port of Kozhikode, where, in the dramatic incident referred to by de la Tour and burnt into the memory of many Malayalis, Eradi, the zamorin, had set fire to the palace and immolated himself.

When Mysore's titular ruler Krishnaraja died that year, Haidar arranged for Krishnaraja's son Nanjaraja to succeed. A year later, in 1767, when the British, the Marathas and the nizam came together to overpower Mysore in what would be called the First Anglo–Mysore War, Haidar first made peace with the Marathas and then sent his young son Tipu plus presents of elephants, horses and jewels to the nizam, who was encamped in Channapatna, 37 miles from Bengaluru. The nizam seemed placated.

Born in Devanahalli on 20 November 1750, Tipu was not yet seventeen when placed at the head of a Mysorean column which dashed towards Madras and surprised the British. In June 1767, this column reached San Thome and indeed 'the very country houses of the Madras councillors', but a defeat for Haidar in Tiruvannamalai (about 115 miles southwest of Madras) forced Tipu and the other Mysoreans to turn around and assist him.

Some months later, Haidar and Tipu were compelled to move to the peninsula's opposite coast, where the British had captured Mangaluru, which, however, they retook in the summer of 1768.

In the following year, Haidar arrived at the gates of Madras and forced a treaty on the British, but he failed in his bid for an Anglo–Mysore alliance against the Marathas. An earlier attempt by him to enlist the nizam in an anti-British drive had also failed.

In the early 1770s, Haidar lost a string of battles against the Marathas but bought peace with money. Suspected of communicating secretly with the Marathas, Mysore's nominal king, Nanjaraja, was executed under Haidar's orders; his brother Chamaraja was placed on the throne.

An astute Brahmin named Apajee Ram represented Mysore in negotiations with an ambassador from the peshwa, the Marathas' chief. When the ambassador insinuated that Haidar had usurped the Mysore king's power, Apajee Ram remarked in response that the Mysoreans were 'merely emulating greater personages elsewhere', a reference to the peshwas' sidelining of the Maratha king.[46]

The Brahmin closest to Haidar was Krishnacharya Purniah, born in 1746 to Krishnacharya and Lakshmi Bai, Vaishnavites of the Madhva[47] sect. Though born and raised in what may be seen as Tamil country—in the village of Tirukambur in Coimbatore district's Kulithalai taluk[48]—Purniah's forebears are said by one scholar to have 'migrated from the southern Maratha districts',[49] but a direct descendant categorically affirms that 'Dewan Purnaiya was Kannada-Madhwa-Brahmin'.[50]

Around 1760, Krishnacharya moved with his family to a town near Coimbatore called Sathyamangalam where the Mysore dalavai, Devaraja, was living with his army. In this town young Purniah found a job with a merchant, Ranga Setty, who supplied goods, clothing and forage to a prominent Srirangapatna merchant named Annadana Setty. Often accompanying Ranga Setty on visits to Srirangapatna, Purniah was recruited there by Annadana Setty, who was providing stores to Haidar.

Another big jump occurred when, noticing Purniah's skills, Haidar's Brahmin treasurer, Krishna Rao, hired him. As Krishna Rao's man, Purniah went at times to Haidar. Taken by Purniah's memory, flair for numbers, and truthfulness, Haidar made him an additional treasurer, almost on par with Krishna Rao, in 1770 or thereabouts.

While Krishna Rao kept accounts in Marathi, Purniah maintained all entries in Kannada. Before long, Haidar gave Purniah the charge of his army's commissariat, sent him to battlefields, and gave him a jagir in Mysore taluka.[51]

Haidar's trust had been won by Purniah, who would become dewan and, after Haidar's death in 1782, Tipu's minister as well.

◆

In the summer of 1779, Christian Frederick Schwartz, a Lutheran evangelizing between Trichy, Thanjavur and coastal Tranquebar, was asked by the Fort St George governor, Thomas Rumbold, to go quietly to Srirangapatna, meet Haidar, gauge his intentions, and report back.

The choice of Schwartz made sense. He had acquired fluency, apart from his native German, in English, Tamil, Portuguese, Hindustani, Persian and Marathi. He also enjoyed wide respect, including that of Tulajaji, the Maratha ruler of Thanjavur, who was a Company vassal. Schwartz would later claim that a weakness for women and liquor had prevented the raja from embracing Christianity.[52]

Though privately viewing Muslims and Roman Catholics as 'the most artful enemies of the Gospel',[53] Schwartz had friends in their circles as well. The Company was confident that Haidar would receive the German missionary.

Setting forth on 1 July, Schwartz found the countryside beautiful, charming, and, to his surprise, hilly. After a pre-dawn climb he wrote: 'The sun rose, and we beheld the numerous heights and depths with astonishment.' Earlier he had noticed 'the streams flowing on each side, and the lofty and branching trees…[that] refresh the eye'.[54]

Arriving in Mysore, Schwartz noticed Dutchmen, Frenchmen and Germans in Haidar's employ, and he also saw that when rain washed away the earth from the sides of a bridge, Haidar's men quickly made repairs. To Schwartz, this contrasted with the Tamil country's European-ruled areas, 'where all is suffered to go to ruin'. Of Srirangapatna, Schwartz would observe,

Here reigns no pomp but the utmost regularity and dispatch.[55]

Schwartz found the illiterate Haidar dictating letter after letter to Brahmin secretaries. The ruler's 'household', by which Schwartz probably meant palace staff, 'consisted chiefly of Brahmins'. He thought that most tax officers, too, were Brahmin. Although at times an officer was rewarded, punishment was the more common prod, and flogging its usual form. However, despite flogging,

Numbers eagerly seek these lucrative employments [as tax officers]. The Brahmins are the worst in this traffic. When one of them has obtained a district, he fleeces its inhabitants without remorse… At length, called upon by Hyder to pay arrears, he pleads poverty. Having undergone a flagellation, he returns to renew his exactions.[56]

Receiving Schwartz courteously, Haidar told him that he wanted friendly relations with the British but also that he remembered their wrongs. Resented more by Haidar, Schwartz felt, was Nawab Muhammad Ali of Arcot.

A few months after Schwartz conveyed his impressions to Fort St George, a big Haidar army attacked Company-dominated Tamil tracts south of Madras. Commencing the Second Anglo–Mysore War, this attack was triggered in part by the East India Company's capture of French-controlled Mahe, the west coast port vital to Haidar's international trade.

From 1780 to 1782, areas around Trichy and Thanjavur saw war and famine. Sluices irrigating the country were destroyed, peasants did not sow, there was nothing to harvest, and large numbers fled the countryside for the towns.

Relief was attempted by Schwartz, including, as he put it, for 'heathens'. Passing through places controlled by Haidar, he found that Mysore's soldiers had been instructed to 'let the venerable padre pass unmolested'.[57]

◆

In the late 1770s, Haidar retrieved some of the lands he had lost to the Marathas and looked interestedly towards the French, whose involvement from 1778 in the American war of independence had sharply divided them from the British. However, while the French wished to recover lost possessions in India through an alliance with Haidar, it was not until February 1782, almost two years after Haidar had invaded the Tamil country, that a French force landed on the Coromandel coast.

It was son Tipu, not an ally, who tipped the scale in Mysore's favour in this 1780 offensive. Supported from the rear by his father, Tipu inflicted, on 10 September 1780, a major defeat in the vicinity of Kanchipuram on a British force led by Colonel William Baillie.

Eighteen months later, in February 1782, Tipu imposed another significant defeat on the British, this time in Kumbakonam in the Thanjavur region. Four hundred Europeans of different kinds, under a Frenchman on Tipu's staff called Lallee, were part of the Mysore army that prevailed over the British, who were led by Colonel John Braithwaite.

Protracted and widespread, this second war with the British proved a burden for Haidar. Though the Mysoreans, using rockets and an energetic cavalry, penetrated several parts of the Tamil country, resentment was caused by soldiers who seized the villagers' food and goods. Meanwhile the East India Company employed its naval power to capture some of Haidar's major possessions on the Malabar coast.

Here is what Haidar apparently told Dewan Purniah in 1782 in a private conversation in an army camp near Kumbakonam:

> Between me and the English there [are] mutual grounds for
> dissatisfaction but not sufficient cause for war... The defeat of
> [the] Baillies and Braithwaites will not destroy them. I can ruin
> their resources on land, but I cannot dry up the sea![58]

We learn of this remark from Wilks, who heard of it from Purniah about
twenty years after it was supposedly made. In that camp conversation
Haidar also spoke, it appears, of his suspicions of the Marathas and
of the French.[59]

After Tipu's fall, and following Purniah's reappointment by the
Company as Mysore's dewan, it was in Purniah's interest to speak
to Wilks of his old master's respect for the British and dislike of
the French and the Marathas. Yet Haidar may well have made the
reported remark.

◆

Annoyed by the delay in the appearance of French troops and their
internal bickering, Haidar drew some cheer from word that Charles
de Bussy, whom he had known from 1750, when the two fought
together for the claims of Chanda Sahib and Muzaffar Jung, was
heading for India.

However, on 7 December 1782, four months before Bussy would
reach India, sixty-year-old Haidar died in an army camp in a village
called Narasingarayanpet near Chittoor, a town about 100 miles east
of Bengaluru.

Haidar's officers (Dewan Purniah among them) tried to conceal
the event. Disguised as treasure, Haidar's body was removed in a large
chest, while bearers carried forward a palanquin festooned to suggest
that the sultan was seated inside. Yet word leaked out.

A bid to prevent Tipu's succession was mounted by a cousin called
Muhammad Amin, ostensibly on behalf of Tipu's younger brother
Abdul Karim. But Purniah and other ministers were alert. Called for
'consultation', Amin was put in chains and removed under guard,
'as if by Hyder's personal orders', for conspiring 'to overthrow the
government while expecting Haidar's death'.[60]

Tipu was on the Malabar coast, trying to win back Kozhikode

from the British, when, on 11 December, a trusty courier brought a letter dictated by Haidar some days before his death, asking the son to return to the sultan's camp.

Always managing to recruit Indian spies, the East India Company in Madras learned of Haidar's death before Tipu did. On 13 December, the governor at Fort St George, George Macartney, wrote to Calcutta: 'We must derive as much advantage out of this as possible'.[61]

A month later, on 13 January 1783, General Sir Eyre Coote[62] observed: 'Many benefits...may be expected to our general interests in India by the important event of Hyder Ali's death. It opens to us the fairest prospect of securing to the mother country the permanent and undisturbed possession of the eastern dominions.'[63]

The man who had confined the British to the two coasts had gone. A Major James Rennell would write of Haidar:

> His military success was founded on the improvement of discipline; attention to merit of every kind; conciliation of the different tribes that served under his banner; contempt of state and ceremony; economy in personal expenses...minute attention to matters of finance and the regular payment of his army. All these together made Hyder as far above the princes of Hindustan as the qualities of Frederick the Great of Prussia raised him above European princes.[64]

Riding long stretches all the way from the west coast towards a distant Chittoor, Tipu reached the camp on 28 December. The next day he was enthroned. The smooth transition broke an India-wide pattern of gory succession battles. It also denied the British the benefits hoped for by Coote.

TIPU (1750–1799)

Shorter than his father, darker in the skin and possessing larger eyes, Tipu wore (Wilks informs us) 'a plain unencumbered attire, which he equally exacted from those around him... He was usually mounted, and attached great importance to horsemanship, in which he was considered to excel... The conveyance in a palankeen he derided' (761).

The tiger was his icon.

Tipu used to say it was better to live for two days like a tiger than drag out an existence like a sheep for two hundred years... He kept six [tigers] in his fortress-city of Seringapatam, where his throne was shaped and striped like a tiger... [T]he hilt of his sword was in the form of a snarling tiger, and his favourite toy was a mechanical tiger straddling a British officer while the victim squealed in terror.[65]

Among dozens of chiefs in eighteenth-century India, Tipu was the only one to have really scared the British. His fame grew, and Tipu found a seemingly permanent place in the pantheon of India's historical heroes. Knowledge that he could be bigoted and ruthless did not dent the image. In the last two decades or so, the scene has changed. 'Tipu was a cruel fanatic' appears to be the only truth for some.

More useful than picking a 'hero' or 'villain' label for a past ruler is to know the issues confronting him and his state, the alignment of forces for and against him, the ruler's responses and initiatives, and the people's reactions at the time.

There is plenty of material to examine, including biographies by two men in his employ, one in Persian by Mir Hussain Kirmani, the other in Marathi by Ramchandra Rao Punganuri (which appears to be based almost entirely on Kirmani's book); and accounts by Britons like Wilks who fought against him, besides dozens of later works.

◆

Although the British briefly took Coimbatore from Tipu, the latter won a bigger prize, the port of Mangaluru, obliging the Company to sign a treaty with him. This March 1784 'Treaty of Mangalore', marking the end of the Second Anglo–Mysore War, restored Coimbatore to Tipu and revived French interest in him.

Blocking the shortest route between Srirangapatna and the Malabar coast, and hosting the spirited Kodava community, the mountains of Coorg were governed by Bidanur-linked rajas until Haidar seized control and imprisoned the ruling family.

Always restive at their subjugation, the proud Kodavas were enraged when, following his victory over the British at Mangaluru, Tipu tightened control over Coorg, strengthened his garrison in its chief fort in Madikeri (Mercara), chastised their chiefs for rising against his late father, and taunted them for their religious beliefs.

The Kodavas again rebelled, and Tipu replied by taking a big army, inclusive of a French battalion, to Coorg. The Kodavas were suppressed, but fury and bigotry joined firmness. A large number of Kodavas were killed or forcibly converted, and many were dragged to Srirangapatna.

When, in a treaty signed in 1783 in Paris, the British recognized American independence, Frenchmen involved with India were emboldened. Bussy wondered whether they could not 'unite the three Indian powers [Marathas, Hyderabad and Mysore] against the English without compromising ourselves'.[66]

But Indians were not interested in allying with one another. The nizam had in fact influenced the Mughal emperor at this time, the feeble Shah Alam II, against recognizing Tipu as Mysore's ruler.

As Bussy himself noted, 'The Marathas and the Nizam have made an alliance to destroy Tipu Sultan. This plan marvellously suits the English.'[67] Moreover, Viscount de Souillac, Governor General of France's eastern territories, regarded Tipu as 'proud, vain, imperious and undependable'. To make Tipu dependent on the French, de Souillac wanted the British to defeat him.[68]

Eventually, however, with Tipu firmly in control in Mysore, and both the Marathas and the nizam reaching an understanding with the English, Governor General de Souillac agreed that Tipu could send an embassy to Louis XVI in Paris. A ship, l'Aurore, was provided for the trip.

On 9 March 1786, four ships including l'Aurore sailed from the Malabar coast carrying three ambassadors, retinues of around 900 persons in all, four elephants (one each for the rulers of Turkey, France and England, the fourth to sell for money), large boxes of personal effects and goods for sale. There was a scramble to get on board, for the intention was to call at Islam's holy places on the return journey.

The mission proved a disaster. Three of the four vessels were destroyed on the voyage and only a handful returned alive. Shipwrecks, plague and the winter in Constantinople (Istanbul) killed hundreds, including women and children.

Sailing first to Muscat and thence to Basra, the party had journeyed by land from there to Istanbul via Mosul and Diyarbakir, often across dangerous terrain. An Indian merchant in Muscat named Maoji Sheth and his agents in Basra, Sewa and Ram, helped, but dissension among the ambassadors damaged commerce as well as diplomacy.

In November 1787 in Istanbul, the Sultan of Turkey, Abdul Hamid I, received what remained of the mission. Tipu's throne was indeed recognized, but this was poor consolation. Fighting the Russians at this time, the Turks had no desire to antagonize the English as well by helping Tipu, and French agents in Istanbul told Tipu's men that the mood in France had changed and they would not be welcome there.

Making an about-turn, the truncated mission left for home, stopping en route at sacred places in Arabia. When the voyage ended on the Malabar coast in December 1789, only a handful were alive to step ashore.[69]

An insistent Tipu had, meanwhile, sent another mission directly to France. This managed to reach Paris and was received in August 1788 by Louis XVI and his queen, Marie Antoinette, in the Salon d'Hercules at the Palace of Versailles.

For a few days the Orientals created a buzz, but the French Revolution was around the corner, even though the king and the queen would not be executed until 1793.

Not recognizing the changes in France, Tipu's envoys asked for 10,000 French soldiers, for whom (they said) Mysore would pay, and they promised the French vast tracts of land in South India (close to Madras and Pondicherry) and also in Bengal and Bihar. The proposals were not taken seriously. The France of 1788 was in no condition to think of helping Tipu.

There were pettier problems. The Mysoreans complained that the palace housing them was not large enough, while French hosts hinted that gifts brought for their king were not valuable enough. Reluctant, it seems, to leave France, the delegation had to be persuaded to depart.

These westward expeditions ordered by Tipu in the second half of the 1780s were ill-conceived, ill-prepared, ill-timed and expensive.

◆

When, in December 1789, the residue of the mission to Turkey returned to the southern Malabar coast, Tipu was close by, trying to breach the so-called Travancore Lines, which had been constructed in the 1760s for Raja Rama Varma of Travancore by his Dutch/Belgian commander-in-chief, the ingenious Eustachius de Lannoy.

We saw de Lannoy in the last chapter as the prisoner enlisted for strengthening Travancore's forces by Rama Varma's predecessor, Marthanda Varma. While protecting Travancore against ground incursions from the north, the Lines were, in fact, built on the land of Travancore's neighbour and frequent rival, Cochin (Kochi). For decades a Dutch possession, Cochin had become a Mysore tributary in the 1770s.

Proceeding for four miles or so from the sea to a river named Chinnamangalam, and another 24 or 25 miles from the river to the hills, the Lines consisted, for much of their length, of a trench or ditch 16 feet broad and 20 feet deep. Bamboo hedges and a rampart protected the trench.[70] Nearby, also in Cochin territory, stood the fort of Cranganore (Kodungallur).

Few traces of the Lines remain today, but in December 1789 these comprised the site for Travancore's successful defence against Tipu's army. Earlier that year, Rama Varma, whose ultimate goal was the 'unification of Malabar under one flag',[71] had bought Cranganore Fort from the Dutch. This transaction between Travancore and the Dutch offended Tipu, who also desired the fort and felt that as Cochin's suzerain he should have been offered it first.

On 28 December, about 800 of Travancore's Nairs, aided by a six-pounder gun, not only stopped the reputed Mysorean army from capturing the Lines, they inflicted a great loss on the attackers, who retreated in panic.

Reports later circulated, to which Wilks would give credence, that Tipu was among the invaders, that he was wounded by a musket ball, and that his palanquin and arms were captured by the Nairs. The story was denied. Though in the vicinity, Tipu, it was said, was not at the Lines that day, and it was reiterated that Tipu never used a palanquin.

Yet the Nair victory of 28 December 1789 was a reality which Malayalis have recalled with pride ever since. In April 1790, the Mysoreans again attacked the Lines and captured them, and in May Cranganore Fort, too, was taken, but when news reached Tipu that the English were ready to invade his kingdom, he marched back towards Srirangapatna.[72]

◆

The British used the Travancore incident to launch an all-out war, known to history as the Third Anglo–Mysore War. Named a British ally in the Treaty of Mangalore, Travancore sought the Company's aid, thereby giving the opportunity for which Lord Charles Cornwallis was waiting.

After fighting unsuccessfully in the western hemisphere against the Americans, Cornwallis had become Governor General in India in 1786. Nursing complaints against Mysore and tempted by its land and money, the Marathas as well as Hyderabad's nizam (Mir Nizam Ali) joined the war on the British side.

Not everyone in the Company favoured a war on Mysore. Controlling a larger territory and capable of mobilizing a much bigger army, the Marathas were seen by many as Britain's primary obstacle in India. However, a twenty-eight-year-old lieutenant called Thomas Munro, posted in Ambur near Vellore to gather intelligence on Tipu's forces, argued for the opposite viewpoint. In January 1790, he wrote to his father:

> It has long been accepted as an axiom...by the directors of our affairs, both at home and in this country, that Tippoo ought to be preserved as a barrier between us and the Mahrattas... [But this] is to support a powerful and ambitious enemy to defend us from a weak one...
>
> [Mysore has] the most simple and despotic monarchy in the world, in which every department, civil and military, possesses the regularity and system [created] by the genius of Hyder...
>
> The other...a confederacy of independent chiefs possessing extensive dominions, now acting in concert, now jealous of each other...and at all times liable to be [swayed] by the most distant prospect of private gain, can never be a dangerous enemy...[And] it maintains no standing army and is impelled by no religious tenets to attempt the extirpation of men of a different belief.

On the other hand, Munro argued, 'Tippoo supports an army of 110,000 men, follows with great eagerness every principle of European tactics...[a]nd he is, with all of his extraordinary talents, a furious zealot in a faith which,' claimed Munro, 'founds eternal happiness on the destruction of other sects.'[73]

The thinking in Munro's letter prevailed, and Tipu was targeted. The allied forces moved in from several points around his domain. Taking personal command of the British force, the battle-seasoned Cornwallis advanced from Fort St George. Coimbatore, lying due south of the Mysore capital, was quickly taken by another British column. Two Maratha armies marched down from the kingdom's northwest, one proceeding south to Dharwad, the other southeast to Kurnool. While the nizam's army also marched southwards on the Deccan Plateau, British units sailing from Bombay captured Calicut and Cannanore on the Malabar coast and lay poised to tighten, from the southwest, the noose around Srirangapatna, which was an island surrounded and protected by the Kaveri.

Tragically for the people trapped in the war, it was also a time of acute scarcity. Nine years later, Buchanan, the Company's doctor/scientist/officer, arriving in a place not far from Chikballapur called Bomma Samudram, would write in his diary:

> *25 July 1800:* [The horrors of famine] were never so severely felt here, as during the invasion of Lord Cornwallis, when, the country being attacked on all sides and penetrated in every direction by hostile armies, or by defending ones little less destructive, *one half at least of the inhabitants perished of absolute want.*[74]

It is a sober truth of history-writing that a phrase like this is located, inserted, italicized—and quietly abandoned.

◆

Gaining Bangalore in March 1791, Cornwallis made it a base to which he returned more than once while attempting junctions with the advancing Maratha and Hyderabad armies. (Italics added) In March 1791, we may mark, 'the town of Bangalore...situated north of the fort...was circular in form and *about three miles in circumference.* Its streets were wide... Few towns in India [had] better houses and richer inhabitants.'[75]

Visiting the city nine years later, here is what Buchanan would say of Cornwallis's attack on it:

> Bangalore, or Bangaluru, [is] a city which was founded by Hyder, and which, during the judicious government of that prince, became

a place of importance. Its trade was then great, and its manufactures numerous.

Tippoo began its misfortunes by prohibiting the trade with the dominions of Arcot and Hyderabad... [His measures] had greatly injured the place; but it was still populous, and many individuals were rich, when Lord Cornwallis arrived before it, with his army in great distress from want of provisions.

This reduced [Cornwallis] to the necessity of giving the assault immediately, and the town was of course plundered. The rich inhabitants had previously removed their most valuable effects into the fort; but these too fell a prey to the invaders, when that citadel also was taken by storm (Buchanan, 193).

In a counter-measure, Tipu retook an unguarded Coimbatore. Penetrating between two British forces, he also reached Pondicherry, but found its French in no state to support him. Revolution in their homeland had paralyzed them.

Trying also to negotiate, Tipu sent to the British camp old Apajee Ram, 'the veteran diplomatist', as Wilks calls him, who twenty years earlier had talked wittily with the Marathas. Cornwallis rebuffed this initiative of February 1791, as also another feeler from Tipu three months later. The Governor General's stand would be sharply criticized by James Mill in his 1817 *History of British India*, for four subsequent decades the standard guide for the Empire's officers in India (Wilks 4: 491fn).

◆

Serving as a soldier in Cornwallis's force, Wilks would later provide eye-witness accounts that reveal the Company's contempt for Indian allies while also providing vivid pictures. Referring to the nizam's army, which joined the English near Bangalore in April 1791, Wilks mentions 'ten thousand men well-mounted on horses in excellent condition' before adding:

It is probable that no national or private collection of ancient armour in Europe contains any weapon or article of personal equipment not [present] in this motley crowd: the Parthian bow and arrow, the iron club of Scythia, sabres of every age and nation, lances of every strength and description, and matchlocks of every form, metallic helmets of every pattern, a steel bar descending diagonally as a protection to the face…complete coats of mail, and quilted jackets, sabre-proof…

To this grand appearance was joined:

> the total absence of every symptom of order, or obedience, or command, excepting groups collected round their respective flags; [with] every individual an independent warrior, self-impelled, affecting to be the champion whose single arm was to achieve victory… (444).

According to Wilks, the British had expected the nizam's army to watch the terrain and provide resources from 'the country to be traversed', but this support was not forthcoming. Worse, the nizam's men consumed forage and grain from grounds on which the English were encamped and plundered villages friendly to the British (445).

In the 1791 summer, as Cornwallis moved west with his army, his goal was to ford the Kaveri along with the nizam's army and, he hoped, the Marathas, and attack the capital. To assure victory, a British force launched by sea from Bombay and moving east from Calicut was also to join the assault.

This cherished plan had to be given up because Cornwallis's army was close to starvation, the Maratha ally seemed nowhere near, and Tipu's soldiers had put up a strong fight at Arakere, 10 miles east of Srirangapatna, before retreating safely to their capital. A British bid to rupture a dam near Arakere to ease the advance of their heavy train was 'abandoned' because of 'the solidity of the work' (453).

In the area around Srirangapatna, Tipu prevented, for a crucial week, the coming together of his foes, a feat accomplished through agile agents on the ground who kept Tipu informed of his enemies' movements while misleading enemy attackers regarding the whereabouts of their allies. Wilks would write:

> With whatever care Lord Cornwallis concealed his intentions…they were distinctly known to the Sultaun… Tippoo's activity against the English army was skillfully displayed in the dissemination of false intelligence (4: 437, 443).

Wilks's sharply negative view, overall, of Tipu lends interest to his observations on the abilities Tipu and his men showed during the 1791 summer. Of the Arakere battle, he says:

> Tippoo Sultaun did not decline the [confrontation], and praise cannot in justice be denied to him...[for] executing his movements with...promptitude and judgment (456).

About the British column advancing from the southwest, which was led by Robert Abercromby, Wilks would write:

> The admirable efficiency of the Sultaun's light troops had prevented all communication of General Abercromby's situation on which Lord Cornwallis's determinations would very materially depend (461).

The long trek towards Srirangapatna from Bangalore had been slow and hard for Cornwallis's British, who faced a great shortage of provisions. Tipu's irregular cavalry had succeeded in cutting off local supplies, and manual support too was absent, for Mysoreans were unwilling to help.

> Many of the heavy guns, as well as the field pieces...and all the battering train and almost every public cart in the army were dragged by the troops (461).

His men exhausted and hungry, and the Marathas conspicuously missing, Cornwallis instructed not only a retreat but also the destruction of his heavy siege equipment. Tipu had won against a Governor General who had graduated from a major war in America.

◆

Three days after that embarrassing order was implemented, the weary British were surprised to face a new body of horsemen. Luckily for Cornwallis, these belonged not to Tipu but to the Marathas. Wilks recorded that Tipu's light cavalry had prevented word of their arrival from reaching the British camp until the Marathas were 'actually in sight' (465).

From Wilks we obtain more pictures, jaundiced perhaps, yet revealing, of scenes from the 1791 summer.

Having not had a wholesome meal for a fortnight, the hungry British and the equally hungry Indian contingents in the Company's force looked with eager eyes at the freshly-arrived Maratha army, but as Wilks put it, 'the inimitable mercantile policy of a Mahratta chief in his own camp was skillfully exhibited in holding up exorbitant prices' (466). The British found some consolation when they saw the nizam's troops also suffering from Maratha 'exactions'.

Wilks contrasted the nizam's 'stately' but lethargic 'cavaliers' with 'the mean aspect and black meagre visage of the common Mahratta horseman' who however 'foraged at large and effectually commanded the resources of the country'. In areas vacated by the retreating British, the Marathas apparently plundered everything 'down to the meanest article of wearing apparel' (468).

But there were impressive features as well. At a 'bazar of a Mahratta camp', its 'famished visitors', of whom Wilks was one, saw:

> the spoils of the east and the industry of the west: English broad cloth, a Birmingham pen-knife, shawls of Cashmire, diamonds, oxen, sheep and poultry; dried salt fish; and the tables of the money-changers overspread with the coins of every country of the east, evidence of mercantile activity inconceivable in any camp excepting that of systematic plunderers (467).

Also available for purchase by British soldiers were 'what their own Indian capitals could not then produce, except as European imports—excellent sword belts' (467).

In the weeks following the retreat, the British noticed quite a few Mysorean accomplishments. Of the Nandidurg Fort, about 31 miles north of Bangalore, Wilks would write:

> Every fortified place the English had hitherto seen in Mysoor exhibited evidence of the extraordinary attention paid by Tippoo Sultaun to [its] repair and improvement, but the works of Nundidroog, a granite rock of tremendous height, seemed to have engrossed in a peculiar degree his design of rendering it impregnable (498).

Wilks refers also to the 'fresh vigour' and 'a very respectable degree of skill' with which Tipu's commander Qamaruddin fought the British in the Coimbatore–Palghat area in October 1791 (507).

◆

Some Maratha units plundering in Tipu's richest province, Bidanur, had meanwhile pillaged the ancient Hindu monastery, possibly founded in the ninth century, at Sringeri, which lay about 75 miles northwest of Srirangapatna. The matha was desecrated, many defenders were killed, and the raiders made off with about sixty lakh rupees in cash or jewels.

The monastery's head, successor to an unbroken line of Sankaracharyas, appealed for aid to Tipu, whose support the matha had evidently received from 1785.

That appeal, and Tipu's positive response, form part of a well-preserved 1791 correspondence, conducted not in Persian but in Kannada, which discloses Tipu's support for the matha, his instruction to the asif or provincial governor of Bidanur to help the Sankaracharya, the latter's appreciation for aid and security received, and also the Sankaracharya's blessings for a Tipu striving to defend his territory.[76]

◆

Alleging that the threat to his capital prompted Tipu to order the execution of twenty English boys who had been detained and trained as 'singers and dancers' in the style of 'Hindoostani dancing girl' (449), Wilks also relates an account of prominent Brahmins around Tipu who were charged with treason and executed.

An unnamed Indian spy recruited by Cornwallis's intelligence chief, Captain William Macleod, was caught by Tipu's men, who found an incriminating letter in Kannada in the spy's hollow walking stick. 'A Muslim official who knew Kannada was ordered to examine the letter,' and the writer was identified and 'seized, a Brahmin forcibly circumcised and now named Mahommed Abbas'.

The letter implicated 'Sheshgere Row, brother of the treasurer Kishen Row'—the long-serving Krishna Rao, who had given Purniah an early break. According to Wilks, not only Seshagiri Rao but also Krishna Rao and two other brothers were 'privately tortured and dispatched' (450).

Writing his account after Tipu's fall, Wilks reported that because a Muslim had inspected the damaging letter, many Brahmins 'continue under the impression' that the alleged involvement of Krishna Rao and his brothers in 'any act of treachery' was a 'calumny' invented by 'Seyed Saheb', the inspector's influential brother-in-law, in revenge for cuts that treasurer Krishna Rao had previously imposed on money going to 'Seyed Saheb' (450). Adds Wilks:

> The Sultaun, in reviewing the measures of his reign, had reasonable cause for distrusting all bramins, and such were all his secretaries for the languages of the south (450).

After Tipu's fall, Wilks discussed with Dewan Purniah, with whom he worked closely, the treason charge against Krishna Rao. He writes: 'I could never get Poornea, his colleague, to give an opinion' (450fn). According to Wilks, Abbas admitted his guilt before Tipu, by whom he was summoned, but refused to implicate others.

> 'And how long,' said Tippoo, 'have you been a traitor?' 'From the period,' replied he, 'that you began to circumcise bramins and destroy their temples.' He was put to death by being publicly dragged at the foot of an elephant (450).

Whether or not Wilks is telling everything truthfully, his narrative reveals a few things. One, throughout his rule Tipu employed Brahmin officers to control funds. Two, punishment for treachery was ruthless. Three, when, some years after Tipu's fall, Wilks was writing his account, Brahmins continued to resent the treachery charge: loyalty to Tipu was a value they still cherished. Four, it was in the British interest to stoke fires of enmity between Muslims and Brahmins. Five, intelligence was a key element in South India's end-eighteenth-century battles. And six, Purniah, working first with one side and then with the other, remained totally discreet with Wilks, a top-level imperial officer.

Travelling across Mysore a few months after Tipu's death, Francis Buchanan was told (he does not state by whom) that Tipu had once asked Purniah to become a Muslim. Apparently Purniah in response merely said, 'I am your slave,' and retired. Thereafter several persons, including Tipu's mother, 'a very respectable lady', told Tipu that he should leave Purniah alone. Pressure on him would 'throw everything into confusion'. Tipu 'very properly allowed the matter to rest' (Buchanan, 61).

From the words quoted it appears likely that Purniah, on whom we know Buchanan had called in Srirangapatna, told the story himself. The 'very respectable lady' was someone who had known and understood Purniah for years.

◆

Eight months after his retreat of May 1791, having secured his supply line for food and forage and strengthened also his network of spies, Cornwallis again attacked Srirangapatna from the east. As before, Abercromby advanced from the southwest. Once more joining the invasion were the Marathas, who had used the interregnum to gain territory in northern Mysore, as also the nizam's troops.

This time Tipu was unable to prevent a confluence of his numerous foes. Facing a massive army outside Srirangapatna, he responded with an unexpected shower of rockets which at first disconcerted the besieging soldiers, but a tight siege was successfully enforced. To furnish timber for the siege, 'the extensive and beautiful garden [in Bangalore] of Lalbaugh', containing every kind of tree, 'a princely nursery for the produce of Mysore', had been cut down, Wilks would admit (547).

The 'rockets were iron tubes a foot long and an inch in diameter filled with gunpowder and attached to [longer] bamboo rods... The tubes were aimed, lit and propelled to distances of up to a thousand yards like fiery arrows. These noisy missiles are said to have skittered and snaked along the ground, some bursting like bombshells, causing panic among the opponents' cavalry.'[77]

Releasing two of his English prisoners, Tipu sent with them a feeler for peace. The Treaty of Seringapatam that quickly emerged included a medieval element on which the British had insisted. Tipu was not only to give the confederates half his territory plus three crore and thirty lakh rupees as damages, he also had to hand over two of his sons to Cornwallis as hostages, to be returned when the damages were fully paid.

On 23 February 1792, Tipu assembled at his capital's main mosque all the principal officers of his army and asked for their frank opinions, sealed by an oath on the Quran, on the peace terms demanded by the confederates. Wilks writes that 'in aftertimes few of the members of that assembly could recite its events without tears' (552).

After Tipu had obtained assent to the terms, the boys were handed over on 26 February. In a solemn ceremony, the two sides exchanging gun salutes, Lord Cornwallis took possession of the Oriental princes, ten-year-old Abdul Khaliq and eight-year-old Moizuddin.

A Scotsman present, Robert Home, painted the scene for posterity.[78] The boys were taken to the Company's secure fort in Vellore, with Lieutenant Thomas Munro (the one who had called Tipu Britain's first enemy in India) commanding the escort, and thence to Fort St George.[79]

While the Marathas and the nizam obtained large tracts from Tipu's domain, the East India Company absorbed Malabar in the west, Bellary and Anantapur in the north, and Salem and Dindigul in the south, attaching these rich districts to its Madras presidency. Tipu also lost Coorg, which became a Company dependency.

◆

Joseph Michaud, a Frenchman familiar with Srirangapatna both before and after Tipu's fall, would write:

> The city of Seringapatam had become one of the most important in Hindustan. The island on which it is situated is three miles and a half long and about a mile and a half broad. It rises to a great height in the middle of the river Cauvery and slopes rapidly to the bank. The fortress occupies a space of a thousand fathoms from the western extremity of the island. The river envelopes it on the north and on the west.[80]

After the 1792 defeat, the capital was strengthened with ramparts, moats and entrenchments, Frenchmen assisting in the work. According to Michaud:

> In times of peace the city was very flourishing. Tippoo Sultan [kept] at his court the sons of the poligars as a pledge of their loyalty [*the medieval element again*]. This made [it] the residence of the most distinguished and the most wealthy families of Mysore and Canara... Gold-work, jewellery and watch-making made remarkable progress in the city...
>
> The population increased considerably under Hyder Ali and Tippoo Saheb. A large number of Frenchmen had settled down in the capital, the majority of whom remained there after its conquest by the English...engaged in mechanical trades such as watch-making and gold-work. The trade of a gun-smith was the

most favoured of all by Tippoo Saheb.

But only the Mussulman religion obtained great prominence and favour.[81]

From notes compiled in the year 1800 by Francis Buchanan, the doctor-traveller, we receive additional pictures of Tipu's administration:

> The people universally accuse Tippoo of bigotry and vain glory; but they attribute most of their misery to the influence of his minister, Meer Saduc, a monster of avarice and cruelty. The Brahmans, who managed the whole of the revenue department, were so avaricious, so corrupt, and had shown such ingratitude to Hyder, that Tippoo would have entirely displaced them, if he could have done without their services; but that was impossible, for no other persons in the country had any knowledge of [the revenue] business (71).

Mysoreans told Buchanan that instead of inspecting his Brahmin bureaucrats, or giving them attractive salaries, Tipu had 'appointed Muslim Asophs [asifs], Lord Lieutenants, to superintend large divisions of the country; and this greatly increased the evil'. These nobles took bribes from Brahmin bureaucrats, who in consequence demanded double the usual bribe from the people (71).

Of Srirangapatna, Buchanan would write:

> The palace at the Laul Baug possesses a considerable degree of elegance and is the handsomest native building that I have ever seen (73).

On the walls of another palace in the capital, Buchanan saw paintings requisitioned by Tipu, including one showing Haidar and Tipu in procession and another capturing the 1782 defeat of Colonel Baillie. Panels portrayed some of Mysore's ethnicities. An intriguing painting taken from one of these panels and published in Buchanan's book is of an unnamed Brahmin with his wife and son. The artist is not named either (74).

◆

A visit to Srirangapatna in January 2017 showed that the Lal Mahal palace admired by Buchanan had long gone, its damaged walls apparently demolished by the British in 1807. The ancient temple of Sri Ranganathaswami, evidently protected by Tipu, was newly painted and thick with devotees, while two similarly ancient temples stood right next to the site of Tipu's residence, one named after Siva in his form as Lord of the Ganga and the other after Narasimha, the half-man-half-lion incarnation of Vishnu.

In the palace with panels that Buchanan had visited (the 'Summer Palace' as it's now called) hang intact wall-portraits including those of Krishnaraja Wadiyar II, Mysore's titular ruler from 1734 to 1766, the period's Hindu rajas of Coorg, Chitradurga and Banaras, the Maratha Peshwa Balaji Baji Rao II, the Muslim Nawab of Arcot, and Kempe Gowda I, the Vijayanagara feudatory who had founded Bangalore in the sixteenth century.

A street now called Purniah (or Purnaiah) Street contained houses where, it seems, only Brahmins reside. Evidently during Tipu's time, too, only Brahmins lived on this street. If, as seems possible, Purniah, too, resided there, it would have been a short carriage ride for him between home and Tipu's palace.

◆

In the six years of peace that followed his treaty with Cornwallis, Tipu fortified his capital, remounted his cavalry, enlarged and disciplined his infantry, suppressed refractory poligars, and encouraged cultivation.[82] The heavy fine to the Company was paid and he recovered his sons. But the 1792 humiliation remained unavenged.

The Marathas, whose rise the British feared, were moving towards disintegration, even though one of their chieftains, Daulat Rao Sindhia, seemed to control Shah Alam II, the Mughal throne's feeble occupant. In Hyderabad, which also seemed disorganized, a group of Frenchmen used the peace to gain influence. Only Mysore looked efficient, even though it had lost half its territory and much of its treasure.

Worried by Mysore's energy, London clamoured in 1797 for a more expansionist India policy, and Richard Wellesley, the Earl of Mornington, an 'imperialist to the core' who disliked France and its radical Jacobins,[83] was named Governor General.

Early that year, the port of Mangaluru, which had remained with Tipu, witnessed the landing of a small ship commanded by a Frenchman,

François Ripaud. Calling himself a Jacobin and an officer in the French navy, Ripaud proceeded to Srirangapatna, where he told Tipu that 10,000 Frenchmen, led by an admiral and a general, had arrived on the Indian Ocean islands of Mauritius (then 'Isle of France') and Reunion (then 'Bourbon'); the French, added Ripaud, wanted Tipu to use this force and overthrow the British.

Perhaps because he was impatient for revenge, and perhaps also because, as Wilks would contend, he was a poor judge of people, Tipu bought the tale. In May 1797, Ripaud and his Jacobin comrades were publicly welcomed, in Tipu's presence, at a Srirangapatna event, where opposition was announced to all kings except Tipu, who was hailed as a 'citizen prince'.

Two officials were asked by Tipu to accompany Ripaud to Mauritius. Arriving in Port Louis on 19 January 1798, they were indeed welcomed by General Malartic, France's Governor General for the two isles, but there was no sign of the 10,000 French fighters.

Unfazed, Tipu's men proposed in Port Louis a treaty with France whereby the French would provide to Tipu thousands of troops whose expenses he would bear, and, secondly, once all English troops were eliminated, territories in India would be equally divided between Tipu and the French.

On 30 January 1798, Malartic issued a proclamation saying that Tipu desired a treaty for expelling the British from India, and that Mysore would look after French fighting men (without, however, serving them wine). Enlisting in Tipu's service, several dozen Frenchmen accompanied Ripaud and the two Mysoreans onto a French frigate, *La Preneuse*, which brought the party back to the Malabar coast by end-April.

Tipu seemed to think that the British would not come to know of these public acts. But the Company's agents had not gone to sleep, and their freshly-named chief in India was eager to act.

On the very day when the French frigate landed in Mangaluru, Mornington, sailing from England, touched Madras. Arriving some days later in Calcutta, he received a report of the Port Louis proclamation, which was followed first by word from the British governor of the Cape of Good Hope that the report was authentic, and next by a ship captain's testimony before the Governor General that he was on shore at Port Louis when the proclamation was made.[84]

Sharpening an unending Anglo–French rivalry, the year 1798 also saw the eastwards advance of Napoleon. In May, Napoleon was in Egypt. In July, he captured Cairo. But in August, the English navy defeated him in the Battle of the Nile.

◆

Reaching India, word of that last result injected confidence in the breasts of the new Governor General in Calcutta and his thirty-year-old younger brother, Colonel Arthur Wellesley, the future victor, in Waterloo, over Napoleon, who had arrived in India a year before his older brother.

The confidence was sorely needed. For through their spies the British had learnt that Napoleon had assured the radicals still in control in Paris that 'as soon as he had conquered Egypt, he will establish relations with the Indian princes and, together with them, attack the English in their [Indian] possessions'.[85]

To a friend, Rear Admiral Charles Magon, Napoleon had evidently exclaimed, 'That's it! It's in India that we must attack English power.'[86]

And Charles Talleyrand, the French foreign minister, had claimed on 13 February 1798: 'Having occupied and fortified Egypt, we shall send a force of 15,000 men from Suez to India, to join the forces of Tipu-Sahib and drive away the English.'[87]

Mornington quickly took military, diplomatic and political steps. Asking Madras and Bombay to quietly assemble forces on both coasts, he also sent Tipu long, stalling letters which betrayed no hint that he was aware of Tipu's Mauritius proclamation or of Napoleon's hopes.

The Governor General also turned his attention to Hyderabad, where, led by a Michel Raymond, 124 French officers, including radical Jacobins, exercised sway over the nizam's 14,000 soldiers. From Madras a force led by a Colonel Roberts was 'secretly but expeditiously dispatched to Hyderabad'.[88]

Arriving there on 10 October, Roberts and his men obtained the surrender, twelve days later, of all the Frenchmen without firing a shot. Fortunately for the British, Raymond had suddenly died that year, before the surrender.

Not only did the nizam consent to this surrender; he agreed by treaty to keep in Hyderabad, at his expense, 6,000 artillery-backed English sepoys and in addition, pay the English an annual subsidy of over 14 lakhs! Why would the nizam not pay for protection from future foes and for the removal of Jacobin influence?

To seal the alliance, Mornington offered to protect the nizam from any new attack by the Marathas, at whose hands Hyderabad had suffered a large defeat in 1795, provided the French-trained army was disbanded.

Accepting the terms, the nizam became possibly the first 'major Indian power' that had 'definitely decided to trust to the British alliance and had for good or evil resolved to throw in his lot with theirs... and to heed their advice'.[89]

While the 124 Frenchmen were sent to Europe as prisoners of war, the Governor General's brother, Arthur, was moved to Hyderabad to head British soldiers poised there for orders to march into Mysore.

To the west, in Poona, 'a treaty was also formed with the Peshwah, the nominal head of the Marhatta empire, which secured the neutrality of that chief'.[90] The peshwa's rival, Daulat Rao Sindhia, who briefly thought of backing Tipu, was threatened that the British would finish him first. Mornington also neutralized the Danish settlement of Tranquebar, where Tipu had found French allies.[91]

On 25 December 1798, Tipu's response to two letters sent by Mornington in November reached Fort St George. Claiming that Mornington's word of Napoleon's defeat in the Nile battle had given him 'more pleasure than possibly be conveyed by writing', Tipu went on to express his wish that 'the French, who are of a crooked disposition, faithless, and the enemies of mankind, may be ever depressed and ruined'.[92]

Knowing what he knew, these sentences from Tipu could not have impressed Mornington.

TIPU FALLS

The Fall of Seringapatam on 4 May 1799 was a huge imperial event, which even Napoleon's later defeat in 1815 would not greatly eclipse. For years afterwards, British novelists (Walter Scott among them) and artists would pair the Corsican and the Mysorean. The siege preceding the fall, a participant, Alexander Beatson, would write, 'has never been surpassed in splendor by any event recorded in the history of the military transactions of the British nation in India'.[93]

By February, when Mornington ordered the attack, about 50,000 soldiers had been assembled to carry it out, mostly at Fort St George (about 350 miles from Srirangapatna) or near Mysore's southern borders (about 130 miles from Tipu's capital).

Headed by General George Harris, this army comprised the Company's units from Madras, Bengal and Bombay, a column from Hyderabad led by Arthur Wellesley, and another contingent sent by the nizam. About 4,000 of this force were white, all of them, apart from a few dozen Swiss mercenaries, British. The rest, a great majority, were native sepoys.

Accompanied by numerous elephants and camels and a vast army of bullocks, the soldiers trekked with big and small guns, batteries for breaching walls, and ladders for scaling them. The starvation that eight summers earlier had forced Cornwallis's retreat was not allowed to recur. Men and animals were fed throughout the long journey, and sustenance left over for enforcing the siege.

The marching mass included 'flocks of sheep and goats to provide meat for the officers, as well as hordes of camp followers and a travelling market selling food and drink for the soldiery'. Adds historian Richard Cavendish:

> Officers took along cooks, grooms, laundrymen and cleaning wallahs, and senior officers like Wellesley, who brought his silver-plated tableware with him, had thirty or more servants in their train. Moving ponderously in the burning heat, the army covered an area of eighteen square miles and on a good day managed to advance ten miles.[94]

A colonial classic, the expedition reached Srirangapatna in the first week of April and placed the city under siege. Though inside the fortress Tipu had around 30,000 soldiers, the British had already won half the battle.

Worse for Tipu, the Kaveri that protected Srirangapatna was almost completely dry: men could walk or even run across it. To delay an attack in hopes of rain, Tipu sent messages to British commanders proposing talks, but the ruse was transparent and the offer spurned.

The spirit inside Tipu's capital was not great. Many residents saw Mir Sadiq, Tipu's chief dewan, as venal and extorting, some as a traitor. Purniah commanded a sizable unit (of over 4,000 men), as did Tipu's son Fateh Haidar and the officer called Qamaruddin Khan, but apart from waiting for an attack all they could do was to randomly fire cannons at a distant enemy.

On 5 April, the defenders succeeded in repelling a night assault, led by Arthur Wellesley, on a village called Sultanpettah. There were twenty-five British casualties; Wellesley himself was injured in the knee and almost captured.[95] The next day, however, the village was easily taken by the British.

Reporting that 'the thunder of the artillery, English and Mysorean, was kept on in the quietness of the night from bank to bank with terrific noise; and the explosion of the mines spread a frightful light over the horizon', Michaud, the Frenchman, would refer to 'the sublime horror of this nightly spectacle'. In his view, 'Tippoo Saheb showed during the siege valour and bravery without parallel' (141).

If Harris waited much longer, his army's stores of food would deplete dangerously, but he wanted a reasonable opening in the fortress's walls before ordering his men to strike. On 28 April and again on 2 May, the attackers' batteries caused breaches in the fortress's walls. The second opening, which the nizam's soldiers had produced, was widened by fresh fire, and on the night of 3 May, Harris decided on storming through it the following day—'in the middle of the day, when the sun was high, and Tipu and his army were taking refreshment'.[96]

David Baird, once a prisoner of Tipu (after the latter's 1782 win over Braithwaite) and now a major general, was asked by Harris to lead the assault. At 1 p.m. on the 4th, 'a dram of whisky and a biscuit were then issued to the European troops [Indians in the army were not entitled to this favour], before Baird drew his sword to signal the attack'.[97]

Evidently 'cheers resounded along the trenches as the storming party dashed across the River Cauvery. Within 16 minutes, they had crossed the river...and...scaled the ramparts...under heavy fire from Tipu's batteries.'[98]

A year later, in April 1800, an *enormous* canvas, 21 feet high and 120 feet long, portraying 'The Storming of Seringapatam' would open in London, done by a young artist called Robert Ker Porter, which Londoners would flock to see over the following nine months.

Many were killed in Srirangapatna that day, hundreds on the British side and thousands on Tipu's, for defence was defiant and brave, and attackers, too, were daring. Rioting by the victorious side took a fresh toll in the forty-eight hours that followed, while some men of Srirangapatna angrily killed Mir Sadiq. After the fall, in apparent confirmation of treachery, his estate received land in Hyderabad from the nizam.[99]

Earlier that morning, when every portent seemed dark, Tipu had given gifts to Brahmin priests of his city's Vishnu temple and asked them to pray for him. In the afternoon, he frontally faced the rush of attackers and kept shooting from his horse. When he was hit himself, aides put him on a palanquin and tried to remove him, but an unidentified British soldier killed Tipu, more, perhaps, for his jewelled sword than in knowledge of who he was.[100]

Tipu's body fell into a pile of other bodies. How it was identified was described in an 'Extract of a Letter from Camp at Seringapatam' in the *Bombay Courier* of 24 August 1799:

> About dusk, General Baird, in consequence of information he had received at the Palace, came with lights to the gate, accompanied by the...Killadar of the fort and others, to search for the body of the Sultaun, and after much labour it was found and brought from under a heap of the slain to the inside of the gate.
>
> The countenance was no ways distorted, but had an expression of stern composure; his turban, jacket and sword-belt were gone, but the body was recognised by some of his people, who were there, to be Padshaw.
>
> An officer who was present, with leave of General Baird, took from his right arm the Talisman, which contained, sewed up in pieces of fine flowered silk, an amulet of a brittle metallic substance of the colour of silver, and some manuscripts in...Arabic and Persian characters [confirming]...the identity of the Sultaun's body.
>
> [The body] was placed on his own palanquin, and by General Baird's orders conveyed to the court of the Palace, where it remained during the night.

A Major Allan who also confronted Tipu's body on the evening of the 4th would write:

> When Tippoo was bought from under the gateway his eyes were open and the body was so warm, that for a few moments Col. Wellesley and myself were doubtful whether he was not alive; on feeling his pulse and heart all doubt was removed... His head was uncovered, his turban being lost in the confusion of his fall...
>
> He had an appearance of dignity or perhaps of sternness in his countenance, which denoted him above the common order of people.

Also near the scene was Alexander Beatson, whose accounts of Tipu's fall were among the earliest to circulate. According to him, 'The Sultaun had been shot, a little above the right ear, by a musquet ball, which lodged near the mouth, in his left cheek: he had also received three wounds, apparently with the bayonet, in his right side.'[101]

◆

Tipu had sent emissaries to France, Turkey and Persia for help. With British ships and spies manning Indian waters, these men were forced to take roundabout routes. Tipu was dead before they returned.

A Tranquebar Frenchman named Dubuc managed to reach France after Tipu's death and told Napoleon that 'it was the knowledge on the part of the English that Napoleon had written to Tipu from Egypt about his plans for the invasion of India that led to Tipu's overthrow'.[102]

Tipu had also tried to persuade the Marathas to mediate between the English and him, sending vakils with money to Poona. When under Company pressure the peshwa ordered them to leave his capital, they did so very slowly, hoping till the last to be recalled for a deal. By the time they reached the Mysore frontier, Srirangapatna had fallen.

◆

Tipu and his father had climbed out of a basket of Indian chiefs to join a global league of famous rulers. In Mysore, their rule gave stability to peasants and merchants for thirty-eight years. Except for months of famine or war, trade and the economy grew, and ports and roads improved. The administration was efficiently organized, with the territory divided into provinces, talukas, groups of villages, and a village. Though justice was severely enforced, magistrates existed, as also rules for customs duties and land revenue. In Thomas Munro's previously quoted words, Mysore had acquired 'a vigour hitherto unexampled in India'.[103]

Tipu innovated widely, not merely in rocketry, guns and coinage, where he acquired fame. Wilks's survey showed, for example, that 'the Sultaun had set his mind on the manufacture of silk', as evidenced by 'the extraordinary attention with which plants of mulberry had been treated' (547fn); and Tipu tried to improve Mysore's sugarcane too.

Also mentioned by Wilks was Tipu's success in 'suppressing drunkenness' and destroying 'the white poppy and the hemp plant even in private gardens' (766, 573).

But he won no Indian allies for his greater goal. Containing an increasingly assertive Company while simultaneously fighting the Marathas and the nizam was an unrealistic plan, as was Tipu's expectation that, forgetting her internal convulsions, France would somehow preserve *his* kingdom.

Fluent in Hindustani, Kannada and Persian and possessing a scholarly side, Tipu liked books, took a refined interest in their binding, and built a large library, yet Wilks's appraisal that he 'neglected the practical study of mankind' was not wrong (762). Tipu failed to read either the wider geopolitical scene or the minds of his own officers. Mir Sadiq was not his only untrustworthy officer. Making money unlawfully had become the norm in Tipu's Mysore.

Stating that Tipu's 'application' was 'intense and incessant' and that he preferred 'to write with his own hand the [rough] draft of almost every dispatch,' Wilks tells a story he may have heard from Purniah.

A secret emissary sent to Poona had evidently informed Tipu in report after report that his cash was expended. After several months of inaction, Tipu finally gave a draft to a secretary, saying, 'Let this be dispatched to [the man] in Poona.' 'Here I am,' said the secretary, who in fact was the former emissary. Having 'returned for some weeks from mere necessity', he had shown up daily at the durbar, but Tipu had not noticed. 'The Sultaun for once hung down his head' (764).

Wilks was not alone in accusing Tipu of 'a dark and intolerant bigotry' (766). We have seen that Munro called Tipu a 'zealot'. That

Muslims received preferential treatment in Tipu's 'Khudadad' or 'God-given' government is undeniable.

In Coorg, Mangaluru and the Malayalam country, many Hindus and Christians were forcibly converted after they had fought or rebelled against Tipu. Yet Islam was not thrust on loyal subjects. The cordiality and durability of his relations with the Sringeri Sankaracharya, his respect until the end for the Sri Ranganathaswami temple in Srirangapatna, and gifts from his government to these Hindu shrines are also undeniable facts.

We may note, too, the nineteenth-century observation of H. K. Beauchamp, Abbé Dubois's editor and translator, that 'not a single priest' of the Catholic mission on whose behalf Dubois had come to South India 'was persecuted by Tippu'.[104]

Certainly Islam was Tipu's preference as also at times his punishment for those offending him, but it was not mandatory under his rule. For some jobs in his government, being a Brahmin may have been more of an asset than being a Muslim. Tipu's large revenue department was staffed wholly by Brahmins, who were employed in other departments as well.

At this chapter's start we recalled the conclusion of Abbé Dubois, whose three decades in the Kannada and Tamil tracts overlapped with Tipu's rule and death, that the people 'cherished and respected' the Indian princes holding sway over them, while hating the native 'administration', and that they 'hated and despised' the British rulers that followed.

Although he did not name him, Tipu was the Indian prince of whom Dubois the eyewitness spoke, one not only respected but cherished by his people, non-Muslims included, despite his brutal harshness towards rebels.

Wilks would call Tipu a defiant soldier unable 'to grasp the plan of a campaign, or the conduct of a war'. Conceding that Tipu 'gave some examples of skill in marshalling a battle' and was courageous at the end, Wilks would add, 'He fell in the defence of his capital; but he fell, performing the duties of a common soldier, not of a general' (764–65).

Yet from the annals of eighteenth-century South India not many persons are better remembered than Haidar (1721–82) and Tipu (1750–

99), for father and son had taken resistance to the British to a new level. There were moments during their rule when Britain's India enterprise seemed shaky indeed. When, in 1799, it was Tipu who expired, London exploded in celebration. Paintings, exhibitions and novels turned the 'Fall of Seringapatam' into a scene of triumph that would abide in English memory.

Rivalry with England had given birth to intermittent French support for Haidar and Tipu, but France's hands were tied first by the 1763 Treaty of Paris, which terminated a seven-year war in Europe with England, and then, in the 1780s and 1790s, by the French Revolution's convulsions. It was essentially on their own that Haidar and Tipu had waged their contests with the British.

◆

For forty-eight hours, Generals Harris and Baird were unable to prevent looting and killing by their triumphant soldiers, but an effort was made to protect Tipu's family. Sons Abdul Khaliq and Moizuddin were recognized and treated courteously by a few Britons, and Purniah boldly suggested that twenty-seven-year-old Fateh Haidar, Tipu's eldest son, should fill Mysore's emptied throne.

A biography of Purniah written by a Kannada historian and published in 1979 by a descendant of the dewan claims that 'during his last battle in 1799, Tipu had entrusted his eldest son and heir apparent Fateh Hyder, who was about 27 years old, to the care and guidance of Purniah'.[105]

According to this biography, the dewan was 'summoned by the English to surrender and assured that he had no cause to be alarmed'. An unnamed 'Maharashtrian envoy' of the British urged Purniah 'to give up his old prejudices and loyalties'. After 'a thorough heart-searching, Purniah decided to surrender himself and to accept the new dispensation'. Since his family were in British custody, the surrender was fully expected (73–78).

'On the 11th May [seven days after Tipu's death], Purniah sent a message to General Harris that he wished to pay his respects'. Called by the general on the 12th, Purniah tried to argue that his surrender had been 'delayed by the Kaveri's rising waters'. Remarking that Muslim rule had become the norm in Mysore, he requested that Fateh Haidar be placed on the throne or given a principality. Otherwise 'it might be difficult to maintain peace' (82).

However, seeing that 'the really powerful Muslim chiefs', including the hated Mir Sadiq, were all dead, Harris, Arthur Wellesley (who would become Mysore's military governor) and Colonel Barry Close (appointed as the Company's first resident in Srirangapatna) concluded that a Muslim rebellion in Mysore was not on the cards. At Fort St George, from where he had overseen the assault on Tipu, Mornington agreed with them.

Reckoning also that a descendant of Haidar and Tipu might one day revolt against the British, whereas Mysore's Hindus would welcome the restoration of the Wadiyars, the Company opted to enthrone Krishnaraja, a five-year-old scion of the displaced dynasty, who was living incognito with a relative (76–82).

Frank discussion inside the Company's governing circles thus produced some astute decisions.

Raja Chamaraja Wadiyar, the boy's father, had expired in 1796. Of that dynasty, the most influential person still alive was Rani Lakshammanni, the old widow of an earlier Krishnaraja Wadiyar, who had died in 1766. To her house went a delegation of the Company's officers, taking Purniah with them. The boy was brought there, and the venerable rani assented to the Company's choice.

PURNIAH

Lakshammanni had, for some time, been in secret contact with Fort St George through an agent called Thirumala Rao, who expected to become the dewan in the new dispensation, but the British not only made Purniah the dewan, they also made him regent during the boy prince's minority.

As for Fateh Haidar, on 18 June he and other descendants and family members were sent out of Mysore, with assurance of pensions, to Vellore in the Madras Presidency, where they were kept under surveillance. Fort St George was given authority over Mysore. Before long, Wilks would write:

> The practical efficiency of the government was secured by the
> uncommon talents of Purniah...and that efficiency was directed to

proper objects by the control reserved to the English government.[106]

For the judicious British, continuity came through Purniah, control through Arthur Wellesley and Barry Close, and popularity through Krishnaraja Wadiyar. An impression in Mysore that 'Hindu Raj' had finally replaced Muslim rule suited the Company. As dewan, the short, plump and light-skinned Purniah would save money, build roads and dams, and win the Company's praise. Visiting Srirangapatna in 1800, Francis Buchanan would find that 'by the inhabitants he is called by the same title as is given to the Peshwa in Poonah'—Srimantha. Added Buchanan: 'Next to Meer Saduc, [Purniah] seems to have [had] a greater power under the late Sultan than any other person; but his authority was greatly inferior [to that of Mir Sadiq]' (Buchanan, 60).

Well-versed in Kannada and Sanskrit, knowing Persian as well as any Muslim noble of the Mysore of Haidar and Tipu, Purniah understood English too but did not speak it (Murthy, 153). Under Haidar and Tipu, his official correspondence was conducted in Persian. Apart from his expertise with money and numbers, he had 'managed the commissariat and raised troops' and also commanded a section of them (153–54).

A story 'current among the people' but lacking a source was that when asked once by Tipu to undertake a tricky diplomatic mission, Purniah told him: 'Neither of us is fit for diplomacy. I will never tell a lie, and you will never tell the truth.' When Tipu's mother heard the reply, she went, it was said, into a fit of laughter (156).

If this story suggests that Purniah enjoyed the privilege of one-on-one conversations with Tipu, as he had earlier with Haidar, it also confirms what was glimpsed earlier, a relationship of understanding between Tipu's mother and this South Indian Brahmin.

Ambitious and bold but prudent as well, aware of political winds, trusted for his integrity and rewarded for his competence, Purniah however was 'ignorant of European politics', Arthur Wellesley would say (154). No wonder he presented no realistic advice when Tipu sent his futile missions overseas. Wellesley also thought that Purniah should have kept better touch with Fort St George and built links to 'the Madras Dubashis, who know everything' (154).

Purniah did not obtain real authority after Tipu's fall.

Frequently overruling him, the British also denied Purniah's request, inspired by Poona's hereditary peshwas, for a continuing dewanship in the family.

He was instead given a jagir rich in timber, plants and water in Yelandur, not very far from the Coimbatore district from where, in his boyhood, he had moved to Srirangapatna. Given in 1807, the lands would stay with the family until the 1970s.

Krishnacharya Purniah died on 27 March 1812 in Srirangapatna, not many months after young Krishnaraja attained maturity and the dewan's regency ended.

◆

A few others who had served Tipu were also given positions in the Company's Mysore, including a man named Khan Jehan Khan. Calling Jehan Khan 'a brave, able and interesting officer under Tippoo' (590), Wilks, who acted as resident after Close and got to know Khan well, tells us that this officer

> was born a bramin and [was] at the age of seventeen a writer in the service of Sheikh Ayaz at Bednore, when it was surrendered to General Matthews. On the recapture of that place by Tippoo, this youth was forcibly converted to Islam and highly instructed in its doctrines. He was soon distinguished as a soldier and invested with high command.
>
> In 1799 he fell, desperately wounded, in attempting to...repel the assault at Seringapatam. He recovered and was appointed to the command of the raja's infantry.

After the restoration of the Wadiyars, Jehan Khan 'made advances through [Purniah] to be readmitted to his rank and caste as a bramin. 'A select conclave' of Brahmin priests held that Jehan Khan could be readmitted but 'with certain reservations to mark a distinction between him and those who had incurred no lapse from their original purity.' Continues Wilks:

> [B]ut the khan would have all or none. 'I prefer,' said he (in conversing with me on the subject), 'the faith of my ancestors, but the fellows wanted to shut up my present road to a better world, and would not fairly open the other... I feel myself more

respectable with the full privileges of a Mussulman than I should as a half-outcaste bramin (590–91fn).

Gathered by Wilks, an earlier story about Jehan Khan throws additional light on his character and his life's complexity. It also brings Khan's unnamed first wife to life.

Before his forcible conversion, [Jehan Khan] was betrothed or married in the usual form, and the lady, on arriving at the proper age, sent a message intimating that notwithstanding his change of religion and marriage with a Mahommedan lady, although she could not be a bramin wife, she could not be the wife of another, and deemed herself bound to regulate her future life according to his commands.

After some further messages, she [entered into] his protection; a separate quarter of the house was allotted for her exclusive use; when he visited her, it was in the braminical costume; and he presented himself to his Mahomedan wife as a true Mussulman.

Another remark by Wilks hints at the emergence of a new community, of unknown size, of the compulsorily converted.

Before I knew [Jehan Khan], he had married [his] Mahommedan daughter to a Mussulman forcibly converted like himself (591fn).

To complete our picture of Tipu and his times, let us take in another story provided by Wilks, this one about one of Tipu's preferred officers, Kadir Khan Keshgee, and a former prince of Coorg named Vira Rajendra.

In the mid-1780s, when young Rajendra and his family were confined by Tipu in Periapatnam Fort on the edges of Coorg, Keshgee, commanding the fort, had quietly allowed Rajendra to hunt in the woods near Periapatnam. In 1788, helped by Kodavas, Rajendra escaped. Tipu's response was to move the rest of the family to Srirangapatna, where two females were 'received into the royal harem'. The third was sent to Keshgee, who, writes Wilks,

had the lady attended by a person of her own caste. [Keshgee] not only never approached her; he sent her secretly to her brother. Later, in Feb–March 1791, when Kadir Khan, leading a body of Mysorean troops, was trapped in Coorg by the raja's forces, who were being supported by a British force sent from Bombay, the raja not only spared Keshgee's life, he gave him his liberty (Wilks, 477–81).

◆

We may conclude this chapter by remembering that if, to Tipu's discredit, he had made the treacherous Mir Sadiq his chief officer, he had also given positions of influence to men like Purniah and Kadir Khan Keshgee.

Chapter 4

ERUPTIONS AND COUNTRY LIFE: 1774–1823

While observing South Indian disquiet before and after Tipu's death, this chapter also tries to look at the land and its people in the last quarter of the eighteenth century and the first quarter of the nineteenth. Drama in the life of Kerala Varma Pazhassi Raja (1753–1805) of the royal family of Kottayam,* in what is now north Kerala's Kannur district, began in 1774, when Haidar moved into Malabar. Unlike many Nair aristocrats (including Kottayam's raja) who escaped that year to Travancore, the twenty-one-year-old Pazhassi stayed put and fought Mysore from his forest hideouts.

Although Haidar was supported by the Hindu raja of nearby Chirakkal and, at this point, also by the ruler of Coorg, Pazhassi Raja successfully defied this triple alliance right until 1780. An understanding with the East India Company enabled Pazhassi to oust the Mysoreans from his area in 1781, and Haidar died the following year.

But the 1784 Treaty of Mangalore between Mysore and the Company, which gave Tipu rights over Malabar, offended Pazhassi, who waged another long guerrilla war, this time against Haidar's son. When the Company and Tipu renewed their clash in 1790, Pazhassi backed the Company, which acknowledged him as Kottayam's ruler.

After Cornwallis clipped Tipu's domain in 1792, the Company acquired direct control over Malabar, inclusive of Kottayam. Many rajas in Malabar accepted the Company's paramountcy but Pazhassi did not. Nor did he appreciate the Company's grant, in 1793, of revenue rights in Kottayam to his uncle Vira Varma, Raja of adjacent Kurumbranad, or the Company's stand that Varma possessed authority over Kottayam as well.

Offended once more, Pazhassi, now forty, opposed Vira Varma's stiff taxes, harassed the British, and enlisted peasants in a widespread revenue boycott. When in reply the Company extended Vira Varma's

---

*Not to be confused with the town of Kottayam to the south of Kochi.

lease by five years, an insurgency was triggered.

Pazhassi Raja and his associates disappeared into the jungles of nearby Wayanad, part of Mysore at this juncture, from where 'they carried out a destructive guerrilla warfare'.[1] In effect, they became Tipu's allies. By a public proclamation in December 1795, the Company forbade help to the rebels, but the 'impenetrable, tract-less forests of Wynad' not only 'proved a safe shelter' for Pazhassi and his band, his rule seemed accepted there.

Something like a broad-based rebellion took place in this hilly and wooded Wayanad area southeast of Madikeri and southwest of Mysore, with Wayanad's tribals and many Malabar Muslims also supporting Pazhassi, who seems to have visited an agent of Tipu's and built a link with the Mysore ruler.[2]

In 1796, Pazhassi evaded a Company bid to arrest him. In the following year, continuing guerrilla warfare forced the Company to sue for peace, enhancing Pazhassi's prestige. In 1800, after Tipu's fall, the conflict was resumed by the British. Remarkably, Pazhassi eluded the Company's soldiers for five more years.

On 30 November 1805, however, he was killed in a Wayanad gunfight across a stream called Kaynara, close to Mysore's border and not very far from Mysore city. The Company officer leading the final hunt, T. H. Baber, left an account:

> Throughout the Northern and Western parts of the Districts, I found the sentiment in our favour [but] at the same time a considerable disinclination to afford the smallest information of the Pychi Rajah or his partisans.
>
> In all classes I observed a decided interest [in] the Pychi Rajah, towards whom the inhabitants entertained a regard and respect bordering on veneration.[3]

The Nair raja had become a hero because, though a prince, he lived in the forest; because tribals, local Muslims and, it seems, Tipu, backed him; and because he stood up to the British.

'Exhortations and occasional presents' (Baber's phrase) finally induced some villagers to inform the British that Pazhassi's men were camping across the Kaynara. After a trek of almost ten hours, Baber and his soldiers found ten or so unsuspecting insurgents including

Pazhassi. The quarries were attacked and all, presumably, were killed. Certainly Pazhassi was, but not before displaying princely contempt. 'Having put his musquet to his breast' (Baber would report), the raja thundered to a man in Baber's posse called Canara Menon, 'Don't touch me!'

> The Raja's body was taken up and put into my palangueen... The following day [it] was dispatched under a strong escort to Manantoddy [Mananthavady], and the Sheristadaar sent with orders to assemble all the Brahmins and see that the customary honours were performed.[4]

Of Pazhassi it has been said, 'This disaffected lion of Kerala alone, even though for purely personal reasons, thought of resisting the British by open rebellion.'[5]

◆

Empire-building posed logistical challenges. Because Haidar, Tipu and the Marathas occupied major portions of South India, the land route for Fort St George's communication with Bombay and London was often blocked.

Mail from Madras therefore went south by land to Palamcottah (Palayamkottai, in Tirunelveli district), thence by land to Anjengo, the Company-controlled port on the South Kerala coast, and from Anjengo by sea to Bombay and thereafter to London. Mail from London took a similar route in reverse.[6]

After Yusuf Khan's 1764 hanging, authority in much of the Tamil country was uneasily shared between its formal ruler, Nawab Muhammad Ali of the Carnatic (or Arcot), and the de facto power, Fort St George.

Inspired by Haidar next door, some local chiefs in the southern districts asserted independence, including poligar Jagaveera Kattabomman of Panchalamkurichi, which lay about 18 miles west of the port town of Tuticorin and about 30 miles northeast of Tinnevelly.

Poligars like Kattabomman were inheritors of a governing structure designed by Madurai's seventeenth-century rulers in which a military camp or fort like Panchalamkurichi was commanded locally by a poligar. For most Europeans, any local chief in South India was a poligar, and sometimes a poligar's soldiers were all called poligars. Writing in the 1870s, Robert Caldwell, missionary, linguist and historian of Tinnevelly, would say:

> [I]t can hardly be said that the idea of governing the country by means of an order of rude, rapacious feudal nobles, such as the Poligars generally were, turned out to be a happy one...
>
> [W]henever they were not at war with the central authority, they were at war with one another, and it was rarely possible to collect from them the tribute or revenue due to the central authority without a display of military force, which added greatly both to the unpopularity and the expense of the collection.[7]

But poligars in the closing decades of the eighteenth century did not think they were less entitled than the nawab or the Company to determine the tax rate on peasants, or to collect and share revenue as they saw fit.

Also active in the region, with Tuticorin as their base and Colombo as headquarters, were the Dutch, who fluctuated in their attitude towards the British. A proposal from Warren Hastings, the Calcutta-based Governor General, for enlisting the Dutch against Haidar by giving them Tinnevelly was successfully resisted by Fort St George and the nawab; and when in 1783 the British captured Tuticorin from the Dutch, they found evidence of a treaty the Dutch had signed with Kattabomman (Caldwell, 143).

That was the year when Kattabomman and other poligars in eastern Tinnevelly, their morale strengthened by Tipu's advance in Mangalore, clashed several times with a British force led by Colonel William Fullarton. Many on both sides were killed.

Fullarton told the vakils of these poligars that unless they came to terms he would vow to Siva, 'whose attribute is vengeance, to spread destruction throughout every possession of the defaulting Poligars' (153). Bringing up Siva was not customary for a Company officer, but the threat seemed to work, and a settlement was reached.

In 1790, after years of dispute between Nawab Muhammad Ali and the Company on who should pay for the costly, and often bloody, exercise of collecting revenue, Fort St George brazenly announced that it had 'assumed the management of the Nawab's country' (159).

Two years later, the nawab conceded that the Company could

collect, at its risk and expense, the revenue of the poligar areas in Tinnevelly, Madurai, Trichy, Ramnad and Sivaganga. Three years thereafter, the old nawab, an ally the British never liked, died, ending a forty-five-year reign on the Arcot throne, to which his son Umdat ul-Umra succeeded.

But Fort St George was finding the southern poligars difficult. Taking over from his father in 1790, Veerapandya Kattabomman emerged as a defiant son of the soil and a poligar independent of the British and the nawab. For nine years the British made intermittent efforts to subdue him but Kattabomman eluded them.

Tipu's fall freed their hands. On 5 September 1799, Major John Bannerman led British units in an attack on Kattabomman, now thirty-nine. While Bannerman was backed by Edward Clive, Governor of Fort St George and son of Robert Clive, Kattabomman was aided by Tinnevelly poligars.

Arriving at Panchalamkurichi with a large force, Bannerman demanded Kattabomman's surrender. When that was not forthcoming, an immediate assault was ordered, but the English, in Bannerman's words, suffered 'very severe' losses. Three days later, Bannerman attacked again with an even larger force, but Kattabomman (called 'the Cat' by British soldiers) and all his men had quietly slipped away the previous night.

The poligar of Ettaiyapuram, the only one in eastern Tinnevelly to ally with the British, pursued Kattabomman. In an engagement both sides suffered losses, but the Cat again escaped, first to Sivaganga, more than 100 miles north, and thence to jungles near Pudukkottai, seat of the Tondaiman Raja who, however, was friendly to the British.

While many of Kattabomman's close associates were killed, Kattabomman himself was seized by the Tondaiman Raja and sent to Bannerman, who had him executed on 16 October 1799. The deed was done near an old fort in the presence of all the poligars of Tinnevelly, who, in Caldwell's words, witnessed the event 'with wonder and silent awe' (Caldwell, 183).

Once again, a British officer praised the foe he had killed. Caldwell quotes Bannerman:

The manner and behaviour of the Poligar during...the examination was undaunted and supercilious. He frequently eyed the Ettiapuram

Poligar, who had been so active to secure his person, with...
indignant scorn; and when he went out to be executed he walked
with a firm and daring air (188).

As, six years later, Pazhassi Raja would, Kattabomman had become
a legend.

◆

Two years after Kattabomman's execution, and within days of the
unexplained death (in July 1801) of Nawab Umdat ul-Umra of Arcot,
the British claimed that Srirangapatna's attics had yielded 'treasonable
correspondence' between Tipu and Arcot. Alleging that the late
Muhammad Ali and his freshly-deceased son were both implicated—a
charge that proved the width of support for Tipu—the Company decided
'to assume the entire possession and government of the Carnatic'
(Caldwell, 169).

The seizure was not challenged. After Tipu's fall the Company had
become South India's undisputed master. The days when it was merely
one contender among many had gone. Red spaces, indicating British
rule, had suddenly expanded on the map. Yet some spirits dared.

On the night of 2 February 1801, two brothers of the dead
Kattabomman, the older one feeble, the younger 'a mere boy' who was
unable to speak, escaped from Tirunelveli's Palamcottah jail. Aided by
supporters who had entered the prison in disguise, they overpowered
the guards.

Joined by hundreds, by dawn they reached Panchalamkurichi,
30 miles to the north, 'making such good use of their heels' that the
British were 'astonished', as James Welsh, staff officer at the time to
the British captain in command, would later admit (196).

Twenty-four hours later, when the British too reached
Panchalamkurichi, they were again astonished on finding that 'the walls,
which had been entirely levelled, were now rebuilt, and fully manned
by about 1500 Poligars' and that 'an entrenchment and breastwork'
protected the mud-fort (197). The Company force was obliged to retreat.

A second assault on the fort, this time joined by a thousand men
provided by the pro-Company poligar of Ettaiyapuram, was also
repulsed. Defenders who were killed were as quickly replaced. But in
May more reinforcements arrived for the British. Attacking the fort

on 24 May with batteries and other arms, they produced a breach in the walls. A Briton called George Hughes would write:

Notwithstanding the strength of the attacking party, with the whole force ready to back them, the defenders shrank not from their duty...the breach was so stoutly defended that it was nearly half an hour before a man of ours could stand upon the summit (204).

Scores of others on the British side also entered the fort, but key leaders escaped. James Welsh, who knew the personalities involved from before the battles, would tell the story. The late Cat's brother, wounded in the assault, was 'a tall slender lad of a very sickly appearance yet possessing an energy of mind which gained pre-eminence in troubled times'. Welsh would term him 'one of the most extraordinary mortals I ever knew'.

This brother, Duraisingam, would direct his soldiers by arranging on his left palm little pieces of straw representing the Company's soldiers. When wanting an attack, he would sweep off the straw soldiers with his right hand, making at the same time a 'whizzing sound' from his mouth. At this signal, his men would mount an attack, which the commander fully joined (206).

After the British wrested the Panchalamkurichi fort, the fleeing Duraisingam and others in his party, most of them also wounded, were pursued by the English cavalry. Three miles on, Duraisingam fell near a small village. One of the village women showing up saw that her son was among the fallen. That young man said, 'O mother, let me die, but try to save the life of Swamy, who lies near me.'

The woman left her dying son and with the help of others took Duraisingam to her home. There, says Welsh, pursuing 'Ettiapureans' showed up. With instant ingenuity, the village women covered Duraisingam with a sheet, 'sent up a shriek of lamentation', and explained that their boy had died of smallpox, at the mention of which the Ettiapureans turned their backs and departed (Caldwell, 206-07).

The escapees eventually found their way to the village of Siruvayal, or 'Sherewele' as the British called it, lying just east of modern Karaikudi and more than a hundred miles north of Panchalamkurichi. Siruvayal contained thousands of rebels linked to the influential Marudu brothers of the Sivaganga palaiyam, to whom the late Cat had been close.

From Siruvayal, home to the Marudu brothers, and, 20 miles away, from Sivaganga, home to fighting Marava clans, the Marudu duo and Kattabomman's brothers harassed English authority for many weeks. Two major chiefdoms in the vicinity, Pudukkottai to the northeast and Ramnad to the southeast, were allied to the British, yet in 1801, Sivaganga, under the de facto rule of the Marudu brothers, raised the banner of independence, even as, it appears, a predecessor of its de jure ruler had joined Haidar Ali in 1773.[8]

For a while in 1801, says Caldwell, the men of Panchalamkurichi held the fort of Tuticorin, having taken it from the English. While not molesting the many Dutch living in the port town, they seized an Englishman called Baggott, but when Mrs Baggott came up to the fort and petitioned for his release, he was set free (81–83).

Of the Marudus, who belonged to lower rungs of the Marava ladder, Welsh would write that while the older brother, Periya Marudu, gave 'his whole time to hunting and shooting' and 'was much esteemed by his European neighbours at Tanjore, Trichinopoly and Madura,' the younger brother, Chinna Marudu,

> was a portly, handsome and affable man of the kindest manners and most easy access...[living] in an open palace without a single guard... [W]hen I visited him in 1795, every man who chose to come in had free ingress and egress...
>
> From a merely casual visit, when passing through his country, he became my friend, and never failed to send me presents of fine rice and fruit... It was he also who first taught me to throw the spear and hurl the Collery stick...to a certainty to any distance within one hundred yards.

According to Caldwell, Chinna Marudu's chief reason for rebellion was being asked by Tinnevelly's first Collector after the British takeover, Stephen Lushington, to show evidence of descent from Sivaganga's ruling family. Unable to produce the documents, Chinna Marudu became an enemy (215).

Also, suggests another historian, the fall of Tipu in 1799 'instilled in [Chinna Marudu] feelings of patriotism and the thought of uniting the patriotic elements of the population'.[9] Open rebellion spread quickly across a wide territory, with Gopala Nayak of Dindigul, among others, playing a major role.

Marudu was put in the position of the chief commissioner of the rebel confederates in the whole of Madurai [division]... Marudu and his followers made the temple of Kalayar Koil [8 miles east of Sivaganga] their strategic centre.[10]

In June 1801, full fifty-six years before the better-known proclamations of 1857 in northern India, the Company's servants found a strongly-worded edict stuck on walls of two contrasting edifices: the nawab's palace in Trichy Fort and, not very far from it, one of India's most hallowed temples, that of Srirangam.[11] It was signed by Chinna Marudu.

This proclamation's raw words included a call to subjugate the 'low wretches', as Europeans were termed. Other phrases, more dignified, seemed designed to appeal to all of South India or even to Indians as a whole. Brahmins, Kshatriyas, Vaisyas, Sudras and Muslims were named separately and implored together.

The people's poverty was mentioned, as also the rights of rajas. The Arcot nawab was referred to with respect but also criticized for foolishly allying with the British. Though issued under Chinna Marudu's name, the proclamation's text and locations hint at collaboration with Muslims identifying with Tipu's fate, or with the nawab whom the Company was about to discard and whose sympathies now lay with the deceased Tipu.

For a while 'the movement attained formidable proportions'. Places like 'Ramnad, Madurai, Kallarnadu and Tanjore' came briefly under Marudu's sway.[12] But by August, British reinforcements had turned the tide.

To undermine Marudu's standing, the Company found a youngster, apparently adopted by an earlier Sivaganga chief and declared him the palaiyam's rightful ruler. On 30 July, Siruvayal was taken, but Chinna Marudu and many others escaped after 'setting their handsome village on fire to prevent its being made use of by the English forces', as Caldwell would write (214).

Chinna Marudu was pursued to his temple stronghold in Kalaiyarkovil. Company forces cut a six-mile path through thick jungle and used field artillery to kill the poligar's fighters, but, numerous and fearless, the latter surrounded the English in the forest, who had difficulty getting out.

On 1 October, however, the English took Kalaiyarkovil; on the 19th a badly wounded Chinna Marudu was captured; on the 24th, he, the older brother and others were executed 'on the highest bastion of the fort of Tirupattur in their own territory'. Welsh would write of the man who had once befriended him:

> Yet this very man I was afterwards destined by the fortunes of war to chase like a wild beast…to see lingering with a fractured thigh in prison; and lastly to behold him, with his gallant brother, and no less gallant son, surrounded by their principal adherents, hanging in chains upon a common gibbet (213–14).

As for the Kattabomman brothers, they were 'brought back to Panchalamkurichi and 'hanged on [a] mound near the fort… Not only was the fort of Panchalamkurichi pulled down and levelled to the ground…the site was ploughed over and cultivated. It was ordered also that the name of Panchalamkurichi should be removed from all maps and accounts.' Loyal poligars, including that of Ettaiyapuram, were rewarded with lands and honours (223–25).

◆

Earlier we noted Caldwell's view of the South's poligars. A few years after that disparagement, the poligars would receive Romesh Chunder Dutt's sympathy in his acclaimed *Economic History of India,* first published in 1901:

> Looking back to these transactions after the lapse of a century, one cannot but regret the harsh policy which led to the extirpation of the Polygars in the Karnatic… It was not a just or wise policy to deprive them of their estates outside their own villages, to demand of them a sudden and exorbitant increase in revenue, or to punish their insurrection by virtually stamping them out.
>
> They had preserved some sort of peace and order in their estates during the harassing and troublesome wars of Southern India in the 17th and 18th centuries; they had protected weavers and manufactures and shielded the cultivators when there was hardly any other constituted authority in the land; they had excavated

great canals and reservoirs for irrigation all over Southern India; and they had given shelter to the British themselves when Madras was taken by the French in the early Karnatic wars...

It is not a humane policy for an alien government to suppress a class, and to confiscate its proprietary rights, in order to add to its income by directly settling with the tillers of the soil.[13]

At least, Dutt pointed out, poligar revenues were spent in South India, whereas what the Company collected went to England, and often to 'the personal safes and coffers' there of the Company's officers rather than to the Company's account, enabling the newly-rich to buy seats in Parliament.[14]

Fighting, killing and extracting did not constitute the whole story of these opening years of the nineteenth century. Caldwell's study mentions Englishmen in southern India in this period who sired children from local concubines or mistresses.

Thus, after citing battle accounts provided by George Hughes 'of Tatchanallur, Translator to the [Company's] force', the historian writes: 'I may add that Mr. Hughes was never married, though he had several children, whom he brought up as Hindus' (194fn).

WHAT THE COUNTRY LOOKED LIKE

Few glimpses of South India's life in the year 1800 are more graphic than those left by Francis Buchanan, who at Mornington's bidding travelled widely across Tipu's late territory, conversed with many (usually through interpreters), learnt a good deal, and jotted it all down.[15] After setting forth from Madras on 23 April, Buchanan noticed, for example, that along the way 'charitable persons [had] built many resting places for porters, who here carry all their burdens on the head. These resting places consist of a wall about four feet high, on which the porters can deposit their burdens, and from which, after having rested themselves, they can again, without assistance, take up their loads' (Buchanan, 1: 2).

Like previous and later European visitors, Buchanan was impressed in his long journey by the number of water reservoirs he saw. He also found areas of good land not cultivated because of a shortage of people. Many villages were fortified; the countryside had seen a lot of fighting. Between Mandya and Srirangapatna, Buchanan saw bones from cattle that had perished during Cornwallis's march nine years earlier.

He felt that villages were rebuilding, canals were being cleared, and 'in place of antelopes and forest guards we have the peaceful bullock returning to his useful labour' (83). Farmers were 'abundantly industrious' but lacking in skills and efficient tools (345). After describing the coconut tree and its manifold uses, Buchanan writes (in Channapatna, 38 miles southwest of Bangalore):

> Although the soil is considered as the property of the government, yet when a man plants a [coconut] palm garden, the trees are considered as his property, and he may at pleasure sell them (157).

As for Bangalore, after the ravages of war, people were

> now flocking to [it] from all quarters; and although there are few rich individuals, trade and manufactures increase apace; and imports and exports are already one-fourth of what they used to be. The manufacturers and petty traders are still very distrustful and timid; but the merchants, many of whom have been at Madras, seem to have the utmost confidence in the protection of our government (194)... Some Gujerati merchants are making the necessary arrangements for opening a trade directly with Madras (200).

Betelnut, pepper, cardamom, sandalwood and other merchandise was being transported by cattle.

> The rate of hire is always fixed on the average load of eight maunds, and never according to time, but always by distance... The carriers are never answerable for any accident that may happen to the goods; the merchant therefore must send with them some trusty person, who is generally a younger branch of the family (205).

Buchanan's impression from towns traversed was that 'the Brahmans appropriate to themselves...generally the best fortified' quarter. 'A Sudra is not permitted to dwell on the same street as a Brahman, while [the Sudra] again exacts the same difference from the parriars and other low casts...who live in wretched huts [outside the town]. A Brahman is considered polluted by merely walking through such a place' (55–56). Also, in different places, though at no great distance, there are considerable variations in the customs of the same [Hindu] tribes [and castes] (79).

Hindu caste groups possessed headmen whose decisions were generally carried out. Being 'outcasted' was the worst form of punishment (81). The amildar who managed a taluka, his assistant the sheristadar, and the village accountant (karnam or shanbag) was almost always a Brahmin; the village headman, usually called patel or gowda, was seen as a Sudra.

Buchanan writes of meat-eating, burying-the-dead, Vishnu-worshipping, 'low-caste' Telugu or Kannada-speaking Sudras in Karnataka who also performed animal sacrifices in which, influenced by local superstition, some Brahmins in difficulty—e.g. with a sick child—would also clandestinely join, e.g. by sending a child who slipped in an offering (242).

Many weavers had learned to read and write accounts and business letters, but evidently this kind of learning was considered undignified. Poetry, not prose, was admired (247).

The men Buchanan ran into seemed able to divorce their women for adultery, not for anything else. But the women had no remedy against their men's infidelity except their tongue. When they overused this weapon, they got a beating (247).

Though southern Brahmins inter-dined across regions, they did not intermarry with Brahmins of another language. There was however a degree of tolerance and even marriage across linguistic divides among other Siva-worshipping and Vishnu-worshipping jaatis. Lower castes seemed as keen on purity as higher castes, married only within their caste, and looked down on some other castes (251–52).

Buchanan concluded that 'Komatis or Vaisyas', dealing in 'cloth, and all sorts of merchandize, especially money and jewels', must be 'found thinly scattered in every part of India'. These Vaisyas appeared to 'interdine and intermarry with Vaisyas of all sects and nations (regions)' and were vegetarians. Their men could marry several wives (256–57).

He likens the Reddis to the Vokkaligas and also to the Kunbis of Maharashtra. In some areas, the Reddis were numerous: they were peasants, or employed to collect taxes, or soldiers. His impression was that the Reddis 'composed the most considerable body in the armies of all native princes' (258).

Buchanan's Reddis ate hogs, sheep, venison and fowl but lost caste if they took liquor. 'The men are allowed polygamy but do not shut up their women, who are very industrious, and perform much of the country labour' (258). Vaishnava and Saiva Reddis married one another. Many were rich or village chiefs (259).

Many Hindu castes buried their dead, and there were many Tamil and Telugu speakers in the Kannada country.

Buchanan described as 'hypocritical cant' the behaviour of 'young men of active professions' who 'frequently turn up their eyes to heaven, and make pious ejaculations, attended with heavy sighs', even when talking of business. And he was surprised that 'being restricted from the pleasures of the world, especially those of the table', 'following no useful employment', and 'being dedicated to what they call piety and learning' were attributes that added status to a caste (254).

He noticed that some 'Brahmans laugh at the prayers of the potters, as being low trash in the vulgar language' (275). When he asks in Chikballapur for 'dates or authority' for events they have described, 'these Brahmins say that they must consult their books, but when I send my interpreter, who is also a Brahman, to copy the dates, the Brahmans here pretend that the books are lost' (July 1800, 336).

But Buchanan was intrigued by a Brahmin he met some miles north of Bangalore who 'believes in a supreme God called Narayana or Para-Brahma, from whence proceeded Siva, Vishnu and Brahma, which still however are all the same God' (304).

Tipu's fall featured in many of Buchanan's conversations. When he reached Bangalore, he noticed many Muslim soldiers in 'great distress' because of 'the change of government'. 'Accustomed to a military life, they do not readily enter into civil occupations, nor are they willing to attach themselves to the military service of the enemies of their late Sultan.' But some 'of the more wealthy among them' were 'betaking themselves to trade'.

'The greatest complainers against the change of government,' Buchanan wrote, 'are certain Brahmins' even though 'by the fall of Tippoo, this cast has been freed from persecution, and is now in the almost exclusive possession of public offices'. Buchanan was told that under Tipu, the persecutions fell chiefly on temple-attached Brahmins who were 'considered as low men' by Laukika or non-priestly Brahmins, and that the latter enjoyed 'full possession of the revenue department' in Tipu's Mysore (lxxv).

In 'Muduru', evidently near Bangalore, he was informed that 'the oppressions of Tippoo and the miseries of war' had 'driven away four-tenths of the cultivators' (1: 55). Added Buchanan:

> Tippoo certainly had considerable talents for war, but his fondness for it, and his engaging with an enemy so much his superior in the art brought on his destruction...

He found, however, that the late ruler had numerous admirers.

> None of his Mussulmans have entered our service, although many of them are in great want; and they all retain a high respect for his memory, considering him as a martyr who died in the defence of his religion (72).

VELLORE MUTINY

Six years after Buchanan's journey through Mysore, a fierce but short-lived mutiny occurred in Vellore Fort, to which Tipu's sons and household had been exiled, and where British and Indian units of the Company's Madras army were garrisoned. Hindus 'formed the bulk of the native troops'[16] but Muslim numbers too were significant.

Before the British took over this supposedly secure fort in the 1760s, it had belonged to the ruler of Arcot, which lay 14 miles east of Vellore, and prior to that to the Marathas. When its Indian sepoys revolted in the pre-dawn hours of 10 July 1806, massacring up to 200 British soldiers and inviting a swift repression, they were venting resentment nursed since Tipu's fall. They were also anticipating, by half a century, North India's Great Revolt of 1857.

Apparent provocations for these far-apart rebellions were eerily similar, including a belief that British rulers desired the conversion of Indians, and rudeness from callow Britons commanding long-serving natives.[17] In Vellore, it was rumoured that a turn-screw issued to the sepoys, meant to be suspended from the neck and therefore capable of contacting the wearer's heart, was actually a cross in disguise.[18]

Coming on top of two hugely unpopular orders, one banning sepoys from displaying ash on the forehead or a beard on the chin (thereby offending Hindus and Muslims both), and another requiring them to replace the customary turban with a round hat topped by a cockade, similar to what some Europeans and Indian Christians were using, the rumour contributed to a mutiny apparently urged by wandering fakirs unreconciled to Tipu's fall.

Instigation may have also come from supporters of the dispossessed Nawab of Arcot.[19]

After the new hat was lampooned by fakirs in streetcorners in Vellore, some of the fort's sepoys and their Indian seniors refused to wear it, whereupon two havildars, one a Hindu and the other a Muslim, were punished with 900 lashes. Mutiny was planned in response, but a sepoy leaked the plot to an English officer. That officer consulted senior native sepoys, who pronounced the informer insane, but the leak forced the mutineers' hand.

They struck at 2 a.m. on 10 July, killing many Britons while they slept and also shooting down others dragged out of the fort's sickrooms. Among those gunned down was the fort's commander, Colonel John Fancourt, though his wife and young children hid themselves and survived. Residing within the fort, Tipu's son Fateh Haidar was declared king and Tipu's flag was raised over the fort.

An escapee, however, alerted the British garrison in Arcot, from where, accompanied by horse-pulled 'galloper' guns, a cavalry squadron led by Colonel Rollo Gillespie rode off at once to Vellore and suppressed the mutiny.

The mutineers and their supporters from Vellore town could have blocked Gillespie's cavalry and the galloper guns at the fort's gates but many of them chose instead to loot its coffers.[20] These guns demolished rebel defences and the cavalry stormed in, cutting down every sepoy in its way. Also, as John Blakiston, an engineer in Gillespie's force who had helped bring down one of the gates, would write,

> Upwards of a hundred sepoys, who had sought refuge in the palace, were brought out...placed under a wall, and fired at... until they were all dispatched.[21]

If about 200 Europeans were slain during the half-day mutiny, nearly 800 sepoys were probably killed in the reprisal, in which Indians among the Company's troops joined.[22] Many of the hundreds who fled from the fort were apprehended in different parts of the peninsula. After a military trial, nineteen 'ring-leaders' were executed in Vellore Fort, some being hanged, some shot, and a few blown from a cannon's mouth (Blakiston, 308–09).

In a book published in 1829 in London, Blakiston would claim as 'a curious fact...well attested by many persons present', that vultures accompanied the condemned men

> to the place of execution, and then kept hovering over the guns till the final flash, which scattered the fragments of bodies in the air, when...they caught in their talons many pieces of the quivering flesh before they could reach the ground (309).

We do not know if stories of this kind discredited the mutiny option, which would not be tried again by southern sepoys. Though not charged with a role in the mutiny, Fateh Haidar and his brothers were sent to Calcutta. Blakiston would write that:

> This was a politic measure in more respects than one; for it not only removed them out of reach of former friends and adherents of their family, but it appeared to throw the odium of the conspiracy upon them, instead of permitting it to rest on the native army, whose loyalty and attachment it would not have been prudent to question (311–12).

Discovering the identities of the Indians in the British force that retook Vellore Fort, or in other British forces of this period, is not easy. Asking why Indians fought 'with such skill and ferocity in the British interest', and also probing their identities, the scholar Vithal Rajan seems to find that recruits were often marked down as 'Telingas', 'Gentoos' or 'Malabars'.

While these labels do not take us very far, many Indian soldiers appeared to bear, according to Rajan, 'the caste names of "untouchables" and a goodly proportion of every regiment seems to have been made up of "Mussalmans", of whom some might have been converts, like Yusuf Khan. Adds Rajan:

> It makes perfect sense...that the men, discriminated against by a caste-ridden society, gravitated to a service that treated them honourably. If they experienced any dishonourable treatment from

any British officer, they [again] fearlessly rebelled even at the cost of their lives.[23]

We may end our glimpse of the Vellore Mutiny by noting that it resulted in the recall of the orders regarding hats, beards and facial ash, as also the recall from India of the Madras Governor, William Bentinck. In 1828, however, Bentinck would return to Calcutta and preside over the legal abolition of sati, with the aid of Raja Ram Mohan Roy.

ABBÉ DUBOIS (1765–1848)

Another scholar portraying this period, including its economic and social life, is Abbé Jean-Antoine Dubois, the French missionary. On the recommendation, it appears, of Arthur Wellesley, Dubois visited Srirangapatna after its fall in order to reconvert around 1,800 Christians who had been absorbed into Islam. They seem to have all returned to the fold of the Catholic Church, with Dubois persuading the regional bishop, a Monsignor Champenois, to accept them.[24]

After the British takeover of Mysore, Dubois started agricultural colonies for the poor in a place about 40 miles northwest of Srirangapatna, and in 1803–04 he probably saved many lives by persuading '25,432' individuals to accept vaccination against smallpox, a novel idea at the time.[25]

Living in southern India from 1792 to 1823, Dubois learnt English, Kannada and Tamil, adopted the clothing of the people amidst whom he lived, observed their condition and customs, tried to be of help, won a few converts, took notes, and drew his conclusions.

The first draft of his book was published in 1816. Dubois revised the text in 1821, which for whatever reason was published only in the 1890s. Dubois's remarks quoted in this chapter are from this later text.[26]

The economic equation between India and Europe altered significantly during the thirty-one years that Dubois spent in India, with India becoming poorer and Europe richer. The change was most dramatic over cloth, to which Romesh Dutt referred in the remarks quoted above. Dubois thought that a major cause for distress was

the decrease in the demand for hand labour, resulting from the introduction of machinery and the spread of manufactures with improved methods in Europe.

Added Dubois:

> Indeed, Europe no longer depends on India for anything, having learnt to beat the Hindus on their own ground... And this revolution [in textiles] threatens to ruin India completely.

> Just before returning to Europe [in 1823] I travelled through some of the manufacturing districts [in the south] and nothing could equal the state of desolation prevailing in them. All the workrooms were closed, and hundreds of thousands of the inhabitants, composing the weaver caste, were dying of hunger... I found countless widows and other women out of work, and consequently destitute, who used formerly to maintain their families by cotton-spinning (94–95).

Also contributing to Indian poverty, Dubois felt, was a population growing 'at an alarming rate' thanks to the peace following Tipu's defeat, the fertility of Indian women, and an Indian father's pride in having numerous children.

Modern researchers have confirmed the Abbé's account of hardship. District records show that 'the Company's investment in Salem had been discontinued' in 1819. Dependent on the Company, weavers were squeezed, being required to pay a loom tax, a house tax, a dye tax, and stamp duty. Unable to pay these taxes, they were forcibly recruited as labourers by the Company, and sepoys supervised production.

Master-weavers, who had moved from representing weavers to serving as the Company's middlemen and later as its henchmen, 'became oppressive and often treated weavers as slaves'.[27]

◆

Expressing the hope that the freshly triumphant British would not deny 'to a subject people' the 'benefits' they enjoyed at home, the French Abbé added a tribute.

> [T]he inviolable respect which [India's British rulers] constantly show for the customs and religious beliefs of the country; and the protection they afford to the weak as well as to the strong, to the Brahmin as to the Pariah, to the Christian, to the Mahomedan and to the Pagan...have contributed more to the consolidation of their power than even their victories and conquests (xxiii–iv).

Recalling the thousands of conversions, mainly from the high castes, that Robert de Nobili had evidently accomplished more than a hundred years earlier, and other conversions achieved by Nobili's contemporaries, Dubois noted that descendants of many of the converts had gone back to Hinduism.

He identified three reasons for the reversal: the venality of many India-based Europeans, unyielding Brahminical opposition, and the conquest of South India by European armies in the late eighteenth and early nineteenth centuries. To him the conquest was 'a disastrous event' for the advance of Christianity. Now, in the 1820s,

> A Hindu who embraces Christianity must make up his mind to lose everything that makes life pleasant. He is henceforth an outcast from society (301).

◆

Dubois recalls that in his first ten to twelve years in southern India he lived 'in abject poverty' with little more than 'the bare necessaries of life' yet aware that 'nineteen-twentieth' of those around him 'were bearing far greater trials of all kinds' (60).

Stating that he was often called upon to offer last rites in a 'Pariah' hut, Dubois adds, 'I was often obliged to creep in on my hands and knees, so low was the entrance door to the wretched hovel'. He would hold to his nose 'a handkerchief soaked in the strongest vinegar' in a vain battle against the 'sickening smell' of carrion, the 'Pariah's' staple. Dubois would leave with his 'body covered in every part with insects and vermin' (59). He adds,

> When a Brahmin doctor wishes to feel the pulse of a sick Sudra, he first wraps up the patient's wrist in a small piece of silk so that he may not be defiled by touching the man's skin. (182)

To this the Editor appended a footnote in 1897, i.e. more than a half-century after Dubois had written his lines: 'And so, too, when a Sudra doctor feels the pulse of a Brahmin patient' (182fn).

Dubois refers, also, to some untouchables in Malabar who were slaves of high-caste landlords and at times sold along with the land. Though lacking the chance to buy their freedom, these enslaved untouchables appeared to Dubois to be content with their fate. Often given the same food as their landlords, physically they looked healthier than free 'Pariahs' (57–58).

As Dubois saw it, 'Pariahs' worked for Europeans as domestic servants only because they were willing to be kicked with the master's leather shoe. Evidently no self-respecting Sudra was willing to be a European's domestic servant, in part because it involved cooking beef or cleaning utensils where beef had been cooked. According to Dubois, close contact between Europeans and 'Pariahs' was one reason why many Indians disliked Europeans (52–53).

Dubois claims he saw sati being performed before his eyes and writes of ceremonies with Brahmins presiding where a goat was sacrificed (509–13). Critical of Buddhism without having met any Buddhists, Dubois seems kinder to Jains, of whom he had met a few.

When a Jain traveller wishes to quench his thirst at a tank or stream, he covers his mouth with a cloth, stoops down and thus drinks by suction, [a] cleanly custom highly to be recommended elsewhere (699).

The Jaina temple at 'Sravana Belgola' impressed Dubois: 'It is between three mountains, on one of which there is an enormous statue, about seventy feet high, sculptured out of one solid piece of rock.' Dubois surmised that those creating the statue 'first levelled the ground from the top of the mountain…leaving in the centre a mass of rock, which was carved into the shape of the statue'—'a tremendous piece of work,' he wrote (699).

◆

Dubois saw merits in the caste system:

I believe caste division to be in many respects the…happiest effort of Hindu legislation…It is simply and solely due to the distribution of the people into castes that India did not lapse into barbarism, and…perfected the arts and sciences of civilization whilst most other nations…remained in a state of barbarism.

In his view, 'a most clear-sighted prudence' assigned to each individual his own profession or calling, ensured continuance 'from generation to generation', and kept Hindus 'within the bounds of duty by the rules and penalties of caste'. The system had its drawbacks but without it Indian society might have become wild and cannibal-like. Acknowledging that other Europeans held opposite views, Dubois stuck to his own (28–32).

The practice of older men marrying very young girls was seen more among Brahmins than among non-Brahmins, writes Dubois, who however adds:

> [Among Brahmins] one hardly ever meets with a woman who is not, or has not been, married. Blind, dumb, deaf, or lame, all find husbands among poor Brahmins... [Also,] I have never yet heard of a divorce being permitted on account of incompatibility of temper, nor have I heard of a man being allowed to put away his wife, however vicious she might be, simply in order to marry another woman.

Relatives would prevent such banishment, which 'would reflect on the whole' caste (210–12).

Dubois praises South India's Brahmins for the chastity of their women, for quickness in arithmetic (in a few minutes, he says on p. 291, Brahmins complete sums that would take European accountants hours), and for their capacity to endure torture (660), and he concedes that Brahmins 'retain a sublime perception' of the Supreme Being (297). But criticisms outweigh praise.

> The Brahmins have also been clever enough to work their way into favour with the great European Power that now governs India... Thus it is nearly always Brahmins who hold the posts of sub-collectors of revenue, writers, copyists, translators, treasurers, book-keepers etc.
>
> Their perfect knowledge of native opinion and of the ways in which it may be guided...account[s] for the readiness with which their services are accepted...in different Government offices.
>
> The Brahmins...do not forget their relatives and friends [... and] usually divide the most lucrative of the subordinate posts among them (289–291).

Dubois claims he found many Brahmins abusing their gods when their petitions were not answered and also openly jesting about the gods (296). 'The Brahmin,' the Abbé thought, 'does not believe in his religion and yet he outwardly observes it,' whereas the European Christian in India believed in his religion, and yet did not outwardly observe it (300).

While acknowledging that some Brahmins had helped him in building and restoring a church, Dubois did not think they would ever give up their 'usages and customs' of diet, washing, and purity while dining with others.

He claims to see a sense of superiority in Hindus generally. They may have lost wars to outsiders, but Hindus have 'always considered themselves infinitely their superior in the matter of civilization'.

> Being fully persuaded of the superlative merits of their own manners and customs, the Hindus think those of other people barbarous and detestable... This ridiculous pride [has] been so deeply ingrained in them that not one of the great dynastic changes that have taken place in India in modern times has been able to effect the smallest change in their mode of thinking and acting...
>
> Ten centuries of Mahomedan rule, during which time the conquerors have tried alternately cajolery and violence to establish their own faith and their own customs amongst the conquered have not sufficed to shake the steadfast constancy of the native inhabitants... Indeed the dominant race has had to yield, and has even been forced to adopt some of the religious and civil practices of the conquered people (302–04).

He compared Muslim pride with that of the Brahmins:

> [T]he haughty Mussulmans can vie with them in pride and insolence. Yet there is this difference: the arrogance of a Mussulman is based only on the political authority with which he is invested... whereas the Brahmin's superiority is inherent in himself, and it remains intact, no matter what his condition in life.
>
> Rich or poor, unfortunate or prosperous, he always goes on the principle engrained in him that he is the most noble, the most excellent, and the most perfect of all created beings, that all the rest of mankind are infinitely beneath him... (304).

Dubois's editor says in a footnote written in the 1890s:

> It must be admitted that the Abbé paints the Brahmins in darker colours than, as a body, they deserve (315fn).

The Abbé describes a conversation on poetics he had with a Brahmin who was 'already somewhat surprised at the facility with which I understood his explanations and I noticed that his professorial tone and arrogant self-conceit were gradually diminishing'.

When Dubois asked whether in a Sanskrit poem a vowel could assume double its size when followed by two consonants joined to each other, e.g. the starting 'a' in 'aksharam', his interlocutor went silent before asking, 'I wonder how such a thought could have occurred to you.' Adds Dubois: 'He found it very difficult to understand how such sublime things could ever have entered the minds of foreigners, and how poets could be found elsewhere than in India' (395).

Chapter 5

SONGS FROM THE SOUL: 1805–1847

Creativity does not require stability. It was while the political pendulum swung violently that Thyagaraja, Muthuswami Dikshitar and Syama Sastri began producing the master songs that, two centuries later, millions in South India love and thousands sing.

When, in 1799, Tipu was killed in his war with the Company and its allies, these three composers were in their twenties or thirties. Starting with Syama Sastri, whose birth occurred in 1762, the three were born within a few years of one another in the same Kaveri delta town of Thiruvarur.

Also noteworthy is the fact that while Thyagaraja's family was Telugu-speaking, and Syama Sastri and Muthuswami were both born in Tamil homes, all three wrote their songs primarily in Telugu or Sanskrit.

But before proceeding further with this famed trio of Brahmin composers, we should enter earlier periods for background.

◆

Between the sixth and tenth centuries, numerous poets in the Tamil country sang of personal devotion to Siva or Vishnu. On occasion, these early Bhakti poets advocated a departure from Vedic rites. At other times, they contested Jaina or Buddhist teaching.

Later, the twelfth-century poet-statesman, Basava, born into a Brahmin family near Bijapur in today's northern Karnataka, popularized through his Kannada songs and vachanas* a radical, caste-free, temple-free and personal devotion to God.

Refusing, it seems, to perform the upanayana ceremony—the traditional rite of passage for a high-caste boy—Basava is said to have left home with an older sister and spent twelve years at a confluence of two rivers, the Krishna and the Malaprabha, where, according to popular belief, he received the insight that as a symbol

---

*A vachana signifies a saying in rhythm.

of an all-pervading God, the linga would protect its wearer from sin.

Support by him for a marriage between an untouchable boy and a Brahmin girl is said to have produced an angry reaction. Tied to an elephant's legs, the fathers of the bridal couple were cruelly killed, it was said.[1]

His Kannada vachanas, free of Sanskrit, have found followers over the centuries. Here are four samples in translation:

Make me an insignificant parrot in this human forest.
Place me in a cage of faith and make me repeat, 'God,' 'God,'
And thus protect me.

O Father, make me lame that I may not walk hither and
thither.
Make me blind that I may not see how to wander and turn
away.
Make me deaf that I may not hear anything
[That pulls me away from] the feet of Thy servants.

If people condemn you behind your back,
Rejoice when you hear of it.
They find pleasure without taking anything from you,
and without giving anything to you.

I am not afraid of the daring serpent,
Of tongues of flames, or the edge of a sword.
But I am afraid of other men's wives.[2]

The Lingayat community initiated by Basava found adherents outside Karnataka as well, especially in the Telugu and Marathi countries.

Also retaining popular favour are three other poets distant from our times, Valluvar, Vemana and Sarvajna. All three caught the attention of Europeans arriving in the eighteenth century.

Describing the three as 'satirical' and 'revolutionary' poets, Dubois claimed that Brahmins were hostile to their poems, a charge later questioned by Henry Beauchamp, Dubois's editor, who was familiar with southern India. 'These authors are held in great respect, and are much read by educated Brahmins,' insisted Beauchamp, writing in 1897.[3] Dubois thought Valluvar was a 'Pariah'. Scholars coming after him have agreed that the poet was a weaver and thus certainly of low caste. Dubois's observation that Valluvar wrote originally in Tamil was factual, but the Frenchman's impression that he belonged to 'recent times' was wide of the mark. Consensus now places the poet's birth in the early common era centuries.

Noting that 'Sarovignaimurti (Sarvajna) was a Lingayat' and that 'his works are in Canarese', Dubois added that among unconventional writers 'one of the most famous' was Vemana, 'whose poems, originally written in Telugu, have since been translated in several other languages'.[4]

◆

Preceding Abbé Dubois into India, the Italian missionary Constanzo Beschi (we met him earlier, in Chapter 2) had composed a Latin translation of Valluvar's *Kural*. French translations of selections from that work were published in Paris in 1767, and a century later the British missionary George Uglow Pope produced *The Sacred Kurral*,[5] as he called and spelt it, which contained his own translation along with an English rendition of Beschi's.

Pope's first teacher in Tamil, described by the pupil as 'a most learned scholar' and 'a profound and zealous Vaishnavite', was a Ramanuja Kavirayar, who died before Pope's work appeared. 'From that noble enthusiastic teacher,' Pope would write, 'I learnt to love Tamil and to reverence its ancient professors.' Pope proceeded to wish 'peace to [the teacher]'s ashes!' Not to the teacher's soul? Reverence notwithstanding, Pope seemed to doubt that a Hindu could possess a lasting soul.[6]

This detail indicates the circumscribed thinking of at least some nineteenth-century Europeans in South India. Nonetheless we should recognize that but for scholars like Pope many an Indian today might have remained unaware of the *Kural*. Thanks in fair part to their exertions, that classic is now available in print or on the net in several Indian and international languages.

Its early circulation was almost entirely oral, and probably confined to southern India. While a Telugu translation was printed in 1887, 'an unpublished manuscript of a Malayalam translation done in 1595

A.D. is reported in the Annual Report of the Cochin Archeological Department for the year 1933–34'.[7]

Surmising from his research that 800-1000 CE was the period encompassing Valluvar's life, Pope detected traces of the Gita and also of Jaina thinking in the *Kural*. Whether Valluvar was a Hindu or a Jaina remains contested to this day; and we may mark also that Pope, who spoke of passages in the *Kural* as being 'Christian in their spirit', speculated that 'the Christian Scriptures were among the sources from which the poet derived his inspiration'.[8]

Pope's view that Valluvar lived in the Mylapore/ San Thome area was taken from long-standing beliefs, and the same was true of assertions regarding the poet's profession as a weaver, his familiarity with the sea and with the world of trade, and his close friendship with a sea captain called Elelasingan (Lion of the Surf).

Contemplating 'the boom of the sea waves' reaching Valluvar's ears, Pope also imagined a 'passer-by' along Valluvar's home 'hearing the click of the shuttle mingling with the low chaunt of his melodious verse'.[9]

Pope found the *Kural*'s 'poetic form' to be 'exquisite'. Each couplet contained 'a complete and striking idea in a refined and intricate metre' and compressed sentences emerged as 'the choicest of moral epigrams'.[10] Valluvar's 'forceful brevity' reminded Pope of the skill ascribed to St Augustine of forging a single phrase into 'a polished shaft, at once pointed to pierce the mind and memory' but also 'barbed', so it would not easily slip out of that mind and memory.[11]

To Pope it seemed a marvel that the *Kural*, 'complete in itself' and 'the sole work of its author', mostly using pure Tamil with occasional words taken from Sanskrit, had 'come down the stream of ages absolutely uninjured' (iii). That its couplets were 'enshrined in the hearts of the whole people' also struck Pope, who wrote:

> Dynastic changes, Muhammadan raids, and irruptions of alien races, through a dozen centuries, have changed many things in the South—'Old times are changed, old manners gone, and strangers fill the Pandyan's throne'—but the Tamil race preserves many of its old virtues... Their English friends, in teaching them all that the West has to impart, will find little to unteach in the moral lessons of the Kurral rightly understood (xii).

On 'the good householder' and his characteristics, Valluvar wrote (Pope's translation):

His wife is the guardian of his fame.

His children are his choicest treasures; their babbling voices are his music; he feasts with the gods when he eats the rice their tiny fingers have played with; and his one aim is to make them worthier than himself.

His house is open to every guest, whom he welcomes with smiling face and pleasant word, and with whom he shares his meal.

He is courteous in speech, grateful for every kindness, with a heart free from envy, speaking no evil of others, refraining from unprofitable words, diligent in discharging all his duties (x).

Pope quoted a Monsieur Ariel, author of a French translation published in Paris in 1848, who found that Valluvar

addresses himself, without regard to castes, peoples or beliefs, to the whole community of mankind...formulates sovereign morality and absolute reason...presents [together] the highest laws of domestic and social life...is equally perfect in thought, language, and poetry; in the austere metaphysical contemplation of the great mysteries of the Divine Nature, as in the easy and graceful analysis of the tenderest emotions of the heart (i).

Pope also picked out the perfect obedience of Vasuki, Valluvar's wife, one-sided though it must appear to the modern mind.

Another day, at noon, when the glaring light was everywhere, the sage, who was at work at his loom, let fall his shuttle, and called for a light to seek it! The wife, with unquestioning obedience, lit a lamp and brought it to him! (vi)

Apparently, when Vasuki's end was imminent,

the dying wife looked wistfully at her husband. 'What is it?' said he. 'When you married me, and on that day I stood and spread the rice for you, you gave me a commandment to place always with your meals a cup of water and a needle. I know not why it was.'

'It was,' he replied, 'that if a grain of rice were spilt, I might

pick it up and purify it.' Satisfied, the meek Vasuki closed her
eyes for ever.

Observes Pope:

She had never during her whole married life questioned her lord's
command. And also, it is clear, no grain of rice had ever been
spilt! (xi)

◆

He has been called 'a poet of the people, a philosopher of freedom
and equality and a fighting saint' whose 'aphorisms are on the lips of
everybody in Andhra', yet until the 1910s Vemana was 'dismissed as
beneath notice by the Telugu literary world', to quote the twentieth-
century scholar-playwright-journalist, Venkateswara Rao Narla.[12]

When in 1824 he read of Vemana in Dubois's book (first published
in 1816), Charles Philip Brown, a Company servant in Kadapa, went
in search of palm-leaf copies of Vemana's verses and found many.
Fluent with languages (he had learnt Telugu, Hindustani, Persian and
Marathi), Brown, born in Calcutta in 1798, then translated the verses
into English.

Five years later, 500 copies of his *Verses of Vemana* were printed
by the Company's college in Madras. Fifty copies were given to Brown
but the remaining 450 disappeared. Ten years later, Brown found the
missing folios in a college backroom, rolled up as wastepaper. Evidently
Verses of Vemana had ended up there with 'the active connivance of
the high-caste pandits of the college board'.[13]

In his preface, Brown wrote, 'These poems have attained very great
popularity and parts are found translated into Tamil and Malayalam
or Canarese.'[14]

The Company's government in Fort St George made Vemana's verses
a textbook in its Telugu schools, but teachers and students evaded
the order. Writing in 1866 in the *Madras Journal of Literature and
Science,* Major R. M. Macdonald of the Madras Staff Corps repeated
Dubois's old charge and asserted that 'Brahmins in particular most
cordially detest this author'.[15]

In 1871, Charles E. Gover produced *The Folk Songs of Southern
India* where Vemana was praised for 'rational' verses written in blunt

language, but Telugu intellectuals withheld appreciation. In *Lives of the Telugu Poets,* first published in 1899, the celebrated nineteenth-century author and social reformer Kandukuri Veeresalingam kept Vemana out. The shroud covering Vemana was taken off only in 1914, when thirty-four-year-old Cattamanchi Ramalinga Reddy, who would gain eminence in education and politics, demanded a place of honour for him.[16]

The ranks of Vemana fans and scholars have grown ever since, yet these scholars disagree on the place, year or even century of his birth. Charles Brown, Vemana's re-discoverer and researcher, seemed over time to alter his own opinion. The poet, he thought, was born in the seventeenth century, or maybe 100 or 200 years earlier, in either Kurnool, Guntur or Cuddapah district, in any case somewhere in the Rayalaseema region.

After examining the arguments of numerous modern scholars, Telugu and European, and scouring Vemana's verses for internal evidence, Narla offers a summary of Vemana's life. Agreeing broadly with Brown's early opinion that the poet was 'born in 1652 and died in the first two decades of the 18th century', Narla believes that Vemana was probably from an influential Reddi (or Reddy) family living close to Kurnool district's Gandicota town, where his brother may have commanded a fort, and that he spent the best part of his life in the districts of Cuddapah and Kurnool (Narla, 19, 23).

Today Kapu and Reddi are seen as different groups in the Andhra/ Telugu country, but until the start of the twentieth century Reddi and Kapu seemed synonymous phrases, the phrase 'Kapu' being used for 'cultivator' while 'Reddi' had the added suggestion of caste. Today Kapu, too, is seen as a distinct caste.

According to Narla's analysis, Vemana's verses reveal that he grew up on a fair-sized farm in a Virasaiva or Lingayat* family, lost his mother while a boy, faced a difficult step-mother, was drawn to a devadasi who, however, found another paramour, ran into debt, was lured by claims of turning base metal into gold, and finally ran into a teacher who showed that base human material can be transformed into something better than gold, viz. a purposeful life (28).

---

*There are wrangles over the connection and/or difference between Lingayat and Virasaiva.

Brought to the Telugu country from Karnataka, Basava's Lingayat outlook seemed at first to equalize all sects and castes, from Brahmin to untouchable. By the time of Vemana, however, the Lingayat movement had ceased to be reformist. Not only had it become merely another sect or caste, or both, it had also split into factions (32). Vemana would warn:

Beware, thousands of cheats trade in religion; They're like a flock of cranes chasing fish (33).[17]

As Saivism and Vaishnavism both got debased, animal sacrifice in the name of Vedic rituals returned to the fore. Vemana's comment was scathing.

Vedic priests, what's your best feat? Killing helpless animals, calling it sacrifice? You wring a poor goat's neck and become a lion? (33)

An iconoclast and a social rebel, Vemana derided religious externals such as wearing the lingam. A belief also existed, which his explicit verses may be seen as supporting, that Vemana was a debauch before he became a detached yogi. Referring together to Vemana and the Kannada country's Sarvajna, Narla would claim: 'As young men, both were philanderers. Both were first much enamoured of, and then disgusted with, devadasis' (53).

Towards the end of his days, 'seeing impostors passing off as religious teachers by putting on the robes of this or that sect', Vemana 'seems to have discarded all clothing' (52).

Attacked for iconoclasm and eccentricities, and for the life he had led before his transformation, Vemana as a poet perhaps suffered even more, Narla tells us, for being a Sudra. 'No less an authority on Telugu poetics than Appakavi,' Telugu's famed seventeenth-century grammarian, 'had laid down...that the work of a Sudra poet should be rejected without examination' (5).

A Vemana verse usually contained two opening lines about a slice of real life, a third line offering an analogy or epigram triggered by the first two, and a never-changing fourth line: Viswadaabhirama Vinura Vema. This last line was the Vemana sign-off or refrain. For example:

You are loved and made much of while your mother is alive. After she is gone, none cares for you. Make good while the time is yet propitious. Viswadaabhirama Vinura Vema (28).

The alliterative and standard final sentence announced Vemana's authorship, but its meaning remains disputed.

Centuries later, some of Vemana's epigrammatic third lines feature in daily conversation among the Telugus.

Does a dog become a lion after a dip in the Godavari?
Does a spoon know the taste of the dish it serves?
Does washing with milk make coal white?
Does a load of perfume on its back make a donkey attractive? (38)

Picturing not golden scenes from the epics but reality at a time when late medieval southern India was coming to an unpleasant close, Vemana's verses suggest, says Narla, 'a decadent age, poor in worldly goods and in spirit, vulgar, and ugly' (31).

His words are tough and bristly. On a traditional belief that a Vedic sacrifice earned the favours of Rambha, the celestial courtesan, Vemana commented,

If father and son perform the sacrifice, both would gain heaven and Rambha's bed; Wouldn't that become incest? (33)

Narla reminds us that in life Vemana was gentle, not harsh. A rotten age that saw weak and mean princes invited his severe words, and he didn't care if he was called mad (34). Of one prince, Vemana says:

His son's a blackguard, friend a tale-bearer; himself he is stupid, and his minister a nincompoop. Verily, a monkey is happiest when baboons surround him (34).

He may not have written a purana blessed by the priesthood, nor composed a classical text with customary features (a prince, a battle, a hunt, the prince's sex life), but in Narla's judgement Vemana's penetrating and bold poetry, independent of school or rules, was innately classical.

Vemana did not write his poetry; he spoke it. It is not 'emotion recalled in tranquillity'; it is emotion in white heat (35–36).

Narla adds that Vemana exploited to the hilt, the ease and rhythm of the ataveladi metre he chose for his verse (37). And he ridiculed superstitions.

If frequent bathing earns salvation, all fishes are saved.

If smearing the skin with ash saves, honour the donkey wallowing in ashes.

If eating plants makes the body perfect, envy the goat.

Vishnu, you say, reposes on an ocean of milk. But as Krishna he steals milk from cowherds' homes. Does a drink on the sly taste sweeter? (40)

You starve and hit a useful bullock; when carved in stone you worship it (58).

Viler than the meanest is he to whom all others are Sudras (59).

Men imagine stones to be Siva and magnify them. Stones are stones and not Siva. And we refuse to discern the Siva who dwells within us (64).

Another Vemana verse derided four orthodox rituals: seclusion, meditation, chanting, bathing.

A dog is often solitary! A crane meditates! An ass chants! A frog bathes all the time! How about knowing your own hearts? (2: 54)

'Vemana's one blind spot,' Narla says, 'is the woman. He gives her an inferior, almost ignominious place... It is best to keep away from her; if you cannot do that, keep her strictly under check.' (47)

We may conclude with two Vemana verses, minus their signature line:

Though a foe worthy of death fall into thy hands, afflict him not. Conciliate him with kindness, and bid him depart. That will be death to him (2: 55).

The rich miser is like the scarecrow in a field; he is amidst plenty, but the field is not his (1: 47).

◆

Almost as radical as Vemana was Sarvajna, who may have been his seventeenth-century contemporary in the Kannada country. Recited by common folk, Sarvajna's verses too were encountered in southern India by Abbé Dubois in the late eighteenth and early nineteenth centuries.

Like Vemana, a product of the Lingayat intervention, Sarvajna also wrote in a popular metre and on worldly subjects. And if it took an

Englishman, C. P. Brown, to collect Vemana verses before they could disappear, a Christian pastor of Indian origin, Chennappa Uttangiri, may have been the first person to enable Sarvajna's verses 'to appear in book form'.[18]

Asserting this, the scholar Jyotsna Kamat stresses that the recluse Sarvajna imagined a humankind beyond boundaries. With a rhythm and rhyme impossible to capture in translation, he wrote:

> The whole town is full of relatives
> Streets brim with kith and kin
> Mother Earth herself is my family Goddess
> Whom can I ignore?

'With begging bowl in hand and a vast land around, with Hara [Siva], the beneficial, at his side, who can be wealthier than an itinerant beggar?' asked Sarvajna.[19] More than three centuries later, the Kannada country echoes with his rhymes.

◆

Old as the hills, the Siva-Vishnu rivalry in southern India was generally friendly. When pressed, both sides usually conceded that Siva, Vishnu and Brahma were only three faces of the same Supreme Being. Vishnu received a boost when Rama and Krishna, deputizing as Vishnu's incarnations, presented irresistible faces via the Ramayana (which told Rama's story) and the Bhagavatham (which related Krishna's). On his part, Siva was powerfully represented by his popular sons, Murugan (or Karthikeyan) and Ganesha.

Exactly when South India was first introduced to Ganesha, Murugan, Rama and Krishna are not questions on which scholars speak with confidence. Long after those early introductions, lasting images of Rama and Krishna were presented by Purandaradasa, who was born in the Kannada country in the last quarter of the fifteenth century.

Growing up to become a rich jeweller, Purandaradasa belonged to a family of Madhva Brahmins who followed the teaching of Madhvacharya, the thirteenth-century Vaishnavite thinker: humans find grace from God by surrendering to him. After his wife gave away her nose-ring to a needy person whose plea for help he had brushed aside, Purandaradasa is said to have found his life's purpose.

The story goes like this. Wanting to sell the ring, the recipient took it to the shop of Purandaradasa, who, intrigued, ran to ask his wife if her ring had been stolen. Minutes earlier, terrified at his likely response to her charity, the wife had prayed to Vishnu and received a replacement. Nervously confessing her deed, she also showed Purandaradasa the new ring.

The miracle, and his wife's compassion that preceded it, changed the jeweller's life. Already well-versed in Sanskrit, Kannada and sacred music, he became a wandering minstrel for the rest of his life and composed a vast number of songs about Krishna and Rama.

The nose-ring story may lack proof. Yet Purandaradasa's songs are not only real and sung daily to this day, those songs and the way in which he sang them are seen as having created what for two hundred years or more the world has called Carnatic or South Indian music, of which Purandaradasa is almost incontestably regarded as the founding father.

He not only wrote the words for these songs of praise, called kirtanas (or keerthanas, in Kannada kirtane), he found (and in some cases founded) the melodies, the beat, and the tempo for singing or playing them, and he also showed how the music now called classical should be taught.

Addressing social issues in addition to extolling Krishna and Rama, he seems to have declared in one of his songs that an untouchable was anyone who did not practise self-discipline, or plotted against his own government, or shrank from charity while possessing wealth, or tried to poison an opponent, or prided himself on the purity of his caste.[20]

Srinivasa, not Purandaradasa, was the name given to him by his father, Varadappa Nayak. Multiplying the wealth bequeathed by the father, the son came to be called 'navakoti narayana', master of nine crores. When, giving away their wealth to the poor, he and his wife Sarasvati took to the street with songs on their lips, he was thirty years old.

Thrice, so it was said, Purandaradasa walked up to the Himalayas and back in his new calling. Treks across the Vijayanagara kingdom took place more often. When he was forty, his gifts were evidently spotted by Vyasaraya, guru to the most reputed ruler in Vijayanagara history, Krishnadevaraya.

It is likely that the name Purandaradasa was bestowed by Vyasaraya. Eventually taking sanyas, Purandaradasa is believed to have died at the age of eighty, having composed a legendary number of kirtane, of which several hundred with clear evidence of his hand survive. Most contain his mudra (vocal signature), 'Purandara Vitthala'.

Given the existence of the famed Vitthala temple in Maharashtra's Pandharpur, the mudra gave rise to suggestions of a possible Maharashtra origin for Purandaradasa, but scholarly consensus favours Karnataka as the region of his birth. Through disciples, his kirtane are said to have reached northern India during Akbar's reign and possibly influenced Hindustani music as well.

The kirtane of Purandaradasa's Kannada contemporary Kanakadasa too are sung to this day. Unlike the jeweller-turned composer, who was a Brahmin, Kanakadasa belonged to a 'low' peasant or warrior caste.

Often depicting real-life scenes, his songs and plays questioned caste's hierarchies, apart from celebrating Krishna and Rama. Paralleling the nose-ring legend associated with Purandaradasa is the belief that, excluded because of his caste from Udupi's celebrated Krishna temple, Kanakadasa entreated the deity from afar with such ardour that the idol swung around by 180 degrees to face him.

Persons like Kanakadasa and Purandaradasa were called haridasas, dasas or servants of Hari. These haridasas created a powerful tradition of devotional music which was reinforced by men like Ramadasu of Bhadrachala, which lay in the Telugu-speaking zone ruled from Golconda by the Mughals' southern viceroy.

In this tradition, which our times too have embraced, the music is at least as important as the devotion. Presenting harikathas (often bhakti stories about Krishna or Rama) through compelling music, these haridasas have also been seen as religious entertainers.

◆

In the chain linking today's music lovers to the haridasas of the sixteenth century, no name is more prominent than that of Thyagaraja (1767–1847), and perhaps no location more central than the Coromandel coast's Thanjavur delta, to which the Kaveri offers its final boons before entering the sea.

In the 1760s, William Fullarton, the Company officer whom we have come across more than once, wrote that the delta, for later cognoscenti the 'most musically rich region in South India', was also the

> most fertile—it is watered by a multiplicity of streams, which by means of embankments and reservoirs are diverted into every field—it annually affords two or three luxuriant crops of rice; the forests abound with valuable trees; the county is overstocked with sheep and cattle...no spot upon the globe is superior in productions for the use of man.[21]

Inevitably attracting outsiders, the delta had seen the sway of Vijayanagara followed by Telugu-speaking nayakas, who fostered Telugu learning in Thanjavur. Maratha chiefs replaced the nayakas, and in the 1760s, when Fullarton wrote those lines, the Carnatic nawab was claiming the delta. Raids from Haidar and Tipu and interventions by the East India Company would soon follow.

Significant Brahmin settlements, dependent on the delta's peasantry, created in Thanjavur a Brahmin percentage larger than anywhere else in the Tamil country.

> Devotion to Siva, Vishnu, Murugan and the Goddess flourished under the brahmins' auspices...and served to unify organically the bonded labourers, vellalas [dominant land-owning peasants who also provided soldiers and bureaucrats], artisans and royalty.[22]

Though obliged to submit to Aurangzeb in 1688, Sahaji II may have been Thanjavur's best Maratha ruler. His brothers Sarabhoji and Tulajaji I, one following the other, succeeded Sahaji II. Tulajaji I promoted music and other arts but a famine in 1730 caused starvation, pestilence, destitution and slavery during his rule, which was followed by the reigns of two sons, the illegitimate Pratap Singh and his successor, Tulajaji II.

Suspecting Tulajaji II of plotting with Haidar and charging him with not paying the tribute demanded by their ally, the Nawab of the Carnatic, the British occupied Thanjavur in 1773. Three years later, however, Tulajaji was restored after he placed himself entirely in their hands. British influence grew, and a few European missionaries, including the previously encountered Charles Schwartz, taught English to Thanjavur's Brahmins and Vellalas aspiring for jobs with the Company.

Tulajaji II's rule was weak, and Haidar attacked Thanjavur twice during his reign, but it was this ruler who granted a house and a land in scenic Thiruvaiyaru to Thyagaraja's parents, Kakarla Ramabrahmam and his wife Sitamma, whose forebears had migrated generations earlier from the Telugu country. Set against the Kaveri, Thiruvaiyaru lay 45 miles west of Thiruvarur, where Thyagaraja had been born.

Ramabrahmam was a Ramayana reciter and music pandit in the Thanjavur court, which employed more than 300 scholars like him who wrote, performed and taught music. The delta had long been a magnet for musicians, and there are records of itinerant musicians bringing and singing compositions there during Purandaradasa's time (38).

If most of these court pandits in Thanjavur were Smartha Brahmins, often called Iyers (of course spelt variously), several of them, including Kakarla Ramabrahmam, were Telugu-speaking (38).

Speaking of 'a bitter rivalry' in the nineteenth century and earlier between Iyers and Iyengars (also spelt diversely), Thyagaraja's diligent biographer, William Jackson, adds that Smartha Brahmins like Ramabrahmam were 'creative synthesizers' who 'Sanskritized bhakti', gave local and folk traditions 'an orthodox aura', and 'toned down Saiva versus Vaishnava bitterness' (31–32).

Ramabrahmam's son Thyagaraja, a Saivite Brahmin singing of Rama and wearing the Vaishnava mark on the forehead, became an archetypical example of a Saiva-Vaishnava synthesis.

◆

Jackson dwells on the 'gruesome harshness of the times' when Thyagaraja was growing up (89). Famine hit Thanjavur in 1776 and again between 1780 and 1783, when Haidar and Tipu attacked the delta.

There was internal turmoil too. After Tulajaji II died in 1787, the German missionary, Schwartz, seems to have rescued his young son Sarabhoji II (also known as Serfoji II) from plots by relatives. Although Sarabhoji recovered his throne in 1798, in 1799 (the year when Tipu died in Srirangapatna and Schwartz in Thanjavur) he surrendered Thanjavur to the Company.

South India's eighteenth-century instability, and how expanding

British rule ended it, were themes portrayed in a Telugu poem, 'The Wars of the Rajas', Brown's translation of which was published in 1853.[23] The poem spoke of Hindu-on-Hindu outrages resulting in Muslim rule, and cruelties by Muslim rulers followed by British rule.

As Thyagaraja grew from teenage into adulthood, Brahmin self-confidence received repeated blows: from the attacks of Haidar and Tipu, from intrigues around the Thanjavur throne, and finally from power over the region going to a beef-eating race of white ship-owners, merchants, bankers, and army or naval commanders.

Yet if some Brahmins in Thanjavur saw British rule as the ruin of tradition, others thought it might eventually bring about justice and peace. In any case, none of them confronted the British.

It was argued that one way of responding to powerful intruders was to ignore them, or treat them as illusory, or, from a long enough perspective, transient. Jackson suggests that the Thanjavur Brahmins' attitude towards the British was marked by superficial 'agreeableness and secret reservations' (96).

The notion that ages come and go was recalled, patience and faith were appealed to, and an inner strength was summoned. Jackson speculates that the new hegemony of the West may even have made the Brahmin in Thanjavur (and elsewhere) more self-aware and eventually prouder of his indigenous heritage.

We do not know for certain what Thyagaraja himself felt about the new white rulers, or about preceding attacks by Haidar and Tipu, or the confusions within Thanjavur. He left no record of his reactions, and his songs transcend such questions.

No song of his refers to the European advent or to any war. As for Muslims, apparently the sole reference in all his songs to them, an indirect one, occurs when Thyagaraja observes that a ritual ceremony of worship cannot take place on a particular street because non-pure 'Turks' inhabit portions of it.[24]

For seeming similarity to the European soldier who was winning South India's battles, a muscular disciple of Thyagaraja was called by him, 'Sojiri' or 'Soldier' Sitaramayya. And the word 'lantern' enters, Telugu-ized, as 'landaru' in one of his songs.

In Thyagaraja's huge linguistic output, these two, it seems, were about the only instances when hospitality was offered to English words.

However, music proved more seductive than idiom. Thyagaraja, worshipper of Rama and Krishna and adorer of Purandaradasa, incorporated English band-tunes into a handful of his songs, while also 'naturalizing' the tunes (Jackson, 92).

Thyagaraja's deepest, strongest and in the end triumphant response to intrusion was to dive into his soul and emerge with everlasting pearls of music. It was an exercise for which, it was said, he had prepared his mind and throat by repeating a Rama line 960 *million* times over a twenty-year period.

Much earlier, as an infant, he would stop breast-feeding when he heard music (3). A pull from infancy, immersion in music became his response to inner calling and outer challenge. His singing-composing was thus a merger of prayer and defiance, or bhakti with a quiet satyagraha component.

This singing-composing was also magical. Melody and words came to him simultaneously, and the musicality of Telugu, where many words end with a flowing vowel, enhanced the power of his creations.

Thyagaraja produced and sang more than 700 exquisite songs, which while highly sophisticated remain popular. Analysing his peninsula-wide appeal, a scholar named S. V. Ramamurti wrote in 1941 in *The Hindu* that Thyagaraja's Telugu speech was 'simple as that of a Telugu country girl returning singing with fresh cut grass', his message in line with the Tamil Nayanars and Alwars of old, and his music 'a continuation of the Kannadiga Purandaradasa'.[25]

The compositions or kritis into which Thyagaraja transmuted his passion 'popularized classical music and classicized popular music'. Through 'hundreds of compact and evocative' kritis, where the singer converses with Rama, Krishna or Siva, Thyagaraja preserved and passed on bhakti to future generations (Jackson, 91). Yet he may have been a composer more of 'art music' than of sacred music.[26]

Renunciation, however, added to the appeal of one who was also a 'brilliant singer', a gifted player of the veena, and a 'great musicologist'.[27] Thyagaraja turned down jewels offered to him by the Thanjavur ruler even though his father and his teacher had accepted the raja's patronage. His soaring kritis were dedicated not to a ruler but to Purandaradasa, Bhadrachala's Ramadasu, and Rama himself; and succeeding generations have pictured Thyagaraja in the simple attire of a haridasa, Rama's slave, not as a companion to any prince.

Near the end of his life, like Purandaradasa, he entered the order of sanyasins. In 1847, he died on a bank of the Kaveri, where, to honour his saintliness, a gravesite was built for him. Not long after his death, there were harikathas about Thyagaraja himself.

Still, influential quarters were slow to recognize him. Brown, who in the first half of the nineteenth century studied a broad range of Telugu poetry, left Thyagaraja out. Compiled studiously by the Company, the *Thanjavur Gazetteer* of 1906—fifty-nine years after Thyagaraja's death—named him merely as 'one of three singers from Thanjavur known widely in the Tamil country'.[28]

◆

Born in Thiruvarur five years before Thyagaraja, Syama Sastri (1762–1827) belonged to a Tamil family that claimed an ancient contact, occurring in Kanchipuram,[29] with the great Sankara, proclaimer of Advaita and creator of that historic renewal whereby Hinduism supplanted Buddhism and Jainism in South India.

Syama Sastri's forebears were priestly Brahmins. Migrating across the Tamil country, with stays in Gingee, around Kumbakonam, and elsewhere, they were welcomed by the Maratha rulers of Thanjavur, who gave them ample lands and temple responsibilities in their domain, including in Thiruvarur.

Syama Sastri's family lived for forty-five years in Thiruvarur, where his father, Viswanatha Iyer, became the priest for worshippers at an ancient idol of Kamakshi, Siva's spouse.

Around 1781, when an attack from Haidar seemed imminent, Viswanatha Iyer obtained Tulajaji II's permission to move with his family to the Thanjavur fortress, which seemed safer than Thiruvarur. Like Thyagaraja, Syama Sastri, too, was thus affected, when he was eighteen or so, by the thrusts of Mysore's ruler.

A maternal uncle had passed on music's rudiments to him, which he swiftly grasped, and he was blessed with a fine voice. Yet Syama Sastri received no proper training in the art until this move to Thanjavur Fort, where a music master suddenly showed up, having journeyed all the way from Varanasi. This man, a Telugu Brahmin, detected the teenager's talents and coached him for a couple of months.

Thanks to his father's tutelage, Syama Sastri was already a brilliant scholar in Telugu and Sanskrit. From the itinerant, he now learnt 'the subtleties of the science of music' and 'soon mastered all the intricacies' of melody, beat, and note permutations.[30]

Before returning to Varanasi, this teacher advised Syama Sastri to approach Pachimiriyam Adiyappayya, then 'adored as the king of musicians' in Thanjavur. Won over by Syama Sastri's virtuosity, this fifty-year-old 'king' gave him lessons, company and confidence.[31]

We are told that even as a youngster the light-skinned Syama Sastri had a 'majestic appearance' and 'a commanding personality'. The older Syama Sastri cut an imposing figure: he is pictured with a necklace of gold-mounted beads, diamond ear-rings, a bright shawl and a silver-mounted walking stick.[32]

The musicologist and music historian P. Sambamoorthy has given an account of a celebrated turn-of-the-century contest between Syama Sastri and Kesavayya from Bobbili in the northern Telugu country, who arrived in Thanjavur not only with cartloads of tamburas surrendered by musicians he had vanquished on his long journey south, but also with signed admissions, complete with date and place, of their defeat.

Armed with the title, 'Bhuloka Chapa Chutti', or 'The Man Who Rolled the World into a Mat', carrying 'a pompous attitude' and decking his personal tambura with 'a challenging flag', Bobbili Kesavayya dared Thanjavur's singers to compete with him. Their confidence shaken by the outsider's parade of strength, Thanjavur's music experts ran to Syama Sastri and begged him to accept the challenge, while the raja set aside a tray of jewels for the winner.

Thanjavur's musical reputation was at stake. Usually disdainful of royal patronage, and seldom in need of it, on this occasion Syama Sastri acceded to the invitation.

Fought on palace grounds, the battle between Thanjavur and Bobbili was witnessed by thousands who craned their necks and adjusted their ears to follow it. Kesavayya's vigorous opening song was answered by one at least as powerful from Syama Sastri, who then asked if Kesavayya could sing without shaking his head. 'Of course,' said the champion from Bobbili, but his head could not stay still while he attempted a tricky number demanded by Syama Sastri.

Sambamoorthy tells us that joyous shouts greeted the proclamation of Thanjavur's triumph. Syama Sastri was given a glittering tray. While Bobbili may recall this battle differently, what is beyond dispute is the pride that musical prowess supplied to South India during a period wanting in self-respect.

Compositions flowed from Syama Sastri, some arriving under inspiration and sung extempore, to be sung two hundred years later with painstaking preparation (81). In his own time, to the thrill of music lovers present, Syama Sastri went on occasion to Thyagaraja's home in Thiruvaiyaru, where the two compared new pieces.

Unlike Thyagaraja, whose more than two dozen scholarly disciples trained hundreds more in their master's compositions, Syama Sastri seems to have had few pupils and little enthusiasm for teaching them. This may help explain the loss of the music for many of his 300 compositions (82).

◆

Ramaswami Dikshitar, the father of the youngest of the Thiruvarur trio, Muthuswami Dikshitar (1776–1835), is credited with the longest composition in Carnatic music.[33] It was said of Ramaswami that he only needed to hear a song once to be able to sing it himself.

Tamil-speaking Smartha Brahmins, the Dikshitars too had moved from place to place, at times because of raids by marauders, before striking roots in the Thanjavur delta.

Ramaswami and his wife, Subbalakshmi, found two girls to marry their son Muthuswami, who was persuaded to go with his pair of wives to Varanasi (again we find a connection with that city) with a yogi of renown who was visiting the delta.

His five years in Varanasi made Muthuswami familiar with Hindustani music and open to northern influences later observed in his compositions. On his way back to the delta, Muthuswami stopped at various shrines; once back, he was mostly found near the entrance of the Thiruvarur temple, playing on his veena and singing.

And he composed. Most lyrics were in Sanskrit. Many were addressed to temples or deities. A famous collection included messages to each planet. In his verses, Muthuswami became a master of rhyme and a creator of 'rhetorical beauties' (138).

Disciples with a range of interests gathered around him. These included male and female (a dancer called Kamalam was one of them, as was a male quartet that sang and danced and became well-known) singers, composers, violin and veena players, and performers with the drum, or with the nadaswaram, the elongated wind instrument. Muthuswami found himself in an unexpected relationship with the raja of an estate far to the south of Thanjavur, Ettaiyapuram near Tirunelveli. We may recall that this place featured, not so proudly, in the story of Veerapandya Kattabomman the rebel, for Ettaiyapuram's raja had helped the British capture and execute Kattabomman.

Somewhere in the 1820s, a brother of Muthuswami found employment with the raja of Ettaiyapuram. Was this the very raja who had joined the Company against Kattabomman? We do not know, but the Company's triumphs had obviously benefited Ettaiyapuram's ruling family.

Making the long trip in a bullock cart to see his brother in Ettaiyapuram, Muthuswami ran first into drought and barren lands, next into a sudden burst of rain, and finally into robbers. The story that has come down has Muthuswami successfully summoning rain through a song and then causing it to stop, again through a song. Terrified at first, the robbers end up escorting Muthuswami to his destination.

Not legend but an undisputed fact is that the Ettaiyapuram raja of the 1820s and 1830s became Muthuswami's friend, admirer and benefactor. It was during another and less dramatic visit to Ettaiyapuram, in 1835, that Muthuswami unexpectedly died.

Three years earlier, in 1832, he had composed, and presumably sung, several Sanskrit verses in what already, in some quarters, were well-known Western melodies. Interestingly, these compositions were dedicated to the Company employee we have already met, Charles Philip Brown, who collected Vemana's verses.[34]

Perhaps (we may speculate) these Sanskrit songs in Western ragas resulted from conversations between Muthuswami and Brown.

That Thyagaraja and Muthuswami both ventured into Western tunes tells us something of what was happening even in Thanjavur's orthodox circles in the first quarter of the nineteenth century. These circles had been shaken by alien ship-owners and cannon-owners who were replacing the country's quarrelling rulers. Nonetheless, aspects of the culture that came with the strangers attracted the natives.

Thus it came about that Vadivelu of the aforementioned Thanjavur Quartet and Muthuswami's brother Baluswami Dikshitar pioneered the use in Carnatic music of the violin, now hardly ever absent from a South Indian music stage. Intrigued by the violin in European bands, men like Vadivelu and Baluswami mastered and adapted it, playing the instrument from a seated, cross-legged position, unlike Europeans who stood while performing with it.[35]

◆

The Thanjavur trio were all alive when a prince ruling close to India's southern-most tip, and not very far to the west from Ettaiyapuram, revealed his musical talents.

Born in 1813 and dying at the young age of thirty-four, Swathi Thirunal Rama Varma II, who reigned over Travancore from 1829, composed around 300 difficult and simple pieces of music. While most of his lyrics were in Sanskrit, some were in Telugu, Malayalam, Marathi, Hindi or Urdu.

A few of the raja's compositions have stood the test of time. Twenty-first-century students of Carnatic music often sing Swathi Thirunal's creation, Chalamela. In the late nineteenth century and during the twentieth, several illustrious musicians offered Chalamela as the first item in their concerts, Sambamoorthy informs us (158).

Evidently a personal disciple of Thyagaraja named Kanniah Bhagavathar journeyed to Travancore and sang many of his teacher's compositions before Swathi Thirunal.

That the Travancore court drew a galaxy of singers and composers is not surprising. More impressive is the fact that the ruler's compositions were quickly taken by musicians to other parts of South India, as also the fact that Swathi Thirunal composed a few pieces in Hindustani ragas.

The Thanjavur Quartet of singers and dancers who were close to Muthuswami Dikshitar—Ponnayya, Chinnayya, Sivanandam and Vadivelu—joined the Travancore court for a while. In recognition of Vadivelu's skill with the instrument, Swathi Thirunal gave him a violin made of ivory (163).

The violinist was sent to Thanjavur to request Thyagaraja to visit Travancore, but in the 1840s Travancore seemed very far from Thanjavur, especially to one in his seventies. The musical prince and the raja of song both died in 1847, without meeting each other.

Chapter 6

STUDY TO RULE: 1800–1855

Tipu's defeat had been a watershed. Apart from assorted poligars, the Vellore rebels, and a handful of other exceptions, South Indians from that moment seemed to give up not only on throwing the Europeans out but also on resisting them. Accommodation with the British, now the sole European power, became the key impulse. No one looked back to ask whether an alliance involving Mysore, Arcot, Hyderabad, Travancore and the Marathas, or some of them, could have been pursued. Enmity in any such grouping was presumed, and British success increasingly accepted as being almost preordained.

Their triumphs changed the British too, bringing them confidence and elation. In England, 103 East India Company merchants sat as members in the House of Commons in 1806.[1] In Madras, the British elite multiplied, along with the locals. Henry Dodwell would write of the city of 1802–03:

How it has grown in these fifty years! Its Indian population, which used to be reckoned at 40,000, is now a quarter of a million, and of the Europeans four or five hundred families think themselves entitled to be asked to Government House... We have ceased to live in the Fort, though we still own 52 houses there.

We now stretch down the Mount Road, beyond the Cooum, where in 1753 there were only three garden-houses besides the governor's. [Now] there are Peter's Gardens, Dent's Gardens, Mackay's Gardens, and many others, each with its wide grounds... North of the river are Haliburton's Gardens, and the Pantheon, and Casamajor's Gardens...

Southwards too by Sulivan's Gardens to Moubray's Gardens on the banks of the pleasant Adyar, and General Braithwaite's mansion at its mouth. In all perhaps nearly a hundred great houses thinly scattered over an area four miles by two, for we like elbow-room, both in our houses and around them.[2]

Complacency was hardly the sole note. The British switched rapidly from conquering to administering, which required studying the land and its inhabitants. Fort St George launched a drive for information. If a Francis Buchanan was instructed to study the plants, cattle and people of Mysore, another gifted Scot, Colin Mackenzie, a soldier-engineer who had served in Hyderabad and fought in Mysore, was asked in 1799 to prepare detailed maps of the territory Tipu had controlled.

Not content with drawing maps, Mackenzie searched for literary, historical and cultural material. Any inscription, manuscript, text, or coin of historical or literary value, be it in Kannada, Malayalam, Marathi, Tamil or Telugu, was wanted by him, along with a translation.

Also, he stretched the exercise to most of the peninsula. Not proficient himself in any of South India's languages, Mackenzie employed talented native assistants who journeyed with or without him to 'almost all the remarkable places between the river Krishna and Cape Comorin...to take copies of all inscriptions, and obtain from the Brahmans of the temples, or learned men in the towns or villages, copies of all records in their possession, or original statements of local traditions'.

The Europe–India equation had altered, yet men like Mackenzie revealed respect for a major if declining power by collecting artefacts for preserving its history. Mackenzie paid Indian aides from his own pocket before London reluctantly agreed to the Company reimbursing him.

The end result was a remarkable archive of '1,568 literary manuscripts, a further 2,070 "local tracts", 8,076 inscriptions, and 2,159 translations, plus seventy-nine plans, 2,630 drawings, 6,218 coins, and 146 images and other antiquities'. It has been called 'the most extensive and the most valuable collection of historical documents relative to India that ever was made by any individual in Europe or in Asia'.[3]

Mackenzie's gathering zeal predated the Company's call for information and continued until his death in 1821, by when he was the Company's Surveyor General for India. In between, from 1811 to 1813, he had also collected archival material in Java where he was chief engineer to an expedition sent to seize the rich island from the Dutch, then allied to Napoleon's France.

When in 1783 he first came to India, Mackenzie's interest (the scholar David Blake informs us) was in Hindu mathematical knowledge. The wife of a Company officer in Madurai introduced Mackenzie to Brahmins familiar with mathematics who, however, 'fired his interest in Indian antiquities'. Asked to survey Mysore, Mackenzie used the opportunity to pursue the antiquities as well.

Procured from villages and towns in South India, taken to England but later returned to India, the Mackenzie collection today forms a core part of Chennai's Government Oriental Manuscripts Library. Not every item in it is an original, or an exact copy, or historically significant. Nonetheless the collection contains genealogies, historical tales, religious legends and records of donations and agricultural production that might have been lost but for the exertions of Mackenzie and his aides at the start of the nineteenth century.

Many records (kaifiyats) collected by Mackenzie and his Indian assistants were from South India's village accountants or karanams, as they were called in the Telugu country. There, and elsewhere in southern India, these village accountants had been 'preserving documents from generation to generation', thereby serving history and acquiring a historical sensibility.[4]

Brothers in a family of Niyogi Brahmins from Eluru in Andhra's West Godavari district, the sons of one Kavali Venkata Subbaiah became Mackenzie's principal aides, especially Kavali Borraiah and Kavali Lakshmaiah, though the oldest brother Kavali Narayanappa was the first to be employed by Mackenzie. Introduced by Narayanappa to Mackenzie, the scholarly Borraiah, who died young, became the first South Indian, it appears, to work in paleography and epigraphy. He may have also been among the earliest Indians, possibly the first, to write journal articles in English, on a range of subjects.

One of these articles, *On the Manners and Customs of the Jains,* was written in 1803 and published in 1810. Another was titled *The Political Conditions of the Carnatic during Mughal Times,* a third dealt with revenue and village administration in the Deccan, while a fourth was *An Account of Srirangapatnam of Mysore!*[5] Says S. Muthiah:

> It is recorded that on Borraiah's death, Mackenzie had a monument to his memory raised on 'the Madras sea shore'. There is mention of the monument as late as 1847, but what happened to it after that is not known.[6]

That young Borraiah and his brother Lakshmaiah were more than assistants to Mackenzie was acknowledged by someone we have met before, Mark Wilks, who knew Mackenzie from 1799, when the two were part of the Company's operations against Mysore. Wilks says that while Borraiah 'had the merit of first tracing the outline of the plan (of collection) which has been so successfully pursued', Lakshmaiah was 'a man of singular literary zeal and scrupulous research'.[7]

Younger than these two, brother Ramaswami wrote at least four books in English, also on diverse subjects: cities in the south, Telugu poets, cooking and caste. These were published in the 1820s and 1830s in Calcutta.[8] Evidently writing chiefly for an audience of India-based Europeans, Ramaswami, who had familiarized himself with European literature, argued that poetry preserved historical knowledge better than inscriptions on stone.

When this gifted individual 'implored indulgence...towards a native who has endeavoured to merit approbation', he was reflecting the literary style as also the new racial equations of his times.[9]

Not many decades earlier, it was the European trader who strove to win an Indian chief's approbation. Now the tables had turned, and they would turn again in the future. In the 1830s, the imploring sentence from Kavali Ramaswami was the done thing. A century later it would be called obsequious.

After Mackenzie's death, the Company was told on his widow's behalf that 'learned natives [had been] very averse' to India's ancient records being 'investigated by any European' and 'very loth to communicate the knowledge they possessed'. However, being 'learned natives' themselves, and possessing 'conciliating manners' as well, the Kavali brothers enabled the Mackenzie enterprise to 'overcome these prejudices' and succeed.[10]

◆

The Kavali brothers represented a new Indian elite of scholars and intellectuals. Their predecessors in the elite category, dubashes and merchants who partnered with the Company in its early phase, and rulers or poligars who fought for or against the Company in the next phase, had belonged to a wealthier league, yet the long-term influence of the 'learned natives' whom the Company employed as translators and teachers early in the nineteenth century would be considerable. Their ranks included Pattabhirama Sastri and Bomakonti Shankara Sastri, also known as Sankaraiah, Telugu-speaking Brahmins who worked with the Company's scholar-officer, Francis Whyte Ellis (1777–1819), to establish what has come down as the Dravidian Proof.

Joining at Fort St George as a nineteen-year-old, Ellis became Collector of Madras in 1810, but what interested him was the language or languages through which young Britons would govern the Company's enlarged territories in the peninsula.

The young civilians would clearly need to learn local languages, but which ones? And should new words required in offices and schools be borrowed from English or from Persian, the official language of the expired Mughal Empire, whose capital, Delhi, had fallen to the British in 1803? Or from Sanskrit, the language declared by scholars in Calcutta, capital of British India, to be the mother of every Indian tongue?

Causing delight and surprise on both sides, the discovery that Sanskrit and European languages employed similar sounds for core words including mother, father, brother, fire and cow was a significant moment in the colonial project, providing a basis, if the parties were willing, for equality and fraternity.

In 1786, the Calcutta-based judge and scholar, William Jones, who was one of the first to probe the similarity between Sanskrit and Latin, expressed these words, later to become famous, about Sanskrit:

> The Sanscrit language, whatever be its antiquity, is of a wonderful structure; more perfect than the Greek, more copious than the Latin, and more exquisitely refined than either, yet bearing to both of them a stronger affinity, both in the roots of verbs and the forms of grammar, than could possibly have been produced by accident; so strong indeed, that no philologer could examine them all three, without believing them to have sprung from some common source...[11]

But was Sanskrit the mother also of Tamil, Telugu, Kannada and Malayalam? Headed by Ellis, a Company committee in Madras went into this and related questions. The opinion of 'learned natives' employed at Fort St George, including Pattabhirama Sastri and Sankaraiah, was sought.

In 1811, Ellis's committee found that different South Indian languages possessed common features. It proposed the creation (at Fort St George) of a Madras College to impart a 'fundamental knowledge of the relative connection and [varied scripts] of the several Southern Dialects...which, as it is always uncertain in what province a Junior Servant may be stationed, would be far more beneficial to the public service than the most intimate acquaintance with one dialect only'.[12]

The intention for the college, which opened in 1812, was to teach new British civilians four courses: the southern scripts, grammars of Sanskrit and Tamil, Oriental literature (including Arabic and Persian), and Hindu and Muslim law.

Also recommended by the Ellis committee was the preparation of grammars in Telugu, Kannada and Malayalam. It was in an introduction to an 1816 text on Telugu grammar written by a protégé, Alexander Campbell, that Ellis offered his 'Dravidian Proof': a conclusion that not Sanskrit but Dravidian Tamil was the foundation for Telugu and the other southern languages.

Comparing the roots of Sanskrit and Telugu, Ellis and his Indian colleagues had found noticeable differences. On the other hand, another table of Tamil, Telugu and Kannada root-words showed similarities. A third exercise where Sanskrit and English passages were translated into Tamil, Telugu and Kannada confirmed that these southern languages were similar in idiom and in syntax. The words were akin, and they were strung into sentences in a like manner.

Since a civil servant was liable at short notice to be transferred from one part of the South to another, he needed familiarity with most of its languages. But if the languages were connected, the challenge was surmountable. This practical recognition triggered the research that found the Dravidian languages to be, first a family, and, second, distinct from the Sanskrit family, and distinct also from 'the Kolarian or Munda or Austroasiatic language family'.[13]

Necessity had become the mother of insight. After delving into these early nineteenth-century probes in Madras, an American scholar from our times, Thomas Trautmann, concludes that the role of men like Pattabhirama Sastri and Sankaraiah was as crucial as that of Ellis, and that language analysis had old roots in India.[14]

On our part, we, too, may concede that some of the young British civilians arriving in Madras were remarkably industrious individuals and, in cases like that of Ellis, who would die in Ramnad in 1819, discerning as well.

◆

Some years older than Ellis was the soldier-administrator Thomas Munro, whose role with Tipu's captive sons we briefly glimpsed. Munro's argument for identifying not the Maratha confederacy but Tipu as the Company's first enemy was also marked by us. Later involved in the Company's victory over the Marathas, who lost their capital, Poona, in 1817, Munro served as Governor of Madras Presidency from 1820 until 1827, when he died of cholera in a tent in Gooty, which lay in the so-called Ceded Districts. Won from Mysore by the nizam in 1792 and surrendered by him to the Company in 1799, these tracts had become part of the presidency governed by Munro.

The presidency's size greatly expanded between 1792 and 1803. Annihilated foes like Mysore and bulldozed allies (the nizam, the Nawab of Arcot and the Raja of Thanjavur) 'ceded' a number of territories to it. Madras now included Malayali Malabar; Tamil places like Thanjavur, Madurai, Trichy, Tinnevelly, Dindigul, Coimbatore and Salem; Kanara in the Kannada country; the Ceded Districts where Telugu and Kannada were spoken; and Coorg and the Nilgiris as well.

Known by the future as the man who set up the ryotwari system where land tax was collected directly from the ryot or peasant, rather than from a poligar or landlord, Munro was good at languages despite being partially deaf. Not long after his arrival in Madras in 1780, and before joining the Company's war against Haidar, this tall Scot had fathered a dark, illegitimate child.

Between 1792 and 1799, Munro was one of four army officers who controlled the so-called Baramahal territory the Company had won from Tipu, which included Salem, Krishnagiri and Dharmapuri and extended towards Srirangapatna. In 1799 and 1800, he ruled over the Kanara area appropriated from Mysore, and from 1800 to 1807 he had charge of the Ceded Districts, which included the old Vijayanagara heartland.

Extending 200 miles from Bellary in the west to Cuddapah in the east, the Ceded Districts measured about 150 miles north-to-south, from the Tungabhadra River to Arcot. Its western hills were high and dense with trees, its eastern ghats were low and scattered, and much of it was an arid plain. Placed around Hampi (Munro's biographer, Burton Stein, would mark) were 'abrupt outcrops of granite rocks stunning in texture and light effects'.[15]

About 30,000 'unsubdued and armed inhabitants', retained by eighty or so poligars, were said to be roaming the Ceded Districts' countryside when Munro arrived there in the year 1800. Though the Company did not explicitly grant him a free hand, the new collector who was also the area's military commander decided to do away with the poligars.

It was in Kanara, his posting before the Ceded Districts, that Munro had reached his policy prescription for Madras presidency: direct Company rule over peasant-proprietors without middle-men zamindars of the sort Governor General Cornwallis had established in Bengal in 1790.

After taking over in the Ceded Districts, Munro issued a revenue demand so high (higher than what the nizam or Haidar ever collected) that 'poligars could not pay their troops and maintain their military capacity and pay the tribute to the company'.[16]

The poligars defaulted and lost their lands but did not fight. South India had changed. Though verbally disapproving of Munro's policy, Company high-ups in Calcutta and London winked at it.[17]

Lauding Munro's ryotwari system 250 years later, the historian C. H. Philips would claim that London 'performed its best and most beneficial work in ensuring that the system of district administration developed not in Bengal but in Madras should become the characteristic mode of administration in India'.[18]

There were excesses. Thus 'European soldiers of the 34th regiment entered the houses of a village in the Ceded Districts, took pots, milk and grain without payment and bayoneted some men attempting to protect their village'.[19]

Some of the area's poligars, elderly and respected, had received the peasants' trust for long periods, but Munro was not swayed. When he deprived an old blind poligar in Pulivendla taluk of his lands in Kadapa district, even colleagues thought the step unworthy. But Munro was set on creating conditions for ryotwari (Stein, 89).

Whether India's people could be administered by the British without the mediation of poligars and chiefs was a question that would dog the British for decades. Earlier we saw the verdict of R. C. Dutt that eliminating or bypassing the poligars was an injurious policy, but contrary opinions also existed. In any case, men like Munro were more than soldiers or district officers. They wished to innovate.

During a long seven-year furlough in Britain (1807–14), Munro found a wife, strengthened connections with persons of influence, and offered to a committee of the House of Lords (on 7 April 1813) an interesting assessment of India's Hindus.

I do not exactly understand what is meant by the civilization of Hindoos; in the higher branches of science, in the knowledge of the theory and practice of good government, and in education… they are inferior to Europeans.

But if a good system of agriculture, unrivalled manufacturing skill, a capacity to produce whatever can contribute to convenience or luxury, schools established in every village for teaching reading, writing and arithmetic; the general practice of hospitality and charity among each other, and above all a treatment of the female sex full of…respect and delicacy are among the signs which denote civilized people, then the Hindoos are not inferior to the nations of Europe; and if civilization is to become an article of trade between the two countries…this country will gain by the import cargo (162).

This was different, it will be observed, from the appraisals provided earlier by Abbé Dubois. For Munro, the India of the first quarter of the 1800s remains a major power with 'unrivalled' creative skills. He may have exaggerated in speaking of 'schools in every village', yet Munro's evidence is not less weighty than the priest's, and was no doubt based on interactions with peasant proprietors and with scholarly Brahmins, including his assistants.

A critical question remains: even if there were schools in many a village, whose children attended them? Those of low-caste parents? Extremely unlikely. Of 'untouchables'? Almost certainly not. Of Brahmins and high-caste non-Brahmins? Very likely.

Brahmin abilities had impressed Munro. Stein tells us that

[along] with others of the Madras establishment, Munro had much praise and admiration for the dewan of [Mysore] state, Purnaiya, under whom the [Mysore] kingdom was administered from the time of restoration under the five-year-old Raja to the time that the latter attained maturity (268).

Steered in fair part by Purniah, Mysore did well for a few years, even though the Company's harsh terms for the old dynasty's restoration included a 58 per cent share of revenue to 'enable to Company to protect Mysore'. Enough revenue was raised by Purniah for this and more.

Later, however, Mysore was poorly administered by its officers. Soldiers were not paid on time and there was a rebellion against the ministers and the raja. In 1831, the British happily took over the state and ran it directly for the next fifty years.

◆

Returning to India in 1814, Munro played a battlefront role in the final defeat, in 1817, of the Marathas. In 1820, he was made Governor of Madras Presidency.

As governor, Munro had the use of three houses in the city: an old one in Fort St George, a new Government House built, following Tipu's fall, on Mount Road (now Anna Salai), and the seventeenth-century Guindy Lodge (today's Raj Bhavan), once owned by the merchant Chinna Venkatadri, who had dealt on equal terms with the Company.

With Tipu gone, the British felt safe to move out of their walled fort, as Dodwell had observed.

One of Munro's predecessors as governor was Robert Clive's son Edward Clive, who served from 1798 to 1803. In 1801, when the incumbent Nawab of Arcot was dispossessed, Governor Clive occupied Madras's grandest edifice, Chepauk Palace, built in 1768 by Arcot's longest-reigning nawab, Muhammad Ali, and possibly designed by Ali's chief creditor, Paul Benfield.[20]

This brazen takeover of the palace of the Company's consistently loyal ally was a tangible expression of British confidence and Indian resignation. But perspective was not wholly absent.

On 31 December 1824, Governor Thomas Munro wrote out a Confidential Minute for himself and senior colleagues of his in Madras,

expressing faith in a direct relationship between the Indian peasant
and the British officer, and envisioning, for a small closed circle, a few
bold if also inconsistent thoughts:

We proceed in a country of which we know little or nothing, as
if we know everything, and as if everything must be done now...

We must endeavour to protect [the peasant] by laws...and for
this we must invest the [European] Collector and Magistrate, the
person most interested in their welfare, with [sufficient] powers...

He who loses his liberty loses half his virtue. This is true
[also] of nations... The enslaved nation loses the privilege...
of taxing itself, of making its own laws, of any share in the
administration...or government of the country. British India has
none of these privileges; it has not even that of being ruled by a
despot of its own...

It is not the arbitrary power of a national sovereign but
subjugation to a foreign one that destroys national character...

We should look upon India not as a temporary possession but
as one which is to be maintained permanently until the natives
shall in some future age have abandoned most of their superstitions
and prejudices and become sufficiently enlightened...

Whenever such time shall arrive it will probably be best
for both countries that the British control over India should be
gradually withdrawn.

Those who speak of the natives as men utterly unworthy of
trust...describe a race of men that nowhere exists... We cannot
easily bring ourselves to take an interest in what we despise.[21]

On 6 July 1827, Governor Munro died of cholera in a tent near Gooty
in the Telugu country; he was touring the Ceded Districts which were
in his charge from 1801 to 1807. A hundred and ninety years after
Munro's death, an Andhra professor based in Chittoor district choked
while recalling, to this writer, the Scotsman's role in southern India.[22]

◆

As the Company moved him from place to place in the presidency,
Brown, the Vemana reviver who was more a scholar than an officer,
wrestled with the perplexity of South India's dates and calendars. In

an 1850 book, Brown noted: 'The Hindus use various methods in recording time.' Referring to 'the Telugu newspapers now printed in Madras', Brown explained how one of those newspapers had presented the date of a past event.

The event occurred, the paper had written, on the '13th of the bright fortnight in the month Sravana in the year Saumya'. Other complex details regarding the date were also provided in the story. With effort and skill, Brown converted the date to '1 August 1849'.[23]

'Printed by Reuben Twigg at the Christian Knowledge Society's Press, Church Street, Vepery (Madras), 1850', Brown's book was called *Cyclic Tables of Hindu and Mahomedan Chronology Regarding the History of the Telugu and Kannadi Countries*. On the title page, the author, who joined the East India Company in 1817, is described as 'Madras Civil Service, Member of the College Board, Telugu Translator to Government, &c.'

Stating in a preface that he and others have 'felt the want of a Key to the various dates in use', Brown attempts in this book to provide a chronology of some of South India's previous rulers. He also discusses the challenge of converting different, at times conflicting, Hindu years, and 'the Hejri' or Islamic ones, into Gregorian dates. Adds Brown:

> In the year 1821 the Bramins in the Madras College, encouraged by the English, began to print Sanscrit Almanacks, as they have done every year since, in the Telugu and Tamil characters; the English dates are also specified; and these manuals have a rapid sale throughout South India. But no Chronological Tables have ever been framed by Bramins.[24]

Observing that 'in every Hindu school' a thirty-six-month cycle of months 'is daily repeated backwards and forwards, along with the names of the months,' Brown adds: 'But in [British-run] schools Hindu lads are allowed to forget the list; and they therefore will find the tables now printed a convenient aid.'[25]

This suggests that elite/educated South Indians of this time, most of them from a Brahmin or a high non-Brahmin caste, as also their young sons, had an acute understanding of an immediate short period, without however connecting that slice of time to earlier periods.

Possessing a clear sense of yesterday, today and tomorrow but not of the previous century or even the previous quarter-century, they were left to imagine the more distant past through the prism of an elongated present.

This may still be an unconscious part of the Indian thought process. Not truly knowing earlier periods, we are liable to project present-day political, ideological or religious contestations into the past, imagining, for example, 'Hindu–Muslim' or 'Indian–European' clashes in previous ages which may have contained different dividing lines.

Brown suggests that despite their complex approach to chronology, the Hindus he was studying were not indifferent or uninformed about the past. Acknowledging, too, that 'royal grants of land engraved on rocks…scattered throughout South India' often mention the year of the grant 'by the Salivahana Calendar', Brown says,

> [T]he oldest existing volumes in the Telugu language are dated after the year one thousand one hundred of the Christian era, at which period the worship of Vishnu was introduced in the Telugu country… After the year A.D. 1590 we frequently meet with dates according to the Musulman reckoning. From that time, therefore, the Hejri year has been duly noticed: and after the year A.D. 1630 the Fasly year is also given.[26]

◆

Because of his exertions over Vemana and Telugu literature generally, Brown is a loved figure in the modern Telugu world, and the subject of a 1978 study[27] that incorporates handwritten autobiographical notes found among his papers.

When a twenty-two-year-old Brown graduated from Madras College in June 1820, he was impacted by a speech given by Governor Munro. Two months later, Brown became assistant to the Collector of Cuddapah, where he started two schools, one for teaching Telugu free of cost, the other for similarly teaching Hindustani.

Sent next to Machilipatnam, Brown read of Vemana in Dubois's book and began collecting palm-leaf copies of his verses and translating them. Reposted to Cuddapah, he bought a bungalow where he kept the manuscripts he had collected and where Telugu pandits hired by him helped translate them into English.

Brown's *Verses of Vemana* came out in 1829, but the Madras College Board kept in cold storage a Telugu dictionary he had produced. In the 1830s, he spent three years in England 'on absentee allowance', worked there on a book on Telugu grammar, and found in London an ignored collection of precious Telugu manuscripts that were brought back to India, along with a catalogue Brown had prepared.[28]

On his voyage back to Madras in 1837, Brown talked at length with Robert Caldwell, whose comments on Yusuf Khan we had seen earlier. For his analysis of Dravidian languages, which built on that of Ellis, Caldwell, who later became Bishop of Tirunelveli, is honoured today in the Tamil country with a statue on the Chennai marina.

Spite existed within India's British society. In a book published before Brown's death, Caldwell claimed, on the basis of interactions with Brown on the journey to India, that knowledge had 'swollen' the latter. Admitting that Brown had 'an immense and impressive mastery of languages —Sanskrit, Telugu, Hindustani, Greek, Latin and French', and 'a very respectable knowledge of English literature', Caldwell added:

Had he been educated at one of the universities and been...in the company of men of real learning and abilities, all would have been well. He would have speedily found his level; his love of display would have been checked...he would have been cut down to an agreeable companion...

But having been in great part self-educated, and afterwards been chiefly in the company of his inferiors in talent and acquirement... the weak points in the mental character swelled out...and those weeds of pedantry...and overbearing dogmatism...luxuriate[d].

The matter [of Brown's conversation] was always strange and startling, and the style broken, rapid, vehement... I was often talked dead, then talked alive again, and finally talked down to my cabin... [Brown gave out] tumults of mighty sounds... War to the knife was waged against my poor thought.

[But] stores of inexhaustible good nature lay hid under [Brown's] obtrusive pedantry and pugnacious dogmatism.

Caldwell finally countered Brown's vehement outpourings with outpourings of his own and thereafter found Brown 'tractable enough and a source of vast amusement'. Conceded the bishop:

I never met with any person who had such an all-grasping all-retaining memory.

In Caldwell's view, Brown had 'a sincere and thorough and well-grounded belief in Christianity...and a very low opinion, I may say a contempt, of Hindooism'. The bishop however added, 'If I have any chance at all of being talked to death, it is neither by infidels nor by Radicals but by my restless "Pandit" Mr. Brown.'[29]

♦

Following his return to Madras in 1838, Brown received a series of postings in that city (with the Madras College, as Persian translator at Fort St George, as a court registrar, as superintendent of lotteries and later of stamps, as collector of sea customs, and finally as postmaster general) before he left for England for good in 1855.

By then he had completed a Telugu translation of the New Testament, his *Telugu Grammar,* the *Dictionaries: Telugu-English and English-Telugu,* his translation from Marathi of the *Memoirs of Hyder Ali and Tippu Sultan* written by Ramchandra Rao Punganuri, who had been employed by both rulers, and *Cyclic Tables.* In an autobiographical note, Brown says:

> As a child I had been taught Hebrew, Syriac, Latin, Persian, Arabic and Greek. Last of all at the age of thirteen I was taught Hindustani: this I retained and forgot the others.

Claiming that in his early years in Madras, 1817–20, he 'practised Hindustani with educated Musulmans' who complimented him on his pronunciation and phraseology, Brown is not complimentary about Telugu dictionaries produced by others: 'My works caused some jealous enmity.'

After repaying a large debt to an English merchant in Madras, Brown evidently gave one thousand rupees to 'an aged Muslim Munshee in my employ', 'one rupee every month to 130 blind, lame and halt', and 4,000 rupees to the Old Church Evangelical Fund, Calcutta, in liquidation of what that fund had given in 1812 to his mother at the death of his father. His notes reveal the hierarchies and vanities among the British of Madras:

Being now [in 1854] in comfortable circumstances, I resumed my old customs of hospitality and often had ladies' parties. I seldom had more than twenty guests but was thought lavish and careless of money. My guests [presumably all British] were chiefly those who never could return my hospitality.

I removed into a large house or palace which I soon adorned with a noble gallery of marble statues and seventy oil paintings, chiefly English, Dutch and Italian landscapes... I had two carriages, six horses and all else my station seemed to require. My table was more splendid than that of the Governor.

That last sentence was scored out after it was written. Added Brown:

When printing my *Grammar* and the *Dictionaries* I worked hard with my Brahmins all the week but always kept the Sabbath holy.

I now made preparations for quitting India, and sold off all my property with about 5000 volumes of European literature. My books went for less than a shilling a volume.[30]

Made professor of Telugu at London University in 1865, Charles Philip Brown, apparently single all his life, died in England in 1884.

◆

What persons like Brown did for Telugu, and men like Ellis (and Beschi, the Jesuit well before Ellis) for Tamil, was done for Malayalam by the grandfather of Hermann Hesse, the modern literature laureate. This was the German missionary, Hermann Gundert, who composed a Malayalam grammar in 1859 and a Malayalam–English dictionary in 1872. Comparable service to Kannada was rendered by another German missionary, Ferdinand Kittel, whose Kannada–English dictionary appeared in 1894.

◆

In the year 1800, the city of Madras contained between 250,000 and 300,000 people, including fisherfolk, artisans, weavers, washermen, the Company's civil servants, their Indian clerks, traders from all over India, lawyers and merchants of many nationalities, British and Indian soldiers, missionaries and 'learned natives'. Schools run by missionaries or the government taught a growing number of children.[31]

New printing presses gradually arrived. The first had come in the 1760s, a church press brought from Tranquebar's protestant mission. In 1785, the four-page *Madras Courier* appeared, British-owned of course, and mostly carrying official notifications, advertisements and excerpts from newspapers in England. A bolder *India Herald* showed up in 1795.

From the 1820s, a few books written by Indian teachers at the Madras College were printed. The college itself moved in 1827 from Fort St George to a building in Egmore and started enrolling fifteen high-caste Indian youths annually.

Examining, in a 2003 study,[32] the connected growth in the Tamil country of printing and Christianity, as also the emergence of printed Tamil literature, Stuart Blackburn has brought to light the Company's attitudes in the first half of the nineteenth century on the Brahmin/non-Brahmin question.

To the European eye, there was a physiognomic and at times skin-colour difference between elements in the South Indian population. At times, castes seemed connected to this racial difference. Yet it was also obvious that down the centuries ethnic mixing had taken place, despite rules against it.

Castes were endogamous; they seemed at times like distinct races. And yet there was overlap; at times groups left one caste and joined another. There was great separation, and—in one of India's annoying yet appealing paradoxes—there was great mixing.

Blackburn's study suggests that for teaching positions, the Company and its college seemed at first to prefer high-caste non-Brahmins from the Mudaliar and Pillai landowning castes over Brahmins. Men from these non-Brahmin high castes wrote a majority of the earliest Tamil books printed in Madras.

In particular, the 1826 publication of a Tamil translation by Tantavaraya Mudaliar, the second of Madras College's head Tamil pundits, of the ancient yet non-religious book of fables, *Panchatantra,* made a considerable impact, turning Tantavaraya into a public figure (Blackburn, 101).

Differing views within the Company kept caste 'preferences' within limits. Also, these preferences could shift. Before Munro would become impressed with Brahmins, Francis Ellis had been warm towards non-

Brahmins. As Blackburn puts it,

> A brilliant linguist...Ellis also equated [a Tamil text's] purity with
> an absence of Sanskrit influence. As Collector of Madras, Ellis
> wrote essays which laid down firm foundations for constructing a
> folk identity for non-Brahmins... He shored up his political base
> among the landowning castes by identifying them as primordial
> sons of the soil (159).

Not knowing how to respond to accusations that so-and-so had violated
caste rules, a Company officer at times asked Brahmins of standing
for their Smartha Vicharam or a process of 'traditional consideration'.
In 1816, when a Brahmin woman in Malabar was accused of liaisons
with men of inferior castes, Company officials evidently detained her
for eight months while Brahmins examined the complaint.[33]

If caste was becoming a tricky issue, so was the appearance of
churches and Christian schools in Hindu localities in Madras, at times
near temples. After Fort St George appeared to abandon a neutral
stance and seemed to support church construction, a Madras Hindu
Literary Society was started in 1833, with, interestingly enough, Kavali
Lakshmaiah, Mackenzie's collaborator, as its first president, and George
Norton, the government's Advocate General, as an active supporter
(Blackburn, 109).

A Saiva Siddhanta Sangam had come up in 1829, and a periodical
called *Desabimani* surfaced to criticize missionary activity in Madras
and Tinnevelly (113).

Ellis may have encouraged the Mudaliars, but that community too
contained opponents of Christian schools, churches and preaching.
To express its opposition, a Mudaliar group started a printing and
publishing house as also the Chatur Veda Siddhanta Society (103–06).
Other Hindu organizations were formed, and public display of sacred
ash was encouraged (113).

A generation after Ellis, Robert Caldwell, a prominent establishment
figure though not part of the government, again advocated the non-
Brahmin position. Writes Blackburn:

> Not only did Caldwell systematize Ellis's 'Dravidian proof' in
> his famous *Comparative Grammar of the Dravidian Family of
> Languages* (1856); he also followed him in championing the

language, literature and religion of non-Brahmins, while not endorsing all their religious practice... (159–60).

In the 1850s and 1860s, the Aryan thesis of a common Indo-European antiquity became popular in some southern circles. Others, however, welcomed a statement made in 1859 by the European scholar of comparative literature, Theodor Benfey, that the non-Vedic *Panchatantra* had inspired European folktales (186). Men like Caldwell focused on the *Panchatantra*'s independent tenor. Caldwell thought that

> the prose of Tantavaraya Mutaliyar's 1826 *Pancatantra* marked the beginning of a modern Tamil literature, 'an entirely new style of composition...[of] good colloquial prose...'

Adds Blackburn:

> But Caldwell also went much further than his predecessors in his anti-Sanskrit, anti-Brahmin rhetoric, and his book on Nadars in Tinnevelly District claimed that northern influences had obscured and defiled a primordial Tamil tradition.
>
> Caldwell also extended the category of non-Brahmin to include Paraiyars, the lowest among the several Tamil Untouchable castes. Ellis, the administrator, had supported the Paraiyars' claim to be 'sons of the soil', but Caldwell, the missionary, confirmed that these people were in fact the original Dravidians (160).

However, human nature curbed Bishop Caldwell's appreciation of Ellis. The American scholar, Thomas Trautmann would write in 2006:

> Caldwell's magisterial comparative study of the Dravidian family has become a classic... But Caldwell was not excessively generous in giving credit to his predecessors, and Ellis in particular gets much less than his due... One notes the minimizing language in which Caldwell [acknowledges Ellis's role].[34]

♦

The Company's Madras Army joined the effort to gather information. In 1843, the army published a report based on accounts received in the late 1830s from medical officers in different parts of today's Kerala and Tamil Nadu.[35] Diseases were part of its focus, but the report also conveys broader facts and appraisals.

Some of the latter are quite subjective, marred by an urge to generalize, and possibly misleading, while several population groups remain out of sight. Still, the report is informative.

We learn that from *Salem* district 'cloth was formerly exported in large quantities to America and the West Indies' (2). Attempts to grow American tobacco and American cotton in the Salem area are not successful.

Parts of the report convey an English wish for an India that competes with the US. However, India's land is different from America's. Most of it is not available for settlement (its people seem unwilling to be driven into reservations). Moreover, not many British, apart from planters of tea and indigo, seem interested in settling on it.

Many weavers live in *Coimbatore*, which possesses numerous comfortable houses. Here the lower castes take more readily to vaccination than the Brahmins, who therefore lose a higher percentage to smallpox when it hits.

Coimbatore's Brahmins perform ceremonies, teach the Vedas, preach pity for the distressed, and recommend salvation by the regular observance of all daily ceremonies, such as bathing and reciting prayers. Their daughters are married before the age of ten. Other castes, lower in status, marry their girls a little later than the Brahmins (49).

In *Travancore*, inhabitants are 'very much attached to their country and can seldom be induced to quit it by any advantages held out to them'. 'Those of the Nair tribe that can afford it eat meat', and 'crimes are not very frequent'. The 'fair' and 'good-looking' Nairs are disciplined in many respects, but their marriages are loose and sexual relations free, causing venereal disease (81–82).

Education in Travancore is fairly wide and in the 1830s the number of English speakers is surprisingly large (82). Europeans reaching a hill-top in Travancore find the view of the sea and the hills 'truly magnificent' (95).

Hindus, Muslims and Christians live in Travancore, the ratio varying by district. Brahmins are 'very numerous' and include local 'Namboories' as well as settlers from the Tamil country. The 'Namboories' are 'the finest looking race and rank first in the estimation of the people, over whom they exercise an influence even greater than is common [for Brahmins] in other parts of India'.

The most numerous, as well as most useful part of the population, are the Nairs, who belong to the Sudra tribe, and are separated into a number of different classes, employed in various occupations: from amongst them are selected the Rajah's troops...

The Shanars [Nadars] who rank very low in the scale of caste, form a numerous body in the south of Travancore, and are chiefly employed in agricultural and other laborious pursuits (80).

The report finds two kinds of Muslims living in Travancore: descendants of Arabs who had landed centuries earlier on the coast, and other Muslims whose more recent forebears, arriving from elsewhere in the peninsula, soldiered for rajas in Travancore.

Christians in Travancore include Protestants, Roman Catholics and Syrian Christians and are 'a considerable part of the population' (80–81).

On *Cochin*:

The houses of the Namboories and Nairs are kept particularly neat while little attention is paid to cleanliness by the Christians or inferior Hindus... There is no middle class here, the people being land proprietors and renters of government lands, or slaves and coolies; labourers are abundant, and wages low (105).

No tables of marriages, deaths or births are kept by the Cochin Sircar (106).

'Namboory' practitioners, we learn, perform bleeding but no surgery (106). Kerala's 'vegetable productions' are mentioned in the report (plantain, breadfruit, jackfruit, mango, pineapple, tamarind, guava, lime, citron, watermelon and pumpkin—among roots the yam, sweet potatoe, and the arrow root) as also 'the articles of merchandize... exported to various foreign marts, principally pepper and cardamoms (both of which are monopolies of the...Rajah of Cochin)' and ginger and turmeric.

Among trees the teak stands pre-eminent... The Malabar teak is well known for its superiority both as regards its specific gravity, and closeness of grain (99).

Labour [in Cochin] is very cheap—the daily hire of the free labourer varying from 2 to 4 annas, according to the nature of the Work, but cultivators of the soil receive only one anna (101).

The Namboories or priests, who maintain an unbounded influence over the inferior castes, have an extraordinary custom with regard to marriage...viz. that of restricting the privilege of marriage to the eldest male member of the family (102).

The [Nairs]...physically considered are a fine race of men; their most striking and obvious characteristic, is a cringing humility towards superiors, or in the presence of those by whom they hope to be benefitted, and a display of arrogance and tyranny, when these qualities can be exercised with impunity.

The marriage ceremony amongst this caste...is very simple, and consists merely of the bride groom...presenting a cloth to the bride, and tieing a string round her neck; the engagement is as easily dissolved as formed, for on either party becoming dissatisfied with the other, they separate...each being then at liberty to enter into a new engagement (102).

In *Madurai*:

Considerable improvement has lately been effected as regards the cleanliness of the town, but there remains still much to be done, owing to the inhabitants having long been permitted to make the space in front of their houses the public necessary...

The bazar is large, and well filled with everything required for native consumption.

The staple manufacture of the place is cloth, and weavers form by far the most numerous body of the inhabitants; they are a peaceable and industrious class of men, but penurious in their habits...the interior court-yard attached to [their houses] is usually wet and miry, no drains being made to carry off the water, which from their occupation, they use in great quantities (128).

Accounts received from *Dindigul* covered many an area of life:

The higher caste Hindoos, who are very numerous, live altogether upon vegetable food of various kinds, with milk and condiments, such as pepper, chillies and pickles. The Musselmans and lower grades of Hindoos eat poultry, fish and eggs, although rice constitutes their principal article of diet...

[A] considerable quantity of mutton is daily consumed, and beef is procurable occasionally, but a large proportion of the labouring people subsist upon raggy [ragi]...made into a paste with buttermilk. Tobacco is used by all classes, and the consumption of arrack is likewise considerable; the spirit is procured by the distillation of jaggery, along with the bark of various trees... (140).

Some silks and muslins are manufactured in the town of Dindigul, and excellent black and white cumblies [blankets] are made by the women, from the Carumber wool, which is abundant; coarse cotton cloths and handkerchiefs are also made in several villages.

At Gootum and Kullumpetty, iron was formerly manufactured upon an extensive scale, but the establishments at which the ore was smelted, are gone to decay, and it is now only produced in a limited quantity in some villages...

Paper is also manufactured, and implements of husbandry, and utensils for household purposes are made in every village, which possesses its own carpenters, braziers, silver smiths and iron workers, though the bulk of the population are cultivators.

The labouring poor are employed chiefly in outdoor work, the wages of a man being three annas per day, and of a woman one anna, and from the cheapness of clothing and food, there are few places where the poor are better off.

From the records of the police it would appear that crime is of less frequent occurrence in this district than in any part of the surrounding country, and the people are for the most part, a moral and well conducted race (141).

Schools are established in every respectable village, where the children of such as can afford to pay a small fee to the teacher are instructed in reading and writing Tamil, in arithmetic, and in religion; they are generally sent to school at the age of 5 years (141).

The native [doctors] are not without skill in the cure of some diseases, particularly the milder forms of leprosy; the most powerful of their remedies is arsenic, which is given in syphilis, fever, and some cutaneous diseases; calomel, jalap, bark, with a few other

European medicines, are in request, and freely used by them, when they can be obtained.

Dietetics form much of their curative plan, upon the supposition that all articles are either of a heating or cooling nature; they have several books upon medicine and surgery, the works of Aghastier [Sage Agastya] being in most estimation...

With regard to the longevity of the inhabitants, no correct information can be obtained, but many persons may be seen upwards of three score and ten (146).

In the district of *Ramnad*:

The population in the interior consists chiefly of Hindoos, who are generally poor, and engaged in agricultural pursuits; but a few of them are occupied in the manufacture of cotton cloth.

In every town there are some Mahomedans, most of whom work in iron; the inhabitants of the towns on the coast are principally Mahomedans ('Lubbays') and Roman Catholic Christians, the former amounting to about 27,000, and the latter to 10,000; the Lubbays are an active and enterprising race, and were formerly possessed of considerable wealth; they are still comparatively independent, their houses being larger, and having more the appearance of comfort, than those of the Hindoos; they are said to be haughty and irascible; but when treated with kindness obliging, communicative and intelligent; they engage in trade both by land and sea, and a few are mechanics.

Many of the Lubbays are acquainted with Arabic, but the Tamil is the language universally spoken by all classes (152).

The army's report confirmed Abbé Dubois's verdict on the dramatic decline of weaving.

It seems to be generally admitted, that the people are in worse circumstances than they were 25, or 30 years ago, when numbers were actively engaged in the manufacture of cotton and silk cloths for exportation, as well as for home consumption; the free admission of English cotton cloths has since seriously injured the commercial and manufacturing part of the community, who are unable to compete with foreign produce; and they are now idle and impoverished, many of them having through necessity become cultivators (152).

◆

It is natural to ask: if the Company's civil and military employees (whatever may be thought of their assessments) were studying the peninsula and its people with such care so as to rule, what were the natives doing to regain self-rule? Studying their new rulers and their psychologies? Showing an interest in fellow-natives?

If the first half of the nineteenth century offers little evidence of their doing any of this, we should recognize that the British takeover had evoked admiration, acceptance—and fear.

Fort St George was exercising its power forcefully, not timidly. In the capital and the districts, its chief officers were generally soldiers. Wielding pens and (from the 1820s) stethoscopes, they also carried guns and were backed by cannons.

In such circumstances, with recent memories of Mysore's defeat, the suppression of poligars, and the crushing of Vellore, and with no broad organization or journal available for airing disappointment or hope, silence was the chief response from hurt native spirits.

Chapter 7

A GIFT FOR THE QUEEN: 1799–1883

To the east of Goa, on an eastern edge of hills that parallel the coastline, lies the small Kannada tract of Kittur. Here a dynasty ruled from 1584 over lands first obtained from the Adilshahis of Bijapur. Though Aurangzeb subjugated Bijapur in the 1680s, the Kittur dynasty retained its lands. One of its rulers, Rudra Gowda, fell for a Muslim beauty who became his second wife. The ruler built a palace for her, she converted to the Virasaiva doctrine, and ballads told her tale into the twentieth century and beyond.

In the second half of the eighteenth century, Kittur had to contend with Marathas coming in from the north, with Haidar and Tipu advancing from the south, and soon with the British as well. Yet it preserved its autonomy and possessions.

In 1778, Kittur agreed to pay tribute to Haidar. The next year its ruler was seized by the Marathas. For a while Kittur was controlled by Dhondu Wagh, the Maratha rebel. Though Tipu took Kittur and imprisoned its young ruler Malla Sarja for about three years, in 1787 the Marathas, obtaining British support, forced Tipu to yield Kittur to them.

During a Maratha–British alliance that lasted for a quarter century from 1792, Malla Sarja placated the British, who in 1804 stonewalled a Maratha demand for his removal. However, in 1809, the Peshwas enforced a yearly tribute of a lakh and three quarter rupees on Kittur while also making Malla Sarja a captive in Poona. When Malla Sarja was about to die, they released him.

His successor from 1816, Shivalingarudra Sarja, helped the British once they broke with the Marathas. But he was weak and ill. In 1818, a year after the British had captured Poona, Thomas Munro, commanding the region around Kittur, compelled Shivalingarudra to give the Company a portion of his territory as also a yearly tribute of a lakh and three quarter rupees.

Emerging from the wings, the ruler's stepmother Chennamma,

second wife to the deceased Malla Sarja, took control in Kittur. When Shivalingarudra died in 1824, Chennamma became the queen.

She had married Malla Sarja—so the story went—after the two first met beside a tiger each claimed had fallen to their arrow; happily for everyone, the tiger displayed two arrows. Marriage resulted, with, predictably, Chennamma promising to treat Sarja's first wife Rudramma as the elder sister.

No average rani herself, Rudramma had learnt Persian and Urdu (evidence of Bijapuri influence in the area) and joined a battle in which Tipu had been driven back.

As for Chennamma, her story is powerful even after dramatic tales are discounted.[1] It reveals a politically shrewd rani—capable of taking decisions on the spur of the moment—who steered Kittur for eight years after her husband's death.

It seems that her stepson Shivalingarudra, who had no son, signed a letter before dying in which he informed the East India Company that he had adopted a distant relative. But by 1824, men like Thomas Munro were looking to do away with rajas and their dynasties.

One of Munro's close associates, St John Thackeray of the Madras Civil Service, was at this point the Company's chief political agent in the area, as also the collector, of nearby, British-run Dharwad. Replying to the Kittur raja's deathbed letter, Thackeray questioned its authenticity and argued that the raja had not taken prior permission for adoption.

Chennamma answered that permission was not required under Kittur's 1818 settlement with Munro.

Thackeray's men then took a detailed inventory of cash and jewels in the Kittur palace, making Chennamma and the family feel they were intruders in their own home. Emissaries she sent to Mountstuart Elphinstone, the Governor of Bombay, returned without cheer.

Rejecting the adoption claim, Thackeray marched on 23 October 1824 from Dharwad to Kittur and tried to take control. To his surprise, the spirited Chennamma had assembled numerous defenders. Thackeray's force was outmanned.

And out-thought, claims Sadashiva Wodeyar, author of *Rani Chennamma*. Her soldiers switched from defence to attack. Sadhunavar Balappa of Amtur shot Thackeray, who fell from his horse. Ram Habshi, an African in Kittur's force, chopped off Thackeray's head, lifted it with his spear, and shouted, 'Thackeray is dead' (Wodeyar, 67). Three other British officers were also killed, and two British civilians, Stevenson and Elliot, taken prisoner.

On 27 October, the adopted boy was crowned. Journeying from Bombay to Poona, Governor Elphinstone discussed Kittur with the Company's commander-in-chief, General Sir Henry Paget, and other British officers. A minute dated 31 October recorded their conclusion that the rebellion's real leader was one 'Sardar' Gurusiddappa, 'although he makes use of the name of Chennamma'.

The minute sagely added: 'Even if Chennamma were equally guilty (of which there is no proof), the punishment of a woman of her rank would be highly unpopular... No notice should, therefore, be taken of the suspicions which exist against her' (100–01).

Hostages Stevenson and Elliot were released by Kittur in hopes of a settlement, but once the two men were back among them, the British launched an overpowering military attack, with units brought from Satara, Poona, Bombay, Sholapur and Bellary. Guided by the Bombay government with support from Fort St George, the Company's troops wanted to show what rebellion would invite.

Breached on the night of 4 December, the Kittur Fort was taken the next morning. Writing a few days later to the Bombay government, William Chaplin, the Company's commissioner for the Deccan, conceded that the 'strong fort of Kittoor' had been 'defended by [a] garrison of an unusually determined character' (130).

Yielding to pressure from gallant aides, Chennamma and her daughters-in-law tried to escape. They were captured by British soldiers. Kept for a week in her own palace, Chennamma was compelled to sign away Kittur before being removed 20 miles north to a fortress in Bailhongal, where, after more than four years of detention, she died on 2 February 1829.

Evidently, she managed from Bailhongal to contact fugitive rebels like Sangolli Rayanna, who continued to fight. Eventually betrayed, Rayanna was brave and defiant when hanged on 28 December 1830. The adopted son, Shivalingappa, would also make several attempts at rebellion, right up to 1857.

Chennamma is a Kannadiga rani in the south who stepped forward and fought the British more than three decades before Jhansi's

Lakshmibai. A post-independence statue in Kittur honours her role, which had been indirectly acknowledged earlier by British-era memorials for Thackeray and the other Britons killed with him.

Later events in Jhansi and elsewhere would confirm that the Company looked forward to the death of rulers lacking a known heir.

◆

Following Krishnaraja Wadiyar's installation, as a five-year-old, on the Mysore throne in 1799, the kingdom paid the Company a large annual tribute. After attaining maturity, Krishnaraja reigned over his titular kingdom from Mysore city, the old Wadiyar base, but he lost prestige with the Company when his officers in the districts failed to collect expected revenues.

This was especially true in fertile Bidnur, where locally powerful men—new poligars—were not inclined to forward the kingdom's share to the capital. Alleging maladministration, and confident of raising large sums on its own, the Company deposed Krishnaraja in 1831.

Whether an able ruler or not, the Mysore raja had done much culturally. Poets, musicians, astrologers and scholars were encouraged by him, and his reign may have witnessed something like 'a renaissance in Kannada language and literature'.[2]

For half a century from 1831, the Company would govern Mysore through commissioners headquartered in Bangalore. In the beginning, Company rule made little impact on the new poligars. Hanumappa Nayak, poligar of Tarikere, offered stiff resistance to the British until 1834, when he was seized and hanged.[3]

Also in 1834, the Raja of Coorg rose in revolt against the British and imprisoned a Company emissary sent to remonstrate with him. In reply, the Company annexed the whole of Coorg in May 1834.

◆

We saw in the last chapter how Madras Presidency had expanded after Tipu's defeat. New Tamil tracts were added in 1801 when the Company stripped the Nawab of Arcot of his lands and eliminated the Tinnevelly poligars. After Mysore was placed under it in 1831, and Coorg as well three years later, the presidency occupied almost the entire lower half of the Indian peninsula, with the Bay of Bengal and the Arabian Sea washing its twin coasts.

With common, and usually humane, rules being applied in all its parts, the enlarged presidency would offer the South an unprecedented yet precarious stability—precarious because the region was now in the hands of officers of an alien race serving a European trading company and a distant monarchy.

In 1816, rupees replaced pagodas and annas were introduced. In 1836, rails were used just outside Madras city for wheeling down carts filled with stones from Little Mount and Red Hills. The first railway service opened, Madras to Arcot, in 1856, a year after the nawabship of the Carnatic was formally abolished. The telegraph had arrived three years earlier, in 1853.[4]

In other signs of confidence, an engineering school started in Madras in 1834, a medical college in 1835, and Madras Christian College in 1837. From 1840, the governor moved for the summer season from Fort St George to Ooty; and in 1857, the University of Madras was incorporated. Four years later, in 1861, an Indian was named to the Madras Legislative Council for the first time: V. Sadagopacharlu.

Most dramatic were two great 'anicuts' built in the Telugu country, in adjacent deltas. The Godavari dam was built, island to island, in the late 1840s near Rajahmundry, the Krishna barrage, in the early 1850s, near Vijayawada. The Krishna dam joined a pair of hills.

South Indian in name and history, anicuts—constructions for storing water—had struck arriving Europeans from the start. Yet these two mid-nineteenth-century incarnations took river harnessing to new levels, bringing vast acreages under cultivation, revenues to Fort St George, and prosperity to farmers.

Their creator, Arthur Cotton (1803–99), was one of eleven brothers. At fifteen, he joined the Company's military academy at Addiscombe. Three years later, he went to Madras as a soldier to join the Company's engineers.

When revenues greatly increased after Cotton had successfully worked on the Kaveri at Mukkombu near Trichy, the way opened for him to face the Godavari and the Krishna. His reply to Company objections over costs was that a day's flow in the Godavari during high floods equalled a year's flow in the Thames.[5]

There were side effects. Soils changed, sometimes deleteriously, cattle faced disease, and swamplands were created. Yet if to this day Andhra farmers speak warmly of Cotton (who became a general as also Sir Arthur), it is because the great anicuts conceived by him and built by thousands of the nameless transformed life along the Telugu coast. On British maps, almost all of South India was now painted colonial red. Immediately to the presidency's north, shown in yellow on the map, lay a large and partially autonomous Hyderabad under a nizam 'protected' and kept in line by the Company's troops.

In the coastal Malayalam country, yellow Travancore was likewise 'autonomous' under British 'protection' from 1795, while Cochin, too, submitted to British supremacy. The status of the hinterland Tamil tract of Pudukkottai, south of Trichy and north of Madurai, was not very different.

VELU THAMPI (1765–1809)

Travancore, the Company's ally against Tipu, had offered dramatic but also brutal scenes in the first decade of the nineteenth century.

While Balarama Varma, reigning from 1798 to 1810 and privately anti-British, was weak, his military and administrative chief for much of this time, Velayudhan Chempakaraman Thampi, known as the dalawa or the dewan, was resourceful and bold.

Hailing from a south Travancore Nair family elevated under the celebrated Marthanda Varma, Thampi possessed two other qualities the times seemed to demand: ruthlessness and the ability to switch allegiances.

Earlier, when Thampi was a tahsildar in charge of a southern Travancore tract, the then dalawa, Sankaran Nampoothiri, had ordered him to raise an impossible sum for a bankrupt treasury. Raising a revolt instead of revenue, Thampi forced Nampoothiri out, replaced him as dalawa, and had two of Nampoothiri's henchmen flogged and their ears sliced off.

But the man with the greatest power in Travancore and Cochin was the Company's resident, a military officer called Colin Macaulay, who chose to live in Cochin. Macaulay not only conveyed the Company's demands to Varma (usually via Thampi), he headed the Company's soldiers stationed in Travancore under a 1795 treaty, and paid for, as the treaty insisted, by the kingdom.

Macaulay, with whom Thampi had built a good relationship, helped Thampi foil a conspiracy for his murder, to which the raja evidently had lent support. As a result of the Thampi–Macaulay alliance, the one who got executed was the conspiracy's organizer, a Travancore official called Kunjunilam Pillai.

Burdened by accumulated debts (some incurred in the war against Tipu), and harassed for payment by the Company, Balarama Varma had not merely dismissed an earlier and much-lauded dewan, the pro-British Kesavadas, it is alleged he had Kesavadas poisoned in 1799.

The severity did not end there. According to the scholar B. Sobhanan, 'the Maharaja and his followers brought about the murder of the remaining members of the late Dewan's family irrespective of sex or age'.[6]

In 1801, the Company compelled the raja to elevate Thampi as dewan. But Thampi's attempt in 1804 to improve the state's finances by reducing the salaries of its soldiers, most of them Nairs, triggered a revolt and a plot to kill both Thampi and Macaulay. Foiling the plot, Thampi also mobilized Christian fishermen from the coast, and hill-men with bows and arrows, against the Nairs.

The revolt was duly suppressed with British support and with great brutality. A leader of the revolt, Krishna Pillai, was gruesomely killed, a pair of elephants pulling his legs in opposite directions.

There was fresh opposition in the following year when Thampi yielded to a new treaty desired by the Company. Providing for a larger British force in Travancore, which the maharaja was required to finance, this 1805 treaty left the kingdom with fewer funds for its own soldiers, which was a bitter blow to Balarama Varma, who prized his throne's armed units.

Thampi's eventual response, secret to begin with, was an anti-British revolt in alliance with Travancore's soldiers, and with the promising backing of a minister in the kingdom of Cochin, the influential Paliath Govinda Achan, whose family owned a good part of that kingdom's lands.

With Cochin's raja neglecting his throne, Achan was the kingdom's dominant figure, except that he had made an enemy of the powerful Macaulay, who had his residence in Cochin. The reason for the Achan–

Macaulay divide was personal: the resident had shielded one of Achan's mortal foes.

Putting up a smokescreen, Thampi offered to resign while quietly planning his revolt and even trying to enlist a French mercenary called Colonel Daly.

Thampi and Achan's men almost killed Macaulay at his residence in December 1808. But the resident escaped, even though a thousand men had surrounded his house all night. 'At day break, on sighting a British ship, the Nayar troops retreated.'[7]

That the mere sight of an English warship could send a thousand soldiers running may say something about the psychological climate of South India in the year 1808.

Shame and disappointment at the failure to finish Macaulay may have been factors in the brutal killing near the end of December, possibly 'on the express orders of the Dewan', of 'Dr. Hume and thirty-three other Englishmen' who were on a ship but 'were driven by bad weather to disembark near Alleppey'. The luckless men were cut down in cold blood, and their bodies thrown into a river 'with heavy stones tied round their necks'.[8]

British atrocities were even more horrific. On 2 January 1809, when 4,000 insurgents were at the receiving end of British fire at Alikkal, possibly 'three to four hundred' of them were shot to death even as they tried to save themselves from drowning in the backwater (Sobhanan, 85).

We should mark a factor once more seen in an Indian revolt's failure: British intelligence. Thampi had planned a 'secret' end-December attack on British soldiers stationed in Quilon (Kollam). Obtaining details of Thampi's 'proposed attack from confidential sources', the Company easily repulsed it (83).

In January 1809, Thampi issued a public call for rebellion from Kundara, about 8 miles northeast of Quilon. Declaring that the British had betrayed the trust of Travancore and the time had come to break with them, Thampi levelled sweeping and rousing charges:

> It is the nature of the English nation to get possession of countries by treacherous means... They will put their own guards in the palaces...destroy the royal seal...suppress the Brahmanical communities and worship in [temples], make monopolies of salt

and every other thing...put up crosses and Christian flags in pagodas, compel intermarriages with Brahman women without reference to caste or creed... (86)

Soldiers in Travancore rose at this call, as did many among the public, but it was an unprepared and uncontrolled rebellion, and several influential figures in the Malayalam country, including the Zamorin of Kozhikode, refused to have anything to do with it.

Previously more suspicious than Thampi of the British, and in fact sympathetic to the revolt, Balarama Varma, however, had no choice but to seek the Company's protection and join in the hunt for Thampi. Soon Paliath Achan also withdrew his support, and there was no sign of the fantasy Thampi had imagined: French aid.

The well-informed British were also swift in moving in from different directions, and they possessed bigger guns. Tens of thousands of soldiers had joined Thampi, but they were disorganized.

On 18 February, a chastened Thampi sought a truce but received no answer from the Company's commanders. On 10 March, the raja was forced to declare that he had signed the hated 1805 treaty with his free will and consent. On 13 March, he named, on British insistence, a new dewan. Before the end of March, the raja coughed up 11 lakh rupees as arrears for the Company.

As the nineteenth century was unfolding, Travancore confirmed that a raja facing the British had to choose between submission and extinction.

Abandoned, fleeing, and often lacking for food, Velu Thampi was cornered on 27 March in a remote temple in Mannadi, 10 or so miles beyond Kundara. When his pursuers knocked, Thampi, it seems, asked his brother to cut his throat.

The brother refusing, Thampi applied the fatal stroke himself, thereby helping to ensure—to quote the words, published in 1955, of the administrator, diplomat and author K. M. Panikkar—that 'his fame still lives...as an unselfish leader of the people, as a lover of freedom who sacrificed himself for it'.[9]

On the orders, presumably, of Macaulay and the new dewan (Ummini Thampi), Velu Thampi's body was brazenly displayed on a hill near Trivandrum on an open gibbet. His house and the houses of close relatives were razed to the ground.

For his part in the failed revolt, Paliath Govinda Achan was kept behind bars for twenty-five years, first in Fort St George and then in Bombay. As for Colonel Colin Macaulay, he would become an MP after returning to Britain.

◆

Initiated in 1826 by Thomas Munro, a survey of education in Madras Presidency showed that out of a total population of 12,594,193, only 188,650 were attending schools, most of them private.

In the presidency's Malabar district, which had a considerable Muslim population, there were 14,153 school students of whom 2,230 were Brahmin boys, five Brahmin girls, 3,697 'Sudra' (i.e. non-Brahmin but not 'untouchable') boys, 707 'Sudra' girls, 3,196 Muslim boys and 1,122 Muslim girls. In 1826, all 75 college students in Malabar were Brahmin boys.[10]

The educational theory of Fort St George was that 'light must first touch the mountain tops before it can pierce to [other] levels'. Seen by themselves and others as the 'top' caste, Brahmins took advantage of available opportunities.

The result, argues T. K. Ravindran, was 'monopolization of education by certain classes who became the beneficiaries of British rule'. With their 'educational qualifications they got a lion's share of public offices'.[11]

Decades after Munro's survey, the Cochin raja would rule that a Brahmin convicted of murder could not be awarded capital punishment. 'Taking a Brahmin's life was an unparalleled sin,' the ruler argued through his dewan in 1871, citing the laws of Manu, and recalling to us what Ananda Ranga Pillai had written in his Pondicherry diary 110 years earlier. Even though its resident in Cochin, George A. Ballard, was unhappy about this, the Raj did nothing.[12]

Ballard wrote in 1870 that outcastes in Travancore faced at least four obstacles. They were barred from public roads, not permitted to come near courts and public offices, excluded from public schools, and blocked from public service. While British policy was to admit all to government schools, Ballard claimed that caste Hindus used social and economic boycott to prevent a lower caste father from sending his children to school.[13]

Likewise, though under British rule the lower castes had the right to use public roads, they hesitated to exercise the right. As for British-run courts, an untouchable required to give evidence usually 'stood afar off' while a go-between took a Brahmin judge's question to the witness and returned with the answers to the judge. This would remain true even in 1924.[14]

HYDERABAD AND THE 1857 REVOLT

Always threatened by stronger powers, Hyderabad's ruling Asaf Jahi dynasty, founded in 1724, had survived by picking the winner in crucial clashes: at first the French over the British, then, when the balance altered, the British over the French, and finally the British over Tipu in 1799.

From 1829, when the dynasty had completed what by prevailing standards was an impressive century, the nizam was Nasir-ud-Daula. He was protected by a Company contingent (maintained by the nizam) of European and Indian soldiers who were based 6 miles away in Secunderabad. Closer at hand was the British Residency, a grand mansion built (with money from an earlier nizam) by James Kirkpatrick, resident from 1795 to 1805, whose wife, Khair-un-Nissa, was Indian.

In an 1817 letter, John Malcolm, diplomat, military officer and future governor of Bombay, described the Residency, which was designed to resemble what at the time was Washington's newly-created White House:

> The present mansion of the British Resident of Hyderabad may well be termed a palace. It is only surpassed in splendour and magnitude by the Government House at Calcutta.[15]

In 1839, one of Nasir-ud-Daula's brothers, Mubariz-ud-Daula, evidently hoped to replace the nizam by riding to the throne on an apparent wave of 'Wahabism', originating in Arabia and finding a response in Hyderabad.[16] Mubariz's ally in the plot against his brother was the Pathan Nawab of Kurnool, but their plans were detected and foiled. Mubariz was sentenced to a cell in the Golconda Fort, where he died in 1854, and Kurnool was formally annexed to Madras Presidency.

In 1853, Nizam Nasir acquired a new minister, Turab Ali Khan (1829–83), who would go on to obtain fame as Salar Jung I. On Nasir's death four years later, on 16 May 1857, his son Afzal-ud-Daula became the nizam.

Within days of his succession, Afzal was confronted by word from upper India of a serious revolt against the British. Sepoys of the Company's Bengal Army, Hindu and Muslim, had mutinied. Reports that beef and pork were mixed in the greased cartridges they opened with their teeth had enraged them. Joined to stories of conversion attempts, the reports lit a fuse. The sepoys found leaders for the rebellion in rajas and ranis prohibited by the Company from adopting heirs.

Worse for the British, Emperor Bahadur Shah Zafar, for decades a nominal ruler under British protection in Delhi's Red Fort, blessed the rebels and declared, on the night of 11 May, that Hindostan was sovereign again. In June, came word that Kanpur and Lucknow were in rebel hands and that many British had been massacred in Kanpur.

Earlier in this book we saw how word of Nadir Shah's invasion of Delhi in 1739 had travelled to Ananda Ranga Pillai in Pondicherry via horses from Delhi to Surat, and thence, at a slightly quicker pace perhaps, by sea along the lengthy coastline. A hundred and eighteen years later, the British in India were in possession of the telegraph, installed from the early 1850s in posts across the land.

Though lines were frequently cut by rebels, the telegraph kept the British and their Indian allies informed of 1857's events almost as they happened. Journeying traders and defecting sepoys also brought the Revolt's excitement to the south.

Once again, a nizam in Hyderabad picked the winning side and saved his throne, this time aided by clarity in his minister, Salar Jung, and firmness in a new British resident, Colonel Cuthbert Davidson. An unnamed British general, described by Davidson as 'the highest military authority at Madras', would say later that summer:

> Hyderabad...is to Southern India what Delhi was to Northern India. All in this quarter look to the Nizam and his capital; and general insurrection here would, I cannot but think, spread like wild fire throughout the Madras Presidency and to Nagpore.[17]

Writing two years later, Davidson would claim that

> every eye [in Hyderabad] was turned towards Delhi and Lucknow,
> and news of every kind was eagerly sought and paid for. Disastrous
> rumours of the wildest kind, hostile to the British Government,
> were prevalent and always acceptable to the fanatical and warlike
> classes of the population; letters of the most treasonable and
> seditious character were intercepted from Aurungabad, Bhopal,
> Ahmedabad, Belgama, Kurnool, and Mysore...
>
> [H]ad a popular leader arisen, Hyderabad would have been
> speedily in a state of insurrection.[18]

That did not happen. On 12 June 1857, Indians in an Aurangabad-
based cavalry unit of the Secunderabad contingent indeed rebelled,
but British officers subdued them with artillery. On 23 and 24 June,
after Company reinforcements arrived from Secunderabad, more than
twenty-five rebel sepoys, most of them Dakhni Muslims, were killed,
either shot by musketry, blown from a gun, or hanged.[19]

Davidson would also claim that, taking a risk, the contingent sent
'half of its numbers' in June and July 1857 to join a British force,
supplied by Bombay, to fight rebels in Central India. He added that
'letters of the men of the Contingent cavalry, mostly Mahommedans
of the Deccan, to their friends and families [in Hyderabad]' described
British victories and 'satisfied the disaffected that the game to subvert
British supremacy was already ended'.[20]

An account of the Hyderabad of 1857 was given four years later
by Henry George Briggs:[21]

> Colonel Davidson was hourly being telegraphed by [British]
> politicals from the north of Central India to as far south as
> Travancore [and urged] to hold to the last, conscious that if the
> capital of the Nizam went, the whole Peninsula would soon rise.
>
> The native mind was in a state of ferment, and it merely
> required some powerful house or great chief to create a flame,
> to make that flame a blaze...
>
> Colonel Davidson from the very onset had trustworthy
> information that the fanatical spirit which prevailed in the city was
> strong against his Government and his country... that a vow had
> been taken to repeat at Hyderabad the scene of Cawnpore; he was

even made aware that he was specially marked for assassination; and he was told that every Sepoy of every arm of our military force had been tampered with... (Briggs, 76–77).

When a few Indian friends urged Davidson to leave 'for his own safety', the resident suspected a design to lower British morale and lift that of the disaffected. Telling one 'well-wisher', 'I have a particular fancy to be buried in the [Residency's] garden', Davidson warned that 'the British Government will hold the Nizam responsible if harm comes to the Resident' (78–78fn).

From the middle of June, 'the tidings from Hindoosthan were daily worse and worse', and there were reports from the city of a plan to attack the Residency. When on 17 July the attack occurred, the Residency was well prepared, thanks to its intelligence network and Salar Jung's counsel, and it was reinforced with troops.

At 5.45 p.m. that afternoon, Salar Jung sent a messenger to warn Davidson that 500 Rohillas* were on their way, with a mob following them, and to request that the resident should defend his place while the minister gathered the nizam's troops (79–80).

'Every gate of the Residency grounds had been closed, and every means of access bristled with bayonets... The Rohillas proceeded to occupy two large upper-storied houses with terraced roofs...facing the western wall of the Residency, belonging to two Soucars, Ubbu Saheeb and Jey Gopall Dass', as also a garden close to the Residency.

'The firing from the two houses was very heavy for about twenty minutes, till it became dusk.' Powerful British guns then responded, and the attackers dispersed, many of them escaping into the city. Thirty-two rebels were killed by the Madras Horse Artillery guns. Rebels 'continued hovering about the Residency all the night long' but by daylight 'they had been completely dispersed' (Briggs, 81).

The British were relieved that the largely Muslim 'Madras native horse artillery' remained 'staunch, and instead of wavering in their duty, opened their guns on the insurgents, although men of their own creed'.[22]

Captured soon after as a leader of the assault, Maulvi Alauddin was sent for life to the Andamans, while another militant, Turebaz Khan, 'was shot by the native government upon refusing to surrender

---

*Urdu-speaking Pathans who had migrated to Hyderabad from the Rohilkhand region of present-day UP.

after escape from confinement' (82).

Davidson would claim that the unsuccessful attack of 17 July was 'the culminating point of our troubles at Hyderabad'. Thereafter, 'no one of rank, wealth and position could rise' (86).

In November 1858—well after the Revolt's suppression and more than a year after Delhi was back in British hands—when whispers warned that daring Tantia Tope, the surviving rebel general, had shown up near the northern frontier of the nizam's dominions, the Hyderabad populace seemed more uneasy than excited.

Memories of Hyderabad's clashes with the Marathas in the eighteenth century had blunted the appeal of Tope's possible entry. In Davidson's view, any

> Mahratta movement having a probability of success would have at once enlisted to our side the old hereditary and ever-cherished 'Moglaee' animosity against their former and national foe, the Mahrattas (85).

Hastings Fraser, who served in Hyderabad, would, however, write eight years after the event that most of the 17 July attackers had escaped along with their wounded, which was taken as 'sufficient proof that the Nizam's own troops were not very warm in our cause'.[23] Recalling 'much uneasiness' in 1857 in Hyderabad, Fraser wrote:

> Rumours of disaster befalling our troops were frequently spread, and as frequently believed.
>
> The prevalent feeling seemed to be one of disappointment, if not of shame, that whilst their brethren in the field had dared the chances of an open conflict with us, the city of Hyderabad was at peace.[24]

When a man imprisoned in Mysore claimed (in 1857) that the rebels enjoyed the nizam's secret support, the Company asked Davidson to enquire whether 'the Nizam was entirely innocent of rebellious intentions'. In his reply, Davidson said that

> he had caused the Nizam to be narrowly watched from quarters and in ways he little suspected, and although emissaries had come to him, he had, after listening to their stories, refused complicity in any movement against the British Government.[25]

Two years later, on 15 March 1859, Davidson came close to getting killed near the entrance to the Nizam's Palace. An armed man on horseback took aim at Salar Jung, with whom Davidson had just emerged. The minister and the resident both escaped, and the assailant, whose hostility towards Salar Jung seemed unconnected to the Revolt, was cut down.

The joint efforts of Salar Jung, the nizam and Davidson had helped secure Hyderabad, and probably other parts of the South, against the Revolt.

◆

Dated 3 September 1857—eleven days before Delhi was retaken by the British—an overview by Fort St George's Judicial Department had communicated serious anxiety:

Hyderabad is always inflammable and was sure to be deeply excited... Our provinces of Kurnool, Caddapah and Malabar contain a large Mussalman population which would participate in these feelings... [A]t Madras itself and the towns of Arcot, Vellore and Trichinopoly, animosity was felt in consequence of the extinction of the Nawabship of the Carnatic...

One newspaper entered into lengthened arguments to prove that greased cartridges of objectionable materials had really been issued... The policy of annexing Native States on the failure of lineal male heirs [has been] discussed in very inflammatory language [in vernacular newspapers]...

In the middle of June, bands of armed Rohillas crossed from the Nizam's country into the Kurnool and Cuddapah district... They were apparently connected with the party who made the attack on the Hyderabad Residency...

In Mysore, about the middle of July, it was found necessary to dispatch some European infantry and guns to overawe the Mahommedans near Seringapatam and Mysore...

In Masulipatam...a green flag and a proclamation urging the slaughter of the English was seized on the 10th of July and it was reported on 15 August that prayers for the success of the King of Delhi were offered up in the Mosques...

In Madras itself the state of feelings in Triplicane...became so suspicious that on 29 June military posts were established in different parts of the town... Proclamations and seditious letters were seized, urging the Nizam and his Minister to start a holy war... The approaching downfall of our power was openly talked of... In Chingleput some seditious plotting was discovered.

Seditious emissaries and Bengal sepoys [were seen] in various parts of the Presidency.[26]

Adding to tensions was a last-minute refusal by units of the 8th Light Cavalry of the Madras Army to board the ship booked to take them to Calcutta to help quell the Revolt.

Riding at the end of July 1857 from Bangalore, where they had been based, the cavalry units reached Sriperumbudur, 20 miles short of Madras, before declaring their unwillingness to proceed further. Following the embarrassment, Fort St George dismissed eight native officers—seven Muslims and a Hindu—for failure to gauge the sepoys' mood.[27]

KARNATAKA DEFIANCE

In the first half of 1858, defiance was displayed in places in the north of present-day Karnataka, including Shorapur, Nargund, Dambal and Koppal. Located about 40 miles south of Gulbarga and 30 miles northwest of Raichur, Shorapur—belonging, like Gulbarga and Raichur, to the nizam's territory—was ruled by Venkatappa Nayak, a young chief from the tribal Bedar community.

After reports of 'Bedars, Arabs and Rohillas' enlisting in an anti-British force in Shorapur had raised suspicion in the Residency in Hyderabad, a clash occurred on 7 February 1858 between a British column and the men of Shorapur, who included Hindus and Muslims, tribals and non-tribals. A Captain was killed, and Venkatappa Nayak escaped, but the Shorapur Fort was taken by the British, who would return it to the nizam in March 1861.

On reaching Hyderabad, which was 160 miles away on horseback, Venkatappa was recognized, arrested, tried, and sentenced to four years' detention in Chingleput in Madras Presidency.

On 11 May 1858, when the English lieutenant escorting him towards Chingleput briefly 'went outside the tent', the twenty-four-year-old chief used the escort's loaded revolver to kill himself. Earlier, in Hyderabad, he had told a former mentor, Meadows Taylor, that he preferred being blown by a gun to being hanged or imprisoned.[28]

Bhaskarrao Bhave, the Konkan-origin Marathi Brahmin chief of Nargund (located about 30 miles northeast of Dharwad/ Hubli), resented a British demand for depositing arms and their refusal to let him adopt a son. During Maratha–Mysore conflicts, the Bhaves had supported the Peshwas. Now, in the late 1850s, Bhaskarrao seemed inspired by the Great Revolt and was in secret correspondence about it with neighbouring chiefs.

Near the end of May 1858, C. J. Manson, political agent for 'the southern Maratha country', stumbled upon letters in which Bhaskarrao had urged rebellion. Finding out that he had been identified, and learning that Manson was moving in his direction, Bhaskarrao and 800 of his men marched on 29 May to stop him. In a village called Sureban, they found Manson hiding in a temple.

One of Bhaskarrao's men cut off Manson's head. Brought to Nargund, the head was stuck on a gate. On 2 June, a force of reprisal arrived. 'Not less than sixty' of Nargund's men were killed in the battle that ensued; 'more than thirty', including Bhaskarrao Bhave, were executed after arrest and trial; and 'about one hundred' were imprisoned for various terms.[29]

Revolt was also pondered, about 30 miles southeast of Nargund, by Bhimrao Mundargi, landlord of the Dambal tract. A Deshasth Marathi Brahmin, Bhimrao had stored arms for potential use in the fortified house of an associate, Kenchangowda, in village Hammigi. When, after a tip-off, a British party raided Kenchangowda's house and found the arms, Bhimrao went on the offensive.

On 24 May 1858, a force of seventy led by him attacked one of the guards the British had placed in Hammigi and recovered the arms. Joined by additional numbers, the force also attacked the treasury in Dambal town, the post and telegraph offices in Gadag, about 10 miles northwest of Dambal, and the fort of Koppal, which stood about 24 miles east of Dambal.

These were daring onslaughts across a sizable area. On 30 May, Bhimrao captured Koppal Fort, which (like Shorapur) lay within the nizam's territory. Two days later, however, a British force assembled from Bellary, Raichur and Dharwad, and led by a Major Hughes, invaded the fort. In an intense battle, about a hundred insurgents were killed, including Bhimrao and Kenchangowda.

In September, Thomas Ogilby, the Dharwad magistrate, informed the Bombay government that Bhimrao's effects included twelve copies of a proclamation by Nana Saheb Dhondu Pant Peshwa, 'under the orders of the Emperor of Delhi', exhorting everyone to 'annihilate the wicked Kaffur English' and 're-establish the Hindoo and Mahomedan kingdoms as formerly'.[30]

Of the rebels captured in Koppal, a British court martial sentenced eighty to death, forty to fourteen years in prison, and twenty others to shorter terms.[31]

A 1993 study would find that ballads in praise of Bhimrao 'are sung to this day in the Dambal area'.[32] However, the Revolt in northern India which Dambal's acts of brave defiance echoed had virtually ended by now. Delhi had been recaptured, and Bahadur Shah imprisoned in September 1857, and the rebels holding Lucknow, the Awadh capital, were defeated in March 1858.

Lakshmibai of Jhansi would indeed remain alive until 17 June 1858 (sixteen days after the death of Bhimrao), and the elusive Tantia Tope until April 1859, but by the summer of 1858 the British victory was more or less complete.

Though many in the south shared the Revolt's temper, the persons who rebelled were not numerous, and they were quickly overpowered by the Company's well-informed officers and well-armed soldiers. Warned through the telegraph and backed by an intelligence network across the south, Governor George Harris at Fort St George, Resident Cuthbert Davidson in Hyderabad, Commissioner Mark Cubbon in Bangalore, and other Company officers prevented rebellion or quickly suppressed it.

INDIA ON A PLATE

What also ended in the 1858 summer was Company rule. In August, the British Parliament and cabinet—serving Queen Victoria, who had ascended the English throne in 1837—took direct control over India. A letter on the occasion from the East India Company's directors to the Queen revealed their understanding of who owned India:

> Let Her Majesty appreciate the gift—let her take the vast country and the teeming millions of India under her direct control, but let her not forget the great corporation from which she has received them.[33]

From August 1858, India's Governor General, Lord Charles Canning, became viceroy as well. On 1 November, he read out, in Allahabad, Queen Victoria's Proclamation in relation to the Revolt, which *The Times* of London interpreted as offering 'royal promises of pardon, forgiveness, justice [and] respect to religious belief'.[34]

In the following year, Canning claimed: 'Order is re-established, and peaceful pursuits have everywhere been resumed.' Two years later, in 1861, he said that Awadh, the heart of the rebellion, was now 'so thriving [and] so tranquil that an English child might travel from one end of it to the other in safety'.[35]

On 1 May 1876, by when a prime minister congenial to Victoria, Benjamin Disraeli, had taken office, the House of Commons resolved to make the Queen the Empress of India as well.

Another outcome of the Revolt was a change in British policy on the thrones and lands of rajas. In 1867, the House of Commons was told that when he came of age, four-year-old Chamarajendra, adopted son of Krishnaraja, the deposed ruler of Mysore, would receive authority over Mysore. Until then the Company commissioner, Mark Cubbon, nephew of the Mark Wilks quoted earlier, would continue to administer it.

In 1857, Krishnaraja, though no longer a ruler, had provided 2,000 men 'for the suppression of [any] Rebellion' and received 'cordial thanks' from Viceroy Canning.[36]

When, in March 1868, Krishnaraja died at the age of seventy-four, the British acknowledged Chamarajendra as his successor, and in 1881, Fort St George formally returned Mysore to the sixteen-year-old prince, who however was required to keep all laws in force and obtain the viceroy's permission for any material changes.[37]

SALAR JUNG (1829–1883)

Descending from an Arab-origin family which in earlier centuries had served the Adilshahis of Bijapur, as also the Mughals, the previously mentioned Salar Jung I, as Turab Ali Khan is known to history, was only twenty-three when in 1853 he became Hyderabad's dewan, a post he held until his death, thirty years later. By then he had given the territory something approaching an efficient administration.

In 1874, he politely but firmly rejected the advice of Lord Northbrook, the viceroy, that the young nizam, Mir Mahboob Ali, should travel to Bombay to welcome the visiting prince of Wales. Grateful for Salar Jung's role in the 1857 Revolt but disliking his independence, the British tried to undermine him.

He was not an ordinary officer. Thanks to him, Hyderabad was for the first time 'divided into clearly demarcated districts with well-defined and identifiable boundaries'. Ownership of lands was carefully recorded, which stabilized the rural economy and simplified the collection of land revenue. Families that had out-migrated for work and food returned. 'Within a few years, 983 villages were repopulated.'

Paid regularly under his stewardship, government servants accepted lower salaries, which reduced Hyderabad's debt. Policing was improved, as also the judiciary. Hating his reforms, well-heeled hangers-on at the nizam's court who had profited from an absence of rules, and moneylenders (Muslim and Hindu) who had made fortunes lending money at usurious rates to the government, tried to destroy Salar Jung. There were at least two unsuccessful attempts to kill him.

Salar Jung's biggest disappointment was his failure, despite repeated efforts and a visit he made to England in 1876, to retrieve for Hyderabad the large cotton-growing tract of Berar, as the Vidarbha portion of modern Maharashtra was called at the time. For inability to pay ever-higher sums demanded for a British force it never asked for, Hyderabad had been compelled in 1850 to cede Berar to a Company hungry to sell cotton to Lancashire's textile mills.

When he arrived in England, Salar Jung was praised for his abilities. Oxford conferred on him an honorary degree. But the bid to regain Berar earned him 'the implacable hostility' of India's British rulers. After serving three nizams, defying narrow interests, and bringing a semblance of order, Salar Jung died in 1883. Assembled in Hyderabad, his collections constitute one of India's finer museums today.[38]

NADARS

Both Malayalam and Tamil are spoken in one of India's southernmost segments, the Thiruvananthapuram-Tirunelveli-Nagercoil triangle, even though the area's bilingual percentage seems to have shrunk in the twenty-first century.[39]

In the 1850s, this area, divided between the ruler of Travancore and the Madras Presidency, saw a bitter controversy over the wish of its Nadar women, many of whom had become Christian, to wear the breast-cloth which custom had long reserved for Nair and other high-caste women. Nadar men worked as palmyra-climbers on lands which were owned either by richer Nadars (called Nadans) or by Nairs.

Of the palmyra and its climbers in the Tamil and Malayalam countries, Robert Caldwell left this nineteenth-century description:

> Almost as straight as the mast of a ship, the palmyra reaches a height of from 60 to 90 feet, with an erect plume of fan-shaped leaves at its top. The leaves are stiff...and of manifold use: in the thatching of houses among the lower classes, in the manufacture of mats, baskets and vessels of almost every description; and the slips of the young leaf form the traditional stationery of southern India.[40]

Most important of all was the sap or juice of the tree. Unfermented, it nourished the tapper and his family. Boiled, it turned into a hard, coarse sugar called jaggery. Distilled, it became arrack, the native gin. The climber

> begins before daybreak, working until noon and then again from late afternoon until night. He will ascend thirty to fifty trees, climbing each twice—sometimes thrice—to extract the juice. During the season in which the sap flows (March-September), the tapper can never leave the trees unattended [i.e. unascended] even for a day.

As a dairy cow cannot be left unmilked, so the palmyra, the tappers' cow, ceased to yield its juice if untapped. The sap was drawn from the flower stalk at the top of the tree, which daily yielded, drop by drop, about three-fifths of a litre. The climber brought it down in earthen pots two or three times a day. Work on the palmyra was arduous and dangerous.

> Each year, many of the climbers, no matter how skilful, fall from the trees to die or to remain crippled for life. In ascending the tree, the climber clasps the trunk with joined hands, supporting his weight with the soles of his feet... Then in a series of springs, in which both hands and feet move together, the climber ascends the tree as rapidly as a man could walk a distance of equal length.

Years of climbing twisted the tapper's body, charred his chest, and turned his hands and feet into paw-like limbs, yet...

> The climber owns neither the land nor the trees which he tapped— only the sharp, tappers' knife, a few earthen pots, and meagre clothing.[41]

Toddy-tapping has greatly declined, but when the nineteenth century began many in the South were engaged in it, even though the climber and his family, whether speaking Tamil or Malayalam, received degrading treatment.

In Travancore, Nadars were required to remain thirty-six paces away from a Nambudiri and at least twelve paces from a Nair. They could not carry an umbrella, or wear shoes or gold ornaments, or live in a house of more than one story. And their women could not carry pots of water on their hips as higher-caste women did—or cover upper portions of their bodies.[42]

In 1812, after Colonel Munro, the Company's resident in Travancore, asked that Christian Nadar women be allowed to cover the upper portion of their bodies, the kingdom's government declared that a short bodice or jacket as worn by Syrian Christian and Muslim Mappila women, could be worn by the Nadar women, but not the full covering used by Nair women.

But the Christian Nadar women chose to wear the breast-cloth freely and fully, which is what their counterparts in Tinnevelly in the Presidency were doing. Though a missionary named Charles Mead asked the Christian Nadar women to be content with the shorter covering, the women continued to wear a fuller one, which led to attacks by Nair groups on Christian Nadar schools. In 1829, some women were beaten.

Despite these incidents, and despite the kingdom asking the women not to wear it, by the 1850s the full cloth had become the norm for most Nadar women in Travancore, whether Hindu or Christian. In October 1858, however, Nadar women were attacked in the bazaar of Nagercoil, then part of Travancore, and stripped of their upper garments.[43] The leading British missionary in the Tamil country, Robert Caldwell, claimed that the Queen's Proclamation of November 1858 assuring respect for Indians' religious beliefs was 'almost universally interpreted by the natives as a declaration in favour of custom and caste'.[44]

Nadars in a village near Nagercoil were again attacked in January 1859, this time with clubs and knives, and the women were stripped of their upper cloths. Attacks elsewhere in the district followed. Evidently nine chapels and three schools were burnt between October 1858 and February 1859.

Following protests, the Travancore government issued a new policy in July 1859, which allowed for freedom with respect to the upper cloth as long as it was not worn in 'the manner of women of high caste'.[45]

◆

As the nineteenth century advanced towards its end, the apparent neutrality, as between native groups, of India's British rulers, their success in putting down the Great Revolt, and the stable rule they provided thereafter should have pleased the woman in England who had received a country as a present.

But that country, we will find out, was changing. No longer content to express itself in isolated military attempts by a small raja here or a nawab there, India's urge for freedom would look for broader and more democratic outlets.

Chapter 8

STUNG TO REFORM: 1877–1901

'What a blazing away of powder there was!' exclaimed a European eyewitness in north Delhi, after cannons had fired 101 rounds on 1 January 1877 in honour of Victoria, who would have imagined the scene from a castle in Britain.

The continual thunder in Delhi was created for a spectacular durbar chaired by the forty-six-year-old Earl Edward Lytton, Victoria's freshly appointed viceroy, and attended by most of India's large and small princes, who also received cannon-fire accolades.[1] Because the rajas of Kashmir and Mysore and the Nizam of Hyderabad were each entitled to a 21-gun salute, the queen in England was offered 101 blasts.

India's privileged ones received a Victoria medal on 1 January, native rajas in gold, British officers in silver. Etched on the obverse of Victoria's face were words calling her 'Empress of India' in three scripts: Roman, Devanagari and Persian.[2] In Devanagari, she was 'Hind ki Kaisar'. In Urdu, too, India was 'Hind'.

Claiming that Victoria's assumption of the elevated title 'conspicuously places her authority upon that ancient throne of the Moguls',[3] the Earl of Lytton showcased Britain's unchallenged power. At the 'Imperial Assemblage', as Lytton described the durbar, that power was underlined in numerous ways. Ancient Mughal buildings in Delhi were commandeered, and 'maharajas were placed at the receiving end of the ceremonies, precisely where their own subjects would have been in traditional durbars'.[4]

Serving as a British diplomat before and after his viceroyalty, Lytton is remembered in today's India as the father-in-law of Edwin Lutyens, colonial New Delhi's famed architect. In his time, Lytton was known mostly for his poems, written under the name Owen Meredith. His tragic poem 'Lucile' became especially popular, American publishers printing it more than two thousand times between 1860 and 1938.[5]

Because 'England's prestige in Asia' was involved in proclaiming Victoria an empress, Prime Minister Benjamin Disraeli evidently felt it 'necessary to have a poet viceroy, and so it came to pass that the author of *Lucile* was intrusted with all the details of the great imperial durbar at Delhi'.[6]

However, the last white word on the India of 1877 would belong not to the poet-viceroy but to a soldier-photographer, Willoughby Wallace Hooper, whose portraits of skeletal South Indian children, women and men trapped in the Great Famine of 1876–78 continue to haunt those that see them.[7]

As drama, the famine would endure better than the durbar.

Starting with the failure in southern India in 1876 of the summer monsoon as also of the one due in late autumn, the Great Famine was made more acute in the following summer by a third consecutive absence of rain. It took more than five million lives across the land, including many in the northern regions from where grain was moved not only to parched places to the south, but also to England.

An 1878 book by William Digby, then a twenty-eight-year-old editor of the *Madras Times*, spells out the Empire's reluctant, and in retrospect callous, response to the tragedy.[8] Both Fort St George and Calcutta, the seat of India's 'Superior Government', as it was called, emerge poorly.

In Madras, attention was first absorbed by the so-called 'Weld' affair, where a British civilian had the body of a Hindu ascetic exhumed from a tank well and buried elsewhere. Then, in October 1876, even as the famine had begun, the Duke of Chandos,* the Governor of Madras (like Lytton a Disraeli appointee), sailed off on a tour of the Andamans, Rangoon (Yangon) and Ceylon (Sri Lanka).

The governor returned soon but only to journey at once for Lytton's Imperial Assemblage. He travelled also to see Lucknow. At least the duke described the scale of the south's crisis to Lytton and his officers, who had dismissed telegrams from Madras as alarmist. In that 1876–77 winter, the telegraph—the weapon that saved British rule in 1857—failed to rouse the Empire to action.

Before the governor began his train journey north, 65,000 had died in the presidency and 13,000 in Mysore (45). These official figures were almost certainly well below the actual.

---

*His full name was Richard Plantagenet Campbell Temple-Nugent-Brydges-Chandos-Grenville, 3rd Duke of Buckingham and Chandos (Wikipedia).

People left their homes and wandered in search of water and food, congregating in public inns, and around dwellings of Europeans, and rushing into Madras city, where, Digby observed, 'ten Hindus were feeding, with one meal per day, 11,400 people' (13).

Bellary, Kurnool and Cuddapah would be revealed as the presidency's worst-hit districts, but even far to their south, in Tinnevelly, the collector saw 'ten females returning home with a few handfuls of grain taken from ant-holes in return for 6 or 8 hours of labour' (14).

The price of grain multiplied, including in districts where famine was not severe, for grain was being sucked out by rail to main depots. The south was now 'a bleak country, no crops, no trees, no water'. An 'occasional patch of withered straw was the only remnant of vegetation' (17).

People ate poisonous roots and leaves, dying parents abandoned dying children, many little ones were sold. In some places cholera and malaria joined famine, and bodies accumulated everywhere.

The contrast between life's last gasps in the south and the hurrahs of imperial Delhi was too strong to be missed, and Digby, for one, underlined it (45). However, relief was crippled by the rigid application of conservative dicta, such as:

> Distributing food creates dependency. Employ able-bodied men for work. Rather than two annas a day for labour, give an anna-and-a-half. Free trade is best, let private merchants move grain across the land. And if England wants grain, let places like Punjab supply it.[9]

Richard Temple, a former Bengal governor sent south by Lytton, articulated some of these policies. Digby remarked that Temple wrote 'numberless memoranda and very long minutes' and took a 'rose-coloured view', which, said Digby, 'the death-rate contradicts' (52).

In that 1877 summer, Madras officials gave up their annual Ooty sojourn, but no steady view was taken of the Presidency's needs. When speakers at a Madras meeting urged England and famine-free parts of India to help, the viceroy and his associates in Calcutta did not like it.

After persistent requests, Lytton finally arrived in Raichur, on the presidency's northern border, on 27 August, and two days thereafter in Madras. Later, in 1880, the Empire would come up with a Famine Commission Report, which said:

The calamitous season of 1877 was accompanied by an extremely high range of prices over all India, due partly to the deficient harvest, and partly to the reduction of the food stocks through export from the Northern Provinces to the south and to Europe. These two causes together prolonged the distress in Madras, Mysore, and part of Bombay over a second year...

The years of famine were also exceptionally marked by great mortality, partly attributable to virulent outbreaks of cholera, small-pox, and fever.[10]

'It can scarcely be asserted,' the report added, 'that the system adopted [in respect of the famine] was altogether satisfactory or efficient.'[11]

Commenting also on pre-colonial India, the report charged that 'in all probability some [old famines] have been altogether forgotten, since the object of Indian historians was generally rather to record the fortunes of a dynasty than the condition of a people' (17).

What the report did not admit was that those responsible in the 1870s for famine relief were distant from ground realities, while those familiar with the latter had no part in governance.

The calamity was huge. Even Lord Sundareswara in his Madurai temple 'pleaded helplessness' before it, said a Tamil satire composed a decade later by poet Villappa Pillai, who lived near Madurai.[12]

◆

In 1878, before the famine ended, Lytton raised a storm with his Vernacular Press Act, which authorized magistrates to fine the printing press of an Indian-language newspaper and confiscate its machinery if in their view the newspaper preached 'disaffection'. In response, Indians in different parts of the country brought out newspapers in English. In Calcutta, the *Amrita Bazar Patrika,* a Bengali weekly started in 1868, became an English-language journal. In Lahore, the Indian-owned *The Tribune* appeared in 1881.

And in Madras, *The Hindu,* a weekly to begin with, was started in 1878. The immediate provocation for its emergence was opposition by British and pro-British elements in Madras to the elevation to the high court of Tiruvarur Muthuswamy Aiyar, a brilliant lawyer from a humble background in Thanjavur. Aiyar was no rebel, he had, in fact, travelled to attend Lytton's Imperial Assemblage. But being Indian seemed flaw enough.

Another Madras-based intellectual from Thanjavur district, G. Subramania Iyer, who was twenty-three, his twenty-one-year-old friend M. Veeraraghavachariar, a city lecturer, plus four law students*— together known as the Triplicane Six—founded *The Hindu*, which would become a daily from 1889. A formidable advocate of Indian rights and of reforms in Indian society, Subramania Iyer would die of leprosy in 1916.

Two years after *The Hindu* appeared in Madras, Benjamin Disraeli was defeated in the British elections, and India unexpectedly found a progressive viceroy, fifty-three-year-old Lord Ripon, whose grandfather had been a Madras governor.

Viceroy Ripon repealed the hated Press Act in January 1882, and in May of that year he announced a policy of local self-government through municipal and rural boards, of which at least two-thirds of the members would be non-officials, chosen if possible by election.

Ripon was aiming at more than local self-government. Privately he told a close friend, Thomas Hughes, the Christian Socialist and author of *Tom Brown's Schooldays*:

I am laying the foundation upon which may hereafter be built a more complete system of self-government for India which may convert what is now a successful administration by foreigners into a real government of the country by itself.[13]

By this time Ripon had found an ally in Allan Octavian Hume, a Scottish civil servant who had been forced out by Lytton and who would enter history for two separate feats: taking the study of India's birds to a new level, and founding the Indian National Congress.

Another Ripon ally was the law member in his cabinet, Courtenay Peregrine Ilbert, who in December 1882 told the imperial legislative council that he welcomed the Indian press as 'the best source of information' on what was happening.

---

*T. T. Rangacharya, P. V. Rangacharya, D. Kesava Rao Pantulu and N. Subba Rao Pantulu.

In February 1883, Ilbert introduced a bill that many Indians had long wanted. It removed the bar on an Indian district magistrate or sessions judge in the hinterland from trying a European accused of a criminal offence. Indian magistrates could do this in a city like Calcutta, but the idea of giving them authority over planters and other whites in the countryside triggered a 'white mutiny'.

India's Britons thought that Ilbert's Bill would destroy the hierarchy that enabled a white minority to dominate a large native population. After Ripon and India's natives were roundly abused at a Calcutta meeting on 29 February 1883, the correspondent of *The Times* reported that 'no such excitement has been witnessed among the Europeans since the time of the Mutiny'.[14]

Inside Britain, the press strongly backed the bill's foes, with the *Daily Telegraph* writing, 'On the day when we surrender the rights and privileges of superior strength and ethnical rank in India we invite our own expulsion', and *The Times* declaring, 'India can be governed by Englishmen only as a conquered country... [T]he privileges of the English who are resident there...are not anomalies at all...'[15]

Ripon's friends in Britain capitulated before the Conservatives, and in India, white solidarity against the Ilbert Bill forced the viceroy to accept a compromise that retained little of what he and Ilbert had put into it. To a friend, Ripon wrote that he had detected in fellow-Britons in India 'the true ring of the old feeling of American slave-holders'.[16]

In September 1884, Ripon left his viceroyalty early to enable Prime Minister William Gladstone to name a Liberal successor in India before new British elections brought Conservatives back in power. Ripon's departure was a triumphal march, with large crowds bidding him farewell as he travelled from Simla to Calcutta and Calcutta to Bombay, the Indian press praising him, and temple priests performing ceremonies for his wellbeing. Some Indians were in tears, and in Bombay no fewer than 154 addresses were presented to him.

Completed in 1913, and housing offices of the city corporation, Chennai's Ripon Building survives against odds to recall his name.

On Ripon's departure, *The Hindu* wrote that thanks to his stances and the Ilbert Bill, 'the first beginning of national life' had been glimpsed in India. The paper added that 'a powerful native opinion' conscious of 'its importance and strength' now existed. '[H]ow to secure this ground' was the question.[17]

◆

A. O. Hume had already answered it. On 1 March 1883, at the height of the white mutiny, he had written a hard-hitting if private letter to 'Graduates of the Calcutta University':

[I]t is to you, her most cultured and enlightened minds, her most favoured sons, that your country must look for the initiative. In vain may aliens like myself love India and her children as well as the most loving of these...they may place their experience, abilities and knowledge at the disposal of the workers, but they lack the essential of nationality, and the real work must be done by the people of the country themselves.

Since individuals could not do what an organization could, Hume proposed, for a start, an association with say fifty 'founders'.

You are the salt of the land. And if amongst even you, the elite, fifty men cannot be found with sufficient power of self-sacrifice, sufficient love for and pride in their country...then there is no hope for India. Her sons must and will remain humble and helpless instruments in the hands of foreign rulers, for 'they [who] would be free, themselves must strike the blow'.

And if even the leaders of thought are all either such poor creatures, or so selfishly wedded to personal concerns, that they dare nor or will not strike a blow for their country's sake, then justly and rightly are they kept down and trampled on... If this be so, let us hear no more fractious, peevish complaints that you are kept in leading strings, and treated like children, for you will have proved yourselves such.[18]

Not published but sent to a circle of friends, this letter from one who had become an Indian in his spirit was an important step in the creation of the Indian National Congress in 1885. But Hume was not alone in thinking in such terms.

A year before Hume had sent out his letter, Calcutta's England-returned Surendranath Banerjee, editor of a new weekly, *The Bengalee*, and prominent leader of a freshly formed 'Indian Association', had publicly asked for 'a great national congress that would meet once a year'.[19]

Dadabhai Naoroji, too, the Parsi who would enter the House of Commons as its first Indian, broached the idea of an annual all-India gathering in December 1884, when Hume and many leading Indians were present in Bombay for Ripon's send-off.[20]

A month later, three barristers practising in Bombay, Pherozeshah Mehta, K. T. Telang and Badruddin Tyabji, each from a different community but jointly called 'the three brothers-in-law', formed a Presidency Association and assured Hume of their support for an annual all-India event.[21] So did Poona's Sarvajanik Sabha (Public Association), principally led by the judge and social reformer, Mahadev Govind Ranade.

The idea crossed provincial boundaries. The Madras Mahajana Sabha, formed in 1884 by P. Anandacharlu, a prominent lawyer, *The Hindu*'s Subramania Iyer and Veeraraghavachariar, and others, also favoured all-India meetings.

'In late December 1884...17 men' apparently 'met at the house of Dewan Bahadur Raghunatha Rao in Mylapore to chart out a plan for the formation of a political national movement.' Among these seventeen were 'delegates to the annual convention of the Theosophical Society that had just concluded at Adyar'.[22]

In any case, *The Hindu* announced on 5 December 1885 that a national gathering would be held at the end of the month in Poona. A cholera outbreak in that city forced a last-minute switch to Bombay, where the first session of the Indian National Congress (INC) was held in a building of the Gokuldas Tejpal Sanskrit College Trust.

Of the 'very close on one hundred gentlemen' who gathered for the opening session, thirty-eight came from Bombay Presidency, twenty-one (including Subramania Iyer and Anandacharlu) from the Madras Presidency, three from Calcutta, three from different Punjab towns, and seven from four towns in what today is Uttar Pradesh. The rest, close to thirty, were Indian officials from different parts of the country, invited to listen and advise, not to speak on record.

Hume's proposal that Calcutta's Womesh Chandra Bonnerjee should preside was unanimously accepted. Proceedings were conducted in camera and only summaries were provided to the press, yet contemporary accounts convey the event's flavour as also the period's idiom.

Writing in the *Bombay Gazette*, a European onlooker referred to 'the men from Madras, the blackness of whose complexion seemed to be made blacker by spotless white turbans', 'bearded, bulky, and large-limbed men' from UP, 'Marathas in their cart-wheel turbans', 'stalwart Sindhis from Kurrachee' and Parsis in a head-dress 'which they themselves have likened to a slanting roof'. A delegate from Bengal would write:

> It was as if every member had inwardly resolved upon having less of words and more of work, every one of them inspired with an inward feeling that it was real work for his country which had called them to that hall...[23]

In his presidential remarks, Bonnerjee refuted the charge that the Congress was 'a nest of conspirators and disloyalists'. To ask to be governed by principles prevalent in Europe was 'in no way incompatible with thorough loyalty to the British Government', he declared. Naoroji said that the Congress was asking for 'the rights of British subjects, as British subjects'.[24]

One Bombay resolution asked for the inclusion of elected members in provincial councils. Another sought a cut in the military budget, which Indian revenues were financing. At the session's end, three cheers were raised for Hume, the lone European in the assembly.[25]

Eight years earlier, another Briton, the viceroy who demoted Hume, had organized a grander event in Delhi. Yet it was of the humbler Bombay occasion that the *Hindustani* of Lucknow wrote:

> When the historian of the future sets himself to write...he will not fail to mention prominently the 28th, 29th, and 30th December 1885, when the various forces of the country were brought together. We have very often used the word 'nation'...and we know also that there are many Anglo–Indians who will not believe that there is anything like a nation in India.
>
> But if any of these gentlemen had been present at the National Congress [in Bombay], he would have been convinced of the existence of something like a nation in India.[26]

A year later, Naoroji presided at the INC's second session in Calcutta. The third session was held in Madras in December 1887 with Badruddin Tyabji in the chair, at Mackay's Gardens, not far from the Thousand Lights Mosque.

Of the 600 who attended this third session, the southern presidency provided 362.[27] The century's remaining years would see several Congress-connected district conferences in Tamil and Telugu areas, stimulating political interest.[28]

Exciting as it was, the visibility of 'a nation' was not welcomed by all. Sayyid Ahmad Khan, founder of what would become the Aligarh Muslim University, warned Muslims against eagerness for an Indian share in government, which he said would strengthen Hindus vis-à-vis less educated Muslims. It was a position that Tyabji, an eminent Muslim, countered at the Madras session.

What sections of society was the Congress speaking for? Asking the question, Maharashtra's Jyotiba Phule, who strove for women's education and the rights of lower castes, said after the Bombay meet that the Congress could become national only if it addressed the hardships of the peasants and the 'untouchables'.[29]

INDULEKHA AND KANYASULKAM

If exclusion of Indians from governance produced the Congress, interaction with Westerners produced a new literature. Enabling South India's society to look at itself during a time of disconcerting change, O. Chandu Menon's Malayalam novel, Indulekha, first published in 1889, and Gurajada Apparao's Telugu play, Kanyasulkam (Bride-price), first staged in 1892, have also lasted as literary texts.

Parenthetically and briefly, Indulekha discussed whether the newly formed Congress was anti-British: being anti-British was seen as a risk or a flaw. For men like Bonnerjee and Naoroji, it was a charge to be refuted.

Yet Indulekha is not a text in colonialism's defence. As the scholar G. Arunima puts it, the novel provides 'a complex engagement with nationalism and colonialism'. Among the questions it touches upon is the equation between one of the Malayali world's most energetic castes, the Nairs (still called Sudras at the time, including by some Nairs), and that world's 'highest' caste, the Nambudiri Brahmins.

The novel's story revolves around a love affair between two Nairs: Indulekha and Madhavan, an English-educated student waiting to graduate from Madras University before starting a legal career. Though not receiving any formal school education, Indulekha is fluent in both English and Sanskrit, having been trained at home by the best teachers.

In Arunima's words, 'By making Indulekha, a Sudra (Nayar) woman, a Sanskrit scholar, Chandu Menon made a serious critique of the caste pretensions of the Brahmins.' Menon also makes Indulekha the winner in an argument she has with a pretentious Nambudiri.

Son of a prosperous Nair tahsildar in Madras Presidency's Malabar district, Chandu Menon went to a school started by the Basel Mission in the coastal town of Talasseri, but he was also taught Malayalam, Sanskrit and Hindustani at home. Learning the law without going to a law college and gaining admiration for acuteness and impartiality, he became, unusually for an Indian in his time, a sub-judge.

Work took Menon to the spaces of British officials, who were appreciative of his abilities, but one of them, G. R. Sharp, went too far when, on one occasion, he caught hold of Menon's kuduma (hair-knot) and suggested its removal. *Indulekha* contains a hint of the offending incident.

Along with colonial rule, shoes and slippers were introduced to the Malabar countryside, but custom forbade footwear before superiors or elders. When Menon saw one day, in front of his house, a subordinate of his, a Tamil Brahmin, carrying something wrapped in paper, he asked, 'Sweets?' 'No, sir,' the man replied, 'these are my new slippers.' This incident too found a place in *Indulekha*.

Recognizing that new customs threatened long-nursed pictures of an Indian self, and of the standing in society of an Indian's caste, *Indulekha* seemed to point out that a native could accept, reject or modify the colonizing world's offerings.

A mixed response was the ground reality. While Western impact caused a few Nairs like Chandu Menon's father to give his son a paternal prefix (Oyyarathu in this case), the great majority chose to remain linked in their names to their mother's taravad, her house and lineage.

Allowing Malayalis to smile at changes in their society and also at the odd ways of their new masters, *Indulekha* captivated Nair households because its Malayalam was closer to the spoken idiom, and because it told a story near to their lives or hopes, not a tale of ages gone by, or of 'the marvels of gods and goddesses, recoverable only through the medium of a pristine, Sanskritized language'.[30]

Even if, as Chandu Menon conceded, there were very few actual Indulekhas in 1889, a great many Malayali young women were willing to imagine themselves as future Indulekhas.

◆

Kanyasulkam's creator was Gurajada Apparao (1862–1915), a Niyogi Brahmin from the princely tract of Vizianagaram in the northern part of the east coast's Telugu country. After graduating from the college created in Vizianagaram by its raja, Ananda Gajapati Raju, Apparao taught there before joining the raja's staff in 1886.

This munificent raja funded several intellectual and cultural efforts in the presidency and also in distant Calcutta. Apparao assisted him in a series of responsible capacities, including as Vizianagaram's epigraphist.

Following the raja's death in 1897, Apparao became assistant, adviser and personal friend to the raja's younger sister, the Maharani of Rewa, a widow who lived in Vizianagaram after the death, shortly after their marriage, of her husband, the Rajput raja of the north Indian principality of Rewa.[31]

Three short lines, translated into English by the poet Srirangam Srinivasa Rao from Apparao's Telugu verse, *Desabhakti*, convey an idea of our artist's outlook:

Never does land
Mean clay and sand
The people, the people, they are the land.[32]

A writer of English poems while a student, Apparao soon switched to Telugu, where he employed words that people actually spoke. Often called the greatest play in Telugu,[33] *Kanyasulkam* was staged for the first time in 1892 and published, with a dedication to the Vizianagaram raja, in 1909.

The play's plot is formed by two intersecting stories. One is the desire of an elderly Brahmin to buy as his new bride Subbi, the very young daughter of another Brahmin who is willing to go through with the deal but whose wife is not, since her older daughter is already a widow and she fears Subbi will become one too.

The other is the love life of a smooth-talking, handsome, English-educated Girish (or Girisham). He has an ongoing secret affair with a young widow who runs an eatery providing meals to employed middle-class Brahmin males. Girish is also involved with a courtesan, Madhuravani, who is anxious to save Subbi.

A recent translator of the play into English, Velcheru Narayana Rao, calls *Kanyasulkam* 'devastatingly honest'. Noting that its thirty-two-strong cast of characters includes Brahmins and non-Brahmins, 'corrupt police officers, idealistic lawyers, smart courtesans, pseudo yogis' and more, Narayana Rao adds: 'Every character in the original speaks in a dialect of Telugu specific to his or her caste, social status, gender, educational level and individual style'.[34]

The contest between an unprincipled Girish and the chivalrous and resourceful prostitute, Madhuravani, has fascinated the Telugu world for more than a century. *Kanyasulkam* is celebrated as a historically powerful voice against the cruel and lifelong widowhoods that were foretold when old Brahmin males procured very young wives and widow remarriage was forbidden.

Narayana Rao, however, questions this standard portrayal of Apparao as a reforming advocate of widow remarriage, suggestive of Bengal's better-known Ishwarchandra Vidyasagar. He asks us to note that *Kanyasulkam*'s characters, 'dynamic, enterprising, creative, funny, intriguing and tough', seem to be having a good time in the play (162).

More importantly, says Narayana Rao, the heated debates over widow remarriage that took place in India around the time of the play's creation involved 'only the small upper-caste layer of Brahmins and an even smaller number of people from Brahminized castes' (166). Those from more populous castes 'did not really need the social reform agenda as most of their women freely married again if a husband died' (166).

Whether Apparao is best seen as a bold reformer or as an uninhibited portrayer of life, the triumphs in *Kanyasulkam* of Madhuravani over Girish, and over the old man thirsty for a child-wife, have been cheered for over a century by the play's audiences and readers.

VIRESALINGAM (1848–1919)

Kandukuri Viresalingam belonged to a family of priestly Saivite Brahmins living in Rajahmundry, an important ancient town on the Godavari's eastern bank, about 30 miles west of the port of Kakınada. For centuries, pilgrims had stopped at Rajahmundry to bathe in the Godavari. Since the poet Nannaya composed (perhaps in the eleventh century) his Telugu Mahabharata there, the town was also seen as the fount for Telugu's literary stream. To Rajahmundry's immediate south lies the Godavari anicut, work for which started in the year preceding Viresalingam's birth.

The 1871 census showed a Brahmin percentage of 5.8 in Godavari district, to which Kakinada and Rajahmundry belonged, but unlike in other districts in the presidency, half of Godavari's Brahmins were owners or tenants of agricultural land.

Though his grandfather too had been a landholder, Viresalingam was raised in hard conditions. His mother Punnamma became a widow when her son was four. The father's brother, who had a wife but no child, took Viresalingam under his roof, but soon died. As an only child growing up under two quarrelling widows, Viresalingam obtained 'first-hand knowledge of some of the problems of Indian women'.[35]

To begin with, Punnamma placed the clearly bright boy in two disappointing traditional schools, the first of which (in Viresalingam's unkind future words) 'was run in a temple by a man with a hare-lip, and the second in an open portico by a hunch-back'.[36] However, in the government district school to which he went next, Viresalingam, it seems, was hailed as 'a wonder boy'.

He also knew what he wanted. Saving half a rupee from his pocket money and using another half-rupee given by Punnamma for school fees, he gave a full rupee to a bookseller as advance for a four-rupee classic that would teach him proper Telugu. However, until the price was fully paid the classic could only be read in the bookshop, so classes had to be missed.

After the truancy was discovered and Viresalingam explained its cause, Punnamma somehow found the three rupees required, and the debt was cleared.[37]

Stories such as this, Viresalingam's lifelong commitment to social reform, including widow remarriage, female education and rationality in religion, and the range of his writing would eventually induce someone like the educator C. R. Reddy, who died in 1951, to say, 'Taken all in all, Viresalingam is the greatest Andhra of modern times'.[38]

He taught for a living (including in a freshly-elevated government college in Rajahmundry and later as first Telugu pandit at Madras's Presidency College) but wrote mostly out of conviction. In 1874, he started *Vivekavardhini*, a Telugu journal initially printed in Madras, and from 1875 at a press installed in his Rajahmundry house. Concluding that simple language made communication effective, he gave up archaic prose.

Reviewing two books by Viresalingam, *The Hindu* wrote in 1878 that at a time when Telugu writers were sacrificing 'ideas at the shrine of jingling words', he had produced a 'style' that was 'pleasant and idiomatic'. There was 'a flow in his works'. There was also force. In the sweeping view of one scholar, *Vivekavardhini*, which folded in 1890, 'made more history than any Telugu journal that preceded or followed'.[39]

In 1878–79, Viresalingam made forthright speeches in defence of widow remarriage, and on 11 December 1881, in the teeth of open threats, he and his wife Rajyalakshmi organized in their Rajahmundry home the marriage of a young Brahmin widow, whose mother wanted her remarried, with a widower, a Brahmin policeman in Vizag.

Admiring Viresalingam's scholarship as also his courage, loyal students joined the presidency's police in protecting the bride and groom and their sponsors from attacks by orthodox bands. A few British officials witnessed the ceremony, and a high fee was paid for the Brahmin priest. Brahmin cooks and water-carriers, and pipers and drummers from the caste of hair-dressers, were all well rewarded. Most of the funding came from a Kakinada merchant, Pyda Ramakrishnayya.

Four days later, Viresalingam held another widow marriage. This time the British collector of Godavari district attended. A parade through town followed, complete with dancing girls. Fellow-reformers had overruled Viresalingam's objections to the dancers' involvement.

Orthodoxy hit back on 31 December with a proclamation issued in Rajahmundry in the name of the Sankaracharya of the Virupaksha seat in Hampi, whose authority was acknowledged by Viresalingam's Brahmin clan. All those who attended or assisted the two weddings stood excommunicated until satisfactory penance was offered, while Viresalingam, his wife Rajyalakshmi and the two couples were expelled without possibility of re-entry.

The blow was sharply felt. A leading supporter of the marriages was unable to enter the temple his grandfather had constructed, the headmaster of the municipal school was driven from his house, and the school itself 'was very nearly abolished'.[40]

Viresalingam and Rajyalakshmi stood firm and aided those affected as best as they could. Students in Rajahmundry and Kakinada backed him, and when the Sankaracharya visited Rajahmundry, student anger forced him to leave the town. A few students went on to marry widows. A price was paid, but the cause had advanced.

Viresalingam himself would go on to perform over forty widow marriages, establish two girls' schools and two homes for destitute widows.[41] His commitment to widow marriage would result in what has been called 'the most intensive campaign in all of India'.[42]

In Rajahmundry and Madras, allies and aides were crucial to his work, but he would be criticized for not giving them a free hand.[43] Some allies stayed with him longer than others. One who never withheld her support was Rajyalakshmi, not even when a remarrying widow made unreasonable demands, saying to her and Viresalingam, 'You married us, now you must help with our children.'

In Viresalingam, self-belief equalled energy. During a seven-year stay, from end-1897, in Madras, he set up his own press in a new house in Purusawalkam where he printed his own collected works, functioning as his own compiler, editor and proofreader![44]

The love of writing never leaving him, he tried almost every form of it. The first Telugu play, the first Telugu novel, the first Telugu autobiography—Viresalingam may have claim to all three. He also translated famous plays from Sanskrit and English. The autobiography, in which he admits 'his quick temper and the diffusion of his energies over too many fields', is perhaps the best remembered of his written works.[45]

With his pen and the spoken word, he fought also for monotheism and reason. In 1906, he 'renounced his caste and with it the sacred thread'.[46] In the following year, when, sparked by the partition of Bengal, that province's great orator, Bipin Chandra Pal, visited Rajahmundry amidst nationalist fervour, Viresalingam refused to join the Vande Mataram movement, as it was called.

Accused of cowardice, Viresalingam, who in 1887 had attended the Madras session of the Congress, held his ground, saying:

> We cannot enjoy the fruits of political independence unless and until we reform our religious and social conditions.[47]

On 27 May 1919, the steadfast man was working in Madras on a new poetical study when the pen suddenly slipped from his hand, announcing his end. Rajyalakshmi had gone ten years earlier. Obstacles to the remarriage of Brahmin widows would take longer to disappear.

UVS (1855–1942)

Recurring frequently in our story, the Tamil country's Thanjavur or Kaveri delta possesses, at its ocean end, a vertical boundary of around 50 miles. Located on this straight stretch are ports like Tranquebar with its Danish links, France-connected Karaikal, and Nagapattinam. Located less than 30 miles inland is the ancient temple town of Kumbakonam.

If Rajahmundry in the similar Godavari delta obtained in 1877 a government college, where Viresalingam taught, Kumbakonam found its government college in 1867, which is where Uttamadhanapuram Venkatasubbaiyer Swaminatha Iyer lectured from February 1880. Of UVS, to use the accepted shorthand for him, an eminent South Indian scholar, K. Swaminathan, has roundly declared:

> No one, anywhere in the world, at any time in history, has rendered to any language the kind of service that Dr. U.V.S. had done to Tamil.[48]

Incomparable or not, UVS, born into a Brahmin family near Kumbakonam, was certainly extraordinary. Near the end of his life, he wrote a much-acclaimed autobiography, which the Tamil weekly *Ananda Vikatan* serialized.

Earlier he had written a similarly praised biography of the Vellala poet Minakshisundaram Pillai (1815–76), the 'polymath genius' who, spending his life in Kaveri delta's towns, mathas and temples, was—in David Shulman's words—'able to create huge numbers of verses in his head and to dictate them to scribes writing on palm-leaf at a pace no human hand could keep up with'[49].

The story behind UVS's greatest achievement, taken from the autobiography, is well known. It begins with his call on 11 October 1880—eight months after his appointment as the Tamil pandit at Kumbakonam's government college—on Salem Ramaswami Mudaliar, a Vellala munsif posted in Kumbakonam, who was known as a Tamil connoisseur.

Asked by Mudaliar to name the Tamil works he had read, the twenty-five-year-old UVS mentioned, one after another, an impressive, even staggering, number of texts, but the munsif merely said, 'Is that all?' When UVS reeled off more names, Mudaliar again responded with 'That's all?'

Finally asking UVS whether he had read Tamil literature's ancient texts, Mudaliar referred to *Chintamani* and *Manimekalai*. The lecturer had heard of the texts but not come across them. In fact, Mudaliar too had not read them.

The next time UVS saw the munsif, the latter gave him a set of palmyra leaves containing a handwritten text of the narrative poem *Chintamani*. Reading it would goad UVS into locating, understanding and sharing as many ignored or lost Tamil texts as he could.

Chintamani being a Jain classic, UVS sought the aid of Jaina scholars for a fuller grasp. He also located other manuscript versions. In 1887, he published his edition of *Chintamani* (Wish-fulfilling Jewel), which was followed by the publication of two other narratives in verse, *Silappadikaram* (Tale of an Anklet) in 1892, and, connected to the anklet tale, *Manimekalai* (named after its beautiful leading character) in 1897. All three were evidently created in the first millennium.

The impact was enormous, even though the first two were written by Jains and the third by a Buddhist. The primary thrust of each was more literary than religious. The verses were compelling. The towns where the stories unfolded seemed sophisticated and held people of different religions. While three ancient kingdoms (Chola, Pandya and Chera) were evoked, women and ordinary men were the stories' heroes.

The Tamil country was filled with pride. In due course, the man who had made the rediscovery possible—journeying to remote corners, on foot if necessary, to obtain crumbling palm-leaf manuscripts and missing pages, deciphering fading words, and producing credible editions of priceless works that appeared lost—would become known as Tamil Thatha—Grandfather Tamil.*

In all, UVS probably reproduced or produced more than a hundred texts. This late-nineteenth-century re-entry into circulation of the classics would 'generate a new literary canon' in the Tamil country.[50] It would also rationalize, we will later see, a new politics.

In 1903, UVS was made Tamil pandit at Presidency College in Madras, rather like Viresalingam, who, we saw, was briefly the Telugu pandit in that college. The years thereafter would see more honours, including posthumous ones, for UVS, who died at a ripe age in 1942.

DIVIDE TO RULE

British awareness of the Brahmin/non-Brahmin divide, and of that divide's potential for strengthening British rule, continued. In 1868, J. H. Nelson, district officer in Madurai, said of the 'Sudra' appellation often given to many other castes by Brahmins:

> The term 'Sudra'...is never used by ordinary natives, who speak of one another as being members of particular tribes, castes and families. [It] would appear to be used by Brahmans alone in speaking of persons of low condition.[51]

Eleven years later, James Duvere, the Tanjore collector, complained of British dependence on Brahmin aides:

> It is one great misfortune of our administration that we should have already made such men our masters to a great extent.[52]

And in 1886, a year after the launch of the Indian National Congress, Governor Mountstuart Grant Duff was directly divisive in remarks to graduates of Madras University:

> You have less to do with Sanskrit than we English have. [Uncouth]

---

*A. R. Venkatachalapathy points out that two Vellala Tamils from Sri Lanka, Arumuga Navalar (1822–79) and C. W. Damodaram Pillai (1832–1901), preceded UVS in bringing out modern editions of Tamil classics (*Then There was No Coffee*, p. 100).

Europeans have sometimes been known to speak of natives of India as 'Niggers' but they did not, like the proud speakers or writers of Sanskrit, speak of the people of the South as legions of monkeys...[or] deliberately grounded all social distinctions on varna, colour.[53]

The line found takers. In 1893, a non-Brahmin writing under the pseudonym 'Fair Play' said that while the British were called the rulers of India, in reality 'the Brahman rules it'.[54]

◆

Meanwhile the printing press was giving Indians new scope. In 1883, the Tamil *Swadesamitran* appeared in Madras, thrice a week to begin with, and edited for twenty years by G. Subramania Iyer, one of the founders of *The Hindu*.

In 1894, G. A. Natesan (once more a Brahmin from Thanjavur) opened a bookselling business in 1894 in Madras's Georgetown, passing up options of government service or law.[55] Three years later, Natesan started a printing press and a publishing company, and in 1900 he came out with an English-language journal, *Indian Review*.[56]

In addition to Viresalingam's *Vivekavardhini* (started in 1874), the Telugu world had the *Andhra Bhasha Sanjivani*, published from Madras for twelve years from 1871 by a Viresalingam critic, Kokkonda Venkataratnam. Brought out from 1885 to 1904 in Nellore, *Amudrita Grandha Chintamani* printed unpublished Telugu classics. Also begun in 1885 was *Andhra Prakasika*, published from Madras by Partha Saradhi Naidu and willing to criticize the government.[57]

The first newspaper to come out in Kannada was *Mangalooru Samachara*, produced in 1843 in Mangaluru by a German from the Basel Mission, Hermann Friedrich. More than half a century later, in 1894, another German missionary, Ferdinand Kittel, compiled the first Kannada–English dictionary.

In Malayalam, the oldest surviving journal is *Deepika*, a Catholic voice first brought out in 1887 in Kottayam. Three years later, in 1890, came *Malayala Manorama,* published, also from Kottayam, by the Kandathil family and continuing, more than twelve decades later, under the family's descendants.

That all their land had been created from the ocean by Parasurama, Vishnu's axe-wielding incarnation, who then gifted it to the Brahmins, remained a firm belief among many in the Malayalam country throughout the nineteenth century and also in the coastal belt to its north, where Kannada, Tulu and Konkani were spoken.

In the Malayalam country, this belief was accompanied by the notion that the so-called Sudras, among whom the Nairs were classed, were created to serve the Brahmin Nambudiris, who were the region's priests as well as its landowners. The rest, forming a majority, were labelled outcastes or avarnas, unlike savarnas who belonged to a caste, high or low.

Though outcast, these avarnas too were assigned a hierarchy that some of them seemed to accept. Some were todil or untouchable, others were tandil or unapproachable, and yet others, the lowest of the low, were unseeable.[58] Published in 1834 in his *Oriental Memoirs*, the following observations of the visiting James Forbes have often been quoted:

> The Pooleahs [pulayas] are not permitted to breathe the same air with the other castes nor to travel on the same road; if by accident they should be there and perceive a Brahmin or Nair at a distance, they must make a loud howling to warn him from approaching until they have retired or climbed up the nearest tree.

Adding that even lower than these Pulayas were the Pariars (with whom the Pulayas did not marry and who, unlike the Pulayas, ate beef and carrion), Forbes went on to charge that Kerala's Brahmins 'have thought proper to place Christians in the same rank with the Pariars'.[59]

Contesting Kerala's Parasurama legend, however, was another popular saying, 'All live as equals when "Mahabali" rules', and a related idea that Mahabali, who 'ruled long, long ago', makes an annual visit to his subjects during the Onam festival.[60]

Ranked highest among Malayali outcastes were people called Ezhava or Thiya,* who in numbers exceeded the Nairs. As it progressed, the nineteenth century found an increasing number of Ezhavas owning land,

---

*There is some disagreement on whether the Ezhavas living largely in the southern half of the Malayalam country are the same as the Thiyas to their north.

engaging in trade and in professions such as teaching and Ayurvedic medicine, and educating their children.

Narayana Asan, Nanoo to his parents, was born on the third day of Onam in 1856 in village Chempazhanthi near Thiruvananthapuram to an Ezhava schoolteacher, Madanasan, and his wife Kuttiyamma, who was the sister of an Ayurvedic physician.

Called Sri Narayana Guru in the future, he insisted on the unity and equality of all human beings, and he succeeded in breaking barriers to Ezhava dignity.

Drawn to languages, he seemed pulled even more by solitude and religious thoughts, which he expressed in Malayalam, Sanskrit or Tamil verses. In 1882 or thereabouts, when he was twenty-five or perhaps a little older, he was married—against his will, some scholars say[61]—to a daughter of one of Madanasan's nieces.

Accounts suggest that within days of the marriage, and possibly even the first time the two met after their wedding, Narayana told the bride, 'I have my path and you have yours, so leave me to pursue mine,' or words to that effect, and departed to wander in the hills and forests of southern Travancore and the Tamil country abutting it.[62]

After living as a renunciate for a few years, including for a while inside a cave, and winning the adulation of many, Narayana did something dramatic in 1888, when he was thirty-two. In Aruvippuram, about twelve miles southeast of Thiruvananthapuram, he installed, as an idol, a stone resembling a Siva lingam, and inaugurated a temple around it.

'How dare an Ezhava instal a Siva lingam!' some Nambudiris seem to have shouted. Narayana's answer was that what he had installed 'was not a Nambutiri Siva'.[63] About his own Siva, Narayana wrote many poems around this time. In *Siva Satakam* (a hundred Malayam verses on Siva), he extols Siva's wonders but also makes a humble personal plea:

> Many are the cruelties I have committed, though in a flippant manner/ And all those falsities were skillfully hidden within/ Such a mean fellow am I/ Knowing me as such, please bless me with due concern and compassion/ O overflowing ocean of mercy.[64]

In a letter written in 1896 after visiting a festival in Aruvippuram attended by thousands, a British evangelist named K. P. Thomas reported that 'Nanen Asan, an Eleven by birth [was] greatly respected for his good behavior and profound study of Hindu Vedas...[and was] very attractive in personal appearance'.[65]

A defiant social message was joined to Narayana's new Siva temple, which, as the evangelist noted, was drawing large crowds. If they were not to be allowed inside existing temples, the outcastes would create new ones, where however they would admit everyone.[66]

Asked by the excluded to create additional temples, Narayana established more than sixty, open to all, in the Malayalam, Tamil and Tulu lands. Later, however, he would say that schools should be the new temples.[67]

Earlier, in 1891, the Maharaja of Travancore had received a petition signed by 10,038 persons, including Nairs, Ezhavas, Christians and Muslims, against the dominance of Tamil Brahmins in his state's staff.[68] Another milestone was a 1903 alliance between Narayana Guru and Dr Padmanabhan Palpu, an England-educated bacteriologist, who had been active over the 1891 petition.

Denied an appointment in Travancore for being an Ezhava, the gifted doctor was serving in Mysore but mobilizing Ezhavas to petition for their rights in the Malayalam country. When he met Swami Vivekananda in Bangalore, the latter, it seems, suggested that the Ezhava movement should find a spiritual leader.[69]

Palpu's subsequent talks with Narayana Guru resulted in the creation of the Sri Narayana Dharma Paripalana Yogam (Association for the Propagation of Sri Narayana's Moral Teachings). Interestingly, the association was registered as a joint-stock company. Its title notwithstanding, SNDP, as it came to be called, was a social not a religious association. It openly sought to advance Ezhava rights.

In 1903, Narayana Guru was chosen as SNDP's permanent chairperson. The brilliant poet Kumaran Asan served as secretary until 1919, and Dr Palpu was the driving force. More than 114 years later, SNDP remains, arguably, 'the largest and most influential social organization' in Kerala.[70]

SNDP's emergence became a signal for other castes. Led by the spirited Ayyankali, who was also born near Thiruvananthapuram, the Pulayas formed their body in 1912. Ayyankali dared to advocate non-cooperation with the upper castes when they refused to concede the primary right 'to walk along public roads, to wear ornaments of their choice and not to be kicked and beaten'.[71]

Strikingly, 'the upsurge of the lower classes in Kerala was spontaneous, and from within, and generated by their own leaders', which was not the case everywhere else.[72]

In 1914, eleven years after the SNDP's emergence, the Nair Service Society was founded by Mannathu Padmanabhan, who would say:

> Seeing Sree Narayana Guru's spiritual utterances and the activities
> of the SNDP Yogam, the other communities also moved step by
> step towards progress, like the Ezhava community.[73]

Was Narayana Guru consciously using spirituality for social justice? A scholar of the Guru's life, Muni Narayana Prasad, holds that 'while a few of the Guru's admirers feel that his main concern was casteism... basically he was a spiritual master...and casteism was the monster he sought to destroy in the fire of wisdom-enlightenment'. Adds Prasad:

> Guru's desire was that [SNDP] should be a social organization
> striving for the benefit of all, irrespective of caste or creed. [It]
> grew very fast, but remained the organization of the [Ezhava]
> community. Guru naturally was very unhappy about it.[74]

Yet Narayana Guru would probably have rejoiced over SNDP's role in creating a pro-equality climate in the Malayalam country. To the Ezhavas, he prescribed education, organization and reform. Marriage ceremonies became simpler and less expensive, and the guru spoke strongly against liquor and toddy-tapping, an occupation for a portion of the community.

Asking for equality in society, Narayana Guru, who lived until 1928, said that his philosophy was Advaita, but joined to unmistakably Hindu words like Siva and Advaita was a refusal to oppose other religions. 'Whatever be the religion, it is enough if the man improves', he would say.[75] Unable to 'love one religion and hate another', he did not join campaigns against conversion, explaining pragmatically and wittily that

> One leaves one's religion as he loses belief in it, and his leaving
> it gives that religion the benefit of getting rid of one non-believer,
> whereas the other religion gets the benefit of gaining one more
> believer.[76]

◆

Exertions by native Christians had contributed to a pro-reform air in the Malayalam country. Born in Travancore's Alappuzha district a half-century before Narayana Guru, Kuriakose Elias Chavara (1805–1871) was a Syrian Catholic priest whom the Vatican would canonize in 2014. A literary scholar versed in Malayalam, Tamil, Sanskrit, Latin, Italian and Portuguese, in 1846 Father Chavara started a printing press from which, four decades later, the journal *Deepika* would emerge. He also opened a convent for sisters. Raised to the office of vicar-general, he insisted on a school in every parish. Songs he wrote would continue to be sung more than a century after his death.

Chavara would be remembered for two other acts. One was the setting up of a space in Alappuzha district's Mannanam monastery where Sanskrit was learnt by seminarians as well as by 'low-caste' students who were not supposed to approach the sacred tongue.

The other was to open, next to a chapel on a hill in Alappuzha, a school where Pulaya children could learn to read and write along with others—and where all children were given a mid-day meal. In many a home connected to the chapel, grains of rice were daily deposited into a pot, which at week's end was used for feeding the school's children.[77] The practice would be emulated in places far from Alappuzha.

◆

As the nineteenth century closes and in January 1901 a distant Empress dies, the onlooker recognizes an advance across South India in education, a growing print culture, and an emerging middle class of small landholders, doctors, lawyers, college teachers, writers, government employees and merchants.

In the realm of ideas, the onlooker discerns a few currents. One is of nationalism. Another is for reform in traditional customs and exclusions. A third is of linguistic pride. And a fourth pursues equality among castes.

Fort St George

Joseph François Dupleix,
Governor of Pondicherry

Ananda Ranga Pillai

Battle of Ambur, 1749

Nadir Shah

Chanda Sahib

Robert Clive

Muhammad Ali, Nawab of Arcot

Haidar Ali

Mark Wilks

Tipu Sultan

Purniah

Governor General Charles Cornwallis

Napoleon Bonaparte

Arthur Wellesley (Duke of Wellington)

Abbé Dubois

General Lord Cornwallis receiving Tipu Sultan's sons as hostages, 1792. Painting by Robert Home.

Killing of Tipu, 1799. Painting by Henry Singleton.

Thyagaraja

Syama Sastri

Muthuswami Dikshitar

Great Famine, 1876–78. An estimated 10.3 million people starved to death. Photo by Colonel Willoughby Wallace Hooper.

Narayana Guru

C. Rajagopalachari with Gandhi

B. R. Ambedkar and Periyar

Annadurai and Periyar

Nizam Osman Ali

M. S. Subbulakshmi

K. Kamaraj

MGR

M. Karunanidhi

J. Jayalalithaa

E. M. S. Namboodiripad

NTR

Devaraj Urs

S. Radhakrishnan

V. V. Giri

N. Sanjiva Reddy

R. Venkataraman

K. R. Narayanan

A. P. J. Abdul Kalam

P. V. Narasimha Rao

H. D. Deve Gowda

Chapter 9

DEFINING THE FOE: 1901–1925

Towards the end of George Nathaniel Curzon's viceroyalty (1899–1905), the presidency of Bengal was partitioned into a Muslim-majority eastern half and a Hindu-majority western half.

Taken as an open display of divide and rule, the move invited indignation across much of India. Punjab's Lala Lajpat Rai, Maharashtra's Bal Gangadhar Tilak and Bengal's Bipin Chandra Pal—the famed Lal-Bal-Pal trio—became household names across India. The south, too, was infected, its disquiet symbolized by Valliappan Olaganathan Chidambaram Pillai (VOC, as he would be called), and the poet Subramania Bharati.

VOC (1872–1936) was born in a Vellala family in Ottapidaram village near Tuticorin town, not far from the scenes of Kattabomman's exploits, in the large Tinnevelly district of the time.

Captured early by Tamil literature and Saivite doctrines, VOC passed a pleadership examination in Tuticorin, made that port town his base, and befriended a young Saivite orator, Subrahmanya Siva. When the Madurai journal *Sen-Tamil* (Classical Tamil), which was started in 1901, wrote an article on India's traditional arts and crafts, VOC complimented the journal in a letter in verse.[1]

Along with Lal-Bal-Pal, persons like VOC and Bharati saw the partition of Bengal as an attack on Indian nationalism and, directly, on the INC, some of whose leaders, including Pal, were born in east Bengal. When, in response, Lal-Bal-Pal urged a boycott of British products and the promotion of Swadeshi, they were wildly cheered.

Uttered by foes of the Bengal partition, the two words, 'Vande Mataram' (I bow to Thee, Mother)—taken from a poem in Bankim Chandra Chatterjee's 1882 novel, *Anandamath*—were quickly adopted by numerous hearers, including VOC and Bharati.

VOC's embrace of political and economic nationalism has been connected to a 1906 meeting he had with the Madras city chief of the Ramakrishna Mission. Taken by the cry of 'Vande Mataram', VOC thought the two words should be the greeting whenever Indians met one another, besides also being an Indian crowd's rallying slogan.

Drawn by the call of Swadeshi and by tales of Tamil seafaring in the past, VOC launched the Swadeshi Steamship Company in October 1906. He wished to compete on the Tuticorin–Colombo maritime route with the British India Steam Navigation Company (BISN). Raising funds and identifying investors, he became the company secretary. In May 1907, two ships ordered by his company arrived at Tuticorin.

However, BISN was too powerful, and the venture would fail. One of the Swadeshi's ships would in fact be sold to BISN. VOC left his company to become an agent from the outside, but had to give up that position too. Nonetheless, the episode earned him the name of Kappalottiya Thamizhan (Ship-steering Tamilian). Independent India would put on the waters a ship called *Chidambaram* to honour him.

Later in 1907, VOC attended the stormy Surat session of the Congress, where the body split into two. To some observers, VOC seemed 'on a par' with Tilak and Aurobindo Ghose in the extremist leadership present at Surat.[2] After the 1907 split, which saw the moderates retaining control of the Congress, a new Nationalist Party formed by the extremists chose a secretary for each presidency: Tilak for Bombay, Aurobindo for Bengal, and VOC for Madras.

Bipin Chandra Pal arrived in Madras in 1907 and made rousing speeches. Whether VOC met him then is not clear. What is known is that VOC and his friend Subrahmanya Siva sowed the seeds in Tinnevelly for a labour movement.

In February 1908, the two addressed workers of the British-owned Tuticorin Coral Cotton Mills. After a strike that began on 27 February, wages were raised, and Sunday was declared a holiday. From Calcutta, Aurobindo praised the successful strike. But after four men were killed in demonstrations and police firing in the wake of a meeting that VOC and Siva had called, the two were arrested, along with a few others.

VOC was awarded bail by the Madras High Court, but since it was withheld from Siva and another arrested associate, he declined the offer. Aurobindo commented that VOC had 'shown us the first complete example of an Aryan reborn'.[3] Trying him in Tinnevelly, a judge called A. F. Pinhey sentenced VOC to forty years of exile and transportation for life—twenty years for seditious speech and another twenty for abetting Siva with his fiery lectures! Siva was adjudged a tool in VOC's hands.

Appeals went to the Madras High Court and to London, where the Privy Council reduced the sentence to six years of rigorous imprisonment. Confined from 9 July 1908, first in Coimbatore Jail and then in Cannanore in Malabar, VOC was placed among criminals. A yoke was tied to him, and he was ordered to do heavy grinding. The Empire's brutal treatment of VOC made him a hero across the presidency.

For a while, the nationalist current flowed strong, but it soon ebbed. In 1909, the Empire doubled down and created a separate Muslim electorate across India, without inviting a strong reaction.

Since imperial strategy required sops to both sides, within two years, in 1911, Bengal was reunified! Simultaneously, the British moved their Indian headquarters from Calcutta to Delhi.

Facing a seemingly unshakeable Empire, nationalist fervour died down. There were no welcoming crowds in December 1912 when, four and a half years into his sentence, VOC was released. His Swadeshi Navigation Company, its ships auctioned to competitors, had been liquidated the previous year.

Barred from his Tinnevelly district, and his law licence revoked, VOC moved with his wife and two young sons to Madras, where this nationalist hero of yesteryears ran a shop selling provisions and another selling kerosene.

VOC had suffered greatly in jail, as had Tilak, who was sentenced in Bombay in 1908 to six years in distant Mandalay for writing in defence of Khudiram Bose, whose bomb had killed two Englishwomen in Bihar. But India was not ready for a revolt. Clandestine groups willing to kill and be killed could create a thrill but not an open movement.

In April 1910 in Tinnevelly district, a twenty-one-year-old Brahmin named Neelakanta, also known as Brahmachari, raised a secret 'Bharatha Matha Association', where, performing rituals before a picture of goddess Kali, members swore to kill European officers.

In the following year, Robert William Ashe, the district collector, was shot while sitting with his wife in a railway compartment at Maniyachi station, about 15 miles inland from Tuticorin and close to where VOC was born.

Minutes later, the assassin, twenty-five-year-old Vanchinathan Iyer, killed himself. Betrayed, caught and later tried, Neelakanta was sentenced to seven years. Shunning violence and politics after his release, he led a sanyasi's life under another name.[4]

When, starting with 1919, the Gandhi-led movements began to enlist large numbers across India, including in the south, VOC did not join. He continued, however, to work for labour unions.

The hero of 1908 was now short of money. Moving to Coimbatore, VOC worked there as a bank manager. A judge named E. H. Wallace granted him permission to practise again as a pleader, and the thankful nationalist named his youngest son Walleswaran.

Years passed in the shadows did not quench an inner flame. When death found him on 18 November 1936, VOC happened to be in the Tuticorin office of the Indian National Congress, pledged by now to the goal of complete independence.

◆

He was born Chinnaswami Subramania (1882–1921) in a Brahmin family in a Tinnevelly town we have encountered before, Ettaiyapuram, but teachers who admired the eleven-year-old's facility for lyrics named him Bharati, a synonym for Saraswati, the goddess of learning.[5]

Interested also in languages, the boy was soon fluent, apart from Tamil, in Sanskrit, English and Hindi, perhaps helped with the last by an early journey to Varanasi.

In 1904, he joined the *Swadesamitran* in Madras, working for eighteen months as a sub-editor and translator under G. Subramania Iyer, the forceful editor. Influenced or encouraged by Iyer, Bharati attended three Congress sessions, in Varanasi in 1905, Calcutta in 1906, and Surat in 1907. In Calcutta, Vivekananda's Irish disciple, Sister Nivedita as she was called, inspired Bharati, and he acquired a smattering of Bengali.

Alongwith Bharati in Surat was VOC, who was older to him by ten years. Sharing similar interests and views, the two had become close friends. When the Congress split in Surat, Bharati had no hesitation in siding with the extremists led by Tilak, Aurobindo and VOC.

In journals, in Madras, now edited by Bharati—interestingly, the Tamil one was called *India* and the English journal *Bala Bharatam*

(Young Bharat)—he defended the extremists and mocked the moderates, including in cartoons. The latter were a new feature in South Indian journalism, with Bharati usually conceiving a cartoon and hiring an artist to sketch it.[6]

Like VOC, Bharati responded with intensity in 1907 to Bipin Chandra Pal's speeches in Madras, and he seems to have made popular orations of his own on the beach. The Tinnevelly artist, a master of romantic and mystical poetry, who 'transmuted vague feelings of Tamil patriotism into lyric expression',[7] was now on fire as an activist.

However, preferring exile in Pondicherry to arrest in Madras, he moved in 1908 to the French territory, where he read, composed anew, or translated texts such as the Gita, Bankim's 'Vande Mataram' song, and pieces by Tagore, into Tamil verse or prose. He remained in Pondicherry during World War I, interacting on occasion with other eminent exiles, including Aurobindo.

The Pondicherry years were financially hard, and callers found Bharati agitated.[8] A correspondent of *The Hindu* who met Bharati in the French territory was struck by the poet's 'manner of speaking'. Apparently Bharati would suddenly stand up in the middle of a conversation, or suddenly sit down, and 'thump' with passion.[9]

In November 1918, when the war ended, he ventured out of the French territory. Detained in nearby Cuddalore, he was released after three weeks—the result, apparently, of an intervention by an Irishwoman who had made India her home—Annie Besant.[10]

In Madras in the following year, when Gandhi visited the south, his host, Chakravarti Rajagopalachari, introduced Bharati to him as 'our national bard'. Patriotic verses, devotional, philosophical and autobiographical ones, verses narrating great stories—Bharati had written them all.

But Madras, where he lived in a house in Triplicane, seemed to neglect him. Bharati was only thirty-nine when he died there in September 1921, the eventual result, it was said, of an injury received from a temple elephant he had regularly fed. Not many mourners joined the funeral of one after whom cities across India would later name streets.

Renaming a street would prove easier than translating the poet. In 2012, his granddaughter S. Vijaya Bharati, a scholar herself, would write in evident distress:

As far as English is concerned, Bharati has never found a good translator. I have been reading translations of Bharati's poems by various authors over the past four decades, and I have yet to see a satisfactory translation of Bharati.[11]

◆

The 1911 census showed that Brahmins were slightly over 3 per cent of Madras Presidency's population, and non-Brahmins 90 per cent. Yet in the ten years from 1901 to 1911, Madras University turned out 4,074 Brahmin graduates compared with only 1,035 non-Brahmin graduates. Numbers for other groups (revealing also how the Empire classified the population at this time) included 'Indian Christian', 306, 'Mohammedan', 69, and 'European & Eurasian', 225.

A little over 22 per cent of Tamil Brahmin males in the presidency were literate in English by 1911. The corresponding figure for Telugu Brahmins was 14.75, for Nairs in Malabar around 3, for Balija Naidus 2.6, and for Vellalas just over two. Among Kammas, Nadars and Reddis, males literate in English were below half a per cent.

Many more had attained mother tongue literacy: 72 per cent of Tamil Brahmins, 68 per cent of Telugu Brahmins, 42 per cent of Nairs, 20 per cent of Indian Christians, and 18 per cent of Nadars.[12]

The span from 1914 to 1918—in Europe the World War I years—saw competition in Madras between nationalists and opponents of Brahmin domination. A small but significant advance for the latter was the opening in 1914 of 'The Dravidian Home' for non-Brahmin students. Financed by men like Panaganti Ramarayaningar (the Raja of Panagal), whose lands lay in the Telugu country to the north of Madras, this hostel was run by C. Natesa Mudaliar, a Vellala doctor in the city.

Leading the Madras nationalists was the Irishwoman Annie Besant (1847–1933), who had arrived in India in 1894 after tumultuous years in England where she announced that she was an atheist before embracing theosophy. Though also spending time in Varanasi, her political base was Madras, where in June 1914 she purchased a newspaper, renaming it *New India*.

Through the paper, she asked for Home Rule for India. That stand, plus Besant's oft-expressed adoration for India's scriptures, her impressive bearing, and her eloquence made her a force to reckon with. The British in Madras, official and civil, responded to Besant with dislike, and *New India* was frequently asked to furnish security, all of which added to her popularity.

On 3 September 1916, she launched the Home Rule League. District centres appeared, and one of Besant's allies, the Congress leader P. Varadarajulu Naidu, an Ayurvedic doctor from a prominent Telugu-origin family near Salem, made speeches in Tamil about Home Rule. There was parallel activity on the other side. On 20 November 1916, around thirty or so eminent non-Brahmins met in Madras's Victoria Public Hall to form the South Indian People's Association (SIPA), a joint-stock company for publishing English, Telugu and Tamil newspapers which would voice non-Brahmin grievances.

A month later, on 20 December, readers of *The Hindu* and of Besant's *New India* were treated to SIPA's 'Non-Brahmin Manifesto', which declared opposition to 'the Indian Home Rule Movement', portraying it as a Brahmin exercise for gaining control over Madras Presidency. It also announced the start of a new political party, the South Indian Liberal Federation (SILF).[13]

Although the manifesto claimed to speak for all non-Brahmins, and its signatories included Telugu, Tamil, Malayali and Kannada names, SILF's first aim was 'not so much to attract a following as to influence the official policy of the British in Madras Presidency'.[14] More places for non-Brahmins in government service and in colleges was the immediate goal.

SIPA's daily newspaper in English, *Justice,* first came out on 26 February 1917. The Tamil daily *Dravidan* appeared in mid-1917. Published from 1885, the Telugu *Andhra Prakasika* was acquired.

Soon SILF became known as the Justice Party. Many of its members took the line that 'Tamil', 'Dravidan' or 'Dravidian', 'non-Brahmin' and 'South Indian' were synonymous terms, as were 'Brahmin', 'Aryan' and 'North Indian'. Their wish was to 'rouse all the non-Brahmanas to a recognition of their past glory with a view to put the haughty Brahmana who is the intruder from the North in his proper place'.[15]

Although it attacked Brahmins, Aryans and the caste system, the Justice Party remained elitist. Moreover, its leaders quarrelled publicly, and the colonial establishment's praise for the party became an embarrassment. Yet the future would identify SILF as the foundation for non-Brahmin political power in the South.

As for Annie Besant, her fame was at its zenith for a year from end-1916, when, at the Congress's Lucknow session, she and two others—Tilak (released in 1914 and back in the Congress) and Muhammad Ali Jinnah (then belonging both to the Congress and the Muslim League)—put together a historic pact where the Congress accepted a separate Muslim electorate and the League joined the Congress in a national demand for self-government.

Grumblings by some in Madras that the pact offered nothing to non-Brahmins were drowned in the protests raised in June 1917 when Besant was ordered not to speak or write politics and interned in Ooty. When she was released in September, there was exhilaration. Returning to Madras, she was taken from the railway station to her home in Adyar in a four-wheeled carriage drawn by white horses.

Mocking her, and clothing her with 'Brahmin-ness', the relentlessly critical *Mail*, which was British-owned, wrote on 21 September 1917:

> A silk canopy, obtained from one of the temples, was held over Mrs. Besant by two students... [T]he procession was preceded by a number of *bhajana* parties chanting hymns... [W]hen the procession reached the Mylapore Tank, it was met by a large number of...Brahmins singing Vedic hymns.[16]

A month earlier, on 20 August 1917, Edwin Montagu, His Majesty's Government's Secretary for State in India, had announced in the House of Commons a new policy of 'increasing association of Indians in every branch of the administration' and of developing 'self-governing institutions' towards the 'progressive realization of responsible government in India as an integral part of the British Empire'.

In London, *The Times* called the statement the 'clearest and most definitive declaration of British aims in India' made since Victoria's proclamation of November 1858.

However, Madras's British businessmen viewed the announcement as the most serious threat to the English position since the Ilbert Bill agitation of the 1880s, and thought that the Justice Party, believing 'in the retention of the British connection', needed their support.

Their sarcastic spokesman was T. Earle Welby, editor of the Madras

Mail, who in 1916 had said of Besant's writings: 'Venom is not made the more acceptable by being mingled with slime' (*Mail*, 22 Jan 1916). In August 1917, the *Mail* asked that she be deported to England.[17] Four months later, Besant would preside over the Congress session in Calcutta.

The Montagu announcement triggered a range of claims. Pointing out that Muslims had received special treatment in 1909, the Justice Party said that non-Brahmins (comprising, it was asserted, 40 million of the presidency's population of 41 million) should have something similar. But separate associations and separate political conferences bothered *The Hindu*, which pointed out that the Congress included many non-Brahmins (14 Sept 1917).

Though unhappy at the Lucknow Pact's silence on non-Brahmin representation, the South's non-Brahmin Congressmen were opposed to the Justice Party for its refusal to ask for self-government. In September 1917, a group of them formed the Madras Presidency Association (MPA), which said that the Lucknow scheme could be modified by adequate recognition of 'the various communities' of South India.[18]

If most zamindars and large landowners seemed to back the Justice Party, well-educated, middle-class non-Brahmins formed the core of the MPA, which, too, started a pair of journals, *Indian Patriot* in English and *Desabhaktan* in Tamil, the latter edited by a young Vellala, T. V. Kalyanasundara Mudaliar, or TVK as he would become known.

As for the Panchamas, the term at the time for the 'untouchables', one of their organizations, the Pariah Mahajanah Sabha, rejected an offer from the Justice Party to 'guide' them. The president, Anchas, said that Home Rule, whether by Brahmins or non-Brahmins, would crush the Panchamas.

Viceroy Chelmsford seemed to put the brakes on Montagu after he landed in India in November. In Madras, where, along with the viceroy, he spent ten days, the Scottish governor, Lord Pentland, and his wife, Lady Pentland, plainly told Montagu that they disagreed with his approach and with Besant's release.

Evidently the Congress, Brahmins and Home Rule, lumped together by the Pentlands, deserved opposition from the Empire and all sensible people, whereas the Justice Party, together with the Madras British, merited warmth.

In his revealing diary (not published until 1930), Montagu spoke of Pentland as 'an early Victorian' serving 'in post-War India'[19] who

talked about the Brahmins bitterly. He assured me that all respect for the Government had gone; that people used to consider all officials, from the Viceroy downwards, as sort of gods not to be... challenged. That had all disappeared (Montagu, 125).

Madras had changed 'appallingly', Montagu thought, from the contented state he had witnessed five years previously, an impression confirmed to him by Mrs Henry Whitehead, the bishop's wife, whom he called 'a very clever woman, very much loved in Madras'. In the Madras of 1917, Mrs Whitehead and Montagu agreed, 'the English hate the Indians, the Indians hate the English, and this new violent opposition of the Brahmans to the non-Brahmans has become the guiding principle' (113–14).

Annie Besant impressed Montagu, who told Chelmsford she should have been invited to a garden party the Pentlands had given. When the viceroy passed on the remark to Pentland, the governor replied, 'Most of the Europeans would have walked off the grounds.'[20]

Led by Welby, the British in Madras distrusted Montagu. His being a Jew was held against him, and he was accused of pro-Brahmin bias (Irschick, 67).

Unsympathetic to communal representation for 'backward' classes, Montagu thought that the Justice Party leaders who called on him did not seem 'backward' in wealth, social standing or education. In his diary, he called one of them, Dr T. M. Nair, the *Justice* editor, 'eloquent and vigorous' but with 'a bee in his bonnet'. In a bizarre gambit, Nair had tried to convince Montagu that 'the Home Rule movement was financed by German money' (Montagu, 127).

Born in a Malayali family in bilingual Palghat (Palakkad) in the presidency's Malabar district, Taravath Madhavan Nair (1868–1919) studied medicine in Madras, Edinburgh and Paris before practising in Madras and entering politics as a Congressman. Holding Brahmins responsible for an electoral reverse, he left the Congress in 1916 and became one of SILF's founders.

Familiar with Sanskrit, a fluent speaker in English, and an excellent Malayalam writer, Nair was always found in Western attire, a practice yet to spread among South Indian men. In a series of articles in *Justice* on 'Political Reconstruction in India', he argued that British authority had kept India united. Demanding its early withdrawal would invite anarchy (Irschick, 73). For months in 1918 and the following year, he lobbied for the non-Brahmin cause in England, where he died of heart seizure in July 1919.

On 2 July 1918, the eagerly anticipated reform scheme had come out, everyone calling it 'Montford', after the secretary of state and viceroy pair. Rejecting proportional communal representation except for Muslims and Sikhs, it proposed for provinces a 'dyarchy' where authority over defence, police, land revenue and other 'reserved subjects' would lie with Empire-appointed officers, while Indians elected under a restricted franchise would look after 'transferred subjects' like local self-government, education and sanitation, all supervised by a governor chosen in London.

It was not Home Rule, only a modest advance towards it. And while the Madras Presidency's non-Brahmins too did not get what they wanted, the scheme gave them scope. In 1920, when the first elections following Montford (and its child, the Government of India Act of 1919) were held in the presidency, 29 out of 98 elected places in a house of 127 were filled from improvised non-Brahmin constituencies.

Only those with land, property or taxable income could vote. Other constituencies, fewer and also improvised, were labelled 'Muslim', 'non-Muslim', 'Indian Christian', 'Anglo–Indian' and 'European'. Of the 29 nominated members, 5 came from designated 'untouchable' castes.

Annie Besant's influence in Indian or Madras politics stopped growing after 1918. Unable to communicate in an Indian language, she did not become a mass leader. Her white skin attracted many Indians for a while until events made it a liability. And the year 1919 would see the inauguration, linked to Madras, of a more dramatic way in which large numbers could directly fight for self-rule.

But even if others led later marches to the Promised Land, those marches would owe something to the 'Home Rule' platform raised by a fearless Irishwoman.

The 'linguistic' current had not stopped flowing. While the Telugu country did not witness any clear counterpart of the bid in the Tamil country to nail its language to South India or its Brahmins to North India, it saw disquiet of a different kind.

Convened in May 1913 in Bapatla, the Andhra Mahajana Sabha (AMS) complained that Fort St George 'did not attend to the needs of the Telugu districts to the same extent as it attended to the Tamil districts'.[21] While a separate province for the Telugu districts was not formally asked for, a separate university for Telugus was demanded.

Unease regarding their future in a coast-dominated Telugu province was expressed in the Rayalaseema districts, but it was allayed. Meeting in Vijayawada in the following year, the AMS resolved in favour of an Andhra province. The resolution was reiterated at AMS gatherings in 1915 (in Vizag) and in 1916 (in Kakinada), hinterland participants from Rayalaseema concurring.

Repeating its request for an Andhra university, the AMS heard in 1916 this prescient statement from K. R. V. Krishna Rao, the zamindar of Polavaram:

> Territorial redistribution of all the provinces of India on linguistic and ethnic basis...for the creation of a federated India...will have to be done ultimately.[22]

During Montagu's 1917 Madras visit, a group of Telugu leaders called on him and on Viceroy Chelmsford to ask for a separate province of the presidency's Telugu districts. The delegation included Nyapati Subbarao Pantulu of Rajahmundry, Konda Venkatappayya of Guntur, Mocherla Ramachandra Rao, and Pattabhi Sitaramayya from Krishna district.[23]

Responding to these sentiments, the Congress created, at its end-1917 Calcutta session, an Andhra Provincial Congress Committee to look after Congress affairs in the Telugu districts.

Inhabiting Mysore and other princely and British-ruled territories, Kannada-speakers found a champion in Bijapur-born Aluru Venkata Rao (1880–1964), who lived in Dharwad in Bombay Presidency and was the author, in 1912, of *Karnataka Gatha Vaibhava,* a book on the Kannadiga past leading up to the Vijayanagara empire.

At the Nagpur Congress of 1920, three years after the emergence of an Andhra Provincial Congress Committee, separate provincial Congress committees for the Karnataka and Kerala linguistic regions were created.

The Tamil world, meanwhile, was hearing calls for linguistic chasteness. Launched in 1915, Maraimalai Adigal's Pure Tamil movement drew on an 1891 Tamil drama, *Manonmaniyam*, 'Madness of the Mind', in which the playwright, P. Sundaram Pillai, praised 'Goddess Tamil' as the 'one primal matter' which remained unchanged even as—claimed the text—'Kannada, joyous Telugu, graceful Malayalam and Tulu' were created out of it.

'The Aryan tongue' would fade away, the play announced, but pure Tamil would endure.

◆

While nationalists debated Montford's pros and cons, or even fancied themselves as ministers in the new councils, the Empire came up with a new 'anti-sedition' law. Named after Sidney Rowlatt, the judge heading the committee that had proposed it, the new law was prompted by fears that Germany, loser in the war that had just ended, or Russia, where the Communist revolution had occurred in 1917, would promote sedition in India.

For times of peace, the Rowlatt law, expressed in two bills, was extreme. Arrests without trial and trials without appeal were authorized, and an Indian with a seditious leaflet in his pocket could face a two-year sentence.

Disturbed as they were by Rowlatt, most nationalist leaders could not take their minds off Montford. But from Ahmedabad in Gujarat, Mohandas Gandhi, who had returned only four years earlier from South Africa, went beyond underlining the threat from Rowlatt. He proposed a precise method for combatting it. In February 1919, he and more than a dozen others* met in Ahmedabad and issued a statement:

> We solemnly affirm that in the event of these Bills becoming law
> and until they are withdrawn we shall refuse civilly to obey these

---

*These included Sarojini Naidu, labour movement pioneer Anasuya Sarabhai, Vallabhbhai Patel, Umar Sobhani (Muslim mill-owner from Bombay) and B. G. Horniman, the British editor of *Bombay Chronicle*.

laws and such other laws as a Committee to be hereafter appointed may think fit, and we further affirm that we will be faithful to truth and refrain from violence to life, person and property.[24]

Gandhi called the signatories 'the Indian covenanters' and their step 'most momentous'. For the first time after 1857, prominent Indians had publicly proclaimed their defiance of British laws. Unlike in 1857, they said it would be nonviolent.

For nonviolent defiance, satyagraha was Gandhi's preferred phrase. Tried by Gandhi and his co-workers in South Africa between 1908 and 1913, in Bihar in 1917 and Gujarat in 1918, satyagraha had fetched fair results. After the Ahmedabad statement on Rowlatt, 'satyagraha sabhas' emerged in many parts of the country.

◆

Wearing khadi, the homespun cloth he was popularizing, Gandhi arrived in Madras in March 1919. He had been invited by Kasturi Ranga Iyengar, *The Hindu*'s proprietor-editor, at the urging of Chakravarti Rajagopalachari or CR, who had recently moved to the city and rented a home owned by Iyengar on Cathedral Road. It was there that Gandhi stayed for five days.

Son of a Brahmin village munsif and educated in Bangalore and Madras, CR (1878–1972) became a successful lawyer in the city of Salem. Like VOC and Bharati, he attended the 1907 Surat Congress and supported Tilak over the moderates' leader, Gopal Krishna Gokhale. Hearing in 1913 of the Gandhi-led struggle of South Africa's Indians, CR sent money for it via Gokhale, who until his death in 1915 was Gandhi's friend and mentor.

In 1916, before Gandhi had tried any satyagraha in India, CR implied in an article in *Indian Review* that it was likely to work in India.[25] Two years later, when he was chairman of the Salem municipality, CR was attacked in letters in *The Hindu* for allowing an 'untouchable' to open the water-tap at the Brahmin quarter. A Brahmin friend asked him, 'Do you wish to kill my grandmother? She has not eaten for two days.' CR did not yield, and resistance died down.[26]

Gandhi had visited Madras before 1919, starting with 1896, when as a twenty-seven-year-old he travelled across India with his 'Green Pamphlet' on the travails of South Africa's Indians. A Madras audience hearing him apparently went 'wild with enthusiasm', *The Hindu* covered his speech at length, and thousands of extra copies of the pamphlet had to be printed.

Almost two decades later, in April 1915, a Gandhi back in India for good spoke to a Madras audience of what South Africa's Tamil and Telugu satyagrahis had accomplished. He added:

> Do you know that in the great city of Johannesburg, the Madrasis look on a [fellow] Madrasi as dishonoured if he has not passed through the jails once or twice? (*Collected Works*, 13: 52)

When in February 1916 he again visited Madras, Gandhi attacked the evil of untouchability in memorable language:

> Every affliction that we labour under in this sacred land is a fit and proper punishment for this great and indelible crime that we are committing.[27]

On 22 March 1919, word reached Madras that, disregarding pleas from eminent Indians, the viceroy had signed one of the Rowlatt Bills into an Act. Early the following morning, Gandhi came up with a response: a Sunday of opposition across India when everyone unhappy with Rowlatt would suspend work or business, fast for the day, and attend protest meetings. Encouraged by CR's positive response to his thought, Gandhi issued a public appeal, and on Sunday, 6 April, many cities across India, including Madras, responded with unprecedented enthusiasm.

Gandhi had read the country's mood. In Calcutta, two lakh gathered. In Delhi, where the protest day was observed a week earlier, Hindus and Muslims showed solidarity, and Mahatma Munshiram, later known as Swami Shraddhanand, was invited to speak in a mosque. In the North-West Frontier Province, twenty-eight-year-old Abdul Ghaffar Khan organized a rally in Utmanzai, about 25 miles east of the Khyber Pass.

As for Madras, an intelligence officer named Moore informed Fort St George that the rally that day on the beach was 'unanimously considered to have been the largest gathering...on such an occasion in Madras'. Moore observed that the humblest obeyed the call: 'Vendors of curd were not seen and even the women who sell rice cakes in the morning did not do so today.'[28]

For perhaps the first time, India had witnessed a nationwide political demonstration. Using an honorific that Tagore had popularized, CR wrote in an article in *The Hindu* published the next day:

> The fiat of the Satyagraha Mahatma has been observed by all of India, by the high and the low, as if he had all the armies and police forces...of the Indian government behind his word.[29]

Since Rowlatt was above all an attack on free speech, an unregistered 'newspaper' called *Satyagrahi* was produced and sold in several cities. Forty-three-year-old Vallabhbhai Patel litho-copied issues of the journal in his home in Ahmedabad, and forty-year-old CR did likewise in his Madras home.

The police commissioner informed Fort St George that CR's home had become the Madras branch of the satyagraha movement and that CR was the secretary of the city satyagraha sabha. Others, the commissioner added, had been 'reluctant to accept the nomination.'[30]

In response to Gandhi's appeal, many men and women fasted, including in Madras. Books banned by the British, including Gandhi's *Hind Swaraj*, first published in 1910, and Thoreau's *Civil Disobedience* (from the previous century), were sold. In Allahabad, twenty-nine-year-old Jawaharlal Nehru, indifferent thus far to Gandhi's approach, joined the local satyagraha sabha.

In a leaflet dated 12 May 1919, CR claimed that the struggle was for long-term principles:

> Let it be clearly understood that we would oppose such legislation vesting in the executive Government the absolute right to suspect and imprison without trial even if the Government is democratic and purely Indian, and not bureaucratic and foreign.[31]

◆

Something ominous was in the air. The Rowlatt Act had only given legal form to the sentiments that persons like Welby and Lord and Lady Pentland had expressed during Montagu's visit. After sixty calm years in much of India, the minds of its white rulers were being invaded by a spectre of violent Indian hostility.

This was particularly true of men like Michael O'Dwyer, the

Governor of Punjab, who claimed that 'the interests of the rural masses' required him to resist political reform. To him, representative government was something which the 'Indian masses...neither desire nor understand'.[32] Montford was a blunder, and any disturbance called for immediate suppression.

In O'Dwyer's Punjab, a dozen cities, including the two largest, Lahore and Amritsar, responded with enthusiasm to the Rowlatt protest day. Hindus, Muslims and Sikhs came together for meetings and processions, with the Punjab police privately noting that 'opposition to the Rowlatt Act and admiration of Gandhi are practically universal'.[33] O'Dwyer's response was to warn in 'most emphatic' terms that the Punjab which did not see disorder during the War 'shall not be disturbed in time of peace'.[34]

Punjabis were indeed restive, partly because the War had raised prices. When, responding to requests from leaders in Lahore and Amritsar, Gandhi journeyed to Punjab to maintain discipline, O'Dwyer had him arrested at the border on the night of 9 April and put on a goods train back to Bombay.

That deportation, and the arrest of leaders in Amritsar and Lahore, sparked off an angry demonstration in Amritsar on 10 April that led to the killing of five Englishmen, including three bank managers and a railway officer, and an equally tragic assault on a British missionary, Miss Marcella Sherwood, while she was cycling to shut down her schools.

Three days later, on Sunday, 13 April, the Jallianwala Massacre occurred, ordered by Brigadier Reginald Dyer. The story of that event, which took at least 379 Indian lives, need not be repeated here.

Governor O'Dwyer gave unhesitating support to the brigadier. The 1925 book in which O'Dwyer would defend his actions, *India As I Knew It*, confirms that in April 1919 it was panic, not facts on the ground, that produced in British eyes the picture of an imminent revolution in which Afghans, Russians and Germans were also supposedly involved. At once 1857 was recalled, and protecting 'threatened' British women and children became the primary concern of civilian and military officers.

He had told the police, writes O'Dwyer, 'that if they had to fire, there was to be no firing in the air'.[35]

Later in the year, when Punjabis seemed afraid to contribute to a Jallianwala memorial, Gandhi said he would, if needed, sell his ashram in Ahmedabad for it. Earlier, when Gandhi learnt that Indians wanting to use the lane where Miss Sherwood had been assaulted had been ordered to crawl on their hands and knees, he said that the crawling order was worse than the massacre.

In December 1919, when the INC met for its annual session in Amritsar,* Gandhi successfully insisted that condemnation of the massacre of 13 April had to be joined by frank acknowledgment of the assault on white lives on 10 April.

In 1919, the Empire stiffened, and Gandhi attained a special place in Indian minds, including in the south. The protest he initiated had become nationwide. Open and announced ahead of time, it was meant to be nonviolent. It bridged divides, enlisting Hindus and Muslims, the rich and the poor. It drew large numbers and upheld Indian self-respect. And it helped Indians, in their contest with the Empire, to occupy the moral high ground.

There was a negative side. Violence had occurred, and hundreds of lives had been lost in Amritsar. In July, Gandhi said in a speech in Gujarat's Nadiad town that launching a satyagraha before training a cadre to keep it nonviolent was 'a Himalayan miscalculation' on his part.[36] That admission seemed to add to Gandhi's stature and strengthen a nationwide belief that a fearless yet dignified way of fighting the Empire had been found.

◆

At the Amritsar Congress, Gandhi, supported by Jinnah, persuaded the Congress to give qualified acceptance to Montford, and the year 1919 passed without Gandhi giving up totally on an Empire in which, relying on its periodic rhetoric of religious liberty and racial equality, he had placed high hopes while in South Africa.

In 1918, he had candidly confessed to his close companion and secretary Mahadev Desai: 'My mind refuses to be loyal to the British Empire and I have to make a strenuous effort to stem the tide of rebellion.' 'But,' he added, 'a feeling deep down in me persists that India's good lies in [the] British connection, and so I force myself to love them.'[37]

---

*Following a schedule set long before the April carnage.

This changed in 1920. One big reason was Britain's refusal to admonish O'Dwyer and a House of Lords resolution defending Dyer. The Empire had become unworthy. The other major reason was England's treatment of defeated Germany's ally Turkey, the world's leading Muslim power.

India's Muslims had been anxious for more than a year about Turkey's future. On 14 May 1920, their worst fears were confirmed. It was revealed that a secret pact between the British and the French would place Islam's sacred sites, Mecca, Medina, Karbala, Najaf and Jerusalem, under a Christian-European umbrella.* Hitherto the suzerain for these Arab sites had been the Turkish Sultan, the khalifa of the world's Sunni Muslims.

To India's shocked Muslims, this transfer of authority seemed a harsh if not hostile act. Their leaders who had celebrated the separate electorate introduced in 1909 thought they had been tricked, and Muslim Indians seemed ready to oppose British rule.

With all Indians feeling let down, even abused, Gandhi sensed a 'once-in-a-hundred-years' opportunity (he used the phrase more than once in speeches in August 1920)[38] to build a Hindu–Muslim alliance and strike for Swaraj, Gandhi's preferred phrase for independence.

If forced to choose between India's Muslims and the imperial power, Gandhi the Hindu was not in any dilemma. Helpful at times, the Briton was always a visitor from afar. Difficult at times, the Muslim was a permanent and close neighbour. Moreover, Gandhi also now saw an opportunity to, as he put it privately to Mahadev Desai, 'win [Muslims] over to love and nonviolence'.[39]

From early 1920 onwards, he presented 'Nonviolent Non-cooperation' as a strategy to all willing to fight, including the Congress, the Muslim League and a Khilafat body formed by indignant Muslim leaders. The last-named body was the first to embrace Non-cooperation, yet before long all were on board.

The range of support for a fight on both issues was remarkably wide, and backers included staunch Hindus such as Lokmanya Tilak, Swami Shraddhanand from Delhi/Punjab, and Lala Lajpat Rai. In the fiercely anti-British climate of 1919 and 1920, the great majority of

---

*The secret Sykes–Picot Pact of 1916 between the British and French foreign ministers was expanded in 1920 into the Treaty of Sevres.

India's Hindus too had no difficulty choosing between their Muslim neighbours and the Empire.

Muslim leaders like the UP's Ali brothers, Shaukat and Muhammad, Calcutta's Abul Kalam Azad, and Delhi's Hakim Ajmal Khan and Mukhtar Ahmed Ansari became popular all-India figures, often speaking at Gandhi's side or along with other Hindu leaders.

◆

Non-cooperation's leading South Indian champion was CR, who shared all of Gandhi's goals and seemed quicker than others to comprehend his strategies and their impact. Two days before the Amritsar massacre, *The Hindu* carried CR's criticism of Gandhi's deportation from Punjab and his remark that if anyone could 'keep the satyagraha movement true to its principles, it is Mr. Gandhi'.[40]

In August 1919, at a conference in Trichy, CR initiated a resolution asking that Islam's holy places remain with the Khalifa, pointed out that some Muslim newspapers in India had been 'gagged', and warned that 'Muslim feeling in India ran high'.[41] In December, he attended the Amritsar Congress. Accompanied by Bihar's Rajendra Prasad and Gandhi's nineteen-year-old son Devadas, he also went to Patna before returning to Madras.

Writing to Devadas on 28 February 1920, CR noted that 'the Khilafat question is assuming most serious proportions',[42] and at a meeting in Madras on 9 April, Muslim merchants gave CR blank cheques for agitations over Khilafat.

In April 1920, Gandhi acknowledged that many leaders attracted by Non-cooperation over Khilafat did 'not believe in my doctrine of nonviolence to the full extent' and that they were not 'free from hatred'. He hoped, however, that by 'joining my love with their hatred' he could 'diminish the intensity of that hatred'[43]. In May, he wrote in a similar vein:

> I told them that non-cooperation would be possible only if they gave up the idea of violence. Even if there was a single murder by any of us or at our instance, I would leave.[44]

What would Non-cooperation entail? Returning the Empire's titles and medals. Boycott of foreign cloth. Boycott also of the Empire's councils, which Montford had made a little more appealing, and of other attractive colonial institutions, including law courts and colleges. Even, at some point, resignation from government offices, and perhaps, at a further point, from the Empire's police and army.

There were positive targets as well. For the Congress, these were two million charkhas, one crore rupees for a Tilak Swaraj Fund, and one crore Congress members.

All this Gandhi indicated as the year progressed. As eager responses piled up, he declared, before Congress took a position on it, that Non-cooperation would be launched on 1 August.

Elections to Montford's new provincial councils were due in November. In Madras Presidency, the Justice Party was keen to contest and win, which to some in the Congress in the south was an additional reason for entering the fray. Yet Gandhi was clear that Non-cooperation applied to councils and could not be postponed.

On 1 August, he and numerous others returned imperial honours— Gandhi had received medals for organizing ambulances in South Africa and in London. Some, including Hakim Ajmal Khan, had returned their trophies well before August.

Earlier, on 1 August, Tilak had died in Bombay, worn out by diabetes and his years in prison. Always watchful on behalf of Hindus, Tilak, too, had said, at the end of May that 'Hindus would support' Muslim decisions on Khilafat.[45] Calling Tilak 'a giant among men', 'the idol of his people' and 'the lion' whose voice was 'hushed', Gandhi, who was in Bombay, shouldered the bier and stood beside the incinerating flames before proceeding to return his medals.[46]

To some, it was a visual transfer of leadership.

From 1 August, many began tossing away their legal careers. In the south, these included CR and a few younger lawyers, and before long, barrister Tanguturi Prakasam from the Telugu country, whose performance as a defence lawyer in the Ashe murder case had won him acclaim. Elsewhere their ranks would include Motilal Nehru, Chitta Ranjan Das, Vallabhbhai Patel, Rajendra Prasad and Jawaharlal Nehru.

There were lifestyle changes, towards simplicity. Despite its roughness and thickness, most Non-cooperators took to khadi, the livery of revolt and identification with the lowly. Often, so did their families.

In September, a special Congress session called in Calcutta debated Non-cooperation. Some of Montford's former foes argued that councils should be entered and wrecked from within. But the national mood was compelling, and younger leaders like Patel, CR, Prasad, Jawaharlal Nehru and Azad were firmly in favour of Non-cooperation, which Calcutta endorsed by a large majority.

Its resolution asked for a surrender of the Empire's honours and titles, a boycott of the Raj's councils and of the elections due in November, a boycott of foreign goods, and a gradual withdrawal by students and lawyers from the Raj's schools, colleges and courts.

Three months later, when the Congress met for its annual session in Nagpur, most seniors too had come around, and Non-cooperation was proclaimed with only a handful of votes against.

Nagpur was notable for three other things. First, Jinnah left the Congress, objecting to a change the session had made in its objective. Instead of 'Self-government within the Empire', the goal now was, simply, 'Swaraj'.

Second, adopting a new structure that Amritsar had asked Gandhi to design, the Congress decided to put in place democratically elected committees at all levels—village, town, taluk, district, province and all-India—and a year-round working committee chosen by an elected president. Provinces were linguistic areas not necessarily coinciding with existing imperial provinces.

Third, the Congress resolved that opposition to untouchability would be part of its political agenda. At the Nagpur session, CR was raised to national leadership and made one of the Congress's three general secretaries, M. A. Ansari of Delhi and Motilal Nehru being the other two.

◆

Another South Indian embracing Non-cooperation was E. V. Ramasami Naicker (1879–1973), born in a merchant family in semi-arid, cotton-growing Erode, which (like CR's Salem) lay in the rocky middle of the lower peninsula's hinterland.

Contemporaries at birth and raised in geographical proximity, CR and EVR (the latter a year behind at both ends of life), were to be comrades for a while, political foes for much longer, and personal friends until the end.

Begun with traditional earnestness, EVR's 1904 journey to Varanasi,

258   MODERN SOUTH INDIA

where he experienced humiliations upon being discovered a non-Brahmin, and witnessed hypocrisies, proved consequential. Joining local politics on returning to Erode, he became (again in parallel with CR) chairman of the town's municipality. Encouraging a widowed young niece to remarry, he signalled what would be an atypical, pioneering, and life-long concern for women's rights.

The spirit of the year capturing him, EVR joined the Congress in 1919 and attended, like CR, the Amritsar Congress at the end of that year. Active in the Madras Presidency Association, in 1920 and 1921 he picketed liquor shops, courting arrest. In 1929, as part of his anti-caste crusade, he dropped the Naicker surname, though others continued to use it for him.

Also prominent in the south were a pair of gifted Brahmin lawyers and orators, S. Srinivasa Iyengar and S. Satyamurti. Some months after Jallianwala occurred, Iyengar, who was the presidency's Advocate General, created a sensation by leaving his prestigious post and joining the Congress. A nationalist from earlier years, Satyamurti felt restricted, as did Iyengar, by the policy of boycotting the Raj's councils.

However, supported by EVR, Varadarajulu Naidu and others, CR ensured that the Madras Congress boycotted the elections held in 1920 for the presidency's first post-Montford council. One result was an easy win for the Justice Party, which the Calcutta-based information bureau of the government of India interpreted as 'a momentous revolution'.

For the first time in the history of India, the lower castes of Madras have asserted themselves against the intellectual oligarchy of the upper, and have seized political power in their own hands.[47]

In September 1921, the Justice ministry, led by the previously mentioned Raja of Panagal, implemented an important electoral commitment. By 'the first Communal G. O.' (Government Order), officers were instructed 'to divide the appointments of all grades in the several departments of government', and in all districts, among the different castes, which were classified as 'Brahmans, non-Brahmans, Indian Christians, Muhammadans, Europeans & Anglo–Indians, and Others'. Henceforth, only one out of seven government jobs could go to a Brahmin.

A year later, a 2nd Communal G.O. directed that the principle of distribution among castes/groups should apply 'both at recruitment and at promotion'.[48]

Although it caused heartburn in Brahmins, communal representation was what the bulk of the people wanted. Speaking for Congress non-Brahmins, the Madras Presidency Association had persuaded the Madras Congress to accept its principle in 1919. In August of that year, *The Hindu* quoted an MPA leader, Kesava Pillai, as saying that CR supported communal representation.[49]

As Non-cooperation unfolded in the south, Srinivasa Iyengar and *The Hindu*'s Kasturi Ranga Iyengar opposed initiatives from CR, who, however, was backed by EVR, Kalyanasundara Mudaliar, Varadarajulu Naidu and the Tamil Nadu Congress Committee. In a ten-day period in the 1921 summer, Congress membership in the Tamil country went up from 8,000 to 30,000.

Large-scale picketing of liquor shops (in Erode led by EVR) produced results. Fort St George informed Delhi in February 1921 of a 'considerable' revenue decrease, and in August of a drop 'through the Presidency' in the demand for toddy-shop licences.[50]

◆

Hindu–Muslim partnership was Non-cooperation's strongest card. Replacing Chelmsford as viceroy in April 1921, Lord Reading wrote to his son of the 'bridge over the gulf between Hindu and Muslim' that was being raised.[51] The bridge was shaken in the second half of 1921 by events in Malabar talukas to the south of Calicut and north of Ponnani: Ernad and Valluvanad.

Combining their version of Islam with violent opposition to the Empire and its supposed allies, the Mappilas of Malabar threw a question mark against the stability of a joint Hindu–Muslim front.

For two centuries after Vasco da Gama's visits in the 1490s, the Malayalam coast had seen continual European–Muslim clashes in which Calicut's Hindu ruler, the Zamorin, often supported the Muslims, many of whom had Arab blood and were called Mappilas, from the Malayalam for son-in-law. These Muslims formed the merchant community in Malabar.

Enjoying the highest social rank, Malabar's Nambudiri Brahmins were landowners as well. Neither they nor the Nairs, who were mostly substantial tenants or soldiers or both, did much trading, whether within or beyond the shores. Muslim communities active in trade grew along the coast and along rivers flowing from the hills into the sea.

Linked to these merchants by their religion and its mosques were much poorer Muslims—peasants, field labourers, porters and others. Also called Mappila, most were descendants of converts from Hindu low castes. Like the latter, these Muslims had little or no land or were tenants removable at will.

Islam had played a conspicuous part in Malabar's political story. Writing *Tuhfat-al-Mujahidin* (Gift to the Holy Warriors) in the 1580s, Zayn al-Din al-Ma'bari said he hoped 'to inspire the faithful to undertake a jihad against the worshippers of the Cross'.[52] His Mappilas must have responded, for a text from Arabia's southern coast described their sea-fight in 1659–60 with European ships and spoke of the former as 'people of great courage and zeal for Islam'.[53]

Later, under Haidar and Tipu, Mappilas found new influence. In Ernad and Valluvanad, where many from poor castes had converted to Islam, they constituted well over half the population. Between 1788 and 1791, before the British forced Tipu Sultan to withdraw from Malabar, tens of thousands of Nambudiris and Nayars fled south to escape the sultan's edict threatening them all with conversion.[54]

After British takeover in the early 1790s, these Hindu high castes returned to Ernad and Valluvanad and regained their lands, estates and social power. Mappilas not only lost the political influence they had won under Tipu, they also lost battles in British-run courts to retain houses, shops, mosques and fields held by them on subordinate tenures from Nambudiris and Nayars.[55]

Bolstered by memories of Mappila dominance, periodic Mappila 'outbreaks' occurred during the British time. Some British officers blamed innate Mappila fanaticism for these violent outbursts, others pointed to the subordination of Mappilas in an area where, socially and economically, Nambudiris were at the top, Nairs in the middle, and Mappilas and the Hindu low castes at the bottom.

◆

Five miles off the coast and 20 or so miles south of Calicut, the town of Tirurangadi had seen many battles. Mappilas sought inspiration there from mosques associated with martyrs and from sites where martyrs were buried. Forced by the British to migrate to West Asia in 1852, one of their heroes, Sayyid Fazl, who died in Istanbul in 1900, had lived in Tirurangadi, where his memory remained alive.

In and around Tirurangadi and Manjeri, which was Ernad's chief town, the soil in 1921 was more than fertile for Non-cooperation and Khilafat, but not for nonviolence.

In August of the previous year, Gandhi had made a visit to Calicut though not to the talukas to its south. With him was Shaukat, the older of the Ali brothers. While Gandhi spoke on Non-cooperation, Shaukat Ali 'connected his appeal with Gandhi's policy of nonviolence'.[56]

A couple of speeches in Calicut were not going to change psychology in Ernad. When, in February 1921, three leaders from Calicut, K. Madhavan Nair (secretary of the Congress in Kerala), U. Gopala Menon and Moideen Koya, and a Madras Khilafat leader, Yakub Hassan, were arrested for objecting to an order against their speaking in Ernad, the reaction was heated.

The public called these men 'the Kerala patriots'. Across Malabar, 230 Congress sabhas emerged to protest the arrests.[57] Other responses were less constructive, in fact ominous. In Calicut, about 12,000 Mappilas, including many from Ernad and some armed with knives and sticks, confronted the district magistrate.

Accompanied by K. P. Kesava Menon, who was practising law in Madras, CR arrived in Calicut on a brief visit. As INC general secretary, he asked Menon to succeed Madhavan Nair as the Congress secretary in Kerala. Returning to Madras, CR urged the public 'not to fall into the trap set by repression and commit violence'[58].

Following the arrests, voices were raised in Malabar for tenants' rights and also on behalf of landlords. Eviction suits against agitating tenants were threatened. In April, Besant made a visit to Malabar but was shouted down by Non-cooperators and Khilafatists. The Madras *Mail* published 'inflammatory' reports, but a pro-British, Malayalam journal in Calicut, *Mitavadi*, asked landlords to see the writing on the wall.[59]

◆

Competing demands and interests were at play, but one collision soon filled the entire Malabar stage. Almost suddenly, Mappilas rose for a religious fight against what they saw as an anti-Muslim colonial government and its presumed allies. Everything else was pushed into the background, including Non-cooperation, the Congress, Hindu–Muslim unity, the cause of Turkey, and tenants' rights.

On 8 June, Ali Musaliyar, a religious teacher in Tirurangadi, took 300 or more agitated Mappilas in a procession from a mosque to a site where martyrs had been buried. On 1 August, thousands of Mappilas assembled threateningly before the palace in Pukkottur (also in Ernad) of the Raja of Nilambur, a Nambudiri landlord.

Local Mappila leaders and a police inspector managed to disperse the crowd, but the district collector, E. F. Thomas, aware of previous outbreaks and of a spurt that summer in the manufacture of swords and knives, informed Fort St George that the situation had gone 'beyond district officials', and he asked for reinforcements.

Early in the morning of 20 August, a detachment of Gurkhas together with the Malabar police swept into Tirurangadi and arrested several men, but Musaliyar escaped. After armed counter-attacks by Mappilas in Tirurangadi and the sacking of a nearby town's railway station and post office, Thomas handed over power to the troops' commanding officer.[60]

The military was in charge now. Obtaining official permission, Kesava Menon, the Congress secretary, met Musaliyar in his hideout. By Menon's account, the meeting took place in 'an atmosphere of fear and uncertainty'. Asked to advise, Menon recommended surrender. Musaliyar remained silent but his 'general', Kunhalavi, 'a strong and sturdy man with a sword in one hand and another one hanging from his shoulder', seems to have said: 'Never. I will die fighting like a man.'[61]

Collector Thomas would write that the 20 August attack on Tirurangadi sparked off 'open rebellion' including 'pillage, looting, murder and forcible conversion' and an 'outburst of fanaticism throughout Ernad, Valluvanad and Ponnani, directed first against European officials and non-officials and latterly against Hindus'.[62]

Summoned from Colombo, the royal navy's *Comus* arrived on 25 August and confronted Calicut. Ninety of its sailors marched in town. If trouble arose in Calicut, the ship, it was decided, would 'at once bombard the Moplah quarter'.[63]

On 28 August, 400 Mappilas were killed in a single battle in Pukkottur, displaying, as a telegram from Fort St George would put it, 'their traditional ferocity and eagerness for death'.[64]

On 30 August, when Tirurangadi was again attacked by the British, Ali Musaliyar was among the thirty-eight who surrendered. Twenty-four were killed. Musaliyar was hanged on 2 November.

Calicut remained free of 'trouble' but rebellion intensified in the two talukas. A few Mappila leaders started calling themselves rajas. One of them, Variakunnath Kunjahammed Haji, declared himself 'Khilafat King' and even issued passports.

Frenzied Mappilas massacred an unknown number of Nambudiris and Nairs, gruesomely in several cases. In Tuvur in eastern Ernad, thirty-three Hindus and two Mappilas were put to death in September for having aided British troops halting there. Other Hindus may have been killed for alleged injustice towards tenants, or in the name of establishing a Muslim kingdom, but terrorizing civilians into refusing to help the government seemed the main motivation.[65]

Many Hindus fled from their homes, but the British named a few Hindus too as associates in Mappila atrocities. A man like M. P. Narayana Menon, head of the Ernad Taluka Congress, was reported to have used his contacts with Mappila leaders to save English lives, but that did not prevent the authorities from arresting him. Menon was imprisoned for thirteen years, until September 1934.[66]

Writing from the war zone, the Madras army chief, General John Burnett Stuart, said on 24 October 1921 that the chase 'may go on in some districts until every Moplah is either exterminated or arrested'.[67] The next day martial law was imposed in the talukas of Calicut, Ernad, Valluvanad and Ponnani. Two days later, Kurumbranad and Wayanad too were brought under the military net.

A forested terrain enabled Mappila militants to hide and continue the ambush for months. Rebellion continued, guerrilla style, and Mappilas found new heroes, but they were up against a well-armed and relentless force. On 20 January 1922, when Variakunnath Haji was hanged, the revolt effectively ended. On 25 February, martial law was allowed to lapse. Hindus had started returning to their homes from December.

Although Mappilas in north Malabar largely stayed out of the six-month rebellion, a great many in the two talukas and in a third,

Ponnani, were actively involved. According to official numbers, 39,348 rebels surrendered before the end, 5,955 were captured, 2,339 killed and 1,652 wounded. Kesava Menon, however, estimated that as many as 10,000 may have died.[68] The British thought that among the rebels were sepoys who had served in World War I campaigns in the Middle East.[69] On the government side, no more than 43, white and Indian, were killed and 126 wounded.[70]

On 19 November, owing to the jails in Malabar being full, ninety-seven Mappilas and three Hindus were packed inside a railway wagon in Tirur (12 miles south of Tirurangadi) to be sent all the way to Bellary. At 7.15 p.m., the wagon was firmly shut from without. A little more than five hours later, at 12.30 in the night, the wagon was opened at Podanur station near Coimbatore, presumably to give the prisoners water. Most prisoners inside were found dead or half-dead from asphyxiation. Thirty survived, but seventy had died.[71].

For many, the death-wagon would remain the symbol of colonial repression and native loss in Malabar in 1921. Others would remember atrocities against Hindus and forcible conversions. The Arya Samaj, which organized relief and re-conversion, claimed that 1,766 were forced to convert.[72]

Re-conversion was arduous. The penance required for having been forcibly polluted included ingesting five cow products (milk, ghee, curd, urine and dung) each day, and repeating the name of Siva or Narayana a few thousand times daily. The number of days and repetitions went up with the seriousness of the pollution, which ranged from tuft removal to reciting the Kalima, circumcision, cohabitation and eating food cooked by Mappilas.[73]

◆

As to why, among Malabar's subtenants and the landless, the Mappila was more active in 1921 than his Hindu counterpart, the Communist leader and future Kerala chief minister, E. M. S. Namboodiripad, would write in 1943 that for the former it was a question of 'sacred war against the desecrator of his creed'.[74]

A religious tinge was also noticeable in the earlier stir in parts of India over Bengal's partition, which invoked Hindu symbols, yet the dominant note in that stir seemed to be of nationalism, and in scale the violence it triggered was minor.

Most Hindu Congressmen in Malabar felt in 1921 that Mappilas had let the nationalist movement down, but there also was Muslim criticism that when relief finally came via the Congress, only Hindus received it.[75]

The shock and tragedy of the Mappila rebellion did not derail Non-cooperation. Wanting to visit Malabar but aware that the Empire would not allow him to do so, Gandhi was on a southbound train, together with Khilafat leader Maulana Muhammad Ali, when, on 14 September, the latter was arrested in Waltair in the Telugu country.

To this, the response of Gandhi and several close colleagues who met in Bombay (including Calcutta's C. R. Das, who had been elected Congress president for the year, Motilal and Jawaharlal Nehru, Punjab's Lala Lajpat Rai, Gujarat's Vallabhbhai Patel, and Madras's CR) was to intensify their nonviolent struggle.

That month the Congress working committee expressed a 'sense of deep regret over the deeds of violence done by the Mappillas in certain areas of Malabar'.[76] Yet there could be no denying that the rebellion had tapped into the nationwide temper of defiance.

The Malayalam country saw at least one positive outcome of Non-cooperation. In February 1922, Kesava Menon, Madhavan Nair and a few others registered a public limited company in Calicut and brought out *Mathrubhumi*, destined to become one of India's most widely read newspapers.

◆

Elsewhere in India, the Non-cooperation train was picking up speed. Foreign clothing, inclusive of shawls and caps, was flung into flames. Khadi spread. Congress membership rose. The Tilak Fund target was reached.

Across the country, more students walked away from colleges and more lawyers from courts. National colleges opened, including one in Madras. In June 1921, CR announced that thirty-six lawyers practising in the Tamil country and Madras city had left the courts.

When the Empire restricted meetings and speeches, orders were calmly defied, first by hundreds, then by thousands. A prison sentence became a badge of honour. Though the Congress was not banned, its volunteer organizations were. By end-December, more than 20,000 civil resisters were in Indian prisons.

When Fort St George forbade meetings, CR announced via leaflets that he would address a public gathering in Vellore on 14 December. Five thousand heard him. 'Hope you will get maximum penalty,' Gandhi wired him. Given a three-month sentence, he wrote Gandhi, 'I feel I am realizing the object of my life'.[77]

Like many other Non-cooperators courting imprisonment in 1921, CR, forty-three at the time, was an admired man in his world and accustomed to living in a decent place. Jail life with its dark cells, unpleasant smells, coarse food containing hair and dirt, cries from deathrow, and rudeness from prison staff was a hard experience for him.

The diary that CR wrote in Vellore jail* describes how he learnt to cope as also his interactions with fellow-prisoners, including Mappilas from Malabar, and with prison staff. Worried about CR's ability to endure prison, the Mappilas evidently said to him, 'We would gladly spend four more years if that would remit your three months' (Diary, 70).

Four on Vellore jail's deathrow were hanged during CR's three months. The diary records 'their foul abuse and oft-repeated attempts at humour', their 'prayers of desperation' and their 'always sitting close against the cell door, for it is the nearest approach to freedom and light', as also CR's outrage that hanging was performed 'with suddenness and dispatch' without 'a single thought' to whether the condemned man 'may not make peace with God before he yields up his life' (71).

In fellow-prisoners and some of the staff CR found 'devotion and brotherliness' but 'no love such as my heart wants'. He treasured the once-a-month interview for which one or more of his sons came, 'chewed and consumed every line and word' of the monthly letter from his children, and resisted homesickness by contrasting his 'insignificant share of suffering' with what others go through.

Without naming her, CR wrote in his diary of his deceased wife. One evening, 'the sweet music of the village nagaswaram from some happy home in the hamlets lying outside the prison walls brought with

---

*C. Rajagopalachari, Jail Diary, Madras: Rochouse, 1922.

it such an irresistible rush of happy recollections of happy youth, of joy and hope' that CR had to check his mind from 'wander[ing] into the garden of sweet flowers that yield only tears' (68).

> All that I shall say to my God is, if she is anywhere and is still subject to pleasure and pain, keep her happy and free from pain or sadness (69).

After the jailor, an unnamed Indian serving under a white superintendent called Major Anderson, hit a fellow-prisoner, Subba Rao, without provocation, CR got the jailor to apologize before witnesses, at which Subba Rao said, 'Providence brought about the incident so that it may change the jailor's heart'.

'How beautiful,' jotted CR, 'is the path of charity and love' (69–70).

Texts such as CR's *Jail Diary* indicated that impressive qualities resided in the movement into which so many had thrown themselves.

> To refuse to cooperate in the process of reducing ourselves to foreign rule…is the natural law and instinct. We forgot this law… and cast our minds into the terrible slough of unfelt slavery (72).

However, the most-quoted lines from the diary, written in the first quarter of 1922, are these:

> We all ought to know that Swaraj will not at once or I think even for a long time to come be better government or greater happiness for the people. Elections and their corruptions, injustice, and the power and tyranny of wealth and inefficiency of administration will make a hell of life as soon as freedom is given to us. Men will look regretfully back to the old regime of comparative justice, and efficient, peaceful, more or less honest administration. The only thing gained will be that as a race we will be saved from dishonour and subordination (72–73).

◆

A place called Bardoli in Gujarat was in CR's thoughts. That was where a major defiance was to take place any day. Participants for that satyagraha had been carefully prepared by Gandhi, Patel and others. Unruliness in Bombay during a boycott of the visit in November of the Prince of Wales raised a question in Gandhi's mind, but he had chosen to go ahead.

By February, the all-India number for arrests had gone up to 30,000. The viceroy and the Indian public were notified that the Bardoli challenge was about to be mounted.

However, when, shortly after raising slogans of 'Victory to Mahatma Gandhi', demonstrators in Chauri Chaura in eastern UP killed twenty-two policemen trapped in a fire, Gandhi knew that Bardoli had to be given up. Not only that: he would suspend all aggressive elements of Non-cooperation and ask the country to focus for a time only on 'the constructive programme'.

On 13 February, EVR came to the Vellore prison for the stipulated monthly interview and informed CR of Gandhi's decision. A shocked CR wrote in his diary:

> In spite of my tenderest and most complete attachment to my master and the ideal he stands for, I fail to see why there should be a call for stopping our struggle for birthrights [because of] every distant and unconnected outburst (*Diary*, 67).

Two mornings later, the jailor roused CR before dawn and rubbed in the humiliation. 'Non-cooperation has gone to sleep,' he announced. When CR's term ended on 20 March, Major Anderson accompanied him through the gates and asked if the jail didn't look nicer from outside. 'The inside is not so bad,' replied CR.

♦

By this time Gandhi was in prison himself, sentenced for six years. Suspension of defiance had proved demoralizing, and the Empire felt it could jail Gandhi without inviting serious unrest.

India's nationalists were not clear about next steps. The constructive programme that Gandhi had urged after Chauri Chaura—promoting khadi and Hindu–Muslim unity, opposing untouchability and liquor—seemed dull to most foes of Empire.

On the other hand, the Empire's councils, where speeches could be made, and headlines earned, looked attractive. The idea of capturing the councils, if only to 'wreck from within', appealed to many leaders who had completed their sentences and were free. C. R. Das, the

Congress president, and Motilal Nehru, who had chaired in Amritsar in 1919, led the bid to change Congress policy. From the south, Srinivasa Iyengar and Satyamurti provided support.

Opposed to a major policy change while Gandhi was behind bars, CR led the 'no changers', as they were called. Confrontation took place in December 1922 at the Congress session in Gaya in Bihar. There, with Das chairing, CR's resolution retaining council-boycott was passed 1,740 to 890.

Also debated at Gaya was a proposal by the so-called 'pro-changers' to boycott British goods, a tactic that had been resisted by Gandhi, who preferred a non-racial boycott of all foreign cloth. Now the mood was more negative, and CR had to fight very hard, but he was successful again, though with a smaller vote margin.

'Great was [the no-changers'] enthusiasm,' Subhas Bose would later comment, 'and the hero of the day was the Madras leader, Mr. Rajagopalachari.'[78]

In February 1924, four years before his sentence was to end, Gandhi was released after surgery for appendicitis. With nationalist fervour dissipated, the Empire felt confident he could do no harm. The freed Gandhi focused on Congress unity and his 'constructive programme', especially the fight against untouchability.

That question was gaining notice. In Madras city, a major strike in 1921 in two British-owned textile mills had sparked off a clash between caste Hindus remaining on strike and 'untouchables' (termed Adi-Dravidas) who had returned to work, followed by a clash between caste Hindu workers and the police. Deaths in the clash prompted *Justice* to accuse the police of 'undue pampering of Adi-Dravidas'.

The charge revealed the fragility of an understanding the Justice Party had tried to build with Adi-Dravidas. In 1923, M. C. Rajah, principal spokesman for the 'untouchables' in the Madras legislative council, alleging 'high-handed poisonous action' against 'the Depressed Classes', announced his Adi-Dravida group's exit from the Justice Party.[79]

◆

Untouchability received greater attention in 1924 and 1925 because of a prolonged and onerous effort in the Travancore principality to let Ezhavas, other 'low' castes and 'untouchables' *merely approach*, without entering it, the hoary Siva temple in Vaikom, about 115 miles north of Thiruvananthapuram.[80]

Travancore's princely family governed this Siva temple and the four roads around it, which were open to caste Hindus, non-Hindus and animals, but not to the Hindu world's low castes and outcastes. Begun on 30 March 1924, the Vaikom Satyagraha, a by-product of the Non-cooperation Movement, witnessed disciplined attempts by Ezhavas and their higher-caste Nair comrades to walk on the prohibited roads. Orthodoxy, led by Brahmin Nambudiris, opposed the satyagrahis, who were arrested by the Travancore police or blocked by barriers on the roads.

In protest, and hoping also to affect orthodox minds, the satyagrahis stood in front of the barriers, plying the charkha. When exceptionally heavy rains inundated the roads, the satyagrahis remained standing in waist-deep water to continue their protest. Accounts of their staying power stirred much of India at a time when the Non-cooperation Movement was no longer making headlines.

Released from prison in February, Gandhi involved himself in the satyagraha on the urgings of, among others, the Ezhava leader, T. K. Madhavan, and a Nair teacher associated with the newly started *Mathrubhumi*, K. Kelappan. Both Madhavan and Kelappan were part of an anti-untouchability committee formed in Vaikom.

Arrests of local leaders and frequent exhaustion of funds tested morale but did not break it. In November 1924, large numbers of Hindus in the Malayalam country marched towards Thiruvananthapuram in two converging processions.

One, going southward, proceeded from Vaikom, and the other, going north, from Kottar. Both marches maintained perfect discipline. In Thiruvananthapuram, twelve of the marchers presented to the Maharani regent a mammoth petition, signed by more than 25,000 persons, for opening Vaikom's temple roads to all.

Unprecedentedly, many Namubudiris and Nairs had joined the march from Vaikom, in organizing which a major role was played by Mannath Padmanabhan, founder, ten years earlier, of the Nair Service Society.

Welcomed on their route by Ezhava women, the marchers ate rice offered by 'untouchable' Pulayas and called, in his ashram, on the venerated Narayana Guru, who blessed their bid. He had visited the satyagrahis' camp a month earlier, made a handsome donation, and apparently offered to be a satyagrahi himself.[81]

In March 1925, Gandhi arrived in Vaikom, held public meetings, bolstered the satyagrahis, met the Maharani regent, and confronted the head of the Nambudiri priests in a three-hour conversation. Before journeying to Vaikom he had written in *Young India* (19 Feb 1925): 'The Vykom satyagrahis are fighting a battle of no less consequence than that of Swaraj' (26: 159).

Having touched several 'untouchable' satyagrahis following his arrival, Gandhi had become polluted. Thus reckoning, the chief priest kept himself at a safe distance throughout the long conversation. The story would endure in the Malayalam country.[82]

On 12 March, accompanied by two southern allies, EVR and CR, Gandhi called on Narayana Guru, who reiterated his endorsement of the satyagraha.

Towards the end of Gandhi's nine-day visit, princely authorities climbed down, yet it was only months later, in November 1925, that all, including Ezhavas and the 'untouchables', were able to walk on the temple roads. Only on three of them, that is. The fourth road was made a 'Brahmins only' path from which Christians and Muslims too were excluded.

Destined to be venerated himself as the rationalist Periyar, EVR played a significant role in the satyagraha and suffered imprisonment for it. In November 1925, he presided at a large public assembly in Vaikom where the struggle's participants and supporters accepted the terms that Gandhi's visit had secured.[83]

Future critics would call the terms inadequate, but the response at the time was of joy and triumph. A year earlier, Dr Bhimrao Ambedkar, thirty-three at the time, called the Vaikom satyagraha 'the most important event' for the country's 'untouchables'.[84]

In 1936, eleven years after the 'three-fourth' victory, Travancore's ruling family would open all its temples, and the roads leading up to them, to all Hindus.

In the Malayalam country, Vaikom helped the freedom and social justice movements to join hands. Elsewhere in India, the news from Vaikom confronted insulated caste Hindus with the ugly realities of untouchability and unapproachability.

There was another consequence. Since the Vaikom struggle took place in the territory of Travancore, 'the princely states were helped onto the map of the national freedom struggle'.[85]

◆

The communities least visible in our glimpses of the South Indian story have been the 'tribals' (as they are often called), or the 'adivasis' (first inhabitants), as they are also called. Scattered across the peninsula, living mostly on forested hills but in some cases in the plains, they have been present in each of the four 'linguistic' zones into which, for want of a better design, we have distributed South India.

This demarcation cannot do justice to smaller linguistic groups, or to areas where no language had clear dominance, or to the 'tribals', who did not see themselves as Malayali, Kannada, Tamil or Telugu, and whose forebears may have inhabited South India before anyone else.

Though, in relative terms, each 'tribal' community was small, each possessed a separate name, home, story and way of life. In many cases it had its own language. A thread common to all was the dislocation caused by the Empire's forest laws, which were influenced by, among other things, the value of timber (teak grew in many tribal areas) and by the perceived disadvantages of podu or shift cultivation.

The intrusion into daily tribal life of forest and other local officers, some of whom laid hands on the tribals' milk and chicken, and commandeered personal service and forest produce, was also a feature common to almost all tribes.

A sizable tribal population, dramatic hills and forests marked Vizag district in the Telugu country, where, as in other places, tribal-dominant areas were demarcated as 'Agencies' within Madras Presidency and administered by special officers. During the Non-cooperation years, Agency tribals in Vizag district became active supporters of a revolutionary group led by a high-caste Telugu, Alluri Sitarama Raju (1897–1924).

Born in a poor rural home near the town of Bhimavaram (170 miles south of Vizag) but raised by an uncle who was a tahsildar, Raju went to different mission schools in Andhra's fertile coastal districts until a slight from the uncle caused the youngster to run away. The asceticism to which he turned became a halfway house to political rebellion.

Supposedly making pilgrimages to different parts of India, in July 1917, Raju found himself in a village called Krishnadevipeta which lay amidst Koya tribals in Vizag Agency's Gudem taluka. Giving the young ascetic food and shelter, the owner of the house where Raju had stopped to ask for water, a non-tribal named Chitikela Bhaskarudu, also showed him a hilltop suitable for meditation.

Raju stayed on in Krishnadevipeta, where his mother and brother joined him. Villagers constructed two huts for them, and Raju and his brother cultivated 30 acres. Raju started a small school, located sites for wells, and prescribed Ayurveda medicines.

Before long he was being viewed as a holy man by the Koyas.

In 1921, when Non-cooperation found an enthusiastic response in Vizag and throughout coastal Andhra, Raju adopted some of its agenda. He 'preached against liquor...urged the agency people not to go to British courts and instead solve their problems in the local panchayats' and 'gained extraordinary influence'.[86]

Wearing 'a flowing beard' and a 'turban, long shirt and knickers all made of red-colour khaddar', he looked, it was said, like a messiah.[87] In a letter sent in 1929 to Mahatma Gandhi, M. Annapurniah, a journalist who had gone to school with Raju, would write that much of Raju's message was spiritual, but 'in the milk of spirituality there was invariably the sugar of patriotism'.[88]

Two non-tribal headmen, brothers Gam Gantam Dora and Gam Mallu Dora, who served as intermediaries between tribals in the hills and zamindars in the plains, became Raju's 'main lieutenants'.[89]

When, in January 1922, a suspicious British police officer asked Raju if he was raising a fituri, using the Urdu word for rebellions the region had seen in the nineteenth century, he denied any such intention. Raju was kept under surveillance, so he asked the divisional magistrate, Fazlulla Sahib, for a site elsewhere to continue his work for the tribals.

Because rebuffing him would annoy the tribals, Raju was allotted 50 acres on a new site. Claiming next, that he wanted to perform a pilgrimage to Nepal, Raju surrendered the land, sent away his mother and father, and clandestinely 'wandered about the agency villages', preparing the ground for a revolt.

Already there was anger against the administration. The Dora brothers were angry because the deputy tahsildar of Gudem taluka, a man called Bastian, had deprived them of their lands and, in the case of one of them, of his office as a village munsif. Tribals who made a hill road from Narsipatnam to Chintapalli were bitter because Bastian and his overseer for roads, Santhanam Pillai, had, it seems, grossly underpaid them.

Raju raised a force. On three successive days, 22, 23 and 24 August, it attacked. Guns and ammunition were seized from police stations in Chintapalli, Krishnadevipeta and Rajavommangi. In the last place, the raiders freed Veerayya Dora, a non-tribal who was a thorn in the administration's flesh.

Fed, lodged and informed by the tribals, the attackers not only evaded arrest for a whole month, on 24 September, they ambushed and killed two British soldiers who had been brought in to deal with them. Christopher Coward, described as 'a renowned shikari', and another marksman, Lionel Hayter, were both gunned down 'by the tribal sharp-shooter Gokiri Erresu'.[90]

Raids persisted, encounters occurred. Ensuring that his men did not loot, Raju preserved tribal sympathy. Food and shelter continued to be supplied. But on 6 December, a Malabar unit seasoned in the Mappila war killed five of Raju's men and captured one. The following night eight more were killed, another four captured, and the rebellion's decline began.

Rewards were announced for the capture of Raju, the Dora brothers and Veerayya. After four months of lying low, in April 1923 Raju moved, into the plains, where he was joined by Vegiraju Satyanarayana Raju of Kumudavalli, a daring rebel who became known as Aggi (fiery) Raju. Taking risks, many in the plains welcomed the fugitives.

September 1923 saw a setback when Mallu Dora was caught while visiting a paramour, but sporadic defiance continued for months. After the administration deployed fresh units, including one from Assam Rifles in January 1924, Aggi was wounded and captured on 6 May. Sitarama Raju was killed the next day, and Gantam Dora a month later.

The rebellion was over, and many participants including Mallu Dora and Aggi Raju were sent to the Andamans, but ballads and other memorials would perpetuate the fame of Sitarama Raju and his band as fearless men who never gave up.

Recording, moreover, that the tribals protected Raju and his men over a prolonged period, and that Raju took care that his force did not oppress their tribal helpers, histories would offer at least faint visibility to South India's tribals. Except, however, for sharpshooter Gokiri Erresu, they remain individually anonymous even in this story.[91]

◆

As the twentieth century's first quarter ended, freeing themselves of the Empire's chains seemed the resolve of a great many Indians in the south and elsewhere. We have seen, however, that other Indians, also in significant numbers, thought that the native society's internal harshness demanded their first attention.

Chapter 10

FROM PRISON TO FORT ST GEORGE: 1920–1939

The CR–EVR relationship is a thread that runs across South India's modern story, here going upward, there going down, but always visible.

In 1920, both men were ardent Non-cooperators, and EVR backed CR in support of defiance.

Personally, too, they were close. It was EVR who in February 1922 called on CR in jail and informed him of Gandhi's suspension of defiance. Since CR had named him as a near one, EVR was able to visit him in prison.

Later in 1922, EVR welcomed CR's opposition to council entry. The Madras legislature would have been Brahmin-dominated had the Congress contested. From October 1923, when, for the sake of Congress unity, CR diluted his opposition to council entry, his bond with EVR started to weaken.

In 1924, however, right after Gandhi's release from prison, EVR and CR worked together in support of the Vaikom Satyagraha, which was followed by a strenuous effort by Gandhi to keep the Congress united. As part of that effort, CR and other 'no changers' were asked to yield political space to the Congress's Swarajists, as 'pro changers' warming towards the councils called themselves. Presiding at the end-1924 Congress session held in Belgaum, Gandhi dropped CR and Patel from his working committee.

Early in 1925, CR started a centre—it was called an ashram—in Tiruchengode, not far from EVR's Erode, for constructive work, with a focus on eradicating untouchability, reviving spinning and weaving, and promoting temperance. What EVR thought of this turn in CR's career is not very clear.

What we know is that in March 1925, a month after CR had started his ashram, Varadarajulu Naidu, born like EVR into the trading Balija caste, wrote an article attacking the Congress around charges that a gurukulam* aided by the party in Tinnevelly district was requiring

---

*residential school

non-Brahmin students to eat separately from Brahmin pupils.

Located in Cheranmadevi, next to a village called Kallidaikurichi, the boarding school was started at the end of 1922 by the ex-militant V. V. S Aiyar (1881–1925), a Brahmin who had spent ten years in exile in Pondicherry, where, among other things, he translated the *Tirukkural* into English. The gurukulam was financed by persons from the merchant community of Nattukottai Chettiars, then flourishing in Burma and Malaya.

In April 1925, after the Tamil Nadu Congress Committee (TNCC) formed a committee to enquire into the charges, Aiyar resigned. Two months later, he met with a tragic end in Tinnevelly district's Papanasam waterfalls.

But the Cheranmadevi issue did not die. Moreover, at a TNCC conference in Kanchipuram in November, EVR demanded a declaration in favour of 'communal', i.e. caste-based, representation, proportionate to numbers, in government jobs and councils. When his resolutions were disallowed by Kalyanasundara Mudaliar, who was in the chair, EVR walked out. A month later, he left the Congress, and before 1925 ended he launched the Self-Respect Movement.[1]

Some months before this, he had started a Tamil weekly, *Kudi Arasu* (Republic), which demanded communal representation and attacked 'Brahminism'. From mid-1927 onwards, *Kudi Arasu* made frontal attacks on religion. Traditionally venerated texts like the Puranas and the Ramayana were 'condemned as irrational and inimical to morals and social justice'. Later, Saivism and its revered texts also received strident criticism.[2]

The Self-Respect Movement avoided the taint of British blessing, which the Justice Party had always carried. Along with his non-cooperation, jail-going, and Vaikom role, EVR's earthy attacks on superstition and hypocrisies, and his demands for equality, including between the sexes, had won him wide popularity, even as his denunciations of loved texts provoked anger in some sections.

In 1926, CR incurred the displeasure of EVR, Varadarajulu Naidu, the Justice Party and the journal *Justice* when he made a deal with the Madras Swarajists, agreeing to back the latter in elections if they supported prohibition. Until this point, so CR claimed, he had been 'a great favourite with the Justice people'.[3]

Nationally, Congress Swarajists faced dissension, sabotage and a loss of reputation when some among them accepted offices under the Raj. Motilal Nehru, who led Congress Swarajists in the central assembly, and Srinivasa Iyengar, who with Gandhi's endorsement was chosen Congress president in 1926, sought CR's help, with Iyengar urging him to counter 'rebellious persons' who were 'deliberately shattering' Swarajist 'prestige in Maharashtra, C.P. and U.P'.[4]

While staying clear of north Indian quarrels, CR issued a strong appeal in support of Congress (i.e. Swarajist) candidates in Madras Presidency. In elections held at the end of 1926, Congress Swarajists won more seats than Justice. Pledged, however, against becoming ministers, the Swarajists backed a ministry of independents led by P. Subbaroyan, who owned lands not from Tiruchengode and was friendly to CR and the Congress.

Growing Congress influence did not go down well with everyone in the south. When Gandhi visited the Tamil country in September 1927, young anti-Brahmin activists in Karaikudi gave him a pamphlet in which CR was attacked. Gandhi not only defended CR, he said that Rajagopalachari would be his successor.

> You do not know the man. If Rajagopalachari is capable of telling
> lies, you must say that I am also capable of telling lies. I do say he
> is the only possible successor, and I repeat it today... The pamphlet
> shows how you are fed on lies... You may offer stubborn battle
> if you like, but build your foundation on truth.[5]

Gandhi was speaking in an all-India context, but in the Tamil country the climate was no longer what it was in the early days of Non-cooperation. To some, the Brahmin was a bigger problem than the British. In June 1927, EVR attacked Gandhi in *Kudi Arasu* for 'giving up his basic principles for the sake of consensus and unity'.[6]

Wanting political independence as well as social equality, Gandhi did not jettison Brahmins valued by him as humans and needed by him for Swaraj. For EVR, however, by 1927 or even earlier, social equality took precedence over national independence. Such a stance was winning a growing constituency.

Yet the urge for freedom and sentiment for Gandhi were strong in South India, as 1930 would soon attest. As for CR, he defended, in October 1929, his own approach to social questions and compared it with that of unnamed others:

> I claim to be a greater changer than many that now beat up a great deal of dust. I have been an outcaste among my relations for the last twenty years. I have done and am doing things which my clamorous friends have not, I believe, in their own persons attempted.[7]

◆

Swarajist experiments failing, there was a yearning across India for another heave at the Empire. Though on occasion feeling old, Gandhi was willing to lead a new all-India fight. Meeting in Calcutta at the end of 1928, the Congress declared that it would ask for complete independence unless dominion status was conceded within a year.

When, at the end of 1929, there was no sign of dominion status, the Congress announced—in Lahore, with forty-year-old Jawaharlal Nehru presiding—that it would launch a struggle under Gandhi's guidance. Swarajists began vacating their council seats.

A new working committee that included CR and Patel asked the people of India to take a pledge on 26 January, drafted by Gandhi, that submission to alien rule was 'a crime against man and God' and that they had the right to disobey laws 'without doing violence, even under provocation' (42: 427–28).

In place after place that Sunday morning, the pledge was read out. No speeches were made, but hands assenting to the pledge were raised everywhere. Important questions remained, however. Which law was to be broken, and where?

How Gandhi, mystifying allies and opponents, settled on defying the salt tax as his strategy and conducted a Salt March from Ahmedabad to Dandi on the shores of the Arabian Sea, setting off nationwide satyagrahas that galvanized Indians, unnerved the Empire, and infuriated Winston Churchill, are oft-told stories that need not be repeated here.

But we should look at a parallel salt march (13 to 30 April) led by CR from Trichy to Vedaranyam, a Thanjavur seaboard town in the Bay of Bengal. With defiance returning as the Congress agenda, the TNCC had asked CR to become its president and organize a campaign in the Tamil country.

He chose Vedaranyam as the destination because of the courage of one its prominent residents, Vedaratnam Pillai, a licensee for a salt factory and secretary of the Thanjavur district Congress. Convincing CR that salt swamps close to Vedaranyam were ideal for scooping up salt, Pillai was also willing to face the consequences of hosting law-breakers.

At dawn on 13 April, singing 'Kathiyinri, Rathaminri' (Sans sword, sans blood), a verse written for the defiance by poet Namakkal Ramalingam Pillai, ninety-eight carefully chosen persons from every Tamil district, nine of whom had given up good jobs to become satyagrahis, stepped forth from the Trichy home of Dr T. S. S. Rajan. Before Gandhi's approach captured him, Rajan, a well-regarded physician-surgeon, had toyed with schemes of assassination in London, where he obtained advanced medical training.

Walking 5 miles in the morning and another 5 miles in the evening, often with the Kaveri flowing seaward to their side, the marchers held meetings in Thanjavur, Kumbakonam, Mannargudi, Thiruthuraipoondi and elsewhere before a mighty crowd greeted them at Vedaranyam on 28 April.

During stops, virtually all of them in Thanjavur district, the marchers fraternized with untouchables, kept clear of temples barred to untouchables, swept village streets, and spoke up for Hindu–Muslim unity and against liquor.

The district's short, astute and energetic collector, John Anderson Thorne, ICS, had promised the march's 'ignominious failure' provided Fort St George authorized him to arrest those housing or feeding the marchers for 'harbouring criminals', and to arrest CR once he entered Thanjavur. The first wish was granted by Fort St George but not the second, as that might 'confer on [CR] the cheap martyrdom that he and Mr. Gandhi desire'.[8]

'I shall take pains to see that [the marchers] meet with increasing difficulties and discomforts,' Thorne assured his chiefs, adding that in Vedaranyam he would 'prevent their getting accommodation'.[9] Via leaflets, loudspeakers and personal appearances, Thorne announced that those feeding or housing the marchers would be imprisoned.

His warnings were defied or foiled. In Koviladi, reached on the second day, the Kaveri's banks were good enough to sleep on after

Thorne's threat had caused the chatram, the pilgrims' inn, to be barred and bolted against the marchers. Food was quietly hung on trees the marchers could not miss.

In Kumbakonam, Pantulu Iyer, a former member of the Madras council, housed and fed all marchers, getting six months in prison. In Thiruthuraipoondi, Ramachandra Naidu, who fed the marchers, was picked up from a public meeting where CR was speaking. The thousands hearing him remained calm while Naidu was carried off.

Earlier, in Thanjavur town, a crowd of 20,000 blessing the march observed complete silence for a whole minute. In Semmangudi, government employees who joined the welcoming crowd lost their jobs.

In Vedaranyam, Thorne's threat failed to materialize. Pillai ensured that all marchers were accommodated. On the 30th morning, CR and fellow marchers bent down and collected salt from pans 2 miles from Vedaranyam. Refusing to surrender the 'contraband' in their fists, they were arrested.

In a quick secluded trial that Thorne arranged under a salt shed near the sea, District Magistrate Ponnuswamy Pillai sentenced CR for six months rigorous, but the magistrate broke down while signing the jail warrant.

Sticks were brought down on fists and salt was forced out, but it continued to be illegally collected for weeks. Thorne ordered wholesale arrests. Including marchers, 375 were picked up in Thanjavur district alone.

One of the hundreds arrested elsewhere in the Tamil country for defying the salt law was twenty-seven-year-old Kumaraswami Kamaraj, son to a coconut-selling Nadar of Virudhunagar, then in Tinnevelly district.

Drawn as a sixteen-year-old into the national movement because of the Jallianwala massacre and specially impacted by a speech by George Joseph, a Congress leader of Malayali origin,[10] Kamaraj (1903–1975) sold khadi and picketed liquor shops in the Non-cooperation stir in 1920–21. In 1924, he joined the Vaikom effort and thereafter involved himself in campaigns led by the Swarajist Congress leaders Srinivasa Iyengar and S. Satyamurti.

In the summer of 1930, Kamaraj was sentenced for two years, Dr Rajan for eighteen months. Rukmini Lakshmipathi, the only woman marcher, got six months. Vedaratnam Pillai, who too received a six-month sentence, was deprived of properties as well. Released in October, CR was sentenced for another year when he refused to pledge 'peaceful behaviour'.

The moral victory had gone entirely to the marchers, with Thorne complaining to Fort St George that he had been right in proposing CR's early arrest and that 'harm to the prestige of Government has been done by the march'.[11]

Acknowledging that CR had achieved 'something of a triumph, even Mohamedans and Adi-Dravidas taking part in the receptions', Thorne said that 'C.R. throughout maintained excellent discipline among his followers...always adhered to nonviolence...and refrained from the arts of demagoguery'. Added Thorne:

> If there ever existed a fervid sense of devotion to the Government, it is now defunct.[12]

◆

Writing more than seven decades later, the scholar C. A. Perumal would appraise the impact of Gandhian strategies:

> The Indian terrorist or revolutionary movement was confined to propertied classes... When Gandhi showed the path of nonviolence, with all the fervour and zeal of a sannyasin, the masses were simply captivated. The terrorist activity lost its appeal...irretrievably.
>
> M. N. Roy turned to radical humanism, and others like Sri Aurobindo became spiritualists. In Tamil Nadu, V. V. S. Aiyer, M. P. B. T. Acharya, T. S. S. Rajan, Gomati Sankara Dikshitar and others joined the Gandhian fold. Neelakanta Brahmachari* became a sannyasin. Thus Gandhi exercised a leavening influence on the revolutionary nationalists either by luring them into his fold or by driving them away from the hotbed of the national movement itself.[13]

Perumal didn't say so directly, but the terrorist movement was a high-caste affair.

◆

*We saw him in the previous chapter.

Among those on whom the salt stir threw a spotlight was a young woman of rare quality and courage, Kamaladevi. Born on 3 April 1903 in a well-off Konkani-speaking family of Mangalore-based Saraswats, Kamaladevi lost her father when she was seven. She and her mother were suddenly disinherited as all the family properties went to a stepbrother, causing Kamaladevi to protest later that women enjoyed 'no rights'.[14]

However, her mother and grandmother were strong figures in the girl's life, as was an unnamed aunt who raised her 'small brood of children' after her husband, 'having become mad', died early.

Yielding to pressure from the deceased husband's 'blindly orthodox' family, this widow (Kamaladevi would later recall in an autobiography) accepted 'the ugly disfigurement' that was insisted upon, including a shaved head, for the 'alternative was quitting the house, leaving the children behind'.

This widowed aunt told young Kamala that she 'felt utterly humiliated but saw no purpose in taking it out on anyone'. The experience had 'burnt into her, leaving a patch of bitterness that was carefully hidden'. Salvaging 'something of her personality', the crushed widow gave 'solace to the disconsolate', including little Kamala, for whom she sang songs in a 'sweet, powerful voice' and narrated 'fabulous stories'.[15]

In her own long life, Kamala, who, too, encountered humiliations, would not only salvage her personality, she would enrich it with multiple talents, and she would help restore other personalities. More than resentment, what seemed burned into her was a passion to make the world nicer.

Travelling across India and beyond, curious always and at home everywhere, she absorbed ideas from an amazing range of persons she met and at times questioned, including Pandita Ramabai of Maharashtra, Annie Besant, Bhikaji Cama, Aurobindo, Tagore and Gandhi, and a host of the less famous.

Married at fourteen, Kamaladevi was widowed in two years, but as a sixteen-year-old she turned up in Bombay to watch Gandhi and his Satyagraha Sabha defy an imperial assault on free speech, the Rowlatt Act.[16]

A spell at Madras's Queen Mary's College led Kamaladevi to marrying, in 1923, the actor and poet Harindranath Chattopadhyay, whose Bengali father was a prominent Hyderabad-based educator. Harindranath's older sister was the already well-known Sarojini Naidu. An older brother was the revolutionary Virendranath, who would be executed in a Stalinist purge in 1937, after three decades of radical activity in Europe. But it was a younger sister, Suhasini, also a student at Queen Mary's, who introduced Kamaladevi and Harindranath to each other.

Endowed with beauty, boldness, and great thirsts, Kamaladevi predictably ignored taunts at her remarriage. At ease, like Harindranath, on a stage, she acted in plays and a few early films. A son was born to them, but the marriage would wither.

Meanwhile, she was pulled by struggles Gandhi was leading. Kamaladevi became active in the Seva Dal, the Congress's volunteer arm, but, being her own person, only after she had studied sociology in England.

In 1926, she ran at the last minute for a place in the Madras Council, encouraged in that bid by an Irishwoman who had made southern India her home: the suffragist and theosophist, Margaret Cousins. The first woman in India to contest an election to a legislature, Kamaladevi, twenty-three at the time, lost by a mere 55 votes.

Three years later, Kamaladevi lobbied in New Delhi's central legislature for the Sarda Bill for preventing child marriages. After making her pitch to Motilal Nehru, she said, 'You will [support the bill], won't you?' Needled by the bluntness, Motilal replied, 'Are you instructing me...how to vote, you chit of a girl?'

'Far from wilting', Kamaladevi stood up and said: 'If your objection is to my age, I will bring a batch of old women to seek your vote.'[17]

She was noticed again in January 1930 in Bombay, when she clung doggedly to a Congress flag that others were trying to remove. It was the Salt March year, and Kamaladevi protested at Gandhi's decision to have only men marching to Dandi.

Shortly before Gandhi's arrest, Kamaladevi was one of a group of women, Hindu, Muslim and Parsi, who conferred with Gandhi on women's participation in national struggles. The outcome was a letter to Viceroy Irwin announcing that women including Kamaladevi and other signatories would picket sales of liquor and foreign cloth.

Once Gandhi was imprisoned, Kamaladevi was among the leaders of defiance in Bombay. When she entered the city's stock exchange and tried to sell contraband salt there, she was arrested and sentenced to a year in prison. She was twenty-seven.

After her release, Kamaladevi would be drawn to the newly formed socialist wing of the Congress. Becoming its chair in 1936, she seemed headed for the centre of India's political leadership.

◆

On 26 January 1931, most prisoners were released before completing their terms, for Irwin wished to explore a settlement. In March, the famous Gandhi–Irwin Pact was signed, and later in the year Gandhi represented the Congress at a London conference where, with Indian parties pressing conflicting proposals, HMG claimed that Indian divisions were delaying political advance.

In January 1932, a new round of struggle ensued, inviting repression from Irwin's successor, Lord Willingdon. Along with thousands across the land, South Indians led by CR were again in prison. From September 1932, however, a fresh front opened for Indian nationalists after Gandhi fasted in jail against a separate electorate for untouchables announced by the Empire.

To Gandhi, a permanent division of society into caste-Hindus and untouchables was unacceptable. Under a mango tree in Yerawada prison, negotiations took place between Gandhi and the 'untouchables' leaders, who were headed by the resolute Bhimrao Ambedkar.

Gandhi's willingness to accept reserved seats for the Scheduled Castes, as the Empire called the 'untouchables', and Ambedkar's willingness, in exchange, to give up a separate electorate, produced the Poona Pact, which the Empire accepted, and which has governed elections in India ever since.

The Congress's president, Vallabhbhai Patel, being behind bars, it was CR, released in July 1932 and named acting president by Patel, who represented the national body in the Poona negotiations. The resulting pact contained his signature as well, and CR exchanged pens with Ambedkar. Also signing the pact were two eminent leaders of the South's Depressed Classes, M.C. Rajah and Rettamalai Srinivasan.

Gandhi's fast prodded caste–Hindus to face the ugliness of untouchability. To save Gandhi's life, temple doors in different parts of the country were opened to Harijans (God's people), the name Gandhi, and others following him, had begun to use for the 'untouchables'.[18] Also prompted by the fast was a public commitment by prominent Hindu leaders, including CR, that removal of discrimination against 'untouchables' would be one of the earliest acts of the parliament of a free India.[19]

Between 1932 and 1934, the Congress was a banned body. Its soldiers were tired, breadwinners had spent repeated spells in prison, and family savings as well as funds for struggle had shrunk. During this phase of repression, the anti-untouchability campaign brought valuable visibility to the Congress.

CR resigned as acting INC president in December 1932 to assist 'untouchable' entry into the famed Guruvayur Temple near Calicut, of which the Zamorin was the trustee. Kelappan, who had played a major role in the Vaikom Satyagraha, wanted to fast to open Guruvayur to all. Asking him to wait, Gandhi said he would fast himself if necessary.

Unlike Vaikom, which was part of Travancore, Guruvayur belonged to Madras Presidency. CR urged caste-Hindus living in the temple's vicinity to express their support for ending the bar. The Zamorin disliked the proposed change, and the Sankaracharyas of the south were totally opposed to it, but Russell, the Calicut collector, informed Fort St George that CR's speeches were 'swinging the mass of popular opinion towards temple entry'.[20]

Held on 24 December, a referendum of caste-Hindus around Guruvayur showed 56 per cent supporting the entry of Dalits (as the Scheduled Castes would eventually come to be called), 9 per cent opposing it, 8 per cent asserting neutrality, and 27 per cent saying nothing. Despite the clear mandate for reform, the temple's doors did not open. Claiming that the shrine was private, the Zamorin also argued that unless the law was changed, even two orthodox opponents could obtain an injunction against temple entry.

The need to change the law over temples was one of the factors forcing a change in the Congress's policy on the Empire's councils. Repression under Willingdon was another factor, and British willingness to enhance the powers of provincial legislatures was a third.

Before 1933 ended, and after CR had served another six-month prison term, he, Gandhi and Patel had come around to considering cooperation with the new councils that seemed to be on the anvil.

In Madras Presidency, no one welcomed a switch in strategy more than Satyamurti, who was demonstrating his debating skills in the conspicuous if largely toothless central legislative assembly. With Srinivasa Iyengar inexplicably opting out of politics in 1930, Satyamurti seemed a natural Congress leader in any empowered Madras legislature.

Gandhi astutely resigned from the Congress in 1934, saying he would help it from without. He wanted to be free himself to put up a struggle against the Empire, if that seemed necessary, even as the Congress cooperated with the proposed new councils.

Efforts to persuade CR to become the INC president were made in 1936 by Patel, who desired support in his equation with Nehru, and by Satyamurti, who hoped that CR's energies would be expended on the national stage, leaving the presidency clear for himself.

In November 1936, Gandhi conveyed Patel's and Satyamurti's urgings to CR, who had been the TNCC chief for five years from 1930, adding, 'I shall be pleased if you will wear [the thorny crown].'[21]

But CR was not willing. The faint possibility of governing Madras appealed more to him, even though he knew that the presidency's imperial governor would retain critical powers. With CR declining the Congress chair, the incumbent president, Jawaharlal, was repeated for another year.

Guilt about his desire for an Empire-related office and memories of his no-changer leadership troubled CR for much of 1935 and 1936. He spoke of his 'fall' in a letter to Devadas Gandhi, who in 1933 had married CR's daughter Lakshmi.[22]

CR's emergence as the Congress leader in the new Madras legislature was clinched in December 1936 when Patel, who headed the Congress parliamentary board, visited Madras.

Patel agreed with people like the influential Kasturi Srinivasan, *The Hindu*'s editor-proprietor, and P. Subbaroyan, the former chief minister who had recently joined the Congress, that only CR could keep persons in the presidency's Congress united. In 1935, the Vellala leader, Muthuranga Mudaliar, had defeated Satyamurti in a contest for the TNCC chair, and it did not seem likely that Prakasam, who led the Congress in the Telugu districts, would serve under Satyamurti.

When the 1937 elections were announced, Patel declared in Bombay that CR would aim to enter the Madras assembly from the university constituency, adding that Satyamurti, expected thus far to contest from that seat, had stepped aside. When, after becoming premier, CR nominated T. S. S. Rajan to Madras's upper chamber and made him a minister, Satyamurti felt betrayed, claiming that CR had assured him the nomination and a place in the cabinet.[23]

November 1936, the month when CR decided to stand for the Madras legislature, was also when the Maharaja of Travancore, supported by his brilliant and controversial dewan, C. P. Ramaswami Iyer, threw open, by proclamation, all the temples under him to the 'untouchables'. Journeying to Travancore, CR took forty young Dalits to the hoary Sri Padmanabhaswami Temple, which had not seen 'untouchables' for hundreds of years.

'God be thanked,' said CR, 'and may your Maharaja live long. This is the happiest day of my life'.[24]

◆

Twelve years after Vaikom, EVR, on his part, no longer seemed very interested in temple entry. 'Reason' was the idol of his Self-Respect Movement, which was allied to the anti-Brahmin drive, of which the Justice Party was the chief political vehicle, even as the Congress was the main vehicle for the freedom drive, with which the temple entry movement seemed allied.

During the winter of 1929–30, EVR visited Malaya and Singapore, and in 1931–32 he spent many months in Egypt, Atatürk's Turkey and seven European countries: Greece, Stalin's Russia, Spain, Portugal, England, France and a Germany about to embrace Hitler. Russia, where he stayed for three months, seemed to make the greatest impact on him, which was seen in the socialistic language in which EVR expressed himself thereafter.

Accompanying him overseas was his articulate younger colleague, S. Ramanathan Pillai (1895–1968), a Vellala who had left the Congress along with EVR and was the movement's ablest communicator in English.[25] On his way back, EVR halted in November 1932 in Ceylon, whose minority Tamils were led by Saivite Vellalas.

For a while it seemed that the Vellala community, which for centuries had produced scholars in Tamil, would continue to have a dominant role in the Justice Party and the Non-Brahmin Movement, but the anti-religious tenor of the Self-Respect Movement and of EVR's speeches and journals clashed with the Saivite beliefs of most Vellalas.

Deriding Sanskrit, the Aryans and 'the north' was one thing, and it seemed possible, if not always simple, to connect Brahmins to all three, but if Saivite belief was to be mocked as part of an anti-Brahmin thrust, the deeply Saivite Vellala community would be offended.

The late 1920s had seen a bitter and almost violent dispute between non-Brahmin Saivites and EVR's supporters from the Self-Respect movement. The erudite Saivite Vellala scholar and Pure Tamil champion, Maraimalai Adigal, who had de-Sanskritized his name from the original R. S. Vedachalam, alleged that criticism of Saivite texts from Self-Respect quarters was secretly Vaishnavite in motivation, and suggested that EVR was not only a Vaishnavite himself but a non-Tamil as well.[26]

While failing to silence EVR's broad criticism of religion, Adigal's comment showed that an ancient Saivite–Vaishnavite divide had not entirely disappeared in South India. It also suggested that any effort to rid the Tamil country of the influence of tradition would invite obstacles. However, the late 1930s would see the Dravidian and Pure Tamil currents coming together to pose joint competition to a dominant independence movement.

In the latter movement, a new strand emerged nationally in 1934, when several jailed Congressmen formed the nucleus of a socialist party within the Congress. Communist groups had begun to be formed in the 1920s, not long after the Bolsheviks had created the Soviet Revolution.

Communism's chief champion in Madras was the affluent M. Singaravelu Chettiar. Embracing Non-cooperation in 1920 before becoming a Communist, Singaravelu would share platforms with EVR in later years.

◆

One of those resigning from imperial legislatures because of the 1930 satyagraha was Dr Muthulakshmi Reddy (1886–1968), born to S. Narayanaswami Aiyer, the Brahmin principal of Pudukkottai's Maharaja's College, and Chandrammal, who belonged to a Devadasi community in the principality.

Muthulakshmi had not married until she was twenty-eight, for the time an exceptionally late age, and that, too, only after the equality she demanded was pledged by the groom, Dr T. Sundara Reddy. After studying medicine in Britain, Sundara Reddy had journeyed from Vizag to ask for Muthulakshmi's hand. In the candid words of her autobiography,

> I gave him my word to marry him on condition that he should always respect me as an equal and never cross my wishes.[27]

Two years earlier, in 1912, she was the first Indian female to graduate with a medical degree from the University of Madras.

Sacrificing a lucrative career in medicine, she mobilized opinion on women's issues: the age of consent, female education, medical aid for women, and more. The first female to be nominated to the Madras Legislative Council, in 1927 she urged the government to put a stop to the practice of dedicating young women as Devadasis in a sacred temple ceremony, which prevented their marriage and set them up for prostitution.

Coming from within the community, Muthulakshmi's initiative—a continuation of earlier activism by outsiders like Viresalingam* against performances by 'nautch girls'—drew considerable attention. Over time, these singing and dancing 'nautch girls' (Bhogamvallu in Telugu) had evolved into exclusive castes in different parts of South India with their own laws of inheritance, customs and rules of etiquette. Some became singers and dancers of great skill, a few became mistresses, but the majority,

> married to a presiding deity...lived by prostitution and were in attendance at private houses on all joyous occasions... To maintain a prostitute and attend a nautch performance became a...mark of social standing.[28]

In 1895, after Mysore's ruling family was censured for engaging dancing girls on festive occasions, the young maharaja had 'issued an order to purify all the temples by driving out dancing girls attached to them'.[29]

Madras Presidency's British officers were more cautious about interfering with temple-connected customs. However, public support for

---

*Another eloquent campaigner was R. Venkataratnam Naidu (1862–1939) of Machilipatnam.

Muthulakshmi's plea compelled the Madras council and the government to agree to make Devadasi pledges in temples unlawful.

Although the law she wanted was finally passed only in 1947, governmental backing for it from 1927 sparked off an immediate controversy within the semi-matrilineal and often literate Devadasi community. Two women wrote to *Swadesamitran*: 'If the Indian Penal Code cannot abolish prostitution, it is inconceivable how banning the practice of [dedication in a temple] will abolish it'.[30]

Opinion outside the community was also divided, but in the 1920s the wish for reform was ascendant.

Among Devadasis working for reform in the 1920s and 1930s were the Telugu country's Yamini Purnatilakam (c. 1890–1950) and the Tamil-speaking Moovalur Ramamirtham (1883–1962). Yamini, who heard Gandhi speak on the Devadasi question in Kakinada in 1921, gave many years to finding alternative occupations and marriage partners for Devadasis, while Ramamirtham worked for similar goals first through the Congress and later via EVR's Self-Respect Movement.

In 1936, Ramamirtham published a novel on the lives into which Devadasis were trapped. In the following year, she was given a six-month jail term for her role in the anti-Hindi movement led by EVR. But when in 1949 Periyar married a woman forty years his junior, Ramamirtham left, along with numerous others, to join a new party, the Dravida Munnetra Kazhagam.

Much earlier, shortly before Muthulakshmi's campaign started, a woman in Madras called Dhanam, whose forebears had danced at the Thanjavur court and who herself was an accomplished veena player, was pestered by a young granddaughter who wished to dance.

We learn from scholar V. Sriram that the granddaughter, Balasaraswati (1918–84), made a hush-hush debut at a Kanchipuram temple in 1925. Before long, she became an admired dancer of Sadir, as the style was called. This was happening even as Muthulakshmi's campaign, including opposition to temple-dancing, was picking up momentum.

Simultaneously, another talented woman, Rukmini Devi Arundale (like Muthulakshmi born in Pudukkottai but to a Brahmin father and a Brahmin mother) was beginning to transform Sadir into what the world would know as Bharatanatyam.

Rukmini Devi (1904–86) was Annie Besant's protégé. In 1920, she married Besant's British associate, George Arundale, who encouraged Rukmini's dancing talents. In 1935, Rukmini Devi gave in Madras her first public performance of Bharatanatyam, a dance form that would spread across the world.

'Temple-dancing' would become respectable again, if on stages far from temples. Bharatanatyam schools would proliferate. In India and beyond, the art would engage numerous teachers, dancers and musicians, and create jobs. But a price was paid. Although some Devadasis found opportunities as teachers, many practitioners faded away into poverty and want. Also,

> With Rukmini Devi as the newfound arbiter of aesthetics, several hand movements, gestures and songs that were found 'unsuitable' were excised.[31]

Balasaraswati herself would fight her way through. Supported by the businessman-politician R. K. Shanmukham Chetty, her partner from 1936, she would become well known in America as a teacher and performer, and eventually receive high honours in Madras.

Others were less fortunate. While scholars have had to work hard to retrieve the stories of some of them,[32] the fame of 'Bangalore' Nagarathnamma (1872–1952) seems assured. Born into a Devadasi family in Nanjangud, south of Mysore, Nagarathnamma performed music and dance in Mysore and Bengaluru before moving to Chennai as a reputed singer in Kannada, Telugu and Sanskrit.

Generosity became part of her image. An orator as well, in 1927 she became the first president of the Madras Presidency Devadasi Association. Earlier, she had taken Viresalingam to task for giving an indecency label to *Radhika Santvanam*, an eighteenth-century Telugu poem by Muddupalani, a Devadasi. Claiming that other writings, including some by Viresalingam himself, were as explicit, Nagarathnamma accused the reformer of applying one norm to men and another to women.[33]

◆

Through elections held in February 1937 under the Government of India Act of 1935, the Madras legislative assembly was chosen by one out of ten in the presidency's population. The limited franchise was however wider than before. Now every literate person could vote.

The house's 215 seats were carefully and elaborately distributed: 116 were 'general' seats, 30 reserved (in line with the Poona Pact) for Scheduled Castes but without a separate electorate, 28 (with only Muslims voting) for Muslims, 8 similarly for 'Indian Christians', 8 for women, 6 for landholders, 6 for commerce and industry, 6 for labour and unions, 3 for Europeans, 2 for Anglo–Indians, 1 for university graduates, and 1 for Scheduled Tribes.

The previous council, chosen under a narrower franchise and boycotted by the Congress, had been controlled by the Justice Party, which enjoyed support from zamindars and industrialists and claimed to represent the presidency's non-Brahmin majority.

John Erskine, governor from 1935, thought that Justice might win again in 1937, since 'the new electorate will be so preponderatingly non-Brahmin'.[34]

Entering the fray for the first time, the Congress however won 159 seats, Justice 16 and the Muslim League 10. In a letter to the king, Erskine conceded that 'the magnitude of the Congress victory was greater than I or anyone else expected.'[35]

That it stood for independence was the Congress's strongest card, while opportunism was seen in support from the 'socialist' EVR to the Justice Party, which was dominated by big landlords.

The Congress was successful also in appealing to Indian unity. When it called Justice 'communal' and an agent of imperialism, Justice responded by uttering weak cries for Swaraj. It was opposed to three B's, the British, the Brahmin and the Bania, said the party. But the open history of collaboration with the British could not be wiped away.

> Support of the British Raj had brought it to power, but with the impact of national consciousness and aspiration of Swaraj, its imperial connections brought it defeat.[36]

Performing very well elsewhere too, the Congress took time to accept office. Caretaker ministries were in charge until July, when, after careful negotiations—including between CR and Erskine—the Congress secured a public assurance from the viceroy that the governor would not 'interfere with the day-to-day administration of a province outside the limited range of responsibilities specially confided to him'.

It was a challenging 'compact'—Gandhi's phrase—between an Empire and its foes, requiring former victims of the Raj to rule a province in conjunction with an alien governor who could, on certain grounds, veto their measures, and through officials who had been their masters and jailors in the past.

While the Congress expected to use ministerial influence to weaken the Empire, the Raj hoped that office would soften recent rebels as they 'become absorbed in the problems of administration,' as the Marquess of Zetland, secretary of state for India, put it to Viceroy Linlithgow.[37]

Winning 5,326 votes in his university seat as against 327 and 270 secured by his two opponents, CR was unanimously chosen as the Congress's leader in the assembly after Prakasam, who was six years older, had proposed his name. His all-male team of ten ministers contained three Telugus: Prakasam, V. V. Giri (a future president of independent India, Giri defeated the outgoing chief minister, the Raja of Bobbili, by over 5,000 votes) and the Santiniketan-educated B. Gopala Reddi from Vijayawada (a future chief minister of Andhra).

The cabinet's five Tamils were CR, P. Subbaroyan, the former first minister who had joined the Congress, Dr T. S. S. Rajan from Trichy, V. I. Munuswami Pillai, a well-regarded Dalit born in the Nilgiris, and S. Ramanathan Pillai, EVR's Vellala colleague who had rejoined the Congress in 1936. K. Ramana Menon from Malabar* and Yakub Hasan Sait, a Congressman from Madras with whom CR had travelled to Malabar in 1921, completed the team.

An immediate bid by CR to increase his influence failed when Erskine rejected his request to see the draft of the governor's opening address. The viceroy supported Erskine in his refusal to show the draft but asked the governor to exclude controversial or argumentative language.[38]

Erskine again held his ground when CR sought the right to advise on the appointment of high court judges, a power the 1935 Act had explicitly reserved for the governor. But when CR, Prakasam and Giri together asked for the transfer of an ICS officer involved in a firing in an Andhra jute mill, the governor yielded.

Governor 'Josh' Erskine, a stocky and bespectacled Scottish

---

*Replaced on his death by C. J. Varkey.

aristocrat, was an MP before Prime Minister Stanley Baldwin sent him to Madras. Nursing hopes of entering the British cabinet, and as jealous as CR of his rights, Erskine was an imperialist to the core. His chief anxiety, he told Linlithgow, was that 'by bad management of our affairs' the British might allow themselves to be 'forced to leave India'.[39]

But imperialists too were divided. Men like Erskine and Samuel Hoare, secretary of state for India until 1935, were bitter foes of Churchill, with Hoare accusing 'Churchill and his friends' of being 'in almost hourly touch with Patiala and other princes' to prevent an all-India federation,[40] and Erskine writing uninhibitedly to Hoare of 'that skunk Winston' who was a 'mongrel of American and English parentage'.[41]

Erskine spent three months in a year in Government House on Mount Road—the house that Robert Clive's son had used as governor—another three in the Guindy mansion which would become the Raj Bhavan for free India's governors, and the remaining six in Ooty.

CR lived in a small house in Mambalam with a widowed daughter and an unmarried son. But as 'prime minister' (heads of previous ministries had humbler titles), he ran the government from Fort St George. Having liked his Scottish teachers while schooling at Bangalore's Central College, he got on reasonably well with Erskine, who wrote in a letter to King George V:

[CR's] main object in life seems to be to get India back to what it was in the days of King Asoka.[42]

The premier's guidelines for friends and relations were quickly established. A relative who had journeyed for favours was instantly shooed away. 'I have come back without opening my mouth,' D. Ramaswami Iyengar told his family in Bangalore.[43]

CR's relationship with the hardworking chief secretary, Sir Cecil Fabian Brackenbury, son of a vicar, became the town's talk after Brackenbury wore a khadi suit presented by CR.

Exactly at eleven in the morning, Brackenbury would walk into CR's office, take instructions and have them carried out.[44]

Within days of assuming office, CR publicly invited cooperation from the Raj's police:

I want the entire service, including the police, to look upon me as a friend.[45]

When radical nationalists mounted an agitation for removing a statue in the city of James Neill, a British hero of 1857 accused of atrocities in Allahabad and Kanpur,* a deft CR had the heavy statue quietly shifted, on a November night, to the interior of a Fort St George museum, where it still stands. 'There are more ways than one of keeping a historical monument,' he minuted.[46]

With a smile, he told Erskine: 'I am the snake charmer of British imperialism.'[47] After a socialist from Bombay, S. S. Batlivala, was arrested in Vellore for allegedly inciting violence, Nehru asked CR whether he too would be arrested for a similar speech. It seems that CR answered in the affirmative.[48]

With excise forming a good part of the government's income, the Congress's prohibition promise was not easy to implement. CR introduced the dry law in stages, starting with Salem district and applying it subsequently to two Telugu districts, Chittoor and Cuddapah, and to North Arcot in the Tamil country.

For enforcing the dry law, CR tasked A. F. W. Dixon of the ICS, 'a tall popular officer determined to make prohibition a success though no teetotaller himself'.[49] Studies by the universities of Madras and Annamalai would indicate improvement in the condition of thousands of households.[50]

Movement towards a separate Telugu province was another Congress promise. Although detractors whispered that CR had sent London a secret letter arguing against it, what in fact had gone was a memorandum, signed by the entire ministry, asking the secretary of state, Lord Zetland, to take steps forcreating Andhra.

When Zetland demurred, CR wrote back: 'There can be no stable administration of the province unless it is divided as desired by the people of Andhra.'[51]

CR's farmers' debt relief bill, cancelling a rural debt when more than twice the principal had been repaid, would be copied by the Congress ministry in Bombay and in Muslim-majority Punjab by pro-

---

*Neill was killed by rebels in Lucknow when a British column he led tried to regain that city.

farmer Unionists, who had captured office defeating both the Congress and the Muslim League. *The Hindu*'s columns were filled with letters calling the measure un-Hindu and predicting the end of credit, but the inflation rate was zero and the prophecies were belied.

W. E. M. Langley, leading the European block, charged that with this bill CR was bringing in 'pale-pink socialism or even communism', while a future finance minister in free India, T. T. Krishnamachari, calling the measure a balm, not a cure, complained that CR had not supplied statistics to justify it.

In reply, CR asked whether 'we should laugh at a bullock cart because it is not a motor car or at our feet because we have bought a bicycle'. As for statistics, 'if mosquitoes had to be escaped in Madras, it was better to buy a net in time before collecting figures as to the distribution of mosquitoes between Mylapore and Triplicane'.[52]

When for his second budget CR obtained 21 lakh rupees as Madras's share of income tax and opposition parties spoke of a 'windfall', he retorted:

> It is return of stolen property. Is the land revenue which comes with the hot tears of the farmer the only legitimate revenue of the province, and not the income tax?[53]

As the replies showed, his interventions were powerful. When, following a blunder by him over Hindi, attacks were hurled at Brahmins and North Indians, he said:

> Is it only this government that is to reap the results of this communal hatred?... Has an earthquake converted Tamil India into an island separated from the rest of India?... When England has forgotten centuries ago the difference between Norman and Saxon and Celt, when we have the standing example of America before us, we are saying this is a dark man; this is a fair man; this is an Aryan, that is a Dravidian; this is a Scythian, that is a Mongolian and that is a Jew.[54]

Criticized for not trying to break the Raj-devised constitution, he said: 'Just as a man does not know exactly when he has cast off his childhood or boyhood or middle age, constitutions do not know when they have been broken.'[55]

CR's 'ability as a parliamentarian among Congressmen' was 'unsurpassed', commented Gandhi,[56] and though Nehru was uncomfortable for a while with CR's concern for order and cordiality with British officers, he would write in 1941: 'It might be said that the Madras Government did more in its brief career than any other provincial government.'[57]

◆

At Fort St George, CR's defects included an itchy pen. He filled pages in files with quotable but avoidable notings. In the assembly, he was apt to rise in a colleague's place, which brightened proceedings but restricted colleagues. More serious was an obstinate attachment to a brainwave or his view on what was best.

The premier 'honestly believes,' said A. T. Pannirselvam, a gifted opposition legislator,* 'that what he has set his mind upon is the will of the country'.[58] Contributing to the caste divide that so troubled CR, this flaw, seen foremost in his Hindi policy, was seized upon by EVR.

We may never know whether this Hindi plan was a brainwave, a move to impress all of India, a compensation for CR's own inability, hurting his right to nationwide leadership, to acquire fluency in the language, or something else.

In any case, in August 1937, within weeks of assuming office, his ministry declared that to equip South Indians for opportunities in the rest of the country, Hindi/Hindustani would be offered in schools. Later, in April 1938, a government order announced that Hindi/Hindustani would be taught in standards six to eight in 125 schools.

Students could choose either Devanagari or Urdu for writing the language, and failing an exam would not block promotion. 'It is chutney on the leaf, taste it or leave it alone,' said CR.[59]

Opponents, however, called it poison, linked Hindi to CR the Brahmin, carried black flags to his meetings, denounced him daily in front of a few schools and his Mambalam home, and took out processions. On one occasion in Trichy, chappals were thrown at him.

---

*Arogyaswami Thamaraiselvam Pannirselvam (1888–1940) was a Justice Party leader who had previously served on Governor Erskine's executive council. In 1937, he defeated George Joseph (INC) in an 'Indian Christian' constituency. Three years later he died in an air crash in the Gulf of Oman.

The Hindi step brought the Justice Party and EVR closer to each other, accelerating a trend that had started in 1935. Pure Tamil advocates alleged that CR's Tamil contained Sanskrit words. EVR and Saivite Vellalas put aside their differences. The Muslim League said that Hindi was Hindu. And EVR bonded with a brilliant young writer and journalist, Conjeevaram Natarajan Annadurai (1909–69).

Born into the Sengundha Mudaliar caste where weaving was the traditional occupation, Annadurai was a writer for EVR's Tamil weekly, *Kudi Arasu,* the Justice Party's Tamil daily, *Viduthalai* (Freedom), which too had been handed over, early in 1937, to EVR, and for the Justice Party's English journal, *Justice.* In 1936, he had stood as a twenty-seven-year-old on a Justice ticket for the Madras municipal corporation but lost.

On 5 September 1937, within weeks of the CR ministry's first announcement that Hindi would be offered, Annadurai claimed at a public meeting at Soundarya Mahal in Madras that if Hindi was taught in the government's 8,000 schools, at least 8,000 teachers of Hindi, all of them Brahmins, would find jobs.[60]

Adding his voice to the agitation, Pannirselvam claimed that Hindi to the Tamilian was 'a foreign language, foreign in words, script, culture and tradition'. Women took part in protest marches.

CR replied that fostering communal hatred injured 'the national heart'. Yet he was unwise in at least two of his responses. Employing a provision in the law the British had used to combat picketing of shops selling toddy and foreign cloth, CR authorized non-bailable arrests of violators of his government's bans.

When CR dismissed his governor's advice against the step, Erskine wrote to the viceroy that it was 'no business of mine to keep the Congress party popular'.[61]*Indian Express* and *Swadesamitran*, both pro-Congress, counselled CR not to copy the Raj, as did Gandhi from afar, but CR was not budging.

A second mistake was to reject advice from Satyamurti and the educator-philosopher Sarvepalli Radhakrishnan to allow a parent to withdraw a child from the Hindi class.

It was in a climate of passion, confrontation and arrests that a Madras meeting called by the women's wing of the Self-Respect Movement resolved that EVR would henceforth be called Periyar, the great or big one.[62] Held in mid-November 1938 and attended by hundreds of women, the meeting was chaired by Neelambigai Ammaiyar, daughter of the Saivite champion of pure Tamil, Maraimalai Adigal.

Yet Adigal's own remarks in 1939 suggested not only aloofness from Hindi but a troubling disdain for other southern languages:

> A language loses its vitality [and] a class of people becomes disintegrated and weak by harmful admixture... The once strong well-knit group of Tamils has, by corruption of their language, become the disjointed and decaying groups of Malayalees, Telugus etc.[63]

By end-January 1939, 683 participants in the anti-Hindi movement, including EVR, Annadurai and 36 women, had been convicted for terms ranging from sixteen weeks to a year. Among them were 173 persons prosecuted for activity in front of CR's house.[64]

Six weeks after being formally addressed as Periyar, EVR, who had received a one-year sentence, was made the Justice Party president in absentia at a convention in Madras, where a fiery message he sent out from Bellary Jail was read out. Calling Brahmins 'mosquitoes', 'bugs' and 'Jews', EVR touched also on the abolition of zamindari proposed by the Congress, which the Justice Party had opposed. Abolishing the reign of priests was more important, EVR said.[65]

The Justice Party asked for 'Tamilnad' to be made a distinct and separate state, loyal to the British Raj, and 'directly under the Secretary of State for India'.[66]

Questioned in the Assembly about EVR's condition in Bellary's prison, CR replied:

> It is a good jail. I claim to be a personal friend of Mr. Naicker, though a very bitter political opponent. He knows that I am, so far as I can be, kind and considerate to him.[67]

CR's repartees in the assembly did not go down well with everyone. Some wanted greater public warmth from the premier for an unwell Periyar.[68]

After months of demonstrations, intensity dropped. In May 1939, EVR was released on medical grounds, and Annadurai and all the others detained were also freed. 'I have received exceptionally kind treatment,' Periyar said when he came out.[69]

◆

When Prakasam, who held the revenue portfolio, presented a bill to protect the rights of the presidency's tenant-farmers—fruit of an eighteen-month effort by a legislative committee he chaired—Congress members gave him an ovation. The Assembly's landlords and Europeans called the bill expropriation, and Erskine told CR that it would never receive assent.

The idea of compensating zamindars at market prices was firmly rejected by CR, who said to the house:

> In the other hemisphere, they once had very valuable properties. Slaves they had. Was compensation paid when slavery was abolished?[70]

In August 1938, the assembly passed a bill for removing social disabilities faced by Dalits. Making discrimination in jobs, wells, public conveniences, roads, transport, schools and colleges a punishable offence, the bill was moved by M. C. Rajah, a fellow-signatory with CR of the Poona Pact and the assembly's leading Dalit, who observed that CR had long wanted such a measure.

But the premier was unable to keep a promise to Rajah to support a blanket temple entry bill prepared by the latter, giving worshippers the right by majority vote to open a temple to Dalits. In 1933, CR had drafted an identical bill after the effort to open the doors of Malabar's Guruvayur temple had failed. However, in 1938 he opted for a measure limited to Malabar, for which he obtained a disappointed Rajah's backing.

Despite strong opposition from orthodox members, the Malabar Temple Entry Bill was passed in September 1938. Ten months later, in July 1939, when trustees and priests of Madurai's prestigious Meenakshi Temple said they wanted to open its doors but feared proceedings for 'offending religious sentiment', CR promised protective legislation if they took the lead.

On 8 July, the temple's priests broke with tradition by allowing entry to Dalits brought by the activist Vaidyanatha Iyer. On the 11th, the draft of an indemnity bill was published by the Madras government. On the 17th an ordinance was issued, replaced later by an Act, indemnifying trustees and priests who opened their temples to Dalits.

Some of the measure's orthodox foes focused on its indirectness. Other critics warned of violence. Krishnamachari recalled Ghazni, the eleventh-century iconoclast, and told CR in the Assembly, 'The blood will be on your head.' There is 'no use my being a minister if I cannot protect the people who brought this about', replied the premier.[71]

In a matter of weeks, hundreds of temples opened their doors to Dalits, including ninety in Thanjavur district. The Congress's stock rose.[72] Tirupati did not open but the Courtallam temple was among those that did. There was no bloodshed.

◆

Earlier in 1939, CR was involved in the national Congress's conflict over its freshly re-elected president, Subhas Bose. Most Congress leaders thought that Bose's advocacy of a mass national struggle for ousting British rule was untimely, and they were troubled by an impression that he wished to sideline Gandhi.

When, in March, the Congress met in Tripuri, not far from Jabalpur in the centre of India, CR seconded, in an astute speech, a resolution asking Bose to 'appoint the Working Committee in accordance with the wishes of Mahatma Gandhi'. Though the UP premier, Govind Ballabh Pant, had moved the resolution, CR may have drafted it.[73] Passed at Tripuri, the resolution triggered Bose's departure from the Congress.

The Muslim League, meanwhile, was getting ready to ask for Pakistan.

The international scene was even more dramatic. In the opening days of September 1939, war erupted in Europe, spelling the end of the Congress–Raj compact and of all the provincial ministries of the Congress, including the one in Madras.

Changing calculations on all sides, the war made Indians keener than ever for independence, in part because England and France had entered it to protect the independence of European lands threatened by Germany. On its part, England hardened its resistance to Indian freedom.

Weeks before the war began, London announced that provincial governments could, as necessary, be overridden or taken over. Once hostilities started, without talking to any Indian leader, the viceroy declared (on 3 September) that India, too, was at war against Germany. What after the war, the Congress asked. Independence? Dominion status? Replying more than a month later, London said, 'Talks.'

Unlike Bose, who was willing to take aid from England's enemies, CR could contemplate Congress giving 'wholehearted support to Britain in the fight against gangsterism personified', which is what he said in a letter on Christmas day to an ICS officer devoted to him, J. B. L. Munro.[74] But England had to commit to dominion status for India at the end of the war and take Congressmen right away into the government in New Delhi.

On 16 September, shortly after the Congress working committee had sought answers on Britain's war aims, Erskine forwarded CR's plea that the viceroy should see Gandhi and Nehru, adding his comment: 'Personally I think we should not enter into any bargain, for if Congress do go out it will be their funeral, not ours.'[75]

Preferring a 'funeral' to humiliation, the Congress exited from office at the end of October. Urged by CR, the Madras assembly had passed a resolution asking his ministry to resign. More than a year earlier, he had said that 'he was ready to retire the next morning if necessary'.[76]

CR's speech on 26 October 1939 was a classic farewell to Empire from a proud antagonist.

> The British are a democratically governed people. But they are an imperialist people... They do not want any other people to rule over them, but the Secretary of State is to govern India...
>
> Has [America] joined the War? No. 'Cash and carry'—that is their formula... Do we say anything so bad? No, we say, 'Let us go not at the end of a leash but as a free people.
>
> We could have had Swaraj in the palm of our hand if the Muslim League had played the game... We could even have fought afterwards among ourselves...

Recalling 'the greatest of the plays of the greatest of poets', CR cited from *King Lear*:

> The eldest daughter said to the king, 'I love you more than words can wield the matter; dearer than eyesight, space and liberty.' Lear

was pleased and said, 'Take this vast portion of my kingdom.' The next girl said she loved him even more; she also got an ample share. But the third said, 'I love you as I should, neither more nor less. I cannot give away all my love to you. I have got to keep a portion of it for my future husband.' Lear got angry…

Congress cannot give all its love to Britain. It must reserve that which is India's share.

Alluding to measures planned but not passed, including the 'law laying down anew the relationship between Zamindars and tenants', CR added:

The house was bedecked. The bride was to come in. But no, we say suddenly. The pandal is to be pulled down.[77]

On the floor of the house, Pannirselvam called it 'one of the most marvellous speeches I have ever been privileged to listen to'.

After resigning on 30 October, *The Hindu* would report, the premier cheerfully signed certificates for drivers, clerks and peons at a desk from which all files had been cleared and the despatch box removed.[78]

◆

As for EVR, he joined two other men with large and devout followings, Jinnah and Ambedkar, to celebrate what Jinnah termed 'Deliverance Day', or freedom from Congress rule. The Empire was sufficiently constitutional not to dissolve elected legislatures, but in Madras Hindi was promptly withdrawn from government schools.

There were larger declarations. On 17 December, EVR demanded 'Dravida Nadu for Dravidians'. In March 1940, the Muslim League formally called from Lahore for a sovereign Pakistan, and Jinnah journeyed to Madras to announce support for an independent Dravida country, which the Justice Party, with EVR as president, formally asked for.

Periyar gave full support to the Pakistan demand and travelled to Bombay to meet Jinnah and Ambedkar, where the three explored possibilities of joint action.[79]

At a conference in Kanchipuram in June 1940, EVR presented a map of a separate Dravida Nadu, taking in the Tamil, Telugu, Kannada and Malayalam areas of Madras Presidency and a few adjoining pieces.[80]

The four southern groups, Periyar argued, were racially different from the Aryan Brahmin.[81]

The war in Europe was destabilizing an India striving to become an independent nation.

Within the southern Congress, CR received a setback in 1940 when, in a keenly contested election for the TNCC presidency, his candidate, Coimbatore's C. P. Subbiah, was defeated by three votes, 103 to 100,[82] by someone watching CR's premiership from close quarters since 1937, the MLA from Sattur, just south of Virudhunagar, Kumaraswami Kamaraj.

Satyamurti had proposed Kamaraj's name for the TNCC chair, worked hard for his victory, and may have had a score to settle with CR, but Kamaraj's success, and growing subsequent strength, was an expression of the Congress's need for a non-Brahmin leader from the grassroots. The need was realized by CR, whose nominee, Subbiah, too was a non-Brahmin. Yet it was the tall, dark and vigilant Kamaraj who found the break.

Ever since his release after the Salt Satyagraha of 1930, when Virudhunagar welcomed him back as a hero, this bachelor who was a ceaselessly travelling, round-the-clock public worker had built a personal link with almost every Congress worker in the Tamil country. He had also filed away in his mind an understanding of how, in different nooks of that country, various castes, sub-castes, classes and personalities viewed one another.

Now, in the summer of 1940, he had found the chance to lead.

Chapter 11

FREEDOM!: 1939–1948

South Indians seemed reluctant to cross the threshold for all-India leadership. In December 1938, two years after turning down pressure from Patel and Satyamurti to accept the Congress presidency, CR told Governor Erskine, who had asked him about new stories of his heading the party nationwide, that he was not drawn to that role.[1]

In the late 1930s, the Congress's national leadership seemed to comprise, Gandhi apart, of six men: Nehru, Patel, Bose, Rajendra Prasad, Abul Kalam Azad and CR. The only South Indian in this circle, CR appeared uninterested in preserving his place there.

By the end of 1939, Nehru, Patel, Bose and Prasad had all served in the Congress chair: Patel once, each of the other three more than once. With Jinnah moving towards the Pakistan demand, Gandhi thought of Azad as the next Congress president. But he gave CR first refusal, asking him, when they talked in Wardha, to mail the Mahatma's offer to Azad, which CR faithfully did.[2]

Within months, however, a period began, which would last for about two years, when events pushed CR to exercise national leadership. In the process, he challenged Gandhi.

Assembling under Azad's presidency in Ramgarh in Bihar in March 1940, the Congress reiterated that it could not join the Empire's war when India's freedom was not promised at its end. Neither could it embarrass an England threatened by Nazi Germany. It resolved the dilemma by deciding to offer selective, disciplined disobedience to the Empire, a stance fully backed by CR.

Within a few days, at a meeting in Lahore, the Muslim League openly demanded Pakistan.

This was followed by Hitler's blitzkrieg of April and May 1940. Most portions of Denmark, Norway, Holland and France were seized by Germany. In CR's mind, this altered the Empire–India equation. To have India as an ally, an England that had lost France might be willing, CR thought, to woo India.

Gandhi was sceptical, the more so as Churchill, replacing Neville Chamberlain, had become England's prime minister. Nonetheless, CR enlisted the support, one by one, of Azad, Patel and Nehru, in that order. In July, meeting in Poona, the Congress offered to join the war if its leaders were taken into the Indian government and the viceregal veto was withdrawn.

The Congress had preferred CR's reasoning to his, but Gandhi did not block its choice. He would be happy, he indicated in *Harijan,* if a Congress leader was invited to lead the government in New Delhi—'one day it may be Rajaji, another day it may be Jawaharlal',[3] he wrote but did not think it likely.

Gandhi's doubts proved correct, and in a declaration in August the Empire, which had been negotiating with Jinnah and other Congress opponents, flatly rejected the Congress offer. Unabashed about divide and rule, the declaration also assured 'elements in India's national life' opposed to the Congress that their 'coercion into submission' would 'never' be allowed.[4]

Having 'taken the lead' in attempting to come to terms with Britain, 'even at the risk of parting with Gandhiji', CR now felt 'completely disillusioned and disappointed'. This, in his words, was Nehru's analysis.[5] However, large crowds heard CR in places like Ellore and Rajahmundry. His message was, 'I am angry. I want you also to feel angry.'[6]

Arthur Hope, Erskine's successor as governor, asked Linlithgow for permission to 'shut up' CR, adding, 'He is obviously angling for the Gandhi succession and is in fact leading Congress throughout India'.[7] Soon CR and hundreds of others in the Congress would themselves court imprisonment. Meanwhile, the ex-premier of Madras made an unexpected move via a reporter of London's *Herald.*

> Let me make a sporting offer. If HMG will agree to a provisional national government being formed at once, I undertake to persuade my colleagues in the Congress to agree to the Muslim League being invited to nominate a Prime Minister and let him form the national government as he would consider best.[8]

Asked in the House of Commons about CR's 'sporting offer', Leopold Amery, the new secretary of state for India, replied that 'no new approach to the Indian question would be considered'.[9]

The Congress returned to Gandhi, and CR too joined its Individual Civil Disobedience campaign of 1940–41, as did thousands of others. The restrained and disciplined campaign—which Gandhi asked a close associate, Vinoba Bhave, to begin—kept the Congress conspicuous at a time when Jinnah was asking for Pakistan and Periyar for Dravida Nadu.

In CR's case, imprisonment came after he declared, in a letter to six MLAs (including some in the opposition) that it was 'wrong to help with men or money' a war for which India's legislatures had not been consulted. On the morning of 3 December, he was picked up from his Bazlulla Road home and taken to the chief presidency magistrate, Abbas Ali, who sentenced him to a year in prison.

Pronouncing the sentence, Ali's voice quavered as he quoted Arjuna's line, 'My body trembles, my breath stops, my bow slips from my hands.' Ali expressed the hope that as a Gita student, CR would recognize a magistrate's duty.

The ten months that CR spent behind bars, most of them in Trichy Jail, were partly devoted to Ramayana studies, but political consultations also occasionally occurred and new thinking emerged.

From distant Lahore, the Unionist Party premier of Punjab, Sikandar Hayat Khan (who had emulated Madras's debt relief law), sent CR the draft of a statement, conciliatory to both the Congress and the League, which he hoped Amery might issue from London, and wanted CR's reaction before sending it to London.

This was in May 1941. Sikandar was the pro-war premier of a province providing Britain with large numbers of Muslim and Sikh soldiers. Recognizing that a message from him to Amery would carry weight, CR told the person bringing the draft to Trichy Jail, *The Hindu*'s editor-proprietor Kasturi Srinivasan, that he was happy with it.

But this peace initiative quickly died. The viceroy expressed his annoyance to Governor Arthur Hope for allowing Srinivasan to meet CR in prison,[10] and Sikandar, warned by the Empire, ceased confabulating with the Congress leadership.[11]

Hope was unaware of Sikandar's bid when he permitted Srinivasan to enter Trichy Jail. Linlithgow's reaction must have puzzled him, for one result of the CR–Srinivasan interview was a *Hindu* editorial advocating the end of disobedience.

The world outside was continuing to change. In December 1940, Hitler had attacked the Soviet Union, hitherto Germany's ally.

CR was looking for a way out of India's political logjam well before his release in October 1941. After release, he met with Gandhi but could not persuade him to resume talks with the Empire, and he failed also with Nehru and Patel. But he won Azad, and once more a world event influenced Congress policy.

Japan having attacked Pearl Harbor on 7 December, America entered the war. Wouldn't America prod England to do something about India?

Despite Gandhi's disagreement, and despite opposition from Patel, Nehru and Prasad, first the Congress working committee and then the All India Congress Committee (AICC), recognizing 'the new world situation', offered cooperation to the allies—Britain, Russia, China and the US—provided India's freedom was declared. It was a big 'if'.

Yet CR had won an important round. He told the AICC, which met in Wardha:

> Our cooperation is available if the British do the right thing. Supposing the central government is placed in my hands, then I would take it. But if the Madras government is given to me without control of the centre, I would not touch it... If I am a hunter, please credit me with being a big game hunter.[12]

Once more Gandhi said he would not stand in the AICC's way. But he made a significant public statement:

> I have said for some years and say now that not Rajaji, not Sardar Vallabhbhai but Jawaharlal will be my successor.[13]

Expressing, for the first time, a readiness to lead an all-India government, CR had also displayed independence and persuasive skills. But not realism. Neither he nor those he persuaded recognized the Indian public's mood of anger towards the British, or the Empire's growing resistance to Indian independence.

Refusing to focus on Gandhi's public elimination of his name, CR spent the following three months rousing public opinion for defence against Japan, which had swiftly seized Hong Kong, the Philippines and Malaya before the dramatic surrender, on 15 February, of Singapore, the Empire's supposed citadel.

Affected by South India's proximity to Malaya and Singapore, CR was on fire. His speeches—in places like Madras, Madurai, Hospet near Bangalore, Ramanathapuram, Virudhunagar and Tinnevelly—were numerous, the crowds huge, the cheers long.

He sounded willing, eager even, to be a war leader, underlining the threat from Japan, recalling heroes like Shivaji, Haidar, Tipu and Ranjit Singh, and criticizing the Empire's refusal to settle with the Congress. Speaking of 'voluntary government' and 'civil defence' if the Empire abandoned South India, he declared:

> *Madras, 21 Jan 1942*: I do not want to surrender to the Japanese. Why should I? I am not carried away by mere hatred... I want to defend my country, and I want to defend it at once.[14]

CR had 'done good in telling the people that India has nothing to gain from the Japanese', observed Hope, writing to the viceroy, but he added that CR's 'attitude that Britain can no longer defend India...is causing a lot of harm'.[15] Significantly enough, CR spoke of Jinnah too.

> *Madras, 21 Jan 1942*: Today the battlefronts include bazaars, the houses of civilians, plantations, fields and factories. Is it good... that there should be a division between government and soldiers on the one hand, and tremendously popular organizations like the Congress and the Muslim League on the other, over whom such illustrious persons as Mahatma Gandhi and Quaid-e-Azam Jinnah preside?... One has become almost as famous as the other.[16]

When CR added that the demand for a separate and sovereign Pakistan was 'an impossible stand', Jinnah publicly asked him to 'define some basis, some common ground' for a Congress–League agreement[17]. CR saw this as an opening.

By this time, Subhas Bose, president of the Congress from February 1938 to the middle of 1939, had slipped out of house arrest in Calcutta and was asking Hitler and Japan to help with Indian independence. There were reports that Bose's supporters would assist any incoming Japanese forces.

Jawaharlal, on the other hand, was recommending a 'scorched-earth policy and guerrilla warfare' in the event of a Japanese invasion, a position supported by the Indian Communist Party.[18]

Gandhi faced his life's biggest challenge thus far: a combination of British inflexibility, bitter divisions inside the Congress, the Pakistan call, the possibility of a Japanese invasion, and a pro-violence fever overwhelming the nonviolent movement he had led from 1915.

The response he came up with was simple. On India's behalf, the Congress should bluntly ask the British to quit.

◆

The Quit India call was preceded by a visit to India in March 1942 by a rising British star, Stafford Cripps, a Labour Party minister in Churchill's coalition government, who offered seemingly promising but in fact unworkable proposals towards independence. Churchill had sent him to India not to return the country to Indians but to placate Franklin Roosevelt, the American president sympathetic to freedom for India. Churchill's glee at the failure of the Cripps Mission is well known.

Working together in Delhi, Nehru and CR tried to reach a deal with Cripps but failed. The British minister was hamstrung by Churchill's written instructions against any terms that Viceroy Linlithgow and Commander-in-Chief Archibald Wavell would not accept. At least partial encouragement for the demands for Pakistan and Dravida Nadu was offered by Cripps's failed proposals, which seemed to give provinces, as well as rajas, the right to join or not join any future Union of India.

Along with three other leaders of the Justice Party, Periyar met Cripps in Delhi at the end of March and asked for Dravida Nadu. However, if we go by Cripps's note about the meeting, the delegation conceded that they could not win a plebiscite for secession.

Evidently EVR and his colleagues asked for a large, separate electorate for the presidency's non-Brahmins, presumably to enable a future Madras assembly to vote for secession. Cripps told the Justice Party leaders that that route did not seem feasible; they had to 'persuade the people of Madras to vote in their favour' under a common electorate.[19]

While concerned over the potential in Cripps's proposals for India's balkanization, the Congress working committee disavowed any wish to coerce crucial sections of the population. A resolution affirmed the Congress's stand against 'compelling the people of any territorial unit to remain in an Indian Union against their declared and established will'.

◆

After Japanese bombs fell in Kakinada and Vizag on 6 April 1942, people in Madras city expected bombs the following morning, but nothing happened, and bombings on the Coromandel coast ceased. Blackouts in the city sufficed, however, for CR to let go of the national scene and concentrate on his province.

Though Congress MLAs were not paid salaries after CR's ministry resigned in December 1939, the legislature had not been dissolved. On 18 April, CR told Hope that he was 'prepared to run an independent show in Madras' for which, in addition to the Congress MLAs, he would enlist the Justice Party and the provincial Muslim League.

What discussion, if any, he had on this with EVR, the Justice Party's head from 1938, is not clear, except that the party had declared its support for the Empire's war.

Six days later, on 24 April, the Congress MLAs met, with CR in the chair, and passed two resolutions. By the first resolution, the MLAs recommended that 'at this hour of peril' the AICC should concede the Muslim League's claim for the separation of 'certain areas'. The second resolution sought the AICC's permission, in the context of the bombings, for inviting the Muslim League's support for a popular government in Madras to organize and defend the public.[20]

Azad, the Congress president,* commented that he was 'greatly astonished' by the resolutions, Patel was furious, and Nehru called the move 'undesirable' and 'extraordinary'.[21] Journeying to Sevagram, CR talked with Gandhi for two hours, after which the Mahatma told his secretary, Pyarelal:

I am wholly opposed to [CR]. But I hold that Rajaji has acted in a wholly constitutional manner. I am a lover of personal freedom and free expression of views... He was hasty in pronouncing his

---

*The campaigns of Individual Civil Disobedience (1940–41) and Quit India (1942–45) preventing changes, Azad remained in the chair from 1940 to 1946.

opinion on vital things before he had consulted his colleagues, but who can help being hasty in these times?[22]

From Sevagram, CR proceeded to Allahabad, where the AICC was meeting. At the station, Hindu Mahasabha men raised black flags against him. In the city, Azad told him that he should have consulted national colleagues before convening the Madras MLAs. Agreeing, CR expressed regret and resigned from the working committee.

Votes at the AICC meeting where CR defended the resolutions of the Madras MLAs went overwhelmingly against him—120 to 15. But he had argued his case with characteristic skill. When with a loud 'No!' Nehru interrupted CR's remark that India's Muslims seemed solidly behind the Muslim League, CR replied: 'I challenge you to produce results. Produce a communal settlement and I will go down on my knees before you'.[23]

He also pointed out that the Madras MLAs had acted in the spirit of the working committee's 'non-coercion' resolution. Though cordially cheered at the end of his intervention, an impulsive CR had isolated himself. After Allahabad, the Madras MLAs began deserting him. Eventually only seven would stand by CR.

EVR, however, seems to have said that 'Rajaji's scheme was not to be condemned outright but might be worth considering'.[24]

Meanwhile Gandhi, too, had dared on his own with the Quit India call. Unlike CR, however, the Mahatma had taken the pulse of the public before moving ahead. Patel, fleetingly, and Azad and Nehru for much longer, tried to resist Quit India, but everyone gave in after encountering Gandhi's conviction and the people's backing for it.

In August, Nehru would move the Quit India resolution in Bombay. CR continued to oppose Quit India and ask for a settlement with the Muslim League. He reached out to the public in Salem, Madurai, Thanjavur and elsewhere, drawing impressive crowds as also bitter opposition and at times hostility. *The Hindu* reported what CR told a knot of violent disturbers at a Madurai meeting: 'If I am to be afraid of you, how am I to face Japanese aggressors if they come?' Added the newspaper:

A missile was thrown at Rajaji. He jumped into the crowd of hostile demonstrators and declared, 'You want to attack me? Come on, here I am'.[25]

For weeks, he held private and public debates with Gandhi until the Mahatma wrote to him:

5 July 1942: Mahadev was telling me how sad you were over my obstinacy in not appreciating what was so plain to you... But I am built that way... I suppose you are of the same build... There seems to be no escape but to suffer each other's limitations.[26]

Public criticism of Congress policies by one seen only a few months earlier as one of Gandhi's likely successors exacted its price. Gandhi advised CR that 'it will be most becoming for you to sever your connection with the Congress and then carry on your campaign', and he added that Patel wanted CR to vacate his assembly seat.[27]

At about the same time, Kamaraj, the thirty-nine-year-old TNCC president, asked CR, who was older by twenty-four years, to show cause within fifteen days why disciplinary action should not be taken against him. To Kamaraj, CR wrote back:

I do seek to convert the Congress from its present attitude. I have done this with the care and caution that may be expected of one who had identified himself for over 30 years with the Congress and who knows the value of discipline as well as the need for liberty of thought in a national organization.[28]

Resigning from the Congress and the assembly, CR continued to urge Gandhi to negotiate with a Jinnah who was denouncing Quit India as a coercive strategy to replace British rule with Hindu Raj. On 7 and 8 August, the AICC endorsed Quit India in Bombay. On 6 August, CR had wired him from Madras:

You should ignore Jinnah's allegations and...offer him such quota of provisional government as he wants... This along with your names on behalf of Congress will rationalize your demand of Britain and force acceptance of proposals.

Replied Gandhi:

Every effort has been and will be made in the direction indicated by you though not identical. Love. Bapu.[29]

Theirs was a tussle out of the ordinary.

◆

The Empire's arrangements for arresting Gandhi and other leaders, suppressing defiance, breaking strikes, and unleashing propaganda were in place well before the Congress tried to organize Quit India, but spontaneity gave the movement its power.

In the pre-dawn hours of 9 August, shortly after an AICC meeting ended on the night of the 8th, Gandhi, Azad, Nehru, Patel and hundreds of others were picked up. But the public was on fire. At the end of a stirring speech, Gandhi had passed on the baton directly to every Indian.

When word of the arrests spread on the 9th, an unplanned explosion seemed to shake India. The shaking continued even after Congress organizations were banned, many more arrests made, and heavy censorship imposed. Demonstrating Indians streamed out of bazaars, colleges and villages, shouting 'Do or Die', and in many cases attacking post and telegraph offices, telephone and railway lines, and police stations. Within four days, 600 Indians were cut down by the Empire's police. By end-November, around 1,000 had been killed, the House of Commons was told. Actual numbers were higher. When August ended, the Empire was out of actual danger, but more than 100,000 Indian nationalists were jailed for indefinite terms in what, in a letter to the king, Linlithgow called 'by far the most serious rebellion since that of 1857'.[30]

There was a core of truth in sweeping generalizations about 1942, like this one from a Bengal politician, Arun Chandra Guha:

> The entire nation...rural and urban, the uneducated and the elite classes, women and men, all came out in rebellion. In many cases women took the lead...in facing the bullets and lathi charges.[31]

Bold things were also done across the south's Malayalam, Tamil, Telugu and Kannada regions, most dramatically perhaps in the latter two. In the course of time, however, another side would be revealed. We may look, first, at this account of a Quit India rebellion in 'Isur, a remote village in Shikaripura taluk of Shimoga district' in the Kannada country.

> On September 25th [1942], when the revenue officials went to the village to collect land revenue, boys and girls shouting patriotic

slogans mobbed them and seized their record books. The following day the village...established a parallel government.

A new law was declared by which everyone had to wear a khadi cap. On September 28th, [when] the government Amildar and his men entered the village, [they] were surrounded...and asked to wear khadi caps. This enraged the police officer accompanying the Amildar...

Lathi charge was followed by firing and the mob become violent. Among the casualties were the Amildar and the police officer...

The Mysore police and military forces descended upon the village... Innocent were tortured, women molested, and houses looted. Charges were filed against many and about five patriots, Gurappa, Mallappa, Suryanarayanachari, Halappa and Sankarappa, were hanged in March 1943.

In response, this website comment was posted on 15 September 2010:

Sir/Mme, The Amildar who was brutally killed by these insurgents was my uncle. He was a gentle, intelligent compassionate human being... My uncle's name was V. N. Chenna Krishnappa, who had finished his Master of Law from Loyola of Madras, coming first...in 1940. He was married in 1941 and left his young widow to mourn for the rest of her life.[32]

◆

Though he had resigned from the Congress, after August 1942 CR was about the only prominent Congress-connected figure not in prison. After the rebellion quieted down, he pushed at the Empire's doors to see if they would yield. He also wrestled with Jinnah's challenge to him to produce a basis for a Congress–League settlement.

A London visit by CR was proposed by Britons friendly to India, but the viceroy and Amery would hear none of it. In November, CR called on Linlithgow and asked for a chance to see Gandhi, who was a prisoner in the Aga Khan's house in Poona. The viceroy rejected the request.

But in February 1943, after Gandhi announced a twenty-one-day fast because he had been barred from answering charges of complicity in Quit India's violence, and three Indians on the viceroy's executive council resigned in sympathy, CR was permitted to meet Gandhi in his confinement.

He described to Gandhi his solution for Jinnah's demands. When Gandhi responded positively, CR wrote his 'formula' down and obtained Gandhi's assent to the written draft, which had four components.

One, the League should endorse the independence demand and cooperate with the Congress in a provisional all-India government. Two, the Congress should agree to post-war plebiscites in contiguous areas, to be identified by a commission, where Muslims outnumbered non-Muslims. Three, the Congress should accept secession if the plebiscites favoured it. Four, in the event of separation, there should be mutual agreements on defence, commerce and communications.[33]

Gandhi's acceptance of his formula was a trump card that CR pocketed. He did not reveal it when, a month later, he talked for ninety minutes with Jinnah in Bombay. But the conversation sufficed for Jinnah to say to the press that he would be open to an initiative from Gandhi.

Learning in prison (from *Dawn*, the League mouthpiece) of Jinnah's 'offer', Gandhi wrote him a letter proposing a meeting. The Raj stopped the letter but informed Jinnah of its contents. The League leader chose to ignore a proposal he had invited but not directly received.

A Congress–League agreement was not a popular goal as 1943 ended, and a Congress–Empire truce seemed nowhere near. Replacing Linlithgow as viceroy, Wavell talked with CR in Madras and told him, without being asked, that he would *not* accept a 'national government' with 'so many nominees of the Congress and so many of the League'.[34]

In April 1944, CR thought the lull might end if he pulled out his trump card. Meeting Jinnah in Delhi, CR described his formula and Gandhi's acceptance of it. It made no impression on Jinnah, who appeared to want all of Punjab and Bengal, not merely their Muslim-majority portions, and Assam as well, and disliked the idea of mutual agreements.

'How did your meeting go?' G. D. Birla asked CR. 'Jinnah is too old,' CR replied.[35]

◆

Not only was Gandhi quite ill by this time but his wife Kasturba, and also Mahadev Desai, his companion-aide, both detained along with him, had died. A rebuke from CR to the Empire for continuing to imprison an ailing Mahatma had just been published when, on 6 May 1944, Gandhi was released.

In July, he asked CR to join him in Panchgani on the hills near Poona. After they conferred, CR wired Jinnah stating that he was releasing his Pakistan formula to the press. Would Jinnah object if he announced the League leader's rejection? He would indeed object, said Jinnah, adding that Gandhi should deal directly with him.

On 17 July, Gandhi wrote to Jinnah. Between 9 and 27 September, the two met fourteen times in Jinnah's Malabar Hill home. Each time Gandhi walked from his lodgings in nearby Birla House. Letters between the two, in all containing more than 15,000 words, recorded their conversations.

Gandhi was not optimistic when the talks began. Neither was CR. An end-July statement by Jinnah that CR's formula only offered 'a maimed, mutilated and moth-eaten Pakistan'[36] was hardly an encouraging signal.

But the exercise was gone through, each hoping to influence the other. On his part, Gandhi also wished to know Jinnah as fully as possible, and he knew that history would not forgive a refusal to attempt agreement.

Excitement in the country joined cordiality between the protagonists. Reporters crowding Jinnah's spacious lawns felt they stood on history's stage. Photographs showed Gandhi and Jinnah smiling. Many in the land prayed.

But the talks failed. Jinnah repeated that he wanted all of Bengal and Punjab. He insisted that in any plebiscites only Muslims would vote. To him the bonds of alliance that Gandhi and CR desired were chains of subjugation. And he wanted separation before the British left, not after.

Gandhi had asked Jinnah to give 'in writing what precisely you want me to put my signature to'[37] but the League leader demurred. What exactly did Jinnah want? Pakistan? Something else?

Joined to his rejection of what seemed a reasonable offer, Jinnah's refusal to spell out his Pakistan left an intriguing question in a corner of Gandhi's mind.

The League leader had turned down a plea from Periyar to raise Dravidastan as well in his talks with Gandhi. Expressing sympathy for 'the non-Brahmins forming 90 percent of the population of Madras', Jinnah however added that Dravidastan was a question for the Madras non-Brahmins to pursue.[38]

◆

In Bombay, Gandhi had given CR daily reports of his talks with Jinnah. Their bond seemed as deep as ever, with no shadows left of their public disputes of 1942. It was a different story in South India. Most Congressmen there, including hundreds still in jail, were not ready to forget CR's absence from Quit India.

Until their release in the 1945 summer, men like Prakasam in the Telugu country, Kamaraj in the Tamil country, and numerous other Congressmen would spend three years in prison for their Quit India activities. Satyamurti had died in March 1943 after suffering a spinal cord injury while being transported to Nagpur as a prisoner. In the mid-1940s' climate of hardship, there was little sympathy for CR in the presidency's large Congress constituency.

In the sidelined Justice Party, members were divided between a minority of pro-Empire elites and Periyar's followers, who comprised the majority. In 1944, the latter converted the Justice Party into a new association, the Dravida Kazhagam (DK), with EVR as their chief, while a small group, led by the England-educated Ponnambala Thiaga Rajan (1892–1974), claimed continuance as the original Justice Party.

Focusing on equality, Periyar's DK asked members to renounce titles given by the British, eliminate caste suffixes from their names, and resign nominated and appointed posts. A key role in the DK's emergence was played by the writer-orator Annadurai, who became general secretary.

Assembling in Trichy in the following year, the DK adopted a black flag ('in mourning for subjected Dravidian people') with a circle in the centre in red (representing hope). It also announced a goal of a sovereign independent Dravidian republic with four linguistic units, each possessing residuary powers.

Four years earlier, addressing an All-India Muslim Conference in Madras, Annadurai had said, 'I shall do all to help...establish Dravidistan', and suggested that 'Muslims are but Dravidians on an Islamic path'. Though Jinnah had gradually distanced himself from Dravidastan, EVR and Annadurai were unwilling to give it up.[39]

In the 1940s, Periyar and Annadurai assailed a centuries' old Tamil classic, Kamban's *Ramayanam*, for allegedly glorifying Aryan supremacy. Helping edit EVR's *Viduthalai* and *Kudi Arasu*, Annadurai, or 'Anna', as he was increasingly called, launched his own weekly, the *Dravida Nadu,* in March 1942. Scripting plays to earn money, he also founded the Dravida Drama Troupe and performed stage roles.

In November 1943, Anna's first drama, *Chandrodayam*, debuted in Erode in EVR's presence. By 1945, EVR was declaring opposition to the British Raj. The change in stance was inescapable if he and the DK wished to retain prestige in post-war South India.[40]

◆

As Hitler neared his end, Viceroy Wavell did what he had expressly and categorically ruled out. He offered the Congress and the League a chance to form a joint national government.

The soldier-viceroy had read the changing world better than Prime Minister Churchill. British soldiers were no longer keen to remain in India, and Britons in the homeland wanted a respite from imperial involvements.

After weeks of lobbying in London, in March 1945 Wavell extracted Churchill's reluctant permission to release imprisoned Congress members, including leaders, and initiate a dialogue on a national government. On his part, the premier urged Wavell to divide India into 'Hindustan, Pakistan and Princestan etc.' Three months later, after British voters had sent Churchill to opposition benches, the ex-premier exhorted Wavell, who was again in London, to 'keep a bit of India'.[41]

At the end of June, released Congress leaders—including Azad, who was still the party president, Nehru and Patel, all of them thin and exhausted after three years in jail—journeyed to Simla to see what the Empire would offer. So did Gandhi, and Jinnah, and premiers or recent premiers of provinces, including CR.

The viceroy's proposal of a joint and autonomous Congress–

League government looked reasonable, and the Congress accepted it. Jinnah did not. He demanded, in Wavell's words, 'the absolute right to select all Muslims' for the government, which to the viceroy was 'entirely unacceptable'.[42] Declaring that his bid had failed, Wavell sent participants home.

On the way back to Madras, CR stopped in Bombay to offer remarks at a women's university that EVR would have approved:

> [I] hope that a large and organized movement may grow for inter-marriages between boys and girls of different castes or religions... Caste can be abolished only by abolishing the very basis of caste, not by eating or working or playing together, but only by inter-marriage.[43]

◆

Though the Simla bid had failed, the Raj announced elections for provincial legislatures to be held in the winter of 1945–46. Meeting in Ariyalur in Trichy district, the Tamil country's released Congressmen voted 670 to 4 to deny roles to those who had stayed out of Quit India.

A defeated Hitler killed himself during that 1945 summer. Some weeks later, Japan surrendered after atom bombs were dropped in Hiroshima and Nagasaki. And Subhas Bose, who had sought German and Japanese help for India's freedom, died in an air crash in Taipei.

In an impressive but flawed exercise in the following year, three members of the British cabinet (secretary of state for India, Lord Pethick-Lawrence, old India hand Stafford Cripps, now president of the board of trade, and first lord of the admiralty, A. V. Alexander) spent three months in India pursuing two difficult aims: installing an interim Congress–League government in New Delhi and resolving the Pakistan demand.

On the latter question, Gandhi's recommendation to the Cabinet Mission, as it was called, was the Pakistan of the CR formula. When the Mission offered this 'small' Pakistan to Jinnah, with the improvement that it could be totally detached from India, the League leader once more rejected it.

The Mission then drafted what *might* have been an acceptable compromise: a large and largely autonomous 'Pakistan area', inclusive of all of Bengal and Punjab and Assam, within an Indian Union. But the Congress opposed the joining of East Punjab, West Bengal or Assam even to a Pakistan-within-India, and the League could not tolerate the slightest association of even 'Big Pakistan' with an Indian Union. For three British cabinet ministers to fail after toiling in India for three months was not an acceptable proposition. The Mission therefore made two clever moves. First, it lured the Congress and the League by announcing that a party or parties accepting their scheme could nominate ministers for an interim government. Second, it tweaked a few words in their scheme to allow the Congress to interpret it one way and the League in a different way.

Both 'accepted' the scheme with their own clashing interpretations.

Wavell did not like the cleverness but went along with the British ministers. Gandhi disliked the ambiguity but went along with Nehru, Patel, Azad, Prasad and CR, all of whom thought that the Congress had earned the right to govern, if need be through ambiguity. Of these five, only CR had dissented from Gandhi in 1942. In 1946, all five dissented.

Gandhi had been isolated.

Both the Congress and the League having 'accepted' the Cabinet Mission's plan, the two parties were invited, in August 1946, to nominate persons to an interim government of India.

◆

In July 1946, Nehru replaced Azad as the Congress president and named CR to the working committee. Azad had previously readmitted him into the Congress.

But CR's heart was in his province, where, as in most other provinces, new elections held early in 1946 had produced a large Congress majority. Though Quit India had not ousted the British, it had strengthened the Congress's bond with the Indian people.

Needing a chief minister, the south's leaders—Kamaraj, the TNCC chief, Prakasam, president of the Andhra Congress, and Madhava Menon, who chaired the Congress in Malabar—sought the Congress high command's advice. With Gandhi's backing, Azad, Patel and Nehru recommended CR's name.

By a large majority of 148 to 38 votes, Madras's newly elected

Congress MLAs rejected the advice. Kamaraj then proposed Muthuranga Mudaliar while Telugu MLAs nominated Prakasam. Winning the votes of 82 MLAs to Mudaliar's 69 (the rest, most of them CR supporters, remaining neutral), Prakasam became the presidency's chief minister on 30 April 1947.

◆

Double-speak from all three sides, the British, the Congress and the League, contributed to the suspicion and bitterness that enveloped India from June 1946. The Congress and the League accused each other of dishonesty and of intriguing with the British.

Insisting that the Cabinet Mission's proposals entitled only the Muslim League to enter the interim government, and alleging a Congress–British plot to foil the League, Jinnah announced 'Direct Action' both by the League and its backers. The result was the Great Calcutta Killings of 16–20 August, in which thousands perished, mostly Hindus on the first day and later a larger number of Muslims.

Calcutta's massacres were followed in October by rape, forced conversion and violence against hundreds from the Hindu minority in Noakhali in east Bengal, which was followed in October–November by the killing of thousands of Muslims in Bihar.

This shedding of blood was accompanied by the empowerment of India's political leaders. Though called 'interim', and though technically chaired by a British soldier-viceroy, an Indian government came into being in Delhi in September and October 1946.

While designated vice-chairman, Nehru was in effect prime minister. In addition to Nehru, who took the external affairs portfolio, the interim government included home member Patel and the League's Liaquat Ali Khan, who became the finance member. Not prepared to serve under Nehru, Jinnah stayed out.

Two South Indians were part of the interim government: CR from the Congress quota and the Malayalam country's John Mathai, a non-politician from the Tata industrial house, who was included for his professional expertise and also to represent the country's Christians.

A constituent assembly in two sections, one for the 'Pakistan area' and another for the rest of India, was part of the Cabinet Mission scheme. Madras Presidency, separately administered Coorg, and before long the princely parts of South India (Hyderabad, Mysore and Travancore-Cochin), all sent members to India's constitution-making body, which first met on 9 December 1946.

CR and Kamaraj, Prakasam and Neelam Sanjiva Reddy, Pattabhi Sitaramayya and N. G. Ranga, Durgabai (later married to C. D. Deshmukh) and Ammu Swaminathan, Dalit leaders P. Kakkan and V. I. Munuswami Pillai (a member of CR's 1937–39 ministry), Father Jerome D'Souza, *Indian Express* owner Ramnath Goenka, and eminent lawyer Alladi Krishnaswami Iyer were among those elected to the constituent assembly by the Madras legislature formed earlier in the year.

Joined by representatives from the princely states, the constituent assembly would also function as the national legislature until independent India's first elections, held in 1952 under universal adult franchise.

Until the League too joined the interim government, CR was its member for industries while Mathai held finance. When, after a few weeks, Liaquat came in as finance member, CR yielded industry to Mathai and became member for education. A few months later, when Azad joined (replacing Asaf Ali, who was named ambassador to Washington) and asked for education, CR reverted to industry.

Not musical chairs, however, but Congress–League friction was the interim government's chief handicap. The League had joined not to share in India's governance but to advance towards Pakistan.

Refusing to acknowledge Nehru's leadership, League members met separately under Liaquat. Officialdom also becoming communally divided, the interim government experience persuaded Nehru, Patel and company that partition might be better.

The Nehru–Patel relationship was another issue. When Patel—a widower like CR and Nehru—suggested to CR that the two might share a home in Delhi, a city not known by either for any length of time, CR declined. He did not wish to appear aligned to one side in any Nehru–Patel dispute.

◆

'We will quit India,' the Empire suddenly announced on 20 February 1947. But there was no handing-over plan. One result was serious violence in the crucial Punjab province, where India's interim government, a divided house, had no capacity to intervene, even as the interim government could do nothing when Bihar had erupted in October–November 1946.

After the 20 February announcement, British officers and soldiers in Punjab and elsewhere started to pack up to go home. Caving in to mounting Muslim League pressure, Punjab's Unionist chief minister, Khizr Hayat Khan, resigned, producing governor's rule under an impartial but hapless Briton called Evan Jenkins.

As hatemongers trumped peacemakers in Punjab, and suspicion turned tragically into hostility, large-scale killings of Sikhs and Hindus occurred in and around the northwestern city of Rawalpindi. This was in the first week of March. The outcome was a resolve in Punjab's Sikh and Hindu leadership for partitioning the province.

In a resolution passed in Delhi on 8 March, the Congress working committee swiftly endorsed this demand by Punjab's Sikhs and Hindus, thereby also endorsing Bengal's partition and accepting India's division.

The 'small Pakistan' that Jinnah had rejected out of hand in 1944 was quickly emerging from blood-soaked events.

Quietly consenting to it, CR, proponent from 1942 of 'small Pakistan', was party to the working committee's resolution, as were Nehru, Patel, Azad and Prasad, and J. B. Kripalani, who had taken over as president from Nehru. But Gandhi, the Congress's guide for more than two decades, had not been consulted. He was in distant Bihar, striving to restore harmony there, but easily reachable from Delhi.

Shaken as he was, Gandhi came up once more with an ingenious response: let the Congress offer India's prime ministership to Jinnah. In 1944, the League leader had refused to touch 'small Pakistan'. Perhaps he would be willing now to lead a united India? If the Congress gave Jinnah the chance and the League leader took it, India's unity might be preserved, and Punjab's peace restored.

Gandhi discussed the idea with the dashing new viceroy who replaced Wavell at the end of March: Lord Louis Mountbatten, a navy admiral related to King George VI. Eager to resolve 'the India problem' quickly and return to England to, as he hoped, lead the Royal Navy, Mountbatten however was by this time committed to the partition solution.

Working briskly to enlist Patel and Nehru, who did not need convincing, he thwarted Gandhi's 'Jinnah card'. Barring Khan Abdul

Ghaffar Khan from the North West Frontier Province, all Congress leaders opposed Gandhi's proposal, which was never put to Jinnah.

In his diary, CR wrote that when Congress leaders discussed the 'Jinnah card', 'Gandhiji's ill-conceived plan of solving the present difficulties' was 'objected to by everybody and scotched'.[44]

Yet that plan was strikingly similar to the 'sporting offer' CR himself had made in August 1940, when for a while he seemed to be leading the Congress nationally, which was that the Muslim League be invited to nominate a prime minister and form a national government[45].

Perhaps, in 1947, practical men triumphed over idealistic ingenuity, but the Congress's ageing leaders, weary from long years in prison and tired of Jinnah, were keen also to occupy seats of authority in an India that was finally independent, if also truncated.

As for CR, he was privately pleased that everyone had finally come around to his scheme. He was also embarrassed by his gladness. To Bangalore's Navaratna Rama Rao, close to him ever since their years together in school, CR wrote:

> 8 June 1947: A great incubus is off India's chest. Yet it is what I asked them to do... The only credit is that I was rash enough to stand up for it. I find a mischievous pleasure in watching and enjoying my colleagues' studied silence on the subject. Vanity all over.[46]

◆

The south's princely portions too were altering. In the all-India hierarchy of princely states, Hyderabad stood at the top.

In earlier times, the Marathas had defied or resisted the British, and so had Tipu. But not Hyderabad. Peace and stability were the other side of the non-resistance coin, yet Hyderabad's society and economy remained markedly feudal, and its nizams co-existed with chiefs and jagirdars, including a few Hindus who controlled autonomous 'Samasthan' tracts.

After Osman Ali Khan, its nizam since 1911 and the seventh in the Asaf Jahi dynasty, made a hefty contribution to the World War I chest, the Empire started calling him His Exalted Highness. But the viceroy in Delhi, guided by the resident in Hyderabad, curbed the nizam whenever he wanted to, and controlled appointments to his executive council.

Osman Ali Khan's request to be raised to the title of a 'king' was rejected by the Empire, and in 1926 Viceroy Reading bluntly asked him not to claim equality with the government of India. Paramountcy, the nizam was told, was not limited by treaties.[47]

Hoping to enhance his dynasty's appeal, the nizam got his two sons married to the daughter and niece of Turkey's exiled caliph in ceremonies arranged in Nice in southern France. The British resident, Terence Keyes, suspected an additional motivation: a wish to be accepted as successor caliphs.[48]

Keyes told the nizam that Hyderabad's Hindus, paying 95 per cent of the state's revenues and constituting 85 per cent or more of the population, would be bitterly opposed to his being called king, not to mention caliph, and that other Indian princes too would be opposed.[49]

Unlike in Mysore, where the raja welcomed a representative assembly in 1881, the nizam resisted the reform. In 1919, a commission appointed by Ali Imam of Bihar, the first sadr-i-azam or president of the nizam's executive council, had proposed an assembly, but the nizam suppressed the recommendation.

One consequence was that many educated and ambitious Hyderabadis sought openings in the Telugu, Marathi or Kannada parts of British India with which they were linguistically connected.

That Hindus possessed but a small share in administration was not the state's only anomaly. Telugu was the population's principal language, while in some parts Marathi and Kannada prevailed, yet Urdu, spoken only in Hyderabad city by a majority, was the state's official language.

Demands for the right to use Telugu led to the creation in 1921 of the Andhra Janasangham (People's Society), which in 1930 changed its name to the Andhra Mahasabha. Especially active in the Telangana region and working also for peasants' rights in areas where zamindars had near-absolute control, the Andhra Mahasabha split in the 1940s into 'communist' and 'nationalist' factions, the latter aligning with the Hyderabad State Congress, which existed from 1938.

A major figure in the Hyderabad Congress was Venkatesh Khedgikar, born in 1903 in a Brahmin family in the largely Kannada district of Bijapur, which the Marathas had captured from Asaf Jahi hands. Later the Marathas were forced to yield Bijapur to the British. A teacher who became an ascetic, Khedgikar, better known as Swami Ramanand Teerth, would struggle for popular and democratic rule in Hyderabad, but some would link him also to an anti-minority outlook.

Forgetting neither his Mughal roots nor the rights conceded to Hyderabad in treaties, Osman Ali Khan continually asserted his claim to Berar and wished to regain the Northern Circars as well. Citing an 1802 accord, he claimed privileges in respect of the port of Machilipatnam.

Later he would try to purchase Goa from the Portuguese and to lay a rail line to Marmagoa (Mormugao). In the early 1940s, when the Nawab of Chhatari was his prime minister, he attempted also to access Bastar's iron ore reserves.[50]

Finding that Osman Ali Khan reinforced Muslim dominance in the state's civil service, judiciary and army, the nizam's biographer, Vasant K. Bawa, adds that

> at a personal level, Mir Osman Ali Khan enjoyed the full support of the Hindu nobility and [of Hindu] officials to whom he had entrusted high offices, and he also treated them with consideration.[51]

Evidently his Parsi officers showed 'reverence' to the nizam, who attended church services at Christmas and did not block Christian activities (Bawa, 400).

Osman Ali appointed some competent officers, but 'he himself always constituted an alternate centre of power', and he was 'widely believed to be parsimonious to the point of miserliness'.

> On ceremonial occasions, he would accept and expect a tribute of gold ashrafis from lower officials and more elaborate presents from higher dignitaries (389).

A few of his subjects were 'bold enough to criticize him in articles published anonymously or pseudonymously in British Indian newspapers but none could dare to do so in the Hyderabad press'. Some who had written negatively of him in the press outside had to leave the state (389).

In 1930, Osman Ali went unannounced to a religious meeting

where he was impressed by a twenty-four-year-old's eloquence on a Muslim ruler's duty. Of Pashtun descent, the speaker, Bahadur Khan, was made Nawab Bahadur Yar Jang by the nizam.

In 1933, the Majlis Ittehadul Muslimeen (Council of United Muslims) was founded in Hyderabad, in part to counter activities of Arya Samaj missionaries from northern and western India. Bahadur Khan soon became the MIM chief and found he could influence the nizam. Thanks to his pressure, in 1941 the nizam replaced Akbar Hydari, the sadr-i-azam, with the Nawab of Chhatari.

Jinnah, meanwhile, named Bahadur Khan as the head of the All India States Muslim League, counterpart of the Congress's body in princely states. Bawa, the nizam's biographer, thinks that consultation between Jinnah, Bahadur Khan and the nizam led to the selection of Chhatari which, however, was followed by dark internal struggles. In 1944, a thirty-eight-year-old Bahadur Khan mysteriously died.[52]

Two years later, in March 1946, a riot was sparked off by an American Christian mission's alleged refusal to let a mosque rise on its grounds in Dichpally, about 90 miles from Hyderabad. The houses in Hyderabad city of Premier Chhatari and the nizam's police minister, a Briton named W. V. Grigson, were vandalized. Since the city's police chief, who reported directly to the nizam, was suspected of complicity, the nizam too faced reproach.[53]

Chhatari soon resigned. He was replaced, to Jinnah's dismay, by someone seen as pro-Congress: Mirza Ismail, former dewan in the princely states of Jaipur and Mysore. The hope that Ismail's connections with the Congress and the British would help over Berar, Goa and Bastar had influenced the nizam.

Jinnah urged Wavell to block Ismail's appointment, but the viceroy did not oblige. In July 1946, even while the Congress and the League were jockeying for influence in Delhi's interim government, Jinnah journeyed to Hyderabad to meet the nizam. Writes Bawa:

> The Nizam took objection to Jinnah...spreading his legs and smoking a cigar before the ruler. The Nizam exploded and demanded angrily, 'Do you know who I am?'... Jinnah was flabbergasted, withdrew his legs, threw away the offending cigar and apologized [but to no effect]... The whole palace resounded

with the Nizam's angry voice and the oldest servants said they had never seen their ruler in such a temper (284).

Hyderabad was polarizing on Hindu–Muslim lines. From 1946, MIM's chief was a fiery orator born in UP, Qasim Rizvi (1902–70). Though Mirza Ismail created a legislative assembly of sorts, an unsatisfied Hyderabad Congress boycotted it. All 42 Muslim seats were won by MIM, and Rizvi became the party's floor leader as well. The Assembly's Hindu seats were filled by independents and new groups, some friendly to MIM. A Depressed Classes Organization led by B. S. Venkata Rao was apparently 'completely under Ittehad influence'.[54]

As the Empire's departure from India neared, MIM's militant wing emerged, the Razakars, aiming at an independent and Islamic Hyderabad, while two elected members of the assembly, MIM's Abdul Rahim and Pingle Venkatrama Reddy, a Hindu landowner, were named to the executive council headed by Ismail.

Much earlier, her suitability vouched for by the British resident, Venkatrama Reddy's daughter, Kumudini Devi, had been appointed companion to Durru Shehvar, the Turkish princess married to Azam Shah, the nizam's eldest son and heir apparent.[55]

As Rizvi's rhetoric escalated, Ismail was increasingly uncomfortable. Unable to control the MIM chief, the nizam was susceptible himself to dreams of independence that Jinnah seemed to encourage.

Finding the nizam and MIM 'hell-bent upon independence', a frustrated Ismail resigned in the summer of 1947, and Chhatari returned as premier to a Hyderabad disquieted by ominous incidents.[56]

At the end of June, a thirty-five-year-old doctor, Narayana Reddy, father of three young boys, was stabbed in Warangal while accompanying a Hindu servant who was too scared to walk alone to his home. When someone in the attacking group shouted, 'Oh, this is Dr. Narayan Reddy!' another replied, 'But he is a Hindu anyway.' The doctor was killed.[57]

◆

Mysore, where Ismail was a popular dewan from 1926 to 1941, had obtained a legislature in 1881, shortly after the Great Famine of 1876–78, under a Tamil Brahmin dewan named C. V. Rangacharlu. Three years later, the much-admired and long-reigning Krishnaraja Wadiyar IV was born.

His mother serving as regent until his maturity in 1902, Krishnaraja lived and reigned until 1940. Mirza, who had been the raja's college-mate, was not his only capable dewan. Another was the remarkable engineer-centenarian Mokshagundam Visvesvaraya (1861–1962), a Brahmin born in Karnataka to a family of Telugu-speaking Brahmins. Among other accomplishments, Visvesvaraya enhanced Mysore's infrastructure during his term from 1912 to 1918.

Big landholders were not numerous or dominant in Mysore. There was also a near-absence, in comparison with other places, of a merchant class capable of influencing the administration or the economy through its money power. Thus a 1954 report on rural credit would find that whereas in West Bengal, Bihar, Madras, Orissa and Hyderabad, 85 per cent of all borrowings had been at rates higher than a stipulated maximum of 12 to 12.5 per cent, in Mysore only a tenth of all rural loans bore this illicit rate.[58]

While a strong agrarian basis for a democratic movement was thus lacking in Mysore, social agitations occurred, mainly via the press, first against 'foreign' dewans imported from Madras Presidency and next against local dewans drawn from the Brahmin caste.

That many in Mysore (and Travancore) saw an Indian from outside their state as a 'foreigner' was a measure of imperial success. The heart of most complaints was that dewans, whether local or 'foreign', were apt to introduce 'their relations and friends, and relations' friends, and friends' friends...into the high offices of the state'.[59]

Charges by Vokkaligas and Lingayats that Visvesvaraya was seeking to 'convert Mysore into a Brahmin colony' made it easier for the maharaja, technically a 'Sudra' himself, to appoint his younger brother as a Sudra representative on his executive council, and later to elevate him to the council's presidency, whereby the brother obtained precedence over Dewan Visvesvaraya.[60]

Though he had tried to address the shortage of non-Brahmins in his administration, Visvesvaraya was obliged to resign. 'No native Brahmin dewan was appointed' thereafter.[61]

Some Mysore dewans were quite close to the INC in the late 1890s and later, and at times even the maharaja was. This took courage, for in 1920 the Empire had set up a 'Chamber of Princes' as a counterweight to the Congress.

All things considered, Krishnaraja stood out as a fair-minded personality, impressing Gandhi as also British politicians. He was liked, too, for his patronage of music, and for his independence in supporting an anti-imperialist cause like khadi.

Unlike Hyderabad, where the Muslim League's Pakistan demand produced tension and uncertainty, Mysore was optimistic as India moved towards independence, but there was a question about the state's future relationship with Kannada-speaking areas in the presidencies of Bombay and Madras.

An Ekikarana (Unification) movement in the Kannada country had received a boost during the Congress's 1924 session held in Belgaum, the only Congress annual where Gandhi presided. The Karnataka Pradesh Congress Committee (headed by Gangadharrao Deshpande, the 'lion of Karnataka' as he was called) hosted this Belgaum session, which was accompanied by a Karnataka unification conference.

Huilgol Narayana Rao's poem, *Udayavagali Namma Cheluva Kannadanaadu* (Let Our Charming Kannada Land Dawn) was sung at this conference. Five years later, the journal *Samyukta Karnataka* was launched in Hubli. Among those who came together to ask for a unified state was Kuppali Venkatappa Puttappa, popularly known as Kuvempu.

Born in a Vokkaliga family in Shimoga district, Kuvempu (1904–1994), often referred to as Karnataka's national poet, was a teacher and writer in English before he composed poetry, plays and novels in Kannada. Displaying an 'extraordinary knowledge of details'[62], Kuvempu's work culminated in *Sri Ramayana Darshanam,* a retelling of the epic in Kannada verse.

Despite its innovations, e.g. in giving Rama a trial along with the test he ordered for Sita, Kuvempu's *Ramayana* would become a classic.

On Krishnaraja's death in 1940, the ruler was succeeded by his nephew, Jayachamaraja Wadiyar. On 9 August 1947, Jayachamaraja signed the instrument of accession to India.

◆

In the Malayalam country, British rule had ended the Nambudiris' political influence over rajas, but unlike Nairs and Ezhavas, who embraced schools started by the British, the Nambudiris, fearful of pollution, had stayed away. Their women stifled and their young men uneducated, the community, more visible in southern Malabar and Cochin than elsewhere in Kerala, was going downhill.

In 1908, reform-minded Nambudiris formed the Yogakshema Sabha, in 1927 its journal *Unni Namboodiri* appeared, and in December 1929 the play *Adukkalayil Ninnu Arangathekku* (From the Kitchen to the Stage) was performed at the sabha's annual gathering in Edakunni in Thrissur.

Written by a brilliant writer-orator, Vellithuruthi Thazhathu Bhattathiripad, or, simply, VT, the play used farce to air the pitiful lives of Nambudiri women suffering from, among other customs, a firm rule banning the community's younger sons, apphans as they were called, from marrying a Nambudiri girl.

In effect banned from marrying, forced into seclusion, obliged to wear a heavy veil, and hide under a large umbrella of matted palm-leaves, single Nambudiri women, the antarjanams, constituted a large portion of the community's females. VT's drama, which they watched from special enclosures, thrilled them.

An apphan himself, VT (1896–1982) had contracted an alliance, a sambandham as it was called, with Madhavikutty Varasyar, who came from a Nair family. Yet like other apphans he had inflicted lifelong spinsterhood on the unknown Nambudiri girl he might have married if allowed.

When Parvathi Manzhi, an antarjanam, appeared unveiled and without the umbrella at the 1929 gathering and the play, it was a daring act. Also associated with the drama, having taken part, in fact, 'in the deliberations of [its] first enactment', was another apphan: Elamkulam Manakkal Sankaran Namboodiripad, better known as EMS (1909–98), who would become one of India's best-known Communist leaders and a two-term chief minister of Kerala.

EMS would later write that, by itself, VT's 'play could bring about changes among the Antarjanams equal to' what 'the decade-long agitation through newspapers and meetings had brought about in the community'.[63]

After watching the first performance, Mannath Padmanabhan, the Nair leader who had played a notable role in the Vaikom Satyagraha, made the same point. He said that 'the drama presentation of a single night' would 'outstrip the cumulative results of all the activities of the past 22 years'.[64]

Staged in nine places in 1929–30 and quickly sold out in print, *Adukkalayil Ninnu Arangathekku* was part of a successful push for legislation to change Nambudiri marriage laws. Because Nambudiris lived all across the Malayalam country, legislatures in Madras, Travancore and Cochin had to be persuaded. Before the end of 1932, Travancore's and Malabar's Nambudiris found significant relief. Cochin would take longer to come around.

By this time, VT had done other interesting things. In 1931, a year after Gandhi's Salt March, VT and his associates, all wearing khadi, conducted a thirty-eight-day march to raise funds for a school for Nambudiri youngsters. Poor Nambudiri women gave money and jewels. Linking himself to VT's march, EMS would soon be arrested for Congress-related activities.

The reformed law enabled apphan VT to marry a Nambudiri woman, Sridevi. As for Madhavikutty, after initial coolness from him, she and VT had come close. Two daughters were born to them. Evidently VT asked Madhavikutty to continue as a co-wife; when she refused, they separated. Not much later, Madhavikutty died.

Enlarging his concerns, VT involved himself in the end-1932 Guruvayur Temple entry campaign (touched upon in the previous chapter). VT's house became the centre of activity for the referendum in which caste Hindus voted to allow Dalits into the temple, and for which, as the acting Congress president, CR had come to Guruvayur. Also joining the Guruvayur effort, which Kelappan (one of the Vaikom initiators) helped organize, was Gandhi's wife, Kasturba.

The Zamorin's refusal to heed the verdict contributed to a bombshell of a statement that VT made in April 1933: he asked for temples to be burnt down. There was a prosecution, a retraction and a fine, but the statement strengthened the image of a passionate individual.

On 13 September 1934, VT conducted, in his home, the first marriage ever, it would seem, of a Nambudiri widow. Nothing like it had been known to occur. However, as had happened forty-three years earlier with Viresalingam in the Telugu country, all who participated in the wedding of Uma Antarjanam were excommunicated.

From 1935, five cast-out families, including VT's, tried to create a new society of equality and bread-labour in a commune about 20 miles north of the Guruvayur Temple. Called Ulbuddha-keralam, the commune or ashram leased 25 acres in Kodumunda near Pattambi in western Palakkad district. But it did not last. Shortage of money and internal dissension brought the commune to an end in less than three years.

In 1940, VT broke another barrier when his sister married a Nair, with Kelappan again playing a role. VT lived for four more decades after that but, almost unbelievably, in virtual silence. If the passion remained, it was firmly suppressed.[65]

◆

Influenced by proliferating print journals, the Malayalam world saw efforts for democratic rule in Travancore and Cochin as also a Communist movement, the latter emerging from the Congress's socialist factions, first formed in 1934.

Fairness in the distribution of government jobs was a live issue. Nairs seemed predominant. In 1882, *Kerala Mitran* pointed out that only 25 Syrian Christians were among 1,424 public servants drawing monthly salaries of Rs 10 or more (43), and a Syrian Christian–Ezhava alliance appeared to emerge.

But behind the famous 1891 Memorial to the Travancore raja was also a sense that the richest slices of the cake of government jobs were going to 'foreigners' from Madras Presidency. 'Of the 16,167 posts in government service', the Memorial asserted, '3,407 posts with [monthly] salaries above 10 rupees, 1,444 were held by foreign Hindus'. The 'average daily salary of a foreign Brahmin was Rs 6.77 ps. as against 12 ps. for Malayali Sudras and 13 ps. for a Christian'.[66]

Newspapers criticizing the appointment of 'foreign' dewans or the performance of 'native' dewans could invite a clampdown in Mysore and Travancore. In 1910, *Swadeshabhimani*, a tri-weekly produced in Travancore by Ramakrishna Pillai, was 'suppressed [and] the press and its accessories confiscated'. Pillai himself was 'arrested and deported' from Travancore via a proclamation from the maharaja.[67]

◆

Two men who would figure in anyone's short list of Malayali

Communists are Ayillyath Kuttiari Gopalan Nambiar (AKG) and EMS. Older by five years, AKG (1904–77) was an elite Nair from Kannur district. Unlike fellow-apphan VT, whose family were poor, EMS was born into a family of Nambudiri landlords in Mappila country. Both AKG and EMS took part in the satyagrahas and anti-untouchability movements of the 1930s, were imprisoned, became active in the Congress Socialist Party, helped found the Communist party in the Malayalam country, and would become famous as parliamentary Communists—AKG in the Lok Sabha, where in 1952 he became the country's first 'leader of the opposition', and EMS as Kerala's two-term chief minister.

In 1936, AKG led a hunger march from Malabar to Madras. EMS used family wealth to finance the party. The Second World War posed difficulties for Communists. Opposing the war at its start, when the Soviet Union was in alliance with Germany, the Indian Communist Party backed the war after December 1940, when Hitler attacked Russia, attracting a 'pro-imperialist' label. During the war years, AKG and EMS spent periods in prison or underground.

Alignments in Malayali politics were influenced by demographic distribution. There was a concentration of Muslims in Malabar, a significant Christian percentage in Travancore/Cochin, and a wide-ranging tussle across the Malayalam country between two large Hindu groups: the Nairs, who had enjoyed political and military dominance in the past, and the steadily rising Ezhavas.

That a Brahmin–non-Brahmin politics, so effective in the Tamil and Kannada countries, did not take hold in the Malayalam country, despite the harshness of its caste-linked restrictions, is in part explained by its ethnic mix.

Moreover, while Saivite heritage was deployed on behalf of the non-Brahmin cause in the Tamil and Kannada countries, that did not happen in the Malayalam country. Though Siva was their most popular Hindu god, Malayalis seemed comfortable worshipping Narayana as well, and named sons after both.[68]

By the 1940s, all political parties in the Malayalam country were opposing bars to temple-entry. Putting atheism and agnosticism to one side, the Communists too supported the restoration of religious shrines at the centre of rural communities. Cutting across caste and ideology, everyone, including those at the margins, gathered at these shrines.[69]

Also, the 'lower castes no longer stepped off the roads at the sight of nayars'. This was 'a significant achievement of political activity over the thirties and the forties', suggesting that in some areas of social life upper-caste power had been checked.[70]

◆

To a growing sentiment in Travancore and Cochin for popular rule was joined an all-Malayali wish, similar to linguistic urges in Karnataka and the Telugu country, for an eventual 'Aikya Kerala', but from the summer of 1945 it was India's march towards independence that provided the dominant political context for the roles of the Travancore Maharaja, Chithirai Thirunal Balarama Varma(1912–91; on the throne 1931–71), and his dewan with a razor-sharp mind, C. P. Ramaswami Iyer (1879–1966).

In 1934, Viceroy Willingdon had called Iyer, a Tamil Brahmin, 'about the ablest Indian in India'.[71] A close Annie Besant associate who left the Congress along with her after Gandhi's ascendancy, Iyer served as law member on the Empire's councils in Madras and Delhi before becoming Travancore's dewan in 1936.

His bond with the ruler was older. In 1931, thanks to Iyer's intervention, the viceroy had accepted Thirunal's right to the throne, rejecting questions about the young prince's mental firmness.

Though it annoyed Travancore's orthodox sections as well as princely establishments in Kochi and Kozhikode, the ruler's 1936 proclamation opening Travancore's public temples to Dalits had brought the throne closer to the people and won credit for the dewan.

But Malayali intellectuals wishing to see freedoms broaden were offended when, in 1937, the dewan made himself the vice-chancellor of a new University of Travancore, and a wider public was alienated by the administration's harshness towards the Travancore Congress, which, after 1938, was demanding popular rule under the leadership of Thiruvananthapuram's Pattom Thanu Pillai (1885–1970).

In October 1946, Iyer's administration did not seem to know what was happening when a large Communist-led workers' agitation in coastal north Travancore turned violent. Reacting in panic, the police killed 200 or more in Punnapra, just south of Alappuzha, on the 24th and, three days later, another 150 in Vayalar, south of Kochi.[72]

These were large numbers. Apparently blind to the ferment under his nose, the dewan also showed a poor understanding of the wider scene when he imagined that he and the ruler could detach Travancore from an India about to reach independence. In other words, dreaming was not confined to Hyderabad.

On 11 June 1947, eight days after the Congress and the Muslim League accepted Britain's proposals for transferring power to India and Pakistan, Iyer announced that Travancore would declare itself an independent state as soon as power was transferred. He also named an agent to a Pakistan that was about to emerge.[73]

A month later, at 8.45 p.m. on 11 July, Maharaja Chithirai Thirunal read out his declaration over the radio: 'On and from 15th August, 1947...Travancore will reassume its independence and sovereignty in full measure.'[74]

Like other parts of the Malayalam country, Travancore had an old, broad connection with the wider world, and princely states had their treaties with the Empire. Yet ancient external contacts, or a treaty with a retreating Empire, could not snap the Kerala–India bond. At last realizing this, on 30 July the maharaja informed Mountbatten, the last British viceroy, that he would sign the instrument of accession to India.

Five days earlier, on 25 July, someone possibly connected to the socialist party had tried to kill the dewan with a knife. Aided by a thick angavastram, Iyer fortunately survived the assault on his neck. On 14 August, he resigned as dewan. Five days later he left the state.

In later acrimony, one side would argue that Iyer had encouraged the ruler's abortive bid for independence, the other that the dewan was following Thirunal's wishes. On 28 July 1947, in a letter contemplating resignation, Iyer had written to the ruler:

> By temperament and training, I am unfit for compromises, being autocratic and over decisive. I don't fit into the present environment.[75]

◆

When independence came to India on 15 August, Madras Presidency was under the chief ministership of Omandur P. Ramaswami Reddiar

(1895–1970), born into a Reddy family long domiciled in the Tamil country's South Arcot district.

In March 1947, after friction between Tanguturi Prakasam and Kamaraj, which bore marks also of Telugu–Tamil tension, OPR had replaced Prakasam at the head of the ministry. At independence in August, the presidency retained the Scotsman Archibald Nye as governor, even as India asked Mountbatten to remain as Governor General.

Urgings from EVR for a free Dravida Nadu paralleled Travancore's short-lived independence excitement and the more substantial separatist bid in Hyderabad. On 11 February 1946, *The Hindu* quoted Periyar 'calling upon the Dravidian peoples of South India 'to guard against a transfer of power from the British to the Aryans' and seek a separate South Indian state.[76]

More than a year later, saying that he wanted British rule to continue, EVR declared 15 August to be a day of mourning. However, the Tamil country was joyful as the day approached. EVR was isolating himself, even as Iyer had done in Travancore.

Observing and sharing the popular mood, Annadurai dissociated himself from Periyar and said he was thankful that with the British going there would now be 'one enemy less'. In his weekly, Anna wrote that 15 August was 'a day of joy'.[77]

That day India, including most South Indians, exploded with happiness. 'The independence of India is a settled fact! I have seen it with my own eyes! I wish I were young again.'[78]

These childlike words with which a sixty-nine-year-old CR expressed his thrill were uttered or echoed by millions who for decades had prayed for the moment, only to be countered by disappointment over Partition, and grief over violence in Punjab and Bengal, provinces suddenly divided into seemingly hostile halves.

At midnight on 14 August, Jawaharlal Nehru gave his Tryst with Destiny speech in a magnificent ring of stone the Empire had built in New Delhi. As undivided India's interim government made way for new governments in India and Pakistan, millions of the uprooted trudged towards a hastily drawn border, many falling before they could cross it.

Struggling to bring peace to a subcontinent he had liberated but failed to keep together, Gandhi spent the nights of transition in an insecure, dilapidated home in Calcutta.

♦

Unexpected in its composition, free India's first cabinet was an attempt at inclusiveness. Nehru, the prime minister, and Patel, the deputy prime minister, led a fourteen-person team that included seven from outside the Congress, including two past and future foes, Ambedkar and the Hindu Mahasabha's Syama Prasad Mookerjee.

On the team were a woman (Amrit Kaur), two Dalits (Ambedkar and Jagjivan Ram), three Brahmins (Nehru, Mookerjee, and Maharashtra's N. V. Gadgil), two Muslims (Abul Kalam Azad and UP's Rafi Ahmed Kidwai), two Christians (John Mathai and Amrit Kaur), a Sikh (Baldev Singh), and a Parsi (C. H. Bhabha).

The two South Indians in the first cabinet were R. K. Shanmukham Chetty, a non-Congress non-Brahmin businessman from the Tamil country, who became finance minister,* and the Malayali John Mathai, the minister for transport.

CR, who had assumed that like Nehru, Patel, Azad and Prasad he would seamlessly slide from the interim government into the new cabinet, was asked by Nehru and Patel to go to Calcutta as governor for Bengal's western half, the eastern half of which had gone to Pakistan. 'Only you can handle Bengal,' said Patel to one who would have preferred to handle not Bengal, not India, but the south.[79] But he went to Calcutta, to live in the historic mansion from where, until 1911, when Delhi became the capital, the viceroy used to run imperial India.

Thirty seconds before 8 a.m. on 15 August, CR mounted a pavilion on the Government House lawns. At the first boom of a 17-gun salute fired from Fort William, he unfurled the tricolour, triggering 'a wild outburst of joy': an invasion of the mansion's grounds and buildings by at least 200,000 Calcuttans, some of whom danced on the sofas of the Empire that had died at midnight.

The next morning, for their first meeting in free India, Bengal's new governor called on Gandhi in his derelict lodgings in Beliaghata, Hydari Manzil. Four months earlier, CR, Nehru, Patel and company had 'scotched' Gandhi's suggestion of a Jinnah premiership to keep India united.

The conversation began in silence, with the old friends holding

---

*We met him earlier when discussing Balasaraswati.

hands, saying nothing. After ninety minutes of talking, the two simultaneously consulted their large pocket watches, and CR left.

Although Calcutta had recovered from the large-scale killings of the previous August, on 31 August 1947 there was a recurrence of violence, to which Gandhi responded by announcing a fast. For three hours CR argued with him, but Gandhi went ahead. In sympathy, 500 policemen, including some Britons and Anglo–Indians, fasted for twenty-four hours.

Weapons were surrendered, peace returned, Calcutta's Hindu and Muslim leaders said they would preserve it at any cost, and Gandhi broke his fast seventy-three hours after starting it. 'Gandhiji has achieved many things,' CR observed on 5 September, 'but in my considered opinion there has been nothing, not even independence, which is so truly wonderful as his victory over evil in Calcutta'[80].

Two days later, Gandhi left for Delhi, on his way, he thought, to Punjab, which had seen horrific massacres, but killings in Delhi detained him. The day after Gandhi left Calcutta, CR reflected on what was happening in Punjab and thought 'India has gone back three centuries to reach independence.'[81]

On 9 October, Nehru wrote to CR: 'All grace, pity and standards... have vanished. The best of us are affected by the prevailing mania... We are living in a war atmosphere and the only thing permitted...is to curse the enemy and cover up one's own errors and sins.'

'Be courageous,' CR wrote back, 'and do not yield to that against which your inner spirit protests... Is it not wonderful that Gandhiji has been spared for us all during this great crisis?' (18 Oct 1947)

For sixteen days in November, when Mountbatten went to England since a cousin, Philip Mountbatten, was getting married to Princess Elizabeth, CR served as acting Governor General in New Delhi. During that period, he met Gandhi seven times, including for an hour on the 26th, when CR returned to Calcutta. A Calcutta newspaper quoted him:

> I saw Gandhiji just before I got into the plane... He is sad beyond words... In his own way, he is suffering as Christ suffered on the eve of the great tragedy recorded in the Gospels.[82]

On 13 January, Gandhi undertook another fast in New Delhi, for, he said, the safety of threatened minorities in Delhi and in Pakistan.

On this occasion, CR did not argue. Asking for prayers in 'temples, mosques, churches and synagogues throughout Bengal', he added:

> The only sane man today is Gandhiji... This time I confess I am not inclined to wrangle.[83]

The people of Delhi acted. The city's Muslims were assured protection, the return of seized mosques, and their right to celebrate a fair held every year from the thirteenth century at Khwaja Qutbuddin's tomb near the Qutb Minar. Angry Hindus and Sikhs had earlier vowed to prevent the fair in a post-Partition Delhi.

Even more importantly, the union cabinet chose to part with Pakistan's share, then in Indian custody, of the sterling balance returned by Britain to undivided India, reversing a previous cabinet decision to withhold it. Matching activity in Delhi, prayers for Gandhi were offered in Pakistan, including 'by Muslim women in the seclusion of their purda'.[84]

On 18 January, Gandhi broke his fast. Two days later, seven men went to his prayer meeting in an assassination bid that failed. One of the seven, who had detonated a grenade, was seized by persons at the scene. The other six slipped away. Ten days thereafter, on 30 January, one of these six, Nathuram Godse, planted himself about three feet in front of Gandhi and fired three bullets into an unprotected chest.

Of the Mahatma's death, CR said:

> [He] was very dear to me, but I do not grieve for him... He was walking to join and lead a prayer... He was a few minutes late and so he was walking fast... How many of you would not like to die when running to pray?

The Gandhi–CR story is a romance. CR would claim that he had 'admired and loved [Gandhi] throughout twenty-eight* rich years of intimate joint labour as never a man admired and loved another'.[85] On 12 February, he emptied an urn containing some of Gandhi's ashes into the Ganga at Barrackpore. Later in the day, he spoke over Calcutta radio:

---

*This was inaccurate by a year. Twenty-nine years had elapsed since Gandhi stayed with CR in 1919.

So it is all over! The world feels so empty!...Do not demand love. Begin to love and you will be loved. This is the law and no statute can alter it. If we do not follow the law, and let the law die with the teacher, we shall indeed become accomplices to the murderer.[86]

♦

The killing had deeply affected Periyar, too, who in an obituary suggested that India should be named 'Gandhi Nadu'.[87] Yet he continued to criticize Gandhi's endorsement of varnashrama dharma. The view that Gandhi condoned only an idealized version of that goal, or did so to retain caste Hindu goodwill, not to divide society hierarchically, did not impress EVR.

Three years after the murder, Periyar offered his analysis of Gandhi's mahatma-hood and assassination. The Brahmins, he wrote, 'made Gandhi a Mahatma because he said he believed in the Vedas, the Epics and in Varnashrama Dharma... The Brahmins assassinated him because he said that Allah and Ram were the same, that it was not the privilege only of Brahmins to be educated, and that the mosques seized by force should be vacated and returned to Muslims.'[88]

Chapter 12

NEW MAPS FOR OLD: 1948–1957

After Gandhi's assassination, Nehru and Patel turned to CR and asked him to become Governor General, for Mountbatten was returning home to steer the Royal Navy. Moving from Kolkata's old imperial mansion to a grander edifice in New Delhi (built in the late 1920s for viceroys), the southerner became the first Indian to head India after Bahadur Shah Zafar, the titular Mughal deposed in 1857.

A successor also to the first Governor General, Warren Hastings, CR imagined himself 'shaking hands with Hastings across the ages and saying, "You were the first and I am the last"'[1]

Neither as weak as the pre-1857 Bahadur Shah Zafar, who was a virtual prisoner of the British, nor as strong as the Hastings who controlled England's possessions in India in the 1770s, Governor General CR was more 'active' than most constitutional heads who followed him as presidents. This was largely because Prime Minister Nehru and Deputy Prime Minister Patel, often disagreeing with each other, sought the Governor General's intervention.

Eight months after he was sworn in, Patel would say about CR: 'He knows how a constitutional Governor-General has...to keep within limits, and yet how to break the limits'.[2] The Sardar was referring to, among other things, CR's involvement over Hyderabad, which began on his first day in office, 21 June, when Ali Yavar Jung, Hyderabad's 'agent-general', as the nizam's representative in Delhi was titled, called on the Governor General.

Remembering Hyderabad's role as England's faithful ally, Mountbatten had urged Nehru and Patel not to intervene against Nizam Osman Ali Khan, even though he had failed to check Razakar activities and Qasim Rizvi's rhetoric, both of which were steadily worsening. Keen to retain Mountbatten's goodwill, and facing a major challenge over Kashmir, Nehru and Patel agreed to hold their horses.

Mountbatten, on his part, obtained an undertaking from the nizam that he would not accede to Pakistan, following which, on 29 November,

Delhi and Hyderabad signed a 'standstill agreement'. K. M. Munshi, the Mumbai-based lawyer and author close to Patel, was appointed India's agent-general in Hyderabad.

But matters did not remain still. Razakar attacks on Hyderabad's Hindus were countered by a trade blockade unofficially enforced by provincial governments surrounding Hyderabad, and by attempts by volunteer groups across Hyderabad's western borders to force the issue.

Before departing, Mountbatten made one final bid, in which Nehru and Patel acquiesced, for a peaceful resolution. In talks in Delhi in the middle of June 1948, the nizam's latest sadr-i-azam, now also called prime minister, Mir Laik Ali (a successful Hyderabad industrialist who had replaced the Nawab of Chhatari) was assured that India would not intervene if the nizam installed an interim government representing all major communities and parties, and if the Razakars were progressively disbanded.

But the nizam, who possessed 'a streak of native shrewdness but [little] understanding of the forces at work in the world', did not act. Perhaps there were moments when he imagined he could revive the Mughal era. Above all he was under enormous pressure from MIM, the Razakars and Qasim Rizvi.

'Please persuade Qasim Rizvi,' the nizam would say if a councillor proposed a conciliatory step. Recalling this later, Pingle Venkatram Reddy, minister on the nizam's council, added that 'Qasim Razvi would barge into council meetings, sit on an arm-rest, and harangue the council.'[3]

To some the nizam indeed conveyed, in biographer Bawa's words, 'the awe of a medieval monarch'. Even those who poked fun at his miserliness, shabby clothes and greed for presents from officers and employees were apparently affected by nizam's 'steely eyes, his kingly hauteur and his commanding presence' (391). But not Qasim Rizvi.

With Hyderabad's rejection of the June offer, the countdown began. Delhi declared official backing for the blockade of goods to the state. When Hyderabad hired two Australian gun-runners who took off at night from Pakistani airports and touched down with arms and ammunition at strips in Bidar and Warangal, the case for intervention became unassailable.

Inside Hyderabad, there was frenzy in the extremist camp, vain dreaming in sections of the regime of aid from a barely-afloat Pakistan or the UN, fear in Hindus of reprisals if Delhi intervened, but also dissent in courageous Muslims.

On 22 August 1948, Shoaibullah Khan, editor of *Imroze*, which was urging democracy, was killed while walking near his home in the city. As they had threatened, the killers severed the editor's hand from his body.

Early in September, Governor General Rajagopalachari formally asked the nizam to ban the Razakars and station an Indian Army contingent in Hyderabad, adding an assurance that 'in any political solution' the nizam's 'prestige and position will be safeguarded'. Rejecting the demands, the nizam said that 'allowing Indian troops to remain in my territory is out of the question'.[4]

Only one course was left open for India, but Nehru and Patel, who was the minister for princely states apart from being deputy prime minister, could not agree on an instant response, whereupon the Governor General, a reluctant convert to military action, stepped in.

According to V. P. Menon, secretary at the States Ministry, after Patel had walked out from a heated discussion with Nehru, CR 'called a meeting in his room of the Prime Minister, Sardar Patel and myself. It was then decided that we should occupy Hyderabad.'[5]

It was obvious that speed of success would minimize two possible reactions: killings of Hindus in Hyderabad and Hindu–Muslim violence across India.

Before dawn on 13 September, the Indian Army's Operation Polo went into effect. In this attack, publicly described as a 'police action', army units moved eastwards into the state from Solapur in the Marathi country, and westwards from Vijayawada in the Telugu country, but, to confuse the enemy, also from half a dozen other points on Hyderabad's long border.

The nizam's army put up no resistance. On the 17th, four days after Indian soldiers had crossed the border, its chief, Major General Syed El Edroos, asked his troops to yield. The next day, Edroos surrendered to Operation Polo's Bengali commander, Major General J. N. Chaudhuri, who became the state's military governor.

Razakar resistance was stiffer. According to the government of India's official history of Operation Polo, 2,727 Razakars were killed,

102 wounded, and 3,364 captured. The Hyderabad Army lost 490 and had 122 wounded. Indian casualties amounted to 42 killed, 97 wounded and 24 missing.[6]

Laik Ali, who 'remained under house arrest for months and years, until he finally escaped, or was allowed to escape, in July 1950',[7] would later provide his account of the regime's final hours.

At 8 a.m. on the 17th, the nizam warned his prime minister of likely bloodshed if the Indian Army entered the capital in war mode, adding, 'Do you not know the fate of the various towns after the Indian armies entered during the past few days?'[8]

A few hours later, when Laik Ali conveyed to his cabinet the nizam's wish for a new ministry willing to obey Delhi, there was, Laik Ali would write,

> complete silence for some minutes. The Deputy Prime Minister, Pingle Venkata Ram Reddy, was the first to break the silence. He said in clear terms that he was even ready to lay down his life for the country and the sovereign. 'I am probably speaking for the last time and in a matter of a few hours I would most likely be shot dead, but in no way would that be a dishonorable death.' It was a brief but stunning speech.[9]

No Hyderabad official would be shot. The nizam, his powers removed, would remain on his throne. Qasim Rizvi would be kept in jail from 1948 to 1957, when he went to Pakistan, which was a condition for his release. Pingle Venkatram Reddy would walk free after a two-year house arrest.

The four-day war saw no massacre of Hindus in Hyderabad and was not followed by Hindu–Muslim violence elsewhere in India.

However, in several Hyderabadi towns and villages through which India's troops passed, Muslims, who were in a minority everywhere, were targeted by local Hindus or, more often, it would appear, by aggressive groups who crossed Hyderabad's western borders in the army's wake, and in some cases by Indian soldiers as well. Rape, forced conversions, abduction of women and looting of property occurred. There were cases when soldiers allowed, encouraged or took direct part in the violence.[10]

Referring to one of the state's towns, Osmanabad, which lay about

30 miles from Solapur, Laik Ali would allege that Indian troops heavily shelled the town even when they knew it was not being defended. After entering the town, the troops, charged Laik Ali, massacred the citizens, 'hunt[ing] down every Muslim in the place, men, women and children, all alike' (256).

Laik Ali's accusation was not quite corroborated by an unofficial committee that was sent following 'reports of killing of Muslims so large in number as to stagger the imagination' and lootings of Muslim property 'on a tremendous scale', to quote from a letter of 26 November from Nehru to the ministry of states.[11] But this committee's report, kept for years under wraps, was damning enough.[12]

Though never released by the government, the report sent by the committee to Nehru and Patel has been in the public domain at least from the start of the twenty-first century and may be viewed on the internet.

Named after the North Indian Brahmin who headed it, Pandit Sunderlal, a Gandhian dedicated to communal harmony,* the Sunderlal Committee, included, among others, a bitter critic of MIM, the journalist Qazi Abdul Ghaffar. Though it was not an official body, the committee's travel from 29 November to 12 December was arranged 'by the military authorities, without [whose permission] no one was allowed to enter or leave the districts of Hyderabad State' (Bawa, 350). Major General Chaudhuri himself journeyed with it for a day or more.

After interviewing military and civilian officers who had taken charge, Congress leaders and numerous citizens, the committee concluded that between 27,000 and 40,000 Muslims may have been killed in violent incidents during and immediately after Operation Polo. Fifty-one villages were evidently visited by the Sunderlal team, and persons from 150 additional villages interviewed. Of the 600 or so interviews conducted, about 200 were recorded.

In the committee's rough estimation, four districts (Osmanabad, Gulbarga, Bidar and Nanded) may have witnessed a total of nearly 18,000 deaths (with Osmanabad town accounting for 725 killings, and Latur around 1000), and four other districts (Beed, Nalgonda, Aurangabad and Medak) nearly 4,000 deaths. Of these eight districts,

---

*In 1970, Sunderlal published a historical study, How India Lost Her Freedom, Bombay: Popular Prakashan.

only Nalgonda lay east of Hyderabad.

Property was looted on a large scale and countless small businesses and homes were destroyed. Women were abducted, though the Chaudhuri administration quickly recovered many abductees. Some women and children were forcibly converted and tattooed with Hindu marks and names. Leaders of the state Congress were implicated in the violence and in extorting protection money from Muslim businessmen.

The team claimed 'absolutely unimpeachable evidence' that some soldiers were involved. While General Chaudhuri was 'without any tinge of communal prejudice', and officers like the one who took the city of Aurangabad prevented lawlessness, in other places 'members of the armed forces brought out Muslim adult males from villages and towns and massacred them in cold blood'. At times Razakar uniforms were fitted on Muslim men before they were shot.

Along with Muslims, Dalits were targeted in the Marathwada area, and a number of them killed, in part because the nizam had gifted land to some of them and also because a Dalit section had supported the call for an Azad Hyderabad.[13]

At a meeting in Hyderabad city, Pandit Sunderlal asked Muslims to respond to allegations of 'murder, looting and rape of Hindus before the Police Action'.

Some others [writes Bawa] kept silent, but a courageous Muslim, Fareed Mirza, replied that Hindus had suffered from atrocities but not as much as the Muslims had after the Police Action (493).

Operation Polo's swiftness and the intercommunal peace that prevailed across India relieved CR. Addressing a thanksgiving rally attended by 20,000 or more at Delhi's Jama Masjid, he spoke frankly of 'the gangsters in Hyderabad' who had 'forced the Nizam' into folly[14]. But we do not know of the Governor General's reaction to the Sunderlal team's grim findings.

How Nehru, Patel and Azad reacted to the report has also not come to light. Whether dictated by fear of inflaming the climate or something else, the report's suppression continues to dismay.[15]

◆

We will shortly look at another struggle waged in Hyderabad before and after Operation Polo, a militant bid to change a landlord-dominated countryside. Here we may note that a majority of Hyderabad's people seemed to regard the entry of Indian troops as an act of liberation. However, there was an element of sadness even among Hyderabad's Hindus, says Bawa, at the state's defeat and the end of the era of the nizams.

Osman Ali Khan's vision was of a benevolent if absolute rule. Possessing sympathy for Hyderabad's common people, he had mixed freely with them. The working class and poor of Hyderabad had treated him with respect and even reverence. Under him a tolerant society had evolved.[16]

The nizam contributed substantially to his downfall. Hopelessly unrealistic, he neither cultivated Hindu support nor built an effective armed force, both necessary for any serious bid for an independent Hyderabad. Equally, he rejected opportunities for an honourable autonomy within India. There was goodwill for him among Hindus, but his weakness before Qasim Rizvi lost him their support.

As his Asaf Jahi predecessors had time and again done, the seventh nizam pocketed the reverse and reconciled himself to the change. When the Governor General visited Hyderabad with his daughter, Namagiri, the nizam gave her a pearl necklace, which was promptly returned. After the nizam said that the wife of the military governor had accepted a similar necklace, CR, working via Patel, got that returned as well.[17]

◆

Fleetingly glimpsed earlier, South India's Communist movement found notable results during the 1946–51 revolt of Telangana's peasants, which is said to have commenced with the killing on 4 July 1946, in Nalgonda district's Kadivendi village, of Doddi Komarayya, a worker of the Andhra Mahasabha. Agents of the area's big landlord, Ramchandra Reddy of Visunur, were blamed for the crime.

Some of the movement's leaders, including Ravi Narayan Reddy and Baddam Yella Reddy, had for years worked with AMS. Founded to preserve Telugu identity, AMS was valuable at a time when autocratic rule prevented direct politics.

Between 1940 and 1942, Ravi Narayan Reddy, Baddam Yella Reddy and some others with AMS joined the Communist Party. In

1944, they and their allies gained control of AMS and turned it into a fighting force. Two years later, in 1946, a militant peasants' movement was launched in the Telangana districts of Nalgonda, Warangal and Khammam.

Widely performed in 1945–46, the play *Ma Bhoomi* or My Land, based on a real story from the 1920s of Bandagi, a Muslim peasantwoman who met her death struggling against the Visunur landlord of her time, assisted the movement, which targeted oppression by landlords and by the nizam's regime.

A high percentage of Telangana's land was owned by a small number of landlords, all from powerful castes. One of them, Jannareddy Pratap Reddy, allegedly owned 150,000 acres and a 750-acre mango orchard. Tax collectors became proprietors of immense tracts.

Practices that made the region fertile for revolt seemed to include coercion of labour, exploitation of tribals, appropriation of girls as slaves or concubines, crushing interest on loans, takeover of lands for non-payment of interest or rent, extortionate taxes on irrigated land, and seizure of sheep or fowl from the poor.

Committed leaders being available from 1946 onwards, militant peasant units were raised, arms were brought in from coastal Andhra or seized from owners, several landlords were driven away from their homes, village committees took charge, and land was redistributed.

Headquartered far from the region and increasingly unpopular, the nizam's regime sent military and police forces but was unable to quell the revolt, in which Hindus, forming a large majority, were joined by minority Muslims.

After Operation Polo, a total of 50,000 men from the armies and police of the Indian union and the Hyderabad government went after the rebels. Around 4,000 were killed, 10,000 or so jailed for three to four years, and another 50,000 dragged for rough treatment into police and military camps.

While, in the wake of Operation Polo, Muslims were attacked in Hyderabad state's western or Marathwada districts (Beed, Nanded, Osmanabad and Aurangabad) and in the southwestern districts of Bidar and Gulbarga, the minority community appeared to find safety in Telangana's Communist-controlled, Telugu-majority areas, where Hindu–Muslim understanding seemed to prevail.

It was claimed that by October 1951, when the revolt was called off, it had impacted around 3 million people living in 3,000 or so villages in an area of about 16,000 square miles, mostly in the districts of Nalgonda, Warangal and Khammam. For twelve to eighteen months, village committees had governed and defended this area with a 12,000-strong security force. One million acres of land were redistributed, many big landlords driven away, and tribals in the forests freed of abuse.

Hard to verify, these claims and figures were reiterated in a 1972–73 appraisal of the rebellion by Puchalapalli Sundarayya (1913–85), secretary of the Communist Party (Marxist) from 1964 to 1978.[18]

Born in Madras Presidency's Nellore district, Sundarayya had changed his name from Sundar Ram Reddy to indicate his anti-caste stand, joined the Salt Satyagraha when he was seventeen, the Congress Socialist Party in the mid-1930s, and the Communist Party soon thereafter, before becoming a guide to the Telangana peasants' movement.

While Sundarayya was thus an interested party, the results of elections held in early 1952 would suggest that a kernel of truth lay behind his claims. Communist candidates performed strikingly well in Telangana, with Ravi Narayan Reddy polling more than 300,000 votes to win the Lok Sabha's Nalgonda seat,* and Reddy's party colleagues entering the Hyderabad state assembly from rebel-area constituencies with equally impressive triumphs.

The movement's impact was also seen in major land-reform laws introduced in Hyderabad state in 1949, and in Vinoba Bhave's remarkable bhoodan or land-gift drive, which began in a Nalgonda village in 1951 and found a response in much of the nation. Moreover, intertwined as it was with Telugu identity, the peasants' movement was a factor in the creation of Andhra in 1953 and in South India's linguistic reorganization in 1956.

Later appraisals would indicate that 'middle' peasants got more out of the reforms prompted by the rebellion than Dalits and tribals, who were much worse off, yet the rebellion's consequential role in the India of the late 1940s and early 1950s seems undeniable.

---

*In these Lok Sabha elections of 1952, Jawaharlal Nehru obtained 230,000 votes to win from a UP constituency.

There was another side. Speaking in January 2017, a Hyderabad professor conceded without hesitation that 'the Telangana armed struggle of mid-1940s was one of South India's most significant historical events', but he spoke also of the blow his own family had taken. Evidently his grandfather, a Brahmin landlord possessing 2,000 acres, was harassed by Razakars during the day and by Communists after dark, until one night when his house was stuffed with straw, set ablaze, and burnt down.

The grandfather restarted life by selling kerosene, earning one paisa per canister when an anna had four paisas and a rupee sixteen annas. Fifty years after being forced out, the grandfather went back to his village. Largely because his sons were well placed, he managed to recover about 100 acres for his big family. He also learnt that a good chunk of the seized land had become the personal property of a local Communist leader.[19]

◆

On 14 May 1949, in the Tamil town of Tiruvannamalai, EVR spent almost two hours with the Governor General, who was on a southern visit, and discussed his wish to marry Maniammai, forty years his junior, who was living with him.

The wedding took place less than two months later and was cited as a reason for a split in the Dravida Kazhagam and the formation of a new party, led by Annadurai, the Dravida Munnetra* Kazhagam, or the DMK.

Some critics accused CR of encouraging the marriage to discredit and divide the Dravida moment, but the truth was very different. Three months before the Tiruvannamalai meeting, EVR had written to CR announcing his intention of marrying Maniammai and requesting CR to participate in the wedding as its sole witness.

In a letter of 21 February, marked 'Confidential',[20] CR replied that he did not think that as Governor General he could quite play the proposed role, and he added advice. EVR should consider, said CR, whether Maniammai was capable, once EVR was no more, of looking after his estate as he would want her to.

---

*Munnetra = progress.

Just what happened in the face-to-face consultation that followed in May in Tiruvannamalai may never be known. Thereafter CR expressed no misgivings. In a letter to EVR dated 12 July, just after the marriage had taken place, CR sent his best wishes to the couple.[21] Philip Spratt, the Chennai-based Cambridge-educated Briton, would state in his *D.M.K. in Power*, published in 1970, when CR and EVR were both living: 'The fact is that Mr. Naicker consulted Rajaji (despite politics they have remained personal friends), and Mr. Rajagopalachari, a good Victorian, replied that...it was his duty to marry her.'[22]

Spratt had come to India as a Communist, served prison terms, married a grandniece of the previously mentioned Singaravelu (possibly the first Tamil Communist), and subsequently rejected Communism. From the late 1950s onwards, Spratt was close to CR.

In June 1949, in an announcement in his paper, Periyar openly referred to CR's role:

Viduthalai, 29 June 1949: As has been explained by me in the last four or five months in various public meetings, in my writings, and in line with my talks with C. R. Achariar... I have decided to make Maniammai, with whom I have been in close association for the last four or five years and who has also identified herself with my own interests and the interests of the movement, as my legal successor.[23]

CR's involvement in his opponent's marriage created as much curiosity as the DK split. A Coimbatore Congress leader, Kovai Ayyamuthu, would later recall a 1949 conference in his city:

Periyar was addressing the gathering. When he had completed his speech, G. D. Naidu* got on to the stage and began to speak.

'Periyar who recommends Valluvar's *Kural* to the people should not lie. He must reveal to the people gathered here what transpired between him and Rajaji at Tiruvannamalai,' said Naidu to laughter from the audience.

'There is nothing that you need to know. I had just made a courtesy call on him. We were speaking about our personal matters,' answered Periyar.[24]

---

*Prominent industrialist and public figure in Coimbatore.

More than the marriage, the idea of Maniammai becoming EVR's successor was resented by his followers, who were increasingly unhappy with his utterances and by his discouragement of electoral politics. The elevation of Maniammai merely advanced the break. On 17 September 1949, Annadurai and his supporters assembled at Robinson Park in north Madras and launched the DMK.

Annadurai was clear that his DMK would pitch its appeal not to the non-Brahmin high castes, or to landowners, or to industrialists who had backed the DK and the Justice Party before that, but 'rather to the masses, the lower castes of the Nadar, Maravar and Adi-Dravida untouchables'.[25] Men between twenty and forty, the lower middle class, workers, petty officials, small traders, the urban unemployed, students—such groups were eyed by Anna and his colleagues, most of whom were writers and journalists like him.

As for CR, his term at the country's head ended on 26 January 1950, when India became a republic. Nehru's wish to have him as the first president was denied by Congress MPs, most of whom preferred Rajendra Prasad, who had served with distinction as the constituent assembly's president.

CR's outstanding performance as Governor General did not suffice. His inadequate Hindi was a handicap, his Quit India abstention was remembered, and Patel, who, at first, also wanted CR as president, soon took the chance to snub Nehru by backing Prasad. The night before he left Delhi, CR spoke at a dinner given by a disappointed Nehru:

> The Prime Minister and his first colleague, the Deputy Prime Minister, together make a possession which makes India rich in every sense of the term. The former commands universal love, the latter universal confidence. Not a tear need be shed for anyone going as long as these two stand four square against the hard winds to which our country may be exposed.[26]

Prasad, Nehru and Patel saw him off. Before entering the two-engine Dakota, CR placed a garland of handspun yarn around President Prasad's neck. On the flight, he penned a letter to his successor, who was younger by five years, requesting Prasad to convey the lines to Patel and Nehru as well:

I go out with joy in my heart at the beautiful manner in which the little changeover has taken place... God bless you all. Yours affectionately, C.R.[27]

◆

On 20 March, after his seventy-three-year-old friend from schooldays, the Bengaluru-based Navaratna Rama Rao, had conveyed an urge for a new assignment, CR wrote back: 'The desire to take up work that haunts the mind of old warriors on their retirement...should be resisted as severely as a desire to marry again and look after a young girl' (20 March 1950).

Within weeks of this pronouncement, CR, now seventy-one, accepted requests from Nehru and Patel to return to Delhi as a minister without portfolio, 'a kind of fifth wheel', as he put it to Rama Rao.

He saw no loss of dignity in joining, in the middle of July, a cabinet that until recently had been 'under' him. Since a cabinet member had to belong to parliament, a unanimous vote of the Madras assembly sent CR to India's upper house.

When Nehru said he wanted Rajaji to take up finance, Home Minister Patel, targeting Nehru's own portfolio, replied, only partially in jest, 'Why not external affairs?' Wishing more than anything else to assist the two and keep them united, CR accepted the 'fifth-wheel' assignment.

Asked by Nehru to head the cabinet's economic affairs committee, CR usually had Chintaman Deshmukh, the finance minister, conduct its meetings. At an early discussion in the external affairs committee, which Nehru chaired, CR disagreed with Patel when, to his and Nehru's shock, the deputy prime minister proposed 'going in' and taking over Goa, a step not taken until 1961.[28]

But over Tibet, which became a live issue before the end of the year, CR and Patel were on the same page. On 1 December, CR wrote to Nehru: 'May God help us from drifting to be just a satellite of China... We do not want any patrons now, do we?'[29]

Another Nehru–Patel conflict occurred over the Congress presidency, for which UP's Purushottam Das Tandon, heading his provincial Congress committee, was once more a candidate. In the preceding election, held in 1948, Tandon had lost to Pattabhi Sitaramayya* of the Telugu country.

Asked by Nehru to stand against Tandon—thus obtaining, in a sequence of spurned opportunities, yet another chance to become Congress president—CR declined once more. Securing Nehru's support, Kripalani contested and lost the election, which was held in August. Patel had backed the winner.

Helped by Maulana Azad, CR succeeded in persuading a hurt Nehru to join Tandon's working committee. On 3 October, when he read Patel's words spoken the previous day, CR was deeply moved. 'Our leader,' Patel had said, 'is Jawaharlal Nehru. Bapu appointed him as his successor in his lifetime... I am not a disloyal soldier.'[30]

A breach had mercifully been averted, but the seventy-five-year-old Patel took ill and never recovered. At Patel's funeral in Mumbai (15 December), tears rolling down his cheeks, CR, older than Nehru and Prasad, who were both present, made the oration.

At Nehru's request, CR now became home minister, saw to the putting down of the Telangana rebellion, which was in its final stages, and steered major legislation. When Nehru was away, he presided at cabinet meetings.

But he took zero interest in creating a political base for himself. The lawns and front rooms of the house allotted to him, 1, York Place,** were free of party persons, lobbyists, or relatives. When a letter arrived charging that an official whose family he had known intimately was corrupt, CR instructed:

> CID must keep watch on his movements... If he is found guilty on enquiry, he must be tried for the offence and dismissed if necessary.[31]

While acquaintances and partymen obtained little encouragement from CR, officials warmed to him, for he 'gave clear and straight answers and left nothing in doubt and never sought to escape responsibility for a mistake'.[32] Aware of the Northeast's complexities, CR asked Assam's

---

*Nine years earlier, Sitaramayya had lost a contest against Subhas Bose for the Congress chair.
**Later to be occupied by Prime Minister Lal Bahadur Shastri and now a Shastri memorial.

chief minister, Bishnuram Medhi, to 'appoint as many of the hill people as possible both in superior and inferior posts'.[33]

Memories of the hostility he had invited over Hindi never leaving him, he spoke out: 'Let me respectfully warn Hindi lovers not to depend upon the coercion of a numerical majority of an ill-knit population.'[34]

Over the Telangana rebellion, Nehru wanted a 'less severe approach, but Rajaji carried the day', B. N. Mullick, chief of intelligence at the time, would later recall. 'In the end, we were able to report to him that the movement had been broken.'[35]

Brought in before his death by Patel, the Preventive Detention Act was extended for a year by a bill that CR piloted. The Communist technique, he charged, was to lure men by the prospect of sacrifice and danger, drive them into 'complete criminal outlawry', and hold them by blackmail. Promising that any officer 'found guilty of misusing his powers under the Act would be regarded as an enemy of the state', he claimed that the Act would be used only against violent persons, blackmarketeers and 'those who continually incite communal passions'.[36]

Did he remember his 1919 statement that he and other foes of the Rowlatt Act would oppose any law 'to suspect and imprison without trial even if the government is democratic and purely Indian'?

◆

The 1st amendment to the Constitution, qualifying rights to property, equality and free speech, came into force while CR was home minister.

Introduced by Nehru on 10 May 1951, the amendment bill was passed on 21 June. A trigger for it was a July 1950 ruling by the Madras High Court in favour of a young Brahmin woman, Champakam Dorairajan, who had been denied a medical college seat under quotas set by the 'Communal GO' of 1927. The quotas were pronounced unconstitutional by the high court, and in April 1951 the Supreme Court confirmed the verdict.

The outcry that followed not only brought EVR and Anna together in the south, it prompted Kamaraj to demand a response. Home Minister CR backed the constitutional amendment authorizing discrimination in favour of the deprived.

The amendment's passing also enabled CR to introduce a

controversial Press Bill, limited to two years, empowering the government to obtain, by court order, security from an indicted publisher or journalist. A proviso gave an accused person the right to insist on a jury of journalists or public persons, and to appeal to a high court.

Claiming that a council of journalists 'inducing the Press to conform to known standards' would make the measure redundant, CR said it would be withdrawn before two years if such a council emerged.

Two journalist members of the house, Deshbandhu Gupta of Delhi's Urdu daily, *Tej*, and Ramnath Goenka of *Indian Express,* mounted a strong attack, but the bill went through, thanks to CR's performance. His interventions over the Press Bill 'excelled in advocacy any ever known in the annals of the central legislature', wrote Durga Das, a seasoned reporter watching the assembly from the 1920s.[37]

'The passage of the bill,' Gupta conceded, 'is a personal triumph of the home minister.'[38] Fortunately, few prosecutions followed the bill's enactment.

Admiration in Parliament House and North Block did not satisfy CR. By September, before the debate on the Press Bill, he had not only decided to leave Delhi, he had also resolved not to contest the elections due in early 1952, which would be the first to be held under the new constitution and, for the first time, with universal adult franchise.

Loathing the compromises with big money, votebanks and party machines that elections seemed to require, and watching ticket-hungry Congressmen captured, as he put it, by 'a fatal ecstasy',[39] CR told himself that enough was enough. But there was another factor.

Nehru was no longer turning to him. The change was not so much in Nehru as in the political landscape. With Patel gone, Nehru didn't need CR any more. Frequent while Patel was alive, Nehru's visits to CR's Delhi home to consult the old colleague had ceased.

CR did not resent Nehru's importance. Still, one who in the 1920s had revelled in uninhibited give and take with Jawahar's father Motilal was not willing, in 1951, to wait or work for the son's attention, no matter how charming, hard-working or popular that son was.

Early in October, when Mountbatten, tipped by Nehru on CR's unhappiness, suggested in a letter from London that CR should come to England as India's high commissioner, the former Governor General vented himself:

8 Oct 1951. You and Edwina are so intensely interested in Jawaharlal Nehru that, may I say, you have no eyes to see or mind to think about any others. Rajaji is just the match-stick to light the cigarette... You throw the match-stick into the ash-tray without a thought after it has served the purpose.

In November, he was back in Chennai, where, retired, CR began work on his version of the Ramayana.

◆

We should not be greatly surprised, however, to learn (*a*) that C.R. was soon back in office, (*b*) that he and EVR resumed a clash, and (*c*) that CR again showed self-destructive stubbornness. The three things happened following elections held in January–February 1952, when the Communists scored significant successes in Madras Presidency's Telugu and Malayalam portions.

In all other provinces, now called states, and in the Lok Sabha, Prime Minister Nehru, who since the previous September was Congress president as well, had led the Congress to impressive victories.

In Madras, however, the Congress won only 43 out of 143 seats in the Telugu region, and only 4 out of 29 in Malabar. In the Tamil country, it got 96 out of 190, in South Kanara 9 out of 11. The Communists won a total 61 seats, there were 63 successful independents, and 9 small parties found representation in a house of 375.

Communist efforts in Malabar and the Telugu country had paid off. A foodgrains crisis, and support in the Andhra area for Prakasam, who had left the Congress to join a new all-India party led by Kripalani, also contributed to the unexpected results.

Even as Prakasam tried to form a front of non-Congress MLAs including the Communists, the thought of recalling CR occurred simultaneously to several influential men in Madras. These included Kumaraswami Raja, the outgoing chief minister who had lost his seat; Coimbatore district's Chidambaram Subramaniam, a Congress leader who had won his seat; Ramnath Goenka, the *Indian Express* proprietor who had lobbied against CR over India's presidency; and A. N. Sivaraman, editor of the Tamil daily *Dinamani.*

Kamaraj, the TNCC chief, and Neelam Sanjiva Reddy, who headed the Andhra Congress, fell in, and Nehru gave consent to their attempt.

On 29 March, after Congress legislators had unanimously resolved to request CR to lead them, a delegation led by Raja (the caretaker chief minister), Kamaraj and Reddy called on him in his home with the resolution.

Since CR wanted to be sure of what the prime minister who was also the Congress president thought, Subramaniam and Soundaram Ramachandran, a leading Congresswoman, flew to Delhi, showed Nehru the resolution, and returned carrying two letters from him. One was to CR, saying 'I naturally accept' the MLAs' wish. The other was to Raja, where Nehru said that 'early steps' would be needed 'for Rajaji's election to the Madras Assembly'.[40]

On CR insisting that he was 'absolutely definite that he would in no circumstances stand for election',[41] the following four things happened in Madras within a single day (31 March):

One, citing a constitutional clause for bringing specialists in literature, science, art or social service to legislatures, Raja advised Sri Prakasa, the governor, to nominate CR to the Madras legislature's upper house. Two, citing Raja's recommendation, Sri Prakasa nominated CR. Three, meeting immediately thereafter, the Congress MLAs formally elected CR as leader. Four, he was sworn in as chief minister!

The next day, 1 April, CR told the press, 'In my private journal I would call this my downfall.'[42] Such qualms were quickly forgotten, however. A thick-skinned CR told the assembly on 9 May:

> Did not the framers of the Constitution imagine that there would
> be circumstances when a man not elected would have to be called
> in for the good of society?[43]

Presented with a fait accompli, Nehru involved himself in discussing ministerial names with CR and did not bring up elections again. Though declining CR's shrewd invitation, the eminent Vellala educator and doctor, Lakshmanaswami Mudaliar, did not join it, the new fifteen-member ministry, which included one non-Congress MLA,* received strong support inside the assembly and from the public for more than a year, until CR pushed his impulsive education scheme.

On the opening day he told the assembly:

---

*Manickavelu Naicker, heading the Commonweal Party.

I am here to save my country from the traps and dangers of the
Communist party (*Applause*). That is my policy from A to Z. I
am placing my cards on the table. I am your enemy number one,
and may I say you are my enemy number one.[44]

This was conviction plus craft: CR was playing on the unease with the
Communists' agenda of many in the opposition. His enemy number
two, CR would declare, was the public works department, notorious
for corruption. Equally popular with the general public was a statement
that he had been 'called to sweep away the cobwebs and clean the
drains' of Congressmen's houses.[45]

For a year, luck was with CR. He asked the public to join with
him in praying for rain: the waters came down. Convinced of stocks
in the countryside, he removed controls on the movement and price
of rice: grain started to flow and queues for rice disappeared. Along
with water levels, the state's coffers rose.[46]

A new law, preceded by an ordinance, banned the eviction of
cultivating tenants in Thanjavur district, which had been hit by agrarian
clashes, and enabled restoration where eviction had occurred. Another
law provided relief for handloom weavers. On the assembly floor, he
again sparkled, over a demand on 28 June 1952 to know what he had
written to Nehru over the creation of an Andhra state.

CR: It is a confidential letter.
Tenneti Viswanatham: Under what provision of the law is the
correspondence treated as confidential?
CR: Gentlemen's correspondence is always private.[47]

At the end of 1952, Potti Sriramulu's death from a fast triggered the
creation of Andhra, which we will soon look at. On 1 October 1953,
Madras was split, Andhra came into being, and Telugu MLAs left to
constitute the first Andhra assembly. The Congress not needing him to
control the residual house, CR thought of resigning and said as much
to Nehru and the governor, but he was dissuaded by both.

'Madras was on the brink of a precipice,' Govind Ballabh Pant,
the central home minister, wrote to CR, 'and has been luckily saved
by you' (3 Sept 1953). 'Rajaji has saved Madras for us,' Nehru told
one of his ministers, Mahavir Tyagi.[48]

Giving the Communists a jolt, Prakasam deserted their company and with Congress support became the new state's first chief minister, a selection that CR had publicly and privately espoused.[49] When Prakasam went to CR's home to share his happiness, CR saw to it that Prakasam, a comrade for decades and older by six years, would not need to step out of his car. Walking up to the visitor's vehicle, CR expressed his joy. 'The eyes of the lion of Andhra became wet.'[50]

◆

'He insists on crucifying me,' jotted CR in his diary in February 1953, referring to a letter in which Nehru had said, 'I am sorry I cannot think of releasing you.'[51] Primarily, however, the death-wish was CR's own. It took the shape of an education scheme.

The reform's core idea was to cut from five hours to three a child's daily time in the government's primary schools. With morning and afternoon sessions, the number of pupils would be doubled. During the two hours freed for them, children would learn creative skills from parents, relations and artisanal neighbours. CR told the assembly:

> It is a mistake to imagine that the school is within the walls. The whole village is the school. The village polytechnic is there, every branch of it: the dhobi, the wheelwright, the cobbler.[52]

The brainwave had a history. As a child, CR had hated the six-hour schoolday. In an article in 1907, he spoke of village teachers as 'angry ill-educated' men 'hammering down' the child's 'human curiosity'.[53] In August 1949, as Governor General, he had painted the village as an idyll where

> the food is grown, the cloth is woven, the sheep are shorn, the shoes are stitched, the scavenging is done, the cartwheels and the ploughs are built and repaired because, thank God, the respective castes are still there, and the homes are trade schools as well, and the parents are masters as well, to whom the children are automatically apprenticed.[54]

Now, as chief minister, he could enact the dream, lighten a child's burden, double literacy, and switch on the village polytechnic, all at no cost! Had this magic ball been thrown at them, a team of educators and administrators might indeed have done something practical with it, but CR insisted on scoring the goal himself and at once.

It was a self-goal, as he always knew it would be. In fact, he had handed the ball to EVR, who ran with it across the Tamil country, declaring: 'Here is proof from the old Brahmin's own mouth. He wants to perpetuate the caste system.'

As had happened over Hindi in his first premiership, CR was unwilling to alter, pause or withdraw. Annadurai and his DMK took to the streets, and Congress MLAs began to desert CR, quietly at first and then openly.

Varadarajulu Naidu, who in 1925 had seized on discriminatory eating practices in a Congress-funded boarding school, asked in November for a new chief minister, claiming that thirty-nine Congress MLAs were with him. Nehru called Naidu's move 'highly improper', but there was no stopping the tide CR had invited. To friend Rama Rao, CR wrote: 'I am not entitled to any pity, for it is all of my own making' (17 Aug 53).

CR and Periyar met cordially at a public occasion in December. 'EVR and I had prophets' meeting', CR wrote in his diary (20 Dec 1953), 'big gathering greatly happy at our being together'. But opposition to his scheme continued to swell. That files at Fort St George were moving without lubricants, and judges were free from interference,[55] no longer mattered.

In March 1954, former chief minister O. P. Ramaswami Reddiar addressed CR in the upper house: 'Please give up the scheme without any more ado. It is a new handle to the blackshirts [DK]. Persistence will only sound the death-knell of our party'.[56]

Most Congress MLAs now wanted Kamaraj to replace CR. A meeting they demanded was fixed for 24 March. On the 23rd, when Kamaraj called on CR, the latter offered to quit if his scheme was continued. 'You stay, Rajaji,' replied Kamaraj, 'but please suspend the scheme.' When CR said that his continuing 'is now impossible', the two agreed to put off the MLAs' meeting by a few days.[57]

On the 25th, a 'weak and pale Rajaji'—affected also by bronchial pneumonia—was 'heard in pin-drop silence' in the assembly as he read a five-minute statement of resignation 'in a calm and clear tone'.[58]

His name proposed by Varadarajulu Naidu, Kamaraj became the new leader of the Congress MLAs on 30 March, receiving 93 votes as against the 41 obtained by C. Subramaniam, contesting at CR's instance. Kamaraj was 'profusely garlanded and lustily cheered' when CR, who chaired the meeting, announced the result.[59] Wisely, Kamaraj retained most of the Rajaji team, including Subramaniam. The education scheme was given up.

Much of the Tamil country was delighted to find at the helm a man of few words who had never gone to university and spoke little English, a bachelor whose sole concern, it seemed, was the ordinary person's well-being, someone personally acquainted, so it appeared, with every Congress worker in the Tamil land.

No one seemed happier, however, than EVR, who called Kamaraj a 'pure' Tamilian and applauded the fact that his cabinet contained no Brahmin.[60] Three year later, in 1957, after new elections made Kamaraj chief minister again, EVR, who had backed Kamaraj as against the DMK, would tell the Coimbatore Congressman, Kovai Ayyamuthu:

I don't meet Kamaraj at all. I don't write to him too. He is a Tamil. Because of that I feel some satisfaction that he annihilated Achariyaar who lorded it over for a long time. That's why I campaigned for him.[61]

We have seen, however, that it was CR who had annihilated himself. As for EVR's backing for Kamaraj, some of it was connected to the DMK's steady growth, which did not seem to please Periyar.

In a major speech in 1950 to about 6,000 men and women, Annadurai had announced his intention to address the Tamil mind, not just the heart. Tamil literature, Tamil linguistics, poetry, plays, films, newspapers and journals were all employed, and the Tamil country was filled with DMK propaganda even during the years of Congress hegemony.[62]

In 1951, a huge meeting on Island Grounds in Madras announced that a new party had arrived. In the following year, a film called *Parasakthi*, written by Muthuvel Karunanidhi (b. 1924) and starring Sivaji Ganesan,* showed Tamils suffering under an indifferent Congress

---

*Ganesan (1927–2001) obtained the name Sivaji from EVR after the latter watched the actor play the Maratha hero in 1946. Quitting the DK in 1949, along with Annadurai and others, to form the DMK, the much-admired actor, who was born into the Kallar caste, became a Kamaraj backer in the mid-fifties.

government. Similar films would soon sweep across the Tamil country's cinema halls, run on electricity generated by Congress ministries.

In 1953, the DMK opened three volleys against the Congress. One, citing a plan to rename a village in Trichy district after the Marwari industrialist, Ram Krishna Dalmia, alleged economic oppression from the north. A second spoke of Nehru's 'Delhi sultanate', while the third attacked CR's education scheme, in demonstrations against which Annadurai and around 6,000 others were arrested.

Two years later, in 1955, a maturing DMK opposed flag burning by the DK.

EVR's support for him was never publicly acknowledged by Kamaraj, who, however, understood the rising importance of the Tamil country's 'backward' castes.[63] The 'Brahmin versus Vellala' debate was out of date by the mid-fifties. When Kamaraj succeeded CR in April 1954, two backward caste leaders were accommodated in his ministry.

POTTI SRIRAMULU (1901–1952)

At the Congress's 1948 session, held in Jaipur and presided over by Pattabhi Sitaramayya, a committee consisting of Nehru, Patel and the party president had been asked to pronounce on the Andhra demand. In April 1949, this J. V. P. committee, as it was called, conceded the strength of the sentiment for a separate Andhra state but advised the Telugus to give up their claim to Madras city.

Although the city's Tamil numbers, constituting a clear majority, were not easy to refute, the rejection of a long and deeply-held wish produced resentment, which was heightened by New Delhi's seeming reluctance to go ahead with an Andhra state even without the city.

Differences among Andhra leaders were cited to justify the centre's hesitation, but hands were forced on 15 December 1952, when Madras-born Pottu Sriramulu died in that city after having fasted for an Andhra state for fifty-eight days.

The trading-caste family into which Sriramulu was born in 1901 had its roots in Nellore district. He went on to become a sanitary engineer and railway officer before joining Gandhi's Sabarmati Ashram and the national movement. In the 1930s and 1940s, he courted prison several times. Prior to his end-1952 fast, he had spent years in Nellore town, demonstrating for Dalit rights on the streets, often by himself.

After forty days of fasting, his situation became perilous. A Madras meeting chaired by Prakasam demanded an immediate declaration of an Andhra state and conversion of the city into a chief commissioner's province. On 9 December, Nehru said in the Rajya Sabha that the centre was willing to go ahead with the Andhra conceded by the J. V. C. committee, but this did not satisfy Sriramulu, who continued his fast and died six days later.

Demonstrators damaged property in Nellore and other towns in the Telugu country, and lives were lost in police firing.[64] Four days after Sriramulu's death, on 19 December, Nehru announced that an Andhra state would be established, without Madras city. It came into being on 1 October 1953.

Researching six decades later in Nellore, an American scholar, Lisa Mitchell, found that residents in the town still 'remembered Sriramulu going about...wearing signboards on his front and back declaring that untouchability was a sin and advocating "Harijana Devalayam Pravesam" (Harijan Temple Entry) and "Sahapankti Bhojanam" (Inter-caste Dining)'.[65]

In the twenty-first century, the four men killed in police firing in December 1952 were thought of in Nellore as martyrs to the cause of Andhra, but little was known about them and even their names were not clearly remembered. One, discovered Mitchell, was a vegetable vendor and the other three were between sixteen to twenty years old. All four were part of a crowd of Hindus, Muslims and Christians converging at the railway station when word arrived of Sriramulu's death. Unruliness occurred, and the police fired.

Not everyone who gathered at the station knew exactly why Sriramulu had died, but all were aware of the dead man's concern for the low of caste and class. Sriramulu had earlier fasted at four different times in Nellore in support of Dalit rights.[66]

◆

Sriramulu's death and the creation of Andhra erased a question mark against linguistic states that Partition-related dislocations had produced. Once the presidency's Telugu portions separated, there seemed little justification for Malabar and South Kanara to continue to be governed from Madras city. Or for all Kannada areas not to come together. Or for all Malayalam areas not to do likewise. Or for a multilingual Hyderabad state to continue.

The transition to linguistic states was not friction-free. A linguistic area was not necessarily homogeneous in economy, terrain or climate. Or in political culture or caste equations. Thus, Telugu-speakers in the Rayalaseema hinterland had to be persuaded to join an Andhra likely to be dominated from its coastal belt. Telangana's politicians too were wary of their linguistic kin on the coast.

Moreover, was it wise to terminate the former princely states of Hyderabad, Mysore, Travancore and Cochin, each possessing a long established regional culture? The question was natural, but movements for linguistic unity won the day, for these had overlapped for almost three decades with struggles for independence and popular rule. Popular rule minus linguistic unity seemed incomplete to many.

In 1956, accordingly, India's internal borders were redrawn, chiefly along linguistic lines.

The governments of Hyderabad, Mysore and Travancore–Cochin came to an end. A large piece of Hyderabad went to Andhra even as Andhra's capital moved to Hyderabad. Another part joined a large Maharashtra. A third portion became part of Mysore, and the enlarged territory was called Karnataka from 1973.

As Hyderabad state disappeared into three other entities, Mysore state expanded, absorbing portions previously belonging to the presidencies of Bombay and Madras and the Asaf Jahi kingdom.

A Tamil-majority piece in southern Travancore was joined to Madras state (it would not be called Tamil Nadu until 1969), but from 1956 the Tamil country was no longer South India's governing base, and Madras city—Chennai after 1996—would not remain the south's undisputed premier city for long.

There were bitter disputes over a few places. In the end, Bellary went to Karnataka, not Andhra; Kasargod to Kerala, not Karnataka; Belgaum to Karnataka, not Maharashtra. In general, however, the redistribution of administrative territories was accepted as people-friendly.

In an interesting intervention, CR asked in November 1955 for a large 'Dakshina Pradesh' inclusive of all Telugu, Malayalam, Kannada and Tamil areas. Such an administrative area would 'retain the political significance of the South' in the Indian union, he claimed.[67]

However, the plea would get no more traction than EVR's older call for an independent Dravida Nadu, which had been interpreted in the south's non-Tamil parts as a euphemism for Tamil dominance. Local rule through the local language seemed the overwhelming preference. Though formally abandoned only in 1963, Dravida Nadu was given a mortal blow when maps were redrawn in 1956.

As for Dakshina Pradesh, the concept did not invite an emotion comparable to what a Telugu, Kannada or Malayalam state evoked. Politically, in fact, neighbours seemed more useful as enemies than as partners.

Despite linguistic unification, minorities of several kinds, including linguistic ones, would remain in each state. Still, linguistic merger conferred benefits. Unification presented Karnataka's writers, poets, playwrights and filmmakers with an enlarged audience freed from walls of separation. The same happened in the Telugu and Malayalam countries.

In architecture, a major accomplishment prior to Mysore's enlargement was Bangalore's Vidhana Soudha, the house of legislature and governance, for which Kengal Hanumanthaiah (1908–1980), Mysore's chief minister from 1952 to 1956, was above all responsible.

Following the 1957 elections, the first to be held after lines were redrawn, the Congress retained office at the centre and in three of the four linguistic states in the south. The only exception was Kerala—now a united Malayalam country, with Malabar and Travancore–Cochin merged—where the Communist Party won and E. M. S. Namboodiripad became chief minister.

The Communists did fairly well in Andhra too, though there, and in Madras and Mysore, 'independents' comprised the largest group after the Congress.

Three non-Brahmin Congress leaders, Kamaraj in Madras, Sanjiva Reddy in Andhra and S. Nijalingappa in Mysore, and Kerala's Brahmin Communist, EMS, formed the league of the south's chief ministers.

A close link had been forged between the Madras chief minister and Nehru, who became prime minister again. The partnership was demonstrated earlier at the Congress's 60th annual session, held in January 1955 in Avadi near Madras city, which Kamaraj organized, and where the Congress declared for the first time that a 'socialistic pattern' of society was its aim.

In the memory of a mentor who had died in 1943, Kamaraj named the venue Satyamurti Nagar.

Chapter 13

EQUATIONS WITH NEW DELHI: 1957–1977

The Communists' electoral success in Kerala in 1957 was an international event. Until then no large region anywhere in the world had *voted* Communists to power.* How did it happen?

For one thing, the Communists benefited from the reordering of South India. The pan-Malayali Kerala created in 1956 included the historically left-leaning Malabar districts, formerly part of Madras Presidency, that had reared Communist stalwarts like A. K. Gopalan and EMS. On the other hand, the largely pro-Congress Tamil-majority talukas from southern Travancore were detached from the new Kerala and merged with Madras state.

Second, the Communist Party's image of unity contrasted favourably with instability in the opposite camp. Between 1952 and 1956, Travancore–Cochin had seen three chief ministers: two Congressmen and one from the Praja Socialist Party (PSP). Third, the Communists promised bold land reforms while also pledging to work within the Constitution.

Moreover, some voters thought the Communists more likely than the Congress to take Kerala to the goal of socialism announced by a popular Jawaharlal Nehru.

There was a 'caste' explanation too. While Christians had voted solidly for the Congress, the more numerous Ezhavas had voted equally solidly for the Communists. The SCs voted 60:40 in favour of the Communists, the Muslims largely preferred the Muslim League, while the Nair vote seemed evenly split between the Congress, the PSP and the Communists.[1]

Winning 60 out of 126 seats (as against the Congress's 43 and the PSP's 9), and backed by five successful independents it had supported, the Communist Party installed a ministry led by EMS, but an education

---

*San Marino, which elected a Communist government in 1945, held fewer than 40,000 people.

measure introduced in its opening weeks invited fierce opposition. Two years later, New Delhi invoked Article 356 and removed Kerala's elected government.

Promised in the party's manifesto and moved by Joseph Mundassery, a literary critic and former college teacher who had become education minister, the Kerala bill authorized the state government to take over government-aided private schools that did not properly manage their teachers or funds. It also seemed to give the government a say in hiring or replacing teachers in private schools.

In 1957, 26.5 per cent of Kerala's schoolchildren were enrolled in government, municipal or local board schools. The remaining 73.5 per cent were in private schools, the great majority of which were run either by Kerala's different churches or by social or religious bodies of Hindus or Muslims.[2]

The Kerala legislature passed the measure in September 1957, but its implementation became problematic when the Catholic church and the Nair Service Society, still led by Mannath Padmanabhan, joined hands to resist it.

No one denied that fees collected from pupils went at times into managers' pockets, or that teachers often signed receipts for salaries they did not get. However, the possibility of a government takeover of schools run by religious organizations produced an outcry that ceased only when the EMS ministry was removed in end-July 1959.

A constitutional question too had arisen. Critics claimed that the education scheme violated Article 30's assurance of protection to minority educational institutions. Barring the Communist Party's organs, all newspapers criticized the scheme, as did virtually every non-Communist party, including most of Kerala's numerous socialist groups. C. H. Mohammed Koya of the Muslim League saw 'Nazism' in it.[3]

Kerala's governor was Burgula Ramakrishna Rao from the Telugu country, who had been chief minister of Hyderabad until that state's dissolution in 1956. When Kerala's Congress leaders urged him to reject the education law, Rao referred it to the centre, which sought the Supreme Court's opinion.

In May 1958, the Supreme Court held that parts of the Act were unconstitutional. The Kerala legislature amended the Act in light of the verdict, but the momentum was very much with its opponents, who found an influential supporter in a woman who, to the surprise of many, became Congress president in February 1959.

At forty-one, Indira Gandhi was a good deal younger than most Indian politicians. Visiting Kerala at the end of April, she concluded that the Communist ministry had to go. Her father hesitated. Having been urged by Kerala's law minister, V. R. Krishna Iyer, to view things for himself, Prime Minister Nehru arrived in the state on 22 June, while a 'liberation struggle'—Vimochana Samaram—was ongoing. Thousands had courted arrest. On 13 June, five were killed in police firing. *Malayala Manorama* ran an editorial demanding the EMS ministry's ouster. For the visiting Nehru's benefit, it was published in English.

Jawaharlal's preferred solution was a mid-term election to be called by the Communist ministry, but he did not block his daughter's more drastic wish. Towards the end of July, EMS and the Kerala Pradesh Congress Committee (KPCC) president, R. Sankar, who was also one of the state's most influential Ezhava leaders, went to Delhi to argue for opposite positions. The EMS government's ouster was announced on 31 July.

No one in India questioned Communism more thoroughly than CR, who by this time had launched a new political party, Swatantra, and was asking Nehru to abandon the socialist goal. However, he too raised his voice against an elected government's dismissal.

'I do not like the Communist party, but this is not the way to deal with it,' CR wrote,[4] even as his Swatantra colleagues, Minoo Masani and K. M. Munshi, joined the 'liberation struggle' in Kerala.

After a spell of President's Rule, elections held in 1960 gave victory in Kerala to an alliance of the Congress, PSP and Muslim League, which won 94 seats with a 54.3 per cent vote share. All ministers connected with the Education Act lost: central intervention had not annoyed the electorate. Still, the Communists obtained an impressive 42.9 per cent of the vote while winning only 29 seats.

Pattom Thanu Pillai of the PSP, chief minister from the victorious alliance, made way after eighteen months for the Congress's R. Sankar, but secession from the Congress of a group of MLAs who called themselves the Kerala Congress* led to the Sankar ministry's fall in September 1964.

---

*Most of them elected from constituencies with a large Christian vote.

Before new elections were held in 1965, the Communists too split, nationally as also in Kerala. Party members were sharply divided over the 1962 Indo–China war, over the Sino–Soviet dispute, which became public by 1962, and over support to the central government.

The 1965 elections gave no party or alliance a majority in Kerala. When, after two years of President's Rule, the Malayalis again voted, they once more chose EMS as their chief minister. EMS represented the larger of the two Communist segments, the Communist Party of India (Marxist), or CPM, as it would become known, but we will find Kerala continuing to see-saw.

TAMIL NADU

In Tamil Nadu,* meanwhile, and not merely there, Kamaraj was enjoying great prestige. Under him, the state was making steady progress in education, rural electrification and employment.

Learning that attendance in Chennai's municipal and 'Harijan Welfare' schools dropped to half on Saturdays, when there was no mid-day meal, Kamaraj steadily expanded the meal program in state-run schools. By 1962–63, 12.65 lakh pupils in 27,256 schools state-wide were receiving the free meal, compared with 2.29 lakh pupils in 1957–58.

The state spent 1.18 crore on this program in 1962–63 (against under 7 lakh five years earlier), but Kamaraj also secured aid from local communities and, with Nehru's help, from the American agency CARE. A prod for the policy was Kamaraj's memory of his childhood school in Virudhunagar, where many families contributed a fistful each of rice for a common school meal.[5]

Listening to officers, reading files with care and penning clear instructions, Kamaraj was, in addition, coming across, in the words of one observer, as

the 'representative' Tamil... His ways of speaking, walking, eating and dress commend themselves to the many millions to whom these are familiar ways, with nothing outlandish about them.[6]

---

*The state was called 'Madras' until 1969.

Yet the 'outlandish' DMK, as some saw it, relying on scriptwriters and actors, was quietly consolidating, assisted by films it was spreading its egalitarian ideology and the party's greater awareness, in comparison with the Congress, of the Tamil country's steady urbanization. Advances in industry, communication and literacy were eroding earlier village-linked clusters of Tamils and creating new communities.

Some of these groups saw the DMK as the truer voice of a changing Tamil nation.[7] In a 1960 book, an American observer, Selig Harrison, wrote of Annadurai as 'the most popular mass figure in the region'.[8] However, most politicians in the Tamil country were slow to notice Anna's strength.

Meanwhile, the Nehru–Kamaraj relationship had strengthened, helped, among other things, by the political rupture between CR and Nehru. In 1961, Jawaharlal unveiled a Kamaraj statue on Chennai's famed Mount Road. Until then no one living had obtained that honour from Nehru, who argued that the exception was deserved.

Careful in speech, Kamaraj usually responded to a tricky question with just one word, 'Parkalaam' (Let's see). When he spoke in public, commonsense was the dominant note, as when, rarely for him, he touched on a religious subject:

> Is Hari great or Siva great? There have been bitter disputations over that question. But the wisdom of the common people resolved the dispute by declaring, 'Hari and Siva are one; woe to the man who does not realize this.'[9]

That was said during the 1962 election campaign, when Kamaraj concentrated on defeating the DMK in the fifteen constituencies it held. The Congress won 14 of those seats, but the DMK won in 49 fresh places, obtaining a tally of 50, even though the party had suffered a split in 1961. Winning 139 seats, the Congress was however confirmed in power, and Kamaraj became chief minister for the third time.

Conscious that Tamil nationalism was a draw even though Dravidastan was being set aside, Kamaraj said that Madras state should be called Tamil Nadu, which however did not happen until 1969.

While CR's Swatantra Party supported the DMK in 1962, EVR openly campaigned for Kamaraj. 'I am old,' said Periyar. 'I may not live very long. After I am gone, Kamaraj will safeguard the interests of the Tamils.' He added:

Vote Congress and you will be well. If you don't, the ingenious Rajaji riding the DMK horse will trample you all without mercy.[10]

The DMK had split because Periyar's nephew E. V. K. Sampath, who in 1949 had left the DK along with Annadurai, broke with him, alleging dictatorial behaviour, an excessive reliance on film stars, and retreat from Dravida ideology.

Yet Anna had a better grasp than Sampath of Tamil opinion, which saw little merit in chasing the Dravidastan daydream. Anna had already clarified, in a 1959 remark, that the DMK wanted nothing more than an 'amendment of the Constitution through perfectly constitutional methods' to end 'North Indian domination'.[11]

Fought in the Himalayas, the Indo–China war of 1962 went poorly for India. After it ended, a constitutional amendment, unanimously passed in March 1963, required every candidate for Parliament or a state legislature to take an oath to preserve India's integrity. Following this 16th Amendment, the DMK removed references to Dravidastan from its declared goals.

In differentiating himself from EVR, Anna was courteous but also clear. For Anna's DMK (as Cho Ramaswamy would later observe), 'it was "one God" in the place of E.V.R.'s "no God"'. It was 'Brahminism which had to be rooted out, not the Brahmins'.[12]

India's setback in the Himalayan war hurt Nehru's prestige and that of his acerbic minister, the brilliant V. K. Krishna Menon, a son of Kerala who had studied in Chennai and London, helped found Pelican Books, mobilized support for Indian independence in the UK, represented India at the United Nations, helped start the Non-Aligned Movement, and served as India's ill-fated defence minister during the 1962 war.

The many Westerners alienated by Krishna Menon's sarcastic interventions at the UN were balanced by Malayalis proud of Menon's nationalist passion, his relentless defence of the 'third world', and his influence, while it lasted, in the chancelleries of non-aligned countries.

Another South Indian who became a central personality during the Himalayan war was Sarvepalli Radhakrishnan, the philosopher-educator from the Telugu country, who had made Indian philosophy accessible to the West as also to Indians unfamiliar with their country's thought or unable to articulate it.

After occupying high positions in universities in Waltair, Oxford and Benares and usually wearing a turban, Radhakrishnan served as India's ambassador to Moscow, where he talked candidly with Stalin. In 1952, he was elected India's vice-president. Ten years later, he succeeded Rajendra Prasad as president.

Later in 1962, when India's battlefront performance embarrassed the country, Radhakrishnan spoke for the people when, shedding the constitutional inhibition associated with a head of state in India, he underlined the government's 'credulity and negligence'.[13]

An eighty-three-year-old CR, meanwhile, had made his first trip abroad. Except for a brief journey to Sri Lanka in 1927, he had not left India's shores before September 1962. Woollen socks and a couple of woollen kurtas were pulled out and dry-cleaned, and knee-length pants stitched into the dhotis of one who had never worn western-style trousers before.

The goal of Rajaji's 1962 trip was to persuade President John F. Kennedy in Washington, Prime Minister Harold Macmillan in London, and Pope John XXIII in Rome to work for nuclear arms control. Earlier, when Nikita Khrushchev visited India, CR had urged the Soviet leader along the same lines.

The meetings with Kennedy and Pope John went particularly well. After the US, Soviet Union and UK reached an agreement on nuclear tests in July 1963, Chester Bowles, the American ambassador in New Delhi, assured CR in a letter that Kennedy would 'stand firm' against US senators opposed to the treaty, adding, '[H]is persistence is, in no small measure, due to your eloquent plea...during your visit.'[14]

KAMARAJ PLAN

Kamaraj too made an unexpected move. Perceiving that the steadily rising DMK was likely to gain from its disavowal of secession, and conscious of danger to the Congress from the DMK's understanding with Rajaji, in 1963 he resigned as chief minister on a symbolically shrewd date, 2 October, in order, he said, to do party work and strengthen the Tamils' link with the Congress.

Consulted beforehand by Kamaraj, a Nehru shaken by the outcome of the war with China and aware, after sixteen years as prime minister, of his diminishing popularity, not only agreed, he took two further steps. One, he ensured that Kamaraj became Congress president. Two, he asked a few other chief ministers and central ministers also to move from government to party work. These included four influential union ministers: Gujarat's Morarji Desai, UP's Lal Bahadur Shastri, Bihar's Jajgivan Ram and Bombay's S. K. Patil.

The turnaround was presented as the 'Kamaraj Plan' for revitalizing the Congress. While CR pointed out that Nehru had exempted himself from the pious switch to party work, EVR, his intuitions intact at age eighty-four, warned Kamaraj in a telegram that the resignation was political 'suicide' for 'the people of Tamilnadu as well as Kamaraj himself'.[15]

For the next three years, though, the opposite seemed to happen to Kamaraj. As Congress president, he was catapulted to the national stage. On 8 January 1964, when, during a Congress plenary held in Bhubaneshwar, Nehru suffered a stroke that partially disabled him, it was Kamaraj who was presiding. Within days, on Kamaraj's urging, Shastri was recalled as a cabinet minister.

When Nehru died in May, Kamaraj interviewed Congress MPs one by one and declared that Shastri, the quiet Congressman from UP, was their preferred choice, not Morarji Desai, who had thrown his crisp white cap in the ring. Shastri became prime minister.

Nineteen months later, when Shastri died in Tashkent in January 1966, it was Kamaraj again who presided over private discussions about a successor among Congress MPs. A contender once more, Desai demanded conventional vote-counting, following which Indira Gandhi emerged as prime minister.

Visible as a king-maker on the national stage and admired for his leadership of the Tamils, the tall, dark and strong-looking Kamaraj knew, however, that he would not sit on India's political throne. Others knew that too. Kamaraj's limitations with Hindi ruled out any direct bond between him and the bulk of the Indian people.

Like CR earlier, Kamaraj had come within reach of national power but was not able to grasp it. There is no indication that he burned to do so.

Preferring silent work to making speeches or composing articles, Kamaraj was also sparing in the letters he wrote. No interesting correspondence between him and Nehru appears to have come to light, even though from 1954 onwards, and possibly from earlier, there was a large degree of trust and understanding between the two.

Asked in early 1975 as to which of the two, Nehru or Patel, he had felt closer to over the years, Kamaraj replied without hesitation, 'Nehru'.[16]

The CR–Nehru relationship saw greater fluctuation and is far better recorded in letters and elsewhere. As political foes, between 1958 and 1964, the two said harsh things about each other. Between 1946 and 1951, they were very close as colleagues charged with governing India. Earlier, from 1919 to 1946, they had marched together towards India's liberty.

Even after CR launched Swatantra in frontal opposition to Nehru's policies, personal warmth remained. In February 1959, CR wrote that it was 'God's grace that there is a good man in India who deserved to be idolized as [Nehru] is. Yet there is nothing more important for the ruler of a great big nation [than] independent, fearless advice.'

Since Gandhi and Patel were there no longer, Rajaji continued, 'I who remain would be untrue to the trust and love they had been bestowing on me if, preferring quiet and ease, I kept silent'.[17] In 1961, he underlined a major disagreement over policy:

> Mr. Jawaharlal Nehru returned from Cambridge with notions of how an all-governing interventionist state can force people into happiness and prosperity through socialism. He sticks to this bias in spite of the demonstration of world experience against it.[18]

Still, when Nehru died on 27 May 1964, CR penned memorable words:

> Eleven years younger than me, eleven times more important for the nation, and eleven hundred times more beloved of the nation...a beloved friend is gone, the most civilized person among us all.[19]

ANNADURAI (1909–1969)

By 1965, EVR was proved right. In the Tamil country, the Kamaraj Plan failed to strengthen the Congress or weaken the DMK. M. Bhaktavatsalam, who became chief minister after Kamaraj resigned, seemed to mishandle agitations spearheaded by the DMK against the union government's language policy.

Unless the law changed, Hindi was going to become India's sole official language from 26 January 1965. To allay fears in non-Hindi regions, Nehru had pushed through an Official Languages Act in 1963 that seemed to provide for the continuing use of English as an additional language for official work. However, as the 1965 deadline neared, the DMK demanded clearer assurances from the centre, where, now, Shastri was prime minster.

Resisted by politicians in the north, the assurances did not come through in time. Starting with a riot in Madurai on 25 January 1965, student protests erupted across the Tamil country. Now eighty-six, CR, the target of anti-Hindi demonstrations in 1937, led the demand for a categorical rejection of a Hindi-only policy.

A costly sequence unfolded: processions, taunts, riots, arrests (in the thousands), lathi charges, police firing, deaths... Bhaktavatsalam was unable to control the spiral. By official figures, around seventy Tamils lost lives in the 1965 agitation. Two Tamils in Shastri's central ministry, C. Subramaniam and O. V. Alagesan, resigned.

The rioting stopped only when Shastri announced that English would remain an official language without an end date, departing only when non-Hindi states wanted it to go.

Later in the year, after the India–Pakistan war of September 1965, CR argued, while addressing the Kashmir issue in his journal *Swarajya,* against 'dogmatism about the liquid truths of political life' (9 Oct 1965). Bhaktavatsalam brought up Defence of India Rules and launched prosecutions against T. Sadasivam, *Swarajya's* publisher (whose wife M. S. Subbulakshmi, through her voice, was raising large sums for the jawans) and Pothan Joseph,* the editor.

Protesting to Chief Minister Bhaktavatsalam, President Radhakrishnan, Prime Minister Shastri and Home Minister Gulzarilal Nanda, CR said, 'Action should be taken against me... The truth of the matter, viz., that I am to be gagged, cannot be hidden from the world by such stratagems.'[20]

Nanda's proposal that Sadasivam call on the chief minister to 'sort

---

*Brother of the George Joseph encountered earlier.

out the matter' was rejected by CR, who indicated he might go to the high court or the Supreme Court. The prosecutions were withdrawn. 'I take it as a victory for dissent,' CR wrote.[21]

◆

Bhaktavatsalam would remain chief minister until the elections in 1967, but the Congress had taken a huge hit in the Tamil country, while the DMK's prestige soared.

In 1967, the Congress was routed. Once more EVR campaigned for the Congress. Once more CR contributed to an anti-Congress alliance. A DMK-led front that included Swatantra and the CPM won 179 seats (DMK 137, Swatantra 20, CPM 11, plus a few others) and a 52 per cent vote-share. The Congress got only 51 seats with a 41 per cent vote.

Except for one member, all in the Bhaktavatsalam ministry lost, including the chief minister. So did Kamaraj himself, beaten in Virudhunagar by a DMK student leader, P. Sreenivasan.

Pushed to the back foot over Hindi, the Bhaktavatsalam ministry was hurt also by corruption allegations, rising prices and a rice shortage. Then, on 12 January 1967, with the election barely a month away, a clinching event occurred.

A pro-DK and pro-Kamaraj male actor, M. R. Radha, attempted, it seemed, to kill the DMK candidate and popular film actor, Marudur Gopala Ramachandran, better known as MGR.[22]

Born in 1917 to Malayali parents in Kandy (Sri Lanka), where his father was a school principal, MGR was only three when his father died. His mother brought him to Tamil Nadu. At six, he joined the 'Madurai Original Boys Company' dramatic troupe and learned dancing, acting and sword-fighting.

Later, when he became a movie actor, his films were all morality plays. On screen, MGR was invariably virtuous: a non-smoking, non-drinking foe of tyrants, a clerk at odds with a corrupt bureaucracy, a cow-herder standing up to a corrupt landlord, or another hero of that sort. In love scenes with the villain's daughter, MGR was usually the pursued, not the pursuer. His films climaxed with 'the defeat of villainy, uplift of the poor, and fulfilled romance in a self-respect marriage'.[23]

A Congress supporter and khadi-wearer to begin with, MGR had switched his loyalty to the DMK in the mid-1950s. Even as Kamaraj scoffed—'How can there be government by actors?'—the DMK rode the rising popularity of films.

Writers and actors from Self-Respect touring companies dominated the Tamil screen. Their Tamil was purged of Sanskritic elements. Golden Tamil ages 'were resurrected on celluloid; Brahmins were portrayed as sinister or foolish'. 'People named their children after the stars instead of the gods, film artists brought glamour and electoral support to the DMK.'[24]

At around 5 p.m. on 12 January 1967, reportedly 'filled with anger and drink' and accompanied by a film producer, Radha enacted in real life the 'bad guy' role he had often played on the screen. He went to MGR's house in Nandambakkam, near St. Thomas Mount, and shot the hero in the neck.

Then Radha tried to kill himself. He and MGR were taken first to a hospital in Royapettah and thence to the General Hospital.

Within hours, 50,000 or so shaken MGR admirers gathered outside the hospital. Twenty devotees pedalled their cyclerickshaws 370 km from Bangalore to be near their wounded hero in Chennai. Other fans went to the Tirupati Temple and shaved their heads to propitiate the gods for MGR's survival.

When it was clear that MGR would live (with a bullet lodged next to his throat), a fan commented that he was greater than Gandhi and Kennedy, for unlike them he had not succumbed to bullets. 'MGR is a god,' actor Asokan told an American scholar, Robert Hardgrave, in December 1969.[25]

Radha, who also survived, was given a seven-year prison term in the trial that ensued, a sentence later reduced to five years.

In the voting in February, MGR won his seat by a landslide. A widely circulated 'iconic picture of MGR sitting on a hospital bed with a heavily bandaged neck'[26] contributed to DMK victories elsewhere in the state. The incident brought a fresh boost to the popularity of MGR, which apparently had begun to sag.

In 1967, Annadurai, who would become chief minister, was the most influential DMK figure, but scriptwriter and filmmaker M. Karunanidhi was also a power in the party. In 1954, failing to enlist Sivaji Ganesan for his film *Malaikallan* (by now Ganesan was moving Congress-ward), Karunanidhi had turned to MGR.

Malaikallan (Mountain Dacoit) became a huge hit and MGR turned overnight into a top star, but the Karunanidhi–MGR link would not endure. Annadurai, on his part, treated MGR with visible regard, 'stopping his speech when M.G.R. entered a meeting, allowing him to be greeted and applauded'.[27]

◆

For Annadurai, the 1967 elections were a dream come true. Five years earlier, while his party did better than expected, Anna had lost his own seat. Now he was chief minister. Moreover, out of Tamil Nadu's 39 Lok Sabha seats, the front led by his party had won 35—DMK 25, Swatantra 6, CPM 4, Muslim League 1.

It was not as if a wave had changed all of the south. In fact, the Congress had done very well in Andhra and Karnataka. In Kerala, on the other hand, the Left for the moment had overcome its divisions, and an alliance that include the CPM, the Communist Party of India(CPI), the socialists and—this time—the Muslim League as well, easily defeated the Congress, which was opposed in many seats by the Kerala Congress too.

While retaining power at the centre, the Congress suffered significant losses in West Bengal (where, in alliance with a dissident Congress faction, the Left did very well), in Orissa, Rajasthan and Gujarat (three states where Swatantra performed impressively, in Orissa forming the government), and in Delhi, where the Jan Sangh, challenging the Congress from the Hindu right, won six out of seven Lok Sabha seats.

In the Tamil country, while Rajaji had been of solid help, the DMK's triumph was essentially its own feat, with welcome aid from the Bhaktavatsalam ministry's failures. 'Assiduously [building] up a party apparatus that spread to every corner of the state through a wide and democratic network of reading rooms that doubled as party offices,' Annadurai personally played the largest part.[28]

Fifty-seven-year-old Anna—a 'barely five-and-a-quarter feet man with a balding pate, tobacco-stained teeth, stubbled chin and a captivating husky voice'[29]—formed an all-DMK ministry, India's youngest at the time, where its chief did not feel threatened by the second line he had groomed.

Within days of the DMK victory, EVR announced his backing for the party he had opposed. When Anna brought in a measure to discontinue the teaching of Hindi in government schools, CR advised Swatantra MLAs to support the change, against which no vote, not even from the Congress, was cast.

Having freed Tamil nationalism from the secessionism he had championed earlier, Anna felt no qualms in organizing a World Tamil Conference in Chennai. During this event in January 1968, MGR gave the city a statue of Annadurai, while Sivaji Ganesan presented one of the everfresh Valluvar.

But in September 1968 Anna, 'an orator of extraordinary brilliance',[30] was diagnosed with advanced cancer in the gullet, apparently caused by tobacco-chewing. Flown to the US for treatment, he returned to Chennai on 6 November. On 20 January, he fell to the floor unconscious, and was moved to the Adyar Cancer Institute. Ramnath Goenka, the newspaper magnate, flew in doctors from the US and funded surgeries, but Anna died on 3 February 1969.

The Tamil country mourned on an unprecedented scale. Anna was buried, not cremated, for Tamils desired a link to him they could physically touch. Rajaji, to whom Anna had come very close, recalled the Socrates story:

> When he said to the jailor that he was ready to drink the potion of death, the weeping friends asked Socrates whether he would like to be cremated or buried. Socrates laughed and [said] they might do whatever they liked if they could catch the bird after it had flown from the cage.[31]

INDIRA (1917–1984)

All-India politics dramatically changed shortly after Anna's death. Picked by Kamaraj and other Congress chiefs for her vote-attracting potential as Nehru's daughter, and in the fond belief that she would act on their guidance, Indira Gandhi revealed a defiant independence as prime minister.

One indication was a statement by her, evidently made at a Congress party meeting and aimed at Kamaraj, that persons defeated in an election should not hold senior party positions.[32] Left with no choice, Kamaraj resigned as Congress president.

With Kamaraj's support and that of Sanjiva Reddy, who was Congress president before Kamaraj and twice chief minister of Andhra, Karnataka's chief minister, S. Nijalingappa, was chosen to succeed Kamaraj in the Congress chair.

Indira offered no resistance to this appointment, but when India's president, Dr Zakir Husain, died in the summer of 1969, and a group of Congress leaders (Kamaraj, Nijalingappa, Reddy, Bengal's Congress chief Atulya Ghosh and Bombay's S. K. Patil) agreed amonst themselves that Reddy should be the Congress candidate to succeed Husain, she not only fought back, she mobilized non-Congress support to overpower her Congress opponents.

Both sides knew that Reddy was intended as a brake on Indira. At a crucial meeting of the Congress parliamentary board, Finance Minister Morarji Desai (who was deputy prime minister as well) and Home Minister Yashwantrao Chavan (dominant in the Maharashtra Congress) backed Reddy, who was chosen as the official Congress candidate over the man Indira suggested: Jagjivan Ram, the Dalit minister from Bihar who had been part of every union cabinet since independence.

After the meeting, Indira uttered only a short sentence: 'There will be consequences.'[33] In line with the board's decision, she first signed Reddy's nomination papers. In the next moment, she struck against him and his allies. Stripping Desai of the finance portfolio, she also, with an instant ordinance, nationalized the country's top fourteen banks.

Emerging overnight as the hero of India's have-nots, and of Communist, socialist and other left-leaning parties, Indira signalled that in the presidential contest, Congress MPs and MLAs should vote for Varahagiri Venkata Giri, India's vice-president at the time, who had entered the lists as an independent.

Giri had been a member, in 1937–39, of the Madras Presidency ministry. Like Reddy, he hailed from Andhra. There was a third candidate, the distinguished former finance minister, C. D. Deshmukh, sponsored by Swatantra, the Jan Sangh and a Congress faction under UP's Charan Singh which had split from Indira.

Led after Anna's death by Karunanidhi, the DMK's MLAs and MPs, constituting a sizeable bloc in the voting college, deserted Rajaji and backed Giri, who won a narrow victory over the Congress's Reddy, with Deshmukh coming third.

There were two Congresses now, an organizational one led by Nijalingappa and a rebelling group rallying around Prime Minister Indira Gandhi, which elected Jagjivan Ram as its leader.

Giri was a Brahmin, as was Indira herself—which was not the case with either Reddy or Deshmukh—yet enough Indians were willing to believe, including in the south, that Indira's Congress was more pro-poor, pro-Dalit and pro-Left than its rival. Sensing the current, many including Chavan mended fences with Indira.

The Left was facing its own difficulties. Accusing the CPM of not being radical enough, many Communists in West Bengal and Andhra had left the party in the late 1960s to join more militant groups. In Kerala, on the other hand, the CPI, which in March 1967 had joined a left ministry led by EMS, now moved closer to the Indira Congress. On 1 November 1969, the CPI's C. Achutha Menon in coalition with the Indira Congress, replaced EMS as chief minister. Eleven months later, after a fresh election, Achutha Menon would lead a CPI–Indira Congress ministry for another six and a half years.

◆

Paralleling the DMK's understanding with the Indira Congress was a movement towards each other between Kamaraj and CR, even though Rajaji was reluctant to break with the DMK, which he had backed for over a decade.

Unhappy, however, with Indira's leftward turn in both internal and external policies, and with the DMK's continuing support for her, he announced at the end of 1970 that Swatantra would support the Kamaraj Congress, not the DMK, in the next round of municipal elections.

Attacking what he had called Indira's 'dictatorial bent of mind',[34] he also expressed disappointment when President Giri promptly signed a cabinet decision to dismiss the UP ministry headed by Charan Singh.

Even though Charan Singh, like Chavan, had switched to supporting Indira—inviting Rajaji's comment that Singh's 'politics are, to put it mildly, curious'[35]—Indira had him removed. It was during a state visit to the Soviet Union that Giri signed an order dismissing the UP ministry. CR noted that the president had put his signature at the point marked in the document sent to him from India without making any enquiry about the other side of the case, and without even caring to go to the office of an Indian ambassador...to affix his formal signature.[36]

◆

By this time, a call from CR for an anti-Indira front had elicited tentative support from Kamaraj. When Nijalingappa, heading the Congress (O), said he was confident that something would 'evolve', CR wrote that 'fellow-Darwinians' could tell Nijalingappa 'how long it took for man to evolve from an ape'.[37]

Before Nijalingappa reacted, Indira charged: on 27 December, the Lok Sabha was abruptly dissolved, and snap elections were ordered. Most of her opponents were caught by surprise. Possessing no common front, leader or programme, they had a hard time collecting funds.

Taking his cue from Indira, Karunanidhi dissolved the Tamil Nadu assembly. In March 1971, elections were held for the Lok Sabha and the Tamil Nadu legislature. Across India, Indira's slogan of 'Garibi Hatao' was countered by a knee-jerk 'Indira Hatao' call. In the Tamil country, the fight became 'Indira–DMK' versus 'Rajaji–Kamaraj'.

Rajaji and Kamaraj? The two had never campaigned together, not even in the decades when both were in the Congress. Because the DMK ministry had attracted corruption charges, and because quite a few in the Tamil country were affronted by Indira's drastic steps, some imagined the Kamaraj–CR duo winning.

'Rajaji, you had better be ready to become chief minister again,' joked Kamaraj, though he and CR had evidently agreed that R. Venkataraman, who had been Kamaraj's ministerial colleague in Tamil Nadu, would make a good head.[38]

The results were stunning. In the Lok Sabha, the Indira Congress won 350 seats, with Swatantra going down from 44 to 8. Most opposition stalwarts—from the Congress (O), Swatantra, the Jan Sangh or the anti-Indira Socialists—lost.

In Tamil Nadu, the DMK won 183 seats as against 21 secured by the Congress (O) and Swatantra together. After recovering from shock, CR, ninety-two, told the press that 'the teacher must go on teaching, whatever be the difficulties'. To Nijalingappa, he wrote:

14 March 1971: The work hereafter is among the people and can no longer be in parliament. We must organize young men and women as when the Gandhian Congress began... The enemy now is totalitarianism and we have to fight it as we fought the British.[39]

There was personal consolation for Kamaraj, who comfortably won the Lok Sabha seat he contested, defeating a DMK rival in Nagercoil. In 1971, Kamaraj was South India's sole Congress (O) entrant in the Lok Sabha.

◆

Indira Gandhi was presented with a tricky challenge in March 1971, when the Pakistani Army cracked down on the people of East Pakistan, who had revolted the previous December after Pakistan's generals and West Pakistani politicians refused to accept the voters' clear verdict in favour of Sheikh Mujibur Rahman's Awami League.

Indira's victorious response added to her popularity across India, including in the south.

Even a sharp critic like CR could not withhold praise for Indira's diplomatic skill in obtaining a treaty with the Soviet Union in August 1971, her clarity in the India–Pakistan war of December 1971, and her sagacity in declaring a unilateral ceasefire on the western front after Pakistani forces had surrendered in the east.

As Indira's star soared, her opponents' solidarity crumbled. When Professor N. G. Ranga, who had served as Swatantra's president, joined the Indira Congress, CR was depressed. But only briefly. He returned to the attack in August 1971, when the 24th amendment to the Constitution, designed to strengthen the Indian state's power to abridge fundamental rights, was passed.

Neither Kamaraj nor the DMK objected to the amendment, but CR asked for a 'Magna Carta Defence League' to protect fundamental rights, vowing:

Even if all others conspire against the Constitution, I shall not ever let Vallabhbhai Patel, Rajen Babu [Rajendra Prasad], K. M. Munshi, Alladi Krishnaswami Iyer and others down, but will protest against the desecration and unwisdom of it as long as my breath lasts.[40]

In March 1972, when he was past ninety-three, CR anticipated the Jayaprakash Narayan-led movement that would surface two years later:

> We must depend upon ways and means not linked to elections and the hope therefore lies in preparing for nonviolent direct action... [to] bring about the change we desire in Smt. Indira Gandhi's convictions.[41]

◆

While much of life and politics was common across India, the South was unique in at least one respect: it turned film stars into politicians and their fan clubs into political pressure groups.

Accusing Karunanidhi of corruption and of betraying Annadurai, MGR—the star actor, member of the Tamil Nadu assembly, and a prominent face in the state's politics—broke with the DMK and formed a new party in 1972, the Anna DMK. He had also been offended, it was said, by an apparent attempt by aspiring actor M. K. Muthu, Karunanidhi's son, to imitate MGR's mannerisms.[42]

Rajaji predicted that the DMK would be 'the loser in this business'.[43]

Two months later, on Christmas day, 1972—a fortnight after his ninety-fourth birthday—CR died in Chennai's General Hospital, where he had been admitted eight days earlier.

President Giri, EVR the Periyar (in a wheelchair), Chief Minister Karunanidhi, a red-eyed Kamaraj, MGR in his trademark cap, Swatantra's Minoo Masani, N. G. Ranga, T. T. Krishnamachari and other figures of Indian politics filled the patient's room, past which plain citizens had for days trudged for a final look at one who for decades had loved and taught his people, and often succeeded in estranging them.

His wheelchair ran down a slope to bring EVR to CR's cremation, where he threw friendly glances at CR's family. The following year, in September 1973, saw a celebration of Periyar's ninety-fourth birthday, and the installation in Erode, Cuddalore, Madurai and elsewhere of his statues, but on 24 December 1973—one year minus one day after CR's death—the Periyar, too, died, in the Christian Medical Hospital in Vellore, his age at death being greater than CR's by a few weeks.

The covered space in Chennai (on Mount Road, renamed Anna Salai) where EVR's body was brought to rest in state, past which great throngs—his people, whom he had taught, loved and rebuked—walked in sorrow and tribute (Kamaraj, Karunanidhi and MGR were among them) bore the name Rajaji Hall.

TELUGU TENSIONS

'Hamko kabza karliya aapne' (Sir, you've subjugated us), said the man in the Andhra city of Kurnool.

These Hindustani words were uttered in 1963 in a hurt if inoffensive tone by a Muslim deputy collector in the Andhra government service. He hailed from the Telangana region. The person he addressed, Sadullah, was the influential personal assistant (PA) to the speaker's boss, the Kurnool collector. Sadullah came from a Telugu area which until 1956 had belonged to Madras Presidency.

A third person heard the remark and remembered it: an IAS beginner named K. R. Venugopal, who, like the other two, was sitting in a room leading to the collector's office.

Since the PA was a Muslim too, Venugopal had assumed an affinity between him and the officer from Telangana, but the latter's remark revealed, seven years after the creation of a single Telugu state, a psychological gulf separating Telangana from other parts of Andhra.[44] This gulf seemed to have little to do with caste, or with the fact that the Telangana region had witnessed an insurgency in the late 1940s, or that a Muslim dynasty had for long ruled Hyderabad.

Other factors had caused it. One was a sense that Telangana was receiving less from the Andhra government than it contributed in taxes. Another was a grievance that outsiders obtained jobs which under a gentlemen's agreement had been reserved for Telangana's sons and daughters. A third was a belief that outsiders armed with insider knowledge were buying prime Telangana land.

Yet Venugopal would later conclude, a role greater than any of these was played by Telangana's urge to defy what looked like 'arrogance bred by better education in Madras presidency and by wealth from wetter lands'.[45]

There was fierce umbrage at an alleged remark by Sanjiva Reddy, the first chief minister of united Andhra, that a deputy chief minister from Telangana (promised under the gentlemen's agreement but not appointed) was an 'unwanted sixth finger of the hand'.[46]

Telangana restiveness showed itself in the late 1960s, when Kasu Brahmananda Reddy from Guntur district became the state's chief minister. Calls at student rallies for moving 'outsider' government employees to their districts on the coast, or to Rayalaseema, were followed in 1969 by violence, police firings and dozens of deaths in Hyderabad and other Telangana towns.

When Indira Gandhi seemed unresponsive to the regional sentiment, a group of prominent Congressmen led by Marri Chenna Reddy formed the Telangana Praja Samithi (TPS). In the 1971 elections, which Indira Gandhi's Congress won overwhelmingly in most parts of India, the TPS was successful in 10 of the region's 14 Lok Sabha seats.

Indira Gandhi's answer was a chief minister for Andhra from the Telangana region. In September 1971, Brahmananda Reddy, who had been chief minister for seven years, was replaced by fifty-year-old P. V. Narasimha Rao, a Brahmin Congressman born in Warangal district.

Well known in party circles but possessing no political base of his own, Narasimha Rao had been an associate in his twenties of Ramanand Teerth. Fluent in several languages, he had translated Nehru's speeches into Telugu at public meetings in the 1950s and 1960s.

Narasimha Rao's appointment as chief minister seemed to defuse tensions until February 1972, when the Andhra High Court held that outsiders could not be denied government jobs in Telangana.

In October of that year, the Supreme Court reversed the high court's ruling, and in December the Narasimha Rao ministry issued a GO extending employment privileges to 'mulkis' or locals, whereupon a 'Jai Andhra' movement erupted in coastal Andhra, in opposition to the 'Jai Telangana' movement that had begun in 1968–69.

Even when treasured, as Telugu certainly was, a common language could not remove material and psychological barriers. More than four decades later, the cycle would be repeated in negotiations and violent agitations that created the new Indian state of Telangana in 2014.

In 1972–73, the army was called in to cope with the violence in the 'Jai Andhra' stir. Narasimha Rao had to leave his post, and for many months in 1973, Andhra was under President's Rule. In December, a new chief minister was installed. Belonging to the land-owning Velama caste, Jalagam Vengala Rao had been reared in Telangana region's Khammam district.

KERALA MODEL

'The major problem of Kerala,' an analyst wrote in 1960, 'is its ever-increasing population, concentrated on a limited area of land.'[47] Occupying 1.18 per cent of India's land area, the state contained 3.43 per cent of the country's population.[48]

In the 1950s, Kerala possessed the country's highest rate of population growth. By the 1970s, it had become the lowest. From 44 per 1,000 in the 1950s, the number would come down to 18 per 1,000 in 1991, and the state would show a female to male ratio of 1.04 to 1, compared with the Indian average of 0.93 to 1.[49]

Accomplished without coercion, these marked improvements seemed connected to policies introduced by the EMS ministry in 1967–69 and continued by a CPI–Congress coalition, led by C. Achutha Menon, which governed Kerala from 1969 to 1977.[50]

What has been described as 'the Kerala model of development' also included the elimination of absentee landlordism. New laws gave tenants full rights to the crop-land they were renting plus full title to their dwellings and to one-tenth of an acre of adjoining land. This last provision was meaningful, for in much of Kerala coconuts, bananas, vegetables, cashews and areca nuts were grown close to dwellings.[51]

Apart from giving Kerala a stable government, the alliance between the Indira Congress and the CPI strengthened the Congress nationally while also deepening the CPI–CPM divide.

Fully matching Kerala's land reforms were radical land policies introduced in Karnataka by Devaraj Urs, the state's chief minister from March 1972 to January 1980. Born into the tiny Arasu caste of Mysore's royal clan of Wadiyars, Urs broke with Karnataka's well-established organizational Congress to side with Indira.

Mobilizing Karnataka's poorer castes and classes, he showed that a Lingayat or Vokkaliga base was not essential to political success in the state. Urs's partnership with Indira produced large victories in Karnataka during the 1971 Lok Sabha contest and again in state elections in 1972.

By 1974, criticism of Indira Gandhi had begun to mount in western, northern and eastern India.

After a long absence, Bihar's Jayaprakash Narayan, or JP, once Gandhi's young and close colleague, re-emerged on the political scene. While much of his focus was on corruption in Bihar's Congress ministry, his call for a 'total revolution' in politics and society attracted a wide following beyond his state, especially of young men and women.

As 1975 unfolded, JP looked like a national leader capable of marshalling the varied groups opposed to Indira Gandhi into a successful force.

Two events occurring on 12 June 1975 made that dream real. The Allahabad High Court invalidated Indira's 1971 election to the Lok Sabha. That very day, news flashed out of Ahmedabad that a front led by Indira's old rival Morarji Desai had defeated the Congress in elections to the Gujarat assembly.

Could Indira survive as a prime minister without being in Parliament? Facing a greater danger than the threat she had repulsed in 1969, Indira responded by imposing a national Emergency. Shortly before midnight on 25 June, without consulting her cabinet, she obtained the signature of the president, Fakhruddin Ahmed, on a formal proclamation. Simultaneously, she ordered drastic steps.

Their electricity cut off, Delhi's newspapers failed to appear the next morning. Early on 26 June, after the Emergency was in place, Indira's cabinet ratified it.

By the 26th morning, hundreds of politicians had been arrested. These included JP, Morarji Desai, Jan Sangh leaders Atal Bihari Vajpayee and Lal Krishna Advani, and Chandra Shekhar and other critics within Indira's party. Press censorship was imposed. Organizations like the Rashtriya Swayamsevak Sangh (RSS), Jamaat-i-Islami and the Anand Marg were banned.

Most of the early arrests took place in north India, although a few like Vajpayee, Advani, the socialist Madhu Dandavate, and the Congress (O) leader Shyam Nandan Mishra were arrested in Bangalore, where a parliamentary committee meeting had been called.

The JP movement had not been conspicuous in the south. Karnataka under Devaraj Urs and Andhra under Vengala Rao, both from the Indira

Congress, faced no political challenges. Kerala's coalition ministry was led by a CPI chief minister dependent on Congress support.

And in Tamil Nadu, the DMK chief minister, Karunanidhi, was one who had unreservedly backed Indira in her clashes with Congress rivals in 1969 before formally allying with her in 1971.

Though taken aback by the Emergency, Urs and Vengala Rao chose to remain silent. To wait and see appeared sensible. In Kerala, Chief Minister Achutha Menon seemed unperturbed by the proclamation. At the all-India level, his party had promptly and loudly defended it.

Indira thus had little cause for anxiety about the South's reaction. True, Kamaraj was around, possessing prestige, a Lok Sabha seat, and control over the organizational Congress in Tamil Nadu. But he had not openly backed JP's movement and was not on Indira Gandhi's list of politicians to be arrested.

Shocked and wounded, he would be quoted as having said, 'Yellaam pochu, yen thappu' (Everything is gone, it's my fault).[52] On his advice, the Congress (O) in Tamil Nadu passed a resolution deploring the Emergency.[53]

Though they had supported Indira's economic policies, Chief Minister Karunanidhi and others from the DMK were shocked by the Emergency, but the press did not publish their pleas for free speech. Pre-censorship was effective and much of the time unnecessary. Some leading newspapers practised self-censorship.

When Karunanidhi was urged to work jointly with Kamaraj against the Emergency, he said the Congress (O) chief should take the lead. Informed of this request, Kamaraj, unwell at the time, indicated from his bed that he would consider doing so.[54]

In the afternoon of 2 October, the seventy-two-year-old bachelor felt uneasy, asked his personal attendant to phone the doctor, took to a bed, and died before the doctor arrived. He had had a massive heart attack. In retrospect, the date seemed fitting.

Hindsight would also cause people to wonder why a broader alliance was not attempted in South India, involving not only Kamaraj and Karunanidhi but also others in the region with a stake in democracy, like Karnataka's Urs.

Such questions were not asked in October 1975, when Indira, widely viewed as the champion of the poor, seemed to be well on top of events. Moreover, she attended Kamaraj's last rites, conferred a posthumous Bharat Ratna on him, and tried to give the impression that on India's political divides he had stood with her.

In some ways, the South India of 1975 was not unlike what it had been in the eighteenth century. Regional chiefs thought less about possible allies next door, more about the big power looming over them, the East India Company in the old case, a prime minister armed with Emergency clouts in the new.

An open fight for democratic rights was however waged by a few writers and artists, while others used a weapon about which authoritarian systems can do little: jokes. Old Acharya Kripalani, Gandhi's colleague from 1915, arrived in Chennai and openly encouraged defenders of democratic freedoms.

Backed by a valiant T. Sadasivam, freedom-struggle veteran K. Santhanam spoke out through *Swarajya*. Cho Ramaswamy's defiant satires in his journal, *Thuglak,* and at small gatherings produced ripples of amusement. Satyamurti's daughter, Lakshmi Krishnamurthy, organized brave get-togethers, even though others remarked, at least in the Emergency's initial phase, that trains and government employees were now punctual.

Activists of different hues, including leftists, Gandhians, those from the banned RSS, and persons like the DMK's Era Sezhiyan and the socialist M. S. Appa Rao, often came together to share concern, but there was not much by way of street protests.

Not even when, citing corruption allegations, Indira Gandhi dismissed the DMK ministry in January 1976. Apart from the climate of caution, MGR's popularity was a factor. His Anna DMK had joined hands with Indira.

After the Karunanidhi ministry's removal, many from the DMK, and some from the Congress (O), the DK and the CPM, were imprisoned under a stiffened Maintenance of Internal Security Act (MISA). In 1977, the Ismail Commission would confirm charges that warders and convicts had beaten Chennai's MISA prisoners.

One such prisoner, forty-one-year-old Chockalinga Chittibabu of the DMK, sitting MP from Chingleput and a former mayor of Chennai, died on 4 January 1977, only a day after a second surgery required to 'relieve anal and urethral constrictions' caused by 'beating and kicking in the abdomen', to quote from the report of the Ismail Commission.[55]

In Bangalore, theatre and cine artist Snehalata Reddy, admired for her roles in Kannada, Telugu and English productions, was jailed shortly before the Emergency for alleged involvement in the Baroda Dynamite Case, which centred around the socialist leader George Fernandes.

In the city's central prison, Reddy 'rallied women inmates to create plays to buoy their spirits',[56] but she may have been ill-treated herself by prison staff. Suffering from a lung disease, she was released on parole on 15 January 1977, but died five days later.

Lawrence Fernandes, a Bengaluru-based brother of George, was tortured in prison by police officers demanding information about his brother, who had gone underground.

Renowned Kannada writers like Shivaram Karanth, U. R. Ananthamurthy and Gopalakrishna Adiga opposed the Emergency, street plays mocking it were performed in Bangalore, and citizens exchanged unhappy sentiments with one another. But Emergency rule was not seriously troubled in Karnataka.

Or in Andhra or Kerala. In the latter state, the remains of two young men, P. Rajan, an engineering student, and Varkala Vijayan, a political activist, both arrested on allegations of involvement in violent activities, both believed to have been tortured to death, were never discovered.

Memories of a Father, written by Rajan's father, T. V. Eachara Varier, recorded the father's unsuccessful effort to have his son's victimizers punished. It also recorded the resignation, following the post-Emergency outcry over Rajan's disappearance, of Chief Minister K. Karunakaran, who was home minister when Rajan vanished after being taken to a police camp.[57]

LITERARY INTERVENTIONS

In the 1960s and 1970s, there were places in south India, the novelist Ananthamurthy would later say, where a youngster crossed several centuries in a day. In the traditional village home where Ananthamurthy grew up, the past was worshipped. In his school, a teacher denounced the Gita. On the way, on someone else's radio, he would hear a discussion on George Bernard Shaw and Bertrand Russell.[58]

A teacher of English at Mysore University, Ananthamurthy (1932–

2014) wrote his classic novel, *Samskara,* in Kannada in 1965, when he was thirty-three. A. K. Ramanujan's translation in English was first published in 1976, a year after the Emergency.

Its story is of a dilemma into which men and women in a rural Brahmin community in western Karnataka are thrown when Chandri, the outcaste concubine of their fallen member Naranappa, announces that Naranappa has died. Anyone cremating Naranappa's body would carry his pollution, but not cremating him would pain ancestors, curse descendants, and become a scandal.

In the end, a Muslim is found to cremate the body of the corrupted Naranappa, but greater tension lies in the vulnerability of the virtuous Praneshacharya, who for twenty years has selflessly cared for an ill wife, and for whom Naranappa had long been the antithesis.

An unexpected affair that Praneshacharya experiences with Chandri (who, earlier, had quietly returned to the Brahmins the gold and silver necklaces Naranappa had given her), and the death of Bhagirathi, Praneshacharya's wife, invite possibilities that the novel does not pursue.

In an afterword, *Samskara*'s interpreter, Ramanujan, notes the shift in 'the arena for battles of tradition and defiance, asceticism and sensuality' from 'a Hindu village community to the body and spirit of the protagonist'—to Praneshacharya's body and soul—and points out that through Chandri, Praneshacharya has merged with his defiant adversary.[59]

Critics questioned whether Praneshacharya, Naranappa and Chandri were typical of their communities. However, the popularity of the novel, the response to the movie that was soon made of it, and the discussion invited by *Samskara* seemed to indicate that South Indians connected themselves to the world it depicts.

Of the fourteen South Indian recipients until the year 2000 of the Jnanpith Award for Literature, seven (including Ananthamurthy) wrote in Kannada,* which was not the primary language in the homes where three of the seven had been raised. The parents of Dattatreya Ramachandra Bendre, a Chitpavan born in Dharwad, spoke Marathi, those of Masti Venkatesha Iyengar, who was born in Kolar district, spoke Tamil, while Girish Karnad, linked like Bendre to Dharwad,

---

*Four wrote in Malayalam, two in Telugu and one in Tamil.

was born to a Konkani-speaking father in Matheran in Maharashtra. Other acclaimed writers in Kannada had Telugu and Malayali origins. Yet there was more to Kannada literature than linguistic surprise. Like their literary counterparts in Konkani, Malayalam, Tamil and Telugu, the Kannada country's poets, novelists and playwrights captured the heroism of the unrecognized. The following lines were written about his rural mother by Palyada Lankeshappa, better known as P. Lankesh (1935–2000) and translated from the Kannada original by H. Y. Sharada Prasad:

> Savitri, Sita, Urmila she was not,
> Or stately Shanta or Sweta of legend.
> She was unlike the wife of Gandhi and Ramakrishna,
> Worshipped no god, heard no epic tales sung,
> Did not even wear vermilion as a married woman.
>
> My mother lived
> For grain and straw, for toil, for children,
> For a roof overhead, for rice, for a blanket,
> For being able to walk head held high among equals.
> To her my salute and tears of thanks,
> For bearing me, rearing me, for living on the earth and going away,
> With cool casual words on her lips,
> As if she went from home to the field.[60]

1977 ELECTIONS

In February 1977, nineteen months after imposing the Emergency, Indira Gandhi unexpectedly lifted it. Most prisoners were released. With complete confidence, she ordered new elections in which she was trounced. Though they had sailed on different political streams, her opponents assembled under the 'Janata' umbrella and chose Morarji Desai as India's prime minister.

But South India voted overwhelmingly in Indira's favour. In Kerala, all 20 Lok Sabha seats were won by a Congress-led alliance, which included the Kerala Congress, the CPI and the Muslim League. In Andhra, the Congress won 41 out of 42 seats, in Karnataka 26 out of 28.

In Tamil Nadu, a Congress–ADMK–CPI alliance won 33 out of 39 seats. Opposing the alliance, the DMK got 2 seats and the Congress (O) 3. The sole Pondicherry seat was won by the ADMK.

The JP–Janata wave which swept across northern and central India, interpreted by many as a choice of democracy over dictatorship, thus left the south untouched. One explanation was that the south had been spared the Emergency excess of compulsory sterilization, which deeply offended the rest of the country.

But a bigger reason for Indira's success with the south's voters was the absence of a compelling southern face to represent her opponents. Karnataka's forceful Urs was with her. Neither Kerala nor Andhra came up with a driven, let alone magnetic, opposition leader. In Tamil Nadu, people seemed to prefer Indira's ally MGR over her opponent Karunanidhi.

Now if Kamaraj had been alive... But he was not. The fates in charge of the South were kind to the defeated Indira Gandhi.

Three months after the Lok Sabha polls, elections for the state legislature were held in Kerala and Tamil Nadu. In Kerala, the Congress-led alliance won 103 out of 140 seats, the CPM 17 and Janata 6.

In Tamil Nadu, demoralized by Kamaraj's death, many Congress (O) members crossed over to the Indira Congress, which with the CPI as minor partner won 32 seats in a house of 234. Contesting on its own, the DMK got 48 seats. Janata, the party in power in Delhi, got only 10.

To placate the new government in Delhi, the ADMK had ended its alliance with the Congress. Even so, with CPM as its minor partner, the ADMK performed strongly, winning 144 of the assembly's 234 seats, and MGR, the hero who brought justice on the screen, entered Fort St George as Tamil Nadu's chief minister.

Chapter 14

PAIN, DRAMA, GRACE: 1980–2000

Her opponents failing to stay together, Indira Gandhi was back in power by January 1980. Before long, a kind of understanding grew between her in New Delhi and MGR in Chennai.

One reason was Sri Lanka, where MGR had been born. The discontent of Sri Lanka's Tamils had enabled the growth of militancy there, spearheaded from 1976 by Velupillai Prabhakaran, founder of the Liberation Tigers of Tamil Eelam (LTTE), which Colombo had proscribed in 1978.

A rude milestone was the burning in the 1981 summer of the Jaffna Library, which housed priceless manuscripts about the island's Tamils. The destruction was apparently connived at by security forces after the LTTE murdered two policemen and a pro-government Tamil politician.[1]

Many in Tamil Nadu felt close to Sri Lanka's Tamils and sympathized with their situation, even if others were troubled by assassinations in the name of the Lankan Tamil cause.

An Indian government facing separatist demands at home—in Kashmir, the Northeast and Punjab—was not going to support secession in Sri Lanka. Still, New Delhi had constantly urged Colombo to do more to satisfy its Tamils.

In addition, Indian authorities and agencies had for some time played a more direct though not open role, organizing camps in Tamil Nadu and elsewhere for training militant Lankan Tamils, including men and women belonging to the LTTE.[2]

This step towards intrusion in Lankan affairs involved Tamil Nadu but also New Delhi. Chief Minister MGR entertained sympathy for the Lankan militants and in particular for Prabhakaran.*

On her part, Indira Gandhi was concerned about 'the external

---

*B. Kolappan, 'When an "arm-twisted" LTTE leaned on a sympathetic MGR', *The Hindu*, 28 November 2017 <https://www.thehindu.com/news/national/tamil-nadu/when-an-arm-twisted-ltte-leaned-on-a-sympathetic-mgr/article21011889.ece>.

political and security equations' that Lankan president Junius Richard Jayewardene was exploring with Pakistan, Israel and the USA. Trained Tamil militants were seen as a potential lever against any anti-Indian build-up in Sri Lanka.[3]

Moreover, as Jyotindra Nath Dixit, India's high commissioner in Colombo during the 1980s, would argue, Indira also wished to guard against Tamil separatism in India. Secessionist talk in Tamil Nadu during the 1930s and 1940s was 'part of Mrs. Gandhi's political memory'. To have 'positive political equations with M.G.R.' therefore became 'important' for her.[4]

Indira may have also hoped that quiet support for a cause resonating in Tamil Nadu would prepare the ground for a Congress revival in the state.

Not easily confined, separatism and militancy may, however, erupt anywhere. In June 1984, Indira Gandhi ordered the Indian Army to enter Amritsar's Golden Temple and take out the Sikh extremists who had gathered there with their weapons. A few months later, on 31 October, she was gunned down at her New Delhi residence by Sikh members of her bodyguard.

The following few days saw terrible violence against innocent Sikhs in Delhi, Kanpur and some other places, but the assassination of a woman prime minister by men sworn to protect her had produced a large sympathy wave. In fresh elections that were soon held, the Congress, now led by Indira's son Rajiv, won an unprecedented 49.1 per cent of the national vote and a huge majority of seats (414 out of 531) in the Lok Sabha.[5]

NTR (1923–1996)

Only one Indian state defied the trend. In Andhra, the Telugu Desam Party (TDP) led by the popular film actor N. T. Rama Rao (NTR), won 30 Lok Sabha seats out of the state's total of 42, with the Congress getting only 2. With that number of seats, the regional TDP became the leading opposition party in the Lok Sabha. For Indian politics, this was a new scenario.

The parlaying of success on the screen to political power, which was the story of MGR, NTR and not long thereafter of J. Jayalalithaa, has been South India's distinctive and well-known contribution to our republic's politics, but we should also absorb the south's ability, glimpsed earlier, to buck a national mood.

We noticed this in the 1977 elections, when the South voted strongly for an Indira who had been trounced nationally. After Indira returned to power in January 1980, the DMK, quickly mending fences with her, persuaded New Delhi to dismiss MGR's ministry in Chennai, citing allegations of corruption. But when, after five months of President's Rule, new elections were held in Tamil Nadu, MGR overcame a DMK–Congress alliance and won a comfortable majority.

It was during his new term as chief minister that New Delhi ran training camps for Lankan Tamil militants. After Indira's assassination, MGR allied himself with the Congress and was easily re-elected as chief minister.

As for NTR, he tasted his first triumph in January 1983, when Indira seemed comfortably placed in New Delhi, but that triumph was achieved by the actor's shrewd political sense, not merely by the hero-with-a-halo image of one who had frequently played Krishna and Rama on the screen.

Born into a family of farmers from the influential Kamma caste in Krishna district and educated in Vijayawada and Guntur, a twenty-four-year-old NTR gave up, in 1947, the valued job of a sub-registrar in the presidency's public service to become a full-time actor in Madras. By 1949 he had made his first movie appearance.

On screen, MGR, older than NTR by six years, was usually a rationalist and reforming hero. In contrast, NTR portrayed incarnations of the divine. For the street, MGR wore a dashing fur hat and dark glasses; NTR put on an ascetic's robes, albeit brightly coloured. In his later films, NTR was at times a Robin Hood figure. The Telugu masses adored him throughout his acting career, which ended only in 1993, when he was seventy.

In the three years between 1980 and 1983, Andhra saw three Congress chief ministers. In February 1982, one of them, Tanguturi Anjaiah, a Dalit who had risen from trade union ranks, took a large group to Hyderabad's Begumpet airport to welcome Indira's Gandhi son, Rajiv, who was arriving on a private visit. Annoyed by the hullabaloo, Rajiv, it was said, lost his cool and rebuked Anjaiah, who soon lost his chief ministership.[6]

Painting the Indira-led Congress as a party that had insulted Andhra pride, NTR formed the TDP in March 1982. Mounting a Chevrolet van converted into a Chaitanya Ratham,* he attacked the Congress in all parts of the state. Within ten months, in January 1983, he was heading Andhra's first non-Congress government, having won for his new party a whopping 54 percent vote share.[7]

In August of the following year, while NTR was in the United States for heart surgery, his finance minister, N. Bhaskara Rao, left the TDP with a group of supporters. Declaring without a floor test that NTR had lost his majority, the Andhra governor, Ram Lal, a Congress politician from Himachal Pradesh, dismissed him and swore in Bhaskara Rao as chief minister.

The Tamil Nadu drama of 1967, when M. R. Radha's bid to kill MGR sky-rocketed the latter's fame, was now replicated in Andhra in September 1984. Returning to Hyderabad after successful surgery, NTR once more rode his Chaitanya Ratham, again tore across Andhra, and shouted that democracy had been destroyed.

The country's non-Congress parties agreed with him, as did a decisive majority of Andhra's TDP MLAs, who were brought to Hyderabad's Raj Bhavan by Rama Rao. Numbers being clearly in NTR's favour, New Delhi was compelled to remove Ram Lal. On 16 September 1984, a new governor, Shankar Dayal Sharma, brought NTR back as chief minister.

A month and a half later, Indira Gandhi was killed, but the pro-Congress sentiment that swept across India as a result did not sway Andhra. In new parliamentary elections, the state voted overwhelmingly for TDP candidates. NTR chose to remain in Hyderabad as chief minister, but he had become a national figure. In 1985, he consolidated himself in Andhra by calling and winning an early election.

India's mood altered in the late 1980s and a National Front of opposition parties took shape in 1989, with NTR as its chairman. For India-wide elections due at the end of the year, a former UP chief minister, Vishwanath Pratap Singh, was projected as a prime minister from the opposition's ranks.

---

*Chaitanya Ratham = chariot of consciousness or awareness.

After an impressive term in UP, Singh (1931–2008) had made a name for himself when, as Rajiv Gandhi's finance minister, he went after suspected tax evaders. Resigning from the Congress and Parliament because of differences with Rajiv, in the summer of 1988 he regained his place in the Lok Sabha in a nationally watched by-election. In the end-1989 general elections, the National Front proved successful, and V. P. Singh (leading a new party, the Janata Dal) became prime minister.

In Andhra, however, NTR's party, hurt by a split and by stories of corruption, lost office, and the Congress regained control. The Telugu state's Lok Sabha seats, too, were mostly back with the Congress. Once more Andhra had diverged from the national mood. It had also shown that though capable in shrewd hands of obtaining power, superstardom did not suffice to retain it.

◆

Tamil Nadu was telling another story. On 1 July 1982, Chief Minister MGR lifted to a new level the mid-day-meal scheme that Kamaraj had introduced a quarter of a century earlier. Now every child in pre-school or in classes one to five in a government or public primary school would get a free nutritious meal. The yearly allocation for mid-day meals went up twenty times, from Rs 6 crore to Rs 120 crore. Two months later, the scheme was extended to urban areas; two years later, to classes six to ten.

On the day of inauguration, eating a meal with children in Trichy district's Pappakurichi village, MGR said:

> This scheme is the outcome of my experience [as a child] of extreme starvation. But for the munificence of a woman next door who extended a bowl of rice gruel to us and saved us from the cruel hand of death, we would have departed this world long ago. Such merciful women folk, having great faith in me, elected me as chief minister of Tamil Nadu...
>
> To picture lakhs and lakhs of poor children who gather to take up nutritious meals in thousands of hamlets and villages all over TN and blessing us in their childish prattle, will be a glorious event.[8]

MGR knew he was drawing fresh popularity, something he had

frequently done, for instance by giving out raincoats to storm-stricken rickshaw pullers. But there was more than political arithmetic to the mid-day-meal scheme. Persons who raised doubts about it in 1982 would later admit their failure to see the scheme's potency.[9] Its contribution to nutrition, school-enrolment, inter-caste dining, and job creation in tens of thousands of new cooking centres would be impossible to deny.

◆

But even as MGR implemented a nutritional and educational policy that much of the country would later adopt, the Tamil world was experiencing tremors from the struggle between Lankan Tamil militants and the Sri Lankan government. Separated only by 18 miles of seawater, the state under him and the land of his birth were both affected.

On 19 May 1982—about six weeks before MGR launched his meals scheme—the city of Chennai saw a shoot-out in Pondy Bazar between the LTTE chief, Prabhakaran, and his former colleague Uma Maheswaran, who had broken off to form the People's Liberation Organization of Tamil Eelam (PLOTE). Along with members of other extremist groups of Sri Lankan Tamils, the LTTE leader and Maheswaran were being hosted, aided and also watched in Chennai.

Both men were arrested but released on bail, and Prabhakaran returned to Sri Lanka. In July of the following year (1983), violence and ethnic polarization escalated after the LTTE killed thirteen Sri Lankan soldiers in a Jaffna ambush. In retaliation, around three thousand Tamils were killed in Colombo and elsewhere, and thousands of Tamil shops and businesses were destroyed.

One fallout was a large flow of Lankan Tamil refugees into Tamil Nadu. Inside Sri Lanka, the LTTE grew in strength and intensity but so did the Lankan government's drive to suppress it.

Hit in October 1984 by kidney failure and a massive stroke, MGR was flown to New York, where he received a kidney transplant and spent months recovering before returning to Chennai in February 1985. By this time Indira had been assassinated. Allying with the Congress, the ADMK won in new elections to the Tamil Nadu assembly, and MGR was sworn in as chief minister for the third time.

In November 1986, when South Asian heads of government including Rajiv Gandhi and Jayewardene met in Bangalore, MGR surprised central leaders by bringing Prabhakaran to that city.[10] According to Natwar Singh, then minister of state for external affairs, MGR thought of Sri Lanka's chief Tamil city, Jaffna, as 'an extension of Tamil Nadu', and was widely believed to be 'covertly financing the LTTE' and arranging military training for its cadres.[11]

While continuing to press Colombo over Lankan Tamil rights, Prime Minister Rajiv Gandhi wanted New Delhi rather than Chennai to control policy towards Sri Lanka. At the end of 1986, he initiated the disarming and deportation of LTTE cadres based in Tamil Nadu. Many made their way to Jaffna, where LTTE rule was proclaimed. To this threat of de facto independence, Colombo replied with a military drive and a stern economic blockade.

Deciding that starvation in and around Jaffna could not be allowed, New Delhi sent five transport aircraft loaded with foodgrains and two fighter planes to that city, a step that angered Colombo but also induced President J. R. Jayewardene, thus far opposed to Indian involvement, to seek New Delhi's help for a resolution of his country's conflict.

Under pressure from New Delhi as well as Colombo, Prabhakaran, too, signalled a readiness to compromise. That the LTTE was 'willing to forego Eelam' was part of a message from its representatives in Singapore, communicated via N. Ram of *The Hindu* between 22 and 24 June 1987 (Dixit, 118).

A 'solution' developed largely from the contents of the LTTE's message was drafted by Indian and Lankan diplomats. Hardeep Singh Puri, first secretary in the Indian high commission, discussed the draft with Prabhakaran in Jaffna, who was stated to be 'generally agreeable' (143).

To clinch the agreement, the LTTE chief was brought in July 1987 to New Delhi in an Indian military aircraft, which stopped en route in Chennai to allow Prabhakaran to talk with MGR.

In Delhi, the LTTE leader expressed reservations. According to Dixit, Indian officials thought that Prabhakaran had 'changed his mind' after the Chennai stopover. Summoning MGR to Delhi, Rajiv 'personally' obtained the chief minister's endorsement for the package that had been put together. MGR asked Prabhakaran to be 'patient' (147, 150).

The Tigers' chief asked Rajiv Gandhi for funds for his hard-up cadres, and Rajiv arranged to provide 3 to 5 crore rupees (158). On 28 July, according to Dixit, Rajiv 'persuaded Prabhakaran to go along with the agreement even if he did not formally endorse it' (150).

Confident that the LTTE had no option except to come on board, Rajiv went ahead with the solution, while also relying on the Indian Army. Responding to a question from Rajiv, General K. Sundarji, the army chief of staff, had replied, 'The Indian armed forces can neutralize the LTTE in a fortnight or three to four weeks' (337).

Moreover, a Research and Analysis Wing chief had assured Rajiv, referring to the LTTE cadres, 'These are the boys whom we know... and so they will listen to us' (155).

In the Rajiv–Jayewardene pact signed in Colombo on 29 July 1987, India reiterated support for a united Lankan state. Conceding, on its part, that the island contained 'a Tamil homeland', Colombo promised devolution of power to it as well as recognition of Tamil as an official language, equal in status to Sinhalese, for all of Sri Lanka.

Colombo also agreed to withdraw to their barracks its troops in the island's Tamil north. And India agreed that it would help, if asked, to disarm the Tamil militants, whose leaders were expected to find political roles in Lanka's Tamil homeland.

With such sensible components, the 'solution' should have worked, except that neither Colombo nor the LTTE was committed to them.

Immediately after the pact was signed, Indian troops proceeded to Sri Lanka to underpin the agreement and keep the peace. To their shock, neither side in the conflict welcomed them, although Jayewardene seemed glad that the Indian Peace Keeping Force, the IPKF as it was called, was likely to protect him from any coup by Sinhala hardliners (161).

Moreover, the IPKF's arrival enabled Jayewardene to move Lankan troops to the island's south, where Colombo was trying to suppress Sinhala militants fighting a class war against their government.

While Sinhala hardliners, including some of Jayewardene's ministers, saw the IPKF as violating their country's sovereignty, the Tigers, from whom the IPKF had expected friendliness, refused to disarm.

After a brief phase of fraternization, the IPKF and the LTTE switched to war mode. In October 1987, after tenacious fighting, the IPKF captured Jaffna from the Tigers, who retreated into jungle sanctuaries from where they continually harassed the Indian force.

Whether coerced or freely given, local support was available to LTTE soldiers. Children and women pressed into shielding the Tigers made the IPKF's task harder.

Sundarji's prediction was blown apart. The war would last for more than two years, involving at its peak around 80,000 Indian soldiers, taking 1,157 Indian lives, and killing a larger if unknown number of Lankan Tamils.

In Tamil Nadu, support for the Tigers grew in the wake of allegations of IPKF excesses, but history provided a sardonic twist in Sri Lanka, where the IPKF's departure was demanded not only by the LTTE but also by Ranasinghe Premadasa, who had succeeded Jayewardene as president in January 1989.

At the end of 1989, when the Congress was defeated in elections to the Lok Sabha by the National Front, the new prime minister, V. P. Singh, announced that the IPKF would return to India. The last contingents left Sri Lanka in March 1990.

Dixit, a principal architect of the Rajiv–Jayewardene pact that inducted the IPKF into Sri Lanka, would later admit that the pact 'did not fulfil its objectives' (338). In fact, these objectives were never quite clear. No one was sure of New Delhi's preference between a Tamil homeland in Lanka and a single Lankan state, if it came down to that.

Poor maps and misleading intelligence hurt the IPKF, but contradictory instructions were a greater impediment. The force was sent to protect Sri Lanka's Tamils but fight the LTTE—fight the LTTE but not emasculate it. India's soldiers in Sri Lanka did not receive a clearly defined task, and commanders did not know the larger intention. Unfair to the IPKF, the confusion flowed from lack of clarity in the central leadership.

Meanwhile Tamil Nadu politicians tapped all the juice they could from Lankan Tamil hardship. As for Rajiv, he possessed (Dixit would later write) 'an innate sympathy' for Lanka's Tamils as well as a 'psychological inhibition to take drastic action against the LTTE' (339). Like his mother before him, Rajiv had to take Tamil politics into account.

As violence in the island took an escalating toll, extinguishing thousands of other lives, including those of Rajiv, Premadasa, and, eventually, Prabhakaran, the future was bound to ask whether alternative paths were sufficiently explored by Sri Lanka's conflicting parties, rival political groups in Tamil Nadu, and policy-makers in New Delhi.

JAYALALITHAA (1948–2016)

In the pre-dawn hours of 24 December 1987, about a month before his seventy-first birthday and five months after the IPKF moved into Sri Lanka, MGR died in his Ramavaram Gardens home in Chennai, having never fully recovered from the 1984 stroke.

Hysteria was set off by the death. Perhaps a million men and women followed the gun-carriage taking his body to the Marina. Around thirty followers committed suicide. Cinemas, shops and buses were attacked, shoot-at-sight orders were issued, schools and colleges shut their gates.

MGR's wife Janaki Ramachandran, a former actress, was with him when he died, but also central to events was thirty-nine-year-old Jayalalitha Jayaram. A Tamil Iyengar Brahmin raised in Karnataka, as a child Jayalalitha was a brilliant student who turned to acting to help her family's strained finances.

In an early film, *Adimai Penn*, made well before MGR broke away from the DMK, young Jayalalitha points to the rising sun, the party's symbol, and says to MGR, 'That is our God.'[12]

Interviewed in December 1969 by American scholar Robert Hardgrave, Jayalalitha spoke of receiving around 200-250 letters from fans every week, seeking photographs, money or, at times, her hand. A college student in Trichy apparently watched her first Tamil film, *Vennira Aadai*, sixty-six times, imagined himself in love with her, came to Madras, and sat outside her door night and day until the police was called to remove him.[13]

Starring in scores of films between 1961 and 1980, and frequently opposite MGR, Jayalalitha became a superstar. In 1982, she joined the ADMK, in the following year she became the party's propaganda secretary, and in 1984 a member of the Rajya Sabha, where her abilities were recognized across party lines.

When MGR died, Jayalalitha's personal relationship with him and her mounting appeal in the party ensured a clash with Janaki, who had her own political aspirations. Millions in Tamil Nadu witnessed images of Jayalalitha standing stoically beside MGR's body in Rajaji Hall, forcing herself onto the gun-carriage taking the body to the Marina, and being forcibly pushed off the vehicle.

Meanwhile, 97 MLAs of the ADMK signed a memorandum to Governor S. L. Khurana supporting Janaki, who was sworn in as chief minister on 7 January 1988. Three weeks later, anarchy engulfed the Tamil Nadu assembly as Janaki tried to prove her majority.

As Jayalalitha's supporters and Congress MLAs accused the speaker of taking Janaki's side, aggressive non-members entered the house. Policemen were summoned. MLAs were being beaten with lathis when the speaker declared that Janaki had proved her majority.

Alleging that democracy had been murdered, Jayalalitha urged the governor to remove Janaki's ministry. Khurana recommended dismissal, and New Delhi, where Rajiv Gandhi was prime minister, imposed President's Rule.

When elections were held a year later, the DMK won a four-horse race against Jayalalitha's ADMK faction, Janaki's ADMK faction, and the Congress.

With a 37.9 per cent vote-share, the DMK won 169 seats, but Jayalalitha's claim that she was MGR's political heir was vindicated. A 25 per cent vote-share gave Jayalalitha 30 seats, including one for herself. Janaki's party got 2 seats, the Congress 26.[14]

'How would a Brahmin woman,' Karunanidhi evidently once asked, 'knowing nothing about Dravida life, be a threat to me in Dravida Nadu?'[15] Part of the answer was provided by an incident occurring two months after his victory. Although the episode hurt his reputation and strengthened that of Jayalalitha, its drama may have been appreciated, at least in hindsight, by Karunanidhi the scriptwriter.

When Chief Minister Karunanidhi, whose portfolios included finance, stood up on 25 March 1989 to read his budget speech, a Congress MLA, Kumari Ananthan, interrupted him with an accusation that the police were harassing Jayalalitha. Repeating the charge herself, Jayalalitha shouted that the chief minister was behind the harassment and her phones were being tapped. 'The head of the government,' she cried, 'is corrupt!'[16]

In the eruption that ensued, abuses were hurled, microphones flung, and papers torn up. The speaker adjourned the house. Then, as Jayalalitha was leaving the chamber, a DMK MLA 'obstructed her path, clutching at her sari as she cried for assistance'.[17]

With its echo of the attack on Draupadi's sari in the Mahabharata, the episode seemed to invite a future retribution of an epic sort, even one where Jayalalitha becomes chief minister. She had come across as a woman of destiny, forged into that role by her will and also by the actions of her political foes.[18]

◆

Many defecting from his party, the Janata Dal, V. P. Singh lost his premiership in eleven months. In November 1990 Chandra Shekhar, another former Congressman leading another Janata Dal faction, became India's prime minister with Congress support. Like Singh, he was from UP.

In January 1991, the Chandra Shekhar government removed Karunanidhi's Tamil Nadu ministry from office. The premier's principal secretary, S. K. Misra, would later claim that intelligence agencies had convinced the prime minister of 'proven links' between Karunanidhi and the LTTE.[19]

Two months after Karunanidhi's dismissal, but for reasons unconnected with it, the Congress withdrew support in Delhi to the Chandra Shekhar government, which fell. On 21 May 1991, after new elections were called, Rajiv Gandhi was campaigning in Sriperumbudur, 40 km from Chennai, when an LTTE suicide bomber killed him.

How the killer and others behind the killing were enlisted may never be fully established. On his part, Dixit would write: 'It was the LTTE's apprehension that Rajiv Gandhi may come back to power and revive the [India–Sri Lanka] agreement, perhaps even reintroduce the IPKF, which led to the LTTE assassinating him' (343).

Helping the Congress return to power at the centre, the assassination also influenced the Tamil Nadu elections held a month thereafter. Contesting as allies, the ADMK and the Congress won a massive 59.8 per cent of the vote and 225 seats out of 234 (164 ADMK, 60 Congress, 1 other).[20]

At the age of forty-three, Jayalalithaa, as she now spelt her name, apparently on astrological advice, became chief minister. The sari episode was avenged. The DMK won only 2 seats, including one where Karunanidhi squeezed through. Its allies got 5.

In the 1991 summer, the Telugu country's Pamulaparti Venkata Narasimha Rao emerged as India's new prime minister, filling the unexpected void created by Rajiv's assassination.

Twenty years earlier, PV, as people in the Telugu country called him, had become the Andhra chief minister, though, as it turned out, only for fifteen months. In that brief period, he had implemented meaningful land reforms. Later, for almost all of the 1980s, he served as a senior central minister, first under Indira and then under Rajiv, holding a major portfolio throughout, either external affairs, home or defence.

But in Andhra he lacked a solid political base. It was from a Maharashtra constituency, Ramtek, that PV had entered the Lok Sabha in 1984 and again in 1989. As a Congress MP sitting on Opposition benches between 1989 and 1991, he had kept only a distant relationship with Rajiv, the ex-prime minister and party president.

Making a long trip to the US, Rao returned quite critical of that country,[21] and as 1991 unfolded he did not ask for a new Lok Sabha term. It seemed that he was fading away.

Sonia Gandhi, the widow born in Italy on whom spotlights stayed after Rajiv's death, had kept clear of politics thus far. PV's low profile was one reason why she wished to see PV succeed Rajiv as Congress president and prime minister.

Rao's innocuous demeanour also scored with the Congress working committee, which unanimously elected him as Rajiv's successor, setting aside the claims of others, chiefly Sharad Pawar, seen as the Maharashtra strongman, and his chief rival, Madhya Pradesh's Arjun Singh. Rao was the compromise candidate accepted by 'stronger' leaders who hoped ere long to replace him.

Installed on 21 June 1991 as India's first South Indian prime minister, Rao won a Lok Sabha by-election in a landslide from an Andhra seat, Nandyal, which was vacated by the Congressman elected from there, Gangula Pratap Reddy.

Telugu pride at PV's ascendancy was considerable. Across India, Congress colleagues, journalists and many others were aware of his fluency in several languages and of his reputation as a 'cerebral' politician, but PV was also spoken of as indecisive. 'When asked "Tea or coffee?" he has difficulty choosing,' C. Subramaniam observed.[22]

Being underestimated was part of his strength. Natwar Singh, a sometime critic who was minister of state for external affairs when PV headed that ministry, would call him, in 2014, 'a thinker of the first order...astute, crafty and patient'.[23]

Reflection and experience had made PV wise as well. He had, for instance, foreseen the weaknesses of the ill-starred Rajiv–Jayewardene Pact of 1987.

When Foreign Secretary K. P. S. Menon and Dixit, high commissioner to Colombo, showed him the draft of that pact, Rao, foreign minister at the time, questioned the need to 'rush into the agreement' and said that rather than sign an agreement with Colombo, India should guarantee an accord between Sri Lankan Tamils and Colombo.

He also wondered whether the LTTE and Colombo 'were genuine' in their reported wish for a compromise and asked if they were not merely making 'interim tactical moves'. In addition, according to Dixit, PV expressed 'reservations about the Indian armed forces moving into Sri Lanka'.[24]

But risk-avoidance went with foresight. As Natwar Singh would write, Rao was 'unwilling' to express his reservations to Rajiv, even though, as foreign minister, he was in Colombo when the pact was signed.[25] Dixit would assert also that he 'did not notice any voice of dissent on any of the important aspects of Rajiv Gandhi's Sri Lankan policies from his political colleagues'.[26]

◆

Though with its 244 seats the Congress was the largest party in the Lok Sabha, it fell 28 seats short of a majority.[27] With the support of a few regional parties, Rao kept his government going for five years.

It was seen as a feat. The two premiers before him, V. P. Singh and Chandra Shekhar, had each lasted less than a year in office.

The 'innocuous' and 'indecisive' Rao quickly showed toughness. Rivals Pawar and Singh were taken into his cabinet, but neither was given a top-tier portfolio. Finance went to an intellectual and former Reserve Bank governor, Manmohan Singh.

Attempts inside the Congress to remove PV failed 'because', as one of those involved would put it, 'he was far cleverer than all of us'.[28]

Accusations that the Rao government bribed a handful of MPs

from Jharkhand to win a crucial no-confidence vote in 1993 were not eventually sustained in the courts, although on dates close to the vote large sums of money had been deposited in the bank accounts of some of the MPs in question. A lower court verdict issued against Rao in the year 2000—four years after the Congress led by him had lost in the 1996 elections—was overturned two years later by the Delhi High Court.

Two things—the Indian economy's liberalization-aided spurt and the Babri Masjid's demolition—will always be joined to PV's name, though some may also remember him for wanting the Congress to have 'a life beyond the Nehru-Gandhi family'.[29] Sonia's initiative had made PV prime minister, and he could never forget her influential, if as yet mostly silent, presence, but for five years from the summer of 1991 the hands around India's levers of power were largely Rao's.

On 1 July, within days of his assuming the premiership, PV and Finance Minister Manmohan Singh devalued the rupee. Though inescapable (exchange reserves had been exhausted), the step took courage. It was followed by equally bold measures to deregulate industry, shrink the licence raj, open doors to foreign investors, and lower taxes on domestic corporations.

Backed by Singh, Rao had placed India on the liberalization-globalization escalator.

◆

The hate-fuelled demolition in December 1992 of Ayodhya's Babri Majid by a mob wielding axes was the culmination of a bid that had begun forty-three years earlier (in December 1949) with the surreptitious insertion, in pre-dawn darkness, of a Rama idol into the mosque.

The carefully planned placement of the idol was portrayed as a miracle. Pressed to undo the insertion, K. K. K. Nayar, the deputy commissioner of the region who was close to UP's Hindu Mahasabha leaders, refused.[30] Prime Minister Nehru urged the UP government to restore the masjid's status, but Lucknow, where the prominent Congress leader, Govind Ballabh Pant, was the chief minister, dilly-dallied.

In 1967, Nayar, a Malayali by birth, entered the Lok Sabha on behalf of the Jan Sangh, from Bahraich in UP. In 1949, he had conceded that the installation of the idol in the mosque has certainly been an illegal act and it has placed not only local authorities but also government in a false position.[31]

Studying the demolition's history, researchers Krishna Jha and Dhirendra K. Jha have linked the 1949 idol insertion to Gandhi's assassination in January 1948, which marginalized Hindu extremists.[32]

To regain popular favour, the extremists evidently came up with a strategy of stoking resentment at Babur's alleged sixteenth-century demolition of a temple in order to build the mosque, and of fusing that resentment with the positive sentiment, existing across India, for the infant Rama.

While admitting in 1949 that the idol insertion was illegal, Nayar contended that he could do nothing about it, which was also the argument that Prime Minister Narasimha Rao would advance before Parliament in December 1992. Rao repeated the explanation in his book on the demolition, which, in line with his wishes, was published only after his death in December 2004.[33]

Prime Minister Rao told the Lok Sabha that UP's government, headed by the BJP, had assured him and also the Supreme Court that the mosque would be protected. He had believed its word. 'I plead guilty for believing a state government,' he said. 'That is the only sin I seem to have committed.'[34]

The prime minister added in explanation that he knew of no legal way in which he could have removed the UP government before the demolition. Helplessness before an illegal act was thus pleaded by Nayar in 1949 and by Rao in 1992. Innovative with the economy, Prime Minister Narasimha Rao seemed inert when communal hatred was let loose.

◆

Exports grew in the 1990s, exchange reserves multiplied, malls appeared across the land, the pursuit of great personal wealth became something to flaunt, not hide, and many Indians lifted themselves out of poverty, but many more remained in misery's grip.

Rao won international plaudits and was praised in India by businessmen and many economists, but his standing was hurt by the demolition and related violence.* There were other damaging factors: the corruption charges mentioned earlier, restiveness among the poor, and the formation of a rebel Congress faction led by Narayan Dutt Tiwari, a former chief minister of UP, and Arjun Singh, who had resigned from Rao's ministry after the demolition.

The result was a decisive defeat for the Congress in the elections of May 1996, which gave 140 seats to the Congress, 161 to the BJP, and the rest—240 or so—to a host of regional or 'third front' parties.[35]

The Congress performed fairly well in Andhra, securing 22 of the state's 42 seats (the TDP got 16), but the Congress–ADMK alliance in Tamil Nadu produced not a single win. The DMK got 17 while its ally, the Tamil Manila Congress, which claimed a link to Kamaraj, won 20.

Although PV comfortably retained his own Nandyal seat, his political career was over. The Congress party offered outside support to a United Front government after a BJP ministry that had been sworn in, led by Atal Bihari Vajpayee, resigned in thirteen days, having failed to muster a majority.

The United Front ministry was headed by Karnataka's H. D. Deve Gowda, India's second prime minister from the south, who took his oath on 1 June 1996.

For five years until 1992, India's president, too, was a southerner, a veteran Congressman born near Thanjavur district, Ramaswamy Venkataraman (1910–2009). One of Kamaraj's close colleagues from the 1940s, RV, as he was known, moved over to the Indira Congress after Kamaraj's death. In the 1980s, he served as Indira Gandhi's finance and defence minister before becoming the nation's vice president and, in 1987, president.

DEVE GOWDA (b. 1933)

Haradanahalli Doddegowda Deve Gowda was born in 1933 in a family of farmers of the caste of Vokkaligas, who had tilled the southern Karnataka countryside for centuries. Before the state's expansion in

---

*The demolition was followed by the killing of hundreds of Muslims in Ayodhya and disturbances elsewhere. Mumbai saw protests by Muslims, riots in January 1993 in which 275 Hindus and 575 Muslims were killed, and retaliatory blasts on 12 March 1993 that took close to 300 lives and destroyed prime properties.

1956, Vokkaligas were Mysore's most influential community. After Kannada-speaking portions of Bombay and Madras presidencies and of Hyderabad state were joined to Mysore, Lingayats outnumbered Vokkaligas in the new Karnataka.

A Congressman since 1953 and from the early 1960s a virtually continuous member of the Karnataka assembly or the national parliament, Deve Gowda stood with the Old Congress in 1969 (when Indira Gandhi broke with it) and later with the Janata Party and the Janata Dal. He had an edgy relationship with Ramakrishna Hegde, chief minister of Karnataka for much of the 1980s, who, too, had progressed from Congress to Janata and Janata Dal.

A lively Brahmin from Uttara Kannada, Hegde (1926–2004) was as comfortable in Hindi and English as in Kannada. Audiences across the country as also visitors who met him privately seemed to like his message of 'value-based politics'. After Hegde's election in 1983 as Karnataka's first non-Congress chief minister, some saw him as a future prime minister of India.

But when Hegde asked a corps of detectives in 1988 to report within a month on corruption charges levelled by a BJP MLA member against Deve Gowda, who was the minister for irrigation and public works, a tussle was set off that Gowda would eventually win.[36]

Divides in the Karnataka Janata Dal helped bring the Congress back to power in the state in 1989. Hegde was isolated in the process, and when in 1994 the Janata Dal regained Karnataka, it was Deve Gowda who became chief minister.

Two years later, when a prime minister acceptable to 'third front' parties, the Left and the Congress was needed, the new chief minister of Karnataka filled the bill, but only after another possible candidate, the West Bengal chief minister Jyoti Basu, was removed from a short list by the central leadership of his party, the CPM.

Hegde, who had 'made no secret of the fact that he believed he was the ideal candidate to head' the new government, spoke out against Deve Gowda's selection and was expelled by the Janata Dal.[37]

Gowda had never held a national-level office before becoming prime minister. He called himself 'a simple farmer'; his Hindi was poor and his English awkward; in Parliament, where on occasion he seemed to doze, he would speak of how things were done in Karnataka, which did not impress northern leaders.

But when, after ten months, he lost the premiership, it was for none of these reasons. Bihar's Sitaram Kesri, Rao's successor as Congress president, asked the United Front to replace Deve Gowda because, alleged Kesri, the prime minister had taken the Congress for granted. He had advised Deve Gowda, said Kesri, to make

> Mayawati the Uttar Pradesh chief minister to keep the communal forces out. But they rejected it [outright]. That was a slap on my face. After all, I am the president of the Congress... Then, I asked [Deve Gowda] to change Romesh Bhandari as Uttar Pradesh governor and he said no.[38]

His refusal to act on UP as the Congress wanted ended Deve Gowda's premiership. The man who moved into the vacated office was his minister for external affairs, Inder Kumar Gujral, an ex-Congressman from Punjab and former ambassador to Moscow, who had joined the Janata Dal in 1989.

Eleven months after becoming premier, Gujral, too, had to go, primarily because he was unwilling to dismiss ministers belonging to the DMK from his coalition government. The demand was made in November 1997, after *India Today* obtained and published the Jain Commission's hitherto undisclosed comment that the DMK 'could be blamed for...facilitating an atmosphere...for the LTTE to carry out' Rajiv Gandhi's assassination in 1991.[39]

In his evidence before the Jain Commission, Karunanidhi had claimed that in the 1980s all parties in Tamil Nadu backed the LTTE. The DMK leader added that he 'withdrew his support' after 19 June 1990, when the LTTE murdered in Chennai a rival leader, K. Padmanabha, and fourteen others.[40]

'Disinclined to believe this', the Commission seemed to lay special blame on the DMK.[41] When the Congress demanded that the premier remove its ministers, Gujral, backed by most United Front partners, refused to do so, whereupon the Congress withdrew its support. The government fell, and new Lok Sabha elections were held in February 1998.

◆

We had left Kerala politics in 1977 when, despite Indira Gandhi's defeat, an alliance led by the Congress and the CPI won all 20 of the state's Lok Sabha seats and 103 of the assembly's 140 seats.[42] In 1980, the CPI abandoned the Congress and returned to an alliance with the CPM. Thereafter, from one election to the next, the Left Front and the Congress-led United Democratic Front have replaced each other with relentless regularity.

As each election brought a change that looked predictable, a kind of reliability if not stability seemed to mark Kerala.[43] But flux within a 'stable' front is also part of the Kerala story. The years between 1977 and 1980, when the Congress and the CPI ran the state, saw five chief ministers, two from the CPI (Achutha Menon and Vasudevan Nair), two from the Congress (K. Karunakaran and A. K. Antony), and one from the Muslim League (C. H. Mohammed Koya, who reigned for all of fifty-one days).

In 1980, when Indira Gandhi returned to power in Delhi, a united Left narrowly defeated the Congress-led front in Kerala, and the CPM's E. K. Nayanar became chief minister. But at the end of 1981, the Congress's Karunakaran—who had been home minister in Kerala's Emergency-era government led by the CPI's Achutha Menon—managed to replace Nayanar.

In less than three months, Karunakaran's ministry fell because one member of a Kerala Congress faction had crossed over, but after fresh polls in 1982, the small-sized, hump-carrying Karunakaran, born in 1918 near Kannur in northern Kerala, was chief minister again, this time for five years.

Recognizing that large numbers in Kerala voted as a caste or as a religious group, Karunakaran had forged an enduring partnership between the Congress and parties linked to Kerala's Muslims and Christians. The United Democratic Front (UDF) he astutely architected would last at least until 2018.

Karunakaran's opposite number in the Left Front was the CPM leader, Nayanar, also born in 1918 and also raised in the Malabar region. Nayanar became chief minister for the second time in 1987 for four years, and again in 1996, this time for five years. No one has served longer as Kerala's chief minister.

Between 1991 and 1996, when it was the UDF's turn to rule,

Karunakaran was chief minister for about four years and his old rival in the Congress, the much younger A. K. Antony, for 400 days.

The need to enlist allies pushed ideology into second place in Kerala. EMS had acknowledged the compulsion: 'Consciousness of one's caste, sub-caste or religious community is still a large force... The party of the working class with its advanced ideology has also to take account of [this] factor.'[44]

Accordingly, the Left's intervention in Kerala has for decades been more parliamentary than militant or ideological. Moreover, the state's rival coalitions have been institutionalized, with constituent parties enjoying long-term support from particular castes and communities. Since four dominant constituencies—Ezhava, Nair, Christian and Muslim—are concentrated in geographical pockets, 'community' politics has made sense.

♦

In Andhra, seventy-one-year-old NTR bounced back in great style in elections held in December 1994, winning 216 seats to the Congress's 26,[45] a result that also revealed the dramatic slide in the fortunes of India's prime minister at the time, Andhra's P. V. Narasimha Rao.

However, NTR's elation was short-lived. In August 1995, he was ousted in a revolt sparked by his marriage in 1993 to a woman younger by thirty-three years, Lakshmi Parvathi, a writer from the Telugu country who had divorced her folksinger husband, V. Subba Rao. Telling NTR that her worship of him began when she was eight, Lakshmi Parvathi added that she wished to write his life story.

NTR was not a radical ideologue like EVR. Other than that, the story of the TDP breakup was similar to that of the much older DK split in the Tamil country, when Annadurai walked out with numerous colleagues after EVR's marriage to Maniammai.

In Andhra, it was NTR's son-in-law, Nara Chandrababu Naidu, who led the revolt, backed by two of NTR's sons, Harikrishna and Balkrishna. However, unlike Annadurai's revolt, which was announced in advance, Naidu's was kept under wraps until the last minute.

Born in 1951 in Chittoor district, Chandrababu Naidu had shown drive from the moment he joined politics. When, as a twenty-eight-year-old, he became a Congress minister in Andhra, cinematography was under his purview. Meetings with NTR followed. In 1980, Chandrababu married one of the superstar's daughters, Bhuvaneswari.

After being defeated as a Congress candidate in the 1983 elections, Chandrababu joined the TDP. In the following year, when NTR had to thwart Bhaskara Rao's bid to replace him, Chandrababu played a critical role in mobilizing MLAs for his father-in-law. His rise in the TDP was steep thereafter.

Within weeks of NTR's marriage to Lakshmi Parvathi, his sons and daughters voiced complaints: the reins of power were in Lakshmi Parvathi's hands, she was appointing favourites to coveted positions, NTR was being shut off from his own children, and so forth.

Privately, most TDP MLAs seemed to agree with Chandrababu that the ageing leader who had created their party and had just given it a resounding victory was no longer physically or mentally capable of guiding it.

They also seemed to agree that Chandrababu, vigorous and modern-minded, was the one to help Andhra's businessmen and politicians profit from the opening up of the Indian economy.

In August 1995, a party coup was quietly and swiftly organized in Hyderabad. NTR was voted out by TDP MLAs, and his son-in-law voted in as chief minister. Though NTR screamed betrayal, he possessed neither the energy nor the friends to fight back.

On 17 January 1996, he told Reuters that he was like Emperor Shah Jahan, who was imprisoned by his son Aurangzeb in the seventeenth-century. Predicting that he would gain his revenge against 'the backstabbers' in his family, he added that Chandrababu Naidu's 'days are numbered'.[46]

The following day, NTR, whose 'voice was stentorian, his gestures grandiose, almost as if every moment of his life was on camera',[47] suffered a heart attack and died. Vast numbers converged on the cricket stadium where his body was laid out beneath a layer of flowers.

Moved mourners took out processions across Hyderabad. 'At street corners, Hindu priests chanted prayers at impromptu shrines where Mr. Rama Rao's portrait had been placed amid statuettes of Hindu gods and burning candles.'[48]

◆

Chandrababu, who would remain in the chief minister's chair until 2004, when he lost to the Congress, transformed Hyderabad into a city of investments from overseas and a high-tech destination. 'Bye-bye Bangalore, Hello Hyderabad', was one of his slogans.

Bill Clinton and Tony Blair called there. Chandrababu said Andhra would become an Asian Tiger. There was a spurt in privatizing healthcare and education in Andhra, and in Telugus moving to the US.

Hyderabad seemed to vibrate. Tall new structures began to fill its skyline. In 1999 Chandrababu was re-elected as chief minister, winning 185 out of the assembly's 294 seats. In the new Lok Sabha, 29 of Andhra's 42 places were held by the TDP, which joined the BJP-led coalition in New Delhi as its second largest member.

Yet if many had become very rich in Andhra as the century drew to a close, many more remained very poor, and hard questions arose about equity and also ethics. For instance, what percentage of the new wealth was legitimate? At a different level, there was friction between Chandrababu and some of his wife's siblings. In 2004, the Congress, led by the driven Y. S. Rajasekhara Reddy from the Rayalaseema country, would replace him.

◆

Born in 1921 in the small thatched hut of an 'untouchable' family in the principality of Travancore, Kocheril Raman Narayanan became India's vice president in 1992 and president in 1997. Perumthanam, the village where he was born, lay in north Travancore, near the small town of Uzhavoor.

Narayanan's 'low-born' father practised Ayurvedic medicine. Innate ability, parental support and scholarships from missionary bodies and the Raja of Travancore saw Narayanan through school and college.

At the London School of Economics, where he studied political science from 1945 to 1948, Harold Laski gave Narayanan a letter of introduction to Jawaharlal Nehru, who urged the young Malayali returning to India to join the foreign service.

After an impressive diplomatic career, in the course of which he met and married Ma Tint Tint (a Burmese Christian who took the name Usha) and served as ambassador to China, Narayanan was made vice-chancellor at Jawaharlal Nehru University in 1979. Joining the

Congress on Indira Gandhi's advice, he was thrice elected to the Lok Sabha from Ottapalam in Palakkad district, and served as a minister of state in Rajiv Gandhi's government.

Narasimha Rao did not include Narayanan in his 1991 ministry, but when the Janata Dal proposed Narayanan's name for vice president, Rao agreed to support him. Narayanan's elevation, in 1997, to the presidency was predictable, but not so his independence in the country's highest constitutional office.

In 1997, he asked the Gujral cabinet to re-examine its decision to remove UP's chief minister, Kalyan Singh of the BJP; and in the following year Narayanan asked the Vajpayee cabinet to reconsider its decision to remove Bihar's chief minister, Rabri Devi of the Rashtriya Janata Dal.

In both cases, the cabinets changed their minds, a tribute to Narayanan's stature and also to his reasoning. Narayanan had reminded the prime ministers of the Supreme Court's 1994 judgment on the centre's powers to dismiss a state government.* That judgment assigned critical weight to a test on an assembly's floor, which was not conducted in Lucknow or Patna.

When India marked the fiftieth anniversary of Independence, and also when the twenty-first century began, the nation's president was Kerala's son, K. R. Narayanan.

◆

As the twentieth century approached its end, the South's eccentricities, extravaganzas and enmities were intact.

Chief Minister Jayalalithaa was deified as Puratchi Thalaivi, the Revolutionary Leader. Party members 'started tattooing Jayalalithaa's image on their bodies'.[49] After a new governor, the Telangana country's Chenna Reddy, arrived in Chennai in 1993, the chief minister 'threw a bombshell in Assembly', alleging that the governor 'had misbehaved with her during her visit to Raj Bhavan'.[50] The legislature was aghast, and not everyone believed Jayalalithaa's allegation.

The 'Mother of All Weddings' was held in 1995 when Chief Minister Jayalalithaa's 'adopted son', as she called V. N. Sudhakaran, the nephew

---

*S. R. Bommai vs the Union of India, 1994.

of V. K. Sasikala* (her 'live-in alter ego', to quote one of Jayalalithaa's biographers),[51] was married to the granddaughter of megastar Sivaji Ganesan, with whom the late MGR enjoyed a screen rivalry.

Two hundred thousand guests were invited though not, of course, Karunanidhi. Workers employed by Chennai city and the State Electricity Board plus many more on the government's payroll were drafted to assist. Arches, viewing galleries, horses, dancers and fireworks filled the processional route, where, loaded with jewels, bride and groom looked like prince and princess, Jayalalithaa like the queen.[52]

It was 'one great blunder', Jayalalithaa would admit eight months later in a rare remark,[53] after her term was over and she had lost to Karunanidhi in new elections. But the fire of revenge burned strongly when, shortly after her defeat, the DMK government authorized Jayalalithaa's arrest on corruption charges. 'Tomorrow will be ours,' she insisted before shaken party workers. She was let out after twenty-eight days.

We saw earlier that Gujral's United Front ministry, dependent on the Congress, fell in end-1997 because he did not dump his DMK ministers. Thanks in part to Jayalalithaa's alliance with it, the Vajpayee-led NDA gained national office in 1998 with a narrow majority.

When, despite Jayalalithaa's urgings, Vajpayee refused to dismiss Karunanidhi's government, she withdrew support, and in April 1999 the NDA government lost a confidence resolution by a single vote.

Once more a Chennai tail had wagged the New Delhi dog.

Arriving in Delhi a few days before the vote, the Tamil lady had signalled her intentions by going to tea with Sonia Gandhi, who, seven years after Rajiv's assassination, had become Congress president.

Hitherto opposed ('on ideological grounds') to the BJP, Karunanidhi however had asked his six DMK MPs to vote to save the Vajpayee ministry. After its fall, Karunanidhi formally joined the NDA, helped it win in fresh polling, and obtained seats for the DMK in the national cabinet.

Seasoned writer of film-scripts and lyrics, known in the Tamil country as Kalaignar, or the artist, Karunanidhi was also a reader of political winds. Three years earlier, backed by Andhra's Chandrababu

---

*The two first became friends in a small video shop that Sasikala ran in Jayalalithaa's Poes Garden locality.

Naidu, Karunanidhi had played a key role in Deve Gowda's elevation as prime minister. Preventing the formation of a BJP government was part of the motivation then. Now, in 1999, Karunanidhi assisted Vajpayee's return to office.

While thus shaping governments in New Delhi, the South's enmities were also eroding ideologies. To counter Jayalalithaa, and to instal DMK members in successive governments in New Delhi, Karunanidhi was prepared to lay aside the doctrines his plays, films, lyrics and speeches had espoused.

Also an NDA ally in 1998–1999, and a minister in Delhi, was Karnataka's Ramakrishna Hegde, his positions influenced by nemesis Deve Gowda's opposition to the BJP.

Following the 1999 elections, the BJP's biggest southern support came from Chandrababu Naidu's TDP, which won 29 seats from Andhra. Unlike the DMK, the TDP chose, however, to remain outside the Vajpayee government, which steered the nation entering a new century.

◆

It is with two of the South's women that this chapter concludes. When we left her way back in 1936, Kamaladevi Chattopadhyay, just emerged from prison terms, had become a leader of India's Congress socialists. Three years later, when Subhas Bose was obliged to leave the Congress, while most other socialists stood with Gandhi, as finally did Nehru, Kamaladevi's sympathies lay with Bose.

A radical with romantic hues, passionate against the oppression of the Global South and of women, Kamaladevi was a ceaseless traveller who sought out, in Europe, the US and elsewhere, foes of colonialism and racial domination. A tour of Japan and China in 1939–40 evoked anxieties about Japanese militarism and admiration for Zhou Enlai and Madame Sun Yat Sen, both of whom she had met.

Her fervour over Quit India attracted, from August 1942, another long prison spell, spent mostly in Vellore. In the 1946 summer, when Nehru succeeded Azad as Congress president, she was named to the working committee, with Gandhi's backing.

However, when in June 1947 the AICC accepted Mountbatten's partition scheme, and an isolated Gandhi acquiesced, as did a distressed JP, Kamaladevi's was one of the small number of hands raised against acceptance.

'With that I broke my link with this political life,' Kamaladevi would later recall. Politics 'was not my vocation', concluded one who had seemed destined for the centre of India's leadership.[54]

She met Gandhi on 29 January 1948, a day before his assassination. On 31 January a shaken Kamaladevi felt another blow when she saw an army truck taking Gandhi's body for cremation.

She lived for four more decades. Refugee resettlement and the revival in remote parts of India of endangered handicrafts, puppetry and folk drama became her dominant concerns.

Kamaladevi proved more than capable in these and other roles, nurturing many an institution (including the All India Women's Conference and the India International Centre, Delhi) and founding some (including the National School of Drama), but her remarkable work with such bodies does not capture the essence of her personality or impact.

More helpful is her autobiography, which she wrote shortly before her death in 1988, even though it does not portray Kamaladevi as much as those she met, the famous and the unknown, who are all described sensitively and also charitably.

The autobiography suggests that this woman of many passions and gifts found her deepest satisfaction not in great accomplishments, or in lasting relationships, but in what she called 'trifles'.

> I seem bold, aggressive, outgoing... In reality, I am shy... [Public work] does not touch my intimate self, it has not satisfied my whole being.
>
> I am very human, I want the trifles, the little things of life—the leisure to dream, to suck in the slow notes of music, to savour in nature the play of light and shadow so reminiscent of life with its joys and sorrows.
>
> [In the end], an individual is a lonely soul, away and apart, holding on only to these little things of life, while all else has faded away.[55]

Making humanity her family and beautiful little things her companions, Kamaladevi died in 1988.

◆

No one ever suggested she was aggressive, and none knowing her could even imagine harshness in Madurai Shanmukhavadivu Subbulakshmi (1916–2004), famous as 'MS' and as Subbulakshmi.

Stunning even while not singing, MS seemed spontaneously graceful in every gesture or movement of hers, whether she was with a prince or a prime minister, an audience or a music critic, her family or friends.

In addition to seeming wholly comfortable with herself, Subbulakshmi was gentle in conduct, modest amidst accolades, and warm in hospitality. Music, however, was her life, and she was blessed with an irresistible voice.

When she sang, listeners felt transported to higher realms. Discipline had kept pace with talent. When people spoke of her 'divine' voice, Subbulakshmi reminded them of the lengthy exercise she daily gave her vocal cords.

Crucially, there was an inner toughness. Her appeal having been discovered early (the Tamil country knew her as a prodigy from when she was ten, and she played film roles in her early teens), her mother Shanmugavadivu, a talented veena artist of Devadasi descent, finally identified, from among an eager range of moneyed suitors, a wealthy Chettiar to whom she would give her daughter.

This would have been in late 1936 or early 1937. Before, however, 'her mother could take any further action', twenty-year-old Subbulakshmi, it seems, 'removed her ornaments, slipped out…quietly one night' from her Madurai home, 'and hopped onto a train to Madras', where, according to her biographer T. J. S. George, she 'knew two trustworthy persons'.[56]

One was a Congress nationalist promoting khaddar. The other, also a Congress nationalist, was Thyagaraja Sadasivam (1902–97), born, like so many in our story, in the Thanjavur delta, whom MS had met in Madras during a 1936 stint in the city.

Sadasivam loved music and was a passionate advocate of Indian independence. After a spell in extremist company, he had become, from 1921, a close associate and follower of Rajaji. In the 1930s, Sadasivam worked for the popular journal *Ananda Vikatan** along with another CR associate, Ramaswamy Krishnamurthy, one of the Tamil country's

---

*Owned by the writer, publisher and filmmaker S. S. Vasan, also originally from Thanjavur.

greatest novelists, who wrote under the pseudonym 'Kalki'.

After reaching Madras, Subbulakshmi found protection in Sadasivam's home. The two married in 1940, following the death of Sadasivam's first wife, Apithakuchambal. Thereafter, Subbulakshmi's career as a singer rose in tandem with the growth of *Kalki*, a new Tamil journal started by Krishnamurthy and Sadasivam.

Inseparable from Subbulakshmi's story are imaginings about what two others must have felt, one a wife, Apithakuchambal, and the other, a mother, Shanmugavadivu. Equally undeniable was the bond between Subbulakshmi and Sadasivam's two little girls, Radha and Vijaya, to whom Apithakuchambal had given birth.

These two grew to sing invariably at their new mother's side, and if any in their audiences wished at times to visualize the mother who was no more, their thoughts always returned to the unison, before their eyes, of the three women singing together, and to the evidence that their harmony extended beyond voice.

Also always at Subbulakshmi's side was Sadasivam. The music and art historian Gowri Ramnarayan ('Kalki' Krishnamurthy's granddaughter), who at times accompanied MS's singing, would later recall:

Subbulakshmi would often say, 'My husband always assured me that if I sang with true feeling, listeners would automatically be drawn to me.' He was particular about diction and sometimes suggested the emphasis in the verses she sang. These verses were chosen by him from the devotional and contemplative lyrics of saint poets from every part of India.

[Sadasivam's] own genuine feeling for [a song, melody or rhythm] influenced his wife's music... He planned every concert of Subbulakshmi to the last detail.[57]

The love of freedom that any artistic genius like MS must possess was astonishingly subsumed in a total and unceasing devotion to Sadasivam, who nurtured her into becoming a world celebrity, which she remained while never losing her beguiling simplicity.

Through him she had found respectability, security, fame. He had taken over but also taken her to the world, structured her but also launched and liberated her for the millions. When, sixty-one years after their first meeting, Sadasivam died in 1997, Subbulakshmi, who would live for seven more years, stopped singing.

MS was an all-India phenomenon from the 1940s, when she acted and sang as *Meera* in a film about the medieval poet-princess from Rajasthan. She sang in numerous south Indian and other Indian languages with impressive diction (but only after absorbing the words' meaning) and became a national symbol.

She sang at a few of Gandhi's prayer-meetings. She sang classical and devotional, in India and the world over, for the initiated and for plain folk, and won immense numbers of lastingly loyal listeners. She sang lyrics by old masters and by contemporaries such as the Kanchi Paramacharya (of whom Sadasivam was a bhakta) and CR, whose *Kurai Ondrum Illai* (No Regrets Have I) in her voice seldom failed to raise tears.

MS raised funds too, for numerous causes. In 1998, she was given the nation's highest award, the Bharat Ratna, the first musician thus honoured. Earlier, while receiving another prestigious medal, the Magsaysay, she had said: 'If I have done something…it is entirely due to the grace of the Almighty who has chosen my humble self as a tool.'[58]

Every day MS's music stops someone somewhere in the world. As for her life, those who observed it can recall an unbroken harmony of goodness and beauty.

Chapter 15

ENDING AN EXCURSION: 2000–2018

Lying on a tiny island called Pamban,* Rameswaram is one of India's holy sites. An isthmus going southeast from Pamban disappears into the sea just before it can reach the larger island of Sri Lanka, where, in the epic, Rama recovered his Sita.

Unsurprisingly, Rameswaram's population (under 50,000 in 2011) is overwhelmingly Hindu, but a few hundred Muslim families have lived there for centuries. Their language is Tamil. In 1931, a woman called Ashiamma from one such family, married to an imam, gave birth to a future rocket scientist who would win the Bharat Ratna in 1997 and, five years later, become India's president.

Dark of skin, short in physical stature, and a lifelong bachelor, Avul Pakir Jainulabdeen Abdul Kalam sported long wavy locks that at times touched his shoulders, and his fingers moved with ease on a veena's strings.

After stints at Trichy's St. Joseph's College and Chennai's Madras Institute of Technology, he did defence and space research for India's armed forces, helping develop, among other devices, the Agni and Prithvi missiles.

Heading, from 1992 to 1999, the government's Defence Research and Development Organisation (DRDO), Dr Abdul Kalam worked in those seven years under many defence ministers and four prime ministers. Narasimha Rao of the Congress, the Janata Dal's Deve Gowda and Inder Gujral, and the BJP's Atal Bihari Vajpayee were the four prime ministers.

It was during this period of Kalam's leadership at DRDO, though without a personal role by him, that the nuclear detonations in Pokhran were accomplished by India's atomic scientists in May 1998. Also striking was our rocket expert's ability to maintain warm relations with political leaders of all hues.

*Attached to Tamil Nadu's Ramanathapuram district.

When President Narayanan's term was ending in 2002 and a successor was needed, Mulayam Singh, the Samajwadi Party head, proposed Kalam's name. As defence minister in the Gowda and Gujral ministries, Mulayam had known and liked his DRDO chief.

The BJP not possessing, in 2002, the numbers to get one of its own elected to Rashtrapati Bhavan, Prime Minister Vajpayee was more than glad to sponsor Kalam, and Sonia Gandhi was willing to support him.

Against him, the Left parties put up another South Indian, Captain Lakshmi Sehgal, born to a Nair mother from Palakkad and an England-educated Tamil Brahmin. Having served in 1944–45 as an officer under Subhas Bose in the Indian National Army, Lakshmi Sehgal possessed vintage value, but Kalam defeated her more than handily.

He became an accessible head of state and a peripatetic one as well, earning the 'people's president' tag. He was in addition an exhorting president, offering unexceptionable and at times quotable advice. Student audiences loved him.

After his presidency ended in 2007, Kalam's enthusiasm for India's classical culture, his liberal praise for leaders of some Hindu religious bodies, and his earlier work for India's defence made him Hindu India's favourite Muslim.

Still, in June 2012, Kalam told a magazine that he performed his morning namaaz 'every day, whenever possible', adding, 'My father was very strict about namaaz and would wake me up at 4 a.m. and take me to the mosque. I also fast... I often visit temples and churches as well. God is everywhere.'[1]

Some political parties, including the BJP and the Trinamool Congress, proposed a willing Kalam for a fresh presidential term in 2012, but the Congress and its allies did not take to the idea. Aware that he lacked the numbers, Kalam did not stand, and Pranab Mukherjee became president.

On 27 July 2015, the former president, now eighty-three, was on his feet in a Shillong auditorium, delivering a lecture on the environment, when, all of a sudden, he collapsed. Taken to an ICU in an adjacent hospital, he was declared dead.

The IAF flew the body of one of the nation's most popular presidents to Pamban Island, where, not very far from Rameswaram's sacred temples, VVIPs and thousands of ordinary Indians saw him being buried with state honours.

◆

Two years after her 1999 switch brought down the Vajpayee ministry in Delhi, Jayalalithaa became chief minister again in Chennai. Within weeks, she had seventy-eight-year-old Karunanidhi dragged out of his bed at two in the morning and arrested on the basis of an FIR alleging irregularities in the construction of flyovers. According to one version, the complaint had been lodged by 'a tainted municipal commissioner'.[2]

Jayalalithaa had again blundered. After being roused in the middle of the night, Karunanidhi managed to summon a TV crew that captured what appeared to be cruelty towards an old man who had just been the state's chief minister.

Within hours, all of Tamil Nadu saw the video clip, as did Indians elsewhere. Arriving from New Delhi, a shocked George Fernandes, the NDA defence minister, called on Karunanidhi in prison and recommended Jayalalithaa's removal from office. Although Prime Minister Vajpayee shrank from that drastic step, the DMK leader was soon released.

Before her death in December 2016, Jayalalithaa would, over different terms, be chief minister for a total of fourteen years and four months. Humbling Jayalalithaa in the 2006 elections, Karunanidhi replaced her for another full term, taking his tally of chief ministerial years to more than eighteen. Although Jayalalithaa would defeat him in 2011 and again, though more narrowly, in 2016, legal proceedings against her (including on how her wealth was acquired and expanded) periodically deprived her of the chief minister's chair.

In September 2014, a trial court in Karnataka found Jayalalithaa, her close aide Sasikala, and two others guilty of amassing resources disproportionate to their incomes. Jayalalithaa went to jail, and her loyal follower, O. Panneerselvam, became chief minister.

In May 2015, however, the Karnataka High Court acquitted the former superstar, who returned to the chief ministerial chair. Those convicted with her were also acquitted.

In February 2016, Jayalalithaa was re-elected as chief minister, but in September of that year an illness hit her from which she would not recover. The circumstances of the illness, presumably known to Sasikala, were not disclosed to the public, and even powerful ministers or party leaders were not permitted inside her hospital room.

The late Jayalalithaa's images linger. She is the imperious woman standing above, and barely noticing, horizontal male ministers as they prostrate at her feet. She is the fair-faced female chief smiling before tens of thousands of Tamils of her gender, all of them poor, thankful and adoring. She is Karunanidhi's vengeful enemy, here successful, there humbled.

She is the courageous politician, too, someone willing in 2004 to authorize the arrest, on a murder charge, of Sri Jayendra Saraswathi, head of the venerable Kanchi matha.*

There was Jayalalithaa's benign face stamped on many a product or service gifted to the needy Tamil, who was also a much-needed voter. Thus emerged the 'Amma canteen, Amma water, Amma baby kit, Amma cement, Amma pharmacies and Amma seeds...the fans, laptops, cycles and grinders that made life so much easier for rural folk'.[3]

She is the accused awaiting with impassive face a court's verdict and the worshipped chief minister dying behind closed doors in a Chennai hospital with everyone watching but no one knowing what was going on. She is the absent face when, after her death, the Supreme Court confirms a lower judge's finding that she and Sasikala had accumulated wealth wrongfully.

Hers was the face too of the woman in command who within hours of the tsunami attack of 26 December 2004 roused the entire Tamil Nadu administration into life-restoring action.[4]

It was a face of one who, with a phalanx of Tamil Nadu MPs behind her, was ready in 2014 to be sworn in as India's prime minister if, as was widely thought, neither the Modi-led NDA nor its opponents obtained a majority. In the event, the Modi wave eclipsed that face, but she still won 37 seats in Tamil Nadu.

With ample reason, many will join her face to that of MGR, while others may remember the strenuous effort she had to make, when MGR died, to snatch his legacy from those set to prevent her. He had not prepared a pathway for Jayalalithaa.

---

*The Kanchi chief was acquitted of this charge in 2013.

Much about this extraordinary woman will never be known. The public figure was totally silent about her private life. The most she said was to *The Hindu* after her 1996 defeat. Involving Sasikala and her husband Natarajan, the remarks were revealing and also sad:

> A male politician has a wife at home and a woman politician has a husband or brother to take care of her personal matters. I have no one. It is only because Sasikala stepped in to take care of my household that I was able to devote my full attention to politics.
>
> After MGR's death, I went through a very traumatic phase and I had no one at home here to help me with anything... [A] t that time Sasikala and Natarajan offered to help... They both came to live here.
>
> But very soon Natarajan overstepped his limits... I asked him to leave my house. But Sasikala opted to stay with me...
>
> Sasikala has sacrificed her whole life in order to be with me and give me moral support and take care of me. In fact, there was an occasion when she saved my life.[5]

What we know of the ups and downs of this extraordinary life is dramatic enough. What we don't know is bound to be richer if also, we can imagine, tragic in places. Perhaps Sasikala will one day share her story.

Far more willing to be interviewed about himself and his equally remarkable life, Karunanidhi also wrote at length about it, and about the Dravidian movement, in his multi-volume autobiography, *Nenjukku Needhi* (Justice to the Heart). An enduring politician who was also an artist with the written and the spoken word, Karunanidhi would die on 7 August 2018 at the age of ninety-four.

◆

After Jayalalithaa's death on 5 December 2016, Panneerselvam again became chief minister, but the party founded by MGR and later commanded by Jayalalithaa was now up for grabs. On 29 December, an ADMK gathering named Sasikala as the party general secretary. Five weeks later, on 5 February 2017, the ADMK MLAs met and 'unanimously' elected her to lead the party.

Sasikala looked ready to replace Panneerselvam as chief minister when, on 14 February 2017, a two-judge bench of the Supreme Court overruled the Karnataka High Court's order acquitting her and Jayalalithaa, and confirmed the earlier guilty verdict. Jayalalithaa was no more, but Sasikala had to proceed to a Bengaluru jail.

Before incarceration, she expelled Chief Minister Panneerselvam from the ADMK, whose MLAs elected E. K. Palaniswami as the new chief minister. After a bitter fight, Panneerselvam and Palaniswami came together to fend off T. T. V. Dinakaran, the jailed Sasikala's brisk nephew.[6]

In December 2017, however, Dinakaran won a by-election in the late Jayalalithaa's constituency (Chennai's Radhakrishnan Nagar) by an overwhelming majority.

Palaniswami became the Tamil Nadu chief minister and Panneerselvam the deputy chief minister. Meanwhile, two superstars, Rajinikanth and Kamal Haasan, jumped into Tamil Nadu's electoral arena, where the DMK remains a major force.

Whatever else Tamil Nadu politics may be, it is not boring.

♦

Partial at best, the story told in the foregoing pages was mostly political. While some artists, including writers, poets, singers, dancers and actors, were encountered, many others were not. For example, though for decades South India provided the country's greatest satirists and cartoonists, men like K. Shankar Pillai, Abu Abraham, R. K. Laxman, Mario Miranda and O. V. Vijayan, we didn't meet them.

And only fleeting impressions, or not even these, were caught of fishermen at sea, or of the entrepreneur's boldness, the pilgrim's penance, or a mother's ingenuity. Or the oppressor's torments and the survivor's strength. Or the mathematician's proofs, the scientist's discoveries and the surgeon's hands.

However, a wanderer can only present the berries (and thorns) *he* has picked on his trails.

As South India's story continues, so does its dark side. In Chapter 13, we looked at a translation of P. Lankesh's Kannada poem about his mother. On the evening of 5 September 2017, Lankesh's daughter, Gauri, fifty-five, was killed in front of her Bengaluru home by a man who drove in on a motorbike, concealing his face under a helmet, shot three bullets into her, and fled. An outspoken editor, Gauri Lankesh had brought together persons from different streams to resist intimidation.*

◆

Even where the South's recent political history was concerned, only portions could be explored on our tour. For instance, the Telangana question (which in 2014 produced a new state, led by Chief Minister K. Chandrashekar Rao) could only be given a brief look.

The terrible cycle of revenge and counter revenge in Kerala's Kannur region received less than that.

The charge that empowered 'backward castes' are giving Tamil Nadu's Dalits a harder time than they previously faced merited attention that could not be given.

The sense of unfairness over resource allocation nursed between Old Mysore, Hyderabad Karnataka and Bombay Karnataka was barely touched upon.

The success in Andhra of Y. S. Rajasekhara Reddy, the Andhra chief minister from 2004 who was killed in 2009 in a helicopter crash, not long after corruption charges were levelled against him, and the more recent political efforts, under a 'YSR Congress' banner, of his son Jagan were not examined.

◆

Before leaving this history of the land south of the Vindhyas, we may look briefly at the story of the BJP and South India, where for decades the party was restricted to a small size. There were three main reasons for this confinement: Brahmin preponderance in the RSS, which had opened branches in the South from the 1920s; the 'Hindi/North Indian' image of the Jan Sangh, the political party that expanded into the BJP; and the BJP's inability to connect itself to the independence struggle.

The Congress's failings, and alleged appeasement of Muslims by successive national and state governments, were the main planks on which the BJP slowly built its southern platform. For a long time, the second charge held little appeal in South India, which had escaped

---

*The manner of her death seemed a replica of the shooting of three other well-known opponents of coercion: Narendra Dabholkar in Pune in August 2013, Govind Pansare in Kolhapur in February 2015, and M. M. Kalburgi in Dharwad in August 2015.

Partition's communal bitterness.

Moreover, the Muslim percentage in the region was small, generally speaking. There were exceptions like Malabar and Hyderabad city, where Muslims were a third or more of the population, or Karnataka's districts of Dakshina Kannada and Bidar, where Muslims comprised about a fifth of the population. In most of South India, however, the so-called 'Muslim question' did not acquire salience.

From the 1980s, the Ram Janmabhoomi movement and the occurrence of Muslim names in terrorist acts in India and elsewhere appeared to give the BJP and its associates opportunities to reach wider audiences.

Suggestions that Muslims had a special tendency to be 'anti-national', and that political parties supposedly pandering to them had to be kept out of power, were circulated. Insinuations of this sort seemed to appeal to a section of South Indians, and many young men were pulled towards extremist Hindu 'senas'.

Some southern Muslim youths, on the other hand, were attracted to militant Islamist outfits, including those operating outside India, worrying their parents and providing Hindu nationalists with fresh ammunition.

In 2004, the BJP emerged as the largest single party in the Karnataka assembly. At first the Congress (which obtained the highest vote share) and Deve Gowda's Janata Dal Secular (JDS) formed a coalition ministry under the Congress's Dharam Singh, but a mid-term deal between the BJP and Deve Gowda ousted Dharam Singh's ministry in 2006.

As part of the deal, Deve Gowda's son H. D. Kumaraswamy became chief minister. A year later, in November 2007, again as agreed under the deal, the BJP's B. S. Yeddyurappa, a Lingayat, replaced Kumaraswamy at the coalition ministry's head, but differences over the distribution of portfolios ended the alliance.

In new elections in 2008, the BJP won 110 seats in a house of 224, enabling Yeddyurappa to lead a purely BJP government. It was a milestone for the BJP, which meanwhile had become an electoral element in some other places in the South. Through local leaders, it had also built strong relations with particular castes, notably with Lingayats in Karnataka.

In 2011, however, court proceedings triggered by corruption charges forced Yeddyurappa to resign both from government and the party. In subsequent elections held in 2013, the Congress comfortably defeated a BJP weakened by Yeddyurappa's exit, but in the 2014 contests for the Lok Sabha, the Modi wave enabled the BJP, which Yeddyurappa had rejoined, to win 17 of Karnataka's 28 seats.

All of India followed Karnataka's state assembly elections of May 2018. Although the BJP won 104 seats out of 224, the Congress, with 79 winners but a vote-share slightly higher than the BJP's, and the JDS, with 37 seats and a 19 per cent vote-share, entered into a post-poll alliance and formed a government headed by Kumaraswamy of the JDS.

The BJP's best results in the elections of May 2018 came in districts like Dakshina Kannada, where direct calls or indirect signals went out for a united Hindu vote to defeat 'pro-Muslim' parties.

◆

Connected to the question of the BJP and South India is an impression that following 2014, when Modi stormed to power at the centre, the South's influence in New Delhi has waned.

The Telugu leader Venkaiah Naidu, a former national president of the BJP, is no doubt India's vice-president, and Nirmala Sitharaman is the country's first woman defence minister.

Yet, Sitharaman apart, no southern BJP leader or ally holds a big portfolio at the centre. As for Sitharaman, she appears to owe her place in Parliament and the cabinet wholly to Modi's goodwill. There is little evidence of political support for her in the state where she was born, Tamil Nadu, or in either of the two states she has represented in the Rajya Sabha, Andhra and Karnataka.

The South's representation in India's governance took another hit in May 2018 when Chandrababu Naidu's TDP, holding the reins of power in Andhra, left the NDA, and that party's ministers resigned from the Modi-led government at the centre.

There appears to be a similar shortage in New Delhi of South Indians in the highest ranks of the civil service and security establishments.

At least to some minds, the days when New Delhi contained heavyweight South Indian politicians and officers seem to belong to a distant past. One that saw an all-India party chief like Kamaraj, cabinet ministers like C. Subramaniam, Krishna Menon, T. T. Krishnamachari,

A. K. Antony, and P. Chidambaram, and presidents like Radhakrishnan, Giri, Sanjiva Reddy, Venkataraman, Narayanan and Kalam, not to mention prime ministers like Narasimha Rao and Deve Gowda.

◆

In our survey of the South's political history, the question of its desire to lead India often came up, and perhaps this study should conclude with a short reflection on it.

We may start by recognizing that the South has seldom been a solid bloc. Today's water disputes between the South's neighbouring states are reminiscent of eighteenth-century clashes, noticed near this volume's start, between adjacent chieftains, like, for instance, the battle between Muhammad Ali and Chanda Sahib in 'the Carnatic'.

'The impossible neighbour', an oft-recurring phrase in current political discourse in Chennai or Bengaluru, may have been a standard refrain 300 years ago on each side of a southern quarrel.

The kind of recent political empires we glanced at in the second half of our study—those, for instance, of Jayalalithaa, Karunanidhi and NTR—resembled the dominant if also unstable principalities of eighteenth-century South India that featured in the first half. Enmity among descendants of political empires, or among claimants to their legacies, also followed an earlier pattern.

At this point of time, about two decades into the twenty-first century, there are not many signs of a joint southern effort for India's leadership. Remarks from individual leaders may occasionally convey aspiration for bigger roles, or alertness to possible opportunities, but the South's political scene does not, at present, communicate a hunger for national leadership.

Or a passion to involve the Indian people in great pursuits, a zeal to enlist southern and other partners for overcoming India's challenges, or find a satisfying global role for India.

Entertained from the 1930s by Periyar followers, the notion that all of the South could unite under a Dravida banner is now rarely articulated. Moreover, venality seems to have replaced ideology in branches of the Dravidian movement, with superstition ousting rationalism.[7]

Yet it may be a mistake to think that the widely accepted belief in a common origin for almost all the languages spoken in the South can provide no psychological or political energy.

Linguistic affinity may prove a useful element in a future geopolitical calculus. So also physical proximity. So, too, the radical idea, nursed for long, that 'the people', all of them, constitute an equal and single community. In some ways, that idea is distinctive to India's South.

While social and political realities have repeatedly mocked it, that notion has not been extinguished, for reformers and poets in different parts of South India have steadily offered it fresh fuel. We can recall, for instance, the pregnant lines, quoted in an earlier chapter, of *Kanyasulkam*'s author, Gurujada Apparao:

Never does land
Mean clay and sand
The people, the people, they are the land.[8]

Lasting until 1956 and taking in pieces from each of the South's principal linguistic areas, Madras Presidency under CR and Kamaraj was an influential player on the all-India scene. When the presidency was broken up in 1956, and new linguistic states created, the predominant reaction was positive, not negative. The sense was of spontaneity and creativity being freed, not of curtailment or of new walls.

However, enemies being useful in politics, the focus shifted from new opportunities to the supposed obstinacy of those across a linguistic border in the South. Moreover, and this was a serious loss, bilingual areas lying along the new borders gradually became more or less unilingual. Palakkad became almost overwhelmingly Malayali, Nagercoil turned predominantly Tamil, Chennai was no longer a hub of Telugu literature, and Bengaluru saw anti-Tamil demonstrations.

Fortunately, reality has frequently been larger than friction. The Malayali MGR was and is loved in the Tamil country. His Tamil fans would like Rajinikanth with his Marathi background to run Tamil Nadu.

When, as happened on occasion, Periyar was attacked for his family's alleged Kannadiga or Telugu origins, the Tamils embraced him the more warmly. Rajaji was always proud of his forebears' links to the Telugu country: his father felt more comfortable in Telugu than in Tamil, and CR himself learnt Telugu before he spoke Tamil.

Then there is the Kannada world's adoration, deep and unceasing, for writers with Marathi, Tamil, Telugu and Malayali backgrounds.

South Indians may in fact be far more charitable than may be suggested by demagogues in their ranks. Many southerners are proudly multilingual, or interested in the neighbour's language, and have been so for centuries.

We may recall the eighteenth-century statement of Abbé Dubois that he had come across Vemana's poems, 'originally written in Telugu... translated in several other [South Indian] languages',[9] as well as the East India Company's dependence, in different parts of South India, on flocks of multilingual dubashes.

Unity, however, is unlikely to come from osmosis, or from precedents alone. It was to be worked for, and it needs champions. Like others thrown together elsewhere in the world, South Indians tend to possess opinions rather than knowledge about their immediate neighbours, and they have but rarely recognized the blessings of solidarity.

Or the power of the native vision of the people, all the people, as a single community.

The last time that the South's political leaders acted together in a significant way was way back in 1969, when Kamaraj, Sanjiva Reddy and Nijalingappa tried to apply the brakes on Indira Gandhi. Although she outsmarted them, at least they joined hands across provincial borders in a bid to give India a lead.

The example of the wide Quit India front that drew men and women from across the South is a quarter century older, while the similarly broad Salt defiance occurred a decade earlier. Still, those wanting to attempt solidarity have instances to draw inspiration from.

A more recent example occurred during Chennai's deluge of December 2015, when, ignoring hardship, Malayalis, Kannadigas and Telugus of different faiths brought food and medicines for strangers marooned in the city. Three years later, Chennai folk can still tear up while recalling the gestures.

That all of today's India can do with initiatives for mutual concern, for respect and reconciliation between communities, for stopping intimidators, and for empowering the vulnerable does not need underlining.

In ending our limited excursion into the history of South Indians, it may be permissible to pray that their children today will recognize the needs of the present—in the region, in India and in the world—and initiate responses.

Warmth for the neighbour was the key. As Valluvar, the *Kural*'s author, wrote a thousand or more years ago,

> To be kind, to care and perhaps to love is to have true wealth;
>
> Even the vile have the other kind that rhymes so well with 'stealth'.[10]

Centuries before him, a line had been sung in India's deep south, 'Yadum Ooru, Yavaram Kelir' (All Towns are One to Us, All People are Our Kin.)[11] The thought refuses to go away.

NOTES

INTRODUCTION

1   W. Francis, ICS, *Vizagapatam District Gazetteer 1907*; Hyderabad: State Editor, District Gazetteers, 1994, p. 3, (repr).

2   Title of Chapter 3 in S. Krishnaswami Aiyangar, *The Beginnings of South Indian History*, Madras: Modern Printing Works, 1918, p. 59.

3   Robert Caldwell, *Comparative Grammar of the Dravidian or South Indian Family of Languages*, Third edition, London: Kegan Paul, Trench, Trubner & Co, 1913; New Delhi: Oriental Books, 1974, pp. xi–xii, (repr).

CHAPTER 1

1   Burton Stein, *Peasant State and Society in Medieval South India*, Delhi: Oxford University Press, 1980, p. 394.

2   Seen as a Dravidian language and in modern times written in the Kannada script, Tulu is presently spoken by about 3 million people, many of whom live in the coastal region of northern Karnataka, and the rest in different parts of southern and western India, in the Gulf, and the Western world.

3   See V. Narayana Rao, David Shulman and Sanjay Subrahmanyam, *Symbols of Substance: Court and State in Nayaka Period Tamilnadu*, Delhi: Oxford University Press, 1992, p. 220, pp. 220–41.

4   Ibid., pp. 84–85, p. 253.

5   Ibid., pp. 113–68.

6   Robert Orme, *A History of the Military Transactions of the British Nation in Indostan, From the Year MDCCXLV, to Which is Prefixed a Dissertation on the Establishments Made by Mahomedan Conquerors in Indostan*, Vol. 2, London: John Nourse, 1778; New Delhi: Today's and Tomorrow's Printers and Publishers, p. 7, (repr).

7   A. V. Williams Jackson, (ed.), Chapter 16, *History of India* (1906 et seq.), p. 367, accessed from <http://www.ibiblio.org/britishraj/Jackson2/chapter16.html>.

8   Report of the Southern Division of the Madras Army, Madras: Government of Madras, 1843; R. W. Thorpe at the Vepery Mission Press, p. 47.

9   Williams Jackson, *History of India*, p. 368.

10 Susan Bayly, *Saints, Goddesses and Kings: Muslims and Christians in South Indian Society*, Cambridge, UK: Cambridge University Press, 1989, p. 74.

11 Cynthia Talbot, *Precolonial India in Practice: Society, Region, and Identity in Medieval Andhra*, New York: Oxford University Press, 2001, citing a 1913–14 translation by E. Hultzsch, p. 73.

12 J. Talboys Wheeler, *Annals of the Madras Presidency, 1639–1702*, Madras,

1861; Delhi: B.R. Publishing, 1985, pp. 3–4, (repr).

13   Quoted in his foreword by Gurcharan Das in Kanakalatha Mukund, *Merchants of Tamilakam: Pioneers of International Trade*, New Delhi: Penguin Books, 2012, p. xvi.

14   Bennet Bronson, 'An Industrial Miracle in a Golden Age: The 17th–Century Cloth Exports of India', written for the exhibition, 'Master Dyers to the World: Early Fabrics from India', opened at Field Museum, Chicago, 29 January 1982 or 1983, <http://iref.homestead.com/textile.html>.

15   Mattison Mines, *Public Faces, Private Voices: Community and Individuality in South India*, Berkeley: University of California Press, 1994, p. 27, quoting David Washbrook, 'Progress and Problems: South Asian Economic and Social History, c.1720–1860', *Modern Asian Studies*, Vol. 22, No. 1, p. 80.

16   Quote in C. H. Philips, *The East India Company, 1784–1834*, Manchester, UK: Manchester University Press, 1968, p. 299.

17   S. Muthiah, *Madras Discovered: A Historical Guide*, Madras: Affiliated East–West, 1987, p. 102.

18   Wheeler, *Annals*, p. 43.

19   Muthiah, *Madras Discovered*, pp. 216–18.

20   Ibid., p. 218.

21   Ibid.

22   Ibid., p. 216, and S. Muthiah in *The Hindu*, 17 March 2003.

23   Henry Davison Love, *Vestiges of Old Madras, 1640–1800*, p. 495; accessed from Internet Archives.

24   Muthiah, *Madras Discovered*, p. 245.

25   Geert de Neve and Henrike Donner, (eds.), *The Meaning of the Local: Politics of Place in Urban India*, New York: Routledge, 2006, p. 98.

26   V. Narayana Rao, David Shulman and Sanjay Subrahmanyam, *Textures of Time: Writing History in South India*, New Delhi: Permanent Black, 2001, p. 115.

27   Abbé J. A. Dubois, *Hindu Manners, Customs and Ceremonies*, London, 1816; Revised edition, Henry K. Beauchamp, (trans.), London 1897–98 (?); Revised edition, Oxford at the Clarendon Press, 1953, pp. 274–75, (repr).

28   Muthiah, *Madras Discovered*, p. 115.

29   Fort St George record quoted in Wheeler, *Annals*, p. 85, (repr).

30   Ibid., pp. 227, 231, 234.

31   Ibid., p. 74.

32   Wheeler, *Annals*, pp. 1–2.

33   Muthiah, *Madras Discovered*, pp. 278–79.

34   *Letters from Fort St George, 1693–1694*, Madras, 1919, pp. 90–91, quoted by S. T. Jeyapandiyan in *South Indian History Congress: Proceedings of the 1982 Conference*, Madurai, 1984, p. 95.

35   Muthiah, *Madras Discovered*, p. 82.

36   K. R. N. Menon in S. Muthiah, (ed.), *Madras: Its Yesterdays, Todays and Tomorrow*, p. 36.

37   Ibid., p. 39.

38   Harry Miller in Ibid., p. 111.

39 V. Narayana Rao, David Shulman and Sanjay Subrahmanyam, *Symbols of Substance: Court and State in Nayaka Period Tamilnadu*, Delhi: Oxford University Press, 1992, pp. 5–8.

40 Ibid., p. 13.

41 Rao, Shulman and Subrahmanyam, *Textures*, pp. 19ff.

42 S. Charles Hill, *Yusuf Khan: The Rebel Commandant*, London, 1914; repr. New Delhi: Asian Educational Services, 1987, p. 3.

43 Talbot, *Precolonial India*, p. 9.

44 Sheldon Pollock, *The Language of the Gods in the World of Men: Sanskrit, Culture, and Power in Premodern India*, Berkeley: University of California Press, 2006, p. 508 and 510.

45 Talbot, *Precolonial India*, p. 73.

46 Ibid., p. 74.

47 Wheeler, *Annals*, p. 187.

48 J. Talboys Wheeler, *India Under British Rule from the Foundation of the East India Company*, London: Macmillan and Co., 1886, p. 22.

49 Ibid., pp. 12–13.

50 Wheeler, *Annals*, p. 99, repr.

51 Ibid., p. 88.

52 Wheeler, *India Under British Rule*, p. 30.

53 Ibid., p. 30fn.

54 B. Sheik Ali, 'History of Karnataka from 1600 AD', in H. M. Nayak and B. R. Gopal, (eds.), *South Indian Studies*, Mysore: Geetha Book House, 1990, pp. 148–49.

55 Historian Rajan Gurukkal to author, Bengaluru, 4 February 2017.

56 Historian J. Devika to author, Thiruvananthapuram, 27 February 2017.

57 Historian Rajan Gurukkal to author, Bengaluru, 4 February 2017.

58 Ibid.

59 Scholars Rajan Gurukkal, Bengaluru, 4 February 2017 and Michael Tharakan, Ernakulam, 2 March 2017 to author.

60 Historian M. G. S. Narayanan to author, Kozhikode, 3 March 2017.

61 Ibid.

62 Historian Rajan Gurukkal to author, Bengaluru, 4 February 2017.

63 P. N. Chopra, T. K. Ravindran and N. Subrahmanian, *History of South India*, New Delhi: S. Chand, 1979, Vol. 3, p. 34. Sibi Joseph writes that Itti Achuthan, an Ezhava scholar and Ayurvedic physician, played a major role in the creation of 'that botanical masterpiece'. See Joseph's 2014 dissertation, 'Socio–cultural dualism: Process of growth of Westernisation and its impact on Kerala economy', p. 59, accessed from <http://shodhganga.inflibnet.ac.in/bitstream/10603/22485/12/12_chapter2.pdf>.

64 Muzaffar Alam, *The Languages of Political Islam: India 1200–1800*, Delhi: Permanent Black, 2004, p. 149, citing several sources including documents in the Andhra Pradesh Archives, Hyderabad.

65 Susan Bayly, *Saints, Goddesses and Kings: Muslims and Christians in South Indian Society*, Cambridge, UK: Cambridge University Press, 1989, pp. 389–90.

66 Ibid., p. 399.

CHAPTER 2

1 S. Muthiah in *The Hindu*, 29 December 2013, quoting a 1914 account by prominent Madras jeweller Ambashankar Tawker (Thakkar?) of his forebears' arrival in the Tamil country with 'Shivaji or his family', which would have been in the 1670s. According to Muthiah's article, Ananda Ranga Pillai's 1759 diary refers to the 'diamond merchant' Nilakanta Tawker.

2 Wheeler, *Annals*, pp. 291–98.

3 Orme, Vol. 1, p. 86.

4 Rao, Shulman and Subrahmanyam, *Textures*, pp. 141–45.

5 Hugh Pearson, *Memoirs of the Life and Correspondence of the Reverend Christian Frederick Swartz*, London: J. Hatchard and Son, 1839, p. 19.

6 The Columbia University website provides direct images of many pages from Pillai's diary; accessed from <http://archive.org/stream/ privatediaryofan01ananuoft/privatediaryofan01ananuoft_djvu.txt>.

7 Susan Bayly, *Saints, Goddesses and Kings*, p. 97, pp. 156–57.

8 Ibid., pp. 156–57.

9 Hill, *Yusuf Khan*, 1914, p. 9.

10 Ibid., p. 12; Orme, Vol. 1, p. 212, 218.

11 Stuart Blackburn, *Print, Folklore, and Nationalism in Colonial South India*, Delhi: Permanent Black, 2003, p. 71.

12 Hill, *Yusuf Khan*, p. 1. Hill cites a Hindu court official in Ramanathapuram confirming the birth details.

13 Ibid., p. 270, where Hill quotes Lawrence's statement from *Orme MSS*, 13, p. 1.

14 Ibid., where Hill quotes Lawrence's statement from *Orme MSS*, 13, p. 16.

15 Ibid., where Hill quotes Lawrence's statement from *Orme MSS*, 13, p. 78.

16 Robert Harvey, *Clive: The Life and Death of a British Emperor*, London: Macmillan, 2014.

17 Pearson, *Memoirs of Reverend Swartz*, pp. 100–02.

18 M. O. Koshy, *Dutch Power in Kerala: 1729–1758*, New Delhi: Mittal, 1989, pp. 5–6. See also <http://dutchinkerala.com/english/1721.php>.

19 Ibid., p. 112.

20 Quoted in Hill, *Yusuf Khan*, p. 100.

21 See Joseph's 2014 dissertation, 'Socio–cultural dualism: Process of growth of Westernisation and its impact on Kerala economy', accessed from <http:// shodhganga.inflibnet.ac.in/bitstream/10603/22485/12/12_chapter2.pdf>.

22 Jake Halpern, 'The Secrets of the Temple', *The New Yorker*, 30 April 2012 <http://www.newyorker.com/magazine/2012/04/30/the–secret–of–the–temple>.

23 Lewis Rice, 'History of Mysore and Coorg', *Imperial Gazetteer of India, Provincial Series: Mysore and Coorg*, Calcutta: Superintendent of Government Printing, 1908, pp. 175–76.

24 Rao, Shulman and Subrahmanyam, *Textures*, pp. 263–70.

25 Ibid., p. 26.

26 Ibid., p. 28.

27 Ibid., p. 29.

28 Ibid., p. 48.

29   Ibid., p. 33.
30   Ibid., p. 80.
31   Ibid., pp. 73–79.
32   Ibid., p. 56.
33   Ibid., p. 60.
34   Ibid., pp. 29–30.
35   Ibid., p. 33.
36   Ibid., p. 53.
37   Ibid., p. 35.
38   V. K. Bawa, *The Last Nizam: The Life & Times of Mir Osman Ali Khan*, Hyderabad: Centre for Deccan Studies, 2010, pp. 15–16.
39   Talbot, *Precolonial India*, p. 41, citing the scholar Parabrahma Sastry.
40   Wheeler, *Annals*, pp. 171–72.
41   Thomas Mullen Jr., in 'Battle of Wandiwash', accessed from <http://www.historynet.com/?s=battle+of+wandiwash>, based on his original article in the February 1994 issue of *Military History*.
42   Orme, Vol. 2, p. 678; Bayly, *Saints, Goddesses and Kings*, p. 194.

CHAPTER 3
1   Chopra, Ravindran and Subrahmanian, *History of South India*, pp. 203–25.
2   Excerpt from *Quarterly Review*, May 1818, quoted in Hill, *Yusuf Khan*, p. 305.
3   Ibid., p. 3.
4   Ibid., p. 37.
5   Bayly, *Saints, Goddesses and Kings*, pp. 195–96.
6   Ibid., pp. 195–96.
7   Hill, *Yusuf Khan*, p. 232.
8   Ibid., p. 52.
9   'Kallar', 'Marava' and 'Thevar' are names for associated pastoral/warrior clans or sub–castes prominent in the southern Tamil country, often allied and at other times rivals.
10   Ibid., p. 59.
11   Ibid., p. 72.
12   Ibid., p. 75.
13   Ibid., p. 88.
14   Ibid., p. 95.
15   Ibid., p. 100.
16   Ibid., p. 35.
17   Ibid., p.101
18   Ibid., p. 101.
19   Bayly, *Saints, Goddesses and Kings*, p. 196.
20   Hill, *Yusuf Khan*, p. 114.
21   Ibid., p. 112
22   Ibid., p. 113.
23   Ibid., p. 138.
24   Ibid., p. 132; p. 139fn.

25 Ibid., p. 142.
26 Ibid., p. 214, citing Charles Campbell.
27 His first name is not found in the records.
28 Ibid., pp. 218–19.
29 Ibid., p. 219.
30 Ibid., pp. 220–21.
31 Marchand's letter is published as Appendix III (a) in Hill, *Yusuf Khan*, pp. 252–55.
32 Hill, *Yusuf Khan*, pp. 230–31.
33 Ibid., p. 306.
34 Bayly, *Saints, Goddesses and Kings*, p. 193.
35 Hill, *Yusuf Khan*, pp. 232–33.
36 Ibid., p. 232.
37 B. A. Saletore in Irfan Habib, (ed.), *Confronting Colonialism: Resistance and Modernization Under Haidar Ali & Tipu Sultan*, New Delhi: Tulika, 1999, p. 130. Another account claims that Haidar was born in Fort Dodballapur in 1721. Mohibbul Hasan, *History of Tipu Sultan*, Calcutta: The World Press, 1971, p. 2.
38 Mark Wilks and Murray Hammick, *South Indian History from the Earliest Times to the Last Muhammadan Dynasty*, 4 Vols., 1817; New Delhi: Cosmo, 1980, Vol. 4, p. 754, (repr).
39 Spelt variously (delavoy, dalawai etc.), the dalavai usually directed the ruler's army as (or through) a commander-in-chief and at times acted as the regent.
40 Hasan, *History of Tipu Sultan*, p. 3.
41 N. K. Narasimha Murthy, *Purniah*, Bangalore: R. Purniah, 1974, p. 15.
42 Francis Hamilton (Buchanan), *A Journey from Madras Through the Countries of Mysore, Canara, and Malabar*, London: T. Cadell and W. Davies, 1807, 3 Vols.; New Delhi & Madras: Asian Educational Services, 1999, Vol. 1, p. 55, (repr).
43 All quotes from Wilks, *South Indian History*, Vol. 4, pp. 754–60.
44 Burton Stein, *Thomas Munro: The Origins of the Colonial State and His Vision of Empire*, Delhi: Oxford University Press, 1989, pp. 20–21.
45 M. M. D. L. T. (Maistre de la Tour), *The History of Hyder Shah, Alias Hyder Ali Kan Bahadur*, London, 1784; Calcutta, 1848.
46 Wilks, Vol. 4, pp. 303–04.
47 Named after the doctrines of Madhvacharya, the thirteenth–century philosopher from Karnataka, who was born near Udupi.
48 Narasimha Murthy, *Purniah*, Bangalore, 1976, p. 18.
49 Burton Stein, *Thomas Munro*, p. 268. However, Francis Hamilton (Buchanan), who travelled to Srirangapatna and places around it in 1800, wrote of Purniah: 'His native language is of course Tamul; but he speaks the Karnataca, the Mussulman, the Marattah, and I believe the Persian.' See Buchanan, Vol. 1, p. 60.
50 Communication to author from Rajeev Purnaiya, 20 January 2016.
51 Murthy, *Purniah*, pp. 20–22.
52 Pearson, *Memoirs of Reverend Swartz*, p. 283.

53   Ibid., p. 233.
54   Ibid., pp. 309–10.
55   Ibid., pp. 313–14.
56   Ibid., pp. 316–17.
57   Ibid., p. 353.
58   Murthy, *Purniah*, Bangalore, 1976, p. 28, citing Wilks.
59   Ibid., p. 28.
60   Ibid., pp. 34–35. The author cites Wilks for the assertion that Purniah 'suggested the arrangement' of concealing Haidar's death.
61   Hasan, *History of Tipu Sultan*, p. 25.
62   Victor over the French in the 1760 Battle of Wandiwash and thereafter an MP in England, Coote was back in Madras at the head of the Company's army.
63   Hasan, *History of Tipu Sultan*, p. 25.
64   Handwritten notings by Rennell in Ram Chandra Rao 'Punganiri', *Memoirs of Hyder and Tippoo: Rulers of Seringapatam*, C. P. Brown, (trans.), Madras: Simkins, 1849, Vol. 4, pp. 59–60. Accessed at Yale University.
65   Richard Cavendish in *History Today*, Vol. 49, 5 May 1999. <http://www.historytoday.com/richard–cavendish/>.
66   Hasan, *History of Tipu Sultan*, p. 113, citing Bussy's letter of August 1784.
67   Ibid., p. 114.
68   Ibid., citing letters from de Souillac in September and November 1785.
69   Ibid., pp. 61–62.
70   Ibid., p. 55, citing description in letter in February 1790 from the Company's agent to Raja Rama Varma.
71   Ibid., p. 153, citing Panikkar, *Malabar and the Dutch*, p. 159.
72   Ibid., p. 167.
73   Quoted in Burton Stein, *Thomas Munro*, pp. 20–21.
74   On 25 July in Bomma Samudram, not far from Chikballapur, Buchanan, *A Journey*, Vol. 1, pp. 390–91.
75   Hasan, *History of Tipu Sultan*, p. 199.
76   See 'The Seringapatnam Times', accessed from <https://toshkhana.wordpress.com/?s=Goddess+and>. Evidently Mysuru's scholar Sheik Ali, too, has published the correspondence.
77   Description in Jackson, *Tyagaraja*, p. 88.
78   See 'The Tiger and the Thistle', accessed from <http://www.tigerandthistle.net/tipu321.htm>.
79   Burton Stein, *Thomas Munro*, pp. 20–21.
80   Joseph Michaud, *History of Mysore under Hyder Ali and Tippoo Sultan*, V. K. Raman Menon, (trans.), Madras: 1924; New Delhi: Asian Educational Service, 1985, p. 144, (repr).
81   Ibid., pp. 146–47.
82   Hasan, *History of Tipu Sultan*, p. 287, citing Martin, *Wellesley's Despatches*.
83   Ibid., p. 286.
84   John Gurwood, (comp.), *Dispatches of the Duke of Wellington*, Vol. 1, London: John Murray, 1834, p. 7.

85 Napoleon's letter to the Directory is quoted in Iradj Amini, *Napoleon and Persia: Franco–Persian relations under the First Empire*, Richmond, Surrey, UK: Curzon 1999, p. 12. Amini citing from Vicomte de Barras's *Memoires*, Paris, 1859, p. 11.

86 Napoleon's remark quoted in Amini, *Napoleon and Persia*, p. 12. Amini citing from *Memoires* of the future Duchess of Abrantes, who was friendly to both Napoleon and Macron, pp. 331–32.

87 Talleyrand's letter is quoted in Amini, *Napoleon and Persia*, p. 12. Amini citing from Lacour–Gayat, *Talleyrand (1754–1838)*, Vol. 1, Paris, 1930, p. 304.

88 John Gurwood, (comp.), *Dispatches of the Duke of Wellington*, Vol. 1, London: John Murray, 1834, p. 8.

89 Bawa, *The Last Nizam*, p. 17.

90 Gurwood, *Dispatches*, p. 8.

91 Hasan, *History of Tipu Sultan*, p. 295.

92 Mia Carter and Barbara Harlow, *Archives of Empire: Volume I. From The East India Company to the Suez Canal*, Durham, NC: University of Duke Press, 2003, p. 183.

93 Alexander Beatson, *A View of the Origin and Conduct of the War with the Late Tippoo Sultaun*, London, 1800, p. 170.

94 Richard Cavendish in *History Today*, Vol. 49, 5 May 1999, accessed from <http://www.historytoday.com/richard–cavendish/>.

95 Lewin B. Bowring, *Haidar Ali and Tipu Sultan, and the Struggle with the Musalman Powers of the South*, Delhi: Idarah–I–Adabiyat, 1974, pp. 84–85. As stated by Wikipedia <https://en.wikipedia.org/wiki/Arthur_Wellesley,_1st_Duke_of_Wellington>.

96 See 'The Tiger and the Thistle', accessed from <http://www.tigerandthistle. net/tipu329.htm>.

97 Ibid, accessed from <http://www.tigerandthistle.net/tipu327.htm>.

98 Ibid, accessed from <http://www.tigerandthistle.net/tipu327.htm>.

99 Ibid, accessed from <http://www.tigerandthistle.net/tipu330.htm>.

100 Richard Cavendish in *History Today*, Vol. 49, 5 May 1999, accessed from <http://www.historytoday.com/richard–cavendish/>.

101 See 'The Tiger and the Thistle', accessed from <http://www.tigerandthistle. net/tipu336.htm>.

102 Hasan, *History of Tipu Sultan*, p. 301fn, citing Archives du Ministere des Affaires Etrangeres, Vol. 2, 1785–1826, ff. 270a–73b.

103 Burton Stein, *Thomas Munro*, pp. 20–21.

104 Beauchamp's introduction in Abbé Dubois, *Hindu Manners, Customs and Ceremonies*, London, 1816; Oxford, 1953, p. xi.

105 Murthy, *Purniah*, p. 37.

106 Wilks quoted in Murthy, *Purniah*, p. 87.

CHAPTER 4

1   Chopra, Ravindran and Subrahmanian, *History of South India*, p. 121.

2   Ibid., p. 121.

3   P. Anima, 'Trailing Pazhassi Raja to his death', *The Hindu*, 5 April 2013 <http://www.thehindu.com/features/friday–review/history–and–culture/ trailing–pazhassi–raja–to–his–death/article4584713.ece>.

4   Ibid.

5   Chopra, Ravindran and Subrahmanian, *History of South India*, Vol. 3, p. 127.

6   Bishop R. Caldwell, *A History of Tinnevelly*, 1881; New Delhi: Asian Educational Services, 1982, (repr).

7   Ibid., p. 58.

8   Colonel Fullarton quoted in Caldwell, *Tinnevelly*, p. 211.

9   Chopra, Ravindran and Subrahmanian, *History of South India*, Vol. 3, p. 125.

10   Ibid.

11   See 'Index of Maruthupandiyar', accessed from <http://www.sivagangaiseemai. com/maruthupandiyar/maruthu–pandiyar–history5.html> and Chopra, Ravindran and Subrahmanian, *History of South India*, Vol. 3, p. 125.

12   Chopra, Ravindran and Subrahmanian, *History of South India*, Vol. 3, p. 125.

13   Romesh Chunder Dutt, *The Economic History of India Under Early British Rule*, London: Kegan Paul, 1901; undated Fourth edition, pp. 131–32.

14   Ibid., pp. 99–100.

15   Hamilton (Buchanan), *A Journey from Madras*.

16   P. Chinnian, *Vellore Mutiny, 1806: The First Uprising Against the British*, Madras: by the author, 1982, p. 109.

17   Vithal Rajan, 'Invisible Invincibility', *Economic and Political Weekly*, 6 September 2014, Vol. 49 No. 36.

18   John Blakiston, *Twelve Years' Military Adventure in Three Quarters of the Globe*, London: Henry Colburn, 1829, Vol. 1, p. 304.

19   Chinnian, *Vellore Mutiny*, p. 114.

20   See article by S. Anand in *Outlook*, July 1906, <http://www.outlookindia. com/magazine/story/july–1806–vellore/231918>.

21   Blakiston, *Twelve Years' Military Adventure*, p. 295.

22   Chinnian, *Vellore Mutiny*, p. 111.

23   Vithal Rajan in *Economic and Political Weekly*, 6 September 2014.

24   Abbé J. A. Dubois, *Hindu Manners*, p. xi.

25   Ibid., p. xii.

26   Ibid.

27   Vijaya Ramaswamy, 'The Genesis and Historical Role of the Master Weavers in South Indian Textile Production', *Journal of the Economic and Social History of the Orient*, Vol. 28, No. 3, 1985, pp. 322–25. Ramaswamy cites *Guide to the Salem District Records*, Vol. 3172, 17 September 1819.

CHAPTER 5

1   C. R. Yaravintelimath, (ed.), *Vacanas of Sri Basaveswara*, P. G. Halakatti, (trans.), Bijapur: BLDE Association, 2003, p. ix.

2   Verses 5, 16, 38, and 42 contained in Yaravintelimath, (ed.), *Vacanas of Sri*

Basaveswara, Slightly edited versions.

3   Abbé Dubois, *Hindu Manners*, pp. 274–75fn.

4   Ibid.

5   G. U. Pope, *The Sacred Kurral of Tiruvalluva-Nayanar*, Oxford, 1886; Asian Educational Service, 1980, (repr).

6   Ibid., p. vfn.

7   See <http://www.oocities.org/nvkashraf/kur–trans/Tel–Int.htm>.

8   Pope, *Sacred Kurral*, p. iv.

9   Ibid., p. ii.

10   Ibid., p. vi.

11   Ibid., p. xv.

12   Back-cover blurbs for V. R. Narla, *Vemana*, Hyderabad: Vemana Foundation, 2006; first published in 1969, New Delhi: Sahitya Akademi, and V. R. Narla, *Vemana Through Western Eyes*, Hyderabad: Vemana Foundation, 2006; first published in 1969, New Delhi: Sahitya Akademi; Narla, *Vemana*, p. 3.

13   Ibid., p. 5.

14   C. P. Brown, (trans.), 'Verses of Vemana', accessed from Sacred Texts <http://sacred–texts.com/hin/vov/vov01.htm>.

15   Narla, *Vemana*, p. 5.

16   Ibid., pp. 9–10.

17   This chapter contains lightly edited versions of Narla's translations.

18   Jyotsna Kamat, 'History of Kannada Literature', accessed from <http://www.kamat.com/kalranga/kar/literature/poet_sarvajna.htm>.

19   Ibid., Kamat's translation slightly edited.

20   See 'Purandara Dasa', *Wikipedia*, <https://en.wikipedia.org/wiki/Purandara_Dasa>. The source cites M. K. V. Narayan, *Lyrical Musings on Indic Culture: A Sociology Study of Songs of Sant Purandara Dasa*, 2010, Read Worthy Publications Private Limited, p. 11.

21   Cited in William J. Jackson, *Tyagaraja: Life and Lyrics*, New Delhi: Oxford University Press, 1991, pp. 38–39.

22   Ibid., p. 46.

23   Ibid., p. 89, citing Brown, *The Wars of the Rajas*, Madras: Christian Knowledge Society Press, p. 67.

24   Ibid., p. 100, citing K. V. Sastri, *Thyagaraja Keertanalu*, Rajahmundry, 1948.

25   Ibid., p. 61, quoting S. V. Ramamurti, *The Hindu*, 4 October 1941.

26   P. Sambamoorthy, *Great Composers*, Chennai: Indian Music Publishing House, 2010, Book 1, p. 9.

27   Ibid., p. 7.

28   Jackson, *Tyagaraja*, p. 94.

29   Sambamoorthy, *Great Composers*, Chennai: Indian Music Publishing House, 2010, Book 1, p. 69.

30   Ibid., p. 79.

31   Sambamoorthy, *Great Composers*, p. 79.

32   Ibid., p. 82.

33   Ibid., p. 123.

34   Ibid., pp. 150–51.

35   Satish Kamath, *The Hindu*, 6 June 2006.

CHAPTER 6

1   C. H. Philips, *The East India Company, 1784–1834*, Manchester, UK: Manchester University Press, 1968, p. 299.
2   Henry Dodwell, *The Nabobs of Madras*, London: Williams and Norgate, 1926, p. 239.
3   David Blake, 'Colin Mackenzie: Collector Extraordinary', a 1991 article in the *British Library Journal*. Accessed from <http://www.bl.uk/eblj/1991articles/pdf/article10.pdf>.
4   See Rama Sundari Mantena, *Origins of Modern Historiography in India: Antiquarianism and Philology, 1780–1880*, New York: Palgrave Macmillan, 2012, pp. 125–28.
5   S. Muthiah, *The Hindu*, 15 June 2009 <www.thehindu.com/todays–paper/tp–features/tp–metroplus/article640362.ece>.
6   Ibid.
7   David Blake, 'Colin Mackenzie: Collector Extraordinary'.
8   Rama Sundari Mantena, *Origins of Modern Historiography in India: Antiquarianism and Philology, 1780–1880*, New York: Palgrave Macmillan, 2012, pp. 110–17.
9   Quoted in Ibid., p. 114.
10   David Blake, 'Colin Mackenzie: Collector Extraordinary'.
11   See 'William Jones', accessed from <https://en.wikipedia.org/wiki/William_Jones_%28philologist%29>.
12   Thomas Trautmann, *Languages and Nations: The Dravidian Proof in Colonial Madras*, New Delhi: Yoda Press, 2006, p. 152.
13   Ibid., p. 76.
14   Ibid., p. 2. See also Rama Sundari Mantena, 'Excavations of British and Indian Intellectual Traditions in Thomas R. Trautmann's *Languages and Nations*' in Cynthia Talbot, (ed.), *Knowing India: Colonial and Modern Constructions of the Past*, New Delhi: Yoda Press, 2011, pp. 394–99.
15   Burton Stein, *Thomas Munro: The Origins of the Colonial State and His Vision of Empire*, Delhi: Oxford University Press, 1989, pp. 74–75.
16   Ibid., p. 88.
17   Ibid., p. 90.
18   C. H. Philips in *The East India Company, 1784–1834*, Manchester: Manchester University Press, p. 304.
19   Burton Stein, *Thomas Munro*, p. 119.
20   Muthiah, *Madras Discovered*, p. 113.
21   Burton Stein, *Thomas Munro*, pp. 291–93.
22   Professor A. R. Ramachandra Reddy during a conversation with the author in Tirupati, 21 January 2017.
23   Charles Philip Brown, *Cyclic Tables of Hindu and Mahomedan Chronology Regarding the History of the Telugu and Kannadi Countries* (Madras: Christian Knowledge Society's Press, 1850); New Delhi: Asian Educational Services, 1994, p. i, (repr).

24 Ibid., p. i.
25 Ibid., p. ii.
26 Ibid., p. iii.
27 G. N. Reddy and Bangorey, (eds.), *Literary Autobiography of C. P. Brown,* Tirupati. Sri Venkateswara University, 1978.
28 Brown, *Cyclic Tables,* p. iii.
29 Caldwell, *Tinnevelly,* pp. 83–97, (repr).
30 Reddy and Bangorey, *C. P. Brown,* pp. 69–77.
31 Blackburn, *Print, Folklore, and Nationalism,* p. 76.
32 Ibid.
33 Chopra, Ravindran and Subrahmanian, *History of South India,* p. 210.
34 Trautmnn, *Languages and Nations,* pp. 74–75.
35 Report on the Medical Topography and Statistics of the Southern Division of the Madras Army, compiled from the records of the Medical Board Office, Madras, 1943. See <http://discovery.nationalarchives.gov.uk/details/rd/4124a368–cbe1–4444–adba–8d190f43cd9c>.

CHAPTER 7

1 Sadashiva Wodeyar, *Rani Chennamma,* New Delhi: National Book Trust, 1977.
2 B. Sheik Ali, 'History of Karnataka from 1600 AD', in H. M. Nayak and B. R. Gopal, (eds.), *South Indian Studies,* Mysore: Geetha Book House, 1990, p. 157.
3 Ibid., p. 155.
4 Much of this information is from S. Muthiah, (ed.), *Madras: Its Yesterdays, Todays and Tomorrows,* Madras: Affiliated East–West, 1990.
5 These comments on the anicuts are drawn from Thangellapalli Vijaya Kumar, 'Irrigation Policies and the Anicuts in Andhra' in Adapa Satyanarayana, (ed.), *Early Modern Andhra, Hyderabad, and Company Rule: AD 1724–1857 (Comprehensive History and Culture of Andhra Pradesh,* Vol. 6, Hyderabad: Emesco, 2016, pp. 132–45.
6 B. Sobhanan, *Dewan Velu Thampi and the British,* Trivandrum: Kerala Historical Society, 1978, p. 8.
7 Ibid., p. 81, citing Company documents.
8 Ibid., pp. 83–84.
9 Ibid., p. 114.
10 Chopra, Ravindran and Subrahmanian, *History of South India,* p. 223.
11 Ibid., Vol. 3, p. 225.
12 Ibid., Vol. 3, p. 213.
13 Ibid., Vol. 3, p. 214.
14 Evidence tendered by O'Malley in 1924 to a commission in Madras. See Chopra, Ravindran and Subrahmanian, *History of South India,* Vol. 3, p. 214.
15 Malcolm's letter to his wife in Henry George Briggs, *The Nizam: His History and Relations with the British Government,* Vol. 2, First Published 1861; Delhi: Manas Publications, 1985, p. 71, (repr).

16 J. D. E. Gribble, *History of the Deccan*, Delhi: Mittal, 1990, pp. 179–80, (repr).

17 Davidson quoted in Henry George Briggs, *The Nizam: His History and Relations with the British Government*, p. 88fn.

18 Briggs, *The Nizam*, p. 86.

19 V. D. Divekar, *South India in 1857 War of Independence*, Pune: Lokmanya Tilak Smarak Trust, 1993, pp. 108–11.

20 Briggs, *The Nizam*, p. 87.

21 Henry George Briggs, *The Nizam: His History and Relations with the British Government*, First published 1861; Delhi: Manas Publications, 1985, (repr).

22 Briggs, *The Nizam*, citing Colonel Montgomerie of the Madras Horse Artillery, p. 86.

23 Hastings Fraser, *Our Faithful Ally: The Nizam*, First Published 1865; New Delhi: Modern Publishers, 1985, p. 288, (repr).

24 Fraser, *Our Faithful Ally*, pp. 289–90.

25 Ibid., pp. 289–91.

26 Quoted in Divekar, *South India*, pp. ix–xi.

27 Divekar, *South India*, pp. 135–39.

28 Ibid., pp. 237–41, citing Meadows Taylor, *The Story of my Life*, pp. 317–18.

29 Ibid., pp. 251–71.

30 Ibid., pp. 327–29.

31 Ibid., pp. 272–84.

32 Ibid., p. 274.

33 Cecil Woodham–Smith, *Queen Victoria: From her Birth to the Death of the Prince Consort*, New York: Knopf, 1972, p. 385.

34 William Howard Russell, *My Diary in India, in the year 1858–59*, London: Routledge, Warne, and Routledge, 1860, p. 181.

35 Quoted in Christopher Hibbert, *The Great Mutiny: India 1857*, London: Penguin, 1980, pp. 389–91.

36 Divekar, *South India*, p. 35.

37 B. Sheik Ali, 'History of Karnataka from 1600 AD', in H. M. Nayak and B. R. Gopal, (eds.), *South Indian Studies*, pp. 158–59.

38 This account of Salar Jung is largely drawn from the article by H. Rajendra Prasad, 'Awakening in Hyderabad State: Salar Jung Reforms', in B. Kesava Narayana, (ed.), *Modern Andhra and Hyderabad: AD 1858–1956 (Comprehensive History and Culture of Andhra Pradesh*, Vol. 7, Hyderabad: Emesco, 2016, pp. 35–54.

39 The scholar A. R. Venkatachalapathy to the author in Chennai, 30 January 2017.

40 Robert L. Hardgrave Jr, *The Nadars of Tamilnad: The Political Culture of a Community in Change*, Berkeley: University of California Press, 1969, p. 26, citing Caldwell, *Lectures on the Tinnevelly Mission*, pp. 31–32.

41 Ibid., p. 26, citing Caldwell, *Lectures on the Tinnevelly Mission*, pp. 34–35.

42 Ibid., p. 57.

43 Ibid., pp. 61–64.

44 Ibid., p. 64, citing Caldwell's letter of 5 February 1859 to Rev. Whitehouse of Nagercoil.
45 Ibid., pp. 65–70.

CHAPTER 8
1   'The Recent Durbar at Delhi', a 1903 article on the Delhi durbar of that year, published on pp. 281–86 of the American journal, *Current Opinion*, Vol. 34, offers first-hand descriptions also of the 1877 Durbar.
2   Medal displayed in the museum at Fort St George, Chennai.
3   Cited in Julie Codell, 'On the Delhi Coronation Durbars, 1877, 1903, 1911', accessed on 24 May 2017.
4   'The Durbar of 1877: A Collision of Classes and Cultures', accessed from <http://www.ago.net/the–durbar–of–1877–douglas–peers>.
5   See 'The Lucile Project', accessed from <http://sdrc.lib.uiowa.edu/lucile/index.html>.
6   *Current Opinion*, Vol. 34, p. 281.
7   'Willoughby Wallace Hooper' on Google.
8   William Digby, *The Famine Campaign in Southern India, 1876–1878*, Vol. 1, London: Longmans, Green, and Co, 1878.
9   These theories are acknowledged in the official *Report of the Indian Famine Commission*, London: Her Majesty's Stationery Office, 1880, prepared by R. Strachey and others.
10 Report of the Indian Famine Commission, p. 31.
11 Ibid., pp. 33–34.
12 Kamil Zvelebil, *Tamil Literature*, Otto Harrassowitz Verlag, 1974, pp. 218; Retrieved 1 January 2013, David Shulman, *Tamil: A Biography*, Cambridge, Mass.: Harvard University Press, 2016 writes on pp. 352–53 of a 'pioneering modernist work', ca. 1899, by Villiyappa Pillai, *A Letter about Famine, in Good Grammar and Meter, by God*, calling it 'a bitter realistic parody'.
13 Letter of 9 January 1883 in S. R. Mehrotra, *The Emergence of the Indian National Congress*, New Delhi: Vikas, 1971, p. 306.
14 Mehrotra, *Emergence*, p. 342.
15 Ibid., p. 344.
16 Letter of 26 March 1883 to W. E. Forster in Mehrotra, *Emergence*, p. 345.
17 Mehrotra, *Emergence*, p. 376.
18 Quoted in Mehrotra, *Emergence*, pp. 354–55.
19 *The Bengalee*, 27 May 1882, quoted in Mehrotra, *Emergence*, p. 318.
20 Mehrotra, *Emergence*, p. 389.
21 Ibid, p. 382.
22 Karthik A. Bhatt, *Madras Musings*, Vol. 21, No. 7, 16–31 July 2011.
23 Mehrotra, *Emergence*, p. 411, p. 415.
24 Ibid., p. 413, p. 417.
25 Ibid., p. 417.
26 Ibid., pp. 419–20.
27 Karthik A. Bhatt, *Madras Musings*, Vol. 21, No. 7.
28 Eugene F. Irschick, *Politics and Social Conflict in South India: The Non–*

Brahman Movement and Tamil Separatism, 1916–1929, Berkeley: University of California Press, 1969, p. 23.

29   Dhananjay Keer, *Mahatma Jotirao Phooley: Father of the Indian Social Revolution*, Bombay: Popular Prakashan, 1964, pp. 219–21.

30   G. Arunima, 'Glimpses from a Writer's World: O. Chandu Menon, His Contemporaries, and Their Times', *Studies in History*, 2004, Vol. 20, pp. 189–214; DOI: 10.1177/025764300402000202

31   Gurujada Apparao, *Girls for Sale: Kanyasulkam, A Play from Colonial India*, Velcheru Narayana Rao, (trans.), Bloomington, IN: Indiana University Press, 2007, p. 168.

32   Pennepalli Gopala Krishna, (ed.), *Diaries of Gurujada*, Hyderabad: Oriental Manuscripts Library and Research Institute, 2009, p. xvi.

33   'Some critics claim that no drama can surpass the popularity of *Kanyasulkam* in the last 100 years', foreword by Jayadhir Tirumala Rao in Gopala Krishna, (ed.), *Diaries of Gurujada*, p. vi.

34   Gurujada Apparao, *Girls for Sale: Kanyasulkam, A Play from Colonial India*, Velcheru Narayana Rao, (trans.), p. xi.

35   John Greenfield Leonard, *Kandukuri Viresalingam*, Hyderabad: Telugu University, 1991, p. 49.

36   V. R. Narla, *Veeresalingam*, New Delhi: Sahitya Akademi, 1968, p. 15.

37   Narla, *Viresalingam*, pp. 15–16.

38   Ibid., p. 81.

39   Ibid., p. 30, p. 49.

40   Leonard, *Kandukuri Viresalingam*, pp. 113–14.

41   Ibid., p. 4.

42   Kenneth W. Jones, (ed.), *Religious Controversy in British India: Dialogues in South Asian Languages*, Albany, NY: SUNY, 1992, p. 163.

43   *The Hindu*, 15 & 21 April, 1911, quoted in Leonard, *Kandukuri Viresalingam*, p. 264.

44   Narla, *Viresalingam*, p. 70.

45   Ibid., p. 65.

46   Ibid., p. 11.

47   Ibid., p. 80.

48   K. Swaminathan quoted by V. Sundaram on <http://www.boloji.com>; retrieved 4 June 2017.

49   David Shulman, *Tamil: A Biography*, Cambridge, Mass: Harvard University Press, 2016, p. 287.

50   Ibid., p. 306.

51   Nelson's *Madura Country* quoted in Irschick, *Politics and Social Conflict in South India*, pp. 11–12.

52   Irschick, *Politics and Social Conflict in South India*, p. 20.

53   Ibid., p. 281, citing Governor Grant-Duff, *An Address Delivered to the Graduates of the University of Madras on 25 March, 1886*, Madras, 1886.

54   Ibid., p. 20, citing unpublished 1966 dissertation by Ramanathan Suntharalingam.

55   CR quoted in Prabha Ravi Shankar, *G. A. Natesan and National Awakening*,

New Delhi: Promilla, 2015.

56 Prabha Ravi Shankar, *G. A. Natesan and National Awakening*.
57 B. Kesava Narayana, (ed.), *Modern Andhra and Hyderabad: AD 1858–1956*, Hyderabad: Emesco, 2016, pp. 890–92.
58 Chopra, Ravindran and Subrahmanian, *History of South India*, p. 207.
59 James Forbes, *Oriental Memoirs: A Narrative of Seventeen Years' Residence in India*, London: R. Bentley, 1834, Vol. 1, pp. 253–54.
60 Muni Prasad, *Narayana Guru: Complete Works*, New Delhi: National Book Trust, 2006, p. xi.
61 E.g. Robin Jeffrey, *Decline of Nayar Dominance: Society and Politics in Travancore, 1847–1908*, New York: Holmes and Meier, 1976, p. 208.
62 Muni Narayana Prasad (trans. and comp.), *Narayana Guru: Complete Works*, New Delhi: National Book Trust, 2006, p. xiii; Vijayalayam Jayakumar, *Sree Narayana Guru: A Critical Study*, K. Sadanandan, (trans.), New Delhi: D. K. Printworld, 1999, p. 49, citing Kumaran Asan's biography of Sree Narayana Guru Swamy, p. 2; also Robin Jeffrey, *Decline of Nayar Dominance*, p. 208.
63 Muni Narayana Prasad, *Narayana Guru*, p. xvi; Jayakumar, p. 63, citing M. K. Kumaran, *Indian Renaissance*, p. 317.
64 Muni Prasad, (trans.), in Prasad, *Narayana Guru*, verse 34, p. 34.
65 Robin Jeffrey, *Decline of Nayar Dominance: Society and Politics in Travancore, 1847–1908*, New York: Holmes and Meier, 1976, p. 209, citing a report of the London Missionary Society.
66 Muni Prasad, *Narayana Guru*, p. xvi.
67 Jayakumar, *Sree Narayana Guru*, p. 103; also Muni Prasad's prologue in this book, p. x.
68 P. N. Chopra, T. K. Ravindran and N. Subrahmanian, *History of South India*, New Delhi: S. Chand, 1979, Vol. 3, p. 219.
69 Most accounts state this.
70 Muni Prasad, *Narayana Guru*, p. xvii.
71 Chopra, Ravindran and Subrahmanian, *History of South India*, p. 220.
72 Ibid.
73 Jayakumar, *Sree Narayana Guru*, p. 68, citing Mannath Padmanabhan, *Narayana Guru*, p. 337.
74 See Muni Prasad, *Narayana Guru*, p. xi and p. xvii, and Prasad's prologue in Jayakumar, *Sree Narayana Guru*, pp. vii–viii.
75 Chopra, Ravindran and Subrahmanian, *History of South India*, p. 245.
76 Jayakumar, *Sree Narayana Guru*, p. xii & p. 75.
77 These lines about Father Chavara are based on Manjula Scaria and Binoy Joseph, 'The Legacy of Kuriakose Elias Chavara as a Social Reformer', *International Journal of Scientific and Research Publications*, Vol. 5, No. 7, July 2015, and the Wikipedia entry on him.

CHAPTER 9

1 J. Parthasarathi, 'The Modern Rediscovery of the Glories of Tamil Literature and Language', in R. Balasubramanian, (ed.), *The Life–world of the Tamils: Past and Present – II*, New Delhi: Centre for Studies in Civilizations, 2009,

pp. 496–99.

2   R. N. Sampath and Pe Su Mani, *V.O. Chidambaram Pillai*, New Delhi: Publications Division, 1992, p. 53.

3   Sampath and Mani, *V.O. Chidambaram Pillai*, p. 75.

4   'The Ashe Murder Case' by 'A special correspondent', *Madras Musings*, Vol. 19, No. 8, Aug. 1–15, 2009. See also C. A. Perumal, 'The Political, Social, and Economic Scenario in Tamil Nadu from A.D. 1900', in R. Balasubramanian, (ed.), *The Life–world of the Tamils: Past and Present – II*, New Delhi: Centre for Studies in Civilizations, 2009, p. 665.

5   Mohan Lal, (ed.), *Encyclopaedia of Indian Literature*, Vol. 5, New Delhi: Sahitya Akademi, 1992, pp. 4190–92.

6   A. R. Venkatachalapathy, *In Those Days There Was No Coffee: Writings in Cultural History*, New Delhi: Yoda Press, pp. 47–49.

7   Irschick, *Politics and Conflict in South India*, p. 285.

8   Mohan Lal, (ed.), *Encyclopaedia of Indian Literature*, Vol. 5, pp. 4190–92.

9   *The Hindu*, 22 September 1916, cited in 'Tagore and Bharati', by A. R. Venkatachalapathy, *Seminar* # 623 (on Tagore), July 2011.

10   Mohan Lal, (ed.), *Encyclopaedia of Indian Literature*, Vol. 5, pp. 4190–92.

11   S. Vijaya Bharati, carried on her blogpost <http://subramaniabharati.com/2012/12/20/translation–or–travesty>.

12   Irschick, *Politics and Social Conflict in South India*, pp. 16–19, citing from the Census of 1921.

13   Ibid., pp. 48–49.

14   Robert Hardgrave Jr, *Essays in the Political Sociology of South India*, New Delhi: Usha Publications, 1979, p. 16.

15   Irschick, *Politics and Social Conflict in South India*, p. 75.

16   Ibid., p. 63.

17   Quotes from Montagu, *The Times* and *The Madras Mail* are in Irschick, *Politics and Social Conflict in South India*, pp. 53–63.

18   *The Hindu*, 14 September 1917; Irschick, *Politics and Social Conflict in South India*, p. 60.

19   Edwin S. Montagu, *An Indian Diary*, London: Heinemann, 1930, p. 136.

20   Montagu, *Indian Diary*, p. 126.

21   P. Krishnamoorthy, 'Formation of Andhra State', in B. Kesava Narayana, (ed.), *Modern Andhra and Hyderabad: AD 1858–1956 (Comprehensive History and Culture of Andhra Pradesh*, Vol. 7, Hyderabad: Emesco, 2016, p. 542.

22   Ibid., p. 546.

23   See *Modern Andhra and Hyderabad*, pp. 538–57.

24   Mahadev Desai, *Day–to–day with Gandhi*, Varanasi: Sarva Seva Sangh, Vol. 1, pp. 298–99.

25   C. Rajagopalachari, 'M. K. Gandhi: His Message to India', *Indian Review*, May 1916, in Mahesh Rangarajan, N. Balakrishnan and Deepa Bhatnagar, (eds.), *Selected Works of C. Rajagopalachari*, Vol. 1, New Delhi: Orient BlackSwan, 2014, pp. 34–40.

26   Masti Venkatesa Iyengar in *Rajaji 93*, pp. 113–14.

27   16 February 1916; *Collected Works of Mahatma Gandhi*, Vol. 13, pp. 232–33.

28   Secret File 271 of 1919, Tamil Nadu Archives, Chennai.
29   *The Hindu*, 7 April 1919.
30   Police Commissioner's report of 25 March 1919 in Secret File 222, Tamil Nadu Archives.
31   Leaflet dated 25 March 1919 in Secret File 271 of 1919, Tamil Nadu Archives.
32   Michael O'Dwyer, *India As I Knew It: 1885–1925*, London: Constable, 1925, p. 449.
33   *Secret Punjab Police Abstract of Intelligence*, 12 April 1919, Vol. 41, No. 15, pp. 152–54, quoted in Ayesha Jalal, *Self and Sovereignty*, p. 205.
34   Quoted by Ravinder Kumar, 'Urban Society and Urban Politics: Lahore in 1919', in Indu Banga, (ed.), *Five Punjabi Centuries*, p. 205. See also O'Dwyer, *India As I Knew It*, p. 270.
35   O'Dwyer, *India As I Knew It*, pp. 275–77.
36   Speech in Nadiad, Gujarat, quoted in Mahadev Desai, *Day-to-day with Gandhi*, Vol. 2, p. 67.
37   Desai, *Day-to-day with Gandhi*, Vol.1, pp. 56–7 and p. 182.
38   In Madras, 12 August 1920, and Calicut, 18 August 1920. *Collected Works*, Vol. 18, pp. 144–45, 180.
39   See Desai, *Day-to-day*, Vol. 1, pp. 56–7 and p. 182.
40   *The Hindu*, 11 April 1919.
41   *The Hindu*, 22 August 1919.
42   Devadas Gandhi Papers.
43   *Navajivan*, 18 April 1920; Vol. 17, p. 320.
44   Ibid., 16 May 1920; Vol. 17, p. 415.
45   Quoted in Dhananjay Keer, *Mahatma Gandhi*, Bombay: Popular Prakashan, 1973, p. 324.
46   *Young India*, 4 August 1920; Vol. 18, No. 110–11.
47   Hardgrave Jr, *Essays in the Political Sociology of South India*, p. 20, citing 'India in 1921–22'.
48   Both Government Orders are reproduced in Irschick, *Politics and Social Conflict in South India*, pp. 369–72. Also reproduced there is the 1851 Standing Order to the Board of Revenue from which the wording of these G.O.s was lifted. See also V. K. Narasimhan, *Kamaraj: A Study*, New Delhi: National Book Trust, 2007, p. 14.
49   *The Hindu* of 14 Aug 1919 is cited in Irschick, *Politics and Social Conflict*, p. 69.
50   Letter of 1 February 1921 from Knapp, chief secretary, Madras, to O'Donnell, officiating home secretary, GOI, in File 43 of 1921; and letter of 28 August 1921 from Marjori Banks, chief secretary, Madras, to home secretary, GOI, in File 18 of 1921, Home (Pol.) Deposit, National Archives, New Delhi.
51   Quoted in Afzal Iqbal, *Mohamed Ali*, Delhi: Idarah-i-Adabiyat, 1978, p. 267.
52   Stephen Frederic Dale, *Islamic Society on the South Asian Frontier: The Mappilas of Malabar, 1498–1922*, Oxford: Clarendon Press, 1980, p. 51.
53   Ibid., p. 53.
54   Ibid., p. 85.

55 Ibid., p. 91.
56 Ibid., p. 196.
57 Robert L. Hardgrave Jr., 'The Mappilla Rebellion, 1921', *Modern Asian Studies*, Vol. 11, No. 1, 1977, p. 69.
58 *The Hindu*, 23 February 1921.
59 Hardgrave Jr., 'The Mappilla Rebellion, 1921', *Modern Asian Studies*, p. 94, p. 70.
60 Ibid., p. 78.
61 Ibid., p. 80.
62 Ibid., p. 81.
63 Ibid., p. 81, citing telegram of 27 August 1921 from viceroy to secretary of state.
64 Ibid., p. 86, citing message from viceroy to secretary of state.
65 Dale, *The Mappilas of Malabar*, pp. 204–05, citing R. H. Hitchcock, *A History of the Malabar Rebellion, 1921*, Madras: Government Press, 1925, p. 65.
66 Hardgrave, 'The Mappilla Rebellion', pp. 82–83, citing A. Sreedhara Menon, *Kerala District Gazetteers: Kozhikode*, Trivandrum: Government Press, 1962, p. 181.
67 Letter of 24 October 1921 in Hardgrave Jr., 'The Mappilla Rebellion, 1921', p. 89.
68 Hardgrave, 'The Mappilla Rebellion, 1921', p. 91, citing Sreedhara Menon, *Kozhikode*, p. 182.
69 Ibid., p. 88.
70 Ibid., p. 91.
71 Ibid., pp.89–90, fn127, citing official report.
72 Ibid., p. 92.
73 Ibid., p. 97, 137fn, citing *West Coast Spectator*, Calicut, 22 August 1921, and Gopalan Nair, *Moplah Rebellion*, pp. 117–188.
74 Ibid., pp. 96–97, citing E. M. S. Nambudiripad, *A Short History of the Peasant Movement in Kerala* Bombay: People's Publishing House, 1943, p. 11.
75 See letter of 7 September 1921 from Abdul Rahman of the Kerala Khilafat Committee in Hardgrave, 'The Mappilla Rebellion, 1921', p. 84.
76 Hardgrave, 'The Mappilla Rebellion, 1921', p. 93.
77 *Young India*, 12 January 1922.
78 Subhas Bose, *The Indian Struggle*, Bombay: Asia, 1964, p. 82.
79 Irschick, *Politics and Social Conflict in South India*, pp. 191–92, citing M. C. Rajah, *The Oppressed Hindus*, Madras 1925, p. 64.
80 See Mary Elizabeth King, *Gandhian Nonviolent Struggle and Untouchability in South India: The 1924–25 Vykom Satyagraha and the Mechanisms of Change*, New Delhi: Oxford University Press, 2015.
81 Mary King, *Gandhian Nonviolent Struggle and Untouchability in South India*, p. 168.
82 Ibid., p. 168fn.
83 Ibid., p. 210.
84 Ibid., p. 200, citing Eleanor Zelliot.

85 Ibid., p. 225.
86 P. Krishnamoorthy, 'Rampa Rebellion, 1922–24' in B. Kesava Narayana, (ed.), *Modern Andhra and Hyderabad: AD 1858–1956 (Comprehensive History and Culture of Andhra Pradesh*, Vol. 7, p. 832.
87 Remark in a thesis for Jawaharlal Nehru University accessed on the net in 2017 but later hard to retrieve. The writer of the thesis could not be identified.
88 Letter published in *Young India*, 18 July 1929; Vol. 41, pp. 193–95.
89 P. Krishnamoorthy in Kesava Narayana, (ed.), *Modern Andhra and Hyderabad: AD 1858–1956*, p. 832.
90 Ibid., p. 836.
91 Much of this account of Sitarama Raju is taken from P. Krishnamoorthy, 'Rampa Rebellion, 1922–24', pp. 829–41 and V. Lalitha, 'Tribes in Andhra Pradesh: Koyas', pp. 785–95, in B. Kesava Narayana, (ed.), *Modern Andhra and Hyderabad: AD 1858–1956 (Comprehensive History and Culture of Andhra Pradesh*, Vol. 7.

CHAPTER 10

1 Irschick, *Politics and Social Conflict in South India*, pp. 269–72.
2 Venkatachalapathy, *There Was No Coffee*, p. 116.
3 Letter of 6 February 1926 to Mahadev Desai, Rajagopalachari Papers, NMML, New Delhi.
4 Letter SN 13274 of 4 October 1926, Gandhi Sangrahalaya, Rajghat, Delhi.
5 On or before 25 September 1927. See *Collected Works*, Vol. 35, p. 32.
6 *Kudi Arasu*, 12 June 1927. Cited in McDermott, Gordon, Embree, Pritchett, and Dalton, (eds.), *Sources of Indian Traditions*, Third edition, Vol. 2, New York: Columbia, 2014, p. 431.
7 Postscript to 'Simplified Marriage', a short story, in Ashram File 'Press: 1929–31', Rajagopalachari Papers.
8 Note by Chief Secretary Charles Cotton on Thorne's letter of 3 April 1930, USS File 687 of 1930, Tamil Nadu Archives.
9 Thorne to Cotton, 3 April 1930, USS File 687 of 1930, TNA.
10 V. K. Narasimhan, *Kamaraj: A Study*, New Delhi: National Book Trust, 2007, p. 9.
11 USS File 687 of 1930, TNA.
12 Confidential Report on the Civil Disobedience Movement (Madras) 1930–31, quoted in B. S. Baliga, *Tanjore District Handbook*, Government of Madras, 1957.
13 C. A. Perumal, 'The Political, Social, and Economic Scenario in Tamil Nadu from A.D. 1900', in R. Balasubramanian, (ed.), *The Life–world of the Tamils: Past and Present – II*, New Delhi: Centre for Studies in Civilizations, 2009, p. 669.
14 Quoted by Vinay Lal, *Indian Express*, 25 October 2015.
15 Kamaladevi Chattopadhay, *Inner Recesses, Outer Spaces: Memoirs*, New Delhi: Navrang, 1986, pp. 6–7.
16 Ibid., pp. 48–49.
17 Ibid., p. 116.

18   Evidently used in the fifteenth century by one of Gandhi's favourite poets, Narsi Mehta, the term 'Harijan' was recommended by one of Gandhi's 'untouchable' acquaintances.

19   *Collected Works*, Vol. 51, pp. 139.

20   Letters of 17 and 23 December 1932 from Russell to the Chief Secretary in File USS 813 of 933, TNA.

21   Letter from Gandhi, 21 November 1936, Rajagopalachari Papers.

22   Letter of 21 January 1937, Rajagopalachari Papers.

23   Narasimhan, *Kamaraj*, p. 23.

24   *The Hindu*, 30 November 1936.

25   See David Arnold, *The Congress in Tamilnad: Nationalist Politics in South India, 1919–1937*, New Delhi: Manohar, 1977, p. 85.

26   Venkatachalapathy, *In Those Days There Was No Coffee*, p. 118.

27   Muthalakshmi Reddy, *Autobiography*, Madras, 1964, p. 19.

28   V. Ramakrishna, *Social Reform in Andhra: 1848–1919*, Delhi: Vikas, 1983, p. 12.

29   Priyadarshini Vijaisri, *Recasting the Devadasi: Patterns of Sacred Prostitution in Colonial South India*, New Delhi: Kanishka, 2004, p. 156, citing *Sanmarga Bodhini*, 17 June 1893.

30   Davesh Soneji, *Unfinished Gestures: Devadasis, Memory, and Modernity in South India*, Chicago: University of Chicago Press, 2012, p. 126.

31   Article by V. Sriram, 'Balasaraswati: The Artist Supreme', in S. Muthiah, V. Sriram and Ranjitha Ashok, (eds.), *Madras Musings: A Silver Jubilee Collection*, Chennai: Ranpar Publications for Chennai Heritage, 2016, pp. 16–18.

32   See Soneji, *Unfinished Gestures*; Vijaisri, *Recasting the Devadasi*, both cited above.

33   Vijaisri, *Recasting the Devadasi*, pp. 264–69.

34   Letter of 15 August 1935 to Zetland, secretary of state for India, EUR D596/12, British Library, London.

35   Letter of 14 April 1937, Erskine Papers, British Library, London.

36   Robert L. Hardgrave, *Essays in the Political Sociology of South India*, New Delhi: Usha Publications, 1979, p. 24.

37   Letter of 28 June 1937, Zetland Papers, Mss. EUR D609/28, British Library, London.

38   Erskine to Linlithgow, 27 August 1937; Linlithgow to Erskine 29 August 1937, Linlithgow Papers, British Library.

39   Letter to Linlithgow, December 1939, Erskine Papers, British Library, London.

40   Letter to Erskine, 5 March 1935, EUR D596/12, British Library, London.

41   Letter 26 March 1935, EUR D596/12, British Library, London.

42   Erskine to George V, 29 December 1937, Erskine Papers, British Library, London.

43   D. Ramaswamy Iyengar to author in 1973 in Bangalore.

44   Krishnaiah, then a member of the Premier's staff, to author in 1973 in Madras.

45   *Indian Review*, Madras, August 1937.

46   Note of 10 November 1937 in File 2602, PWD, of 13 December 1937, Tamil Nadu Archives.

47   CR's remark to Erskine is quoted in a letter dated 30 June 1938 from the

governor's political secretary, T. G. Rutherford, to Frederick Puckle, senior intelligence officer, Government of India, Erskine Papers, British Library, London.

48   CR's remark to grandson, Gopalkrishna Gandhi.

49   W. G. Lamarque of the ICS, who served in Madras in the late 1930s, to author in 1973 in London.

50   A. Ramaswami, *District Gazetteer (Salem)*, Madras 1967, pp. 596–97.

51   Letter of 21 December 1938 in Erskine Papers, EUR D596/12, India Office Library, London.

52   Madras Legislative Assembly Debates (Government of Madras), or MLAD, Vol. 4, pp. 104ff, pp. 598–99.

53   MLAD, Vol. 5, p. 344.

54   MLAD, Vol. 11, pp. 370–78.

55   MLAD, Vol. 11, pp. 370–78.

56   *Harijan* 10 September 1938.

57   S. Gopal, (ed.), *Selected Works of Jawaharlal Nehru*, Vol. 2, pp. 799–800.

58   MLAD, Vol. 13, p. 312.

59   *The Hindu*, June 1938.

60   Kasinath Kavlekar, *Non–Brahmin Movement in Southern India, 1873–1949*, Kolhapur: Shivaji University Press, 1979. Author cites *Justice*, Madras, 6 September 1937.

61   10 June 1938 & 19 October 38, Erskine Papers, British Library.

62   Accessed from <http://shodhganga.inflibnet.ac.in/bitstream/10603/72904/10/10_chapter2.pdf>, citing *Viduthalai*, 16 December 1938.

63   Cited by Blake Wentworth in Yigal Bronner, Whitney Cox and Lawrence McCrea, (eds.), *South Asian Texts in History: Critical Engagements with Sheldon Pollock*, Primus: New Delhi, 2016, p. 155.

64   Figures from File (GO) 597 of 13 April 1940, TNA, quoted in Marguerite Ross Barnett, *Politics of Cultural Nationalism in South India*, Princeton, NJ: Princeton University Press, 1976, p. 52.

65   *The Hindu* 29 December 1938.

66   Hardgrave, *Essays in the Political Sociology of South India*, p. 27.

67   MLAD, Vol. 11, pp. 369–70.

68   Appraisal offered by historian A. R.Venkatachalapathy, Chennai, 30 January 2017.

69   *The Hindu* 23 May 1939

70   MLAD, Vol. 9, p. 588, pp. 703–07.

71   MLAD, Vol. 13, p. 44ff & 109; and *The Hindu*, 22 July 1939.

72   See, for instance, Hardgrave, *Essays*, p. 139, for the positive impact of temple entry on the Nadars in 1939–40.

73   J. B. Kripalani to author in Chennai, 1975.

74   Letter of 25 December 1939 to J. B. L. Munro, shown in 1973, in his home in England, by Munro. The former officer cried while speaking of CR.

75   Telegram from Erskine to Linlithgow, 16 October 1939, Erskine Papers, British Library.

76   MLAD, Vol. 5, p. 57.

77   MLAD, Vol. 14, pp. 36–128.
78   *The Hindu*, 31 October 1939
79   Hardgrave, *Essays*, p. 27.
80   See 'Dravida Naidu' <https://en.wikipedia.org/wiki/Dravida_Nadu>, accessed 10 July 2017.
81   Hardgrave, *Essays*, p. 27.
82   See 'Vamanan's Sight'. Carried on his blog <https://vamanan81.wordpress.com/tag/rajaji/>, accessed 10 July 2017.

CHAPTER 11
1   Erskine to Linlithgow, 21 December 1938, Erskine Papers, British Library, London.
2   CR to author in Chennai in the 1960s.
3   *Harijan*, 22 September 1940.
4   *The Hindu*, 7 August 1940
5   S. Gopal, (ed.), *Selected Works of Jawaharlal Nehru*, Vol. 11, p. 800.
6   *The Hindu*, 12, 13 and 15 August 1940.
7   Hope to Linlithgow, 9 September 1940, Linlithgow Papers, British Library.
8   *The Hindu*, 23 August 1940.
9   *The Hindu*, 6 September 1940.
10   Linlithgow to Hope, 8 May 1941, Linlithgow Papers, British Library.
11   Statement to author in 1974 by B. Shiva Rao, *The Hindu*'s special correspondent in Delhi and intermediary between Sikander and Srinivasan.
12   *The Hindu*, 18 January 1942.
13   *Harijan*, 25 January 1942.
14   C. Rajagopalachari, *Defence of India Speeches*, Madras: Rochouse, 1942.
15   Hope to Linlithgow, 22 March 1942, Linlithgow Papers, British Library.
16   C.Rajagopalachari, *Defence of India Speeches*.
17   *The Hindu*, 23 February 1942.
18   *Collected Works*, Vol. 76, p. 40, 109.
19   N. Mansergh and E. W. R. Lumby, (eds.), *The Transfer of Power*, London: Her Majesty's Stationery Office, 1970–83, Vol. 1, Note 446, p. 555.
20   *The Hindu*, 25 April 1942.
21   *The Hindu*, 26 and 27 April 1942.
22   Pyarelal to Devadas, 27 April 1942, Devadas Gandhi Papers.
23   *The Hindu*, 3 May 1942.
24   Ross Barnett, *Politics of Cultural Nationalism in South India*, Calcutta, 1976, p. 83, cited in <http://shodhganga.inflibnet.ac.in/bitstream/10603/133437/9/09_chapter%202.pdf>.
25   *The Hindu*, 22 May 1942.
26   Rajagopalachari Papers, 5 July 1942.
27   Gandhi to CR, 5 July 1942, Rajagopalachari Papers.
28   *The Hindu*, 10 July 1942.
29   Rajagopalachari Papers.
30   Linlithgow to Churchill, 31 August 1942. Linlithgow Papers, F 125/58, British Library.

31 Arun Chandra Guha, *India's Struggle: Quarter of a Century, 1921–46*, New Delhi: Publications Division, 1982, Vol. 2, p. 562.

32 See 'Itihas', <https://ithihas.wordpress.com/2009/06/18/history–of–freedom–movement–7/>.

33 C. Rajagopalachari, *Reconciliation*, Bombay: Hind Kitabs, 1945, pp. 17–19.

34 Penderel Moon, (ed.), *Wavell: The Viceroy's Journal*, London: Oxford University Press, 1973, p. 57.

35 Account of CR–Jinnah talk based on J. Ahmad, (ed.), *Speeches and Writings of Mr. Jinnah*, Vol. 2, Lahore: Ashraf, 1947, S. S. Peerzada, (ed.), *Leaders' Correspondence with Mr. Jinnah*, Bombay: Taj Office, 1944, and letter from G. D. Birla to Devadas Gandhi, 14 April 1944, Devadas Gandhi Papers.

36 Quoted in G. Allana, *Quaid-e-Azam Jinnah*, Lahore: Ferozsons, 1967, p. 362.

37 A. H. Merriam, *Gandhi vs. Jinnah*, Calcutta: Minerva, 1980, p. 102.

38 *The Madras Mail*, 23 September 1944, cited in <http://shodhganga.inflibnet.ac.in/bitstream/10603/133437/9/09_chapter%202.pdf>.

39 Hardgrave, *Essays*, p. 31.

40 Ibid., p. 28.

41 Penderel Moon, (ed.), *Wavell: The Viceroy's Journal*, London: Oxford University Press, 1973, p. 120, p. 168.

42 Moon, (ed.), *Wavell*.

43 To SNDT University. In C. Rajagopalachari, *University Addresses*, Bombay: Hind Kitabs, 1949, pp. 55–57.

44 Diary, 13 April 1947, Rajagopalachari Papers.

45 *The Hindu*, 23 August 1940.

46 Text provided by Navaratna Ram, Rajagopalachari Papers

47 Bawa, *The Last Nizam*, p. 388.

48 Ibid., pp. 398–99.

49 Ibid., pp. 157–88.

50 Ibid., p. 388.

51 Ibid., p. 399.

52 Ibid., p. 253, 434.

53 Ibid., pp. 278–80.

54 Ibid., p. 286, citing Ali Yavar Jang, *Hyderabad in Retrospect*, p. 11.

55 Vikram Rao, grandson of Pingle Venkatram Reddy, to author, Hyderabad, 5 December 2015.

56 Bawa, *Last Nizam*, p. 290.

57 Dr T. Dharma Reddy, 95, to author, Hyderabad, 3 December 2015.

58 Vanaja Rangaswami, *The Story of Integration: A New Interpretation*, New Delhi: Manohar, 1981, p. 13.

59 Ibid., p. 31.

60 Ibid., *The Story of Integration*, p. 43.

61 Ibid., *The Story of Integration*, p. 43.

62 H. Y. Sharada Prasad, 'A few inches of ivory: A profile of modern Kannada literature', *IIC Quarterly*, Vol. 14, No. 2 (Summer 1987), p. 127.

63 M. R. Manmathan, 'The rebel and the reformer: V.T. Bhattathiripad in

historical perspective', Thesis, Department of History, University of Calicut, Kerala, 2007, p. 274, accessed from <http://shodhganga.inflibnet.ac.in/bitstream/10603/19905/10/10_chapter%204.pdf>.

64   Ibid.

65   This account of V.T.'s life is drawn almost entirely from M. R. Manmathan, 'The rebel and the reformer'.

66   Rangaswami, *Story of Integration*, pp. 31–32.

67   Rangaswami, *Story of Integration*, p. 37.

68   Historian Rajan Gurukkal to author, Bengaluru, 4 February 2017.

69   Dilip M. Menon, *Caste, Nationalism and Communism in South India: Malabar, 1900–1948*, Cambridge, UK: Cambridge University Press, 1994, p.192.

70   Ibid., p. 192.

71   Letter to Erskine, Governor of Madras, 2 November 1934, Erskine Papers, MSS EUR D596/8, British Library.

72   For conflicting accounts, see M. K. Nidheesh, *Livemint*, 28 October 2016 <http://www.livemint.com/Politics/Gbimy6vm42wFeDe851AOEN/A–veteran–recounts–the–1946–PunnapraVayalar–uprising–70–ye.html> and *The Hindu*, 8 June 2008, <http://www.thehindu.com/todays–paper/tp–national/tp–kerala/Punnapra–Vayalar–uprising–a–historical–blunder–Hassan/article15237821.ece>.

73   Quoted in A. G. Noorani's article in *Frontline*, Vol. 20, No. 13, 21 June–04 July, 2003, accessed on 6 August 2017. <http://www.frontline.in/static/html/fl2013/stories/20030704000807800.htm>.

74   Ibid.

75   Ibid.

76   Hardgrave, *Essays*, p. 1.

77   A. R. Venkatachalapathy, *India Today*, 10 April 2008; V. Sriram in S. Muthiah, V. Sriram and Ranjitha Ashok, (eds.), *Madras Musings: A Silver Jubilee Collection*, Chennai: Ranpar Publications for Chennai Heritage, 2016, p. 32.

78   *Hindustan Times*, 15 August 1947.

79   CR to author in Chennai.

80   *Statesman*, 6 September 1947.

81   In a letter to A. K. Chanda, 8 September 1947, Rajagopalachari Papers.

82   *Amrita Bazar Patrika*, 29 November 1947.

83   *Statesman*, 15 January 1948.

84   Pyarelal, *Last Phase*, Vol. 2, p. 713.

85   *Harijan*, 30 January 1949.

86   C. Rajagopalachari, *Speeches*, Calcutta, 1948, pp. 118–19.

87   This remark is found on several websites offering Periyar's thoughts, including <https://arxiv.org/ftp/math/papers/0511/0511559.pdf>, where W. B. Vasantha Kandasamy, Florentin Smarandache and K. Kandasamy analyse Periyar's views on untouchability.

88   McDermott, Gordon, Embree, Pritchett, and Dalton, (eds.), *Sources of Indian Traditions*, Third edition, New York: Columbia University Press, 2015, p. 431, citing *Viduthalai*, 12 April 1951.

CHAPTER 12

1   *Statesman*, 9 June 1948.
2   *Hindustan Times*, 23 February 1949.
3   Pingle Venkatram Reddy to Dr T. Dharma Reddy, as recalled by the latter to the author in Hyderabad on 3 December 2015
4   *Hindustan Times*, 9 September 1948.
5   V. P. Menon, *An Outline of Indian Constitutional History*, Bombay: Bhavan, 1965, p. 74.
6   S. N. Prasad, *Operation Polo: The Police Action Against Hyderabad, 1948*, New Delhi: Ministry of Defence, 1972, pp. 209–10.
7   Bawa, *The Last Nizam*, p. 349.
8   Mir Laik Ali, *Tragedy of Hyderabad*, Hyderabad: Deccan Archaeological and Cultural Research Institute, 2011, p. 274.
9   Laik Ali, *Tragedy of Hyderabad*, pp. 274–75.
10 Report of the Sunderlal Committee, available on the internet and reproduced as Appendices 14 and 15 in A. G. Noorani, *The Destruction of Hyderabad*, London: Hurst & Co, 2014.
11 Bawa, *Last Nizam*, p. 349.
12 Report of the Sunderlal Committee.
13 Dalit killings are recounted in Sharan Kumar Limbale's autobiography, *Akkarmashi*, Pune: Dilipraj Prakashan, 1984. A paper by Vinod K. Jairath and Huma R. Kidwai, 'Violence of Silence: "Police Action" in Hyderabad and its Aftermath', provides several troubling images, including of threats in Osmanabad to Pandit Sunderlal.
14 *Hindustan Times*, 27 September 1948.
15 Interviewed in December 2015, a Hyderabad doctor, a Hindu, observed, 'I doubt that so many would have been killed. But we did hear of bodies thrown into wells in the Latur region.' A Hyderabad–based Hindu scholar described the Sunderlal report as 'credible', while another Hindu, asked to comment on the seeming shortage of accounts of killings from relatives of victims, observed, 'Who was prepared, relatives included, to speak of their tragedies in the 1948 climate?' Interviewed in Mumbai in January 2018, a Maharashtrian scholar spoke of his grandmother's recollection of an unbearable stench from dead bodies as she journeyed by bullock cart on the road used by Indian soldiers moving north from Solapur.
16 Raghu Cidambi to author, 5 December 2015, Hyderabad.
17 Related to author by Dr T. Dharma Reddy, 95, Hyderabad, 3 December 2015.
18 P. Sundarayya, 'Telangana People's Armed Struggle, 1946–1951', *Social Scientist*, Vol. 1, No. 7, February 1973, pp. 3–19, accessed from <http://www.jstor.org/stable/3516269>.
19 In interview with author.
20 Photocopy, seen by the writer, of letter made available to Gopalkrishna Gandhi by K. Veeramani of the DK.
21 Ibid.
22 Philip Spratt, *D.M.K. in Power*, Bombay: Nachiketa, 1970, p. 38.
23 Ross Barnett, *Politics of Cultural Nationalism in South India*, Princeton, NJ:

Princeton University Press, 1976, p. 70, citing T. M. Parthasarathy, *Ti Mu Kalaka Varalaru*, p. 30.

24 See <https://vamanan81.wordpress.com/tag/g–d–naidu/>.
25 Hardgrave, *Essays*, p. 35.
26 *Hindustan Times*, 26 January 1950.
27 Letter of 26 January 1950 in Durga Das, (ed.), *Sardar Patel's Correspondence*, Ahmedabad: Navajivan, Vol. 10, pp. 77–78.
28 K. P. S. Menon in *Rajaji 93*, put together in 1971 by T. Sadasivam and published by Bharathan, Madras, p. 130.
29 Rajagopalachari Papers.
30 *Hindustan Times*, 3 October 1951.
31 File 7/18/51, Home Pol, National Archives, New Delhi.
32 B. N. Mullick to author, 1973.
33 Minute in File 12/1//51, Home Pol, National Archives, New Delhi.
34 *Hindustan Times*, 28 December 1950.
35 Mullick to author, 1973.
36 *Hindustan Times* 10 & 20 February 1951.
37 *Hindustan Times*, 7 October 1951.
38 *Hindustan Times*, 8 October 1951.
39 From lines written by CR in October 1951, reproduced in *Swarajya*, 14 June 1975.
40 Rajagopalachari Papers.
41 Letter from Sri Prakasa to Prasad and Nehru, 1 April 1952, Rajagopalachari Papers.
42 *The Hindu*, 2 April 1952.
43 9 May 1952, Madras Legislative Assembly Debates, Tamil Nadu Archives.
44 Madras Legislative Assembly Debates, Tamil Nadu Archives.
45 *The Hindu*, 2 April 1952.
46 Letter from the governor of the Reserve Bank quoted by Governor Sri Prakasa to President Rajendra Prasad, 16 May 1954, Rajagopalachari Papers.
47 28 June 1952. MLAD, Vol. 2, pp. 340–41.
48 Tyagi to CR, 6 September 1952, Rajagopalachari Papers.
49 See speech by C. Subramaniam, 6 March 1954, MLA, Vol. 12, p. 651.
50 Eye-witness Pattabhirama Rao, CR's and Prakasam's ministerial colleague, to author in Madras, 1973.
51 Letter of 12 February 1953, with jotting, in Rajagopalachari Papers.
52 29 July 1953; MLAD, Vol. 9, p. 1736.
53 *Hindustan Review*, Patna, June 1907.
54 On 8 August 1949, C. Rajagopalachari, *Speeches*, New Delhi: Governor General's Press, 1950, pp. 257–59.
55 Justice P. Chandra Reddy in *Rajaji 93*, p. 263.
56 *Indian Express*, 10 March 1954.
57 Accounts provided by Subramaniam and Pattabhirama Rao to author, Madras, 1973.
58 *Indian Express*, 26 March 1954.
59 *The Hindu*, 31 March 1954.

60   Ross Barnett, *Politics of Cultural Nationalism in South India*, p. 80.
61   See blogpost 'Vignettes from Kovai Ayyamuthu's reminiscences of 'Periyar' — III', <https://vamanan81.wordpress.com/tag/rajaji/>.
62   See Barnett, *Politics of Cultural Nationalism in South India*, p. 82.
63   Ibid., p. 81.
64   P. Krishnamoorthy, 'Formation of Andhra State, 1953', in B. Kesava Narayana, (ed.), *Modern Andhra and Hyderabad: AD 1858–1956*, pp. 538–57.
65   Lisa Mitchell, *Language, Emotion, & Politics in South India: The Making of a Mother Tongue*, Ranikhet, Uttarakhand: Permanent Black, 2010, p. 205.
66   Mitchell, *Language, Emotion, & Politics in South India*.
67   *Indian Express*, 27 November 1955.

CHAPTER 13
1   Jitendra Singh, 'Communism in Kerala', *Political Quarterly*, Vol. 31, No. 2, 1960, pp. 188–92 <http://onlinelibrary.wiley.com/doi/10.1111/j.1467–923X.1960.tb00401.x/pdf>.
2   D. Dhanuraj, 'Story of 1957 Education Bill in Kerala', Centre for Public Policy Research, Tripunithura, Kerala, 2006 <https://www.slideshare.net/cppr123/education–bill–1957–24014348>.
3   Ibid.
4   *Swarajya*, 20 June 1959.
5   N. Sivakumar's 2014 thesis on Kamaraj's Rule, pp. 67–73, <http://shodhganga.inflibnet.ac.in/bitstream/10603/30267/8/chapter2.pdf>.
6   R. Bhaskaran quoted in <http://www.perunthalaivar.org/english/2008/01/25/kamaraj–as–chiefminister/>.
7   Hardgrave, *Essays*, pp. 8–10.
8   A.R. Venkatachalapathy in *India Today*, 10 April 2008, <http://indiatoday.intoday.in/story/Letter+and+spirit/1/6878.html>.
9   Narasimhan, *Kamaraj*, p. 174.
10   Robert L. Hardgrave, Jr., 'The DMK and the Politics of Tamil Nationalism', *Pacific Affairs*, Vol. 37, No. 4, Winter, 1964–65, p. 408, citing *Link*, 26 November 1961.
11   Ibid., p. 405, citing *Link*, 27 December 1959 and 3 July 1960.
12   Article in *India Today*'s 2000 number, <http://www.india–today.com/itoday/millennium/100people/durai.html>.
13   B. G. Verghese, *Tehelka*, 5 October 2012.
14   Rajagopalachari Papers, 9 August 1963.
15   N. Sivakumar citing A. Gopanna, *Periyarum Perunthalaivarum*, Chennai, Nava India Publishers, 2007, p.6. Accessed from <http://shodhganga.inflibnet.ac.in/bitstream/ 10603/30267/7/chapter1.pdf>.
16   In response to a question asked in Chennai by the author.
17   *Swarajya*, 28 February 1959.
18   Ibid., 21 November 1961.
19   Ibid., 6 June 1964.
20   To Radhakrishnan, 1 December 1965, to Nanda 15 December 1965,

Rajagopalachari Papers.

21 *Swarajya*, 1 January 1966.

22 See <https://www.thehindu.com/news/cities/chennai/radha–pleaded–innocence–was–found–guilty/article4232721.ece>.

23 Hardgrave, *Essays*, p. 104.

24 Ibid., p. 93.

25 Ibid., p. 108.

26 A. Srivathsan in *The Hindu*, Chennai, 23 December 2012 <http://www.thehindu.com/news/cities/chennai/the–day–mr–radha–shot–mgr/article12059018.ece>.

27 K. R. Venugopal, IAS, to author, Hyderabad, 16 January 2017.

28 A.R. Venkatachalapathy in *India Today*, 10 April 2008 <http://indiatoday.intoday.in/story/Letter+and+spirit/1/6878.html>.

29 Ibid.

30 Cho   Ramaswamy,   <http://www.india–today.com/itoday/millennium/100people/durai.html>.

31 *Swarajya*, 8 February 1969.

32 Supported in the stand by Morarji Desai, Indira thought that 'people who had lost in the elections should not be appointed to important posts'. Morarji Desai, *The Story of My Life*, Delhi: Macmillan, 1974, Vol. 2, p. 246.

33 Inder Malhotra, 'A Populist Move', *Indian Express*, 10 Jan 1914 <http://indianexpress.com/article/opinion/columns/a–populist–move–a–party–chasm/>.

34 *Swarajya*, 18 November 1969.

35 Ibid., 21 February 1970.

36 Ibid., 28 February 1970.

37 Ibid., 28 November 1970.

38 CR to grandson Gopal Gandhi, as related by the latter.

39 Rajagopalachari Papers.

40 *Swarajya*, 25 September 1971.

41 Ibid., 18 March 1972.

42 Hardgrave, *Essays*, p. 111.

43 *Swarajya*, 21 October 1972.

44 K. R. Venugopal to author, Hyderabad, 16 January 2017.

45 Ibid.

46 Report of Justice B. N. Srikrishna Committee, 2010, <http://pib.nic.in/archieve/others/2011/jan/d2011010502.pdf>.

47 Jitendra Singh, 'Communism in Kerala', *Political Quarterly*, Vol. 31, No. 2, 1960, p. 186, <http://onlinelibrary.wiley.com/doi/10.1111/j.1467–923X.1960.tb00401.x/pdf>.

48 Govindan Parayil, 'The "Kerala model" of development', *Third World Quarterly*, Vol. 17, No. 5, 1996, p. 942.

49 Ibid.

50 Ibid., pp. 942–45.

51 Ibid.

52 M. G. Devasahayam, 'The Kamaraj Legacy', *The Hindu*, 30 November 2014   <http://www.thehindu.com/opinion/open–page/the–kamaraj–legacy/

article6646815.ece>.

53 Though widely blacked out by censorship, this author viewed the resolution in Chennai in June 1975. See, too, P. Kandaswamy, *The Political Career of K. Kamaraj*, New Delhi: Concept, 2001, p. 130, citing J. S. Bright, *One Year of Emergency*, New Delhi, 1977, p. 14, also Kandaswamy's interview with P. Ramachandran, Congress (O) leader in 1975.

54 Remarks from Karunanidhi and indication from Kamaraj to the author in Chennai in 1975.

55 'Jail Brutality: Ismail Commission's indictment', *Economic & Political Weekly*, 22 April 1978.

56 Aditi De, *The Hindu*, Bengaluru, 1 December 2003.

57 T. A. Eachara Varier, *Memories of a Father*, trans. from Malayalam by Neelan, Hong Kong: Asian Human Rights Commission, 2004.

58 Paraphrase of Ananthamurthy's remarks cited by Ratik Asokan in *The Nation*, 20 March 2017.

59 U. R. Ananthamurthy, *Samskara*, trans. from Kannada by A. K. Ramanujan, Delhi: Oxford University Press, 2012.

60 Excerpted from 'A few inches of ivory: A profile of modern Kannada literature' by H. Y. Sharada Prasad, *IIC Quarterly*, Vol. 14, No. 2, Summer 1987, p. 131. Reproduced by permission of Kavitha Lankesh and the *IIC Quarterly*.

CHAPTER 14

1 Committee for Rational Development, *Sri Lanka: The Ethnic Conflict*, New Delhi: Navrang, 1984, p. 79.

2 'Ominous presence in Tamil Nadu', article by Shekhar Gupta in *India Today*, 31 March 1984: 'Quietly and methodically, Sri Lankan Tamil rebels have been acquiring arms and training for what they claim will be an attempt to carve out an independent Tamil Eelam in northern Sri Lanka.'

3 Jyotindra Nath Dixit, *Assignment Colombo*, Delhi: Konark, 1998; Colombo: Vijitha Yapa Bookshop, 1998, pp. 329–30.

4 Ibid., pp.328–29.

5 'Indian general election, 1984', *Wikipedia*, <https://en.wikipedia.org/wiki/Indian_general_election, 1984>.

6 Sagarika Ghose, 'Don't take us for granted', *Hindustan Times*, 9 October 2009.

7 'Andhra Pradesh Legislative Assembly election, 1983', *Wikipedia*, <https://en.wikipedia.org/wiki/Andhra_Pradesh_Legislative_Assembly_election, 1983>.

8 Srinivasan Ramachandran, *Times of India* blog, 14 March 2016 <https://blogs.timesofindia.indiatimes.com/tracking–indian–communities/mid–day–meals–high–noon–of–welfare–2/>.

9 Including the present writer, who at the time wondered in a newspaper article whether the scheme would not encourage dependency. See also Anita Pratap, *Outlook*, 18 August 2003.

10 K. Natwar Singh, *One Life is Not Enough: An Autobiography*, New Delhi: Rupa Publications, 2014, pp. 252–53.

11   Ibid., p. 254.

12   Hardgrave, *Essays*, p. 111.

13   Ibid., pp. 123–24.

14   Statistical Report on General Election, 1989 to the Legislative Assembly of Tamil Nadu, accessed from <https://eci.nic.in/eci_main/StatisticalReports/SE_1989/StatisticalReportTamilNadu89.pdf>.

15   Vinod K. Jose, 'The Last Lear', *Caravan*, 1 April 2011.

16   Ibid.

17   Ibid.

18   According to one version, Jayalalithaa publicly vowed to 'never step foot inside the House until conditions are created for a woman to attend the Assembly with dignity', See Vinod K. Jose, 'The Last Lear', *Caravan*, 1 April 2011.

19   S. K. Misra, principal secretary to Chandra Shekhar, writing in *Flying in High Wind*, New Delhi: Rupa Publications, p. 270, quoted in *The Hindu*, 14 April 2016.

20   Statistical Report on General Election, 1984 to the Legislative Assembly of Tamil Nadu, accessed from <https://eci.nic.in/eci_main/StatisticalReports/SE_1984/StatisticalReportTamilNadu84.pdf>.

21   In remarks to author at a Rashtrapati Bhavan lunch in 1990.

22   To author in Chennai.

23   Natwar Singh, *One Life is Not Enough*, p. 290.

24   Dixit, *Assignment Colombo*, p. 160, pp. 219–20.

25   Singh, *One Life is Not Enough*, p. 259.

26   Dixit, *Assignment Colombo*, p. 345.

27   Statistical Report on General Elections, 1996 to the Eleventh Lok Sabha, accessed from <https://www.eci.nic.in/eci_main/StatisticalReports/LS_1996/Vol_I_LS_96.pdf>.

28   Singh, *One Life is Not Enough*, p. 294.

29   Sanjaya Baru, *The Accidental Prime Minister: The Making and Unmaking of Manmohan Singh*, New Delhi: Penguin India, 2014, p. 63.

30   Nayar's relationship with the Mahasabha leaders is described in detail in Krishna Jha and Dhirendra K. Jha, *Ayodhya: The Dark Night*, New Delhi: HarperCollins, 2012.

31   Letter from Nayar to chief secretary, UP, quoted in P. V. Narasimha Rao, *Ayodhya: 6 December 1992*, New Delhi: Penguin India, 2006, p. 18.

32   Jha and Jha, *Ayodhya*.

33   Narasimha Rao, *Ayodhya*. The book opens with the line, 'Published posthumously in accordance with the author's wishes'.

34   Remarks in Lok Sabha, 21 December 1992, in Narasimha Rao, *Ayodhya*, p. 260.

35   Statistical Report on General Elections, 1996 to the Eleventh Lok Sabha, accessed from <https://www.eci.nic.in/eci_main/StatisticalReports/LS_1996/Vol_I_LS_96.pdf>.

36   Parvathi Menon's obituary on Hegde, *Frontline*, Vol. 21, No. 3, Jan. 31– Feb. 13, 2004, <http://www.frontline.in/static/html/fl2103/stories/20040213005712300.htm>.

37 Parvathi Menon, *Frontline*, Vol. 21, No. 3, 31 January–13 February 2004.
38 Kesri responding to Harinder Baweja, *India Today*, 19 January 1998 <https://www.indiatoday.in/magazine/interview/story/19980119-sonia-gandhi-has-come-as-a-saviour-sitaram-kesri-828188-1998-01-19>.
39 Vaasanthi, *Cut-outs, Caste and Cine Stars: The World of Tamil Politics*, New Delhi: Penguin India, 2006, p. 173, referring to the Jain Commission Report.
40 Ibid., p. 175.
41 Ibid., p. 175.
42 'Indian Parliament Elections : Kerala State–1977', accessed from <http://keralaassembly.org/lok/vote_share.php4?year=1977>.
43 Girish Menon, 'An Architect of Bipolar Coalition Regime', *The Hindu*, 23 December 2010.
44 Bidyut Chakraborty, *Communism in India: Events, Processes and Ideologies*, New York: Oxford University Press, 2014, p. 62.
45 Statistical Report on General Election, 1994 to the Legislative Assembly of Andhra Pradesh, accessed from <https://www.eci.nic.in/eci_main/StatisticalReports/SE_1994/StatisticalReport-AP94.pdf>.
46 John F. Burns citing the Reuters interview in his obituary on N.T.R. in the *New York Times*, 19 January 1996.
47 *India Today*, 15 Feb 1996 <https://www.indiatoday.in/magazine/obituary/story/19960215-n.t.-rama-rao-a-quiet-ending-for-an-enigmatic-personality-834350-1996-02-15>.
48 John F. Burns in the *New York Times*, 19 January 1996.
49 Vaasanthi, *Amma: Jayalalithaa's Journey from Movie Star to Political Queen*, New Delhi, Juggernaut, 2016, p. 79.
50 Ibid, p. 90.
51 Vaasanthi, *Cutouts*, p. 159.
52 Ibid., pp. 158–63.
53 Interview to *India Today* cited in Vaasanthi, *Cutouts*, p. 158.
54 Kamaladevi Chattopadhay, *Inner Recesses, Outer Spaces: Memoirs*, New Delhi: Navrang, 1986, p 305.
55 Ibid., pp. 401–02.
56 T. J. S. George, *M. S. Subbulakshmi: The Definitive Biography*, New Delhi: Aleph Book Company, 2016.
57 Gowri Ramnarayan in *Frontline*, Vol. 13, No. 25, 13–26 December 1997.
58 In 1974. 'M .S. Subbulakshmi, "Nightingale" of Carnatic Music', *PTI*, <http://www.rediff.com/news/2004/dec/11ms2.htm>.

CHAPTER 15

1 In interview to M. J. Akbar, *India Today*, 30 June 2012 <https://www.indiatoday.in/magazine/interview/story/20120709-abdul-kalam-presidential-elections-2012-new-book-turning-points-758940-2012-06-30>.
2 Vaasanthi, *Amma*, p.134.
3 Ibid., p. 170.
4 Ibid., pp. 143–44.
5 Ibid., pp. 84–85.

6   T. S. Sudhir, 'AIADMK crisis: Palaniswami, Panneerselvam join hands but ousting Dinakaran won't be easy', *Firstpost*, 10 August 2017, <https://www.firstpost.com/politics/aiadmk–crisis–palaniswami–panneerselvam–join–hands–but–ousting–dinakaran–wont–be–easy–3915083.html>.

7   See, for instance, this comment by Cho Ramaswamy on Periyar in 'E.V. Ramaswami Naicker and C.N. Annadurai', *India Today*, millennium issue, January 2000: 'He broke the idols of Vinayaka; today the Vinayaka procession is a gala event in Tamil Nadu. He tore pictures of Rama and applied the chappal to it; a few years ago, Tamil Nadu sent a strong contingent of devotees of Rama carrying bricks for the shilanyas at Ayodhya. He fought superstitions; his followers in the AIADMK tonsured their heads for the good health of their leader, J. Jayalalitha,' accessed from <http://www.india–today.com/itoday/millennium/100people/durai.html>.

8   From Gurujada's *Desabhakti*, Srirangam Srinivasa Rao, (trans.), p. xvi in Pennepalli Gopala Krishna, (ed.), *Diaries of Gurujada*, Hyderabad: Oriental Manuscripts Library and Research Institute, 2009.

9   Abbé Dubois, *Hindu Manners*, pp. 274–75, footnote.

10   Verse 241, Gopalkrishna Gandhi, (trans.), *The Tirukkural*, New Delhi: Aleph Book Company, 2015, p. 27.

11   Kanniyan Pungundranar, G. U. Pope, (trans.), accessed from <https://en.wikipedia.org/wiki/Kaniyan_Pungundranar>. Pope's 'men' has been altered here to 'people'.

BIBLIOGRAPHY

Achaya, K. T., *Indian Food: A Historical Companion*, Delhi: Oxford University Press, 1994.

Alam, Muzaffar, *The Languages of Political Islam: India 1200–1800*, Delhi: Permanent Black, 2004.

Alavi, Seema, (ed.), *The Eighteenth Century in India: Debates in Indian History and Society*, New Delhi: Oxford University Press, 2002.

Amini, Iradj, *Napoleon and Persia: Franco–Persian relations under the First Empire*, Richmond, Surrey, UK: Curzon 1999.

Ananthamurthy, U. R., *Samskara*, A. K. Ramanujan (trans.), Delhi: Oxford University Press, 1978.

Apparao, Gurujada, *Girls for Sale: Kanyasulkam, A Play from Colonial India*, Velcheru Narayana Rao (trans.), Bloomington IN: Indian University Press, 2007.

Arnold, David, *Police Power and Colonial Rule: Madras, 1859–1947*, Delhi: Oxford University Press, 1986.

———, *The Congress in Tamilnad: Nationalist Politics in South India, 1919–1937*, New Delhi: Manohar, 1977.

Arunima, G., *Glimpses from a Writer's World: O. Chandu Menon, His Contemporaries, and Their Times*, New Delhi: Sage, 2004.

Baker, C. J., Washbrook, D. A., *South India: Political Institutions and Political Change, 1880–1940*, Madras: Macmillan, 1975.

Balasubramanian, R., (ed.), *The Life-world of the Tamils: Past and Present–II*, New Delhi: Centre for Studies in Civilizations, 2009.

Barnett, Marguerite Ross, *Politics of Cultural Nationalism in South India*, Princeton, NJ: Princeton University Press, 1976.

Baru, Sanjaya, *The Accidental Prime Minister: The Making and Unmaking of Manmohan Singh*, New Delhi: Penguin/Viking, 2014.

Bawa, V. K., *The Last Nizam: The Life & Times of Mir Osman Ali Khan*, Hyderabad: Centre for Deccan Studies, 2010.

———, *Hyderabad Under Salar Jung I*, Delhi: S. Chand & Co, 1986.

Bayly, Susan, *Saints, Goddesses and Kings: Muslims and Christians in South Indian Society*, Cambridge, UK: Cambridge University Press, 1989.

———, *Caste, Society and Politics in India from the Eighteenth Century to the Modern Age*, Cambridge, UK: Cambridge University Press, 1999.

Blackburn, Stuart, *Print, Folklore, and Nationalism in Colonial South India*, Delhi: Permanent Black, 2003.

Blakiston, John, *Twelve Years' Military Adventure in Three Quarters of the Globe*, 2 Vols., London: Henry Colburn, 1829.

Bowring, Lewin B., *Haidar Ali and Tipu Sultan, And The Struggle With The Musalman Powers Of The South*, Delhi: Idarah-I-Adabiyat, 1974.

Briggs, Henry George, *The Nizam: His History and Relations with the British Government*, Published in 1861; Delhi: Manas Publications, 1985, (repr).

Brittlebank, Kate, *Tiger: The Life of Tipu Sultan*, New Delhi: Juggernaut, 2016.

Bronner, Yigal, Whitney Cox and Lawrence McCrea (eds.), *South Asian Texts in History: Critical Engagements with Sheldon Pollock*, New Delhi: Primus, 2016.

Brown, Charles Philip, *Verses of Vemana*, Madras, 1829; New Delhi: Asian Educational Services, 2003, (repr).

———, *Cyclic Tables of Hindu and Mahomedan Chronology Regarding the History of the Telugu and Kannadi Countries*, Madras: Christian Knowledge Society's Press, 1850; New Delhi: Asian Educational Services, 1994, (repr).

Caldwell, Robert, *Comparative Grammar of the Dravidian or South Indian Family of Languages*, Third edition, London: Kegan Paul, Trench, Trubner & Co, 1913; New Delhi: Oriental Books, 1974, (repr).

———, *A History of Tinnevelly*, 1881; New Delhi: Asian Educational Services, 1982, (repr).

Cariappa, M. P. and Cariappa, Ponnamma, *The Coorgs and Their Origins*, Mysore: Geetha Publishing House, 1981.

Chakravarthy, N. Manu, (ed.), *U. R. Ananthamurthy Omnibus*, Gurgaon: Arvind Kumar Publishers, 2007.

Chattopadhyay, Kamaladevi, *Inner Recesses, Outer Spaces: Memoirs*, New Delhi: Navrang, 1986.

Chinnian, P., *Vellore Mutiny, 1806: The First Uprising Against the British*, Madras: by the author, 1982.

Chopra, P. N., Ravindran, T. K. and Subrahmanian, N., *History of South India*, 3 Vols., New Delhi: S. Chand, 1979.

Cohen, Benjamin B., *Kingship and Colonialism in India's Deccan, 1850–1948*, New York: Palgrave Macmillan, 2007.

Dale, Stephen Frederic, *Islamic Society on the South Asian Frontier: The Mappilas of Malabar, 1498–1922*, Oxford: Clarendon Press, 1980.

Das, Durga, (ed.), *Sardar Patel's Correspondence*, 10 Vols., Ahmedabad: Navajivan.

Digby, William, *The Famine Campaign in Southern India, 1876–1878*, Vol. 1, London: Longmans, Green, and Co., 1878.

Dirks, Nicholas, *Castes of Mind: Colonialism and the Making of Modern India*, Princeton, NJ: Princeton University Press, 2001.

Divekar, V. D., *South India in 1857 War of Independence*, Pune: Lokmanya Tilak Smarak Trust, 1993.

Dixit, Jyotindra Nath, *Assignment Colombo*, Delhi: Konark, 1998; Colombo edition: Vijitha Yapa Bookshop, 1998.

Dodwell, Henry, *The Nabobs of Madras*, London: Williams and Norgate, 1926.

Dos Santos, Anne Noronha, *Military Intervention and Secession in South Asia: The Cases of Bangladesh, Sri Lanka, Kashmir and Punjab*, Westport, CT: Praeger, 2007.

Dubois, Abbé Jean-Antoine, *Hindu Manners, Customs and Ceremonies*, London, 1816; Oxford, 1953; New York: Cosimo, 2007.

Dutt, Romesh Chunder, *The Economic History of India Under Early British Rule*, London: Kegan Paul, 1901; updated Fourth edition.

Eaton, Richard M., *A Social History of the Deccan, 1300–1761*, Cambridge, UK: Cambridge University Press, 2005.

Francis, W., *Vizagapatam District Gazetteer 1907*, Hyderabad: State Editor, District Gazetteers, 1994, (repr).

Fraser, Hastings, *Our Faithful Ally: The Nizam*, 1865, New Delhi: Modern Publishers, 1985, (repr).

Gandhi, Gopalkrishna, *The Tirukkural: A New English Version*, New Delhi: Aleph, 2015.

George, T. J. S., *M. S. Subbulakshmi: The Definitive Biography*, New Delhi: Aleph, 2016.

Gilmour, David, *The Ruling Caste: Imperial Lives in the Victorian Raj*, New York: Farrar, Straus and Giroux, 2005.

Pennepalli, Gopalakrishna, (ed.), *Diaries of Gurujada*, Hyderabad: Oriental Manuscripts Library and Research Institute, 2009.

Gowda, Chandan, (ed.), *The Way I See It: A Gauri Lankesh Reader*, New Delhi: Navayana, DC Books, 2017.

Goyal, Shankar, *Studies in the History of the Deccan and South India*, Jodhpur: Kusumanjali, 2009.

Guha, Arun Chandra, *India's Struggle: Quarter of a Century, 1921–46*, 2 Vols., New Delhi: Publications Division, 1982.

Gundajois, Keladi, *Glorious Keladi: History and Culture*, Mysore: Directorate of Archaeology & Museums, 2011.

Gurwood, John, (comp.), *Dispatches of the Duke of Wellington*, Vol. 1, London: John Murray, 1834.

Habib, Irfan, (ed.), *Confronting Colonialism: Resistance and Modernization under Haidar Ali & Tipu Sultan*, New Delhi: Tulika, 1999.

Habib, Irfan, (ed.), *State and Diplomacy under Tipu Sultan: Documents and Essays*, New Delhi: Tulika, 2001.

Hamilton (Buchanan), Francis, *A Journey from Madras through the countries of Mysore, Canara, and Malabar*, London: T. Cadell and W. Davies, 1807, 3 Vols., New Delhi & Madras: Asian Educational Services, 1999, (repr).

Hancock, Mary, *Politics of Heritage from Madras to Chennai*, Bloomington, IN: Indian University Press, 2008.

Hardgrave Jr., Robert L., *The Nadars of Tamilnad: The Political Culture of a Community in Change*, Berkeley: University of California Press, 1969.

———, *Essays in the Political Sociology of South India*, New Delhi: Usha Publications, 1979.

Hasan, Mohibbul, *History of Tipu Sultan*, Calcutta: The World Press, 1971.

Hayavadana Rao, C., (ed.), *Mysore Gazetteer*, Bangalore, 1926; Delhi: B. R. Publishing, 1984, (repr).

Hill, Samuel Charles, *Yusuf Khan: The Rebel Commandan*, London, 1914; New Delhi: Asian Educational Services, 1987, (repr).

Irschick, Eugene F., *Dialogue and History: Constructing South India, 1795–1895*, Berkeley: University of California Press, 1994.

———, *Politics and Social Conflict in South India: The Non-Brahman Movement and Tamil Separatism, 1916–1929*, Berkeley: University of California Press, 1969.

Jackson, William J., *Tyagaraja: Life and Lyrics*, Delhi: Oxford University Press, 1991.

Jafri, S. Z. H., (ed.), *Recording the Progress of Indian History: Symposia Papers of the Indian History Congress, 1992–2010*, Delhi: Primus, 2012,

Jayakumar, Vijayalayam, *Sree Narayana Guru: A Critical Study*, K. Sadanandan (trans.), New Delhi: D. K. Printworld, 1999.

Jayewardene-Pillai, Shanti, *Imperial Conversations: Indo–Britons and the Architecture of South India*, New Delhi: Yoda Press, 2007.

Jeffrey, Robin, *Decline of Nayar Dominance: Society and Politics in Travancore, 1847–1908*, New York: Holmes and Meier, 1976.

Jha, Krishna and Jha, Dhirendra K., *Ayodhya: The Dark Night*, New Delhi: HarperCollins, 2012.

Kamath, Suryanath U., *Krishnadevaraya of Vijayanagara and his Times*, Bangalore: IBH Prakashana, 2009.

Kamath, Suryanath U., *A Concise History of Karnataka*, Bangalore: Jupiter, 1997.

Kandaswamy, P., *The Political Career of K. Kamaraj*, New Delhi: Concept, 2001.

Kapur, R. P., *Kamaraj: The Iron Man*, New Delhi: Deepak Associates, 1966.

Karashima, Noboru, (ed.), *A Concise History of South India: Issues and Interpretations*, Delhi: Oxford University Press, 2014.

———, *Ancient to Medieval: South Indian Society in Transition*, New Delhi: Oxford University Press, 2009.

———, *History and Society in South India: The Cholas to Vijayanagar*, New Delhi: Oxford University Press, 2001.

Kate, P. V., *Marathwada under the Nizams, 1724–1948*, Delhi: Mittal Publications, 1987.

Kavlekar, Kasinath, *Non-Brahmin Movement in Southern India, 1873–1949*, Kolhapur: Shivaji University Press, 1979.

Kesava Narayana, B., (ed.), *Modern Andhra and Hyderabad: AD 1858–1956 (Comprehensive History and Culture of Andhra Pradesh)*, Vol. 7, Hyderabad: Emesco, 2016.

Koshy, M. O., *The Dutch Power in Kerala: 1729–1758*, New Delhi: Mittal, 1989.

Krishnaswami Aiyangar, S., *Beginnings of South Indian History*, Madras: Modern Printing Works, 1918.

Kolharkulkarni, Krishna, *Bijapur: The Wonder Land*, Bijapur: District Administration, 2007.

Kunjukuttan, Matampu, *Outcaste*, Vasanthi Shankaranarayanan (ed. and trans.), Madras: Macmillan India, 1996.

Laik Ali, Mir, *Tragedy of Hyderabad*, Hyderabad: Deccan Archaeological and Cultural Research Institute, 2011.

Leonard, John Greenfield, *Kandukuri Viresalingam*, Hyderabad: Telugu University, 1991.

Ludden, David, *Peasant History in South India*, Princeton, NJ: Princeton University Press, 1985.

Madhavan, Chithra, *History and Culture of Tamil Nadu: As Gleaned from the Sanskrit Inscriptions*, New Delhi: D. K. Printworld, 2007.

Mahalingam, T. V., (ed.), *Mackenzie Manuscripts: Summaries of the Historical Manuscripts in the Mackenzie Collection*, 2 Vols., Madras: University of Madras, 1976.

———, *Readings in South Indian History*, Delhi: B. R. Publishing, 1977.

Mantena, Rama Sundari, *Origins of Modern Historiography in India: Antiquarianism and Philology, 1780–1880*, New York: Palgrave Macmillan, 2012.

Menon, Dilip M., *Caste, Nationalism and Communism in South India: Malabar, 1900–1948*, Cambridge, UK: Cambridge University Press, 1994.

Michaud, Joseph, *History of Mysore under Hyder Ali and Tippoo Sultan*, V. K. Raman Menon (trans.), Madras: 1924; New Delhi: Asian Educational Service, 1985, (repr).

Mills, Margaret, Claus, Peter and Diamond, Sarah, (eds.), *South Asian Folklore: An Encyclopedia*, New York: Routledge, 2003.

Mines, Mattison, *Muslim Merchants: The Economic Behaviour of an Indian Muslim Community*, New Delhi: Shri Ram Centre, 1972.

———, *The Warrior Merchants: Textiles, Trade, and Territory in South India*, Cambridge: Cambridge University Press, 1984.

———, *Public Faces, Private Voices: Community and Individuality in South India*, Berkeley: University of California Press, 1994.

Mitchell, Lisa, *Language, Emotion, & Politics in South India: The Making of a Mother Tongue*, Ranikhet, Uttarakhand: Permanent Black, 2010.

M. M. D. L. T. (Maistre De la Tour), *The History of Hyder Shah, Alias Hyder Ali Kan Bahadur*, London, 1784; Calcutta, 1848.

———, *The History of Hyder Shah and of his son Tippoo Sultaun*, 1855; Delhi: Cosmo, 1976, (repr).

Montagu, Edwin S., *An Indian Diary*, London: Heinemann, 1930.

Moon, Penderel, (ed.), *Wavell: The Viceroy's Journal*, London: Oxford University Press, 1973.

Muddachari, B., *Mysore–Maratha Relations in the 17th Century*, Mysore: University of Mysore, 1969.

Mukherjee, Rila, (ed.), *Beyond National Frames: South Asian Pasts and the World*, Delhi: Primus, 2015.

Mukund, Kanakalatha and Sundari, B. Syama, *Traditional Industry in the New Market Economy*, New Delhi: Sage, 2001.

Mukund, Kanakalatha, *Merchants of Tamilakam: Pioneers of International Trade*, New Delhi: Penguin Books, 2012.

Muthanna, I. M., *Karnataka: History, Administration and Culture*, Bangalore: Lotus Printers, 1977.

Muthiah, S., *Madras Discovered: A Historical Guide*, Madras: Affiliated East-West, 1987.

———, *Tales of Old and New Madras*, Madras: Affiliated East-West, 1989.

———, (ed.), *Madras: Its Yesterdays, Todays and Tomorrows*, Madras: Affiliated East-West, 1990.

———, Sriram, V. and Ashok, Ranjitha, (eds.), *Madras Musings: A Silver Jubilee Collection*, Chennai: Ranpar Publications for Chennai Heritage, 2016.

Murthy, Narasimha N. K., *Purniah*, Bangalore: R. Purniah, 1974.

Nair, A. A., *Peeps at the Press in South India*, Madras: A. A. Nair, 1966.

Narasimha Rao, P. V., *The Insider*, New Delhi: Penguin, 2000.

———, *Ayodhya: 6 December 1992*, New Delhi: Penguin/Viking, 2006.

Narasimhan, V. K., *Kamaraj: A Study*, New Delhi: National Book Trust, 2007.

Narayan, R. K., *The Emerald Route*, Mysore: Indian Thought Publications, 1977.

Rao, V. Narayana, *Twentieth Century Telugu Poetry: An Anthology*, Delhi: Oxford University Press, 2012.

———, Shulman, David and Subrahmanyam, Sanjay, *Symbols of Substance: Court and State in Nayaka Period Tamilnadu*, Delhi: Oxford University Press, 1992.

———, *Textures of Time: Writing History in South India*, New Delhi: Permanent Black, 2001.

Narla, V. R., *Veeresalingam*, New Delhi: Sahitya Akademi, 1968.

———, *Vemana*, 1969, New Delhi: Sahitya Akademi; Hyderabad: Vemana Foundation, 2006, (repr).

———, *Vemana Through Western Eyes*, 1969, New Delhi: Sahitya Akademi; Hyderabad: Vemana Foundation, 2006, (repr).

Singh, K. Natwar, *One Life is Not Enough: An Autobiography*, New Delhi: Rupa Publications, 2014.

Nayak, H. M. and Gopal, B. R., (eds.), *South Indian Studies*, Mysore: Geetha Book House, 1990.

Sastri, K.A. Nilakanta, *A History of South India*, 1955, Madras: Oxford University Press, 1976; Fourth edition, (repr).

Orme, Robert, *A History of the Military Transactions of the British Nation in Indostan, From the Year MDCCXLV, to Which is Prefixed a Dissertation on the Establishments Made by Mahomedan Conquerors in Indostan*, Vol. 2, London: John Nourse, 1778; New Delhi: Today's and Tomorrow's Printers and Publishers, (repr).

Panikkar, K. N., *Culture, Ideology, Hegemony: Intellectuals and Social Consciousness in Colonial India*, London: Wimbledon Publishing Company, 2002.

Parthasarathy, R., *A Hundred Years of The Hindu: The Epic Story of Indian Nationalism*, Madras: Kasturi & Sons, 1978.

Pearson, Hugh, *Memoirs of the Life and Correspondence of the Reverend Christian*

Frederick Swartz, London: J. Hatchard and Son, 1839.

Philips, C. H., *The East India Company, 1784–1834*, Manchester, UK: Manchester University Press, 1968.

Pillai, P. Chidambaram, *Right of Temple Entry*, Chennai: MJP Publishers, 2008, (repr).

Pope, G. U., *The Sacred Kurral of Tiruvalluva–Nayanar*, Oxford, 1886; New Delhi: Asian Educational Service, 1980, (repr).

Prasad, Muni Narayana, (trans. & comp.), *Narayana Guru: Complete Works*, New Delhi: National Book Trust, 2006.

Rao 'Punganiri', Ram Chandra, *Memoirs of Hyder and Tippoo: Rulers of Seringapatam*, C. P. Brown (trans.), Madras: Simkins, 1849.

Rajaram, Nyapathy and Srinivas, Nyapathy, *Life & Times of 'Andhra Bheeshma' Shri Nyapathy Subba Rao Pantulu*, Chennai.

Ramachandramurthy, S. S., *A Study of Telugu Place–Names*, Delhi: Agam Kala Prakashan, 1985.

Raman Pillai, C. V., *Marthanda Varma*, B. K. Menon (trans.), 1936; New Delhi: Sahitya Akademi, 1998, (repr).

Ramaswami, N. S., *Political History of the Carnatic Under the Nawabs*, New Delhi: Abhinav, 1984.

Rangarajan, Mahesh, Balakrishnan, N. and Bhatnagar, Deepa, (eds.), *Selected Works of C. Rajagopalachari*, Vol. 1, 1901–21, New Delhi: Orient BlackSwan, 2014.

Rangaswami, Vanaja, *The Story of Integration: A New Interpretation*, New Delhi: Manohar, 1981.

Ravi Shankar, Prabha, *G. A. Natesan and National Awakening*, New Delhi: Promilla, 2015.

Reddy, G. N. and Bangorey, (eds.), *Literary Autobiography of C. P. Brown*, Tirupati: Sri Venkateswara University, 1978.

Reddy, V. Ramakrishna, (ed.), *Contemporary History of Andhra Pradesh and Telangana* (*Comprehensive History and Culture of Andhra Pradesh*), Vol. 8, Hyderabad: Emesco, 2016.

Reddy, S. Muthulakshmi, *Autobiography*, Madras: 1964.

Robertson, S., *Approaching Religion in a Pluralistic Context*, Bengaluru: BTESSC/ SATHRI, 2009.

Sambamoorthy, P., *Great Composers*, Chennai: Indian Music Publishing House, 2004; 2010, (repr).

Sampath, R. N. and Mani, Pe Su, *V.O. Chidambaram Pillai*, New Delhi: Publications Division, 1992.

Satyanarayana, Adapa, (ed.), *Early Modern Andhra, Hyderabad, and Company Rule: AD 1724–1857* (*Comprehensive History and Culture of Andhra Pradesh*), Vol. 6, Hyderabad: Emesco, 2016.

Sethu, *Aliyah*, Catherine Thankamma (trans.), New Delhi: HarperCollins, 2016.

Shulman, David, *Tamil: A Biography*, Cambridge, Mass: Bellnap Press of Harvard University Press, 2016.

———, *More than Real: A History of the Imagination in South India*, Cambridge, Mass: Harvard University Press, 2012.

Sivaraman, Mythily, *Haunted by Fire: Essays on Caste, Class, Exploitation and Emancipation*, New Delhi: LeftWord, 2013.

Sobhanan, B., *Dewan Velu Thampi and the British*, Trivandrum: Kerala Historical Society, 1978.

Soneji, Davesh, *Unfinished Gestures: Devadasis, Memory, and Modernity in South India*, Chicago: University of Chicago Press, 2012.

Sreenivasa Murthy, H. V., Rao, B. Surendra, Veluthat, Kesavan and Bari, S. A., (eds.), *Essays on Indian History and Culture* (in honour of Prof. B. Sheik Ali), New Delhi: Mittal Publications, 1990.

Srinivas, M. N., *The Remembered Village*, Delhi: Oxford University Press, 1976.

Stein, Burton, (ed.), *Essays on South India*, Honolulu: University Press of Hawaii, 1975.

———, *Peasant State and Society in Medieval South India*, Delhi: Oxford University Press, 1980.

———, *Thomas Munro: The Origins of the Colonial State and His Vision of Empire*, Delhi: Oxford University Press, 1989.

Strachey, R. and Others, *Report of the Indian Famine Commission*, London: Her Majesty's Stationery Office, 1880.

Sudhakar, G. J., (ed.), *Popular Uprisings in India with Special Reference to Tamil Nadu, 1750–1857*, Chennai: C. P. R. Institute of Indological Research, 2015.

Sullivan, Robert E., *Macaulay: The Tragedy of Power*, New Delhi: Orient BlackSwan, 2010.

Sunderlal, Pandit, *How India Lost her Freedom*, Bombay: Popular Prakashan, 1970.

Talbot, Cynthia, (ed.), *Knowing India: Colonial and Modern Constructions of the Past*, New Delhi: Yoda Press, 2011.

———, *Precolonial India in Practice: Society, Region, and Identity in Medieval Andhra*, New York: Oxford University Press, 2001.

Thomas, Daniel, *Sree Narayana Guru*, Bangalore: Christian Institute for Study of Religion & Society, 1965.

Thompson, Edward, *A History of India*, New York: Doubleday, 1928.

Trautmann, Thomas, *Languages and Nations: The Dravidian Proof in Colonial Madras*, New Delhi: Yoda Press, 2006.

Vaasanthi, *Cut-outs, Caste and Cine Stars: The World of Tamil Politics*, New Delhi: Penguin/Viking, 2006.

———, *Amma: Jayalalithaa's Journey from Movie Star to Political Queen*, New Delhi, Juggernaut, 2016.

Venkatachalapathy, A. R., *In Those Days There Was No Coffee: Writings in Cultural History*, New Delhi: Yoda Press, 2006.

Vijaisri, Priyadarshini, *Recasting the Devadasi: Patterns of Sacred Prostitution in Colonial South India*, New Delhi: Kanishka, 2004.

Vizagapatam District Gazetteer 1907, Hyderabad: State Editor, District Gazetteers, 1994, (repr).

Wheeler, J. Talboys, *Annals of the Madras Presidency, 1639–1702*, Madras, 1861; Delhi: B. R. Publishing, 1985, (repr).

———, *India Under British Rule from the Foundation of the East India Company*, London: Macmillan and Co., 1886.

Wilks, Mark and Hammick, Murray, *South Indian History from the Earliest Times to the last Muhammadan Dynasty*, 4 Vols., 1817; New Delhi: Cosmo, 1980, (repr).

Wodeyar, Sadashiva, *Rani Chennamma*, New Delhi: National Book Trust, 1977.

INDEX

politics, 113
powers, xxii, 3, 63
priests, 26
soldiers, 17, 61, 170
tactics, 90
trader, 8, 167
trading, 20, 21, 192
Europeans,
    India-based, 136, 166
    in Haidar's service, 78
    polluters, not liberators, 56
    Europeans
Europe–India equation, 164
EVR (see Ramasami, E. V.)
exports, 6, 52, 128
extremists, 238, 240, 241, 402, 416
Ezhavas, 23, 232-35, 271-72, 334, 336-37,
    372, 374, 421

fakirs, 132
famine, 83, 91, 108, 154, 155, 213, 214,
    215, 332
Famine Commission Report, 215
fanaticism, 261, 263
Fazl, Sayyid, 262
Fernandes, George, 397, 433
Fernandes, Lawrence, 397
Fishery, 4, 5
Fishing, 27, 28
    village, 27, 28
Folk drama, 427
Folklore, 32, 47
Folktale, 15, 181
    European, 181
    Tamil, 15
    The Subahdar of the Cot, 15
Folk traditions, 155
Folk traditions, 155
Forts
    George, 17
    Gingee 12, 31, 32
    Golconda, 24
    Kittoor, 190
    Mahe, 5
    St David, 13, 39, 40, 61
    Tellicherry (Thalassery), 50
    Trichy, 45, 46, 47, 125
    Tuticorin, 124
    Wandiwash, 62
    Fort St George, xx, xxii, 7-14, 16-19, 30-
        33, 38, 40, 46, 64, 68, 81-82, 85, 91,
        99, 104, 105, 112-13, 119, 120-21, 146,
        164, 167-68, 172, 177-80, 187, 190,
        192, 197, 203-07, 213, 248, 251-52,
        260, 263-64, 267, 277, 281, 283, 282,
        296-97, 299, 365, 400
    Britons at, 8
    confidential records, 12

French capture of, 38
    minute of 16 June 1690, 10
    records, 9, 10
Fort St George museum, 297
Fraser, Hastings, 202
French, xx, 1, 2-3, 6, 10, 12-13, 25, 27-29,
    32-50, 53-57, 61-63, 67, 68-69, 73-74, 83,
    84, 86-88, 92, 102, 104, 111, 127, 134-
    35, 143, 145, 176, 195-98, 241, 255
    capture of Fort St George, 38
    factory in India, 27
    Gingee captured by, 45
    in South India, 41
    military expeditions to India, 39
    navy, 102
    settlement, 34, 36
    ships, 25, 38, 39
    support for Haidar and Tipu, 111
    threw the English out of Fort St George, 13
    traders, 2
French East India Company, 27, 34, 43, 45,
    48, 62
French Revolution, 88, 111
Friedrich, Hermann, 232
Fryer, Dr, 19
Fullarton, William, 68, 120, 154
fundamental rights, 390

Gadgil, N. V., 342
Gajapati Raju, Ananda, 224
Ganapati, Kakatiya king, 5
Gandharvas, 15
Gandhi, Devadas, 256, 288
Gandhi, Indira, 374, 379, 385-406, 413, 417-
    18, 420, 424, 442
    assassination, 403
    convictions, 390
    economic policies, 395
Gandhi–Irwin Pact, 286
Gandhi, Mohandas, 240-41, 249-58, 262,
    266-74, 277, 279-88, 292, 295, 299-27,
    333, 335, 338, 341-45, 367, 380, 383,
    394, 396, 399-02, 406, 416, 420, 424-27,
    430, 432, 442
    death/assassination, 343, 345, 416, 427
    Hind Swaraj, 252
    imprisoned, 286
    policy of nonviolence, 262
    release from prison, 277
    suspension of defiance, 277
    visited
        Calicut, 262
        Madras, 250
        south, 242
        Tamil country, 279
        Vaikom, 272
        Yerawada prison, 286
Gandhi, Rajiv, 402-19, 424-25

assassination, 412-13, 425
  Sri Lankan policies, 414
Gandhi, Sonia, 413, 425, 431
Ganesan, Sivaji, 366, 383, 385, 425
George V, King, 296
George VI, King, 327
George, T. J. S., 428
George Town, 11
Ghaffar, Qazi Abdul, 349
Ghosh, Atulya, 386
Gillespie, Colonel Rollo, 132
Gingee, xvii, 2, 12, 31, 32, 33, 34, 45, 158
Giri, Varahagiri Venkata, 295-96, 386-87
Gita, 11, 144, 241, 309, 397
Gladstone, William, 217
Godse, Nathuram, 343
Goenka, Ramnath, 325, 360-61, 385
Gokhale, Gopal Krishna, 250
Gokuldas Tejpal Sanskrit College Trust, 219
Golconda (Hyderabad), xv, xvi, xxii, 1, 4, 9,
  12-13, 19, 24-26, 29, 31-32, 36, 40, 43-
  45, 53-56, 73, 87, 90-92, 101-107, 153,
  164, 165, 193, 198-209, 212, 285, 325-
  33, 339, 340, 345-54, 369, 373, 391-92,
  403-04, 418, 422-23, 437-38
  agents and spies in, 12
  court of, 12
  dominion over San Thome, 12
  fall of, 12
  official language, 25
Golden Temple, Amritsar, 402
Gopala Menon, U., 262
Gopalan, A. K., 372
Gopala Reddi, B., 295
Gover, Charles E., 147
  Lives of the Telugu Poets, 147
  The Folk Songs of Southern India, 147
Government of India Act of 1919, 247
Government of India Act of 1935, 294
Government Oriental Manuscripts Library,
  Chennai, 165
Gowda, Kempe I, 101
Grammars, xxi, 47, 167, 168, 176, 177, 178,
  180
  Malayalam, 178
  Telugu, 168, 176
Great Calcutta Killing, 324
Great Famine, 213, 332
Great Mogul, 49, 60
Great Revolt, 131, 205, 211
Green Pamphlet, 250
Grigson, W. V., 330
Guerrilla warfare, 117, 118, 312
Guha, Arun Chandra, 316
Gujaratis, 21, 29, 68
Gujral, Inder Kumar, 419, 424-25, 431-32
Gulbarga, xvi, xxii, 204, 349, 352
Gundert, Hermann, 178

Gunpowder and weapons, 7, 9, 17, 18, 30,
  49, 51, 63, 65, 94, 98, 105, 109, 132,
  133, 187, 196, 201, 203, 275
Gun salute, 9, 212, 341
Gupta, Deshbandhu, 360
Gurukkal, Rajan 445, 467
Gurusıddappa, 190
Guruvayur temple, 287, 302, 335, 336
  entry campaign, 335
  entry of Dalits, 287

Habib, Irfan, 74
Haidar army, 82
Haidar Ali, xviii, 53, 54, 62, 64-68, 71-86,
  100, 110-13, 117, 119-20, 124, 154-58,
  169-70, 188, 261, 311
  anti-British drive, 80
  arms and horsemanship, 72
  captured Sira, 79
  court and administration, 76
  death of, 77, 81, 84, 85, 117
  defeat in Tiruvannamalai, 80
  interest in Coorg, 79
  international trade, 83
  military skills, 73
  speaking and writing capacities, 75
Hamilton, Francis, 74, 449, 452, see also
  Buchanan, Francis
Hampi, xvii, 2, 19, 170, 226
Hanumanthaiah, Kengal, 370
Hardgrave Jr., Robert, 383, 410, 456, 460,
  461, 462, 464, 465, 466, 467, 468, 469,
  470-74
Haridasas, 153, 154, 158
Harijan, 308
Harijana Devalayam Pravesam, 368
Harijan Temple Entry, 368
Harikathas, 153, 158
Harris, General George, 105, 106, 111, 112,
  206
Harrison, Selig, 376
Hasan Khan, 9
Hasan, Mohibbul, 74, 449, 450, 451
Hassan, Yakub, 262
Hastings, Warren, 120, 345
Hayavadana Rao, C. (ed.), 30, 30*(fn)*
  Mysore Gazetteer, vol. 1, 30*(fn)*
Hegde, Ramakrishna, 418, 426
Herald, 308
Higginson, Nathaniel, 13
Hill, Samuel Charles, xx, 16, 48, 66-72, 446,
  447, 448, 449
Himalayas, xviii, xix, xxi, 153, 377
Hinduism/Hindooism, 27, 136, 158, 177
Hindu Mahasabha, 314, 341, 415
Hindu–Muslim, 56, 63, 75, 168, 199, 255,
  260, 263, 269, 281, 331, 342, 347, 348,
  352

alliance, 255
partnership, 260
prejudice, 56
understanding, 352
unity, 263, 269, 281
violence, 347, 348
Hindu/Hindus, 50, 171, 184, 185-86, 206
castes, 130
chief, 31
Malayalis, 23
Rajas, 61
sense of superiority in, 139
Hindustan/Hindostan, 6, 44, 85, 99, 199, 321
Hindustani, 220
Hindu, The, 215-16, 219, 231, 243, 245,
250-52, 256, 260, 288, 298, 305, 309,
314, 340, 401, 407
Hitler, 289, 307, 310-11, 321-22, 337
Hoare, Samuel, 296
Holland, 6, 307
foreign trade of, 6
Home, Robert, 99
Home Rule, 243, 245-47
Home Rule League, 243
Hooper, Willoughby Wallace, 213
Hope, Arthur, 308, 309, 311
Horniman, B. G., 249*(fn)*
House of Commons, 163, 207, 219, 244,
308, 316
House of Lords, 171, 255
Hoysalas, xvii, xxi
Hughes, George, 123, 127
Hughes, Major, 206
Hughes, Thomas, 216
Tom Brown's Schooldays, 216
Hume, Allan Octavian, 195, 216, 218, 219,
220
Humiliations, 37, 101, 259, 269, 284, 304
Humility, 39, 184
Hunas, 15, 19
Husain, Dr Zakir, 386
Hydari, Akbar, 330
Hyderabad
killings of Hindus in, 347
Hyderabad armies, 91, 348
Hyderabad Congress, 329, 331
Hyder, Fateh, 106, 111-12, 132-33

Ideology, 15, 339, 376-77, 421, 426, 440
Dravida, 377
radical, 421
Ilbert, Courtenay Peregrine, 216, 217, 244
Ilbert's Bill, 217, 244
Imperial Assemblage, 212-13, 216
imperialism, 294, 297
imports, 6, 17, 95, 128
Imroze, 347
Independence movement, 290

India
eighteenth-century, 86
exports, 6, 52
first joint-stock company, 9
French empire in, 44
French factory in, 27
French military expeditions to, 39
imports, 6
independence of, 340
language policy, 381
mode of administration in, 170
Muslim rulers, 14, 64
Partition, 340
peninsular, xvii
pre-colonial, 215
terrorist acts in, 438
trade, 4
India, 241
India As I Knew It, 253
India–China war, 375, 377
India Herald, 179
Indian textiles, dominance of, 6
Indian
agents and spies, 12
antiquities, 165
chiefs, 3, 60, 63, 65, 108
Christians, 132, 242, 247, 259, 294, 299
cloth, 6, 7
dubash, 9
economy, liberalization of, 415
exports, 6, 52
independence, 307, 310, 311, 322, 377,
428
labour, 7
merchants, 1, 7, 8, 10, 12, 34, 50, 63, 88
nationalism, 237
peasants, 55, 172
politics, 247
princes, 42, 63, 103, 110, 328
sepoys, 46, 48, 61, 64, 131
revolt of, 131
spy, 96
textiles, 7
troops, 347, 349, 351, 408
Indian Army, 17, 46, 58, 347, 348, 402, 408,
414
Operation Polo, 347, 349, 350, 351, 352
Indian Association, 219
Indian Communist Party, 312, 337
Indian Express, 300, 325, 360, 361
Indian National Army, 432
Indian National Congress (INC), 216, 218-21,
230, 237, 240, 254, 262, 287-88, 299-
300, 333, 385, 417
annual session, 254, 258
leadership, 309
national leadership, 307
policy, 270, 310

Kanpur (Cawnpore), 199, 200, 297, 402
Massacre in, 199
Karanth, Shivaram, 397
Karnataka, xxii, 2, 19, 24, 30-31, 52, 129,
141-42, 148, 153, 204, 248-49, 332-33,
338, 369-70, 384, 386, 393-400, 410,
417-19, 426, 433, 435, 437-39
Maratha incursions, 52

Karnataka defiance, 204
Karnataka Janata Dal, 418
Karnatic wars, 127
Karunakaran, K., 398, 420-21
Karunanidhi, Muthuvel, 366, 383-91, 395-96,
400, 411-12, 419, 425-26, 433-35, 440
Kashmir issue, 212, 345, 381, 401
Kasturba, 319, 335
Kattabomman, Jagaveera, 119-121,
Kattabomman, Veerapandya, 121-126, 161,
237
Kaur, Amrit, 341
Kavali brothers, 166
Kavali Venkata Subbaiah, 165
Keladi rulers, 20
Kelappan, K., 271, 287, 335-36
Kenchangowda, 205, 206
Kennedy, John F., US President, 378, 383
Kerala, xxi, xxii, 1, 20-24, 27, 50-52, 117,
119, 181, 183, 232-35, 249, 262, 265,
334-39, 369, 370-77, 384, 387, 393, 395,
397, 399-400, 420-24, 437
Communists' electoral success in, 372
Education Act, 374
land reforms, 393
Left's intervention in, 421
model of development, 393
President's Rule, 374
upsurge of the lower classes in, 235
Kerala Congress, 374, 384, 399, 420
Kerala Mitran, 336
Kerala Pradesh Congress Committee (KPCC),
374
Kesavadas, 194
Kesava Menon, K. P., 262-66
Kesava Pillai, 260
Kesavayya, Bobbili
Bhuloka Chapa Chutti, 159
Keshgee, Kadir Khan, 115, 116
Kesri, Sitaram, 419
Keyes, Terence, 328
khadi, 250, 257, 266, 269, 282, 296, 317,
333, 335, 382
Khammam, 352-53, 393
Khan, Abdul Ghaffar, 251, 327
Khan, Anwaruddin, 'Nabob' of Arcot, 38,
42, 44, 45
Khande Rao, 74, 79
Khan, Dilavar, 52

Khan, Dost Ali, 40
Khan, Hakim Ajmal, 256, 257
Khan, Khizr Hayat, 326
Khan, Liaquat Ali, 324
Khan, Muhammad Yusuf, xx, 38, 47-48, 64-
72, 119, 133, 177
1764 hanging, 119
assistance to the British, 66
bid to rescue, 70
conspiracy against, 69-70
defeated Varma's army, 69
fighting skills, 67
fiscal skills, 67
taken over Madurai, 66
visit to Meenakshi temple, 66
Khan, Nizam Osman Ali, 328, 329, 345, 351
Khan, Sayyid Ahmad, 221
Khan, Shams-ud-daula Husain Dost, 40
Khan, Sher Muhammad, 53
conquered Srikakulam, 53
Khan, Shoaibullah, 347
Khan, Sikandar Hayat, 309
Khan, Zulfiqar, Mughal commander, 12
siege of Gingee Fort, 12
Khedgikar, Venkatesh, 329
Khilafat, 255-57, 262-66
Khudadad, 110
Khurana, S. L., 411
Kidwai, Rafi Ahmed, 341
Kirkpatrick, James, 198
Kirmani, Mir Hussain, 86
Kittel, Ferdinand, 178, 231
Kochi (Cochin)
Dutch capture of, 23
Kodava(s), xvii, 86, 87, 115
Kodumunda, 336
Kolappan, B., 401*(fn)*
Komatis (Komutis, Komuttis) 37, 43, 129
Koya, C. H. Mohammed, 373, 420
Koya, Moideen, 262
Koyas, 274
Kripalani, Acharya J. B., 326, 358, 361, 396
Krishnadevaraya, Vijayanagara's emperor, 2,
52, 153
Krishnadevipeta, 274, 275
Krishna Iyer, V. R., 374
Krishnamachari, T. T., 298, 303, 390, 439
Krishna Menon, V. K., 377, 439
Krishnamurthy, Lakshmi, 396
Krishnamurthy, Ramaswamy, 429
Kalki, 429
Krishna Pillai, 194
Krishnaraja, 73, 80, 101, 112-14, 191, 207,
333-34
Krishna Rao, K. R. V., 81, 96-97, 248
Krishnaswami Aiyangar, S., xviii
*South India: A Distinct Entity in Indian
History*, xviii

Mudali, Kanakaraya, 35, 37
Mudali, Tittarappa, 66
Muddupalani, 293
  Radhika Santvanam, 293
Mughal Delhi, 15
Mughal Empire, xxii, 1, 36, 59, 167
Mughal hegemony, 56
Mughal pride, 25
Mughal(s), xv, xvi, xvii, xxii, 1, 3-4, 12, 13,
  15-20, 25-32, 36, 39, 44-45, 52-53, 56,
  59-60, 72, 74, 87, 101, 153, 165, 167,
  208, 212, 329, 345, 346
  armies, 32
  court, 13, 27
  paramountcy over India, 18
  southern successes of 26
  viceroy, 74
  victories over Deccan, 17, 29
Muhammad Ali, Nawab, 32, 44-46, 47, 49,
  62, 65-74, 82, 101, 119-22, 132, 154,
  169, 172, 191, 439
Muhammad, Fath, 72
Muhammad Shah, Emperor, 36
Mukherjee, Pranab, 432
Mukkombu, 192
Mullen, Thomas, Jr., 61
Mullick, B. N. 359, 470
Mundargi, Bhimrao, 205, 206
Mundassery, Joseph, 373
Muni Narayana Prasad, 235
Munro, J. B. L., 304
Munro, Thomas, 77, 90-91, 99, 109, 169-
  175, 179, 188-89, 197, 210
  about strength of Mysore, 77
  Confidential Minute, 172
  educational theory, 197
  policy, 170
  survey of education, 197
Munshi, K. M., 346-74, 389
Munuswami Pillai, V. I., 295, 325
Musaliyar, Ali, 263, 264
Music, xix, 145, 152-62, 268, 293, 333,
  427-30
  Carnatic, 160, 162
  classical, 157
  devotional, 153
  Hindustani, 153, 160
  sacred, 152, 157
Murthy, N. K. Narasimha 448, 449, 451
Muslim League, 244, 255, 294, 298, 300,
  303-08, 311-14, 324-327, 330, 333, 339,
  372-74, 384, 399, 420
  Pakistan demand, 307, 333
Muslim chiefs, 112
Muslim traders, 5
Muslims and Brahmins
  enmity, 97
Muslim warriors, 22

Muthiah, S., xx, 166, 445, 454, 455, 464
Muthulakshmi Reddy, Dr, 290-93
  campaign, 292
  on women's issues, 291
Muthu, M. K., 390
Muzaffar Jung, 42, 44-45, 73, 84
Mylapore, ix, 11, 19, 144, 219, 244, 298
Mysoor, 95
Mysore,
  autonomy, 20
  Company's operations against, 166
  defeat, 187
  ethnicities, 100
Maratha incursions into, 73
Muslim rebellion in, 112
Muslim rule, 111
Mysorean army, 66, 72-73, 83, 89
Mysore University, 397

Nabi Khan Khattack, 66
attack on the temple of Srivilliputtur, 66
Nadars, 181, 183, 209-11, 243, 356
Nadir Shah, Emperor, 36-37, 199
  invasion of Delhi, 199
Nagabattan, 7, 9
Nagarathnamma, 293
Naicker, Manickavelu, 362*(fn)*
Naidu, Partha Saradhi, 231
Naidu, P. Varadarajulu, 243
Naidu, Ramachandra, 282
Naidu, R. Venkataratnam, 291*(fn)*
Naidu, Sarojini, 249*(fn)*, 285
Naidu, Varadarajulu, 243, 259-60, 277-78,
  365
Naidu, Venkaiah, 439
Nair, Dr T. M., 246
Nair(s) (Nayars), 50, 51, 79, 89, 117-18,
  182-84, 193-94, 209-11, 221-23, 232-35,
  242, 246-47, 260-66, 271, 333-38, 372-
  73, 420-21, 432
  aristocrats, 117
  victory of 28 December 1789, 89
Nair Service Society, 235, 271, 373
Nair, Vasudevan, 420
Nambiar, Ayillyath Kuttiari Gopalan (AKG),
  337
Namboodiripad, Elamkulam Manakkal
  Sankaran (EMS), 265, 334-37, 370-75,
  387, 393, 421
Namboories, 182, 183, 184
Nambudiri(s), 21, 23, 210, 222, 232-33, 260-
  64, 271, 272, 334-37
  priests, 272
Nampoothiri, Sankaran, 193
Nana Saheb Dhondu Pant Peshwa, 206
Nanda, Gulzarilal, 381
Nandidurg Fort, 95
Nandyal, 413, 417

Nanjaraja, 72, 73, 80
Naoroji, Dadabhai, 219-21
Napoleon, 74, 103-04, 108, 164
Narasimha Rao, Pamulaparti Venkata, 392,
    413-17, 421, 424, 431, 440
Narasingarayanpet, 84
Narayana Guru, Sri, 232-36, 272
    Siva Satakam, 233

Narayana Menon, M. P., 264
Narayanan, Kocheril Raman (K. R.), 423-24,
    440
Narayanappa, Kavali, 165
Narayana Rao, Huilgol, 333
    Udayavagali Namma Cheluva
        Kannadanaadu, 333
Narayanaswami Aiyer, S., 291
Narayan, Jayaprakash (JP), 390, 394-95, 400,
    427
Narayan Reddy, Ravi, 351, 353
Narla, Venkateswara Rao, 146-50
    analysis of Vemana's verses, 147
Nasir Jung, 42-45, 73
Nasir-ud-Daula, 198
Nasrani (Christian) Jaati Aikya Sangha, 22
Natesan, G. A., 231
National Front, 404, 405, 409
nationalism, 221, 236-37, 266, 376, 385
    economic, 237
    political, 237
    Tamil, 376, 385
national leadership, 258, 307, 440
national movement, 219, 282-83, 286, 303,
    367
National School of Drama, 427
Nattukottai Chettiars, 278
Nautch girls, 291
Navaiyats, 40
Nawab of Chittoor, 72
Nawab of Kadapa, 45
Nawab of Sira, 72
Nawab of Surat, 36
Nayadu, Shayappa, 52, 53
Nayakas, xvii, 1, 2-4, 8, 15, 26, 32, 40, 65,
    154
    Hindu, 40, 65
    lands, 26
    of Gingee, 2
    of Madurai, 2
    of Thanjavur, 2
    rulers, 3, 65
    territories 2,
Nayak, Gopala, 125
Nayak, Hanumappa, 191
Nayak, Varadappa, 152
Nayak, Venkatappa, 204
Nayanar, E. K., 420
Nayanars, 157, 420

Nayar, K. K. K., 415
NDA, 425-26, 433-34, 439
Neelakanta, 239-40, 283
Nehru, Jawaharlal, 252, 257-58, 266, 280,
    288, 297, 299, 304, 307-16, 322, 323-27,
    341-53, 356-81, 385, 415, 423, 426
death of, 379, 380
Nehru–Kamaraj relationship, 376
Nehru, Motilal, 257-58, 266, 270, 279, 285,
    360
Nehru–Patel, 325-26, 357
Neill, James, 297
Nellore, xvii, 16, 30, 48, 231, 353, 367-68
Nelson, J. H., 230
Nenjukku Needhi, 435
New India, 242, 243
Nijalingappa, S., 370, 386-88, 442
Nilgiris, 169, 295
Nivedita, Sister, 240
Nizam(s) of Hyderabad, 31, 36-37, 40, 42-45,
    51, 54, 56, 73-74, 80, 87, 90-95, 98, 99,
    103-09, 169-70, 194, 198, 199-208, 212
Nizam Ali, Mir, 90
Non-Aligned Movement, 377
Non-Brahmin Movement, 290
Non-Brahmins, 19, 62, 75, 138, 171, 174,
    179-181, 197, 224, 230-31, 242-47, 259-
    60, 278, 290, 294, 306, 312, 320, 333,
    337-38, 341, 356, 370
high-caste, 62
Non-cooperation, 234, 255-63, 266, 269-74,
    278-79, 282, 290
Nonviolence, 255-56, 262, 283
Nonviolent movement, 312
Nonviolent Non-cooperation, 255
Northern Circars, 329
North-West Frontier Province, 251, 327
Norton, George, 180
Novel(s), 134, 221-22, 227, 237, 292, 398
    Malayalam, 221
    Telugu, 227
Nuclear detonations, 378, 431
Nye, Archibald, 340

O'Dwyer, Michael, 252-55, 460
Official Languages Act, 381
Ogilby, Thomas, 206
Old Church Evangelical Fund, Calcutta, 177
Oppression, 352, 367, 426
    economic, 367
Oriental Memoirs, 232
Orme, Robert, 4, 38-49, 57-60, 444, 447,
    448
    about
        custom in an Indian army, 58
        defeated soldiers, 58
        Indian chiefs, 60
        non-combatants, 58

Saivism, 148, 278
Saivites, 155, 225, 237, 290, 300, 301, 337
  non-Brahmin, 290
Salabat Jung, 45
Salar Jung, 199, 201, 203, 208, 209
  role in the 1857 Revolt, 208
Salar Jung I, 199, 208
Salt Satyagraha, 280, 285, 306, 335, 353
Salt tax, 280
Samajwadi Party, 432
Sambamoorthy, P., 159, 162, 453
Sampath, E. V. K., 377
Sampati Rao, 51
Samyukta Karnataka, 333
Sandalwood, 20, 128
Sanjiva Reddy, Neelam, 325, 361, 370, 386,
  391, 440, 442
Sankaracharya, 96, 110, 226, 227
Sankaraiah, 167, 168
Sankar, R., 374
Santhanam, K., 396
Santhanam Pillai, 275
San Thome, xv, 11-12, 39, 80, 144
  Portuguese established, 11
Sarabhai, Anasuya, 249(*fn*)
Sarabhoji II (Serfoji II), 154, 155
Saraswathi, Sri Jayendra, 434
Sarda Bill, 285
Sarovignaimurti (Sarvajna), 142-43, 148, 150,
  151
Sarvadevavilasa, 10
Sasikala, 425(*fn*), 433, 434, 435, 436
Sastri, Natesa, 15
The Subahdar of the Cot, 15
Sastri, Pattabhirama, 167, 168
Sastri, Syama, 141, 158, 159, 160
Sati, 9, 134, 137
Satyagraha, 157, 250, 252, 254, 256, 269-72,
  277, 285, 287, 290, 306, 335, 353
Satyagraha movement, 252, 256
Satyagraha Sabha, 252, 285
Satyamurti, S., 259, 270, 283, 288-89, 301,
  306-07, 320, 371, 396
Satyanarayana Raju, Vegiraju, 275
Scheduled Castes (SCs), 286-87, 294, 372
Scheduled Tribes, 294
Schwartz, Charles Frederick, 50, 81-83, 155,
  156
Scott, Walter, 104
Sehgal, Lakshmi, 432
Self-government, 216, 244, 245, 247, 258

Self-respect, 160, 254, 382, 383
Self-Respect Movement, 278, 289, 290, 292,
  301
Sen-Tamil, 237
Separatism, 402
sepoys, 46-48, 61, 64, 71, 104-05, 131-35,

199-200, 204, 265
  English, 104
  southern, 133
Seshagiri Rao, 96
Settlements, 10-11, 13, 17, 34, 36, 62, 104,
  120, 182, 189-90, 286
  agrarian, 17
  Brahmin, 154
  Danish, 104
  French, 34, 36
Setty, Annadana, 81
Setty, Ranga, 81
Setupati of Ramnad, 27
Seva Dal, 285
Sevagram, 313, 314
Seven-year war, 111
Sezhiyan, Era, 396
Shah Alam II, 87, 101
Shanars [Nadars], 183
Shankar Pillai, K., 436
Sharada Prasad, H. Y., 399
Sharma, Shankar Dayal, 404
Sharp, G. R., 222
Shastri, Lal Bahadur, 358, 358(fn), 379, 381
  death of, 379
Shaukat Ali, 256, 262
Sherwood, Miss Marcella, 253, 254
Sheth, Maoji, 88
Ships, 1, 5, 7, 8, 14, 18, 20-25, 38-39, 63,
  87, 108, 238, 239, 261
  Danish, 14
  Dutch, 8, 20
  French, 25, 38, 39
  Portuguese, 20, 24
  Turkish, 22
Shivaji, 12, 24-29, 32, 312
  captured Bijapur, 28
  captured Gingee, 12
  died in 1680, 29
Shivalingarudra Sarja, 188, 189
Shivamogga (Shimoga), xvii, 317, 333
Shorapur, 204, 206
Shraddhanand, Swami, 251, 255
Shrines, xvii, 15, 110, 160, 338, 422
Shulman, David, 11, 15, 53, 56, 229
Sikhs, 247, 253, 309, 326, 341, 343, 402
  violence against, 402
Silappadikaram, 229
Sindhia, Daulat Rao, 101, 104
Singh, Arjun, 413, 417
Singh, Baldev, 341
Singh, Charan, 386, 387
Singh, Dharam, 438
Singh, Dr Manmohan, 414-15
Singh, Kalyan, 424
Singh, Mulayam, 432
Singh, Natwar, 407, 414
Singh, Ranjit, 311

Viceroy Linlithgow, 295-96, 308-09, 312, 318, 318
Viceroy Reading, 328
Viceroy Ripon, 216, 217, 219
Viceroy Willingdon, 338
Victoria, Queen & Empress, 207
  Proclamation, 207
Viduthalai, 300, 321, 355
Vijaya Bharati, S., 242
Vijayanagara Empire xv-xviii, xxii, 1-3, 8-9, 13, 15, 19-20, 25, 32, 52, 101, 153-54, 169, 248
  defeat of, xvi, 1, 2, 8, 9
  feudatory, 101
Vijayan, O. V., 436
Vijayan, Varkala, 397
Villappa Pillai, 215
Vimochana Samaram, 374
Vindhya mountains xviii, 436
Viranna, Kasi, 9
Viranna, Mudda, 13
Virasaiva, 147, 188
Vira Varma, 117
Virendranath, 285
Viresalingam, Kandukuri, 147, 225-31, 291, 293, 336
  Telugu Mahabharata, 225
Visvesvaraya, Mokshagundam, 332, 333
Viswadaabhirama Vinura Vema, 148, 149
Vithal Rajan, 133
Vitthala temple, Pandharpur, 153
Vivekananda, Swami, 234, 240
Vivekavardhini, 226, 231
Vizianagaram, 53-55, 223
  ruler, 55
Vokkaligas, 129, 332-33, 393, 417-18
Vyasaraya, 153

Wadiyar, Jayachamaraja, 334
  signed instrument of accession to India, 334
Wadiyar, Raja Chamaraja, 112
Wadiyars, 112, 114, 393
  restoration of, 112, 114
Walajah, Muhammad Ali, 44-47, 62
  failure of, 47
Wallace, E. H., 240
Waltair, 266, 378
Wandiwash, 41, 61, 62, 68
Wavell, Archibald, 312, 318-23, 327, 330
Wayanad, 118, 264
  tribals, 118
weaving, 34, 186, 277, 300
  decline of, 186
Welby, T. Earle, 244

Wellesley, Colonel Arthur, 103, 105, 106, 112-13, 134
Wellesley, Richard, the Earl of Mornington, 74, 101
  expansionist India policy, 101
Welsh, James, 122-26
  about Chinna Marudu, 126
  about Marudu brothers, 124
Wheeler, James Talboys, 17, 30, 61, 444, 445, 446, 447, 448
  Annals of the Madras Presidency, 1639–1702, 30
White Town, 17, *see also* Fort St. George
widow remarriage, 224, 226
Wilks, Mark, 74-77, 84-89, 92-98, 102, 109-16, 166, 207
  about
    Haidar, 75-76
    Jehan Khan, 115
    Mahratta camp, 95
    Tipu's fall, 96, 97
    Tipu's preferred officers, 115
  survey, 109
Willingdon, Lord, Viceroy, 286
Winter, Sir Edward, 18
Wodeyar, Sadashiva, 189
  Rani Chennamma, 189
Women,
  age of consent, 291
  education, 221
  laws of inheritance, 291
  medical aid for, 291
  Nadar, 209, 210, 211
  Nambudiri, 334, 335
World Tamil Conference, 385
World War I, 241, 242, 265, 328
World War, Second, 337

Yale, Elihu, 13
Yeddyurappa, B. S., 438, 439
Yella Reddy, Baddam, 351
Yogakshema Sabha, 334
Young India, 272
YSR Congress, 437

Zafar, Bahadur Shah, Mughal Emperor, 200, 345
Zamindari, abolition of, 301
Zamindars, 53-54, 56, 170, 245, 248, 274, 294, 302, 305, 329
Zamorin, 1, 20, 22, 51, 79-80, 196, 260, 287, 335
Zayn al-Din al-Ma'bari, 261
  Tuhfat-al-Mujahidin, 261
Zetland, Lord, Secretary of State, 295, 297